POLITICS IN STATES
AND
COMMUNITIES

POLITICS IN STATES AND COMMUNITIES

THIRD EDITION

Thomas R. Dye

Florida State University

PRENTICE-HALL, INC., ENGLEWOOD CLIFFS, NEW JERSEY

Library of Congress Cataloging in Publication Data

Dye, Thomas R. (date)
    Politics in States and communities.

    Includes bibliographical references and index.
    1. State governments. 2. Local government—
United States. I. Title.
JK2408.D82   1977   320.4'73   76-18290
ISBN 0-13-686360-4

Printed in the United States of America
10 9 8 7 6 5 4 3 2 1

PRENTICE-HALL INTERNATIONAL, INC., *London*
PRENTICE-HALL OF AUSTRALIA PTY. LIMITED, *Sydney*
PRENTICE-HALL OF CANADA, LTD., *Toronto*
PRENTICE-HALL OF INDIA PRIVATE LIMITED, *New Delhi*
PRENTICE-HALL OF JAPAN, INC., *Tokyo*
PRENTICE-HALL OF SOUTHEAST ASIA PTE. LTD., *Singapore*
WHITEHALL BOOKS LIMITED, *Wellington, New Zealand*

TO JOANN

Contents

Chapter Three
PARTICIPATION IN STATE POLITICS 56

Chapter Four
PARTIES IN STATE POLITICS 92

Chapter Five
LEGISLATORS IN STATE POLITICS 117

Chapter Six

GOVERNORS IN STATE POLITICS   162

Chapter Seven

COURTS, CRIME,
AND CORRECTIONAL POLICY   186

Chapter Eight

COMMUNITY POLITICAL SYSTEMS   220

Chapter Thirteen
BLACK POLITICS, CIVIL RIGHTS, AND PUBLIC ORDER 360

Chapter Fourteen
THE POLITICS OF EDUCATION 397

Chapter Fifteen
THE POLITICS OF TRANSPORTATION, HOUSING, AND URBAN AFFAIRS 419

Foreword

If this book has a theme, it is that states and communities in America play an important role in the political life of the nation. State and local governments do more than merely provide certain services such as education, road building, or fire protection. They also perform a vital political function by helping to resolve conflicts of interest in American society. The concern of this book is with "politics," that is, conflicts over public policy in American states and communities and the structures and processes designed to manage these conflicts.

This book not only attempts to *describe* politics and public policy in American states and communities, but, more important, it attempts to *explain* differences that are encountered from state to state and community to community by means of comparative analysis. In the past the phrase "comparative government" applied to the study of foreign governments, but the American states and communities provide an excellent opportunity for genuine comparative study. By that we mean the comparison of political institutions and behavior from state to state and community to community for the purpose of identifying and explaining existing similarities or differences. Only by comparing politics and public policies in different states and communities can we arrive at any explanation of political life.

No longer is the field of state and local government a "lost world" to students of politics. Today, some of the most intellectually exciting and theoretically significant research in political science is focused on American states and communities. This book tries to summarize the results of recent systematic, comparative research in political science and incorporate these results into a comprehensive analysis of politics in states and communities.

The author of a textbook is deeply indebted to the research scholars whose labors produce the insight and understanding that a text tries to convey to its readers. There is no way to adequately express this indebtedness.

POLITICS IN STATES
AND
COMMUNITIES

Politics
in states and communities

A POLITICAL APPROACH TO STATES AND COMMUNITIES

States and communities do more than provide public services such as
education, highways, and police protection. They also play an important
role in managing conflicts of interest in American society. It is appropriate for a book on "politics" in states and communities to consider
important conflicts in American life, for "Politics arises out of conflicts,
and it consists of the activities—for example, reasonable discussion, em-
passioned oratory, balloting, and street fighting—by which conflict is
carried on." [1] The concern of this book is therefore with "politics," that
is, conflicts over public policy in American states and communities, and
the structures and processes designed to manage these conflicts.

There are various approaches to the study of state and local government. Many books emphasize basic structure, organization, and practice
of government; other books suggest that the key to understanding lies in
the mastery of the constitutional relationships between national, state,
and local governments; still other books concentrate on the administration of state and local governments. No one denies that the organizational,
constitutional, or administrative aspects of state and local government

---

[1] Edward C. Banfield and James Q. Wilson, *City Politics* (Cambridge: Harvard–
M.I.T. Press, 1963), p. 7.

Chapter one

are important, but the really critical problems facing American communities, such as education, welfare, racial hatred, slum housing, and financial crises cannot be solved through organizational reform, constitutional change, or administrative efficiency. The obstacles to the solution of these problems are primarily *political* in character; that is, people have different ideas about what should be done, or if anything should be done at all. Only when everyone agrees on a solution can the problem be entrusted to lawyers, accountants, or technicians. In American politics, this agreement seldom exists. Even if there is "only one way to pave a street," political questions remain, "Whose street shall be paved?" "Who will get the paving contract?" "Who will bear the cost?" "Why not build a school gym instead of paving the street?"

The management of conflict in society is one of the basic purposes of government. The Founding Fathers were very much aware that the control of "factions" was the principal function of government. Moreover, they defined faction as a number of citizens united by common interests that oppose the interests of a number of other citizens. James Madison thought that regulating such conflict was "the principal task of modern legislation." [2] To paraphrase Madison, the management of conflict is a principal task of state and local government.

A political approach to states and communities does not ignore the organization of state and local government, the constitutional limitations upon them, or their administrative problems, for the principal responsibility for managing conflict falls upon government institutions. Governments manage conflict by (1) establishing and enforcing general rules by which conflict is to be carried on, (2) arranging compromises and balancing interests in public policy, and (3) imposing settlements which the parties in the disputes must accept. In other words, governments must lay down "the rules of the game" in political activity; they must make decisions which allocate values among competing interests and then see that these decisions are carried out. The organization of a government, its constitutional limitations, and the administrative arrangements under which it operates, all vitally affect the way it performs political functions. In considering the constitutional, organizational, and administrative aspects of state and local government, we should focus our attention on their impact on political questions.

A COMPARATIVE APPROACH TO STATES AND COMMUNITIES

The task of political science is not only to *describe* politics and public policy in American states and communities but, more importantly, to

[2] James Madison, *The Federalist,* No. 10.

explain differences encountered from state to state and community to community by means of comparative analysis. We want to know "what" is happening in American politics, but we also want to know "why" it is happening. In the past, the phrase "comparative government" applied to the study of foreign governments, but American states and communities provide an excellent opportunity for genuine comparative study, that is, the comparison of political institutions and behavior from state to state and community to community for the purposes of identifying or explaining the similarities or differences that are found. Studies that merely describe governmental agencies or political events, without identifying or explaining their similarities or differences, cannot really contribute to the explanation of politics and public affairs. Comparison, in other words, is a vital part of explanation. Only by comparing politics and public policy in different states and communities with different socioeconomic and political environments can we arrive at any comprehensive explanations of political life. Comparative analysis helps us answer the question "why."

The American states provide an excellent opportunity for applying comparative analysis. These fifty separate political systems share a common institutional framework and cultural background. All states operate under written constitutions, which divide authority between executive, legislative, and judicial branches. All states function within the common framework of the American federal system. All states share a national language, national symbols, and a national history. Thus, some important institutional and cultural factors can be treated as constants in the comparative study of state politics.

Of course, American states and communities are not entirely alike in their social and economic environments, the nature of their political systems, or their public policies. These differences, however, are important assets in comparative study because they enable us to search for relationships between different socioeconomic environments, political system characteristics, and policy outcomes. For example, if differences among states and communities in educational policies are closely associated with differences in economic resources or in party systems, then we may assume that economic resources or party systems help "explain" educational policies.

By way of example, let us pose some specific questions about state and community politics which a comparative approach will help us answer. Are single-industry states more likely to have powerful pressure groups dominating the state legislature than multi-industry states? Are governors generally more powerful in the urban industrial states than in the rural agricultural states? What effect does urbanization have on party competition in the states? Is one-partyism a product of ruralism, poverty, or a lack of industrial development? What is the impact of educational levels on voter participation rates? Do states with competitive parties and high voter turnout have more generous welfare programs than one-party states with low voter turnout? What factors affect crime rates in states and cities, and what forces operate to shape state prison and parole programs? How do income levels in the states affect spending for education, welfare, highways, and so forth? Are tax burdens significantly heavier in some states than in others? Does a large black population improve the chances for civil rights legislation and desegregation, or does it strengthen the position of political forces resisting social change? What kinds of cities are likely to have strong political party organizations ("machines") dominating local government in contrast to reform-minded, "do-good" administrations? Are "machine" cities more responsive to the demands of ethnic or black populations than "reformed" cities? Is city-manager government more common among middle-sized cities than big cities, and, if so, why? What is the effect of increasing black populations in the nation's largest cities? Where has metropolitan government been successful and what factors contribute to its success or failure? What is the impact of federal programs on states and cities? Do federal grants-in-aid operate to reduce inequalities among the states in educational opportunities? What is the effect of federal money on housing, urban renewal, planning, transportation, and poverty programs in the nation's cities? These are the kinds of questions that can be approached from a comparative viewpoint.

SETTINGS FOR STATE POLITICS

State politics are often affected by unique historical circumstances. (See Figure 1–1, Table 1–1.) Louisiana is distinctive because of its French-Spanish colonial background, and the continuing influence of this background on its politics today. For nine years Texas was an independent republic (1836–45) before it was annexed as a state by Congress. California was the scene of a great gold rush in 1849. Eleven southern states were involved in a bloody war against the federal government from 1861 to 1865. Hawaii has a unique history and culture, combining the influence of Polynesian, Chinese, Japanese, and hoalie civilizations. Alaska's rugged climate and geography and physical isolation set it apart. Wisconsin and Minnesota reflect the Scandinavian influences of their settlers, and Utah reflects the religious influences of its Morman settlers. The states of the Deep South—South Carolina, Georgia, Alabama, Mississippi, Louisiana—still reflect their plantation cultures. Life in Florida is more tourist oriented than anywhere else. Michigan is noted for its

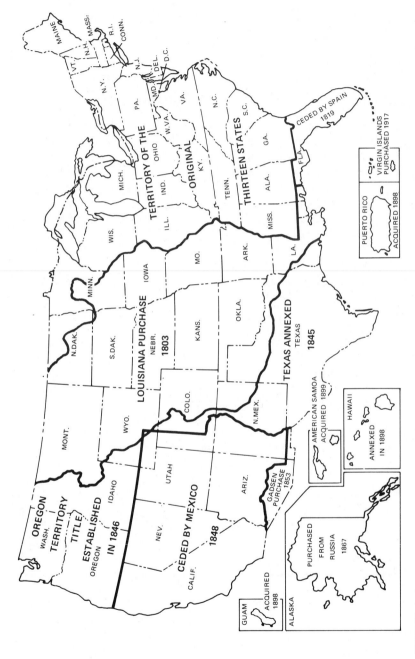

FIGURE 1-1
Source: U.S. Bureau of the Census.

5

TABLE 1.1 The States of the Union—Historical Data

State or Other Jurisdiction	Capital	Source of State Lands	Date Organized as Territory	Date Admitted to Union	Chronological Order of Admission to Union
Alabama	Montgomery	Mississippi Territory, 1798(a)	March 3, 1817	Dec. 14, 1819	22
Alaska	Juneau	Purchased from Russia, 1867	Aug. 24, 1912	Jan. 3, 1959	49
Arizona	Phoenix	Ceded by Mexico, 1848(b)	Feb. 24, 1863	Feb. 14, 1912	48
Arkansas	Little Rock	Louisiana Purchase, 1803	March 2, 1819	June 15, 1836	25
California	Sacramento	Ceded by Mexico, 1848	(c)	Sept. 9, 1850	31
Colorado	Denver	Louisiana Purchase, 1803(d)	Feb. 28, 1861	Aug. 1, 1876	38
Connecticut	Hartford	Royal charter, 1662(e)		Jan. 9, 1788(f)	5
Delaware	Dover	Swedish charter, 1638; English charter 1683(e)		Dec. 7, 1787(f)	1
Florida	Tallahassee	Ceded by Spain, 1819	March 30, 1822	March 3, 1845	27
Georgia	Atlanta	Charter, 1732, from George II to Trustees for Establishing the Colony of Georgia(e)		Jan. 2, 1788(f)	4
Hawaii	Honolulu	Annexed, 1898	June 14, 1900	Aug. 21, 1959	50
Idaho	Boise	Treaty with Britain, 1846	March 4, 1863	July 3, 1890	43
Illinois	Springfield	Northwest Territory, 1787	Feb. 3, 1809	Dec. 3, 1818	21
Indiana	Indianapolis	Northwest Territory, 1787	May 7, 1800	Dec. 11, 1816	19
Iowa	Des Moines	Louisiana Purchase, 1803	June 12, 1838	Dec. 28, 1846	29
Kansas	Topeka	Louisiana Purchase, 1803(d)	May 30, 1854	Jan. 29, 1861	34
Kentucky	Frankfort	Part of Virginia until admitted as State	(c)	June 1, 1792	15
Louisiana	Baton Rouge	Louisiana Purchase, 1803(g)	March 26, 1804	April 30, 1812	18
Maine	Augusta	Part of Massachusetts until admitted as State	(c)	March 15, 1820	23
Maryland	Annapolis	Charter, 1632, from Charles I to Calvert(e)		April 28, 1788(f)	7
Massachusetts	Boston	Charter to Massachusetts Bay Company, 1629(e)		Feb. 6, 1788(f)	6
Michigan	Lansing	Northwest Territory, 1787	Jan. 11, 1805	Jan. 26, 1837	26
Minnesota	St. Paul	Northwest Territory, 1787(h)	March 3, 1849	May 11, 1858	32
Mississippi	Jackson	Mississippi Territory(i)	April 7, 1798	Dec. 10, 1817	20
Missouri	Jefferson City	Louisiana Purchase, 1803	June 4, 1812	Aug. 10, 1821	24

TABLE 1.1 The States of the Union—Historical Data (Cont.)

State or Other Jurisdiction	Capital	Source of State Lands	Date Organized as Territory	Date Admitted to Union	Chronological Order of Admission to Union
Montana	Helena	Louisiana Purchase, 1803(j)	May 26, 1864	Nov. 8, 1889	41
Nebraska	Lincoln	Louisiana Purchase, 1803	May 30, 1854	March 1, 1867	37
Nevada	Carson City	Ceded by Mexico, 1848	March 2, 1861	Oct. 31, 1864	36
New Hampshire	Concord	Grants frmo Council for New England, 1622 and 1629. Made royal province, 1679(e)		June 21, 1788(f)	9
New Jersey	Trenton	Dutch settlement, 1618; English charter, 1664(e)		Dec. 18, 1787(f)	3
New Mexico	Santa Fe	Ceded by Mexico, 1848(b)	Sept. 9, 1850	Jan. 6, 1912	47
New York	Albany	Dutch settlement, 1623; English control, 1664(e)		July 26, 1788(f)	11
North Czrolina	Raleigh	Charter, 1663, from Charles II(e)		Nov. 21, 1789(f)	12
North Dakota	Bismarck	Louisiana Purchase, 1803(k)	March 2, 1861	Nov. 2, 1889	39
Ohio	Columbus	Northwest Territory, 1787		March 1, 1803	17
Oklahoma	Oklahoma City	Louisiana Purchase, 1803	May 2, 1890	Nov. 16, 1907	46
Oregon	Salem	Settlement and treaty with Britain, 1846	Aug. 14, 1848	Feb. 14, 1859	33
Pennsylvania	Harrisburg	Grant from Charles II to William Penn, 1681(e)		Dec. 12, 1787(f)	2
Rhode Island	Providence	Charter, 1663, from Charles II(e)		May 29, 1790(f)	13
South Carolina	Columbia	Charter, 1663, from Charles II(e)		May 23, 1788(f)	8
South Dakota	Pierre	Louisiana Purchase, 1803	March 2, 1861	Nov. 2, 1889	40
Tennessee	Nashville	Part of North Carolina until admitted as State	(c)	June 1, 1796	16
Texas	Austin	Republic of Texas, 1845	(c)	Dec. 29, 1845	28
Utah	Salt Lake City	Ceded by Mexico, 1848	Sept. 9, 1850	Jan. 4, 1896	45
Vermont	Montpelier	From lands of New Hampshire and New York	(c)	March 4, 1791	14
Virginia	Richmond	Charter, 1609, from James I to London Company (e)		June 25, 1788(f)	10
Washington	Olympia	Oregon Territory, 1848	March 2, 1853	Nov. 11, 1889	42
West Virginia	Charleston	Part of Virginia until admitted as State	(c)	June 20, 1863	35
Wisconsin	Madison	Northwest Territory, 1787	April 20, 1836	May 29, 1848	30

TABLE 1.1 The States of the Union—Historical Data (Cont.)

State or Other Jurisdiction	Capital	Source of State Lands	Date Organized as Territory	Date Admitted to Union	Chronological Order of Admission to Union
Wyoming	Cheyenne	Louisiana Purchase, 1803(d,j)	July 25, 1868	July 10, 1890	44
American Samoa	Pago Pago		Became a Territory, 1899		—
Guam	Agana	Ceded by Spain, 1898	Aug. 1, 1950		—
Puerto Rico	San Juan	Ceded by Spain, 1898		July 25, 1952(l)	—
TTPI	Saipan	Administered as trusteeship for the United Nations, July 18, 1947			—
Virgin Islands	Charlotte Amalie	Purchased from Denmark, January 17, 1917			—

(a) By the Treaty of Paris, 1783, England gave up claim to the thirteen original Colonies, and to all land within an area extending along the present Canadian border to the Lake of the Woods, down the Mississippi River to the 31st parallel, east to the Chattahoochie, down that river to the mouth of the Flint, east to the source of the St. Mary's, down that river to the ocean. Territory west of the Alleghenies was acquired by various States, but was eventually all ceded to the Nation. Thus, the major part of Alabama was acquired by the Treaty of Paris, but the lower portion from Spain in 1813.

(b) Portion of land obtained by Gadsden Purchase, 1853.

(c) No territorial status before admission to Union.

(d) Portion of land ceded by Mexico, 1848.

(e) One of the original thirteen Colonies.

(f) Date of ratification of U.S. Constitution.

(g) West Feliciana District (Baton Rouge) acquired from Spain, 1810, added to Louisiana, 1812.

(h) Portion of land obtained by Louisiana Purchase, 1803.

(i) See footnote (a). The lower portion of Mississippi was also acquired from Spain in 1813.

(j) Portion of land obtained from Oregon Territory, 1848.

(k) The northern portion and the Red River Valley were acquired by treaty with Great Britain in 1818.

(l) On this date Puerto Rico became a self-governing Commonwealth by compact approved by the United States Congress and the voters of Puerto Rico as provided in U.S. Public Law 600 of 1950.

SOURCE: *The Book of the States 1972-73* (Lexington, Ky.: Council of State Governments, 1972).

automobile industry, Pennsylvania for its steel industry, and West Virginia for its coal mines. Nevada is most conspicuous for its legalized gambling.

These unique historical and cultural settings help to shape state political systems and public policies; however, students of state politics must search for social and economic conditions that appear most influential in shaping state politics over time in all the states. Despite the uniqueness of history and culture in many of our states, we must still search for generalizations which will help to explain why state governments do what they do. Since it is impossible to consider all the environmental conditions that might influence state politics, we must focus our attention on a limited number of environmental variables.

Economic development is one of the most influential environmental variables affecting state politics. Economic development is defined here to include three closely related components; urbanization, income, and education. *Urbanization* is an integral part of economic development. Industrial activities require the concentration of people in urban centers, whereas agricultural activities spread population over larger land areas. It is possible for a population center to grow without industrialization, but industrialization requires urbanization. A common definition of urbanization is the percentage of population living in urban areas, that is, in incorporated cities of twenty-five hundred or more or the urban fringe of cities of fifty thousand or more. This is the standard Census Bureau definition. In 1790 the urban population of the United States was only 5 percent of the total population. By 1900 this figure had grown to 40 percent, and in 1970, 73.5 percent of the population lived in urban areas. Yet here again not all the states share this high degree of urbanization. Vermont has the smallest proportion of urban residents of any state in the nation (32.2 percent), and California has the highest proportion (90.9 percent). The distribution of states according to the percentage of their population living in urban areas is shown in Figure 1–2.

Rising *income* is also a basic component of economic development. An industrial economy means increased worker productivity and the creation of surplus wealth. Per capita personal income in the United States grew from $1,500 in 1950 to $2,200 in 1960 and to $3,900 in 1970. This wealth was not evenly distributed throughout the states (see Figure 1–2). Per capita personal income in Connecticut was over $4,800, but it was only $2,500 in Mississippi.

An economically developed society requires educated, rather than uneducated, workers. Many economists have asserted that economic growth involves an upgrading of the quality in the work force, the development of professional managerial skills, and an increase in the volume

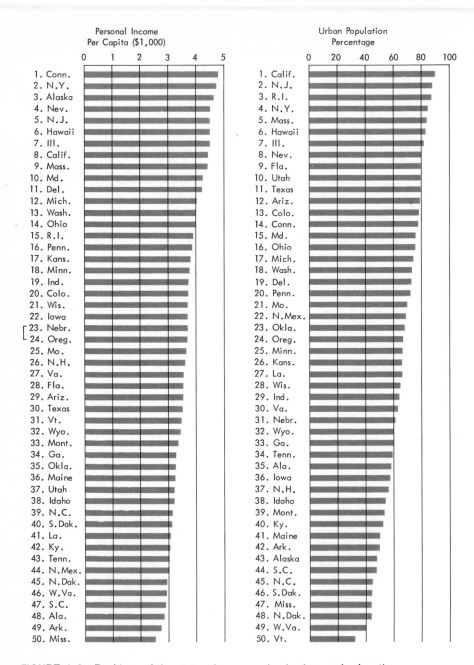

FIGURE 1–2 Rankings of the states: income, urbanization, and education.

Median School Year
Completed by Adult Population

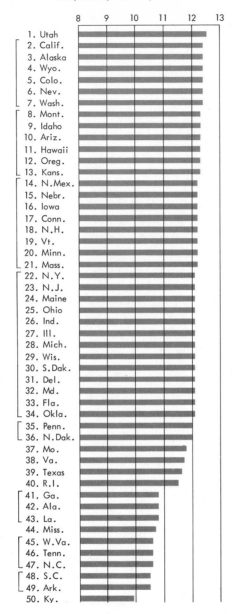

FIGURE 1–2   (cont.)

of research. These developments obviously involve a general increase in the *educational levels* of the adult population. In 1940 the median school year completed by the adult population of the United States was 8.6. By 1970 the median school year had advanced to 12.0. This generally high level of educational attainment did not prevail uniformly throughout the states (see Figure 1–2).

The extent to which economic development—urbanization, income, and education–affects the politics of the states is an important question, which we will return to again and again in the chapters that follow.

STATES AND COMMUNITIES IN THE AMERICAN POLITICAL SYSTEM

At the beginning of the twentieth century, most government activity in America was carried on at the *local* level. Table 1–2 reveals that local governments once made about 59 percent of all government expenditures in the United States, compared to 35 percent for the federal government and 6 percent for state governments. Yet by the 1970s centralization in the American federal system had proceeded to the point where local governments were making only 23 percent of all government expenditures, compared to 64 percent for the federal government and 13 percent for state governments.

Wars and the depression had a great deal to do with the shift away from local reliance in American government. During national emergencies, both foreign and domestic, Americans have turned to the federal government for help. After the emergency, federal activity decreases somewhat in relation to state and local activity, but federal activity never returns to the precrisis level. Thus, during World War I and World War II, and the Korean and Vietnamese wars, the federal government increased its percentage of total government activity, while local and state government percentages declined. Since the federal government has the primary responsibility for national defense, this is what we would expect to occur during wartime. But the federal government also expands its activities in response to domestic crisis; it was during the 1930s that federal expenditures surpassed the combined expenditures of all states and communities.

While foreign and domestic crises have brought about increasing centralization in American government, it should be noted that expanded federal activity has *not* come at the expense of state and local activity. Federal power and state-local power are not at the opposite ends of a seesaw; the growth of federal power has not necessarily curtailed the power of states and localities. National activity has expanded in the twentieth century, but so has the activity of state and local governments.

The extent of centralization of government activity in the American federal system varies widely according to policy area (see Table 1–3). In the fields of national defense, space research, and postal service, the federal government assumes almost exclusive responsibility. In all other fields, state and local governments share responsibility and costs with the federal government. State and local governments assume the major share of the costs of education, highways, health and hospitals, sanitation, and

TABLE 1.2   A Comparison of the Expenditures of Federal, State, and Local Governments over Seven Decades

	Percentages of Total General Expenditures of Governments in the U.S.[3]		
	Federal[1]	State[2]	Local[2]
1902	35%	6%	59%
1927	31	13	56
1936	50	14	36
1944	91	3	7
1950	64	12	24
1960	62	13	25
1970	64	13	23
1975	61	18	21

[1] Figures include social security and trust fund expenditures.

[2] State payments to local governments are shown as local government expenditures; federal grants-in-aid are shown as federal expenditures.

[3] Figures may not total correctly because of rounding.

SOURCE: Standard sources of data on American states and communities in tables throughout include: U.S. Bureau of the Census, *Statistical Abstract of the United States,* published annually by the U.S. Government Printing Office, Washington, D.C.; U.S. Bureau of the Census, *Census of Governments,* published after each five-year governmental census (1967, 1972, etc.) by the U.S. Government Printing Office, Washington, D.C.; U.S. Bureau of the Census CENSUS OF POPULATION 1970, including individual state volumes on "Numbers of Inhabitants," "General Population Characteristics," and "General Social and Economic Characteristics," as well as individual reports on Standard Metropolitan Statistical Areas, published by the U.S. Government Printing Office, Washington, D.C.; *The Book of the States,* published biennially by the Council of State Governments, Lexington, Kentucky; *Municipal Yearbook,* published annually by the International City Managers Association, Washington, D.C.; U.S. Bureau of the Census, *City-County Data Book,* published every five years by the U.S. Government Printing Office, Washington, D.C.; and *America Votes,* edited by Richard Scammon, and published periodically by the Governmental Affairs Institute, Washington, D.C. Unless otherwise indicated, the social, economic, governmental, and electoral data presented in this volume are drawn from these sources.

TABLE 1.3   Federal and State-Local Shares of Expenditures by Policy Areas, 1927-75

	1927		1938		1970		1975	
	Federal[1]	*State and Local*	*Federal*[1]	*State and Local*	*Federal*[1]	*State and Local*	*Federal*[1]	*State and Local*
National defense	100%	0%	100%	0%	100%	0%	100%	0%
Space research	100	0	100	0	100	0	100	0
Postal service	100	0	100	0	100	0	100	0
Education	1	99	6	94	10	90	18	82
Highways	1	99	23	77	29	71	28	72
Welfare	6	94	13	87	58	42	63	37
Health and hospitals	18	82	19	81	33	67	32	68
Natural resources	31	69	81	19	80	20	82	18
Housing and urban renewal	–	–	–	–	82	18	85	15

[1] Federal grants-in-aid are shown as federal expenditures.
SOURCE: U.S. Bureau of the Census, *Statistical Abstract of the United States.*

fire and police protection. Welfare costs are gradually being shifted to the federal government, and the federal government assumes the major share of the costs of natural resource development and social security.

POLICY RESPONSIBILITIES OF STATES AND COMMUNITIES

States and communities in America operate the world's largest public school system and highway network. They operate most of the nation's judicial, welfare, police, health, correctional, and recreational facilities. Most regulation of industry, banking, commerce, utilities, labor, and protection of public safety is in the hands of state and local governments. Their programs in conservation, sanitation, social work, housing, and urban planning are vital to the day-to-day lives of all Americans. Even when the national government is involved in these programs, states and communities must decide whether to participate in national programs, and if they participate, they must administer the programs within their jurisdictions. Despite the glamour of national politics, states and communities carry on the greatest volume of public business, settle the greatest number of political conflicts, make the majority of policy decisions, and direct the bulk of public programs. They have the major responsibility for maintaining domestic law and order, for educating the children, for moving Americans from place to place, and for caring for the poor and the ill. They regulate the provision of water, gas, electric, and other public utilities, share in the regulation of insurance and banking enterprise, regulate the use of land, and supervise the sale of ownership of property. Their courts settle by far the greatest number of civil and criminal cases. In short, states and communities are by no means unimportant political systems.

Education. Education is the most important responsibility of state and local governments and the most costly of all state-local functions. States and communities are responsible for decisions about what should be taught in the public schools, how much should be spent on the education of each child, how many children should be in each classroom, how much teachers should be paid, how responsibilities in education should be divided between state and local governments, what qualifications teachers must have, what types and rates of taxes shall be levied for education, and many other decisions which affect the life of every child in America. Support for higher education, including funds for state colleges and universities, is one of the most rapidly increasing expenditures of state governments. The promise of equal access to a college degree for all qualified students is proving to be a heavy burden on states and communities. The federal government is currently contributing about 10 percent of the total expenditures for education.

Transportation. Transportation—more particularly highways—is the second most costly function of state and local governments. There are over two million miles of surfaced roads in America, and nearly one hundred million registered motor vehicles in the nation, almost one for every two persons. States and communities must make decisions about the allocation of money for streets and highways, sources of funds for highway revenue, the extent of gasoline and motor vehicle taxation, the regulation of traffic on the highways, the location of highways, the determination of construction policies, the division of responsibility between state and local governments for highway financing administration, the division of highway funds between rural and urban areas, and other important issues in highway politics. While the federal government is deeply involved in highway construction, federal grants for highways amount to less than 30 percent of all expenditures for highways.

Health and welfare. States and communities continue to carry a heavy burden in the field of health and welfare—despite an extensive system of federal grants-in-aid for this purpose. States and communities must make decisions about participation in federal programs and allocate responsibilities among themselves for health and welfare programs.

Within the broad outlines of federal policy, states and communities decide the amount of money appropriated for health and welfare purposes, the benefits to be paid to recipients, the rules of eligibility, and the means by which the programs will be administered. States and communities may choose to grant assistance beyond the limits supported by the national government, or they may choose to have no welfare programs at all. Moreover, states and communities must maintain institutions for the care of persons who are so destitute, alone, or ill that federal payments are not sufficient. These are the state orphanages, homes for the aged, and state and county hospitals and homes for the physically and mentally ill.

Crime. States and communities have the principal responsibility for public safety in America. Crime is increasing at a much greater rate than the population. The federal government, through the Federal Bureau of Investigation, has limited jurisdiction over certain crimes, such as kidnapping, bank robbery, and espionage. State police have important highway safety responsibilities and cooperate with local authorities in the apprehension of criminals. But community police forces continue to be the principal instrument of law enforcement and public safety. Local governments employ over a quarter of a million policemen in the United States today, and approximately the same number of firemen. The sheriff and his deputies are still the principal enforcement and arresting officers in rural counties. States and communities also have the principal responsibility for maintaining prisons and correctional institutions. Each year, over two million Americans are prisoners in jails, police stations, juvenile homes, or penitentiaries. More than 90 percent of these prisoners are at state and local rather than federal institutions.

Civil rights. The national government has defined a national system of civil rights, but these rights cannot become realities without the support of state and local authorities. States and communities must deal directly with racial problems, such as desegregation in the public schools, job discrimination, and the existence of segregated housing patterns or ghettos in the cities. They must deal with the consequences of racial tension, including violence.

Physical environment. Local governments have the principal responsibility for our physical environment. They must plan streets, parks, and commercial, residential, and industrial areas and provide essential public utilities for the community. The waste materials of human beings —rubbish, garbage, and sewage—exceed one ton every day per person. The task of disposal is an immense one; the problem is not only collecting it but finding ways to dispose of it. If it is incinerated, it contributes to air pollution; and if it is carried off into streams, rivers, or lakes, it contributes to water pollution. Thus, communities are largely responsible for two of the nation's most pressing problems—air and water pollution.

Taxation. To pay for these programs, states and communities must make important decisions about taxation: they must decide about levels of taxation and what tax burdens their citizens can carry. They must determine what reliance shall be placed upon income, sales, or property taxation. States and communities must raise nearly $200 billion per year and at the same time compete with each other to attract industry and commerce.

While it is true that the decisions of states and communities are at times heavily influenced by decisions made at the national level, states and communities continue to bear the major responsibility for policy making and finance in domestic affairs. States and communities are important political systems with the legal authority, money, manpower, and policies and programs which touch the lives of all Americans.

THE CONSTITUTIONAL FRAMEWORK OF STATE GOVERNMENT

Probably no other people in the world are more devoted than the American people to the idea of written constitutions. This devotion has deep roots in American national traditions. In 1215 a group of English lords forced King John to sign a document, later known as the Magna Carta, which guaranteed them certain feudal rights and set a precedent for constitutional government. Although the British political tradition eventually rejected the formal written constitutions, the idea of a written constitution was strongly reinforced by the experience in the American colonies. The American colonies were legally established by charters given to companies establishing settlements here. These charters became more elaborate as the colonial ventures succeeded, and the habit of depending upon a written code for the regulation of governmental organization and operation became strongly entrenched in the American colonies.

The charters, or "constitutions," were granted by royal action, either by recognizing proprietary rights, as in Maryland, Delaware, and Pennsylvania, or by granting royal commissions to companies to establish governments, as in Virginia, Massachusetts, New Hampshire, New York, New Jersey, Georgia, and North and South Carolina. Only in Connecticut and Rhode Island was there much popular participation in early constitution making. In these two colonies, royal charters were granted directly to the colonists themselves, who participated in drawing up the charter for the submission to the Crown. The important point is that these charters, whatever their origin, were present in all the colonies, and many political traditions and expectations grew up around them. All the colonies and charters were subject to royal control. Colonists looked to these charters for protection against British interference in colonial affairs. This was particularly true in Connecticut and Rhode Island, which were organized along popular principles with elected governors and legislatures whose acts were not subjected to a royal governor's veto, nor sent to England for approval. The political importance of these early charters is illustrated by the conflict over the Fundamental Orders of Connecticut. In 1685 King James issued an order for the repeal of Connecticut's charter. The colony offered its submission, and in 1687 Sir Edmund Androse went to Hartford and in the name of the Crown declared the government dissolved. The charter was not surrendered, however, but hidden in an oak tree, which is now displayed for sightseers. Immediately after the English revolution of 1688, people returned to exercising all the powers of the original charter. Succeeding British monarchs silently permitted this without struggle or resistance. After the Declaration of Independence, new constitutions were written in eleven colonies; Connecticut retained her charter as the fundamental law until 1818, and Rhode Island kept her charter until 1842. The colonial experience, together with the earlier English heritage, had firmly implanted the tradition of written constitutions.

Constitutions govern governments. They prescribe the essential structure and organization of government, and they distribute powers among the various branches of government. Constitutions both authorize governments to exercise power and place prohibitions on the exercise of governmental power. Constitutions provide for stability and continuity in government by providing for terms of offices and for orderly replacement of political leaders. They provide the opportunity for orderly change. Since constitutions govern the activities of governments themselves, they are considered more fundamental than the ordinary laws and statutes passed by governments. State *constitutions* take precedence over any state *law* in conflict with them. Since constitutions are more fundamental than ordinary law, they cannot be changed by the routine methods employed to amend ordinary laws. Constitutional amendments generally require some special legislative procedures together with popular referendum. (See Table 1–4).

State constitutions take precedence over state law, but they are subordinate to the U.S. Constitution and the laws of the United States. The United States Constitution mentions state constitutions only once, and it does so to assert the supremacy of the U.S. Constitution and the laws and treaties of the United States. Article VI states:

TABLE 1.4   General Information on State Constitutions

State or other jurisdiction	Number of constitutions	Dates of adoption	Effective date of present constitution	Estimated length (number of words)	Number of amendments Proposed	Number of amendments Adopted
Alabama	6	1819; 1861; 1865; 1868; 1875; 1901	1901	106,000	497	326
Alaska	1	1956	1959	12,000	12	11
Arizona	1	1911	1912	18,500	141	77
Arkansas	5	1836; 1861; 1864; 1868; 1874	1874	40,170	(a)	53
California	2	1849; 1879	1879	68,000	667	392
Colorado	1	1876	1876	40,190	147(b)	53(b)
Connecticut	4	1818(c); 1965	1965	7,959	5	4
Delaware	4	1776; 1792; 1831; 1897	1897	22,000	(a)	83
Florida	6	1839; 1861; 1865; 1868; 1885; 1968	1969	21,286	15	10
Georgia	8	1777; 1789; 1798; 1861; 1865; 1868; 1877; 1945	1945	500,000	1,016	767
Hawaii	3	1950; 1958; 1968	1968	11,904	41	38
Idaho	1	1889	1890	22,280	125	85
Illinois	4	1818; 1848; 1870; 1970	1971	17,500	0	0
Indiana	2	1816; 1851	1851	11,120	52	29
Iowa	2	1846; 1857	1857	11,200	41	36(d)
Kansas	1	1859	1861	14,500	93	65(d)
Kentucky	4	1792; 1799; 1850; 1891	1891	21,500	47	20
Louisiana	10	1812; 1845; 1852; 1861; 1864; 1868; 1879; 1898; 1913; 1921	1921	256,000	749	498
Maine	1	1820	1820	20,000	143	123(e)
Maryland	4	1776; 1851; 1864; 1867	1867	37,300	199	160

TABLE 1.4 General Information on State Constitutions (Cont.)

State or other jurisdiction	Number of constitutions	Dates of adoption	Effective date of present constitution	Estimated length (number of words)	Number of amendments Proposed	Number of amendments Adopted
Massachusetts	1	1780	1780	36,000	115	97
Michigan	4	1835; 1850; 1908; 1963	1964	19,867	13	6
Minnesota	1	1858	1858	20,080	186	100
Mississippi	4	1817; 1832; 1869; 1890	1890	25,742	106	37
Missouri	4	1820; 1865; 1875; 1945	1945	33,260	52	37
Montana	2	1889; 1972	1973	11,250	0	0
Nebraska	2	1866; 1875	1875	19,975	238	164
Nevada	1	1864	1864	17,270	117	70
New Hampshire	2	1776; 1784(f)	1784	12,200	135(f)	61(f)
New Jersey	3	1776; 1844; 1947	1947	16,030	23	17
New Mexico	1	1911	1912	26,136	185	88
New York	5	1777; 1822; 1846; 1849; 1894	1894	47,000	249	172
North Carolina	3	1776; 1868; 1970	1971	17,000	5	5
North Dakota	1	1889	1889	31,470	(a)	90
Ohio	2	1802; 1851	1851	30,000	195	110
Oklahoma	1	1907	1907	63,569	196	85
Oregon	1	1859	1859	23,000	284	143
Pennsylvania	4	1776; 1790; 1838; 1873; 1968(g)	1873; 1968	24,750	9	6
Rhode Island	1	1843(c)	1843	21,040	79	42
South Carolina	6	1776; 1778; 1790; 1865; 1868; 1895	1895	45,740	430	417
South Dakota	1	1889	1889	24,000	161	82
Tennessee	3	1796; 1835; 1870	1870	15,150	34	19
Texas	5	1845; 1861; 1866; 1869; 1876	1876	54,000	343	218
Utah	1	1896	1896	20,990	103	60

TABLE 1.4 General Information on State Constitutions (Cont.)

State or other jurisdiction	Number of constitutions	Dates of adoption	Effective date of present constitution	Estimated length (number of words)	Number of amendments	
					Proposed	Adopted
Vermont	3	1777; 1786; 1793	1793	7,600	200	44
Virginia	6	1776; 1830; 1851; 1868; 1902; 1970	1971	8,000	2	2
Washington	1	1889	1889	26,930	103	61
West Virginia	2	1863; 1872	1872	22,970	74	42
Wisconsin	1	1848	1848	17,966	127	98(d)
Wyoming	1	1889	1890	23,170	67	36
American Samoa	2	1960; 1967	1967	5,000	9	5
Puerto Rico	1	1952	1952	9,338	6	6

(a) Data not available.
(b) Information only available from 1912 to present.
(c) Colonial charters with some alterations, in Connecticut (1638, 1662) and Rhode Island (1663), served as the first constitutions for these States.
(d) Amendments nullified by Supreme Court. Iowa: three on procedural grounds; Kansas: one; Wisconsin: two.
(e) One adopted amendment will not become effective until the Legislature enacts further legislation.
(f) The constitution of 1784 was extensively amended, rearranged and clarified in 1793. Figures show proposals and adoptions since 1793.
(g) Certain sections were revised by limited convention.

SOURCE: *Book of the States, 1974-75* (Lexington, Ky.: Council on State Governments, 1975).

> This constitution, and the laws of the United States which shall be made in pursuance thereof; and all treaties made, or which shall be made, under the authority of the United States, shall be the supreme law of the land; and the judge in every state shall be bound thereby, anything in the constitution or laws of any state to the contrary notwithstanding.

All state constitutions have a bill of rights, which asserts the basic freedoms of speech, press, religion, and assembly. There are frequent references to basic procedural rights, such as the writ of habeas corpus, trial by jury, protection against double jeopardy and self-incrimination, prohibitions against ex post facto laws, imprisonment for debt, unreasonable searches and seizures, and excessive bail. Frequently one finds in the state constitutions interesting "rights," which are not found in the national Constitution. The right of private clubs and fraternal organizations to sell alcoholic beverages is specifically enumerated in the Oregon Constitution. The Florida Constitution incorporates a "right to work" provision barring union shops.

All state constitutions reflect the American political tradition of separation of powers, with separate legislative, executive, and judicial articles establishing these separate branches of government. Generally, however, state constitutions emphasize legislative power over executive power. The historical explanation for this is that governors were appointed by the king in most colonies and the early constitutions reflected the colonists' distaste for executive authority. Yet the fact that constitutions are usually written by legislatures, legislative commissions, or constitutional conventions which resemble legislatures may also explain why legislative power is emphasized. Finally, the curtailment of executive power may reflect the desires of important interest groups in the states, who would prefer to deal with independent boards and commissions in the executive branch rather than a strong governor. (See Chapter 6 for further discussion of this point.)

Whether the reasons are historical or political, the executive branches of most state governments are weakened and divided by state constitutions. Executive powers are divided between the governor and many separately elected executive officers—attorney general, secretary of state, treasurer, auditor, lieutenant governor, state school superintendent, and others. State constitutions also curtail executive authority by establishing a multitude of boards or commissions to head executive departments. Membership on these boards and commissions is generally for long overlapping terms, which are not coextensive with the term of the governor.

Only the Nebraska Constitution provides for a unicameral legislature. All other state legislatures are divided into an upper and a lower chamber—making a total of ninety-nine state legislative bodies. In many states the basis for apportioning these bodies is set forth in the state constitution. However, since the guarantee of the U.S. Constitution that no state shall deny to any person the "equal protection of the laws" takes precedence over state constitutions, malapportionment embodied in a state constitution is no more acceptable to federal courts than malapportionment by state law. (See Chapter 5.)

All state constitutions provide for revision by amendment, but the difficulty of amending constitutions varies widely. Some states require a constitutional amendment to be passed in not one but two successive legislative sessions, in addition to being submitted to the electorate for its approval in a referendum. In the states requiring only one legislative session to propose an amendment, some permit a constitutional amendment to be proposed by a simple majority vote but others require either a two-thirds or a three-fifths vote. Every state except Delaware requires constitutional amendments proposed by the legislature to be submitted to the voters for approval in a referendum. Some states require an approval by a majority of all voters participating in the general election, rather than a majority of those voting on the amendment. This presents an additional obstacle to ratification of constitutional amendments, since voter participation in the choice of candidates is generally greater than participation in constitutional amendments. *The most common means of amending state constitutions is to provide for approval by a two-thirds vote in the legislature and then by a majority of the people voting on it in the next election.* In all but a few states, constitutions can also be changed by calling a constitutional convention. This is a very cumbersome procedure, although it can result in more extensive rewriting than the process of single amendments would achieve. Generally, the legislature must first submit to the voters the issue of calling a convention; if the voters approve, the convention must convene, draw up its revisions, and submit its revisions again to the electorate in a referendum.

All state constitutions have provisions regarding the organization and powers of local government. Local governments are really subdivisions of state governments; they are not legally independent governmental bodies. State constitutions generally describe the organization of counties, cities, towns, townships, boroughs, school districts, and special districts. They may delegate responsibilities to them for public safety, police, fire, sanitation, sewage and refuse disposal, hospitals, streets, and public health. State constitutions may establish tax and debt limits for local governments, describe the kinds of taxes they may levy, and prescribe a way in which their funds may be spent. In the absence of constitutional provisions governing local governments, these subordinate units must rely upon state legislatures for their organization and powers.

In recent years there has been a movement toward greater home rule for communities. More than half the states have provided for some semblance of home rule, which removes some of the internal affairs of communities from the intervention of state legislatures. Of course, when a "home rule" charter is granted to a community by an act of the legislature, it can be readily withdrawn or revised by the legislature. But when the authorization for municipal home rule is part of the state's constitution, it is somewhat less subject to state legislative intervention. Constitutional home rule is a more secure grant of power to communities than legislative home rule. (See Chapter 8 for further discussion.)

THE POLITICS OF STATE CONSTITUTIONS

The U.S. Constitution is a relatively brief document, which sets forth the fundamental structure of the government and the important limitations placed upon its power. It is simple and brief; it leaves to the Congress, the president, and the courts the power to determine public policy. But very few state constitutions are simple or brief, and most of them set forth many details of public policy.[3] Such constitutional detail makes the need for amendment quite frequent. Unlike the U.S. Constitution, state constitutions are too detailed and specific to permit much change through interpretation. Hence, most existing constitutions have been amended many times, and few elections are held in which voters are not asked to vote on constitutional amendments.

What is the political significance of these constitutional restraints on state power? It appears that lengthy detailed constitutions tend to *strengthen the position of conservative interests,* those who wish to preserve the status quo. It also tends to *strengthen the role of the courts,* since an abundance of constitutional detail leads to decision making through court litigation.

Professor Lewis A. Froman has argued convincingly that lengthy and detailed state constitutions reflect the strength of organized interest groups in the states.[4] He reasons that in states where interest groups are stronger, a larger number of special privileges and advantages will be granted in state constitutions. The stronger the interest groups in the state, the greater the length of the state constitution, the greater the number of proposed amendments, and the greater the number of amend-

[3] See Robert B. Dishman, *State Constitutions: The Shape of the Document,* rev. ed. (New York: National Municipal League, 1968).

[4] Lewis A. Froman, Jr., "Some Effects of Interest Group Strength in State Politics," *American Political Science Review,* 60 (December, 1966): 952–62.

ments adopted. To test his theory about state constitutions, he used the judgments of political scientists about which states had strong, moderately strong, or weak interest groups, and he then compared the constitutions of each of these three groups of states. The results are shown in Table 1–5. States with strong interest groups tend to have long constitu-

TABLE 1.5   Relationships Between Strength of Interest Groups and Three Dependent Variables

Strength of Interest Groups	Average Length of Constitution	N^1	Average No. of Proposed Amendments per Year	N^2	Average No. of Adopted Amendments per Year	N^3
Strong	33,233	24	2.97	19	1.58	22
Moderate	17,985	14	1.14	12	.76	14
Weak	14,828	7	.68	5	.41	7

[1] Alaska and Hawaii are excluded from this table. In addition, Idaho, New Hampshire, and North Dakota were not classified by strength of interest groups.

[2] Arkansas, Colorado, Connecticut, Delaware, Iowa, Michigan, North Carolina, Utah, and Washington are excluded for lack of data.

[3] Michigan and North Carolina are excluded for lack of data.

SOURCE: Lewis A. Froman, Jr., "Some Effects of Interest Group Strength in State Politics," *American Political Science Review,* 60 (December 1966), 956.

tions, which deal directly with questions of public policy (labor practices, regulation of utilities, transportation problems, and so on). Typically interest groups press for constitutional provisions to protect their interests because they are unwilling to trust future legislatures in matters of public policy. Thus, strong interest group states are likely to have lengthy constitutions, which, among other things, specify public utility tariffs and charges, limit the taxing powers of the states and communities, place restrictions on state debt, specify the duties and powers of public service commissions and the regulation of utilities, set forth regulations on insurance companies, specify the duties of local government officials, set the salaries of the state and local officeholders, exempt certain industries from taxation, regulate school systems, and so on. He concludes that constitutions are one of the means by which advantages and disadvantages are distributed in political systems and that the strength of interest groups in gaining special constitutional advantages can be observed in the length of state constitutions and in amending activity.

Important political interests are at stake in constitutional revision. Legislatures are understandably hesitant about calling constitutional conventions. A "runaway" convention may rearrange the balance of political power in the state. It may strengthen the governor at the expense of the legislature, authorize new taxes, eliminate the earmarking of certain revenues, or allocate greater power over urban affairs to cities. In other words, a constitutional convention may seriously alter the status quo. Interest groups that presently enjoy special privileges or exemptions from taxation in the state constitution have reason to fear a constitutional convention. They may stress the expense involved in such a convention or the danger that "radical reformers" may foist their dangerous ideas upon an unsuspecting public. Taxpayer groups may fear that constitutional limitations on taxing powers may be removed. Public officials may be concerned that their offices will be abolished. In other words, constitutional revision is a political thicket which discourages all but the most courageous of men.

Reform interests—good-government groups, the League of Women Voters, and political science professors—argue that the constitution and the structure of state and local government should be simple, brief, and understandable. It should permit the legislature and the governor to make public policy. It should allocate power to the governor and the legislature commensurate with their responsibilities, and it should enable the voters to hold elected officials clearly accountable for public decisions. It should permit local governmental consolidation and community home rule. The need for frequent amendment should be eliminated.

These ideas are not received with enthusiasm by organized interests in the states, but they do appeal to many voters. The idea of successful constitutional revision appeals to an ambitious governor with aspirations to higher office. A favorite device for constitutional revision is the establishment of a constitutional revision commission. A typical commission is created by an act of a legislature, and its membership usually includes legislators, executive officials, and prominent citizens. Legislatures generally prefer such a commission to a constitutional convention, because a commission can only study and report to a legislature on the changes it deems necessary. Such recommendations are usually handled like regular constitutional amendments, although they may be more sweeping than ordinary amendments.

POLITICS IN CONSTITUTIONAL CONVENTIONS

While there has been only one national Constitutional Convention, in 1787, there have been many state constitutional conventions—over 200 in all and more than a dozen in the last decade.[5] These conventions

---

[5] Albert L. Sturm, "Constitutions," in *Book of the States, 1974–75* (Lexington: Council of State Governments, 1975), p. 9.

generally come into being in response to demands by reform-oriented "good-government" interest groups, often with the assistance of aspiring politicians who are seeking higher office and want to use the convention as a stepping-stone. But the activities of constitutional reformers usually spark counteractivities from interests desiring to preserve the status quo —political officeholders, party politicians, bureaucrats, and business interests, particularly those subject to state regulation.

Participants in state constitutional conventions can be categorized as follows: [6]

> *Reformers,* who are active in civic organizations and generally recruited from upper-class segments of society. Their motivation is ideological— they are interested primarily in "good government."

> *Aspirants* for higher political office, who are often young lawyers seeking a reputation for reform and innovation. Their motivation is career advancement—they are generally but not always on the side of reform.

> *Chieftains* with high public office in the state, who frequently exercise internal convention leadership. Their motivation is the preservation of their leadership in state affairs—they are generally fluid on the issue of reform.

> *Statesmen,* who have previously held high public office (ex-governors, senators, etc.) or who currently hold judgeships. Their motivation is prestige—they are to be found on either side of major issues.

> *Stand-ins* for party leaders or officeholders, who are selected for their past party loyalty and who generally follow the advice of those who selected them. They are motivated by recognition they receive by being there— they are likely supporters of the status quo.

> *Standpatters* are middle-level or minor officeholders or bureaucrats, who enter the convention to protect a present position in the government structure. They are motivated by a desire to preserve their political position—they are consistent opponents of major reforms.

Membership in constitutional conventions is generally weighted in the direction of reform, since the calling of the convention itself indicates the strength of reformers in the state political system. There is a relationship, however, between the type of election for delegate and the type of delegate selected. Partisan elections (delegates run under party labels) with small-size districts maximize the selection of party activists, current officeholders, and bureaucrats interested in preserving the status quo. Nonpartisan elections (delegates run without party designation)

---

[6] For a test of these categories in Maryland, Rhode Island, and New York, see Elmer E. Cornwell, Jr., Jay S. Goodman, and Wayne R. Swanson, "State Constitutional Conventions: Delegates, Roll Calls and Issues," *Midwest Journal of Political Science,* 14 (February, 1970): 105–30.

with at-large or multimember constituencies maximize the number of "reformer," "good-government" types.

A special study of the Illinois Constitutional Convention of 1970, to which delegates were selected on a nonpartisan ballot, reported "muted partisanship" and "bipartisan accommodation."[7] While roll-call voting still reflected party identification, as well as the influence of the powerful Chicago mayor, Richard J. Daley, other voting dimensions also emerged. These included: "status quo versus progressives"; "Jacksonians versus Whigs" (appointment versus election of public officials); "cosmopolitans versus locals" (delegates concerned with statewide versus local interests); "fundamentalists versus modernists" (school prayer, abortions, etc.); "human rights versus property rights" (death penalty, free speech, etc.); and "expansion versus restriction of state tax power." Interestingly, occupation, region, age, race, or sex did not significantly divide delegates on roll-call votes. Nor was there a clear-cut liberal-conservative division. The Illinois convention was an example of moderation; only modest changes were made in the constitution itself. Both parties endorsed the product and it was approved by the electorate.

The basic division within most conventions is between reformers versus preservers of the status quo. This line of division is often more pronounced than the division between Republicans versus Democrats, urban versus rural, a governor's supporters versus his opponents, legislators versus nonlegislators, and so forth. Reformers in recent state conventions have pressed for many of the same provisions—shorter constitution, reduced size of the legislature, executive officials, municipal home rule, removal of limitations on taxing authority, removal of special constitutional provisions dealing with business and industry, court reform, and so forth.[8]

Despite the influence of reformers at constitutional conventions, the final outcome of constitutional revision through the convention method has been mixed. While new constitutions have generally moved states closer to the "reform model," the extent of change has not been very great.[9] Since new constitutions must go to the voters for approval, reform-oriented constitution makers must be careful not to offend voters with controversial innovations. They must also try to satisfy all major

[7] See Jack R. Van Der Slik et al., "Patterns of Partisanship in a Nonpartisan Representational Setting: The Illinois Constitutional Convention," *American Journal of Political Science*, 18 (February, 1974): 95–116.

[8] For an excellent political analysis of constitutional conventions in Maryland, Rhode Island, and New York, see Cornwell et al., "State Constitutional Conventions."

[9] Reformers do not always agree on what the "ideal" state constitution should look like. For a close approximation of the reform model, see *Model State Constitution* (New York: National Municipal League, 1968).

blocs at the convention in order to avoid their leaving the convention only to work against ratification. New constitutions are very vulnerable at the polls. Generally voters must vote yes or no on the whole document; voters who are offended by a single provision may vote no even when all other provisions are acceptable. Different voters may be voting no for different reasons, but a cumulation of specific no votes on separate provisions may spell defeat for the whole document. Provisions that frequently prove controversial include state aid to parochial schools (see Chapter 14), legislative pay increases (see Chapter 5), state civil rights guarantees (see Chapter 13), and welfare reform (see Chapter 16). (In the past voters also tended to defeat constitutional clauses aimed at lowering the voting age; but now that this reform has been incorporated into the Twenty-sixth Amendment of the U.S. Constitution, the issue has been removed from state politics. See Chapter 3.)

Ratification of new state constitutions is by no means assured. A careful study of ratification voting on nine recent state constitutions reveals that three were approved by the voters and six rejected.[10] Generalizations about factors affecting voter support or opposition to new constitutions are difficult to derive, even on close examination of voting results. There is some evidence that higher socioeconomic groups give greater support to ratification than lower socioeconomic groups. But special "contextual variables" usually explain ratification outcomes more successfully than socioeconomic or partisan factors. For example, in Arkansas opponents of ratification convinced voters the new constitution was "atheistic" and would lead to new taxes. In Maryland the new document was portrayed as "elitist, intellectual, and pro-black." In Kentucky there were partisan divisions over ratification as well as opposition from rural residents and local officeholders whose jobs would lose constitutional protection in the new document. In New York there was fear of higher taxes, partisanship, and scandal over the pay the constitution delegates received ($15,000 for five months' part-time work). In the successful states, partisanship was carefully avoided, the changes proposed were very modest, and state leaders of both parties publicly supported the document. Moreover, some of the less popular items proposed were separated from the main document for separate voting.

Of course, reform interests have not yet succeeded in simplifying state constitutions or in eliminating the special privileges and exemptions contained in them. Newer constitutions, however, are somewhat

[10] Jay S. Goodman et al., "Public Responses to State Constitutional Revision," *American Journal of Political Science*, 17 (August, 1973): 511–96. Approved were Connecticut (1965), Hawaii (1968), and Illinois (1970). Rejected were Kentucky (1966), Rhode Island (1968), New York (1967), Maryland (1967), New Mexico (1969), and Arkansas (1970).

shorter and more streamlined than the average state constitution. All the newer documents tend to strengthen the executive, provide for more equitable apportionment, and remove limitation on legislative power. But most state constitutions are still very conservative documents. There is not much hope that state constitutions will be simplified in the near future or that special exemptions and privileges will be eliminated.

States, communities, and American federalism

THE POLITICS OF DECENTRALIZATION

Why have state and local governments anyway? Why not have a central-ized political system with a single responsible government accountable to national majorities in national elections—a government capable of implementing uniform policies throughout the country?

Over a century ago Alexis de Tocqueville, in a haunting, perhaps prophetic, passage in his *Democracy in America*, described a nation of people "equal and alike," totally dependent upon a single centralized government. His melancholic vision is worth quoting at length:

> I seek to trace the novel features under which despotism may appear in the world. The first thing that strikes the observation is an innumera-ble multitude of men, all equal and alike, incessantly endeavoring to procure the petty and paltry pleasures with which they glut their lives. Each of them, living apart, is as a stranger to the fate of all the rest; his children and his private friends constitute to him the whole of mankind. As for the rest of his fellow citizens, he is close to them, but does not see them; he touches them, but does not feel them; he exists only in himself and for himself alone; and if his kindred still remain to him, he may be said at any rate to have lost his country.

Chapter two

Above this race of men stands an immense and tutelary power, which takes upon itself alone to secure their gratifications and to watch over their fate. That power is absolute, minute, regular, provident, and mild. It would be like the authority of a parent if, like that authority, its object was to prepare men for manhood; but it seeks, on the contrary, to keep them in perpetual childhood: it is well content that the people should rejoice, provided they think of nothing but rejoicing. For their happiness such a government willingly labors, but it chooses to be the sole agent and the only arbiter of that happiness; it provides for their security, forsees and supplies their necessities, facilitates their pleasures, manages their principal concerns, directs their industry, regulates the descent of property, and subdivides their inheritances: what remains, but to spare them all the care of thinking and all the trouble of living? . . .

After having thus successively taken each member of the community in its powerful grasp and fashioned him at will, the supreme power then extends its arm over the whole community. It covers the surface of society with a network of small complicated rules, minute and uniform, through which the most original minds and the most energetic characters cannot penetrate, to rise above the crowd. The will of man is not shattered, but softened, bent, and guided; men are seldom forced by it to act, but they are constantly restrained from acting. Such a power does not destroy, but it prevents existence; it does not tyrannize, but it compresses, enervates, extinguishes, and stupefies a people, till each nation is reduced to nothing better than a flock of timid and industrial animals, of which the government is the shepherd.[1]

Let us describe some of the political advantages in decentralized government.[2]

1. Political decentralization frequently reduces the severity of conflict in a society. Decentralization is a classic method by which disparate peoples can be brought together in a nation without engendering irresolvable conflict. Conflicts between geographically defined groups in America are resolved by allowing each to pursue its own policies within the separate states and communities; this avoids battling over a single national policy to be applied uniformly throughout the land.

Of course, denationalizing conflicts sometimes maintains the stability of the national political system at the price of "sweeping under the rug" very serious conflicts. Certainly this was the case with regard to the questions of slavery and segregation. For long periods of American history these issues were cast out of national politics in an effort to reduce conflict and achieve unity between North and South. For more than

---

[1] Alexis de Tocqueville, *Democracy in America*, trans. by Reeve, Bowen and Bradley (New York: Random House—Vintage Books, 1955), II 336–37.

[2] For a full discussion of the advantages and disadvantages of decentralization, see Norman Furniss, "The Practical Significance of Decentralization," *Journal of Politics*, 36 (November, 1974): 958–82.

sixty years after the Constitutional Convention, national conflict over slavery was reduced by denationalizing the conflict. When the question of slavery did emerge as a national issue in the 1850s, nationalization of the conflict led directly to Civil War. A decade after the end of the Civil War the issue of segregation was denationalized, and for another sixty years or more national conflict over the issue was avoided. But the price of denationalizing the issue was paid by black Americans. It was not until the question was nationalized again in the 1950s and 1960s that blacks began to make significant progress.

2. Decentralization distributes power more widely among different sets of leaders. The widespread distribution of power is generally thought to be a protection against tyranny; a plurality of leadership is generally believed to be more democratic than a single set of all-powerful leaders. To the extent that pluralism exists in America, state and local governments have undoubtedly contributed to it. Robert Dahl observes that "state and local governments have provided a number of centers of power whose autonomy is strongly protected by Constitutional and political traditions. A governor of a state or the mayor of a large city may not be the political equal of a president (at least not often); but he is most assuredly not a subordinate. In dealing with a governor or mayor, a president rarely if ever commands; he negotiates; he may even plead. Here then is a part of the intermediate stratum of leadership that Tocqueville looked to as a barrier to tyranny." [3] It should be added that state and local governments provide a political base of offices for the opposition party when it has lost national elections. In this way state and local governments contribute to party competition in America by helping to tide over the losing party after electoral defeat so that it may remain strong enough to challenge incumbents at the next election. And finally, of course, state and local governments provide a channel of recruitment for national political leaders. National leaders can be drawn from a pool of leaders experienced in state and local politics.

3. Decentralization allows more people to participate in the political system. There are nearly eighty thousand governments in America— states, counties, townships, municipalities, towns, special districts, and school districts. Nearly a million people hold some kind of public office. The opportunity to participate doubtlessly contributes to popular support of the political system. Many people are given the opportunity to exercise political leadership; moreover, state and local governments are widely regarded as being "closer to the people." Survey data reveal that Americans look upon local governments as being more manageable

[3] Robert A. Dahl, *Pluralist Democracy in America* (Chicago: Rand McNally & Co., 1967), p. 189.

and more responsive to individual desires than the national government. Thus, by providing more opportunities for direct citizen involvement in government, state and local governments contribute to the popular sense of political effectiveness and well-being.

4. Decentralization makes government more manageable and efficient. Frequently we are told that our present system of multiple state and local governments is inefficient and unmanageable and in need of reform. And certainly there is much room for improvement. But imagine the bureaucracy, red tape, and confusion if every government activity in every local community in the nation—police, schools, roads, fire fighting, garbage collection, sewage disposal, and so forth—were controlled by a centralized administration in Washington. If local governments did not exist, they would have to be invented. Even in the Soviet Union—where centralized discipline and policy control are a matter of political ideology—national leaders have been forced to resort to decentralization simply as a matter of practical expediency. Government becomes arbitrary when a bureaucracy far from the scene directs a local administractor to proceed with the impossible—local conditions notwithstanding. Decentralization softens the rigidity of law and makes unpopular laws more tolerable.

THE STRUCTURE OF AMERICAN FEDERALISM

In deciding in 1869 that a state had no constitutional right to secede from the union, Chief Justice Salmon P. Chase described the legal character of American federalism:

> The preservation of the states and the maintenance of their governments, are as much within the design and care of the constitution as the preservation of the union and the maintenance of the national government. The constitution, in all of its provisions, looks to an indestructible union, composed of indestructible states.[4]

What is meant by "an indestructible union, composed of indestructible states"? The American federal union is an indissoluble partnership between the states and the national government. The Constitution of the United States allocated power between two separate authorities, the nation and the states, each of which was to be independent of the other. Both the nation and the states were allowed to enforce their laws through their own officials and courts directly on individuals. The Constitution itself was the only legal source of authority for the division of powers

---

[4] *Texas* v. *White*, 7 Wallace 700 (1869).

between the states and the nation. The American federal system is a strong national government, coupled with a strong state government, in which authority and power are shared, constitutionally and practically.

The framework of American federalism is determined by (1) the powers delegated by the Constitution to the national government; (2) the constitutional guarantees given to the states; (3) the powers denied by the Constitution to the national government and to the states; (4) the constitutional provisions giving the states a role in the composition of the national government; (5) the subsequent interpretation of these constitutional provisions by the courts; and the practices that evolved for the settlement of disputes between the nation and the states.

1. Article I, Section 8, of the U.S. Constitution lists eighteen grants of delegated power to Congress, including authority over matters of war and foreign affairs, the power to declare war, raise armies, equip navies, establish uniform rules for naturalization, and so on. Another series of delegated powers are related to control of the economy, including the power to coin money, to control its value, and to regulate foreign and interstate commerce. The national government has been given independent powers of taxation "to pay the debts and provide for the common defense and general welfare of the United States." It has the power to establish its own court system, to decide cases arising under the Constitution and the laws and treaties of the U.S. and cases involving certain kinds of parties. The national government was given the authority to grant copyright patents, establish post offices, enact bankruptcy laws, punish counterfeiting, punish crimes committed on the high seas, and govern the District of Columbia. Finally, after seventeen grants of express power, came the power "to make all laws which shall be necessary and proper for carrying into execution the foregoing powers, and all other powers vested by this constitution in the government of the United States or in any department or officer thereof." This is generally referred to as the Necessary and Proper Clause.

These delegated powers, when coupled with the National Supremacy Clause of Article VI, insured a powerful national government. The National Supremacy Clause was quite specific regarding the relationship between the national government and the states. In questions involving conflict between the state laws and the Constitution, laws, or treaties of the U.S.:

> This constitution, and the laws of the United States which shall be made in pursuance thereof; and all treaties made or which shall be made under the authority of the United States shall be the supreme law of the land; and the judges in every state shall be bound thereby, anything in the constitution or laws of any state to the contrary notwithstanding.

2. Despite these broad grants of power to the national government, the states retained a great deal of authority over the lives of their citizens. The Tenth Amendment reaffirmed the idea that the national government had only certain delegated powers and that all powers not delegated to it were retained by the states:

> The powers not delegated to the United States by the constitution, nor prohibited by it to the states, are reserved to the states respectively, or to the people.

The states retained control over the ownership and use of property; the regulation of offenses against persons and property (criminal law and civil law); the regulation of marriage and divorce; the control of business, labor, farming, trades, and professions; the provision of education, welfare, health, hospitals, and other social welfare activities; and provision of highways, roads, canals, and other public works. The states retained full authority over the organization and control of local government units. Finally, the states, like the federal government, possessed the power to tax and spend for the general welfare.

3. The Constitution denies some powers to both national and state governments; these denials generally safeguard individual rights. Both nation and states were forbidden to pass ex post facto laws or bills of attainder. The first eight amendments to the Constitution, "the Bill of Rights," originally applied to the federal government, but the Fourteenth Amendment, passed by Congress in 1866, provided that the states must also adhere to fundamental guarantees of individual liberty. "No state shall make or enforce any law which shall abridge the privileges or immunities of the citizens of the United States; nor shall any state deprive any person of life, liberty or property without due process of law; nor deny to any person within its jurisdiction equal protection of the laws."

Some powers were denied only to the states, generally as a safeguard to national unity, including the powers to coin money, enter into treaties with foreign powers, interfere with the obligations of contracts, levy duties on imports or exports without congressional consent, maintain military forces in peacetime, engage in war, or enter into compacts with foreign nations or other states.

4. The states also play an important role in the composition of the national government. U.S. representatives must be apportioned among the states according to their population every ten years. Governors have the authority to fill vacancies in Congress, and every state must have at least one representative regardless of population. The

Senate of the United States is composed of two senators from each state regardless of the state's population. The times, places, and manner of holding elections for Congress are determined by the states. The president is chosen by electors, allotted to each state on the basis of its senators and representatives. Amendments to the U.S. Constitution must be ratified by three-fourths of the states.

THE EVOLUTION OF AMERICAN FEDERALISM

The importance of formal constitutional arrangements should not be underestimated; however, the American federal system is a product of more than formal constitutional provisions. It is also shaped by the interpretations placed upon constitutional principles and the way in which disputes over state and national authority have been resolved.

The real meaning of American federalism has emerged in the heat of political conflict between states and nation. In the formulative days of the new Republic, Chief Justice John Marshall, who presided over the Supreme Court from 1801 to 1835, became a major architect of American federalism. Under John Marshall, *the Supreme Court assumed the role of arbiter in disputes between state and national authority.* It was under John Marshall that the Supreme Court in *Marbury* v. *Madison* assumèd the power to interpret the U.S. Constitution authoritatively. Nothing in the Constitution explicitly vested the Supreme Court with the power to render authoritative interpretations of the Constitution; from time to time Congress, the president, and the states have laid claim to this power. But John Marshall argued forcefully that Article III of the Constitution, which says that "the judicial power of the United States shall be vested in one Supreme Court," made the Court the final arbiter in conflicts over the meaning of the Constitution. Marshall argued that the "the judicial power" historically meant the power to interpret the meaning of the law, and since the Constitution was the supreme *law* of the land, it was the legitimate duty of the Supreme Court to interpret that law. This meant that the Supreme Court assumed the role of umpire of the federal system and referee of conflicts between nation and states.

The fact that the referee of disputes between state and national authority has been the *national* Supreme Court has had a profound influence on the development of American federalism. Since the Supreme Court is a *national* institution, organized and staffed by national authority, one might say that in disputes between nation and states, one of the members of the two contending teams is also serving as umpire.

Constitutionally speaking, then, there is really *no* limitation on national as against state authority *if* all three branches of the national government —the Congress, the President, and the Court—act together to override state authority. The Constitution and the laws of the United States "made in pursuance thereof" are the supreme laws of the land, "anything in the constitution or laws of any state to the contrary notwithstanding." And the Supreme Court, a national institution, through its "judicial power" interprets the Constitution and decides what laws are "made in pursuance thereof." Thus, *Marbury* v. *Madison* paved the way for the development of national power.

Chief Justice John Marshall was also responsible for making the *Necessary and Proper Clause* the most significant grant of constitutional power to the national government. Political conflict over the scope of national power arose before the new Republic had been in operation for a year. In 1790 Alexander Hamilton, as Secretary of the Treasury, proposed the establishment of a national bank. Congress acted on Hamilton's suggestion in 1791, establishing a national bank to serve as a depository for national money and to facilitate federal borrowing. Jeffersonians considered the national bank dangerous centralization in government and objected that the power to establish a national bank was nowhere to be found in the enumerated powers of Congress. Thomas Jefferson contended that Congress had no constitutional authority to establish a bank because a bank was not "indispensably necessary" in carrying out its delegated functions. Hamilton replied that Congress could easily deduce the power to establish a bank from grants of authority in the Constitution relating to currency and other aspects of national finance, backed by the clause authorizing Congress "to make all laws which will be necessary and proper for carrying into execution the foregoing powers." Jefferson interpreted the word "necessary" to mean "indispensable," but Hamilton argued that the national government had the right to choose the manner and means of performing its delegated functions and was not restricted to employing only those means considered indispensable in the performance of its functions. The question eventually reached the Supreme Court in 1819 when Maryland levied a tax on the national bank and the bank refused to pay it. In the case of *McCulloch* v. *Maryland*, Chief Justice John Marshall accepted the broader Hamiltonian version of the Necessary and Proper Clause:

> Let the end be legitimate, let it be within the scope of the Constitution, and all means which are appropriate, which are plainly adopted to that end, which are not prohibited but consistent with the letter and the spirit of the Constitution, are constitutional.[5]

[5] *McCulloch* v. *Maryland*, 4 Wheaton 316 (1819).

The *McCulloch* case firmly established the principle that the Necessary and Proper Clause gives Congress the right to choose its means for carrying out the enumerated powers of the national government. Today Congress can devise programs, create agencies, and establish national laws on the basis of long chains of reasoning from the most meager phrases of the constitutional text because of the broad interpretation of the Necessary and Proper Clause. The Supreme Court has generally, although not universally, acceded to broad exercises of congressional power under the Necessary and Proper Clause.

Another major contribution of the Marshall Court was its interpretation of the *National Supremacy Clause*. In *McCulloch* v. *Maryland*, the Court held Maryland's tax on the national bank to be unconstitutional on the grounds that the state tax interfered with a national activity which was being carried out under the Constitution and laws "made in pursuance thereof." Maryland's state taxing law was declared unconstitutional because it conflicted with the federal law establishing the national bank. From Marshall's time to the present, the National Supremacy Clause has meant that states could not refuse to obey federal laws. States have no right to disobey or resist the application of valid federal laws.

Of course it was one thing to announce that the state had no constitutional right to resist federal authority, but it was quite another thing to establish this principle as a political reality. In the famous Virginia and Kentucky Resolutions, the early Jeffersonians devised a doctrine of state "interposition" to resist enforcement of the national government's Alien and Sedition Acts of 1798 which were passed by a Federalist Congress. The Jeffersonians argued, rightly no doubt, that the Alien and Sedition Acts violated the Constitution's guarantees of free speech and press. But the "interposition" argument went on to assert that when the national government acted "unconstitutionally" in the eyes of a state, a state could "interpose" itself between its people and the operation of an unconstitutional federal law. Since the Jeffersonians captured the presidency in 1800, and a Jeffersonian Congress repealed the Alien and Sedition Acts in 1801, the interposition argument in the Kentucky and Virginia Resolutions was never formally challenged in the courts.

The *Civil War* was, of course, the greatest crisis of the American federal system. Did a state have the right to oppose national law to the point of secession? In the years preceding the Civil War, John C. Calhoun argued that the Constitution was a compact made by the *states* in a sovereign capacity rather than by the *people* in their national capacity. Calhoun contended that the federal government was an agent of the states, that the states retained their sovereignty in this compact, and that the federal government must not violate the compact, under the penalty of state nullification or even secession. Calhoun's doctrine was embodied in the Constitution of the Confederacy, which begins with the words "We, the people of the Confederate States, each state acting in its sovereign and independent character, in order to form a permanent federal government . . ." This wording contrasts with the preamble of the United States Constitution, "We, the people of the United States, in order to form a more perfect union . . ." The difference emphasizes Calhoun's thesis that the central government should be an agency of the states rather than of the people.

The issue was decided in the nation's bloodiest war. What was decided on the battlefield between 1861 and 1865 was confirmed by the Supreme Court in 1869: "Ours is an indestructible union, composed of indestructible states." [6] Yet the states' rights doctrines, and political disputes over the character of American federalism, did not disappear with Lee's surrender at Appomattox. The Thirteenth, Fourteenth, and Fifteenth Amendments, passed by the Reconstruction Congress, were clearly aimed at limiting state power in the interests of individual freedom. The Thirteenth Amendment eliminated slavery in the states, the Fifteenth Amendment prevented states from discriminating against Negroes in the right to vote; and the Fourteenth Amendment declared that "No State shall make or enforce any law which shall abridge the privileges or immunities of citizens of the United States; nor shall any state deprive any person of life, liberty, or property without due process of law; nor deny to any person within its jurisdiction the equal protection of the laws." These amendments delegated to Congress the power to secure their enforcement. Yet for several generations these amendments were narrowly construed and added little, if anything, to national power. By tacit agreement, after southern states demonstrated their continued political importance in the disputed presidential election of 1876, the federal government refrained from using its power to enforce these civil rights.

But after World War II, the Supreme Court began to build a national system of civil rights based upon the *Fourteenth Amendment*. In early cases, the Court held that the Fourteenth Amendment prevented states from interfering with free speech, free press, or religious practices. But not until 1954, in the Supreme Court's desegregation decision in *Brown* v. *Board of Education* in Topeka, Kansas, did the Court begin to call for the full assertion of national authority on behalf of civil rights.[7] When the Court decided that the Fourteenth Amendment prohibited the states from segregating the races in public schools, it was asserting national authority over deeply held beliefs and long-standing practices in many of the states.

---

[6] *Texas* v. *White*, 7 Wallace 700 (1869).

[7] *Brown* v. *Board of Education of Topeka, Kansas*, 347 U.S. 483 (1954).

The Supreme Court's use of the Fourteenth Amendment to insure a national system of civil rights supported by the power of the federal government is an important step in the evolution of the American federal system. Of course, the controversy over federally imposed desegregation in the southern states renewed the debate over states' rights versus national authority. The vigorous resistance of southern states to desegregation in the decade following *Brown* v. *Board of Education* testified to the continued strength of the states in the American federal system. Despite the clear mandate of the Supreme Court, the southern states succeeded in avoiding all but token integration for more than ten years.[8] Yet only occasionally did resistance take the form of "interposition." Governor Faubus used the Arkansas National Guard to prevent the desegration of Little Rock Central High School in 1957, but this "interposition" was ended quickly when President Eisenhower ordered the National Guard removed and sent units of the United States Army to enforce national authority. In 1962 President Kennedy took similar action when Governor Ross Barnett of Mississippi personally barred the entry of a black student to the University of Mississippi, despite a federal court order requiring his admission. Governor George Wallace of Alabama "stood in the doorway" to prevent desegregation but left his post at the doorway several hours later when federal marshals arrived. These actions failed to alter the principle of national supremacy in the American political system.

The growth of national power under the *Interstate Commerce Clause* is also an important development in the evolution of American federalism. The Industrial Revolution in America created a national economy with a nationwide network of transportation and communication and the potential for national economic depressions. In response to the growth of the national economy, Congress progressively widened the definition of "interstate commerce" to include the regulation of interstate transportation (particularly the railroads) and of communication (particularly telephone and telegraph). Industrialization created interstate businesses, which could only be regulated by the national government; this was recognized in the passage of the Sherman Anti-Trust Act in 1890. Yet for a time, the Supreme Court placed obstacles in the way of national authority over the economy, and by so doing created a "crisis" in American federalism. For many years, the Court narrowly construed interstate commerce to mean only the movement of goods and services across state lines, and until the late 1930s, the Supreme Court insisted that agriculture, mining, manufacturing, and labor relations were outside the reach of the delegated powers of the national government. But when con-

---

[8] See Chapter 13, "Black Politics, Civil Rights, and Public Order."

fronted with the depression of the 1930s and the threat of presidential attack on the membership of the Court itself, the Court yielded. In *National Labor Relations Board* v. *Jones and Laughlin Steel Corporation* in 1937, the Court recognized the principle that production and distribution of goods and services for a national market could be regulated by Congress under the Interstate Commerce Clause. The effect was to give the national government effective control over the national economy, and today few economic activities are not within the reach of congressional power.

THE GROWTH OF POWER IN WASHINGTON

Over the years the national government has acquired much greater power in the federal system than the Founding Fathers originally envisioned. The growth of power in Washington has not necessarily meant a reduction in the powers of states and local governments—in fact, *all* governments have vastly increased their powers and responsibilities in the twentieth century. But today the national government is no longer really a government with only "delegated" or "enumerated" powers. The delegated powers of the national government are now so broadly defined —particularly the power to tax and spend for the general welfare and the interstate commerce power—that the government in Washington is involved in every aspect of American life. There are really no segments of public activity "reserved" to the states or the people.

It is possible to argue that even in the earliest days of the Republic, the national government was deeply involved in public activities that were not specifically delegated to it in the Constitution.[9] The first Congress of the United States in the famous Northwest Ordinance, providing for the government of the territories to the west of the Appalachian Mountains, authorized grants of federal land for the establishment of public schools, and, by so doing, showed a concern for education, an area "reserved" to the states by the Constitution. Again, in 1863 in the Morrill Land Grant Act, Congress provided grants of land to the states to promote higher education.

Many commentators feel that the date 1913, when the Sixteenth Amendment gave the federal government the power to tax income directly, was the beginning of a new era in American federalism. Congress had been given the power to tax and spend for the general welfare in

---

[9] See Daniel J. Elazar, *The American Partnership: Inter-governmental Cooperation in Nineteenth-Century United States* (Chicago: University of Chicago Press, 1962).

Article I of the Constitution. But the Sixteenth Amendment helped to shift the balance of financial power from the states to Washington, when it gave Congress the power to tax the incomes of corporations and individuals on a progressive basis. The income tax gave the federal government the power to raise large sums of money, which it proceeded to spend for the general welfare as well as for defense. It is no coincidence that the first major grant-in-aid programs (agricultural extension in 1914, highways in 1916, vocational education in 1917, and public health in 1918) all came shortly after the inauguration of the federal income tax.

The federal "grant-in-aid" has become a principal instrument in the expansion of national power. It should be noted that there is no general grant of power to the national government in the Constitution to protect and advance the public health, safety, welfare, or morals. Theoretically, the national government may not enact laws dealing directly with housing, streets, zoning, schools, health, police protection, fire fighting, crime, and so on, simply because such a law might contribute to the general welfare. However, it may *tax* or *borrow* or *spend money* for the general welfare, even though it has no power in the Constitution to regulate welfare activities directly. This is a subtle distinction, but it is an important one. For example, Congress cannot outlaw billboards on highways, because billboard regulation is not among the enumerated powers of Congress in the U.S. Constitution. But the federal government, through its power to tax and spend, can provide financial assistance to the states to build highways and then pass a law threatening to withdraw financial aid if the states do not regulate billboards themselves. Thus, the federal government can involve itself in billboard regulation through its taxing power and financial resources, even though this field is "reserved" to the states.

The Great Depression of the 1930s brought pressure upon the national government to use its tax and spending powers in a wide variety of areas formerly reserved to states and communities. The federal government initiated grant-in-aid programs to states and communities for public assistance, unemployment compensation, employment services, child welfare, public housing, urban renewal, and so on; it also expanded federal grant-in-aid programs in highways, vocational education, and rehabilitation. The inadequacy of state and local revenue systems to meet the financial crisis created by the depression contributed significantly to the expansion of federal power.

During World War II and the cold war that followed, federal grant-in-aid programs contrived to expand while taking on labels that made them appear to be part of the defense effort. Aid to public schools came in a program to assist school districts experiencing rapid population growth because of military bases, defense industries, or federal installa-

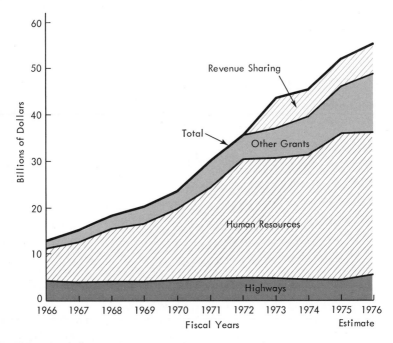

FIGURE 2–1   Federal aid to state and local governments.

tions. In 1956 the Interstate and *Defense* Highway Act greatly expanded federal aid for the construction of the interstate highway system. In the National *Defense* Education Act of 1957, federal grants and loans were authorized for higher education. How important these highway and education programs were to the defense effort is debatable, but identifying them with defense made them more attractive to Congress and expanded future federal activity in domestic affairs. The "Great Society" programs of the 1960s brought a myriad of new federal grant programs in urban affairs, education, economic development, manpower, and education. Figure 2–1 shows the expansion of federal grant programs in a single decade.

FEDERAL GRANTS-IN-AID: PROS AND CONS

Today grant-in-aid programs are the single most important source of federal influence over state policy. Approximately one-fifth of all state and local government revenues are from federal grants. This money is paid out through a staggering number and variety of programs. There are probably five hundred different federal grant programs in existence today. So numerous and diverse are federal aid programs that substantial information gap surrounds their availability, purpose, and requirements. Learning about the availability of federal grants, and mastering the art of grant application, places a heavy burden on state and local officials. Moreover, the problem of program coordination, not only between levels of government but also among federal agencies, is a difficult one.

Federal grants are available in nearly every major category of state and local government activity. Federal grants may be obtained to assist in everything from the celebration of the American Revolution Bicentennial to the drainage of abandoned mines, riot control, and school milk. Federal aid for welfare and highways, however, accounts for over two-thirds of total federal aid money.

Not only have federal grants-in-aid to the states expanded rapidly in terms of the number of programs and the dollar amounts involved; states and communities have also come to *rely* on the national government for an ever-increasing share of their total revenues (see Table 2–1). Before the New Deal, federal grants amounted to only 2 or 3 percent of total state-local revenue. The New Deal itself, in spite of all of its in-

TABLE 2.1   Federal Grants-in-Aid and State-Local Finances

	Total Federal Grants-in-Aid (In Millions)	Federal Grants as a Percentage of State Local Revenue
1902	$ 7	*
1913	12	*
1922	118	2.1
1927	123	1.6
1932	232	2.9
1938	800	7.2
1940	945	8.1
1944	954	6.8
1948	1,861	8.6
1950	2,486	9.7
1955	3,131	8.3
1960	6,974	11.6
1962	7,871	11.3
1967	15,366	14.0
1970	25,029	14.8
1972	36,080	16.6
1976	55,632	22.2

*Less than 1 percent.
SOURCE: U.S. Bureau of the Census, *Statistical Abstract of the United States.*

novations in federal aid programs, only raised this proportion to 7 or 8 percent. State-local reliance on federal aid has continued to increase, from 8 percent over total state-local revenues in 1946 to over 22 percent today. Thus, no matter how it is measured—increased numbers of programs, increased dollar amounts, increased reliance by states and communities—federal aid has grown into a major influence over state and local governmental activity.

There are several reasons for this growth of federal aid. First of all, these grants permit the federal government to single out and support those state and local government services in which it has a particular interest. Grants permit the national government to set national goals and priorities in all levels of government without formally altering the federal structure. Thus, as problems of public assistance, urban renewal, highway construction, education, poverty, and so on, acquire national significance, they can be dealt with by the application of national resources.

Second, the grant-in-aid system helps to overcome the inadequacies of state-local revenue resources. Contrary to the political rhetoric charging the states with fiscal conservatism, the states have actually demonstarted a great deal of fiscal courage, effort, and ingenuity in trying to cope with money problems. In the last two decades state-local expenditures have risen at a faster *rate* than federal expenditures. These fiscal efforts have meant increased income or sales tax rates in nearly every state in the past ten years as well as increased liquor and gasoline tax rates. Yet in spite of these efforts by states, their fiscal problems continue to multiply.

States and communities must raise revenue and at the same time carry on interstate and interlocal competition for industry and wealth. While the influence of tax considerations on industrial locations decisions may be overstated by most lawmakers, this overstatement itself is part of the political lore at statehouses and courthouses and operates to impede revenue raising.

A third general argument on behalf of federal grants-in-aid centers about the greater progressivity of the federal tax structure. If a particular government program is funded through state and local taxes, it is funded on a tax structure that is regressive or only mildly progressive. In contrast, if a particular program is funded out of federal taxes, it is funded on a more progressive basis. This may help to explain the "liberal" predisposition for federal financial involvement.

Finally, grants-in-aid provide an opportunity for the national government to insure a uniform level of public service throughout the nation as a minimum or foundation program—for example, federal grants-in-aid to help achieve equality in educational opportunity in all parts of the nation or to help insure a minimum level of existence for the poverty stricken regardless of where they live. This aspect of federal policy assumes that in some parts of the nation, state and local governments are unable, or perhaps unwilling, to devote their resources to raising public service levels to minimum national standards.

Whenever the national government contributes financially to state or local programs, state and local officials are left with less freedom of choice than they would have had otherwise. Federal grants-in-aid are invariably accompanied by federal standards or "guidelines," which must be adhered to if states and communities are to receive their federal money. The national government gives money to states and communities only if they are willing to meet conditions specified by Congress. Often Congress delegates to federal agencies the power to establish the "conditions" that are attached to grants.

No state is required to accept a federal grant-in-aid. Thus, states are not required to meet federal standards or guidelines, which are set forth as conditions for federal aid; states and communities have the alternative of rejecting the federal money, and they have sometimes done so. But it is very difficult for states and communities to resist the pressure to accept federal money. It is sometimes said that states are "bribed and blackmailed" into federal grant-in-aid programs. They are "bribed" by the temptation of much needed federal money, and they are "blackmailed" by the thought that other states and communities will get the federal money if they do not, money contributed in part by their own citizens through federal taxation.

In short, through the power to tax and spend for the general welfare, and through "conditions" attached to federal grants-in-aid, the national government has come to exercise great powers in many areas originally "reserved" to the states—highways, welfare, education, housing, natural resources, employment, health, and so on. Of course, federal grants-in-aid have also enabled many states and communities to provide necessary and desirable services that they could not have afforded had it not been for federal aid. Federal guidelines have often improved standards of administration, personnel policies, and fiscal practices in states and communities. More importantly, federal guidelines have helped to insure that states and communities do not engage in racial discrimination in federally aided programs.

Yet the centralization of power in Washington has created some serious problems in the implementation of public policy. First of all, federal grant programs frequently work at cross-purposes, reflecting fragmentation of federal programs. For example, urban renewal grants attempt to save central cities from deterioration and population loss, while federal highway grants have built expressways to make possible the suburban exodus. The federal public housing programs have tried to increase the supply of low-rent housing for the poor, but federally funded urban renewal and highway programs have torn down low-rent housing.

Second, the federal government has never set any significant priorities among its hundreds of grant programs. The result is that too few dollars chase too many goals. Cities are pressured to apply for funds for projects they do not really need, simply because federal funds are available, while they may receive little or no federal assistance for more vital programs. Federal grant money is frequently provided for "new" or "innovative" or "demonstration" programs, when the real crisis facing states and communities may be in traditional public services—police, sewage, sanitation, and so forth.

Third, the administrative quagmire created by the maze of separate federal grant programs threatens to drown state and local officials in red tape. The five hundred separate federal grant programs with separate purposes and guidelines are uncoordinated and bureaucratic. State and local officials spend a great deal of their time in "grantmanship"—learning where to find federal funds, how to apply, and how to write applications in such a way as to appear to meet purposes and guidelines.

Finally, the current grant-in-aid system assumes that federal officials are better judges of goals and priorities at all levels of government than state or local officials. State and local officials do not determine what activities in their states and communities will receive federal money— federal officials determine these priorities. Moreover, federal officials must approve each federally funded project—a public housing project in Des Moines, an airport in Pittsburgh, a new set of welfare regulations in California, a sewage disposal system in Baton Rouge, an urban renewal project in Atlanta, highway in North Dakota, and so forth. Whether federal officials or state and local officials are better judges of public goals and priorities is, of course, a political question.

REVENUE SHARING—
A NEW DIRECTION IN FEDERALISM

The many dissatisfactions with the conditional grant-in-aid system led to appeals for a new approach to federal financial assistance to state and local governments—unrestricted federal grants with no strings attached. For many years Congress debated the idea of "revenue sharing"— the turnover of federal tax dollars to state and local governments for use as they see fit. The idea of revenue sharing assumes that the federal government is better at *collecting* revenue than state or local govern-

ments, but state and local governments are better at *spending* it. Consequently, revenue sharing was said to combine the best features of each
level of government. More importantly, revenue sharing promised to
reverse the flow of money and power to Washington, to end excessive
red tape, and to revitalize state and local governments.

The State and Local Fiscal Assistance Act of 1972 authorized
general revenue sharing—the distribution of over five billion dollars per
year of federal monies to states and communities with very few restrictions on its use. Revenue sharing under this act does *not* replace any
existing grant-in-aid programs, but does provide states and communities
with new unrestricted revenues. Revenue sharing promised to check the
trend toward centralization of power in Washington. Of course, it still
is too early to judge whether revenue sharing will accomplish such a
bold objective. Congress will always be under pressure to attach restrictions to the use of any money coming out of the federal treasury. We will
return to the specific issues posed by revenue sharing in the final chapter
of this book (Chapter 17). But revenue sharing may mark the beginning
of a new phase of American federalism—one in which states and communities acquire new resources and new power to cope with the challenges of the 1970s.

THE EROSION OF LOCAL AUTONOMY

Accompanying the growth of power at the national level has been a
centralization of power *within* states in state capitols. Local governments
are gradually losing power in relation to state governments. This is
true whether one chooses to measure power in terms of financial resources, responsibility for governmental services, or the size of bureaucracies.

Let us first consider overall changes in state versus local financial
resources and manpower levels. Table 2–2 shows the percentage distribution of federal, state, and local revenues, expenditures, and manpower,
for 1902 and 1970. Over time there has been a marked shift toward
greater power at higher levels of government, with greatest relative
losses sustained by local government. Early in the twentieth century,
local governments raised the bulk of governmental revenue, spent the
most money, and employed the most people. Today, the nation's 18,000
local governments raise less money than the nation's 50 state governments, and a great deal less than the national government. Because of
grants-in-aid from both state and federal governments, local governments still spend more than state governments, and they still employ

TABLE 2.2   Federal, State, and Local Revenues, Expenditures, and
Manpower, 1902-1970

	Percentage Distributions 1902	1970
Revenues From Own Sources		
Federal	38	62
State	11	20
Local	51	18
Total Direct Expenditures		
Federal	34	55.5
State	8	17
Local	58	27.5
Public Employment		
Federal	31.5	39
State	10	16
Local	58.5	44

SOURCE: U.S. Bureau of the Census, *Historical Statistics of the United States* (Washington, D.C.; Government Printing Office, 1960); updated from *Statistical Abstract of the United States.*

more people in "labor-intensive" fields—police and fire protection, sanitation, etc. But the direction of change is clear.

States vary in their degree of centralization. Centralization can be measured by financial responsibility (the percentage of state/local expenditures paid at the state level); by responsibility for governmental services (the number of major functions performed by the state rather than by local governments); and by manpower (the percentage of total state/local public employees employed by the state).[10] These measures are closely interrelated,[11] and it is possible to construct a composite index of centralization in the states. Such an index is shown in Table 2–3. Highly-centralized states such as Hawaii and Alaska have higher percentages of state expenditures, more state services, and proportionately larger state bureaucracies, than the decentralized states such as New York and New Jersey. Note that there is a tendency for larger states to be decentralized, while smaller states are more centralized.

[10] See G. Ross Stephens, "State Centralization and the Erosion of Local Autonomy," *Journal of Politics,* 36 (February, 1974): 44–76.

[11] The simple correlation coefficient for the relationship between financial responsibility and service responsibility is .64; service responsibility and manpower is .87; and financial responsibility and manpower is .78. Ibid., p. 65.

TABLE 2.3   Centralization Within the States

A Composite Ranking of States Based Upon State versus Local Proportions of Financial Resources, Services, and Manpower

Centralized

1. Hawaii	4. West Virginia
2. Alaska	5. Delaware
3. Vermont	6. Rhode Island

Partly Centralized

7. New Mexico	12. Oklahoma
8. South Carolina	13. Maine
9. Kentucky	14. Idaho
10. Utah	15. North Dakota
11. Louisiana	

Balanced

16. Montana	28. Georgia
17. Mississippi	29. Wyoming
18. Connecticut	30. Virginia
19. Washington	31. Arizona
20. Pennsylvania	32. Nevada
21. South Dakota	33. Missouri
22. Alabama	34. Texas
23. Arkansas	35. Massachusetts
24. New Hampshire	36. Iowa
25. North Carolina	37. Colorado
26. Tennessee	38. Florida
27. Oregon	39. Michigan

Partly Decentralized

40. Illinois	43. Wisconsin
41. Maryland	44. Minnesota
42. Indiana	45. Kansas

Decentralized

46. Ohio	49. New Jersey
47. California	50. New York
48. Nebraska	

SOURCE: Derived from data provided in G. Ross Stephens, "State Centralization and the Erosion of Local Autonomy," *Journal of Politics,* 36 (February, 1974); 67.

POLITICS OF FEDERALISM

What politicial interests are likely to support the rights of states in contrast to national authority?

Interests that constitute a majority at the national level assert the supremacy of the national government and extol the virtues of national regulation. Interests that are minorities in national politics, but compose local or statewide majorities in one or more states, continue to see merit in the preservation of the rights of states.

Today, the prevailing philosophy of America's liberal leadership includes a commitment to use governmental power to correct perceived wrongs done to others. It is a philosophy of reform, public-regarding-ness and do-goodism. The liberal believes that men's lives can be changed by the exercise of governmental power—to end discrimination, abolish poverty, eliminate slums, insure employment, uplift the poor, educate the masses, and cure the sick. The government in Washington has more power and resources than state and local governments have, and the liberal has turned to it, rather than to state and local governments, to cure America's ills. State and local governments are regarded as too slow, cumbersome, weak, and unresponsive. The government in Washington is seen as the principal instrument for liberal social and economic reform. Thus liberalism and centralization are closely related in American politics.

Federal aid programs have created a vast bureaucracy in Washington which has acquired great power over a wide variety of public activities in America—education, welfare, health, transportation, natural resources, housing, urban affairs, civil rights. This bureaucracy, together with the congressional committee members who oversee its activities and appropriate its funds, has come to believe that it knows more about national needs than do state and local officials. This bureaucracy had become the important force in the movement toward centralization in the American federal system. As federal programs expand, the bureaucracy expands, which in turn provides a thrust for further program expansion.

Nonetheless, public confidence in state and local government is very high. National surveys show that Americans believe state governments spend taxpayers' dollars "more wisely" than the federal government. (Question: "Which do you think spends the taxpayer's dollar more wisely—the state government or the federal government? Answer: state—49 percent; federal—18 percent; neither—17 percent; no opinion—16 percent.[12]) Of course, public opinion may or may not be "right"

---

[12] *Congressional Record*, February 15, 1967.

about which level of government spends money "more wisely," but the confidence expressed in state government is itself a source of power for the states in their relations with the national government.

What kind of people pay the most attention to state and local politics? Jennings and Zeigler studied the characteristics of people who indicated in a national survey that they "pay more attention" to state politics than to national or international affairs.[13] Although the "attentive public" for state and local politics "is not particularly large," these authors speculate that state and local politics may tend to reflect the values of these attentive people more than the values of the public at large. Jennings and Zeigler found that the attentive public for state politics was concentrated in small-town and rural environments, possessed less education than the attentive public for national politics, and had lived in the same state or county for most of their lives. Southerners and westerners were more attentive to state politics than midwesterners or easterners. Moreover, the attentive public for state politics evidenced somewhat more conservative values than the attentive public for national politics. The former were less trusting and more suspicious of people and governments, particularly the government in Washington.

INTERSTATE RELATIONS

The U.S. Constitution provides that "full faith and credit shall be given in each state to the public acts, records, and judicial proceedings of every other state." As more Americans move from state to state, it becomes increasingly important that the states recognize each other's legal instruments. This constitutional clause is intended to protect the rights of individuals who move from one state to another, and it is also intended to prevent individuals from evading their legal responsibilities by crossing state lines. Courts in Illinois must recognize decisions made by courts in Michigan. Contracts entered into in New York may be enforced in Florida. Corporations chartered in Delaware should be permitted to do business in North Dakota. One of the more serious problems in interstate relations today is the failure of the states to meet their obligations under the Full Faith and Credit Clause in the area of domestic relations, including divorce, alimony, child support, and custody of children.[14] The result is now a complex and confused situation in domestic relations law.

[13] M. Kent Jennings and Harmon Zeigler, "The Salience of American State Politics," *American Political Science Review*, 64 (June, 1970): 523–35.
[14] *Williams* v. *North Carolina*, 325 U.S. 226 (1945).

The Constitution also states: "The citizens of each state shall be entitled to all privileges and immunities of citizens in the several states." Apparently the Founding Fathers thought that no state should discriminate against citizens from another state in favor of its own citizens. To do so would seriously jeopardize national unity. This clause also implies that citizens of any state may move freely about the country and settle where they like, with the assurance that as newcomers they will not be subjected to unreasonable discrimination. The newcomer should not be subject to discriminatory taxation, he should be permitted to engage in lawful occupations under the same conditions as other citizens of the state, he should not be prevented from acquiring and using property, or denied equal protection of the laws, or refused access to the courts. However, states have managed to compromise this constitutional guarantee in several important ways. States establish residence requirements for voting and holding office, which prevent newcomers from exercising the same rights as older residents. States often require periods of residence as a prerequisite for holding a state job or for admission into professional practice such as law, medicine, and so on. States discriminate against out-of-state students in the tuition charged in public schools and colleges. Finally, some states are now seeking ways to keep "outsiders" from moving in and presumably altering the "natural" environment.

The Constitution also provides that "A person charged in any state with treason, felony, or other crime who shall flee from justice and be found in another state, shall on the demand of the executive authority from the state from which he fled, be delivered up, to be removed to the state having jurisdiction of the crime." In other words, the Constitution requires governors to extradite fugitives from another state's justice. But the Supreme Court conceded that it has no power to compel the governor of a state to fulfill this constitutional obligation. Governors have not always honored requests for extradition, but since no state wants to harbor criminals of another state, extradition is seldom refused. Among reasons advanced for the occasional refusals are (1) the individual has become a law-abiding citizen in his new state; (2) a northern governor did not approve of the conditions in Georgia chain gangs; (3) a black returned to a southern state would not receive a fair trial; (4) the governor did not believe that there was sufficient evidence against the fugitive to warrant his conviction in the first place.

The Constitution provides that "No state shall without the consent of Congress . . . enter into any agreement or compact with another state." Over one hundred interstate compacts now serve a wide variety of interests, such as interstate water resources; conservation of natural resources, including oil, wildlife, fisheries; the control of floods; the development of interstate toll highways; the coordination of civil defense measures; the reciprocal supervision of parolees; the coordination of welfare and institutional care programs; the administration of interstate metropolitan areas; and the resolution of interstate tax conflicts. In practice, Congress has little to do with these compacts; the Supreme Court has held that congressional consent is required only if the compact encroaches upon some federal power.

States are not supposed to make war on each other, although they did so from 1861 to 1865. They are supposed to take their conflicts to the Supreme Court. The constitution gives the Supreme Court the power to settle all cases involving two or more states. In recent years the Supreme Court has heard disputes between states over boundaries, the diversion of water, fishing rights, and the disposal of sewage and garbage.

Participation
in state politics

THE NATURE OF POLITICAL PARTICIPATION

Popular participation in the political system is the very definition of democracy. There are many ways that individuals can participate in politics. They may run for, and win, public office; participate in marches, demonstrations, and sit-ins; make financial contributions to political candidates or causes; attend political meetings, speeches, and rallies; write letters to public officials or to newspapers; wear a political button or place a bumper sticker on a car; belong to organizations that support or oppose particular candidates or take stands on public issues; attempt to influence friends while discussing candidates or issues; vote in elections; or merely follow an issue or a campaign in the mass media.

This listing probably constitutes a ranking of the forms of political participation in their ascending order of frequency. (See Figure 3–1.) Less than one percent of the American adult population runs for public office. Only about 5 percent are active in parties and campaigns, and about 10 percent make financial contributions. About 15 percent wear political buttons or display bumper stickers. Less than 20 percent ever write their congressman or contact any other public official. About one-third of the population belongs to organizations that could be classified as interest

Chapter three

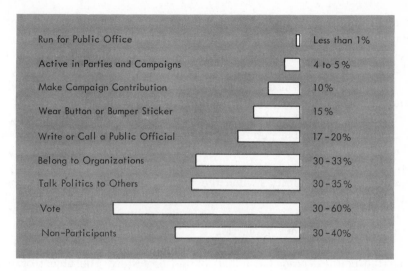

FIGURE 3–1   Political participation.

groups, and only a few more ever try to convince their friends to vote for a certain candidate. About 60 percent of the American people will vote in a hard-fought presidential campaign; but far fewer vote in state and local elections. Over one-third of the population is politically apathetic: they do not vote at all, and they are largely unaware of the political life of the nation.

ORGANIZED PROTEST AS POLITICAL PARTICIPATION

Organized protests—marches, demonstrations, disruptions, civil disobedience—have grown in importance in recent years as forms of political activity. Beginning with the civil rights movement and followed by the Vietnam War protests and campus disruptions, the strategy of organized protest has spread to nearly every sector of American political life. Protest marches and demonstrations are now nearly as frequent at state capitols and city halls as in Washington.

It is important to distinguish between *protest, civil disobedience,* and *violence,* even though all may be forms of political activity. Most *"protests"* do *not* involve unlawful conduct and are protected by the constitutional guarantee of the First Amendment to "peaceably assemble and petition for redress of grievances." A march on city hall or the state capitol, followed by a mass assembly of people with speakers, sign-waving, songs, and perhaps the formal presentation of grievances to whichever brave official agrees to meet with the protestors, is well within the constitutional guarantees of Americans.

Protest refers to many types of direct, collective activity by persons who wish to obtain some concessions from established power-holders. Often the protest is a means of acquiring bargaining power by those who would otherwise be powerless. The protest may challenge established groups by threatening their reputations (in cases in which they might be harmed by unfavorable publicity), their economic position (in cases in which the protest calls for an economic boycott), their peace and quiet (in cases in which noise and disruption upset their daily activity), or their sense of security (when the threat exists that the protest may turn unruly or violent). The strategy of protest may appeal especially to powerless minorities who have little else to bargain with except the promise *not* to continue protesting.

Protests may also aim at motivating uncommitted "third parties" to enter the political arena on behalf of the protesters. The object of the protest is to call attention to the existence of some issue and urge others to apply pressure on public officials. Of course, this strategy requires the support and assistance of the news media. If protests are ignored by television and newspapers, they can hardly be expected to activate support. However, the news media seldom ignore protests with audience interest; protest leaders and newsmen share an interest in dramatizing "news" for the public.

Civil disobedience is a form of protest which involves breaking "unjust" laws. Civil disobedience is not new: it has played an important role in American history, from the Boston Tea Party to the abolitionists who illegally hid runaway slaves, to the sufferagettes who demonstrated for women's voting rights, to the labor organizers who picketed to form the nation's major industrial unions, to the civil rights workers of the early 1960s who deliberately violated segregation laws. The purpose of civil disobedience is to call attention, or to "bear witness" to, the existence of injustice. In the words of Martin Luther King, Jr., civil disobedience "seeks to dramatize the issue so that it can no longer be ignored." [1] There should be no violence in true civil disobedience, and only "unjust" laws are broken. Moreover, the law is broken "openly, lovingly" with a willingness to accept the penalty. Punishment is actively sought rather than avoided, since punishment will help to emphasize the injustice of the law. The object is to stir the conscience of an apathetic majority, and win

---

[1] For an inspiring essay on "nonviolent direct action" and civil disobedience in a modern context, read Martin Luther King, Jr., "Letter From Birmingham City Jail," April 16, 1963, reprinted in Thomas R. Dye and Brett W. Hawkins, eds., *Politics in the Metropolis* (Columbus: Charles E. Merrill, 1967).

support for measures which will eliminate the injustices. By willingly accepting punishment for the violation of an unjust law, the person practicing civil disobedience demonstrates his sincerity. He hopes to shame public officials and make them ask themselves how far they are willing to go to protect the status quo.

As in all protest activity, the participation of the news media, particularly television, is essential to the success of civil disobedience. The dramatization of injustice makes news; the public's sympathy is won when injustices are spotlighted; and the willingness of demonstrators to accept punishment is visible evidence of their sincerity. Cruelty or violence directed *against* the demonstrators by police or others plays into the hands of the protestors by further emphasizing the injustices they are experiencing.[2]

Violence can also be a form of political participation. To be sure, this form of political participation is a criminal one, and it is generally irrational and self-defeating. But political assassination, bombing and terrorism, and rioting, burning, and looting have occurred with uncomfortable frequency in American politics.

It is important to distinguish violence from protest. Peaceful protest is constitutionally guaranteed. One careful study of protest activity in American cities estimates that only six percent of the reported protest involved violence of any kind.[3] Occasionally there is an implicit *threat* of violence in a protest—a threat that can be manipulated by protestors to help gain their ends. But most protests harness frustrations and hostilities, and direct them into constitutionally acceptable activities. Civil disobedience should also be disinguished from violence. The civil disobedient breaks only "unjust" laws, openly and without violence, and willingly accepts punishment without attempting escape. Rioting, burning, and looting—as well as bombing and assassination—are clearly distinguishable from peaceful protest and even civil disobedience. Later we will examine the ghetto riots of the 1960s as an example of violence expressing hostility toward established authority. (See Chapter 13, "Black Politics, Civil Rights, and Public Order.")

Only a small proportion of citizens have ever participated in any protest activity. A study of Buffalo residents in 1968 reported that only

[2] For more detailed examination of the purposes, functions, and rationale of civil disobedience, see Paul F. Power, "Civil Disobedience as Functional Opposition," *Journal of Politics,* 34 (February, 1972): 37–55; and "On Civil Disobedience in Recent American Thought," *American Political Science Review,* 64 (March, 1970): 35–47.

[3] Peter K. Eisinger, "The Conditions of Protest Behavior in American Cities," *American Political Science Review,* 67 (March, 1973): 11–29.

about two percent of white citizens had ever attended a protest meeting, although the same study reported that 11 percent of blacks had done so.[4] Even in the spectacular Watts ghetto riot in 1964, only about 20 percent of the area's residents participated. Many Americans believe that protest activity is "wrong," although blacks and whites differ significantly in this regard. For example, the Buffalo study reported the following percentages of people who believe it is "wrong" to take various actions: [5]

	Blacks	Whites
Attend Protest Meeting	8%	29%
Join Protest March	14	52
Join Public Street Demonstration	21	62
Refuse to Obey Unjust Laws	21	41
Riot to Correct Political Wrongs	62	83

Certain conditions in cities affect the frequency of protest activity; we will return to this topic in Chapter 10, "Participation in Community Politics."

Are protests effective? It is difficult to provide a clear-cut answer to this question. Several conditions must be present if there is to be any likelihood of success.[6] First of all, there must be a clear goal or objective of the protest. Protestors must aim at specific concessions or legislation they desire; generally, complex problems or complaints which cannot readily be solved by specific governmental action are not good targets for protest activity. Secondly, the protest must be directed at some public officials who are capable of granting the desired goal. It is difficult to secure concessions if no one is in a position to grant them. Thirdly, the protest leaders must not only organize their masses for protest activity, but they must also simultaneously bargain with public officials for the desired concessions. This implies a division of labor between "organizers" and the "negotiators." [7]

Finally, we might note in this discussion the strategies available to public officials who are faced with protest activity. They may greet the

[4] Lester W. Milbrath, "Individuals and Government," in Herbert Jacob and Kenneth N. Vines, *Politics in the American States*, 2nd ed. (Boston: Little, Brown and Company, 1971), p. 56.

[5] Ibid., p. 59.

[6] See Michael Lipsky, "Protest as a Political Resource," *American Political Science Review*, 62 (December, 1968): 1144–58.

[7] For an example of how protest leaders and established bargainers worked in tandem to desegregate public facilities in Atlanta in 1960, see Jack L. Walker, "Protest and Negotiation: A Case Study of Negro Leadership in Atlanta," *Midwest Journal of Political Science*, (May, 1963): 99–124.

protestors with smiles and reassurances that they agree with their objectives. They may dispense *symbolic* satisfaction without actually granting any tangible pay-offs. Once the "crisis" is abated, the bargaining leverage of the protest leaders diminishes considerably. Public officials may dispense *token* satisfactions by responding, with much publicity, to one or more specific cases of injustice, while doing little of a broad-based nature to alleviate conditions. Or public officials may *appear to be constrained* in their ability to grant protest goals by claiming that they lack the financial resources or legal authority to do anything—the "I-would-help-you-if-I-could-but-I-can't" pose. Another tactic is to *postpone action* by calling for further study while offering assurances of sympathy and interest. Finally, public officials may try to *discredit* protestors by stating or implying that they are violence-prone or unrepresentative of the real aspirations of the people they seek to lead. This tactic is especially effective if the protest involves violence or disruption or if protest leaders have "leftist" or criminal backgrounds.

POLITICAL ALIENATION AND CYNICISM TOWARD GOVERNMENT

Nonparticipation is sometimes viewed as a reflection of "alienation" from the political system. Political alienation involves a feeling that voting and other forms of participation are useless, that nothing is really decided by an election, and that the individual cannot personally influence the outcome of political events. The fact that nonvoting occurs most frequently among those at the bottom of the income, occupation, and education ladder in America tends to substantiate this view. Nonvoting is also more frequent among blacks than whites. (See Table 3–1.) Alienation occurs more frequently among those groups who have not shared in the general affluence of society. This interpretation is discouraging for those who cherish the democratic ideal, because it suggests that not all groups in society place a high value on democratic institutions.

The exact percentages may change from one election to another, but the general pattern remains very stable. The percentages of nonvoters shown in public opinion surveys are lower than the real percentages of nonvoters. For example, actual votes cast in the 1972 presidential election indicate that 44.3 percent of the population fail to vote, yet the percentages of nonvoters reported in polls are generally lower than this figure. One reason for this discrepancy is that many interviewees exaggerate their political activity when questioned.

Political cynicism has been on the upswing in the last decade. Distrust of government and related feelings of helplessness and inability to

TABLE 3.1   Characteristics of Nonvoters

	Percentage of Nonvoters in Presidential Elections			
	1960	1964	1968	1972
Total	37.2	38.2	39.1	44.3
Education				
Grade school	33	32	37	48
High school	19	22	21	34
College	10	11	16	21
Occupation				
Professional and managerial	12	14	12	19
Other white collar	18	15	13	21
Skilled and semi-skilled	24	26	29	34
Unskilled	31	32	35	45
Farm	18	19	13	20
Community				
Metropolitan area	19	18	21	35
Towns and cities	22	20	21	38
Rural areas	22	26	26	41
Race				
White	19	21	22	36
Black	47	35	32	48

SOURCE: Data drawn from elections studies of the Survey Research Center, University of Michigan, and *Statistical Abstract of the United States 1974,* p. 437.

influence political events have risen steadily throughout the Vietnam and Watergate era. General trust in government is declining, the belief that "a few big interests" run the government is increasing, the belief that government "wastes a lot of money" is held by seventy percent of the electorate, nearly half of the electorate believe that the people running the government "don't know what they are doing," and almost one-third believe that "quite a few" public officials are "crooked." [8] Blacks were more trustful of government than whites in the 1960s, but blacks are less trustful of government than whites today, even though trust among both blacks and whites has declined. Closer analysis reveals that increased cynicism can be attributed to increases in both "cynics of the left" (who want more social change) and "cynics of the right" (who perceive government to be too liberal on many social issues).

There is some dispute about how serious or lasting this increased cynicism may be. Certainly, Watergate did little to dispel cynicism in the

[8] Arthur H. Miller, "Political Issues and Trust in Government," *American Political Science Review,* 68 (September, 1974): 951–72.

early 1970s. But a combination of political circumstances—the ending of the Vietnam War, the passing of the Watergate affair, the end of the recession, and more favorable media reporting of the presidency—may reduce cynicism significantly. Moreover, political cynicism as an *attitude* is not closely related to nonparticipation as a *behavior*.[9] Persons low-in-trust vote almost in the same proportion as persons high-in-trust. (For example, reported nonvoting in 1972 presidential election for persons with *low* trust in government was 30.3 percent, *middle* trust—24 percent, *high* trust—24.9 percent). This suggests that cynicism is simply an expression of dissatisfaction with current policies and/or officeholders, and not necessarily any deep-seated hostility toward the political system itself.

How are feelings of political alienation and cynicism reflected in state and local politics? Interestingly, most of the current distrust of government in public opinion is directed at the *federal* government. The public appears to have greater confidence in state and local government than in the federal government, and to believe that federal government is more to blame for "making things worse" than state and local governments. Cynicism toward local government has been expressed as follows: "Sure around election time, the politicians promise us a city like we've never seen. But after the election all the promises are empty and we go into four more years of decay." "You can bet on one thing: local government will attract people who are not well-trained, are political hangers-on, and are more interested in collecting their pay than anything else." Regarding state government cynicism has been expressed as: "we have Watergates right here in our own state." "The Governor seems more intent on reaching higher places in political life than helping people. He just wants to feather his own nest and couldn't care less about what kind of nests we live in." [10]

VOTING IN THE STATES

Voting is the central form of popular participation in a democracy. Voting requires an individual to make not one, but two decisions. He must choose between rival parties or candidates, and he must choose whether or not to cast his vote at all. This latter decision is just as important as his selection of parties or candidates, because his selection is not effective if he fails to vote. Decisions about whether or not to vote can clearly influence the outcome of elections, yet nonvoting is widespread. Presidential elections may

[9] See Jack Citrin, "The Political Relevance of Trust in Government," *American Political Science Review*, 68 (September, 1974): 973–88, particularly Table 5.

[10] Quotations are from *Report to Government Operations Committee, U.S. Senate*, by Louis Harris Associates, Inc., pp. 44–45.

inspire sixty percent of the voting age population to go to the polls, while elections to statewide offices usually turn out less than fifty percent of the eligible voters. State elections held in nonpresidential years inspire even fewer voters, and only a very small minority (25 to 30 percent) cast votes in local elections held at times other than national or statewide elections. The idea behind "off-year" elections was to separate state and local issues from matters of national concern. Such off-year elections may succeed in insulating state and local politics from national trends, but they also significantly reduce the number of voters participating in state and local elections.

There is a great deal of variation among the states in voter participation rates (see Figure 3-2). The turnout in presidential elections ranges from less than 40 percent of the voting population in several southern states to nearly 70 percent. Voter participation is notably higher in states with higher median famliy incomes and well-educated adult populations. The states with the lowest turnouts are the Deep South states; the next lowest turnouts are found in the border states. Midwestern, New England, and Mountain states rank very high in voter turnout. The urban industrial states, with large metropolitan populations, tend to cluster around the middle of the rankings.

Most of the variation among the states in voter turnout can be explained by *socioeconomic characteristics* of their population. Indeed, educational level, urbanization, median family income, and percentage black, considered together, can explain about 85 percent of the variation in voter turnout in presidential elections.[11] This means that most of the differences among states in voter turnout is explained by the socioeconomic characteristics of individuals living in the states.

However, *legal factors* also affect voter turnout. Turnout is affected by laws of the states, which define registration procedures; residency requirements, literacy tests, poll taxes, voting hours, absentee-ballot rules, and so on. Indeed, some political scientists have cited these legal factors as paramount: "Differences in the turnout for elections are to a large extent related to local differences in registration, and these in turn reflect to a considerable degree local differences in the rules governing . . . and . . . handling . . . the registration of voters." [12] However, these legal factors themselves may be a product of the socioeconomic character of the state; wealthy urban states with well-educated adult populations have

[11] For a complete discussion of the factors affecting voter turnout in the states, see Jae-On Kim et al., "Voter Turnout in the American States: Systemic and Individual Components," *American Political Science Review,* 69 (March, 1975), 107–23.

[12] Stanley Kelley et al., "Registration and Voting: Putting First Things First," *American Political Science Review,* 61 (June, 1967): 359–77.

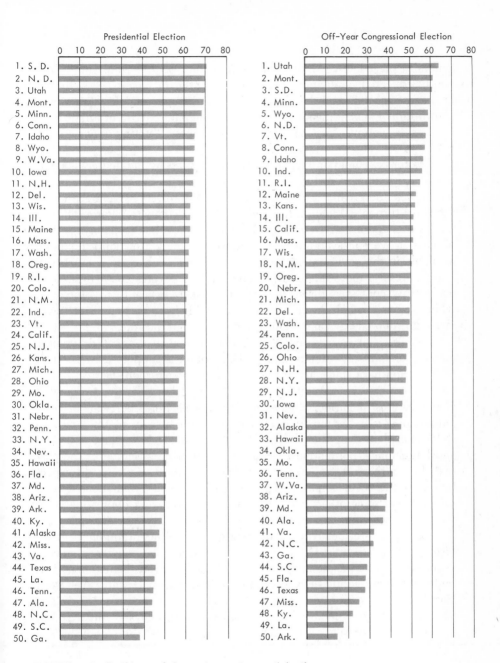

Presidential Election

	0 10 20 30 40 50 60 70 80
1. S. D.	
2. N. D.	
3. Utah	
4. Mont.	
5. Minn.	
6. Conn.	
7. Idaho	
8. Wyo.	
9. W.Va.	
10. Iowa	
11. N.H.	
12. Del.	
13. Wis.	
14. Ill.	
15. Maine	
16. Mass.	
17. Wash.	
18. Oreg.	
19. R.I.	
20. Colo.	
21. N.M.	
22. Ind.	
23. Vt.	
24. Calif.	
25. N.J.	
26. Kans.	
27. Mich.	
28. Ohio	
29. Mo.	
30. Okla.	
31. Nebr.	
32. Penn.	
33. N.Y.	
34. Nev.	
35. Hawaii	
36. Fla.	
37. Md.	
38. Ariz.	
39. Ark.	
40. Ky.	
41. Alaska	
42. Miss.	
43. Va.	
44. Texas	
45. La.	
46. Tenn.	
47. Ala.	
48. N.C.	
49. S.C.	
50. Ga.	

Off-Year Congressional Election

	0 10 20 30 40 50 60 70 80
1. Utah	
2. Mont.	
3. S.D.	
4. Minn.	
5. Wyo.	
6. N.D.	
7. Vt.	
8. Conn.	
9. Idaho	
10. Ind.	
11. R.I.	
12. Maine	
13. Kans.	
14. Ill.	
15. Calif.	
16. Mass.	
17. Wis.	
18. N.M.	
19. Oreg.	
20. Nebr.	
21. Mich.	
22. Del.	
23. Wash.	
24. Penn.	
25. Colo.	
26. Ohio	
27. N.H.	
28. N.Y.	
29. N.J.	
30. Iowa	
31. Nev.	
32. Alaska	
33. Hawaii	
34. Okla.	
35. Mo.	
36. Tenn.	
37. W.Va.	
38. Ariz.	
39. Md.	
40. Ala.	
41. Va.	
42. N.C.	
43. Ga.	
44. S.C.	
45. Fla.	
46. Texas	
47. Miss.	
48. Ky.	
49. La.	
50. Ark.	

FIGURE 3–2   Rankings of the states: voter participation.

generally placed fewer barriers to voting than poorer, rural states with poorly educated populations. More importantly, in recent years, the influence of legal factors has been diminished by federal legislation and constitutional amendments which have eliminated most of these local barriers to voting. (See section in this chapter, "Voting Laws in the States.")

Voter participation rates can also be affected by the degree of *interparty competition* in a state. The more vigorous the competition between the parties, the greater the interest of citizens in elections, and the larger the voter turnout. When parties and candidates compete vigorously, they make news and are given a large play via the mass media. Thus a setting of competitive politics tends to have a greater amount of political stimuli available in the environment than does a setting with weak competition. People are also more likely to perceive that their votes count in a close, competitive contest, and thus they are more likely to cast them. Moreover, when parties are fighting in a close contest, their workers tend to spend more time and energy campaigning and getting out the vote.[13]

Some scholars have cited *region* as an explanation of differences among the states in voter turnout.[14] This notion is supported by the fact that the Southern states are at the bottom of voter turnout figures. But to cite "region" as an explanation of voter turnout begs the question: what characteristics of various regions explain the electoral behavior of their populations? For the most part, the lower voter turnout of the Southern states is explained by their lower educational levels, lower income levels, and larger black populations. However, it has been observed in the past that the Southern states have even lower turnouts than we would expect based on the socioeconomic characteristics of their populations.[15] This suggests that some other unidentified factors are at work depressing voter turnout in these states.

Finally, voter behavior in some states is a product of *unique political history*. West Virginia has experienced considerable poverty in recent years—its adult educational level is one of the lowest in the nation and its registration and voting laws are similar to those of most states. Yet West Virginia voters insist upon going to the polls in large numbers. For many years this apparent inconsistency defied political analysts. But a recent intensive study of West Virginia politics suggests that the bloody history

---

[13] Studies of voter turnout *within* states, e.g., studies of voter turnout by county, confirm the importance of competition in increasing turnout. See C. Richard Hofstetter, "Inter-Party Competition and Electoral Turnout: The Case of Indiana," *American Journal of Political Science*, 17 (May, 1973): 351–66.

[14] Robert H. Blank, "Socio-economic Determination of Voting Turnout," *Journal of Politics*, 36 (August, 1974): pp 731–52.

[15] Jae-On Kim et al., "Voter Turnout in the American States," pp. 121–23.

of organizing miners' unions in that state established a tradition of active political participation among West Virginians. "Contrary to what was taking place in other border and southern states, in West Virginia that group that was least likely to participate in politics—the lower socio-economic status group, the 'working man'—was being motivated and 'organized' to participate [by the United Mine Workers]." [16]

SECURING THE RIGHT TO VOTE

The only mention of voting requirements in the Constitution of the United States as it was originally adopted is in Article I: "The electors in each state shall have the qualifications requisite for electors for the most numerous branch of the state legislature." Of course, "electors" (voters) for the most numerous branch of the state legislature are determined by *state* laws and constitutions. The effect of this constitutional provision was to leave to the states the power to determine who is eligible to vote in both state and federal elections. Over the years, however, a combination of constitutional amendments, congressional actions, and Supreme Court decisions have largely removed control over voting from the states and made it a responsibility of the national government.

Early in American history, the states chose to enact very restrictive voter eligibility standards: suffrage was limited to males over twenty-one years of age, who resided in the voting district for a certain period and owned a considerable amount of land or received a large income from other investments. So great was the fear that "the common man" would use his franchise to attack the rights of property that only about 120,000 persons out of 2 million were permitted to vote in the 1780s. Men of property felt that only other men of property had sufficient "stake in society" to exercise their franchise in a "responsible" fashion. But Jeffersonian and Jacksonian principles of democracy, including confidence in the reason and integrity of the common man, spread rapidly in the new Republic. Soon property qualifications were eliminated, and suffrage was extended to great masses of people by state law.

The first important limitation on state powers over voting came with the ratification of the Fifteenth Amendment: "The right of the citizens of the United States to vote shall not be denied or abridged by the United States or any state on account of race, color, or previous condition of servitude." The object of this amendment, passed by the Reconstruction Con-

[16] Gerald W. Johnson, "Research Note on Political Correlates of Voter Participation: A Deviant Case Analysis," *American Political Science Review*, 65 (September, 1971): 768–76.

gress and adopted in 1870, was to extend suffrage to former black slaves and prohibit voter discrimination on the basis of race. The Fifteenth Amendment also gives Congress the power to enforce black voting rights "by appropriate legislation." Thus, the states retained their right to determine voter qualifications, *so long as they do not practice racial discrimination,* and Congress was given the power to pass legislation insuring black voting rights.

It is a tribute to the ingenuity of southern politicians that they were able to defeat the purpose of this amendment for almost a century. While social and economic pressures and threats of violence succeeded in intimidating many thousands of would-be voters, there were also many "legal" methods of disenfranchisement.

For many years the most effective means of banning black voting was a technique known as the "white primary." So strong was the Democratic party throughout the South that the Democratic nomination for public office was tantamount to election. This meant that *primary* elections to choose the Democratic nominee were the only elections in which real choices were made. If blacks were prevented from voting in Democratic primaries they could be effectively disenfranchised. Thus southern state legislatures resorted to the simple device of declaring the Democratic party in southern states a private club and ruling that only white persons could participate in its elections, that is, in *primary* elections. Blacks would be free to vote in "official," general elections, but all whites tacitly agreed to support the Democratic, or "white man's" party, in general elections, regardless of their differences in the primary. Not until 1944, in *Smith* v. *Allright,* did the Supreme Court declare this practice unconstitutional: "When primaries become part of the machinery in choosing officials, state and national, as they have here, the same tests to determine the character of discrimination . . . should be applied to the primary as are applied to the general election." [17]

Black voting in the South increased substantially after World War II. From an estimated 5 percent of voting age blacks registered in southern states in the 1940s, black registration rose to an estimated 20 percent in 1952, 25 percent in 1956, 28 percent in 1960, and 39 percent in 1964. This last figure was a little more than half of the comparable figure for white registration in the South. However, most of this increase in black registration occurred in urban areas of the South. Prior to 1965, in hundreds of rural counties throughout the South, no Negroes had ever been permitted to vote. Despite the Fifteenth Amendment, local registrars in the South succeeded in barring Negro registration by means of an endless variety of

[17] *Smith* v. *Allright,* 321 U.S. 649 (1944).

obstacles, delays, and frustrations. Application forms for registration were lengthy and complicated; even a minor error would lead to rejection, like underlining rather than circling in the "Mr.-Mrs.-Miss" set of choices as instructed. Literacy tests were the most common form of disenfranchisement. Many a black college graduate failed to interpret "properly" the complex legal documents that were part of his test. In the unlikely event that a black succeeded in passing such tests, he would then be required to convince the registrar that he was of "good character" and that he had paid his poll taxes. Needless to say, white applicants for voter registration were seldom asked to go through these lengthy procedures.

The Civil Rights Act of 1964 made it unlawful for registrars to apply unequal standards in registration procedures, or to reject applications because of immaterial errors. It required that literacy tests be in writing and made a sixth-grade education a presumption of literacy. The Twenty-fourth Amendment to the Constitution was ratified in 1964, making poll taxes unconstitutional as a requirement for voting in national elections. In 1965 the Supreme Court declared poll taxes unconstitutional in state and local elections as well.[18] Yet in Selma, Alabama, in early 1965, civil rights organizations effectively demonstrated that local registrars were still keeping large numbers of blacks off the voting rolls. Registrars closed their offices for all but a few hours every month, placed limits on the number of applications processed, went out to lunch when black applicants appeared, delayed months before processing black applications, and discovered a variety of other methods to keep blacks disenfranchised. It became apparent that a registrar who wanted to keep blacks from voting could always find a way to do so if he tried hard enough, regardless of the law.

In response to the Selma episode, Congress enacted a strong Voting Rights Act in 1965 designed to fulfill the Fifteenth Amendment's promise that the right to vote shall not be denied because of race. The act applied to any state or county where (1) the literacy test or similar qualifying device was enforced as of November 1, 1964, and (2) fewer than 50 percent of voting age residents either were registered or cast ballots in the 1964 presidential election. In these areas, the Attorney General upon evidence of voter discrimination was empowered to replace local registrars

18 *Harper* v. *Virginia State Board of Elections*, 383 U.S. 663 (1966). Opponents of the new law argued that it interfered with the historic right of states to determine voter qualifications. However, a constitutional amendment by definition takes precedence over earlier language in a constitution. The Fifteenth Amendment prohibited racial discrimination in voting and gave Congress the power to enforce this prohibition "by appropriate legislation." In 1966 the Supreme Court took notice of the long history of discrimination by southern voting registrars and upheld the Voting Rights Act of 1965 as "appropriate legislation" in the fight against voter discrimination.

with federal registrars, abolish literacy tests, and register voters under simplified federal procedures.[19] It turned out that federal registrars were sent to only a small number of southern counties. Many southern counties which had previously discriminated in voting registration hurried to sign up black voters just to avoid the imposition of federal registrars.

The black voter is now very important in southern state and local politics. By 1970 it was estimated that 65 percent of eligible blacks in the southern states were registered to vote, compared with 70 percent of eligible whites.[20] Most of the remaining difference between blacks and whites is attributable to the generally lower economic and educational levels of black populations in the South rather than to race itself. Blacks and whites at the same socioeconomic level register and vote with the same frequency.[21] Blacks sit in every southern state legislature and hold important political office in local governments throughout the South.[22] There are many southern towns and counties where blacks outnumber whites, and where in recent years black local officials have replaced traditional white leadership. Perhaps the best known example of black success in local southern politics is the election of a black mayor, Maynard Jackson, in Atlanta.

Despite this evidence of progress in black political participation in the South, there is still concern over the extent of intimidation of black voters in counties of the deep South. Intimidation may no longer occur in the form of physical violence, but instead in the form of subtle pressures against blacks who are *economically vulnerable*. For example, political scientists Lester M. Salamon and Stephen Van Evera measured black vulnerability in 29 Mississippi counties in terms of the percentage of blacks who were farm laborers or service employees, and the percentage of blacks who were renters or tenant farmers.[23] Their theory was that blacks who were economically dependent upon white employers or landlords would be less active politically than blacks who were self-employed and owned their own homes. It turned out that in these Mississippi counties economic vulnerability was more closely related to nonvoting among blacks than either income or education.

[19] *South Carolina* v. *Katzenbach,* 383 U.S. 301 (1966).

[20] U.S. Bureau of the Census, *Statistical Abstract of the United States, 1970,* p. 369.

[21] Anthony M. Orum, "Social and Political Participation of Negroes," *American Journal of Sociology,* 72 (July, 1966): 44.

[22] See Metropolitan Applied Research Center, *National Roster of Black Elected Officials,* annual.

[23] Lester M. Salamon and Stephen Van Evera, "Fear, Apathy, and Discrimination: A Test of Three Explanations of Political Participation," *American Political Science Review* 67 (December, 1973): 1288–1307.

Continued nonparticipation among some segments of the Southern black population may also be a product of apathy produced by generations of poverty and poor schooling. This explanation is supported by evidence showing that black voting does indeed correlate with black educational levels.[24] Moreover, the percentage of blacks casting votes increases dramatically in counties where blacks constitute more than 50 percent of the population, and therefore have a real chance of winning office. In short, apathy disappears when education and a chance of winning office motivates political organization and activity. However, evidence of white reaction can often be found in Southern counties where blacks appear to be organizing themselves and actively seeking to increase black voting. *White* voter turnout in Mississippi counties has been shown to *increase* with increases in *black* voter turnout. Thus, black-voter mobilization in many deep-South counties has the side effect of increasing white-voter turnout.

It is important to remember, however, that blacks are a minority in every state in the nation. Unless black candidates can win some white support, they cannot achieve success in *statewide* elections. In any statewide election in which blacks and whites divide strictly along racial lines, the black candidate will be defeated. (See Table 3–2.) Thus, black

TABLE 3.2   The Black Potential for Electoral Influence in the South

	Black Percentage of Total Population	Registered Voters		Percent Black
		White	Black	
Alabama	26.4	1,311,000	315,000	19.4
Arkansas	18.6	728,000	153,000	17.4
Florida	15.5	2,495,000	302,000	10.8
Georgia	25.9	1,615,000	395,000	19.7
Louisiana	29.9	1,143,000	319,000	21.8
Mississippi	36.8	690,000	286,000	29.3
North Carolina	22.4	1,640,000	305,000	15.7
South Carolina	30.5	668,000	221,000	24.9
Tennessee	16.1	1,600,000	242,000	13.1
Texas	12.7	3,599,000	550,000	13.3
Virginia	18.6	1,496,000	269,000	15.2

SOURCE: U.S. Bureau of the Census, *Statistical Abstract of the United States, 1975,* p. 436.

[24] Sam Kernell, "A Re-evaluation of Black Voting in Mississippi," *American Political Science Review,* 67 (December, 1973): 1307–18.

separatism offers little hope of acquiring real power in America, but increased black participation in coalitional politics offers a path to black political influence in the South and in the nation. We will return to the topic of black politics and the struggle for equality in Chapter 13.

VOTING AND AMERICAN YOUTH

Before 1970 only three of the fifty states permitted persons eighteen to twenty-one years of age to vote—Georgia, Kentucky, and Alaska. All other states, in the exercise of their constitutional responsibility to determine the qualifications of "electors," had set the voting age at twenty-one. The movement for eighteen-year-old voting had received its original impetus in Georgia in 1944 under the leadership of Governor Ellis Arnal, who argued successfully that eighteen-year-olds were then being called upon to fight and die for their country in World War II and therefore deserved to have a voice in the conduct of government. But this argument failed to convince adult voters or leaders in other states; qualifications for military service were not regarded as the same as qualifications for rational decision making in elections. In state after state, voters rejected state constitutional amendments designed to extend the vote to eighteen-year-olds.

In the Voting Rights Act of 1970, Congress intervened on behalf of eighteen-year-old voting. In this act, Congress asserted very far-reaching authority over the conduct of elections in America by (1) extending the suffrage to persons eighteen to twenty-one years of age regardless of state law, (2) abolishing residency requirements of more than thirty days for voting in national elections, and (3) suspending all literacy tests. This action by Congress immediately raised serious constitutional questions about the extent of congressional power over voting. There was no doubt that Congress could, under the Fifteenth Amendment, end *racial* discrimination in state electoral laws or practices, but extending the suffrage by act of Congress to young people was another matter. The Constitution vests the authority to determine general voter qualifications in the states, and all previous restrictions on state power over the suffrage had come by constitutional amendment—the Fifteenth Amendment barring racial discrimination (1870), the Nineteenth Amendment dealing with women's voting rights (1920), and the Twenty-fourth Amendment eliminating poll taxes (1964).[25]

[25] The constitutional question of congressional power to determine voter qualifications came before the Supreme Court in *Oregon* v. *Mitchell* in 1971. In a controversial five to four decision, the Court held that Congress had acted constitutionally in extending the vote to eighteen-year-olds in *federal* elections, but not in *state* or *local* elections. The reasoning of the judges was complex, and no one was really satisfied with the outcome of the case.

The constitutional debate prompted Congress to pass and send to the states the Twenty-sixth Amendment to the Constitution extending voting rights to all persons over eighteen years of age in all federal, state, and local elections. The legislatures of three-fourths of the states promptly ratified the amendment, perhaps more out of a desire to end confusion than out of a genuine enthusiasm for eighteen-year-old voting. Thus, Congress succeeded in extending the vote to America's youth, although the states had declined to do so themselves.

VOTING LAWS IN THE STATES

Voting laws in the states are now heavily circumscribed by national authority:

Fifteenth Amendment—No denial of voting because of race

Nineteenth Amendment—No denial of voting because of sex

Twenty-fourth Amendment—No poll taxes

Twenty-sixth Amendment—No denial of voting to persons eighteen or over

Civil Rights Act of 1964—No discrimination in the application of voter registration laws

Voting Rights Act of 1965—Attorney general may replace local voting officials with federal examiners on evidence of voter discrimination in southern states

Voting Rights Act of 1970—No denial of voting to persons eighteen or over; no residency requirements in national elections; no literacy tests

The states, however, continue to administer national, state, and local elections. All but four states (Alaska, Arkansas, North Dakota, and Texas) have established a system of voting *registration*. Presumably, registration helps to prevent fraud and multiple voting in elections. Registration may be either permanent (once a voter is on a registration list, he remains there until he leaves the district) or periodic (voters must register at periodic intervals ranging from one to ten years). Some states will accept a record of having voted sometime during the registration period as a substitute for reregistration. This system requires no initiative on the part of the voter in keeping his name on the list of eligibles. As a matter of practice, registration lists are usually out of date whether registration is permanent or periodic. Registration procedures can be employed to facilitate or to hinder voting. In many localities registration is inconvenient. It may require a trip to the county courthouse, and registration forms may be complicated. In contrast, many communities have adopted mobile registration systems, where registrars canvass door to door or booths are conveniently established in shopping centers on well-publicized days preceding elections.

Congress has threatened to remove all control over elections from the states by establishing a national post-card registration system administered by a federal voter-registration agency.[26] Support for this proposal comes from representatives of labor and minorities who argue that registration is cumbersome and restrictive, and that it tends to discourage voting among blacks, poor people, working-class, and highly mobile persons. Opponents argue that the proposal would establish a new federal bureaucracy to oversee elections, further erode the role of state government in the federal system, and lead to large-scale vote fraud. It would be easy, opponents say, for individuals to register and vote many different times with little chance of detection.

Do state registration requirements depress voter turnout? Consider the 1972 presidential election, which produced the lowest voter turnout of recent times—55.7 percent. Although this was the first presidential election in which 18-year-olds could vote, 73.9 percent of the voting age population *was* registered. But one out of every four persons who were registered failed to vote! Automatic or post-card registration might increase turnout somewhat, but there would still be many nonvoters.[27] It is sometimes argued that registration filters out the disinterested citizen whose vote would be cast haphazardly anyhow. A free society should respect the decision of those who choose not to vote, as well as those who desire to participate and make the effort to do so.

PUBLIC OPINION AND PUBLIC POLICY

The problem in assessing the independent effect of public opinion on the actions of decision makers is that the actions of decision makers help to mold mass opinion. Public policy may accord with mass opinion, but we can never be sure whether mass opinion shaped public policy or public policy shaped mass opinion. In V. O. Key's most important book, *Public Opinion and American Democracy,* he wrote:

> Government, as we have seen, attempts to mold public opinion toward support of the programs and policies it espouses. Given that endeavor, perfect congruence between public policy and public opinion could be government *of* public opinion rather than government *by* public opinion.[28]

While V. O. Key himself was convinced that public opinion did have some independent effect on public policy, he was never able to demonstrate this in any systematic fashion.

[26] See *Congressional Quarterly Weekly Report,* May 11, 1974, pp. 1274–75.

[27] For a contrary argument that attributes nonvoting primarily to state registration requirements, see Stanley Kelley, Jr. et al., "Registration and Voting: Putting First Things First," *American Political Science Review,* 61 (June, 1967): 359–77.

[28] V. O. Key, Jr., *Public Opinion and American Democracy* (New York: Alfred A. Knopf, Inc., 1967), pp. 422–23.

There is very little *direct* evidence in the existing research literature to support the notion that public opinion is an important influence over public policy. Many surveys reveal the absence of any knowledge or opinion about public policy on the part of masses of citizens. This suggests that mass opinion has little influence over the content of public policy. How can mass opinion be said to affect public policy when there *is* no mass opinion on a great many policy questions? Studies suggesting that the masses of people have little knowledge of, or interest in, or opinion about, a great many policy questions clearly imply that public opinion has little impact on the content of public policy. Likewise studies indicating that public opinion is unstable and inconsistent also imply that public opinion has little policy impact.

Public opinion *in the states* is much more difficult to study than *national* opinion. National opinion polls require about 1,500 interviews nationwide, but a fifty-state survey would require 1,000 to 1,500 interviews in each of the fifty states—a fifty-times increase in effort. However, Professor Frank Munger devised a method of converting national survey data about public opinion into *estimates* of opinion within the separate electorates.[29] His work allowed him to examine the impact of public opinion on state policy by considering five state policies about which most people have opinions of some kind—legal lotteries, capital punishment, right-to-work laws, antidiscrimination laws, and gun controls. He was able to designate the states in which a majority supported legislation on these topics and the states in which a majority opposed such legislation. Then he examined the laws of the states to ascertain the congruence between majority opinion and public policy.

The really startling fact about public policy in these five issues is the general lack of congruence between public policy and public opinion. On the question of state lotteries, public opinion supported public policy in 32 of the 50 states (64 percent); on the question of capital punishment, public opinion supported state policy in 25 states (50 percent); on state right-to-work laws, public opinion supported state policy in 34 states (68 percent); on gun-control laws, public opinion supported state policy in only eight states (16 percent); but on antidiscrimination laws, public opinion supported public policy in 46 states (92 percent). Munger concludes: "There are substantial discrepancies between electoral preferences and state policies; and there are great variations among the five policy areas in the closeness of fit between opinions and actions." The overall figure for policy-opinion congruence is only 58 percent; this means that the

[29] Frank J. Munger, "Opinions, Elections, Parties, and Policies: A Cross-State Analysis," paper delivered at the annual meeting of the American Political Science Association, New York, 1969.

chances of a state's policy matching the preferences of its citizens are only a little better than the fifty-fifty ratio generated by chance! Of course, it is true that these five policy areas are by no means a representative sample of all public policy. And it is also interesting to note that in the area of civil rights—where many studies have suggested that public opinion is well-defined and intense—state policy conforms with public opinion in the states. But on such seemingly important questions as lotteries, capital punishment, right-to-work laws, and gun controls, public opinion has little relationship to public policy. Another attempt to link public opinion to public policy in the states using correlation analysis was equally disappointing.[30] Despite the authors' stated *belief* that opinion preferences should be important determinants of public policy (because traditional democratic theory assumed this to be true), it turned out that only in the area of civil rights was there a close relationship between opinion and policy in the states. Using Munger's state-opinion estimating technique, political scientists Rober Weber and William Schaffer presented data showing that socioeconomic variables were *better* predictors of state policy in parochial school aid, right-to-work laws, teacher unionization, and gun control, than popular opinion. Undaunted by their own findings, however, they concluded that public opinion *must* be considered as a factor influencing public policy. But certainly we have no evidence to support the assertion that public opinion is an *important* independent influence over public policy.[31]

When V. O. Key wrestled with the same problem confronting us—namely, the determination of the impact of popular preferences on public policy—he concluded that "the Missing Piece of the Puzzle" was "that thin stratum of persons referred to variously as the political elite, the political activists, the leadership echelons, or the influentials." As he wrote,

> The longer one frets with the puzzle of how democratic regimes manage to function, the more plausible it appears that a substantial part of the explanation is to be found in the motives that activate the *leadership echelon*, the values that it holds, the rules of the political game to which it adheres, in the expectations which it entertains about its own status in

[30] Ronald E. Weber and William R. Schaffer, "Public Opinion and American State Policy-Making," *Midwest Journal of Political Science,* 16 (November, 1972): 683–99.

[31] An alternative view is that majority opinion (over 50%) is the wrong "threshold" of opinion support required for policy enactment. Different "thresholds" exist for different policy areas. Of course, the notion that any "threshold" other than 50% should be required for policy enactment runs contrary to common understanding of democratic theory. But see Anne H. Hopkins, "Opinion Publics and Support for Public Policy in the American States," *American Journal of Political Science,* 18 (February, 1974): 167–78.

society, and perhaps in some of the objective circumstances, both material and institutional, in which it functions.[32]

In short, it is not really the opinions of the *general* public that influence public policy, but rather the opinions of state and community leaders, inside and outside of government.

When state legislators are asked to name individuals whom they regard as knowledgeable about public affairs, and whose advice they might seek out about public issues or problems, they tend to name wealthy, well-educated, and prestigiously employed individuals who are politically active in their states and communities.[33] They name individuals who meet frequently with public officials, who understand public issues, who hold public office, and who tend to believe that the state legislature and other governing bodies are doing a "good job." In brief, state legislators interact *with people like themselves*, and not with the general public. The "attentive constituents" differed from the general public in their awareness of public issues, their activity and experience in politics, and in their loyalty to, and support for, governing institutions.

INTEREST GROUPS IN STATE POLITICS

Membership in a political interest group is an important form of political participation, and interest group activity is an important aspect of political life.[34] Political interest groups arise when individuals with a common interest decide that by banding together and by consolidating their strength, they can exercise more influence over public policy than they could as individuals acting alone. The impulse toward organization and collective action is particularly strong in a society of great size and complexity. As societies become more urban and industrial, individual action in politics gives way to collective action by giant organizations of businessmen, farmers, professionals, and laborers, as well as racial, religious, and ideological groups. As Earl Latham explained: "Organization represents concentrated power, and concentrated power can exercise dominating influence when it encounters power which is diffused and not concentrated and therefore weaker." [35]

[32] Key, *Public Opinion and American Democracy*, p. 537.

[33] R. Boynton, Samuel C. Patterson, and Ronald D. Hedlund, "The Missing Links in Legislative Politics: Attentive Constituents," *Journal of Politics*, 31 (August, 1969): 700–21.

[34] See Harmon Zeigler, *Interest Groups in American Society* (Englewood Cliffs, N.J.: Prentice-Hall, Inc., 1964).

[35] Earl Latham, "The Group Basis of Politics," *American Political Science Review*, 46 (June, 1952): 387.

Groups may be highly organized into formal organizations with offices and professional staffs within the state capitals of every state: the National Association of Manufacturers, the AFL–CIO, and the National Education Association are examples of highly organized interest groups that operate in every state. Other groups have little formal organization and have been unable to organize themselves very effectively for political action: an example of such a group would be parents opposed to busing for racial integration. Political interest groups may be organized around occupational or economic interests (for example, the American Farm Bureau Federation, the National Association of Real Estate Boards, the United States Chamber of Commerce), or on racial or religious bases (for example, the National Association for the Advancement of Colored People, the National Council of Churches, the Anti-Defamation League of B'nai B'rith), or around shared experiences (for example, the American Legion, the Veterans of Foreign Wars, the League of Women Voters, the Automobile Association of America), or around ideological positions (for example, Americans for Democratic Action, Common Cause, Americans for Constitutional Action). Government officials and governments themselves organize to help exert pressure on higher levels of government (for example, the National Governors' Conference, the Council of State Governments, the National League of Cities, U.S. Conference of Mayors, and National Association of Counties). Even the recipients of government services are organizing themselves (for example, the National Welfare Rights Organization).

Many scholars believe that economic interests tend to exercise more influence in American politics than noneconomic interests. But certainly the proliferation of active noneconomic groups in America, from the American Legion to the Sierra Club, the League of Women Voters and the liberal-oriented Common Cause, testifies to the importance of organization in all phases of political life. Particularly active at the state level are the businesses subject to extensive regulation by state governments. The truckers, railroads, insurance companies, and liquor interests are consistently found to be among the most highly organized groups in state capitals. State chapters of the National Education Association are also active in state capitals, presenting the demands of educational administrators and teachers. Even local governments and local government officials organize themselves to present their demands at state capitals.

It is very difficult to get a comprehensive picture of interest group activity in state capitals. Many organizations, businesses, legal firms, and individuals engage in interest group activity of one kind or another, and it is difficult to keep track of their varied activities. Many states require the registration of "lobbyists" and the submission of reports about their membership and finances. These laws do not restrain lobbying (that would probably violate the First Amendment freedom to "petition" the government for "redress of grievances"). Rather, they are meant to spotlight the activities of lobbyists. However, many hundreds of lobbyists never register under the pretext that they are not *really lobbyists,* but, instead, businesses, public relations firms, lawyers, researchers, or educational people. Thus, only the larger, formal, organized interest groups are officially registered as lobbyists in the states.

Many smaller businesses maintain part-time lobbyists or contract with law firms that specialize in representing businesses in government. These lobbyists and business representatives help to sell their company's services or products to government agencies, handle their company's relations with administrative and regulatory agencies, and attempt to influence legislation in which their company has an interest. In almost every state, there are hundreds of professional organizations, from accountants to undertakers, and most of these have engaged in lobbying activity from time to time. State chapters of the National Education Association and the American Medical Association are perhaps the most influential of these professional groups. In addition to the activities of the AFL–CIO, individual labor unions—United Automobile Workers, United Steel Workers, International Association of Machinists, International Brotherhood of Teamsters, United Mine Workers, and so on—are also active in state capitals on behalf of working men and women. American farmers generally have a number of trade associations speaking for them in specialized fields —cattlemen, sheepmen, poultry producers, and citrus growers, for example —and three organizations attempt to speak for all farmers at both the state and national level—the American Farm Bureau Federation, the National Grange, and the National Farmers Union. State chapters of the Sierra Club and the Audubon Society have become increasingly influential as issues in pollution, ecology, and environmental protection have become popular.

There is also considerable agreement among the state legislators about which types of interest groups are most powerful. Business interests were named in *The Legislative System* study as "most powerful groups" more often than any other interests in all four states.[36] Educational interests rank second in three states and tie for third in the fourth, and labor interests rank third in all four states. Agricultural interests, government interests (the associations of city, county, and township governments and government employee associations), ethnic and demographic interests, and religious, charitable, and civic interests were given some mention as powerful interests.

[36] John C. Wahlke et al., *The Legislative System* (New York: John Wiley & Sons, Inc., 1962), pp. 311–42.

FUNCTIONS AND TACTICS
OF INTEREST GROUPS

Both interest groups and political parties organize individuals to make claims upon government, but these two forms of political organizations differ in several respects. An interest group seeks to influence specific policies of government—it does not seek to achieve control over government as a whole. A political party concentrates on winning public office in elections and is somewhat less concerned with policy questions. An interest group does not ordinarily run candidates for public office under its own banner, although it may give influential support to candidates running under a party banner. Finally, the basic function of a political party in a two-party system is to organize a *majority* of persons for the purpose of governing. In contrast, an interest group gives political expression to the interests of *minority* groups.

In a democracy, where decisions are made by majority rule, it is particularly important that minorities have a means of expressing themselves. Organized interest group activity offers a form of protection for minorities when the faint preferences of a majority threaten the vital interest of a minority. The threatened minority can be expected to engage in intense political activity and, in so doing, ward off the threat to its vital interest. In short, interest group activity can function to represent intensity of feelings in minorities and to blunt the effects of majoritarianism.

Interest groups are also essential in representing interests that are not geographically defined in American society. The formal structure of American government does not recognize functional interest groupings—such as businessmen, laborers, farmers, blacks, Catholics, and so on—but territorial divisions instead—such as cities, counties, legislative districts, and states. Interest groups supplement the formal system of territorial representation in American government by providing for an internal system of functional representation.

Interest groups also function to stimulate interest and participation in politics among their members. They often pressure candidates to clarify their stands on issues in an election, and they perform an important information and education function for public officials and citizens alike.

Interest group techniques are as varied as the imaginations of their leaders. Groups are attempting to advance their interests when a liquor firm sends a case of bourbon to a state legislator; when NOW (National Organization of Women) marches on the state capital in support of the Equal Rights Amendment; when the League of Women Voters distributes biographies of political candidates; when an insurance company argues before a state insurance commission that insurance rates must be increased; when the National Education Association provides state legislators with information comparing teachers' salaries in the fifty states; when railroads ask state highway departments to place weight limitations upon trucks; when the American Civil Liberties Union supplies lawyers for civil rights demonstrators; or when theater owners testify in legislative committee hearings against the adoption of daylight savings time. Let us try to classify the many techniques of interest groups under three major headings—public relations, electioneering, and lobbying.

Most people think of interest group tactics as direct attempts to influence decision makers, but these groups spend more of their time, energy, and resources in general public relations activities than anything else. The purpose of a continuing public relations campaign is to create an environment favorable to the interest group and its program. It is hoped that a reservoir of public goodwill can be established, which can be relied on later when a critical issue arises. Generally, business interests have a distinct advantage over nonbusiness interests in public relations. Business interests already have at their disposal public relations skills of their advertising departments. The cost of business public relations campaigns can be regarded as tax-deductible operating costs.

Electioneering is a common practice among interests groups. If a candidate who is already favorably inclined toward a particular interest can be elected, the group is reassured that its interests will be protected once he has taken office. On the whole, it is a good strategy for interest groups to remain in the background during campaigns—making monetary contributions to their favorite candidates, offering their public relations skills to them, or exhorting their own members to support them. Political campaigns are very expensive, and it is always difficult for a candidate to find enough money to finance his campaign. This is true for officeholders seeking reelection as well as new contenders. It is perfectly legal for an interest group to make a large contribution to a candidate's campaign fund. Ordinarily, a respectable lobbyist would not be so crude as to exact any specific pledges from a candidate in exchange for a campaign contribution. He simply makes a contribution and lets the candidate figure out what he should do when in office to assure further contributions for his next campaign.

It is considered bad taste for an interest group to make a campaign contribution to a state legislator at the very time that a bill in which the group is interested is being considered. However, interest group activity in state capitals may be somewhat cruder—if not actually corrupt—than interest group activity in Washington. In interviewing lobbyists and legislators in Washington, Lester Milbrath found that they considered state lobbying much more corrupt than national lobbying: "Lobbying is very different before state legislators; it is much more individualistic. Maybe this is the reason they have more bribery in state legislatures than in Congress." "In the state legislatures, lobbying is definitely on a lower plane. The lobbyists are loose and hand out money and favors quite freely." "Lobbying at the state level is cruder, more basic, and more obvious." "Lobbying at the state level is faster and more freewheeling and less visible; that is why it is more open to corruption." [37]

Needless to say, it is difficult to document such activity. However, it seems reasonable to believe that state legislators are more subject to the pressures and appeals of organized interest groups than congressmen. State legislators meet less often and for shorter periods of time than Congress, and, consequently, most state legislatures have not developed the formal and informal rules governing their behavior that exist in the U.S. Congress. State legislators are less likely to assume the "professional" attitude that characterizes many congressmen; state legislators are more likely to regard their legislative careers as secondary aspects of their lives. Moreover, state legislators make less money than congressmen and may therefore be more vulnerable to the appeals of interest groups offering financial support.

Lobbying is defined as any communication, by someone acting on behalf of a group, directed at a government decision maker with the hope of influencing his decision. Direct persuasion is usually more than just a matter of argument or emotional appeal to the lawmaker. Often it involves the communication of useful technical and political information. Many public officials are required to vote on, or decide about, hundreds of questions each year. It is impossible for them to be fully informed about the wide variety of the bills and issues they face. Consequently, many decision makers come to depend upon the skilled lobbyists to provide technical information about matters requiring action and to inform them of the policy preferences of important segments of the population. A state legislator or administrator may call upon the Chamber of Commerce, the AFL–CIO, or the National Education Association to inform him about the views of businessmen, labor, or teachers on a particular issue. Indeed, legislators *use* lobbyists, just as lobbyists use legislators:

> Whatever their image of lobbyists, legislators are more likely to look on them as service agents than as opinion manipulators . . . . Typically, legislators utilize lobbyists as sources of influence in three ways: by calling upon lobbyists to influence other legislators, by calling upon lobbyists to help amass public opinion in favor of the legislator's position, and by

[37] Lester Milbrath, *The Washington Lobbyists* (Chicago: Rand McNally & Co., 1963), pp. 241–43; also cited by Harmon Zeigler, "Interest Groups in the States," in *Politics in the American States*, ed. Herbert Jacob and Kenneth Vines (Boston: Little, Brown and Company, 1965), p. 104

including lobbyists in planning strategy in an effort to negotiate a bill through the legislature." [38]

It is unwise for lobbyists to try to threaten legislators, for example by vowing to defeat them in the next election. This is the tactic of an amateur lobbyist, not a professional. It usually produces a defensive response by the legislator. As one lobbyist put it: "Once you have closed the door you have no further access to the individual. Once you've threatened an individual, there is no possibility of winning in the future." [39] Even the publication of voting records of legislators by interest groups is considered an implied threat and generally disregarded by legislators.

Testimony at legislative committee hearings is the most common form of information exchange between lobbyists and legislators. Legislators in four states reported that this was their primary source of information about legislation.[40] Direct meetings in legislators' offices are also frequent and effective. Social gatherings (where the liquor is usually furnished by the lobbyist) are more important in establishing friendships; professional lobbyists seldom bring up "business" on such occasions. Legislators are wined and dined so much during legislative sessions that attendance at social functions is sometimes viewed as a chore. The least effective method of lobbying is the submission of long letters or reports.[41] One form of lobbying that is growing rapidly in importance is communication with legislative *staff* personnel. As state legislatures acquire more full-time staff for their standing committees, House and Senate leaders, and majority and minority party caucuses, professional lobbyists are coming to recognize that these staff people can have as much or more to do with the specific content of bills as legislators themselves. Many of the more "modernized," "professional," state legislatures rely heavily on the advice of professional staffs (see Chapter 4). The wise lobbyist in these states cultivates friendships among staff personnel.

INTEREST GROUPS IN THE STATES:
A COMPARATIVE VIEW

How can states be compared in terms of the strength of their interest groups? Some measure of "strength" must be developed by which the

---

[38] Harmon Zeigler and Michael A. Baer, *Lobbying: Interaction and Influence in American State Legislatures* (Belmont: Wadsworth, 1969), p. 107.

[39] Ibid., p. 121.

[40] Ibid., p. 163.

[41] Ibid., p. 169.

states can be ranked. But it is very difficult to measure the "strength" of interest groups, since this is a function of many factors including size, resources, organization, leadership, prestige, unity or "cohesion," and "access" (contacts) to decision makers. Thus, a strictly objective measure of interest group strength in each state is exceedingly difficult to obtain. However, some years ago the American Political Science Association sent questionnaires to political scientists located in several states, asking them to judge whether interest groups in their respective states were strong, moderately strong, or weak.[42] These judgments by political scientists are open to challenge, but they are probably the best available estimate of interest group strength in the states.

Harmon Zeigler used this "classification" to show that states with stronger interest groups are also more likely to be (1) one-party states in contrast to competitive two-party states, (2) states in which parties in the legislature show little cohesion or unity, and (3) states that are poor, rural, and agricultural.[43] Zeigler notes that states that are wealthy, urban, and industrial have *more* interest groups, but it is in these states that interest groups are more likely to balance each other and less likely to dominate the political scene. Poor, rural, agricultural states may have *fewer* interest groups, but it is in these states with relatively backward economies that strong interest groups exercise considerable power over public policy. (See Table 3–3.)

Zeigler also identified several "pressure group patterns" in the states.[44] The first pattern, "an alliance of dominant groups," was the typical pattern in rural, agricultural states with one party politics and weak legislative unity among the parties. This pattern was descriptive of the southern states and of nonsouthern states without industrial economies, such as Maine.

> A good sample of this pattern is Maine. . . . Specifically, power, timber, and manufacturing—the big three—have proven to be the catalysts for much of the controversy in the state. While other interests occasionally voice demands, the big three clearly out-distance any rivals in political activity and power. Certainly the key position of these interests in the economy of the state contributes to their crucial position in the decision making process of the state. Over three-fourths of the state is woodland and most of this land is owned by a handful of timber companies and paper manufacturers. These interests, combined with power companies and textile and shoe manufacturers, are able—in so far as their well-being is directly involved—to "control Maine politics." [45]

[42] Belle Zeller, ed., *American State Legislatures* (New York: Thomas Y. Crowell Company, 1954), pp. 190–91.

[43] Harmon Zeigler, "Interest Groups in the American States."

[44] Ibid., pp. 117–28.

[45] Ibid., p. 118.

TABLE 3.3   The Strength of Pressure Groups in Varying Political and
Economic Situations

Social Conditions	Types of Pressure System[a]		
	Strong [b]	Moderate[c]	Weak[d]
Party competition	(24 states)	(14 states)	(7 states)
One-party	33.3%	0%	0%
Modified one-party	37.5%	42.8%	0%
Two-party	29.1%	57.1%	100.0%
Cohesion of parties in legislature			
Weak cohesion	75.0%	14.2%	0%
Moderate cohesion	12.5%	35.7%	14.2%
Strong cohesion	12.5%	50.0%	85.7%
Socio-economic variables			
Urban	58.6%	65.1%	73.3%
Per capita income	$1900	$2335	$2450
Industrialization index	88.8	92.8	94.0

[a]Alaska, Hawaii, Idaho, New Hampshire, and North Dakota are not classified or included.

[b]Alabama, Arizona, Arkansas, California, Florida, Georgia, Iowa, Kentucky, Louisiana, Maine, Michigan, Minnesota, Mississippi, Montana, Nebraska, New Mexico, North Carolina, Oklahoma, Oregon, South Carolina, Tennessee, Texas, Washington, Wisconsin.

[c]Delaware, Illinois, Kansas, Maryland, Massachusetts, Nevada, New York, Ohio, Pennsylvania, South Dakota, Utah, Vermont, Virginia, West Virginia.

[d]Colorado, Connecticut, Indiana, Missouri, New Jersey, Rhode Island, Wyoming.

SOURCE: Harmon Zeigler, "Interest Groups in the American States," in *Politics in the American States,* ed. Herbert Jacob and Kenneth Vines (Boston: Little, Brown and Company, 1965), p. 114.

A second pattern of "a single dominant interest" is found in rural nonindustrial states with two-party politics and moderate legislative unity, such as Montana. About Montana, Zeigler writes:

In a state in which the extraction of minerals is the major nonagricultural source of personal income, Anaconda is the largest employer. While "the company," as it is known in Montana, began its operations in mining for copper, it now owns mills, aluminum companies, railroads, fabricating plants, and forests. The enormity of the Anaconda empire is described by Thomas Payne: "Its strength rests not only in its wealth and resources, but also with its elaborate network of relationships with key citizens, banks, legal firms, and business organizations throughout the state. Rare is that unit of local government—county, city, or school district—that does not have among its official family an associate, in some capacity, of the Anaconda Company." [46]

[46] Ibid., pp. 119–20; quotation from Thomas Payne, "Under the Copper Dome: Politics in Montana," in Frank Jonas, *Western Politics* (Salt Lake City: University of Utah Press, 1961), pp. 197–98.

The position of Anaconda in Montana is not much different from the position of oil companies in Texas or Du Pont in Delaware. Of course, there is a difference between reputation for control and actual control of public policy. No doubt the reputation for control exceeds the actual control that these interests exercise over public policy. Undoubtedly, in large areas of state policy, these dominant groups have little interest and exercise little influence.

A third pattern described by Zeigler was that in which there is a "conflict between two dominant groups." This pattern is found in a non-diversified industrial economy with strong two-party politics and legislative unity within the parties. Michigan is a prime example of this bipolar interest group pattern. Joseph LaPalombara writes: ". . . No major issues of policy (taxation, social legislation, labor legislation, and so on) are likely to be decided in Michigan, without the intervention, within their respective parties and before agencies of government, of automotive labor, and automotive management." [47] The United Automobile Workers union is deeply involved in the affairs of the Democratic party, while the automobile manufacturers are deeply involved in the Republican party. In other words, labor and management in Michigan each have "their" political parties.

Another pattern of interest group activity was described by Zeigler as the "triumph of many interests." This pattern is found in urban states with industrial economies but relatively weak political parties. Party loyalty has never been strong in California, with many legislators and voters crossing party lines in their political activity. The lack of any effective and disciplined party organization in California paved the way for interest groups to exercise relatively unchecked influence in California politics. No one interest group dominates California politics, but the initiation of public policy appears to be largely the responsibility of organized groups in that state. The railroads, the California State Brewers Institute, the race tracks, motion pictures, citrus growers, airplane manufacturers, insurance companies, utilities, and a host of other interests maintain offices in Sacramento, financially support many state legislators, and exercise important influence in legislative affairs.

What is the impact of interest groups on the structure of state government? Lewis A. Froman used the same classification of states by interest group strength that Zeigler employed in an interesting attempt to answer this question.[48] He found that the stronger the interest groups, the

[47] Joseph LaPalombara, *Guide to Michigan Politics* (East Lansing: Michigan State University Press, 1960), p. 104; also cited by Zeigler, "Interest Groups in the American States," p. 123.

[48] Lewis A. Froman, "Some Effects of Interest Group Strength in State Politics," *American Political Science Review*, 60 (December, 1966): 952–62.

greater the number of state-elected officials, and the greater the likelihood that state agencies would be headed by elected rather than appointed officials. He concluded that states with stronger interest groups are better able to isolate government agencies and officials from executive and legislative influence than states with weaker interest groups. Interest groups strive to isolate administrative agencies from the governor and the legislature in order to strengthen their own influence with these agencies. By weakening gubernatorial and legislative control over state administration, interest groups feel that they are more likely to be successful in exercising influence in administrative agencies.

WOMEN IN POLITICS: MARRIAGE, ABORTION, AND THE EQUAL RIGHTS AMENDMENT

Potentially the largest interest group in American politics is women. The earliest active "feminist" organizations grew out of the pre-Civil War antislavery movement. The first generation of feminists, including Lucretia Mott, Elizabeth Cody Stanton, Lucy Stone, and Susan B. Anthony, learned to organize, to hold public meetings, and to conduct petition campaigns as *abolitionists*. After the Civil War, women were successful in changing many state laws which abridged the property rights of married women and otherwise treated them as "chatel" (property) of their husbands. Women were also prominent in the Anti-Saloon League which succeeded in outlawing prostitution and gambling in every state (except Nevada) and providing a major source of support for the Eighteenth Amendment ("Prohibition"). In the early twentieth century the feminist movement concentrated on "women suffrage"—the drive to guarantee women the right to vote. The early "suffragettes" employed mass demonstrations, parades, picketing, and occasional disruption and civil disobedience—tactics not dissimilar from those of the civil rights movement of the 1960s. The culmination of the early feminist movement was the passage in 1920 of the Nineteenth Amendment to the Constitution: "The right of citizens of the United States to vote shall not be denied or abridged by the United States or by any state on account of sex." The more moderate wing of the American suffrage movement became the League of Women Voters; in addition to women's vote, they sought protection of women in industry, child welfare laws, and honest election practices.

Renewed interest in feminist politics came after the Civil Rights movement of the 1960s. The "women's liberation" movement of recent years has worked in the states and in Congress on behalf of a wide range of reforms—from the Twenty-seventh (Equal Rights) Amendment to the Constitution, equal employment opportunities for women, reform of marriage and divorce laws, more convictions in rape cases, and liberalization of abortion laws, to the promotion and the use of *Ms.* in place of *Miss* or *Mrs.* New organizations have sprung up to compete with the conventional activities of the League of Women Voters by presenting a more militant and activist stance toward women's liberation. The largest of these new organizations is the National Organization of Women (NOW) founded in 1966, which promises to change "the false image of women now prevalent in the mass media and in the texts, ceremonies, laws and practices of our major social institutions," which "perpetuate contempt for women by society and by women for themselves." [49]

Until recently, the legal status of women in society has been determined largely by *state* laws, particularly laws governing marriage, divorce, employment, and abortion. State laws frequently differentiated between the rights and responsibilities of men and women. Women had many special protections in state laws, but often these protections limited opportunities for advancement and encouraged dependence upon men.

For example in *marriage*, most states require that a woman: give up her "maiden" name and assume the last name of her husband; adopt her husband's place of living as her own "domicile"; give up the right to sue her husband; and exchange sexual relationships for financial support. Divorce is granted in most states to a male for his wife's failure to allow sexual contact, but it is not granted to the male for his wife's failure to provide financial support when he is disabled. In contrast, divorce is not granted to a wife for her husband's failure to provide sexual contact, but it is granted to a wife for her husband's failure to support her. Women are generally required to follow their husbands if their husbands move, but husbands are not required to follow their wives. Divorce in most states requires a finding of "fault" of one of the partners—adultery, cruelty, nonsupport, desertion, etc.—and the "guilty" party is treated harshly when the alimony and child support are decided. Only a few states have added "irreconcilable differences" or "incompatibility" as grounds for divorce. In 1970, California achieved a break-through by eliminating "fault" proceedings altogether and substituting "irreconcilable differences" as the sole grounds for divorce. Under California's "no fault" proceedings, alimony, child support, and property division are determined by the relative economic circumstances of the partners and not on "fault." A wife capable of supporting herself will receive no alimony; custody of children will be given to the parent best able to play the parental role; and the wife may even be required to support an ex-husband who is unable to support himself. Nonetheless, there remains

---

[49] Congressional Quarterly, *The Women's Movement* (Washington: Congressional Quarterly, 1973), p. 14.

today a complex web of contradictory state laws covering marriage and divorce.

Until recently, most state laws governing *employment* considered women as frail creatures in need of special protections against long hours, heavy work, night work, and so on. Moreover, states did *not* guarantee equal pay and promotion opportunities for women or bar sexual discrimination in employment. But the federal Civil Rights Act of 1964, Title VII, prevents sexual (as well as racial) discrimination in hiring, pay, and promotions. The Equal Employment Opportunity Commission (EEOC), which is the federal agency charged with eliminating discrimination in employment, has established guidelines barring stereotyped classifications of "men's jobs" and "women's jobs." State laws and employer practices which differentiate between men and women in hours, pay, retirement age, etc., have been struck down. Under active lobbying from feminist organizations, federal agencies, including the U.S. Office of Education and the Office of Federal Contract Compliance, have established "affirmative action" guidelines for government agencies, universities, and private businesses doing work for the government; these guidelines set goals and timetables for employers to alter their work force to achieve higher female percentages at all levels.

At the center of feminist group activity in recent years is the *Equal Rights Amendment* to the Constitution (ERA) which would strike down *all* existing legal inequalities, in state and federal laws, between men and women. The amendment states simply: "Equality of rights under the law shall not be denied or abridged by the United States or by any state on account of sex." ERA passed the Congress easily and was sent to the states for the necessary ratification of three-fourths (thirty-eight) of them. The amendment won quick ratification by half of the states, but a developing "Stop-ERA" movement slowed progress and threatened to defeat the amendment itself. Debate over ratification of ERA in the states has suggested that it may eliminate many legal protections for women— financial support by husbands, an interest in the husband's property, exemption from military service, and so forth. In addition to these specific objections, opposition to "women's liberation" in general has charged that the movement weakens the family institution, demoralizes women who wish to devote their lives to their family and children, and even encourages men to assert their masculinity in antisocial ways. It is argued that there are indeed physiological differences between men and women which account for differential sex roles. The women's role in reproduction and care of the young is biologically determined. To the extent that she seeks to protect her young, she also seeks family arrangements which will provide maximum security and support for them. It is also argued that men are physically stronger than women, and their role as economic providers is rooted in this biological difference. Despite sometimes heated debate, it is impossible to predict exactly what impact ERA will have on state and federal laws,[50] much less the general condition of women in society.

Potentially the most important and far-reaching decision in the recent history of the Supreme Court is its action in the *legalization of abortion.*[51] Historically, abortions for any purpose other than saving the life of the mother were criminal offenses under state law. About a dozen states acted in the late 1960s to permit abortions in cases of rape or incest, or to protect the physical health of the mother, and in some cases her mental health as well. Relatively few abortions were performed under these laws, however, because of the red tape involved—review of each case by several concurring physicians, approval of a hospital board, and so forth. Then, in 1970, New York, Alaska, Hawaii, and Washington enacted laws that in effect permitted abortion at the request of the woman involved and the concurrence of a physician. New York, unlike the other states enacting such laws, did *not* establish a state-residency requirement for patients.

Abortion is a highly sensitive issue. It is not an issue that can easily be compromised. The arguments touch on fundamental moral and religious principles. Proponents of liberal abortion laws argue that a woman should be permitted to control her own body and should not be forced by law to have unwanted children. They cite the heavy toll in lives lost in criminal abortions and the psychological and emotional pain of an unwanted pregnancy. Opponents of abortion generally base their belief on the sanctity of life, including the life of the unborn child, which they believe deserves the protection of law—"the right to life." Many believe that the killing of an unborn child for any reason other than the preservation of the life of the mother is murder.

The movement for liberal abortion laws in America, which began with a struggle for the liberalization of state laws, won a *national* victory when the Supreme Court ruled that the Constitutional guarantee of personal liberty in the First and Fourteenth Amendments included a woman's decision to bear or not to bear a child. In the *Row* v. *Wade* and *Doe* v. *Bolton* decisions, the Supreme Court ruled that the word *person* in the Constitution did *not* include the unborn child. Therefore the Fifth and Fourteenth Amendments to the Constitution, guaranteeing "life, liberty and property," did not protect the "life" of the fetus. The court also ruled that a state's power to protect the health and safety of the mother could

---

[50] See Shana Alexander, *Shana Alexander's State-by-State Guide to Women's Legal Rights* (New York: Wollstone Craft, 1975).

[51] *Row* v. *Wade*, 410 U.S. 113 (1973); *Doe* v. *Bolton* 410 U.S. 179 (1973).

not justify *any* restriction on abortion in the first three months of pregnancy. Between the third and sixth months of pregnancy, the state could set standards for how and when abortions can be performed, in order to protect the health of the mother; but the state cannot prohibit abortions in this period. Only in the final three months of pregnancy, the Supreme Court said, can the state ban all abortions to safeguard the life and health of the mother. Thus, the Supreme Court set national standards for state laws governing abortions.

Nonetheless, there are still many unresolved issues in state abortion laws.[52] "Right-to-life" groups have sprung up in many states to continue the fight against legalized abortion, as well as to push for a Constitutional amendment to define the fetus as a "person." Some states have passed legislation protecting doctors and nurses from loss of jobs or other penalties for refusing to carry out abortions because of their moral and religious convictions. State laws are ambiguous about efforts to save aborted fetuses which emerge alive; it is still possible to convict a doctor of manslaughter if he fails to save a live aborted fetus. The Supreme Court has struck down state laws requiring husband or parental approval for abortions. However, state laws are still very restrictive in their definition of an "approved facility" for an abortion. Another unresolved problem is whether hospitals can refuse to allow abortions on their premises. In summary, abortion legislation is still an important item on the agenda of state legislatures and state courts.

The percentage of women who vote is only slightly lower than the percentage of men who vote. However, there have never been more than 19 women among the nation's 535 members of Congress. Many of them gained their seats through widowhood, having been appointed or elected to fill the term of a deceased husband. There have been four women governors in the states, but only one of these, Ella Grasso of Connecticut, did not serve in the shadow of her husband. Approximately 350 of the nation's 7,800 state legislators are women.[53]

[52] Orma Linford and Naomi B. Lynn, "The Impact of the Abortion Decision: The States Respond," paper delivered at the Southern Political Science Association meeting, 1974.

[53] Congressional Quarterly, *The Women's Movement,* pp. 56–59.

Parties in state politics

PARTIES IN THE FIFTY STATES

Decentralization of power is the most important characteristic of American party organizations. These organizations are built around public offices at the federal, state, and local level. Organizationally, the Democratic and Republican parties consist of a national committee; a House and Senate party conference; various national clubs, such as Young Democrats and Young Republicans, and Democratic and Republican Women's Federations; and fifty state parties, which in turn are composed of state committees and county and city organizations. This structure is tied together very loosely. State parties are not very responsive to national direction, and in most states, city and county organizations operate quite independently of the state committees. State committees are generally involved in important statewide elections—governors, U.S. senators, and congressmen in the smaller states. City and county committees are generally responsible for county and municipal offices, state legislative seats, and congressional seats in the larger states. The Democratic and Republican National Committees exist primarily for the purpose of holding national conventions every four years to select the presidential candidate. Since each level of party organization has "its own fish to fry," each operates quite independently of the other levels.

Chapter four

State parties are by no means merely local representatives of national firms. In fact, the national Democratic and Republican parties are often described as confederations of fifty distinct party organizations. It is not surprising in the American system of federalism—where only the president and the vice-president have *national* constituencies, and senators, congressmen, governors, state legislators, county and municipal officials all have *local* constituencies—that the American parties would be decentralized in their organization. Parties function to capture control of public office for their nominees, and most elective offices in the American political system are chosen by state and local constituencies rather than national constituencies. (One might say *all* elected offices in the U.S. are chosen by state or local constituencies, since the president and the vice-president are really elected by the electoral votes of the states rather than the popular vote of the nation.)

Party affairs are governed largely by the laws of the states. Each state sets forth the conditions that an organization must meet to qualify as a political party and to get its candidates' names printed on the official election ballots. Each state sets the qualifications for membership in a party, and the right to vote in the party's primary election. State laws determine the number, method of selection, and duties of various party officials, committees, and conventions. The states, rather than the parties themselves, decide how the parties shall go about nominating candidates for public office. Most states require that party nominations be made by direct primaries, but several states still nominate by party caucuses or conventions. Most states also attempt to regulate party finances, although with little success.

Since party organizations in the states are relatively autonomous from the national Democratic and Republican parties, we can expect a great deal of variation in party systems from state to state. First of all, the comparative strength of the Republican and Democratic parties obviously differs from state to state. States can also be differentiated by the level of interparty competition and by the strengths and functions of their party organizations. Some states can be characterized as one-party states, while in other states more competitive situations exist. In some states, the Republican and Democratic parties offer substantially different policy positions on education, welfare, taxation, highways, and other important public issues. In other states, it is more difficult to distinguish a clear party position on these issues. In some states, the Democratic and Republican parties represent separate social and economic groups in the states: the Democratic party may be composed of central-city, low-income, ethnic, and racial constituencies, while the Republican party represents middle-class, suburban, small-town, and rural constituencies. However, in other states both parties may attempt to represent the same groups, and it is then difficult to detect any socioeconomic differences between Democrats and Republicans.

The wide range of differences between state party systems means that state party organizations with the same party label may be quite different from one another. Often, state Democratic parties are further apart on policy matters from each other than from Republicans. The Minnesota and Mississippi Democratic parties, for example, have little in common except the party label. Variations in state Republican parties may be just as great: certainly the New York and Arizona Republicans are quite different from one another, not to mention the Alabama Republicans. Each of these Republican and Democratic state parties is more a product of its statewide constituency than of any national Democratic or Republican organization. State parties are more inclined to fit their programs to popular demands within their states than to offer significantly different policy alternatives derived from national party differences. Democratic and Republican parties within a state are competing in the same vote market, and hence their policy positions have more in common with each other than with those of their counterparts in different states. In short, parties in each state tailor their policies to local conditions.

In this chapter we will endeavor not only to describe the structure and activities of state party systems but also to compare state party systems and identify some of the causes and consequences of variations among the states.

ONE-PARTY AND TWO-PARTY STATES

Interparty competition has received a great deal of attention from political scientists studying state politics. Many political scientists have contended that competitive, responsible parties are necessary for effective democratic control of government in modern society. The ideal "responsible" party system is said to be one in which competitive parties present alternative programs in election campaigns, and the party winning the majority of votes captures all the power it needs to write its program into law. Moreover, in the responsible party system, the party's elected officials act cohesively, so the voters can hold the party collectively responsible for public affairs at the end of its term of public office. The key to this ideal party system is the existence of competitive parties which are roughly balanced in strength.

In reality, however, the degree of party competition among the states varies a great deal. In the past, the Republican party in the Deep South states was practically nonexistent, and even today, despite some Republican successes in the South, the Republican party frequently fails to run candidates for governor, U.S. senator, Congress, and the state legislature. Even though these southern states may be competitive in presidential elections, Democrats have continued to win state office by wide margins and dominate southern state legislatures by heavy majorities. The party systems in these states have been termed "one-party Democratic." Republican domination in the midwestern and upper New England states has never been so complete that it warrants the designation of a "one-party system" (see Figure 4–1).

There are several important differences between one-party states and two-party states. Voters in two-party states use party labels to help them identify the politics of candidates. The fact that a candidate runs under a Republican or Democratic label does not guarantee his stand on every public issue, but it indicates with which broad coalition in American politics a candidate has associated himself. Party labels carry meaning for most voters, even though individual candidates may be "disloyal" to their party on occasion. At the very least, a party label in a two-party state tells more about a candidate's politics than a strange name on a ballot with no party affiliation indicated.

A party label in a competitive state is a very conspicuous attribute of a candidate. One-party states may have important "liberal" or "conservative" factions of some durability. But in two-party states, the party label can be seen by every voter on election day. A party label is not so obscure as an alignment with a liberal or conservative faction. Most students of state politics feel that it is more difficult to hold factions responsible. Factions are even more fluid, and change personality and policies more frequently than parties. V. O. Key argues that southern factional systems obscure politics for most voters and permit conservative interests to manipulate the voters.[1] A large number of people who have very little knowledge about the policies or memberships of various factions are easily misled. This does not mean that many voters are not confused about party policies in competitive states or that competitive parties can always hold their legislators responsible, but it does mean that party competition is more likely to clarify things for the voter than factional politics. Even if policy differences between the parties are vague, there is at least an "in-party" and an "out-party," which can be identified at election time. Finally, in one-party states, and even in states with limited competition, the minority party often fails to run candidates for many offices. Under these circumstances, the party out of office is unable to perform the important role of criticizing officeholders. The existence of a competitive

[1] V. O. Key, Jr., *Southern Politics in State and Nation* (New York: Alfred A. Knopf, Inc., 1949). See also Alan P. Sindler, "Bifactional Rivalry as an Alternative to Two-Party Competition in Louisiana," *American Political Science Review*, 46 (1955): 641.

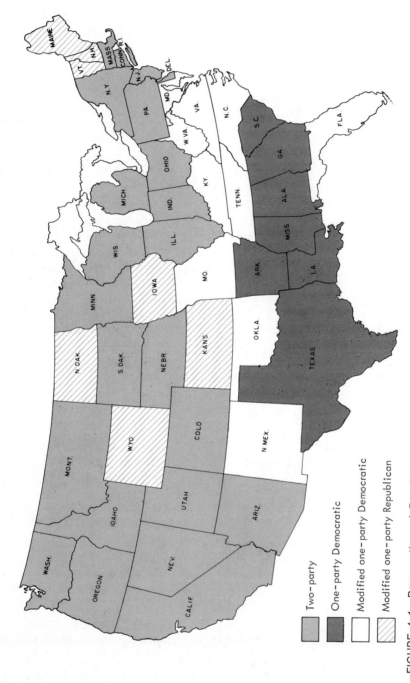

FIGURE 4–1 Democratic and Republican success in state offices, 1954–75.
NOTE: Hawaii and Alaska, not shown, are two-party states.

Two-party

One-party Democratic

Modified one-party Democratic

Modified one-party Republican

party *outside* of government, a party that has a real chance of replacing officeholders at the next election, can help to make officeholders more aware of their responsibilities to the voters. In a competitive two-party system, the party out of power has the strongest kind of incentive for exposing the weaknesses of the ruling party.

In recent years political scientists have developed various ways of measuring interparty competition in the states.[2] Figure 4–1 shows the distribution of the fifty states by levels of interparty competition in lower and upper houses of state legislatures and in governors' elections. This distribution of states by level of party competition focuses upon *state* offices and not upon a state's congressional delegation, its U.S. senators, or its vote in presidential elections. Other students of state politics have included a wider range of offices in their measures of party competition, but these measures of party competition are directly related to the study of *state* government.

CAUSES AND CONSEQUENCES OF PARTY COMPETITION

Why do some states have competitive two-party systems and others do not? Slavery and the subsequent status of blacks in society had a great deal to do with one-partyism in the South.[3] A majority of white southerners were Democrats before the Civil War, and the Republican party was founded to resist the spread of slavery. A Republican president wrote the Emancipation Proclamation and a Republican Congress wrote the Thirteenth, Fourteenth, and Fifteenth Amendments and supervised the military occupation of the South. One-partyism is characteristic of political systems in which large numbers of people are united in opposition to a perceived serious threat. Historically, one-partyism helped to exclude blacks from effective political participation. Whites would handle their own squabbles within the Democratic party primary and unite behind the "white man's party" in the general election.

But this explanation, while helpful in understanding southern politics, fails to explain the lack of effective party competition in many states outside the South. Party competition also appears to be closely related to socioeconomic conditions in the states. Party competition is greater in those urban, industrial states in which separate socioeconomic groups re-

---

[2] See David G. Pfeiffer, "The Measurement of Inter-Party Competition and Systemic Stability," *American Political Science Review*, 61 (1967): 457–67; Paul T. David, "Party Strength in the United States," *Journal of Politics*, 36 (August, 1974): 785–96.

[3] See Key, *Southern Politics in State and Nation.*

side. Rural agricultural states with homogeneous populations do not provide enough social division to support well-organized, disciplined, and competitive parties. It is not surprising, then, that competitive states tend to be those urban and industrial states with heterogeneous populations.

In large states, such as New York, Pennsylvania, and Illinois, the parties are first divided along rural-urban lines, and, within urban areas, they are further divided on socioeconomic bases. Republicans dominate in rural areas and in the wealthier urban areas (upper-middle-class suburbs and "silk-stocking" districts in the cities). Democratic districts are found predominantly in the less wealthy, urban areas of the state. A similar pattern emerges if occupational, religious, or racial characteristics are considered. Republican districts within urban areas prove to be the districts with greater concentrations of professional, managerial, sales, and clerical jobs. Republican candidates fare badly among black voters. The Democrats dominate in the ethnic districts with southern and eastern European, Irish, and Catholic voters. These are frequently the big-city, mining, and mill districts. The Republicans draw heavily in the Anglo-Saxon, northern and western European, Protestant districts of these states. A high degree of party competition results from these socioeconomic conditions within a state's electorate. In contrast, the less competitive states —for example, Maine, Kansas, Vermont, New Hampshire, North and South Dakota—are more homogeneous in their social composition.

Table 4–1 confirms our reasoning that party competition is related to urbanization, income, and education in the states. The two-party states are more urban, wealthy, and well educated than either the one-party Democratic or the modified one-party Republican states. It is also interesting to note that the two-party states and the Republican states have much smaller proportions of blacks in their populations. In contrast, the one-party Democratic states have larger proportions of blacks in their populations.

What difference does it make in public policy whether a state has competitive or noncompetitive parties? Do states with a competitive party system differ in their approach to education, welfare, health, taxation, or highways from states with noncompetitive party systems? This is not an easy question to answer. Since competitive states tend to be wealthy, urban, industrial states, and noncompetitive states poorer, rural, agricultural states, it is difficult to sort out the effects of party competition from these other socioeconomic variables. Several scholars have asserted that a competitive party system leads to more liberal education, welfare, and taxation policies and that one-partyism strengthens conservative views; however, available evidence suggests that interparty competition does not play a really influential role in determining public policies in these fields. As we shall see in later chapters, education, welfare, taxation, and highway programs appear to be more closely related to socioeconomic

TABLE 4.1   Social and Economic Characteristics of the States and Party Competition

	One-Party Democratic[1] (7 states)	Modified One-Party Democratic[2] (11 states)	Two-Party[3] (25 states)	Modified One-Party Republican[4] (7 states)
Urbanization	58%	65%	72%	53%
Income	$2363	$2743	$3199	$2797
Education	10.7 yrs.	11.2 yrs.	12.2 yrs.	12.0 yrs.
Black Population	26%	11%	5%	1%

[1] Alabama, Arkansas, Georgia, Louisiana, Mississippi, South Carolina, Texas.

[2] Florida, Kentucky, Maryland, Missouri, Oklahoma, New Mexico, North Carolina, Rhode Island, Tennessee, Virginia, West Virginia.

[3] Alaska, Arizona, California, Colorado, Connecticut, Delaware, Hawaii, Idaho, Illinois, Indiana, Massachusetts, Michigan, Minnesota, Montana, Nebraska, Nevada, New Jersey, New York, Ohio, Oregon, Pennsylvania, South Dakota, Utah, Washington, Wisconsin.

[4] Iowa, Kansas, Maine, New Hampshire, North Dakota, Vermont, Wyoming.

SOURCE: U.S. Bureau of the Census, *Statistical Abstract of the United States.*

factors in the states than to the degree of party competition itself.[4] However, as we have already observed, a lack of party competition can seriously affect the degree of popular control over state government and the ability of individuals to hold public officials responsible for the state of public affairs. Also, as we observed in Chapter 3, the lack of party competition appears to reduce voter participation in state politics.

The ideal "responsible" party model, with its emphasis on unity and discipline, may be ill suited to a complex, pluralistic society such as the

[4] The traditional assumption that party competition had an important liberalizing effect on public policy is found in V. O. Key, Jr., *American State Politics: An Introduction* (New York: Alfred A. Knopf, Inc., 1956); Duane Lockard, *The Politics of State and Local Government* (New York: The Macmillan Company, 1963); John H. Fenton, *People and Parties in Politics* (Glenview: Scott, Foresman & Company, 1966). The effect of party competition on public policy was shown in statistic analysis to be *less* influential than economic conditions in Thomas R. Dye, *Politics, Economics, and the Public* (Chicago: Rand McNally & Co., 1966); Richard E. Dawson and James A. Robinson, "Inter-Party Competition, Economic Variables, and Welfare Policies in the American States," *Journal of Politics*, 25 (May, 1963): 265–89; Richard I. Hofferbert, "The Relation between Public Policy and Some Structural and Environmental Variables in the American States," *American Political Science Review*, 60 (March, 1966): 78–82. However, party competition combined with voter participation was found to have *some* effect on certain welfare policies in Ira Sharkansky and Richard I. Hofferbert, "Dimensions of State Politics, Economics and Public Policy," *American Political Science Review*, 63 (September, 1969): 867–79. For a full discussion of the impact of economic and political variables in shaping public policy, see Thomas R. Dye, *Understanding Public Policy* (Englewood Cliffs, N.J.: Prentice-Hall, Inc., 1972), Chap. 11.

United States. A large nation with many diverse interests might not be accommodated by a two-party system in which the parties were highly centralized and disciplined. It is the relative irresponsibility of our parties, and the generality and ambiguity of their party platforms that make compromise possible in this nation. Neither party is so different from the other that members of the losing party will fail to support candidates of the winning party after they are elected to office. Austin Ranney has argued that an increase in responsibility, discipline, and unity in American parties might destroy the system rather than improve it: "To the extent that this [party irresponsibility] is an accurate description of our present national party system, it results not from any mere organizational deficiency in our national party machinery, but rather from the diversity and multiplicity of our interest groups and the heterogeneity and complexity of the political conflict they express. As long as the basic nature of the American community remains the same, therefore, centralizing and disciplining our national parties would very likely result in a multiple party rather than a two-party system." [5]

REPUBLICAN AND DEMOCRATIC PARTY FORTUNES IN STATES

In recent years the Democratic party has held a decided edge in American state politics. Table 4–2 shows the number of upper and lower houses in state legislatures controlled by Democrats and Republicans from 1954 through 1974; with the number of Democratic and Republican governors. For most of this period the Democratic party has held control of a majority of state legislatures and governorships.

Because of these Democratic successes, any distribution of states according to the degree of Democratic or Republican party success will be skewed toward the Democratic party. A state's political coloration in national politics may be quite different from its statewide political affiliations. In 1964 five Democratic states of the Old Confederacy (Alabama, Georgia, Louisiana, Mississippi, and South Carolina) voted for Republican presidential candidate Barry Goldwater, largely on the basis of his vote against the Civil Rights Act of 1964. Yet in these states, over 90 percent of both houses of the legislature were Democratic. In 1968 only one (Texas) of the eleven southern states cast its electoral votes for the Democratic presidential nominee, Hubert Humphrey. Five states cast their vote for George C. Wallace (Alabama, Arkansas, Georgia, Louisiana, and Mississippi), and the remainder for Republican Richard Nixon

[5] See Austin Ranney, *The Doctrine of Responsible Party Government* (Urbana: University of Illinois Press, 1954).

TABLE 4.2   Governorships and State Legislative Chambers Controlled By
Democrats and Republicans, 1954-1974

	Upper Houses			Lower Houses			Governorships	
	Dem.	Rep.	Tie	Dem.	Rep.	Tie	Dem.	Rep.
1974	40	7	2	42	7	0	37	12*
1972	29	19	1	31	17	1	32	18
1970	26	21	1	22	25	1	29	21
1968	25	22	1	23	25	0	16	34
1966	29	18	1	25	22	1	24	26
1964	34	12	2	39	9	0	33	17
1962	28	20	0	27	29	1	33	17
1960	30	18	0	31	17	0	34	16
1958	31	17	0	28	9	1	35	15
1956	25	21	2	28	20	0	31	19
1954	20	25	1	26	20	0	27	21

*Maine elected an Independent governor in 1974.
SOURCE: U.S. Bureau of the Census, *Statistical Abstract of the United States.*

(Florida, North Carolina, South Carolina, Tennessee, and Virginia). And in 1972, every southern state gave the Republican President a heavy majority. Yet all these states were strongly (although not exclusively) Democratic in state and local politics. The 1974 election in the states, coming on the heels of the Watergate scandal, was a disaster for Republican party fortunes. Republican strength in state legislatures and governorships was reduced to a new low.

Historically, southern states have accounted for much of the Democratic party's strength in state politics, while midwestern and New England states have accounted for many of the Republican party's victories. It is not really surprising that this regional factor is reflected in Democratic and Republican party successes. The Republican party was founded in 1854 to resist the spread of slavery, which, at the time, was the principal labor source in the southern region. The Civil War was the deepest political cleavage in American history; seventeen states fought for the Union and eleven states for the Confederacy. Of course, the Civil War ended over a century ago, but these party identifications linger on in state politics as a product of the way in which individuals acquire party affiliations from their parents. A few individuals change party affiliation as a result of changes in their social or economic position in life, or a move to another community. But massive party switches take place only under crisis circumstances, such as the Civil War, the Great Depression, or, perhaps, the civil rights revolution of the 1960s.

Democratic and Republican states differ significantly with respect to income and educational levels. Democratic states tend to have lower income and educational levels than Republican states. However, this relationship between Democratic success and state politics in lower income and educational levels depends upon the eleven southern states, which are both Democratic and at the bottom of state rankings on income and education. If we remove the eleven southern states, we find that there is really no relationship in the thirty-nine nonsouthern states between Democratic or Republican party success and urbanization or income or education. There is, however, a significant relationship between Democratic success and industrialization in nonsouthern states: an increase in industrialization leads to an increase in Democratic success.[6]

One interesting trend in party fortunes in recent years has been the rise of Republican voting in a number of southern and border states. Before the Eisenhower years, both southern and border states merited the phrase "the Solid South." Eisenhower made the original inroads into the Solid South by carrying Texas, Virginia, and Florida. When Barry Goldwater cast his vote against the Civil Rights Act of 1964, Republican party fortunes soared in the Deep South states. While it is true that a majority of both Republicans and Democrats in Congress supported the Civil Rights Act, many Deep South voters held the Democratic party responsible, since the act was passed by a Democratic Congress with the support of a Democratic president. Goldwater won electoral votes of five Deep South states—Alabama, Georgia, Louisiana, Mississippi, and South Carolina. George C. Wallace blunted Republican hopes of winning over the entire region in 1968 by winning five Deep South states (Alabama, Arkansas, Georgia, Louisiana, and Mississippi). But in 1972, Republican Richard Nixon's majorities in the southern states were far greater than the national majority. Indeed, the southern states led the Nixon landslide.

But Republican success in southern states in *presidential* elections has not significantly altered the Democratic grip on southern state capitals. Republicans have experienced only a modest increase in their representation in southern state legislatures. Republican Claude Kirk was elected governor of Florida in 1966 and Republican Winthrop Rockefeller was twice elected governor of Arkansas. (Republican Howard "Bo" Calloway won a plurality of votes in the Georgia gubernatorial election of 1966, although he failed to win a majority, and, as prescribed by the state constitution in such cases, the Georgia Legislature picked conservative Democrat Lester Maddox as Governor.) But these flirtations with Republicanism in southern state politics of the late 1960s were blunted with the rise of a

[6] Dye, *Politics, Economics, and the Public*, p. 53.

number of young, moderate, and charismatic southern state governors in the 1970s, including Jimmy Carter of Georgia, Reuben Askew of Florida, and Dale Bumpers of Arkansas. It is likely that the southern states will remain solidly Democratic in state and local politics.

DEMOCRATS AND REPUBLICANS—
WHAT'S THE DIFFERENCE?

It is sometimes difficult to define the meaning of party labels in state politics. The Democratic and Republican party organizations in the fifty states are devoid of any common ideology and very often lacking in clear and consistent policy positions. The Democratic and Republican parties within a state are competing in the same vote market, and, hence, both must tailor their policies to local conditions.

Does this mean that there are no real differences between Republican and Democratic parties in the states? Certainly at the national level, it is not difficult to see the different coalitions of groups that compose the Democratic and Republican parties. While the moderate viewpoints of American parties insure that major social groups are seldom wholly within one party or the other, differences between the Democratic and Republican parties at the national level are revealed by different proportions of votes given by major groups in the electorate to the Democratic and Republican parties.[7] The Democratic party receives a disproportionate amount of support from Catholics and Jews; blacks; lower educational and income groups; younger people; skilled, semiskilled, and unskilled laborers; union members; and big-city residents. The Republican party receives disproportionate support from Protestants; whites; higher educational and income groups; older people; professional, managerial, and other white-collar workers; nonunion members; and rural and small-town residents. (See Table 4–3.)

The differing group bases of the Democratic and Republican parties at the national level are reflected in the policy positions of Democratic and Republican leaders. Herbert J. McCloskey and his associates presented a series of policy questions to over three thousand delegates at the Democratic and Republican National Conventions.[8] McCloskey found that there were substantial differences between Democrats and Republicans

---

[7] See Frank J. Sorauf, *Party Politics in America* (Boston: Little, Brown and Company, 1972).

[8] Herbert J. McCloskey et al., "Issue Conflict and Consensus among Leaders and Followers," *American Political Science Review*, 54 (1960): 426.

TABLE 4.3 Vote by Groups in Presidential Elections (Based on Gallup Poll Survey Data)

	1956		1960		1964		1968			1972	
	Dem Steve.	Rep Ike	Dem JFK	Rep Nixon	Dem LBJ	Rep Gold.	Dem HHH	Rep Nixon	Ind Wallace	Dem McG.	Rep Nixon
NATIONAL	42.2%	57.8%	50.1%	49.9%	61.3%	38.7%	43.0%	43.4%	13.6%	38%	62%
SEX											
Men	45	55	52	48	60	40	41	43	16	37	63
Women	39	61	49	51	62	38	45	43	12	38	62
RACE											
White	41	59	49	51	59	41	38	47	15	32	68
Non-White	61	39	68	32	94	6	85	12	3	87	13
EDUCATION											
College	31	69	39	61	52	48	37	54	9	37	63
High School	42	58	52	48	62	38	42	43	15	34	66
Grade School	50	50	55	45	66	34	52	33	15	49	51
OCCUPATION											
Prof. and Business	32	68	42	58	54	46	34	56	10	31	69
White Collar	37	63	48	52	57	43	41	47	12	36	64
Manual	50	50	60	40	71	29	50	35	15	43	57
AGE											
Under 30 years	43	57	54	46	64	36	47	38	15	48	52
30-49 years	45	55	54	46	63	37	44	41	15	33	67
50 years and older	39	61	46	54	59	41	41	47	12	36	64
RELIGION											
Protestants	37	63	38	62	55	45	35	49	16	30	70
Catholics	51	49	78	22	76	24	59	33	8	48	52

TABLE 4.3   Vote by Groups in Presidential Elections (Based on Gallup Poll Survey Data) (Cont.)

	1956		1960		1964		1968			1972	
	Dem Stev.	Rep Ike	Dem JFK	Rep Nixon	Dem LBJ	Rep Gold.	Dem HHH	Rep Nixon	Ind Wallace	Dem McG.	Rep Nixon
POLITICS											
Republicans	4	96	5	95	20	80	9	86	5	5	95
Democrats	85	15	84	16	87	13	74	12	14	67	33
Independents	30	70	43	57	56	44	31	44	25	31	69
REGION											
East	40	60	53	47	68	32	50	43	7	42	58
Midwest	41	59	48	52	61	39	44	47	9	40	60
South	49	51	51	49	52	48	31	36	33	29	71
West	43	57	49	51	60	40	44	49	7	41	59
MEMBERS OF LABOR											
Union Families	57	43	65	35	73	27	56	29	15	46	54

on important public issues, including public ownership of natural resources, government regulation of economy, equalitarianism, tax policy,
and foreign policy. McCloskey concluded:

> Although it has received wide currency, especially among Europeans, the
> belief that the two American parties are identical in principle and doctrine
> has little foundation in fact. Examination of the opinions of Democratic
> and Republican leaders shows them to be distinct communities of co-
> believers who diverge sharply on many important issues. Their disagree-
> ments, furthermore, conform to an image familiar to most observers and
> are generally consistent with differences turned up by studies of congres-
> sional rollcalls. Republican and Democratic leaders stand furthest apart
> on issues that grow out of their group identification and support—out of
> the managerial, proprietary, and high status connections of the one, and
> the labor, minority, low status, and intellectual connections of the other.[9]

McCloskey went on to identify the different policy positions of his Democratic and Republican leaders:

> Democratic leaders typically display the strongest urge to elevate the low-
> born, the uneducated, the deprived minorities, and the poor in general;
> they are more disposed to employ the nation's collective power to advance
> humanitarian and social welfare goals (for example, social security, im-
> migration, racial integration, a higher minimum wage, and public educa-
> tion). They are more critical of wealth and big business and more eager
> to bring them under regulation. Theirs is the greater faith in the wisdom
> of using legislation for redistributing the national product and for furnish-
> ing social services on a wide scale. Of the two groups of leaders, the
> Democrats are the more "progressively" oriented toward social reform
> and experimentation. Republican leaders, while not uniformly differ-
> entiated from their opponents, subscribed in greater measure to the simple
> practices of individualism, laissez faire, and national independence. They
> prefer to overcome humanity's misfortunes by relying upon personal
> effort, private incentives, frugality, hard work, responsibility, self denial
> (for both men and government), and the strengthening rather than the
> diminution of the economic and status distinctions that are the "natural"
> rewards of the differences of human character and fortunes.[10]

These differences between the Democratic and Republican parties at
the national level can be observed in the politics of some states but not in
others. Certainly, differences between the Democratic and Republican
parties in the large urban industrial states tend to resemble the differences
between the national Democratic and Republican parties. William J. Keefe
reported that Democratic and Republican parties in the Pennsylvania and
Illinois state legislatures differed substantially in questions involving labor

[9] Ibid., p. 426.
[10] Ibid., p. 428.

minorities, social legislation, and the role of government in the economy.[11] On the other hand, the Democratic party in the southern states has *not* typically represented the "lowborn, the uneducated, the deprived minorities, and the poor in general," nor has it advocated the use of national power to advance racial integration. While it is true that the Democratic party in the southern states has supported national efforts to redistribute wealth and furnish social services on a national scale, one suspects that the southern Democrats have done so for the very practical reason that the southern states stand to gain the most by such redistribution. Nor has the Republican party in New York always conformed to the symbols and practices of individualism and laissez faire to the same extent as the national Republican party. New York Republicans have rather consistently supported social welfare measures at both the state and the national level. In short, the national images of the Democratic and Republican parties are not always the images that these parties reflect in the politics of individual states.

State Republican and Democratic parties resemble the national Republican and Democratic parties only in those states where each party represents separate socioeconomic constituencies. Party conflict over policy questions is most frequent in those states in which the Democratic party represents central-city, low-income, ethnic, and racial constituencies, and the Republican party represents middle-class, suburban, small-town, and rural constituencies.[12] In these larger urban industrialized states, the Democratic and Republican parties will tend to disagree over taxation and appropriations, welfare, education, and regulation of business and labor —that is, the major social and economic controversies that divide the national parties.

In contrast, state parties do not necessarily reflect national party differences in homogeneous states, where there are no major social divisions in the electorate. For example, the Democratic party does not fully reflect the views of labor groups, Catholic voters, and racial and ethnic minorities in those midwestern and New England states that do not have large numbers of these kinds of voters. In these states the Democratic party will tend to be atypical of the national Democratic party and will tend to represent the attitudes of small-town and rural residents, farmers,

[11] William J. Keefe, "Comparative Study of the Role of Political Parties in State Legislatures," *Western Political Quarterly,* 9 (1956): 535–41.

[12] See Thomas A. Flinn, "Party Responsibility in the States: Some Causal Factors," *American Political Science Review,* 58 (1964): 60–71; Duncan MacRae, Jr., "The Relation between Roll Call Votes and Constituencies in the Massachusetts House of Representatives," *American Political Science Review,* 46 (1952): 1046–55; and Thomas R. Dye, "A Comparison of Constituency Influences in the Upper and Lower Chambers of a State Legislature," *Western Political Quarterly,* 14 (1961): 473–80.

and shopkeepers. Similarly, the Republican party in New York cannot afford the image of a party devoted to the interests of white, Protestant, middle-class, small-town, rural people. New York's large number of Catholics and Jews, ethnic groups, Negroes and Puerto Ricans, low-income, urban dwellers make the New York state Republican party something different from the national Republican party. Traditionally, the Democratic party in southern states did not represent urban, ethnic, or racial minorities; quite the contrary, it was the party of the "establishment." The fact that the national Democratic party has been associated at various times with the aspirations of minorities in America, including blacks, has caused quite a bit of confusion and frustration among the ranks of traditional southern Democrats.[13] Many white *rural* southern Democrats go to great lengths to disassociate themselves from the national Democratic party. Increasingly, in *urban* areas of the South, however, the Democratic and Republican parties are coming to represent the separate socioeconomic constituencies described above.[14]

Nonetheless, *national* party affiliations of voters do affect their voting in *state* elections.[15] Basic party identifications of voters operate in state elections in spite of statewide issues, candidate images, and other local factors. National surveys reveal that Democratic party identifiers tend to vote Democratic in state as well as national elections and Republican party identifiers show the same voting consistency. This is true even though candidates of different parties frequently win statewide majorities in the same election, owing to split-ticket voting. These results can occur when only five or ten percent of the national party identifiers defect from their party in a statewide election. Interestingly, such defections are attributable more to the effects of *incumbency* than any other local factor.[16] Generally, an incumbent running for re-election can count on winning a small but significant number of votes from persons who identify with the opposition party.

NATIONAL TIDES AND STATE POLITICS

National political tides can have an important bearing on party fortunes in states and communities. National issues, personalities, and party loyalties

[13] For a description of contrasting views of the national Democratic party and the Mississippi Democratic party, see F. Glenn Abney, "Partisan Realignment in a One-Party System," *Journal of Politics,* 31 (November, 1969): 1102–6.

[14] See Jerry Perkins, "Bases of Partisan Cleavage in a Southern Urban County," *Journal of Politics,* 36 (February, 1974): 208–14.

[15] For an interesting documentation of the relationship between national and state party voting, see Andrew Cowart, "Electoral Choice in the American States," *American Political Science Review,* 67 (September, 1973): 835–53.

[16] Ibid.

TABLE 4.4   Governorship Won by Democrats and Republicans

	Eisenhower v. Stevenson 1956		Off-Year 1958		Kennedy v. Nixon 1960		Off-Year 1962		
	Dem	Rep	Dem	Rep	Dem	Rep	Dem	Rep	
	17	14	30	9	16	12	25	14	

Johnson v. Goldwater 1964		Off-Year 1966		Nixon v. Humphrey 1968		Off-Year 1970		Nixon v. McGovern 1972		Off-Year 1974		
Dem	Rep	Dem	Rep	Dem	Rep	Dem	Rep	Dem	Rep	Dem	Rep	Ind
18	8	13	24	8	13	22	13	11	7	28	6	1

can affect voting for state and local offices, particularly in presidential election years. Of course, one way of trying to insulate state elections from national influences is to hold state elections at times other than the dates of national elections. About half of the states elect their governors in off years, that is, years in which no presidential election takes place. Eleven states elect their governors for two-year terms in even-numbered years and alternate gubernatorial elections between presidential years and off years. Twelve states elect their governors for four-year terms in presidential years, and, theoretically, these states are most subject to national tides in their gubernatorial politics. It is difficult to measure the effect of a president's "coattails" in state politics. Eisenhower did not appear to help Republican officeholders in the states in 1956; yet in 1958, without Eisenhower at the head of the Republican ticket, Republicans fared even worse. In 1960 the Kennedy-Nixon battle was so close that no national trends were apparent, although Kennedy helped many local Democratic candidates in big-city, Catholic areas. Johnson was influential in sweeping many state and local candidates into office in 1964 (although it may have been that Goldwater was influential in keeping many Republican candidates out of office). Republicans fared much better in the off years 1962 and 1966 when Johnson was not a candidate (and Goldwater was not leading the Republican ticket). Nixon appeared to help GOP candidates for governor in 1968. In 1970 Nixon campaigned for Republican candidates, but they fared badly nonetheless; and Nixon's landslide in 1972 provided little or no help to state GOP candidates. Republican candidates suffered badly from the stigma of Watergate in the 1974 off-year elections. The GOP won only six of thirty-five governorships up for election, and lost control of the governors' offices in the nation's two largest states, New York and California, when Rockefeller and Reagan left office and were succeeded by Democrats. Voter disillusionment with both parties was reflected in the election of an independent candidate in Maine, the first independent candidate elected governor of a state in nearly fifty years.

Republican party identification among the nation's voters is at a low ebb. Opinion polls report party identifications of the national electorate as:

Republicans	23%
Democrats	47%
Independents	30%

Democrats have maintained their two-to-one margin over Republicans for many years, despite Republican victories in Presidential elections. However, in recent years both parties have lost to the rise of "Independents"

—individuals who decline to identify themselves with either party. The reluctance of voters to identify with the GOP is particularly frustrating to Republican leaders, who view their party as a vehicle of conservatism. Opinion polls report that "conservative" is a more popular political label than "liberal":

Conservative	40%
Liberal	30%
No Opinion	30%

But the Republican party has failed to convince many "conservative" Democrats and Independents to affiliate with the GOP. The Democratic party is clearly the majority party nationally, and its success in state politics is evident.

THE STRUCTURE OF
STATE PARTY ORGANIZATIONS

State party organizations generally consist of a "state committee," a "state chairman," and perhaps a small office staff working at the state capitol. Democratic and Republican state committees vary from state to state in composition, organization, and functions; they are generally controlled by state law. Membership on the state committee may range from about a dozen up to several hundred. The members may be chosen through party primaries or by state party conventions. Generally, representation on state committees is allocated to counties, but occasionally other units of government are recognized in state party organization. A state party chairman generally serves at the head of the state committee; state chairmen are generally selected by the state committee, but their selection is often dictated by the party's candidate for governor.

State committees are supposed to direct the campaigns for important statewide elections—governors and U.S. senators, and congressmen in the smaller states. They are supposed to serve as central coordinating agencies for these election campaigns and to serve as the party's principal fund-raising organization in the state. However, the role of the state committee very often depends upon the preferences of the party's statewide candidates regarding the handling of their campaigns. Often candidates have their own campaign organizations to plan and execute campaign strategy. State party organizations may or may not play an effective role in the candidate's campaign, depending upon the candidate's preferences. State committees are not very responsive to the direction of the national committee, and in most states, city and county party organizations operate quite independently of the state committees. In other words, there is no real hierarchy of authority in state party systems. As V. O. Key explained: "The party organization is sometimes regarded as a hierarchy, based upon the precinct executive, and capped by the national committee, but it may be more accurately described as a system of layers of organization. Each successive layer—county or city, state, national—has an independent concern about elections in its geographical jurisdiction. Yet each higher level of organization, to accomplish its ends, must obtain the collaboration of the lower layer or layers of organization. That collaboration comes about, to the extent that it does come about, through a sense of common cause rather than by the exercise of command." [17]

Party organizations at the city and county level are probably the most cohesive organizations within the parties. Yet these organizations are far from a disciplined, cohesive group. Frank Sorauf describes the "average" city or county party organization as follows: [18]

1. An active chairman and executive committee, plus a few associated activists, who in effect make most of the decisions in the name of the party, who raise funds, who seek out and screen candidates (or approve the candidates who select themselves), and who speak locally for the party.
2. A ward and precinct organization in which only a few local committeemen are active and in which there is little door-to-door canvassing or other direct voter contact.
3. The active participation in organizational matters of some of the party's elected public officials, who may share effective control of the organization with the official leadership of the party organization.
4. A distinctly periodic calendar of activities marked by a watchful waiting or general inactivity at other than election times.

Nonetheless, the nation's three thousand Republican and three thousand Democratic county chairmen probably constitute the most important building blocks in party organization in America. City and county party officers and committees are chosen locally and cannot be removed by any higher party authority. City and county committees are elected by the voters in their constituency, and they cannot be removed by state committees or national committees of their party, even if they decide to campaign for the opposition party. In short, authority is not concentrated

[17] V. O. Key, Jr., *Politics, Parties, and Pressure Groups* (New York: Thomas Y. Crowell Company, 1964), p. 316.

[18] Frank J. Sorauf, *Party Politics in America*, 2nd ed. (Boston: Little, Brown and Company, 1972), p. 72.

in any single statewide organization but is divided among many city and county party organizations.

State party organizations have also been weakened by our system of primary elections for determining the party's nominee for statewide office. State party organizations were very powerful in the nineteenth century, when state party *conventions* made the nominations for statewide office. But with the advent of the *primary system,* support from party leaders was no longer a prerequisite for a party nomination, and anyone who wished to run for governor, senator, or other statewide offices could organize a group of supporters to place his name on the party's primary ballot. The state party organization or convention may give an "official" endorsement to a candidate in the primary, but such an endorsement may or may not carry weight with the party's rank-and-file voters.

Although state party organizations are weakened by decentralization, state party chairmen are by no means political hacks. Most state chairmen have been successful businessmen, lawyers, or public officials, who serve in their posts without salaries to satisfy their interest in politics and public affairs.[19] Republican chairmen are more likely to have held important positions in business and management, while Democratic chairmen are more likely to be lawyers who have previously held political office.

City and county, rather than state, party organizations are the most cohesive levels of organization. City machines and bosses are discussed at length in Chapter 9, together with the reform movements which have attempted to counter their power. There are very few *statewide* machines headed by *state* bosses that command the loyalties of their county chairmen and direct party affairs from a statewide perspective. Huey Long's organization in Louisiana in the 1920s and 1930s and the Harry Byrd organization in Virginia from the 1930s to the 1960s could be classified as statewide machines. They were tightly disciplined party organizations, held together and motivated by a desire for tangible benefits rather than by principle or ideology. They established a system of rewards and punishments in which votes were obtained by trading off social services, patronage jobs, and petty favors; these were, in turn, paid for by kickbacks from public contractors, bribes from holders of business franchises, contributions from persons with an interest in specific public policies, and other proceeds from the sale of government benefits. It is not a coincidence that most statewide machines developed in the poor rural states, particularly in the South. It is in these states, with their rural economies, lower family income, and poorly educated work forces, that patronage looks most attrac-

[19] See Charles W. Wiggins and William L. Turk, "State Party Chairmen: A Profile," *Western Political Quarterly,* 23 (June, 1970): 321–32.

tive, and local pork barrel projects are most important. "Ole Gene" Talmadge found that Georgia's county chairmen could be bought relatively cheaply; all that was required was a firm grip on the state highway department, which acted as the chief dispenser of patronage and pork in the Talmadge organization. It is also in the poorer rural states where demagoguery can be an important instrument of power, supplementing the use of patronage and pork. A demagogue plays upon racial and religious prejudice and fear to attract uneducated masses to his cause. However, statewide political machines are highly exceptional, and on the whole, state party organizations are quite decentralized. (See Chapter 9 for further discussion.)

STATE PARTY ORGANIZATIONS IN DISARRAY

While national party *conventions* still nominate the presidential candidates, party *primary* elections nominate most other candidates for public office in America. For the nation's first century, candidates were nominated by party conventions, not primary elections, and as a result party organizations were far more influential then than they are today. Primary elections were a key reform in the "progressive" movement of the early twentieth century. Primaries "democratized" the nomination process and reduced the power of party "bosses."

Primary elections in 41 states are "closed"—that is, only voters who have previously registered as members of a party may vote in that party's primary. Only registered Democrats vote in the Democratic primary, and only registered Republicans vote in the Republican primary. Primaries in nine states are "open" [20]—voters can choose when they enter the polling place which party primary they wish to vote in. (In Alaska and Washington, voters can vote in *both* party primaries simultaneously.) Party leaders generally prefer the closed primary because they fear "cross-overs" and "raiding": *cross-overs* are voters who choose to vote in the primary of the party that they usually do not support in the general election; *raiding* is an organized attempt to cross over and try to defeat an attractive candidate running for the opposition party's nomination. But there is no evidence that large numbers of voters connive in such a fashion.

State party conventions continue in a handful of states. New York and Connecticut parties hold statewide conventions and nominate candidates; however, these nominations can be "challenged" in a later primary election, with the winner becoming the official party nominee.

---

[20] Alaska, Michigan, Minnesota, Montana, North Dakota, Utah, Vermont, Washington, and Wisconsin.

Primaries, then, reduce the influence of party organizations in the political process. It is possible, of course, for party organizations at the city, county, or state levels to "endorse," officially or unofficially, candidates in primary elections. The importance of endorsements varies with the strength and unity of party organizations. Where party organizations are strong at the city or county level (where "machines" are still alive), the word can be passed down to ward chairmen and precinct committeemen to turn out the party's faithful for the endorsed candidate. But party endorsement in a statewide race appears to have less value.

The failure of statewide organizations to have much influence over primary outcomes is due in part to changes in the styles of political activity in recent years. First of all, party organizations are weak or nonexistent in many counties: there are *no* ward or precinct-level workers. (Reasons for the decline of city and county party organizations are discussed in Chapter 9.) More importantly, traditional "grass-roots" efforts—telephoning, door-knocking, riding voters to the polls—which are usually handled by party organizations, have given way to mass-media techniques. Television appearances, radio commercials, and mass mailings, permit a candidate to take his case directly to the voters, without the party organization as intermediary.

A classic case of contrasting political styles—"exposure versus organization"—is reported by Frank Sorauf in the defeat of the powerful Democratic party organization of Pennsylvania by millionaire industrialist Milton Shapp.[21] In 1966, the state Democratic organization endorsed a youthful state legislative leader, Robert P. Casey, for governor, and few observers gave much chance to Milton Shapp, an older, wealthy, Philadelphia industrialist who had not held any previous elective office. But Shapp spent an estimated one million dollars, largely from his own personal fortune, for 34 half-hour, prime-time television shows, thousands of radio commercials, and the mailing of an impressive brochure to one and a half million voters. Shapp's campaign was directed by a professional campaign management and public-relations firm. The result was an upset victory for Shapp and a stunning defeat for organizational politics in the primary election. Democrat Shapp lost the *general* election in 1966, but went on to defeat the Democratic organization again in 1970 and win the governorship for two consecutive terms with the same methods.

Mass-media campaigns, directed by professional public-relations specialists, have also replaced the party organizations' role in the *general* election. Few candidates for governor or U.S. senator rely exclusively on the party organization to handle their campaigns. Most statewide candidates create their own campaign organizations, and increasingly these can-

[21] Frank J. Sorauf, *Party Politics*, pp. 230–31.

didates are relying on professional public-relations firms or consultants to manage a mass-media campaign. Both Nelson Rockefeller in New York and Ronald Reagan in California relied heavily on professional mass-media campaigns, and both of these Republicans won election and re-election in heavily Democratic states. It is doubtful that they could have achieved such success if they relied on the sickly Republican party organizations in these states. Thus, the new "image industry" is gradually replacing the role of party organizations in campaigns. As one candidate explains:

> With mass media which use a common language that everyone can read, people no longer need party workers to advise them how to vote. When a citizen can see and hear a candidate on a screen at home, and read news, written by the best journalists from a variety of points of view, about the candidate's public and private life, he does not heed what is told him by the precinct captain on his block. . . . A candidate now pays less attention to district leaders than to opinion polls.[22]

---

[22] Stimson Bullit, *To Be A Politician* (New York: Anchor, 1961), p. 65.

Legislators in state politics

FUNCTIONS OF STATE LEGISLATURES

If you were to ask state legislators what the job of the legislature is, they might say: "Our job is to pass laws," or "We have to represent the people," or "We have to make policy." All the answers are correct. But none by itself tells the whole story of the role of the legislature in state politics.

It is true that, from a legal viewpoint, the function of state legislatures is to "pass laws," that is, the enactment of statutory law. In the early 1950s American state legislators considered about 25,000 bills a year, but by the 1970s this figure had grown to over 150,000. The total number of state legislative enactments grew from approximately 15,000 to over 50,000 in that same twenty-year period.[1] As our society grows more complex and becomes increasingly urban and industrial, the need for formal statutory control seems to grow. Legislatures in urban industrial states will enact more than 1,000 laws in a legislative session, while legislatures in rural agricultural states will enact fewer than 500.

The range of subject matter of bills considered by a legislature is enormous. A legislature may consider the authorization of a billion dollars

[1] Council of State Governments, *Book of the States*. Published biennially by the Council of State Governments, Chicago.

Chapter five

of state spending, or it may debate the expansion of the hunting season on raccoons, or it may increase teachers' salaries, or it may argue whether or not inscribing license plates with "The Poultry State" would cause the state to be called "chicken." Obviously, these considerations range from the trivial to the vital; yet every bill that comes into the legislature is important to someone. In addition to the enactment of statutory law, legislatures share in the process of state constitutional revision, approve many of the governor's appointments, establish U.S. congressional districts, and consider amendments to the U.S. Constitution. But perhaps their single most important legal function is the passage of the appropriation and tax measures in the state budget. No state monies may be spent without a legislative appropriation, and it is difficult to think of any governmental action that does not involve some financial expenditure. Potentially, a legislature can control any activity of the state government through its power over appropriations, but as a practical matter, this legal power over fiscal affairs does not amount to political control.

From a political viewpoint, the function of state legislatures is to resolve conflicts over public policy. But it is misleading to say merely that the legislature "makes policy." Obviously, the legislature is not the only group that helps to make policy. The governor, the courts, executive agencies, interest groups, the press, political parties, and many other groups of individuals share in the making of public policy. How, then, do we distinguish the role of the legislature from that of other groups? For example, does the legislature merely "rubber stamp" the decisions of a strong governor or of the influential leaders of powerful interest groups? Or are legislatures themselves an important part of the process of proposing and deciding public policy? Does the legislature merely referee political struggles between organized interests in the state, recording the terms of surrender, compromises, or conquests in the form of statutes, or does the legislature exercise independent influence over policy? Are legislatures "initiators" of public policy, or do they merely express public sentiment in favor of or in opposition to policies initiated by others?

It is true, from the point of view of representation, that the legislature functions to "represent the people." But the question remains, "How does a state legislature go about representing the people?" Do legislators simply "mirror" the views of their constituents, or do they exercise independent judgment in determining policy judgments? In "representing the people," does a legislator reflect the views of his state, his constituency, interest groups, his party, or his own conscience? We hope in this chapter to explore some of the forces influencing the way in which legislators "represent the people."

THE MAKING OF A STATE LEGISLATOR

People need not be physically represented in a legislature in order for their interests to be recognized. State legislators are not "representative" of the population of their states in the sense of being typical cross sections of them. On the contrary, the nation's 7,800 state legislators are generally selected from the better-educated, more prestigiously employed, middle-class segments of the population. Yet our system of popular elections requires these legislators to "represent" the interests of their constituents, even though they do not share the same social background as their constituents.

However, evidence indicates that legislators generally mirror their constituents in certain "birthright" characteristics—race, religion, and ethnic and national background. In a thorough study of the Pennsylvania state legislature, for example, Frank Sorauf found that religious composition of constituencies had a distinct impact on both Democratic and Republican candidates.[2] Protestant candidates came from Protestant districts, and Catholics tended to win in Catholic districts. These religious differences parallel ethnic differences. Catholic candidates seldom won in the Protestant "Bible Belt" counties of Pennsylvania, nor did Lutherans or Presbyterians win in the Irish and Italian wards of Philadelphia.

Another social characteristic in which the constituencies demand conformity is race. Of the nearly eight thousand state legislators in the nation, no more than two hundred are black. Blacks are reasonably well represented in the legislatures of northern urban industrial states where the black population is concentrated in core areas of large cities. Blacks are seriously underrepresented in the legislatures of southern and border rural states. This underrepresentation occurs primarily because blacks are spread out in rural areas rather than concentrated in black urban constituencies. The vast majority of the nation's black state legislators are Democrats elected from ghetto areas of large cities. For the near future, it is very likely that all, or nearly all, black state legislators in the nation will come from majority black constituencies. From the viewpoint of representation, the ghettos, with their concentration of black voters, grant blacks an advantage in capturing legislative seats. This advantage is lost when the black vote is spread out and diluted. For the same reason, single-member legislative districts give blacks an advantage in capturing legislative seats over multimember districts which dilute the black vote to the point where it is less than a majority.

[2] Frank J. Sorauf, *Party and Representation* (New York: Atherton Press, 1963), pp. 89–94.

Legislators are far less mobile than the population as a whole. They tend to have deep roots in their constituencies. One study reported that 83 percent of the state legislators of New Jersey had been born in the district they represented or had lived there over thirty years; in Tennessee this figure was 76 percent and in Ohio it was 88 percent. Even in California, one of the states with the highest population mobility, 56 percent of the legislators had been born in their district or had lived there thirty years, and only 10 percent had lived in their districts less than ten years.[3]

Certain social characteristics, however, escape the constituencies' demand for conformity. More than three-quarters of the nation's state legislators have been exposed to a college education, a striking contrast to the educational level of the total population. Legislators are also concentrated in the occupations with more prestige. A great majority of legislators are either engaged in the professions or are proprietors, managers, or officials of business concerns. Farmers constitute a sizable minority of legislators in all but the most urban states. Lawyers are the largest single occupational group.

Women in our population are seldom represented by more than 5 percent of the members of any state legislature. Sorauf reports that the legislative chambers bear the signs of the male club—highly burnished cuspidors, for example; the lady legislator "may be viewed as an intruder in the smoking-room company." [4] Women are somewhat better represented (up to 18 percent) in the less populous New England and western states with less "professional" legislatures; the large urban industrial states with more "professional" legislatures have few female representatives.[5]

Social background information on state legislators also indicates that legislators tend to come from the "upwardly mobile" sectors of the population.[6] This places many of them among the "second-rung" elites in the

[3] John C. Wahlke et al., *The Legislative System* (New York: John Wiley & Sons, Inc., 1962), p. 488.

[4] Sorauf, *Party and Representation*, p. 67.

[5] For an excellent survey of women in state legislatures from 1921 to 1964, see Emmy F. Werner, "Women in State Legislatures," *Western Political Quarterly*, 21 (March, 1968): 40–50.

[6] The data on social characteristics of state legislators are voluminous. More useful studies include Charles S. Hyneman, "Who Makes Our Laws," *Political Science Quarterly*, 55 (1940): 556–81; Paul Beckett and Celeste Sunderland, "Washington State Lawmakers," *Western Political Quarterly*, 10 (1957): 180–202; Joseph A. Schlesinger, "Lawyers and American Politics," *Midwest Journal of Political Science*, 1 (1957): 26–39; David Derge, "The Lawyer as Decision-Maker in American State Legislatures," *Journal of Politics*, 21 (1959): 408–33; Victor S. Hjelm and Joseph P. Pisciotte, "Profiles and Careers of Colorado State Legislators," *Western Political Quarterly*, 21 (December, 1968): 698–722; Wahlke et al., *The Legislative System*, pp. 489–90; and Sorauf *Party and Representation*, pp. 75–81.

status system rather than the established wealth. Although the sons and grandsons of distinguished old families of great wealth are increasingly entering presidential and gubernatorial politics in the states, they seldom run for the state legislature. In contrast, state legislators have tended to take up occupations with more prestige than their fathers. Legislators are frequently among the middle or upper-middle status groups for whom politics is an avenue of upward mobility. Constituencies accept higher educated, more "prestigiously" employed candidates in the name of success, status, and the popular conceptions of "qualifications" for the legislative job.

In general, constituencies seek socially rising men from the prevailing racial, religious, and nationality groups of the district. Candidates should be "respectable" in whatever ways the local mores define that term. The voters seem to want candidates typical of themselves in religion, race, and ethnic background, but with education, occupation, and social status above the average. In short, constituents seem to prefer that their legislators be "local boys made good." [7]

Occupational data also clearly indicate that the state legislator's job is a part-time one. Legislators must come from occupational groups with flexible work responsibility. The lawyer, the farmer, or the business owner can adjust his work to the legislative schedule, but the office manager cannot. The overrepresented occupations are those involving extensive public contact. The lawyer, insurance agent, farm implement dealer, tavern owner, and undertaker establish in their businesses the wide circle of friends necessary for political success. In short, the legislator's occupation should provide free time, public contacts, and social respectability.

The overrepresentation of lawyers among state legislators is particularly marked. It is sometimes argued that the lawyer brings a special kind of skill to politics. The lawyer's occupation is the representation of clients, so he makes no great change in occupation when he moves from representing clients in private practice to representing constituents in the legislature. A lawyer is trained to deal with public policy as it is reflected in the statute books, so he may be reasonably familiar with public policy before entering the legislature. Also, service in the legislature can help a lawyer's private practice through free public advertising and opportunities to make contacts with potential clients.[8]

There are also important structural advantages for lawyers to enter state politics—specifically, the availability of a large number of highly valued "lawyers-only" posts in state government, such as judge and

---

[7] Sorauf, *Party and Representation*, p. 91.

[8] Schlesinger, "Lawyers and American Politics," pp. 26–39; Derge, "The Lawyer as Decision-Maker in American State Legislatures," pp. 408–33.

prosecuting attorney. Lawyers are eligible for many elective and appointive public jobs from which nonlawyers are excluded. State legislative seats are viewed by lawyers as stepping stones to these posts—appellate court judge, Supreme Court justice, attorney general, regulatory commissioner, etc. Examination of postlegislative careers of lawyers show that over half go on to other public offices, compared to less than one-third of the nonlawyer legislators.[9] Moreover, available evidence suggests that lawyers in the legislature are more likely to entertain conscious aspirations for advancement than nonlawyers.

We know, then, that legislators differ from their constituents in certain *socioeconomic* background characteristics—social class, education, occupation. But are there *psychological* differences between legislators and their constituents which are independent of these socioeconomic differences? Years ago, political scientist John B. McConaughy succeeded in getting South Carolina state legislators to submit to extensive psychological testing.[10] The results suggested that legislators were more self-sufficient, more self-confident, more extroverted, slightly more dominant, less neurotic, and less fascistic than the average American. A more recent study of Iowa state legislators found that legislators are generally more tolerant toward others, less authoritarian, and more favorably disposed toward minority groups than a cross-section of Iowa voters, even when the effects of socioeconomic backgrounds are controlled.[11] In short, there is some evidence that psychological predispositions—self-confidence, gregariousness, tolerance toward others—operate as self-selective factors in determining who will choose to make a career in political life.

GETTING TO THE STATE CAPITOL

The state legislature is a convenient starting place for a political career. About one-half of the state legislators in the nation have never served in public office before their election to the legislature, and a greater percentage of new members are in the lower rather than upper chambers. The other half had only limited experience on city councils, county commissions, and school boards. The record of turnover of state legislators

---

[9] See Paul J. Hain and James E. Pierson, "Lawyers and Politics Revisited: Structural Advantages of Lawyer-Politicians," *American Journal of Political Science*, 19 (February, 1975): 41–51.

[10] John B. McConaughy, "Some Personality Factors of State Legislators," in John C. Wahlke and Heinz Eulau, eds., *Legislative Behavior: A Reader in Theory and Research* (Glencoe, Ill.: Free Press, 1959).

[11] Ronald W. Hedlund, "Psychological Predispositions: Political Representatives and the Public," *American Journal of Political Science*, 19 (August, 1973): 489–505.

suggests that returning to office is not particularly important to many of them. Thus, in many ways the state legislatures appear "amateurish" in comparison with Congress, where turnover is low and members acquire more parliamentary skills. The high turnover clearly is *not* a product of competition for the job; only a very small proportion of state legislators are rejected at the polls. Most simply do not seek re-election and quit because of dissatisfaction: "Being in the legislature has hurt my law practice and cost me money"; "Any way you look at it, the job means a sacrifice to you, your home, and your business"; "It's a nervous life"; "The more service a man has, the more enemies he makes." [12]

Why does a legislator decide to run for office in the first place? It is next to impossible to determine the real motivations of political office seekers—they seldom know themselves. Legislators will usually describe their motivations in highly idealistic terms: "I felt that I could do the community a service"; "I considered it a civic duty." [13] Only seldom are reasons for candidacy expressed in personal terms: "Oh, I just think it's lots of fun." Gregariousness and the desire to socialize no doubt contribute to the reasons for some office seekers. Politics can have a special lure of its own: "It gets into your blood and you like it." Particular issues may mobilize a political career but ideological involvement occupies a relatively unimportant place in a candidate's motives. Activity in organizations that are deeply involved in politics also leads to candidacy: "When I decided to run, I was quite active in the union." There is some evidence that political activists, including legislators, from middle- and upper-class districts are more *ideologically motivated* (running for office to correct perceived wrongs, do good, resolve issues, etc.) than political activists from working-class districts, who are more *personally motivated* (running to achieve prestige, recognition, or material rewards).[14]

An individual faces two important obstacles when he decides to run for the state legislature: the primary and the general election. His seat in the legislature depends on how much competition he meets in these elections. First, let us consider competition in the primary elections. Available evidence indicates that more than half of the nation's state legislators are unopposed for their party's nomination in primary elections. Many legislators who do face primary competition have only token opposition. V. O. Key has shown that most primary competition occurs

---

[12] Quotations from state legislators interviewed by Wahlke et al., *The Legislative System*, pp. 95–134.

[13] Ibid.

[14] For a more detailed analysis of why people "get into politics," see Margaret Conway and Frank B. Feiget, "Motivation, Incentive Systems and Party Organization," *American Political Science Review*, 62 (December, 1968): 1159–73.

in a party's "sure" districts, some competition occurs in "close" districts, and there is a distinct shortage of candidates in districts where the party's chances are poor.[15] In other words, primary competition is greater where the likelihood of victory in the general election is greater. Exceptions to this generalization are found in districts where the incumbent legislator is so strong that he discourages prospective competitors, even though chances for the party's success in the general election may be good.

The culmination of the recruitment process is in the general election, yet in many legislative constituencies one party is so entrenched that the voters have little real choice at the general election. In many one-party states, the minority party is so weak that it fails to run candidates for many legislative seats. In the southern and border states where the legislatures are heavily Democratic, there often is no competition in the general election for legislative seats. (Of course, in these states primary competition in the majority party is frequent.) More seats are contested in states with close two-party competition, but even in a hotly contested state such as Pennsylvania, nominations to the state legislature occasionally will not be filled because of a collapse in local party organization in certain districts. "Competition" implies more than a name filed under the opposition party label. Generally a competitive election is one in which the winning candidate wins by something less than two to one. In light of this more realistic definition of competition, the absence of truly competitive politics in state legislative elections is striking. Even in Pennsylvania, over half of the state legislators are elected by margins in excess of two to one.[16] Similar findings are reported for competitive Massachusetts and Michigan.[17]

Turnover in state legislatures is considered high—the overall rate in recent years for fifty state senates is 30.4 percent; for forty-nine state houses, it is 36.1 percent.[18] This means that about one-third of all state legislators are new-comers at any legislative session; there is widespread speculation that such turnover weakens state legislatures and reduces their effectiveness. However, turnover rates vary by state, ranging from below 20 percent to above 50 percent. Interestingly, it is *not* party com-

---

[15] V. O. Key, Jr., *American State Politics: An Introduction* (New York: Alfred A. Knopf, Inc., 1956), pp. 171–81.

[16] Sorauf, *Party and Representation*, p. 117.

[17] Duncan MacRae, "The Relations between Roll-Call Votes and Constituencies in the Massachusetts House of Representatives," *American Political Science Review*, 46 (1952): 1046–55; Robert W. Becker et al., "Correlates of Legislative Voting," *Midwest Journal of Political Science*, 6 (1962): 384–96.

[18] Alan Rosenthal, "Turnover in State Legislatures," *American Journal of Political Science*, 18 (August, 1974): 609–16.

petition that increases turnover; far more legislators voluntarily quit than are defeated for re-election. A careful study of factors affecting turnover indicates that the frequency of elections is the most important factor. The more often one has to go through the work and expense of a campaign for re-election, the more likely one is to voluntarily give up the seat. Reapportionment also contributes to turnover, but this should occur only after each ten-year census. (In 1971–72, reapportionment resulted in an average turnover of 43 percent in state senates and 38 percent in state houses.[19]) There is *less* turnover in the larger states, which have longer legislative sessions and pay their legislators more money. In other words, more "professional" legislatures have lower turnover rates than the "amateur" legislatures.

Over time, legislative turnover appears to be decreasing, as state legislatures become more professional.[20] Higher pay, greater prestige, more professional staff assistance, and increased perquisites of office may reduce voluntary retirements, even though sessions are longer and more work is required. An increasing percentage of legislators are seeking re-election in urban, industrial states, and despite greater party competition, these incumbents are remaining in office. It is still an open question, however, whether increased experience and seniority lead to more effective legislatures.

"LEGISLATORS REPRESENT PEOPLE, NOT TREES OR ACRES"

The politics of representation center about the size and composition of legislative districts and who gains and who loses from the variations. Inequality of representation, or "malapportionment," is claimed when there are differing numbers of people in districts that receive the same number of representatives in the legislature. For example, if one legislator represents a district of ten thousand inhabitants and another a district of forty thousand, it is said that the right to vote in the smaller districts is worth four times as much as it is in the larger district.

Prior to 1962 malapportionment was widespread in American state legislatures. Small minorities of the population could elect a majority of the house or senate or both in most of the states. Generally it was the rural voters in a state who controlled a majority of legislative seats, and

[19] Council of State Governments, *Book of the States, 1974–1975*, p. 69.
[20] David Ray, "Membership Stability in Three State Legislatures: 1893–1969," *American Political Science Review*, 68 (March, 1974): 106–12.

it was the urban voters who were discriminated against in the value of their vote.[21]

For many years the federal courts avoided the distasteful task of compelling legislative reapportionment by asserting that this was a legislative rather than a judicial function. Underrepresented populations were told by the courts that their remedy was to elect a legislature that would do its duty, a worthless prescription, of course, since electing a legislature was the very thing underrepresented populations could not do.[22] The position of the courts changed radically, however, after the U.S. Supreme Court decision in *Baker* v. *Carr*.[23] This case involved the complaint of urban residents in Tennessee where the largest district in the lower house was twenty-three times larger than the smallest district. The Supreme Court decided that such inequalities in state apportionment laws denied voters "equal protection of the laws" guaranteed by the Fourteenth Amendment and that the federal courts should grant relief from these inequalities.

Reaction to the decision was immediate and widespread. Underrepresented voters throughout the nation petitioned federal courts to order state legislative reapportionment on the basis of the equal protection clause of the Fourteenth Amendment. Federal courts found themselves struggling with the mathematics of apportionment. The courts did not decide on any firm mathematical standard of correct apportionment, holding only that "as nearly as practicable, one man's vote should be equal to another's." [24] State after state was induced to reapportion its legislature under the threat of judicial intervention. In addition to requiring population equality in legislative districting, the Supreme Court also required population equality in congressional districting by state legislatures [25] and threw out the county unit system of voting in statewide elections.[26] The philosophy underlying all these decisions was expressed by the Court: "The conception of political equality from the Declaration of Independence to Lincoln's Gettysburg Address, to the Fourteenth, Fifteenth, Seventeenth, and Nineteenth Amendments, can mean only one thing—one person, one vote." [27] The Court made no

---

[21] Paul T. David and Ralph Eisenberg, *Devaluation of the Urban and Suburban Vote* (Charlottesville: Bureau of Public Administration, University of Virginia, 1961). See also Manning J. Dauer and Robert G. Kelsay, "Unrepresentative States," *National Municipal Review*, 44 (1955): 551–75.

[22] *Colegrove* v. *Green*, 328 U.S. 549 (1946).

[23] *Baker* v. *Carr*, 369 U.S. 186 (1962).

[24] *Westberry* v. *Sanders*, 84 S. Ct. 526 (1964).

[25] Ibid.

[26] *Gray* v. *Sanders*, 83 S. Ct. 801 (1963).

[27] Ibid., p. 809.

distinction between malapportionment that was a product of state law and malapportionment that was embodied in state constitutions; both forms of malapportionment were declared to be in violation of the Fourteenth Amendment.

Two years after *Baker v. Carr*, the Supreme Court decided that representation in the second house of a state legislature also had to be based on population. Most state constitutions based representation in the upper chamber upon some unit of local government, rather than upon population. The justifications for such an arrangement are rooted deep in American democratic theory. The idea of bicameralism was based in part upon the advantages of having two separate systems of represenation in a legislature. *The Federalist Papers* vigorously defend a second chamber capable of checking the popular majority which was represented in the lower chamber and protecting interests which may be threatened by that majority. In 1964, however, the Supreme Court in *Reynolds v. Sims,* a case involving Alabama's attempt to base representation in its senate on counties, the Court decided that *both* houses of a state legislature must be fairly apportioned according to population.[28] In the words of Chief Justice Earl Warren, writing for the Court: "Legislators represent people, not trees or acres. Legislators are elected by voters, not farms or cities or economic interests. . . . The complexions of societies and civilizations change, often with amazing rapidity. A nation once primarily rural in character becomes predominantly urban. Representation schemes once fair and equitable became archaic and outdated." [29] The Court dismissed the federal analogy as "irrelevant" because "political subdivisions of states . . . never have been considered as sovereign entities." [30] The Court argued that requiring both houses to have the same basis of representation did not make bicameralism meaningless, because differences between the houses in numbers, terms of office, and size of constituencies would still remain.

Today there is very little malapportionment in any state, and "one man, one vote" is the prevailing style of representation. The percentage

[28] *Reynolds* v. *Sims,* 84 S. Ct. 1362 (1964).

[29] Ibid., p. 1381.

[30] Apparently representational schemes once fair and equitable can grow archaic very rapidly, for it was as late as 1948 that Earl Warren, the governor of California, wrote: "The agricultural counties of California are far more important in the life of our state than the relationship their population bears to the entire population of the state. It is for this reason that I never have been in favor of redistricting their representation in our state senate on a strictly population basis. It is the same reason that the founding fathers of our country gave balanced representation to the states of the Union, equal representation in one house and proportionate representation based on population in the other." Quoted in *Time,* June 26, 1962, p. 22.

deviation of actual districts from absolute equality (an ideal model in which every district in the state has the same number of people) generally clusters between 2 and 6 percent.[31] The federal courts have permitted limited deviation from absolute equality by permitting legislatures to give *some* consideration to preserving existing political subdivision lines in constructing legislative districts. The Supreme Court also ordered federal district courts not to get "bogged down" in reapportionment cases which involved only "minor deviations" from absolute equality.

THE IMPACT OF REAPPORTIONMENT

What has been the impact of reapportionment on state legislative politics? Reapportionment has significantly increased the representation afforded urban interests. Of course, this is what reapportionment was expected to do. But it is still interesting to observe the full impact of reapportionment in increasing the representation afforded urban constituencies and decreasing rural representation. Table 5–1 is illustrative of what happened in many states. The percentage of the state's population living in various types of communities is shown in the left column; these figures are compared with the percentage of house and senate seats afforded these communities "before" and "after" reapportionment. Georgia's urban counties, which contain 53.3 percent of the state's population, increased their representation in the Senate from 28.7 to 52.0 percent and in the

TABLE 5.1   The Effects of Reapportionment on the Representation Afforded Urban Communities in Georgia

	Percentage of State Population	Percentage of Representation Senate "Before"	Senate "After"	House "Before"	House "After"
Atlanta metropolitan area	20.0	6.0	24.3	6.3	12.2
All metropolitan areas	39.0	14.3	44.3	15.1	29.1
All non-metropolitan areas	61.0	85.7	55.7	84.9	70.9
Urban counties (over 50% urban population)	53.3	28.7	52.0	24.9	43.8
Rural counties (less than 50% urban population)	46.7	71.3	47.9	75.1	51.2

[31] Council of State Governments, *Book of the States, 1974–75*, p. 54.

House from 24.9 to 48.8 percent. Rural counties, which contain 46.7 percent of the state's population, decreased their representation from 71.3 to 47.9 percent in the Senate and from 75.1 to 51.2 percent in the House.

Finally, there is evidence that reapportionment has a significant impact on the kinds of people who are winning seats in state legislatures. Reapportionment seems to bring younger, better-educated, more prestigiously employed men into the legislature. It also brings many "new" people into legislative politics—men who have had little or no previous experience in public office. This, however, may be a temporary effect which will diasppear after reapportionment legislatures have been functioning over time.

What has been the impact of reapportionment on the policy choices of state legislatures? There is no doubt that significant political differences exist between big-city and small-town or rural legislators and that malapportionment granted a real political advantage to the latter. If the perceptions of state legislators themselves about legislative conflict are to be given any weight, then rural-urban conflict not only is discernible but is the most important conflict in American state legislatures. Rural-urban conflict was the only type of conflict rated "important" by over half of the legislators interviewed in four separate states. [32] It seems safe to say that legislators from large central cities and those from rural areas and small towns differ over the following: housing and welfare measures, aid for urban renewal and mass transit, the division of the state's tax dollar, state aid to schools, the location of highways, and the regulating authority granted cities. [33] In some southern states, urban legislators represent a "moderate" approach to race relations, while segregationists remain strong in rural areas.

One must be cautious, however, in estimating the policy consequences of reapportionment. In the past proponents of reapportionment were overly enthusiastic about its expected consequences. Having attributed a lack of party competition, unfair distribution of state funds, conservative tax schemes, unprogressive education policies and penny-pinching welfare programs to rural overrepresentation, they naturally expected to see these policies change significantly with reapportionment. Yet there is little in the way of empirical evidence to support such hopes.

In the first place, even before *Baker* v. *Carr* there was no evidence that the policy choices of well-apportioned states differed significantly from the policy choices of malapportioned states. There were no sig-

---

[32] Wahlke et al., *The Legislative System*, p. 425.

[33] See Malcolm Jewell, *The State Legislature* (New York: Random House, Inc., 1962), pp. 17–33; Loren P. Beth, *The Politics of Misrepresentation* (Baton Rouge: Louisiana University Press, 1962); and Gordon E. Baker, *Rural versus Urban Political Power* (New York: Doubleday & Co., Inc., 1955).

nificant differences between well-apportioned and malapportioned states in the levels of expenditures for welfare and education, the quality of public education, the tax burden, the revenue structure, the liberality of welfare benefits, or the extent of state participation in education, health, and welfare.[34] Most of the differences among the states in these kinds of policies were accounted for by differences in socioeconomic environment; apportionment practices seem to have little direct impact on these policies. Of course, it is possible that the policy impact of reapportionment will be subtle and diverse and that reapportionment will have a greater impact on the rural-urban division of *marginal increases* in public expenditures in contrast to *overall levels* of public expenditures, sources, or benefits. But there is little evidence that the "one man, one vote" movement will solve any of the pressing problems of the nation's cities—poverty, racial tension, slum housing, congestion, and so forth. Indeed, a careful study of state aid to metropolitan governments before and after reapportionment in the fifty states showed that reapportionment did *not* significantly increase the amount of state aid flowing to urban areas.[35]

If reapportionment does increase urban representation, why does it not lead to major policy changes? Within urban areas there are many real conflicts of interest between city and suburbs based upon the different attributes of persons living in each area. Crowded slum dwellers living in the central city have different opinions about public policy than inhabitants of suburban split-levels on half-acre lots. Blacks in ghettos have different policy positions than whites in suburbs. Often there are differences between the residents of medium-sized cities and the residents of a large central city in a metropolitan area. In contrast, rural legislators are much more likely to agree on policy issues and to vote in a bloc. On some issues we find a conservative coalition of suburban and rural legislators. Several studies of legislative voting have indicated that urban legislators have difficulty in agreeing on policy positions and voting as a bloc.[36]

[34] Thomas R. Dye, "Malapportionment and Public Policy in the States," *Journal of Politics,* 27 (August, 1965): 586–601; Herbert Jacob, "The Consequences of Malapportionment: A Note of Caution," *Social Forces* (Winter, 1965): 256–61.

[35] Robert E. Firestine, "The Impact of Reapportionment Upon Local Government Aid," *Social Science Quarterly,* 54 (September, 1973): 394–402.

[36] David Derge, "Metropolitan and Outstate Alignments in the Illinois and Missouri Legislative Delegations," *American Political Science Review,* 52 (1958): 1052–65; Richard T. Frost, "On Derge's Metropolitan and Outstate Legislative Delegations," *American Political Science Review,* 53 (1959): 792–95; and Robert S. Friedman, "The Urban Rural Conflict Revisited," *Western Political Quarterly,* 14 (1961): 495.

Before reapportionment, Florida was one of the most malapportioned states in the nation, and many observers expected dramatic changes with reapportionment. There were many policy changes in Florida in the 1960s, perhaps even some that could be attributed to reapportionment. But as one Florida solon explained:

> The fellows from the upstate counties control the state's politics, no matter what happens with one-man one-vote law. Those fellows work together and vote together whenever there's something really important coming up. They can stop the big cities cold whenever they want to.

> Here's why: Take Dade County [Miami] for example. They've got 22 representatives in Tallahassee and you'd think that would give them a lot of power, but they're always fighting among themselves. When they split down the middle, they end up with a majority of one. That gives Dade County one vote while the Porkchoppers [rural legislators] are putting up a couple of dozen solid votes all one way.[37]

LEGISLATIVE ORGANIZATION AND PROCEDURE

The formal rules and procedures by which state legislatures operate are primarily designed to make the legislative process fair and orderly. Without established customs, rules, and procedures it would be impossible for fifty, one hundred, or two hundred men to arrive at a collective decision about the thousands of items submitted to them at a legislative session. State legislatures follow a fairly standard pattern in the formal process of making laws. Table 5–2 provides a brief description of some of the more important procedural steps in lawmaking.

What are the political consequences of the legislative procedures described in Table 5–2? Obviously, it is a very difficult process for a bill to become a law—legislative procedures offer many opportunities to defeat legislation. Formal rules and procedures of state legislatures lend themselves easily to those who would delay or obstruct legislation. Table 5–2 illustrates the deliberative function of legislatures and the consequent procedural advantages given to "conservative" forces; that is, those who would defend the *status quo.* Moreover, these procedures imply that the legislature is structured for deliberation and delay in decision making, rather than speed and innovation. This suggests that the legislature functions as an arbiter, rather than an initiator, of public policy, since its procedures are designed to maximize deliberation, even at the expense of granting advantage to those who oppose change.

---

[37] Tallahassee *Democrat,* October 26, 1969, p. B1.

TABLE 5.2   Summary of Legislative Procedure for Bill Passage

1. INTRODUCTION OF BILL	One or more members file bill with Clerk or presiding officer who gives it a number and refers it to a committee. This constitutes the first reading.
2. COMMITTEE HEARINGS	Important bills may be given public hearings at which all interested persons or groups may testify. Committee may speed or delay hearings.
3. COMMITTEE REPORT	Committee meets in executive (closed) session. Bills may be amended or pigeonholed or reported favorably or unfavorably.
4. BILL PLACED ON CALENDAR	Bills reported by committee are placed on calendar for floor consideration. Urgent or favorite bills may get priority by unanimous consent or informal maneuvering; other bills may be delayed, sometimes indefinitely.
5. FLOOR DEBATE, AMENDMENT, VOTE	The second reading of the bill before the entire chamber is usually accompanied by debate and perhaps amendments from the floor. Often the crucial vote is on an amendment or on second reading.
6. THIRD READING AND PASSAGE	Usually a bill is delayed one calendar day before it is brought to the floor for third reading. On third reading debate is not customary and amendments usually require unanimous consent. After final vote, bill is certified by presiding officer and sent to second house.
7. REFERRAL TO SECOND CHAMBER	Biil is sent to second chamber where steps 1 through 6 must be repeated. Bills must pass both chambers in identical form before going to governor.
8. CONFERENCE COMMITTEE	If there are differences in wording in the bills passed by each house, one or the other house must accept the wording of the other house or request a conference committee. This committee is made up of members of both houses and it arrives at a single wording for the bill.
9. VOTE ON CONFERENCE COMMITTEE REPORT	Both houses must vote to approve conference committee wording of bill. Bills may be shuttled back and forth and eventually die for lack of agreement between both houses.

TABLE 5.2 (Cont.)

10. GOVERNOR'S SIGNATURE OR VETO	An identical bill passed by both houses becomes law with the governor's signature. It may also become law without his signature after a certain lapse of time (e.g., 10 days) if the legislature is still in session. If the legislature has adjourned during this time, the governor's failure to sign is the same as a veto. A governor may formally veto a bill and return it to the house of origin for reconsideration. An unusual majority is generally required to override a veto.

INFORMAL RULES OF THE GAME

Partly to counteract the impact of formal rules and procedures, legislatures have developed a number of informal "rules of the game." These unwritten rules are not merely quaint and curious folkways. They support the purposes and functions of the legislature by helping to maintain the working consensus among legislators so essential to legislative output. Some rules contribute to the legislative task by promoting group cohesion and solidarity. In the words of legislators themselves: "Support another member's local bill if it doesn't affect you or your district"; "Don't steal another's bill"; "Accept the author's amendments to a bill"; "Don't make personal attacks on other members." [38] Other informal rules promote predictability of behavior: "Keep your word"; "Don't conceal the real purpose of bills or amendments"; "Notify in advance if you cannot keep a commitment." Other rules try to put limits on interpersonal conflict: "Be willing to compromise"; "Accept half a loaf"; "Respect the seniority system"; "Respect committee jurisdiction." Finally, other rules are designed to expedite legislative business: "Don't talk too much"; "Don't fight unnecessarily"; "Don't introduce too many bills and amendments"; "Don't point out the absence of a quorum"; "Don't be too political."

A most important informal device is unanimous consent for the suspension of formal rules; this permits a legislature to consider bills not on the calendar, pass bills immediately without the necessary three readings, dispense with time-consuming formalities, permit nonmembers to speak, and otherwise alter procedure. Another informal rule is the practice

[38] Quotations from state legislators interviewed by Wahlke, *The Legislative System*, pp. 146–61.

TABLE 5.3   Informal Legislative Norms*

"Highly undesirable" legislative behavior
1. Concealing the real purpose(s) of a bill or purposefully overlooking some portion of it in order to assure its passage.
2. Dealing in personalities in debate or in other remarks made on the floor of the chamber.
3. Being a thorn to the majority by refusing unanimous consent, etc.
4. Talking about decisions which have been reached in private to the press or anyone else.
5. Seeking as much publicity as possible from the press back home.
6. Being generally known as a spokesman for some special-interest group.
7. Introducing as many bills and amendments as possible during any legislative session.
8. Talking on a subject coming before the legislature about which you are not completely informed.
9. Giving first priority to your re-election in all of your actions as a legislator.

*Items which at least 40 percent of Iowa House and Senate members checked as "highly undesirable." See F. Ted Hebert and Lelan E. McLemore, "Character and Structure of Legislative Norms," *American Journal of Political Science,* 17 (August, 1973): 506-27.

in many states of passing "local bills" that would affect only one area of a state without debate or opposition when the delegation in that area unanimously supports that bill.

Most of these rules are enforced by informal sanctions. The most frequently mentioned sanction involves obstructing the bills of an errant legislator by abstaining or voting against him, keeping his bills in committee, and amending his bills; or more personal sanctions, such as using the "silent treatment," not trusting him, and removing patronage and good committee assignments. Other sanctions include denial of legislative courtesies and occasionally even overt demonstrations of displeasure, such as ridicule, hissing, or laughing. The observance of rules, however, is not obtained primarily through fear of sanction so much as the positive recognition by legislators of the usefulness of rules in helping the legislature perform its chores.

LEGISLATIVE COMMITTEES

While it is most convenient to study legislative decision making by observing floor actions, particularly the division of ayes and nays, the floor is not the only locus of important legislative decisions. Many observers and legislators feel that committee work is essential to the legislative process. It is here that public hearings are held, policies pleaded and debated, legislation amended and compromised, bills rushed to the floor or pigeonholed. Harmon Zeigler writes: "The committee hearing is generally the most important source of information for legislators, and lobbyists tend to flock to the committee rooms as the focal point of their contact with legislators." [39] The function of the committee system is to reduce legislative work to manageable proportions by providing for a division of labor among legislators. But by so doing the committees themselves often come to exercise considerable influence over the outcome of legislation. Another opportunity is provided for delay and obstruction by less than the majority of legislators, sometimes by a single committee chairman. Duane Lockard reports: "What a new legislator soon finds is that there is no choice but to depend upon his colleagues to inform him about issues assigned to their committees, and, like it or not, he is reduced to following their advice unless he knows the subject well enough to have an opinion. It is a source of surprise to many new members how many issues they are too ignorant to have an opinion about. . . ."[40]

A typical legislative chamber will have between twenty and thirty standing committees which consider all bills in a particular field, such as revenue, appropriations, highways, welfare, education, labor, judiciary, or local government. Many houses operate with a rules committee which governs house proceedings and determines the priority given the bills on the legislative calendar. Committees may prevent the bill from coming to the floor for vote by inaction ("pigeonholing"), although twenty states require every committee to report on every bill either favorably or unfavorably.

The importance of committee systems seems to vary from state to state. Yet Malcolm Jewell argues effectively that state legislative committees do not exercise the independent influence over legislation that congressional committees enjoy. He offers several reasons "why legislative standing committees are but pale shadows of their Congressional counterparts." [41] Most state legislatures meet only a few months every other year, giving committees very little time for any careful review of bills. Committees seldom have good staff assistance, legislative turnover is high, a seniority system is not as prevalent as it is in Congress, and committee members seldom acquire the experience and expertise of

[39] Harmon Zeigler and Michael Baer, *Lobbying: Interaction and Influence in American State Legislatures* (Belmont: Wadsworth Publishing Co., 1969), p. 126.

[40] Duane Lockard, *The Politics of State and Local Government* (New York: The Macmillan Company, 1963), p. 28.

[41] Jewell, *The State Legislature*, p. 93.

their congressional counterparts. In most state legislatures the rules committee does not have the power to determine what bills will reach the floor as does the Rules Committee of the U.S. House of Representatives. Of course, the fact that legislative committees in the states are not as powerful as in Congress does not mean that they are never used as important instruments of party or factional control.[42]

Studies suggest the following explanations for variations among the several states in the strength of their committee system:

1. Committees exercise less independent influence over legislation in two-party states where party discipline is high.
2. Committees exercise less influence in states where the governor is strong and the legislature is of the same party as the governor, but exercise more influence under divided government.
3. In states where the governor, the party, or a faction exercises strong influence over the legislature (for example, by appointing committee chairmen), committees are not likely to play an independent role.
4. In contrast, committees are more likely to be influential in one-party states where the governor does not exert strong leadership.
5. Committees are more effective when they are fewer in number and characterized by a more rational division of labor.
6. Committees are more influential in more "professional" legislative settings.[43]

LEGISLATIVE PROFESSIONALISM

Some state legislatures are highly professional, while others are not. By *professional* we mean that in some legislatures the members are well-paid and tend to think of their jobs as full-time ones; members and committees are well staffed and have good informational services available to them; and a variety of legislative services, such as bill drafting and statutory revision, are well supported and maintained. In other legislatures, members are poorly paid and regard their legislative work as part time; there is little in the way of staff for legislators or committees; and little or nothing is provided in the way of legislative assistance and services.

The Citizens Conference on State Legislatures has undertaken to rank the states according to their idea of legislative professionalism. This organization is a reform-oriented good-government group which has

[42] See Loren P. Beth and William C. Havard, "Committee Stacking and Political Power in Florida," *Journal of Politics*, 23 (1961): 57–83. In contrast, see Gilbert Y. Steiner and Samuel K. Gove, *Legislative Politics in Illinois* (Urbana: University of Illinois Press, 1960), pp. 12–13.

[43] See Alan Rosenthal, "Legislative Committee Systems," *Western Political Quarterly*, 26 (June, 1973): 252–62.

studied and evaluated various aspects of legislative life in the states, as described in Table 5–4. Note that this table does *not* rank state legislatures according to the wisdom of their legislation, but only according to their institutional character.

The pay, perquisites, and working conditions of legislators vary a great deal from state to state. In general, the more populous urban industrial states provide more comfortable environments for their legislators than do the smaller rural states. California legislators receive annual compensation in excess of $25,000, and legislators in Illinois and New York receive compensation in excess of $20,000 per year. In contrast, New Hampshire pays its legislators $200 for the biennium. It is not surprising that turnover is higher among legislators in rural than in the urban states. The larger urban states, however, tend to consider more legislation, remain in session longer, and demand more time of their legislators. This means that their legislators probably devote a smaller proportion of their time to private business and become more dependent on their legislative salary.

ROLE PLAYING IN LEGISLATURES

Roles are expectations about the kind of behavior people ought to exhibit. Expectations are placed upon a legislator by his fellow legislators, his party, the opposition party, the governor, his constituents, interest groups, and his friends, as well as by himself.

Perhaps the most distinctive roles in the legislative process are those of the leadership. A typical legislative chamber has a presiding officer, a majority and a minority floor leader, a number of committee chairmen, and a steering committee. These leaders perform functions similar to the functions of rules. First of all, leaders are expected to help make the legislative system stable and manageable. They are expected to maintain order, to know the rules and procedures, to follow the rules, and to show fairness and impartiality. Leaders are also expected to help focus the issues and resolve conflict by presenting issues clearly, narrowing the alternatives, organizing public hearings, and promoting the party or administrative point of view on bills. The majority leader is supposed to "get the administrative program through," while the minority leader "tries to develop criticism," "find party issues," and "develop a constructive opposition." [44] Leaders are also expected to administer the legislature and expedite business. This includes "promoting teamwork,"

[44] Quotations from state legislators interviewed by Wahlke et al., *The Legislative System*, pp. 170–90.

TABLE 5.4   Rankings of State Legislatures

Major factors considered under the five categories:

Functional—time and its utilization, availability of staffing physical facilities such as office space, size of the legislature, number of committees, organization, and procedures.

Accountable—districting, method of leadership selection, adequacy of information necessary for lawmaking, public access to voting records and actual deliberations, character and quality of bill drafting, leadership constraints, and treatment of minority party.

Informed—amount of time devoted to legislative process, number of standing committees, handling of testimony, staffing between sessions, reports filing, form and character of bills, and professional staff resources.

Independent—independence of legislative from state's executive branch, frequency and duration of sessions, compensation of members, regulating of special interest groups and lobbyists, control of conflicts of interest.

Representative—qualification, compensation, and voting requirements of legislators; size and complexity of each legislative body; diffusion and restraints on the leadership; relationship of members and constituents.

Overall Rank	State	Functional	Accountable	Informed	Independent	Representative
1	California	1	3	2	3	2
2	New York	4	13	1	8	1
3	Illinois	17	4	6	2	13
4	Florida	5	8	4	1	30
5	Wisconsin	7	21	3	4	10
6	Iowa	6	6	5	11	25
7	Hawaii	2	11	20	7	16
8	Michigan	15	22	9	12	3
9	Nebraska	35	1	16	30	18
10	Minnesota	27	7	13	23	12
11	New Mexico	3	16	28	39	4
12	Alaska	8	29	12	6	40

TABLE 5.4 Rankings of State Legislatures (Cont.)

Overall Rank	State	Functional	Accountable	Informed	Independent	Representative
13	Nevada	13	10	19	14	32
14	Oklahoma	9	27	24	22	8
15	Utah	38	5	8	29	24
16	Ohio	18	24	7	40	9
17	South Dakota	23	12	15	16	37
18	Idaho	20	9	29	27	21
19	Washington	12	17	25	19	39
20	Maryland	16	31	10	15	45
21	Pennsylvania	37	23	23	5	36
22	North Dakota	22	18	17	37	31
23	Kansas	31	15	14	32	34
24	Connecticut	39	26	26	25	6
25	West Virginia	10	32	37	24	15
26	Tennessee	30	44	11	9	26
27	Oregon	28	14	35	35	19
28	Colorado	21	25	21	28	27
29	Massachusetts	32	35	22	21	23
30	Maine	29	34	32	18	22
31	Kentucky	49	2	48	44	7
32	New Jersey	14	42	18	31	35
33	Louisiana	47	39	33	13	14
34	Virginia	25	19	27	26	48
35	Missouri	36	30	40	49	5
36	Rhode Island	33	46	30	41	11
37	Vermont	19	20	34	42	47
38	Texas	45	36	43	45	17
39	New Hampshire	34	33	42	36	43
40	Indiana	44	38	41	43	20

TABLE 5.4   Rankings of State Legislatures (Cont.)

Overall Rank	State	Functional	Accountable	Informed	Independent	Representative
41	Montana	26	28	31	46	49
42	Mississippi	46	43	45	20	28
43	Arizona	11	47	38	17	50
44	South Carolina	50	45	39	10	46
45	Georgia	40	49	36	33	38
46	Arkansas	41	40	46	34	33
47	North Carolina	24	37	44	47	44
48	Delaware	43	48	47	38	29
49	Wyoming	42	41	50	48	42
50	Alabama	48	50	49	50	41

SOURCE: Citizens Conference on State Legislatures.

"being accessible," "cracking the whip in the interest of time and smooth operation," starting the sessions on time, keeping them on schedule, and distributing the workload. It involves communication, coordination, and liaison with the governor, the administrative departments, and the other chambers.

The role of legislative leaders varies from state to state, and there appears to be a relationship between "professionalism" and leadership roles. In more professional legislatures, there is less turnover in legislative leadership; the leaders serve a longer apprenticeship before becoming leaders; there is more likely to be an established line of succession to leadership positions (from party whip, to floor leader, to speaker); and there are fewer open contests for leadership positions.[45]

Another set of legislative roles that are commonly encountered and which make important contributions to the legislative process are the "subject-matter experts." Unlike leadership roles, the roles of subject-matter experts are not embodied in formal offices. The committee system introduces specialization into the legislature, and the seniority system places at the head of the committee those persons longest exposed to the information about the committee's subject matter. Thus, subject-matter experts emerge among legislators in the fields of law, finance, education, agriculture, natural resources, local government, labor, transportation, and so on. There is some evidence to support the view that subject-matter experts exercise more influence over bills within their fields than nonexperts.[46]

Legislators might also be classified according to the way in which they see the legislative function—in other words, according to the expectations they place upon their own behavior. *The Legislative System* study found four types of self-conceptions among legislators—the ritualist, the tribune, the inventor, and the broker.[47] The *ritualist* sees his job in a technical fashion as one of "making laws." The ritualist is concerned with the mechanics of legislative operations, parliamentary rules and routine, and committee work. The technical perfection of a law seems almost as important to him as its policy implication. The *tribune* perceives his role as the discoverer of popular needs and the defender of popular interests. He sees his task as one of understanding his constituents' problems, making himself available to them, and keeping track

[45] See Douglas Camp Chaffey and Malcolm E. Jewell, "Selection and Tenure of State Legislative Party Leaders: A Comparative Analysis," *Journal of Politics*, 34 (November, 1972): 1278–86.

[46] William Buchanan et al., "The Legislator as Specialist," *Western Political Quarterly*, 13 (1960): 636–51.

[47] The discussion that follows relies upon Wahlke et al., *The Legislative System*, pp. 245–60.

of public opinion. The *inventor* sees himself as the initiator and creator of public policy. He wants to see the legislature take the lead in solving important problems in his state—welfare, education, highways, taxes, and so on. Only a few legislators consider themselves inventors. The fact that few legislators even claim to approach their task in a creative manner is further evidence that legislators themselves realize that policy initiation has shifted from the legislature to the governor, executive agencies, and interest groups. The true inventors of legislatures are probably frustrated men, since seldom does the legislature do anything but respond to the governor, civil servants, or active pressure groups. Finally, some legislators see their role as that of referee or *broker* in the struggle between interest groups, constituencies, and executive agencies. The broker's task is to balance, to compromise, to arbitrate between conflicting interests. It is interesting that legislative leaders are more likely to see themselves in this role than nonleaders.

Still another way of describing characteristic behaviors in a legislature is to discover the legislators' orientations toward the expectations of constituents and party. Legislators have been classified as *trustees* (those who are guided in legislative affairs solely by their personal conscience), *delegates* (those who are guided by instructions or wishes of their constituents), or *partisans* (those who look to the party leadership for guidance).[48] Despite the concern of many political scientists with the classic question of whether legislators should represent their party, their constituency, or their own conscience, few legislators actually exhibit in their behavior a firm commitment to any one of these. Most legislators when facing specific issues do not see any conflict between the wishes of their constituents, their party, or their own judgment. Even where such conflict is perceived, most legislators attempt to find a compromise between conflicting demands rather than choose one role or the other exclusively. One legislator even denied that such a question would ever arise: "A representative's judgment should arise from knowing the needs and wants of his district and state."[49] Of course, if legislators are asked how they make their decisions, they *claim* to be guided solely by their own conscience. But this is little more than a verbalism; it reflects a heroic image of the courageous defender of the public interest, who acts out of personal virtue and conviction regardless of the consequences.

The more politically experienced legislator is more likely to assume the role of a trustee. There is some evidence that legislators who come to the office with little prior experience as public officials, and those with less service in the legislature, are more likely to respond in the

---

[48] Sorauf, *Party and Representation*, pp. 121–46; and Wahlke et al., *The Legislative System*, pp. 281–86.

[49] Sorauf, *Party and Representation*, p. 125.

FIGURE 5–1 The many roles of a state legislator.
Source: The *Atlanta Journal and Constitution*, January 23, 1966. Reproduced by permission.

manner of a "delegate" or politico, while their more experienced colleagues give "trustee" responses to interviewers.[50]

The future political ambitions of legislators also influence their legislative roles and behavior. Legislators who express the desire to remain in the legislature for several terms and those who express a desire to run for higher public office are more likely to see themselves as "trustees" who use their own judgment in reaching legislative decisions.[51] In con-

---

[50] Charles G. Bell and Charles E. Price, "Pre-Legislative Sources of Representational Roles," *Midwest Journal of Political Science*, 13 (May, 1969): 254–70.

[51] John W. Soule, "Future Political Ambitions and the Behavior of Incumbent State Legislators," *Midwest Journal of Political Science*, 13 (August, 1969): 439–54. These findings are confirmed at the level of city councilmen by Kenneth Previtt and William Noulin, "Political Ambitions and the Behavior of Incumbent Politicians," *Western Political Quarterly*, 22 (June, 1969): 298–308.

trast, legislators who express little desire to remain in public office are more likely to see themselves as "delegates" who represent their constituents' opinions. Furthermore, the more ambitious legislators are more likely to express a "state orientation" to legislative issues in contrast to a "district orientation." Apparently the politically ambitious legislator seeks to broaden his constituency in legislative affairs and assume a more state-oriented role.

Finally, there is evidence that the *non*ideological legislators—those who are willing to bargain, accommodate, and negotiate and who are not intensely issue-oriented—are more likely to acquire seniority, good committee appointments, and leadership position than their more ideological, programatic brethren.[52] Thus, there is an informal bias in legislatures favoring moderation and compromise and disfavoring controversial, high-risk innovation.

CONFLICT IN STATE LEGISLATURES

Many decisions made by state legislatures do not involve conflict, and most bills are enacted into law without a single negative vote. This does not mean, however, that the legislative chambers are free from conflict; unanimous bills are generally local bills or minor bills involving decisions that are not deeply divisive.

What kinds of issues generate conflict in legilsatures? Wayne L. Francis reports that a national sample of legislators rank as "important" issues those that fall into the following categories: taxation, apportionment, education, finance, labor, health, business, and civil rights.[53] If legislators are asked to indicate what kinds of issues generate various types of conflict—party, factional, regional, or interest group—the results turn out as shown in Table 5–5. Party conflicts occur in issues touching on elections, state administration, and apportionment, as well as on broader social issues of labor, land, finance, taxation, and welfare. Certain kinds of issues bring dissension *within* parties more frequently than *between* parties: liquor regulation, constitutional revision, agriculture, business regulation, and gambling. Regional conflicts occur most frequently on apportionment, powers of local governments, and constitutional revision. Interest group divisions are most frequently observed as labor legislation, liquor and business regulation, civil rights, gambling,

---

[52] See Corey M. Rosen, "Legislative Influence and Policy Orientation in American State Legislatures," *American Journal of Political Science*, 18 (November, 1974): 681–91.

[53] Wayne L. Francis, *Legislative Issues in the Fifty States* (Chicago: Rand McNally & Co., 1967).

TABLE 5-5   Legislative Issues Arranged by Types of Conflict

| | | Types of Conflict | | | |
Ranking	Party	Factional	Regional	Interest Group	Issue "Importance"
1	Elections	Liquor	Apportionment	Labor	Taxation
2	Labor	Constitutional revision	Local government	Liquor	Apportionment
3	Land	Agriculture	Constitutional revision	Business	Education
4	Finance	Civil rights	Social welfare	Civil rights	Finance
5	Administration	Business	Civil rights	Gambling	Labor
6	Apportionment	Apportionment	Gambling	Natural resources	Health
7	Taxation	Gambling		Agriculture	Business
8	Social welfare	Taxation		Taxation	Civil rights

SOURCE: Derived from Wayne L. Francis, *Legislative Issues in the Fifty States* (Chicago: Rand McNally & Co., 1967).

145

natural resources, agriculture, and taxation. Of course, these rankings are the product of a national sample (838) of state legislators from all fifty states; issues and conflicts will vary from state to state in importance.

PARTY POLITICS IN STATE LEGISLATURES

There are ninety-six partisan legislative chambers in the United States; Nebraska and Minnesota legislatures are elected on a nonpartisan ballot.[54] The influence of parties in legislative decision making in the fifty states is by no means uniform. First of all, it is obvious that parties in one-party states do not exercise tight party discipline over the voting of legislators. In terms of legislative behavior, one-party states are really no-party states.

However, within the competitive states, party divisions on roll-call votes are more frequent than any other divisions, including rural-urban divisions.[55] One common measure of party influence on voting is the percentage of nonunanimous roll-call votes on which a majority of Democrats voted against the majority of Republicans. The compilations by the *Congressional Quarterly* show that the proportion of congressional roll calls in which the two parties have been in opposition has ranged from 35 to 50 percent. Table 5–6 suggests that party voting may be higher in the state legislatures of New York, Pennsylvania, Ohio, Delaware, Rhode Island, Massachusetts, and Michigan than it is in Congress. Party voting is also common in Indiana, New Hampshire, New Jersey, Washington, and West Virginia. Parties appear less influential in Idaho, Kansas, Nevada, Utah, and California.

Party cohesion is the tendency of legislators to vote with their own party majority on roll calls in which a majority of one party voted in opposition to a majority of the other. The party cohesion of individual legislators is measured by the percentage of roll calls in which parties were in opposition and on which the legislator sided with his own party; the average party cohesion of Democratic or Republican legislators is

---

[54] The special conditions affecting legislative affairs in these nonpartisan legislatures are discussed in Susan Welch and Eric H. Carlson, "The Impact of Party on Voting Behavior in a Nonpartisan Legislature," *American Political Science Review*, 67 (September, 1973): 854–67. This research concludes, among other things, that in the nonpartisan Nebraska Legislature there are no cohesive reference groups and the voting behavior of members is highly unpredictable. This makes it difficult for voters to make a rational choice at election time.

[55] See Glenn T. Broach, "A Comparative Dimensional Analysis of Partisan and Urban-Rural Voting in State Legislatures," *Journal of Politics*, 34 (August, 1972): 905–21.

TABLE 5.6   Party Voting in State Senates

State	Party Votes: Percentage of Nonunanimous Roll Calls with Party Majorities in Opposition *	Mean Index of Cohesion on Party Votes Democrats	Republicans
California	17	48	57
Connecticut	50	90	67
Delaware	62	84	87
Idaho	30	58	62
Illinois	27	75	63
Indiana	51	65	68
Iowa	39	69	60
Kansas	35	49	82
Kentucky	39	51	59
Massachusetts	74	78	77
Michigan	58	81	75
Missouri	35	49	63
Montana	37	54	56
Nevada	28	70	43
New Hampshire	62	63	38
New Jersey	46	85	90
New York	70	76	88
Ohio	69	83	71
Oregon	29	55	64
Pennsylvania	82	82	90
Rhode Island	100	99	96
South Dakota	44	67	67
Utah	26	41	53
Vermont	40	63	41
Washington	50	60	78
West Virginia	54	85	73

*All roll calls in which at least 10 percent of those voting dissented from the majority position.

SOURCE: Derived from Hugh L. LeBlanc, "Voting in State Senates: Party and Constituency Influences," *Midwest Journal of Political Science,* 13 (February 1969), p. 36.

simply their mean party cohesion scores. In a comprehensive analysis of roll-call voting in state legislatures, Hugh L. LeBlanc computed the mean party cohesion of Democrats and Republicans in twenty-six state senates in a single session. The results are presented in Table 5–6. Party cohesion is high in Connecticut, Delaware, Ohio, Massachusetts, Michigan, Pennsylvania, Rhode Island, and West Virginia. It is low in Idaho, Kansas, Kentucky, Missouri, Utah, and California.

On what types of issues did the parties exercise great influence? Minor bills involving the licensing of water well drillers, beauticians, or barbers do not usually become the subject matter of party votes, and only infrequently will the parties divide over such matters as the designation of an official state bird. In the more urban and industrialized states, parties usually display the greatest cohesion on issues involving taxation and appropriations, welfare, and regulation of labor—in short, the major social and economic controversies that divide the national parties. Party influence in budgetary matters is particularly apparent, since the budget often involves issues of social welfare and class interest on which parties in urban states are split. In addition, the budget is clearly identified as the product of the governor and carries the label of the party of the governor. Appeals are made for legislators to support the budget of the governor of their party, while opposition legislators are stimulated to force changes in the budget in order to create issues for coming elections. Another type of bill that is often the subject of party voting is one involving the party as an interest group. Parties often exhibit an interest in bills proposing to transfer powers from an office controlled by one party to an office controlled by the other, or bills proposing to create or abolish non-civil-service jobs. Parties display considerable interest in bills affecting the organization of local government, state administration, the civil service, registration and election laws, and legislative procedure. On issues that directly affect the party organization and prestige, the parties react in a manner characteristic of interest groups.

What factors distinguish those states in which the party substantially influences legislative decision making from those states in which it does not? First of all, party cohesion is found in the competitive states rather than in the noncompetitive states. Since the noncompetitive states are the rural nonindustrial states, party voting appears related to urbanism and economic development if all fifty states are considered. There are, however, some urban states in which party voting is not a frequent occurrence; California is a notable example. *Party cohesion is strongest in those urban industrial states in which the parties represent separate socioeconomic constituencies.* Party voting occurs in those competitive states in which Democratic legislators represent central-city, low-income, ethnic, and racial constituencies, and Republican legislators represent middle-class, suburban, small-town, and rural constituencies. Party cohesion is weak in states where party alignments do not coincide with socioeconomic divisions of the constituencies.[56]

56 Perhaps the best systematic comparative study of party voting in state legislatures is Hugh L. LeBlanc, "Voting in State Senates: Party and Constituency Influences," *Midwest Journal of Political Science,* 13 (February, 1969): 33–57; Malcolm Jewell also provides useful comparative data on party voting in state legislatures—see *The State Legislature,* p. 52, and "Party Voting in American State Legislatures," *American Political Science Review,* 49 (1955): 773–91.

Party cohesion is not related to the majority or minority status of parties in the legislature. On the basis of his twenty-six state study, LeBlanc concludes that party cohesion was no greater among minority party legislators than among those of the majority party. Nor was the level of cohesion obtained by a party affected by whether or not it controlled the office of the governor.

What then is the basis of party cohesion in the states where it exists? Is party cohesion a product of effective party organization and discipline? Or is it really a result of similarities in the constituencies represented by each party? For example, is Demorcatic party cohesion in industrial states a result of party organization pressures? Or is it because Democrats are typically elected from metropolitan centers with strong labor groups, many Catholic voters, racial and ethnic minorities, and persons with few skills and poor education, and is it really constituency similarities that hold the Democratic legislators together? Can it be that Republican cohesion in these states occurs because Republicans typically represent middle-class suburbs, small towns, and rural areas, and these types of constituencies have similar ideas about public policy?

CONSTITUENCY INFLUENCE
IN LEGISLATIVE POLITICS

It is unlikely that party organization and discipline alone are the cause of party voting, for organization and discipline can be effective only under certain conditions. The weight of evidence seems to support the hypothesis that party influence is most effective where the parties represent separate and distinct socioeconomic coalitions. Where the constituencies of a state are divided along social and economic lines and where the party division coincides with these constituency divisions, then party program and discipline will be effective in shaping policy in legislative chambers.

After investigating the correlations between party cohesion and constituency characteristics in twenty-six state senates, LeBlanc found that (1) senators were more loyal to their party when their constituents voted heavily for their party in gubernatorial and presidential elections; (2) senators were more loyal to their party in partisan states where the Democratic party was heavily supported in constituencies of racial and ethnic minorities, low-income groups, and the poorly educated; (3) senators were less loyal to their party in states where a more ambiguous relationship existed between the Democratic party and socioeconomic constituencies. He observed:

It is understood, of course, that constituency influences on legislative voting are sometimes difficult to disentangle from party influences and the dictates of the legislator's own conscience or convictions. Often the several influences reinforce one another. Thus an individual of liberal convictions is politically involved in the Democratic party for that reason and, as the Democratic party's candidate for senator, is victorious at the polls in a constituency conventionally associated with Democratic party success— perhaps a racially mixed, low income, urban constituency, heavily populated with industrial workers. In voting to increase workmen's compensation payments, the senator could be said to vote his convictions, his party's program, and his constituency.[57]

Pennsylvania is an excellent example of a state in which Republican and Democratic legislative districts are clearly differentiated by socioeconomic variables. The parties are first divided along rural-urban lines, and within urban areas they are further divided along indices of socioeconomic status. Republicans dominate in rural areas and in the wealthier urban areas (upper-middle-class suburbs and several "silk-stocking" districts in Philadelphia and Pittsburgh). Democratic districts are predominantly found in the less wealthy urban areas of the state. A similar pattern emerges if occupational, religious, or racial characteristics are considered. Republican districts within urban areas prove to be the districts with greater concentrations of professional, managerial, sales, and clerical jobs. Republican candidates fare badly among black voters. The Democrats dominate the southern and eastern European, Irish, Catholic districts which are frequently the big-city, mining, or mill districts. The Republicans draw heavily in the Anglo-Saxon northern and western European, Protestant districts of the state. This same sort of party division of legislative districts has been documented in other northern, urban, industrial states. In short, the Democratic and Republican division of legislative constituencies in these states follows the socioeconomic divisions of national party politics.

It is this division of constituencies that is the basis of party cohesion and influence in the legislature. One of the more rigorous investigations into the causes of party voting in a state legislature is Thomas A. Flinn's study of party voting in Ohio.[58] Flinn expresses the constituency basis of party cohesion in the following hypothesis: ". . . legislators from similar constituencies will vote together and in opposition to legislators from constituencies with contrasting characteristics. To the extent that parties find their support in contrasting constituencies, party responsibility is the consequence." Flinn argues that constituency factors alone do not fully

[57] LeBlanc, "Voting in State Senates," p. 45.
[58] Thomas A. Flinn, "Party Responsibility in the States: Some Causal Factors," *American Political Science Review,* 58 (1964): 60–71.

explain party cohesion, since members of the same party representing dissimilar districts show greater cohesion than members of the rural and urban blocs. On the other hand, the experience in Ohio does indicate a relationship between constituency and party loyalty. Within each party, members from districts typical of their party in socioeconomic attributes support the party position more often than members from districts atypical of the party. Flinn concludes:

> Party responsibility is a consequence of party competition. . . . Various factors may intervene to inhibit or promote party responsibility, but the only important one located with substantial confidence . . . is constituency. Prospects for increased party responsibility depend, therefore, on the spread of party competition and upon a sorting out of legislative constituencies so that the districts represented by the respective parties are more homogeneous.[59]

Constituency characteristics, then, help to explain not only the outcome of elections but the behavior of the elected.

ARE LEGISLATORS RESPONSIBLE POLICY MAKERS?

A classic dilemma of representative government is whether the legislator should vote his own conscience—"the trustee"—or vote his constituency's wishes—"the delegate." Good philosophical arguments can be found to support either of these guiding principles. Nearly two hundred years ago the English political philosopher Edmund Burke confronted this question directly and urged representatives to vote their own conscience about what is right for society. Burke believed that the voters should elect wise and virtuous men to govern *for* them—to use their own judgment in deciding issues regardless of popular demands. Even today the term *Burkean representation* refers to the willingness of a representative to ignore public opinion and decide public issues on the basis of his own best judgment about what is right for society.

Other political philosophers stress *responsiveness* of representatives to the views of their constituents. Consider, for example, philosopher Hanna Pitkin's definition of representation: "Representation means acting in the interest of the represented, in a manner responsive to them."[60] Responsiveness connotes a deliberate effort by the legislator to match his votes on public policy issues to his constituency's preferences. But to be

---

[59] Ibid., p. 71.
[60] Hanna Pitkin, *The Concept of Representation* (Berkeley: University of California Press, 1967), 154–55.

"responsive" to his constituents two conditions must be met: (1) the legislator must correctly perceive his constituents' views on the issues; and (2) he must act in accord with his perceptions of these views.

Let us consider the first condition: Do legislators know the views of their constituents on public issues? Unfortunately, the evidence is mixed. When Iowa legislators were asked to predict whether their own district would vote for or against some proposed constitutional amendments, the resulting predictions were good on some issues but poor on others.[61] The legislators were better predictors of the more politically charged issues of home rule (91.5 percent accurate) and reapportionment (81.7 percent accurate), than the less controversial items such as annual sessions (58.9 percent) and the item veto (64.3 percent). Only one-third of the Iowa legislators correctly predicted which way their district would vote on all four issues. (Interestingly, the poorest predictions came from legislators from poor districts, suggesting that legislators have less understanding of the views of poor constituents than affluent ones.) In contrast, when Florida legislators were asked to predict how both their state and district would vote on referenda on school busing and school prayer, nearly all of them made accurate predictions for both their district and the state.[62] Indeed, even their estimates of the percentage of the vote were very close to mark (against busing consensus prediction—73.1, actual—74.1; for school prayers: consensus prediction—75.5, actual—79.4). Perhaps one explanation for these apparently conflicting findings is that legislators know their constituents' views on well-publicized, controversial, emotionally charged issues; but that legislators are poor predictors of constituent opinion on other kinds of issues.

Do legislators deliberately vote their constituents views on public issues coming before the legislature? Most legislators *claim* to side with Burke's classic argument that the representative should be guided *not* by "local purposes" or "local prejudices," but by "his unbiased opinion, his mature judgment, his enlightened conscience." Sixty-three percent of the legislators in four states identified themselves with the Burkean position, rather than subscribe to the role of district delegate or even admit to balancing personal views with those of constituents.[63] It is not surprising that most legislators perceive themselves as unfettered decision makers drawing their wisdom chiefly, if not completely, from their own virtue,

[61] Ronald D. Hedlund and H. Paul Friesma, "Representatives Perceptions of Constituency Opinion," *Journal of Politics*, 34 (August, 1972): 730–52.

[62] Robert S. Erikson, Norman R. Luttbeg, William V. Holloway, "Knowing One's District: How Legislators Predict Referendum Voting," *American Journal of Political Science*, 19 (May, 1975): 231–41.

[63] Wahlke et al., *The Legislative System*, pp. 267–86.

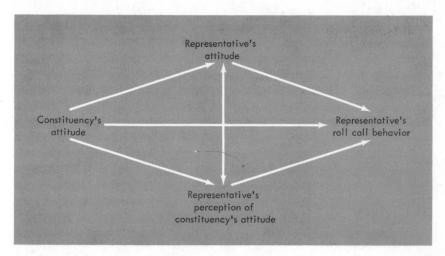

FIGURE 5–2 A model of constituency influence.[64]

knowledge, and experience. But these formal-interview claims to independence may be mere rhetoric; party and constituency influences may
push individual principles aside more often than legislators are willing
to admit.

In a study of congressional voting behavior, Warren Miller and
Donald Stokes constructed the following model to clarify the linkages
between the constituency's attitude, the legislator's perception of his
constituents' attitude, his own attitude, and his roll-call vote. Their research suggested that constituency attitude, congressional perception of
it, and congressional voting, were closely linked on civil-rights issues,
but *not* on foreign affairs or social-welfare issues. On these less visible
and controversial issues, the linkage between a congressman's own attitude and his vote were strongest.

State legislators may indeed vote their own attitude on *most* issues
coming before the legislature. A careful study of voting on welfare, tax,
and consumer issues in the Texas legislature revealed that: "In both
houses, in every issue-area examined, the path connecting the representative's attitude with his roll-call vote is far more important than the path
linking his perceptions of his constituency's attitude with his voting." [65]
The explanation offered was that activities of the governor and his staff,

[64] See Warren E. Miller and Donald E. Stokes, "Constituency Influence in
Congress," *American Political Science Review,* 57 (March, 1963): 45–56.
[65] Bryan D. Jones, "Competitiveness, Role Orientations, and Legislative Responsiveness," *Journal of Politics,* 35 (November, 1973): 924–47.

other legislators and legislative leaders, and outside-interest groups, create "the din of the immediate legislative struggle" which "muffles" the voices from the home district. Even legislators from competitive districts were seemingly unaffected by their views of their constituents' attitudes. As expected, legislators who opted for the role of "delegate" voted what they believed to be their constituents' attitudes more than legislators who opted for the role of trustee.

In summary, the absence of direct evidence that (1) legislators know their constituents' views, and (2) vote their constituents' views rather than their own views, creates difficulties for the "responsiveness" theory of democracy. There is a great deal of "noise" along the lines from constituents' views to their legislator's roll-call vote.

However, the classic choice posed by Burke between district demands and personal judgment is an artificial issue to most legislators. They are products of their constituency and they share its goals and values. Conflicts between their district's views and their own are rare. We have seen that legislators have roots deep in their constituencies—many organizational memberships, lifetime residency, shared religious and ethnic affiliations, for example. The party with which the legislator identifies is also a creature of the constituency; it accedes to local interests, local political mores, local political style. The legislator is so much "of" his constituency that he needs little direct prompting or supervision. As one discerning legislator commented: "Basically you represent the thinking of the people who have gone through what you have gone through and who are what you are. You vote according to that. In other words, if you come from a suburb you reflect the thinking of people in the suburbs; if you are of depressed people, you reflect that. You represent the sum total of your background." [66]

INTEREST GROUPS IN STATE LEGISLATURES

The character and influence of organized groups in legislative decision making varies from state to state. Chapter 3 discussed interest groups in state politics and gave an analysis of their relative influence in the fifty states. It is difficult to measure the effects of lobbying in the legislative process. We can ask legislators what they perceive to be the impact of lobbying activity. This was the approach of Harmon Zeigler and Michael Baer in their study of lobbying in four states.[67] They asked legislators to

[66] Ibid., p. 253.
[67] Zeigler and Baer, *Lobbying: Interaction and Influence in American State Legislatures.*

evaluate the worth of the information they received from lobbyists and the degree to which they depended upon this information, and they asked legislators how much they believed they had been influenced by lobbyists. The results are shown in Table 5–7. Note that there are considerable differences among legislators in different states in their estimate of the effects of lobbyists. Only about one-fifth of the legislators in Massachusetts and North Carolina admitted that lobbying activity "frequently" or "occasionally" changed their position on an issue, while closer to one-half of the legislators in Oregon and Utah made such an admission. Note also that the legislators in Massachusetts and North Carolina had less confidence in the information supplied by lobbyists than legislators in Oregon and Utah. Zeigler and Baer report that, generally, the greater the number of contacts between legislators and lobbyists, the greater the degree of influence enjoyed by the lobbyists. They also report that lobbyists and legislators tend to share similar socioeconomic backgrounds; many lobbyists, like legislators, are lawyers and have held previous governmental positions.

Legislators disagree about the usefulness of interest groups in the legislative process. *The Legislative System* [68] study classified 36 percent of the legislators interviewed in four states as "facilitators" (those having

TABLE 5.7   Perceived Effect of Lobbying By Legislators in Four States

	Mass.	No. Car.	Ore.	Utah
Persuasion				
Percentage of legislators believing they have been influenced to the extent of:				
Changing from one position to another	20%	18%	51%	42%
Leaning more to the news of lobbyist	31	20	42	38
Questioning a previously held opinion	34	22	45	32
Information				
Percentage of legislators indicating they:				
Depend upon information from lobbyists	50	41	83	80
Have confidence in information from lobbyists	55	56	88	70
Find information from lobbyists helpful	41	28	61	43

SOURCE: Derived from data supplied in Harmon Zeigler and Michael Baer, *Lobbying: Interaction and Influence in American State Legislatures* (Belmont: Wadsworth Publishing Co., 1969).

[68] Wahlke et al., *The Legislative System*, pp. 311–42.

knowledge of group activity and a friendly attitude toward it); 37 percent
of the interviewees were classified as "resisters" (those having knowledge
of group activity but a hostile attitude toward it); 27 percent were classified as "neutrals" (those having either little knowledge about group
activity or no strong favorable or unfavorable attitudes toward it). Facilitators were more ready than neutrals or resisters to attribute importance
to the views of interest groups and were more ready to use the aid of
lobbyists in drafting bills and lining up support for their own bills. Resisters and neutrals were less likely to feel that the views of interest groups
were important in shaping the opinions of legislators. Facilitators and
resisters could not be differentiated with regard to income or occupational
status or rural-urban residence or age. Better-educated legislators, however, tended more than others to be facilitators. This finding suggests that
increased knowledge of the complexity of society is associated with greater
realization and acceptance of interest-group activity.

On what kinds of decisions are interest groups more likely to exercise
influence? Party and constituency interests are most apparent on broad
social and economic issues. On narrower issues parties are less likely to
have either an interest or an opinion. The legislator is, therefore, freer to
respond to the pleas of organized groups on highly specialized topics than
he is on major issues of public interest. The absence of both party and
constituency influences on certain types of issues contributes to the effectiveness of organized interests. Economic interests seeking to use the law
to improve their competitive position are a major source of group pressure
on these specialized topics. Particularly active in lobbying are the businesses subject to extensive government regulation. The truckers, railroads,
insurance companies, and liquor interests are consistently found to be
among the most highly organized and active lobbyists in state capitals.
Organized pressure also comes from associations of governments and
associations of government employees. State chapters of the National
Education Association are persistent in presenting the demands of educational administrators and occasionally the demands of the dues-paying
teachers as well. Lobbying is largely unregulated except for registration
requirements established by about half of the states.

THE GOVERNOR IN THE LEGISLATURE

The responsibility for the initiation of major statewide legislative programs falls upon the governor, and he relies heavily upon his staff and
executive personnel to fulfill this responsibility. The governor's programs
are presented to the legislature in various governor's messages and in his
budget. Through his power of policy initiation alone, the governor's im-

pact on the legislature is considerable. The governor sets the agenda for public decision making; he largely determines what the business of the legislature will be in any session. Few major state undertakings ever get off the ground without gubernatorial initiation. And in setting the agenda of legislative business, he frames the issues, determines their context and decides their timing. These functions have a great deal to do with the outcome of issues. As influential as a governor can be through policy initiation alone, however, few governors seem content with the role of "initiator" and most act to interject themselves into the role of "arbiter" as well.

A variety of formal and informal powers accrue to governors which enable them to directly involve themselves in legislative decisions.[69] Among the formal powers is the governor's right to call special sessions; by utilizing this power a governor can focus attention on an issue and intensify pressure on the legislature. Another formal power is the veto which every governor has, except in North Carolina; in thirty-five states it requires a two-thirds vote to override a veto rather than a simple majority. The governor has an item veto on appropriations measures in forty-one states. The closing days of any legislative session generally see a flurry of bills passed. A governor can exercise his veto on these measures after the legislature has adjourned and for all practical purposes foreclose the opportunity of being overridden. Overriding vetoes is a difficult process, since a governor is seldom so weak that he cannot count on at least one-third of the legislature to sustain his veto. The mere threat of a veto can also operate to change the course of legislative action. The state constitution may limit or strengthen the governor's influence in the legislature by determining his frequency of election and ability to succeed himself. All other things being equal, a governor with a four-year term and an opportunity to succeed himself should be in a stronger position than a governor who faces election every other year or one who cannot serve more than four years.

The governor's informal powers over legislatures center around his role in the state political system. The governor's office carries prestige in any state; no man becomes governor without considerable political resources of one kind or another. It is natural that a governor will attempt to use his prestige and resourcefulness to influence legislatures. The governor is the most visible state official. His comments are more newsworthy than those of legislators. He is much more sought after for television, and public appearances. As a consequence, he is able to focus public attention on issues that he deems important. There is no assurance that he will always be able to influence public opinion, but there is little doubt that he has

[69] For a discussion of the governor's legislative powers, see Jewell, *The State Legislature,* pp. 105–27; and Coleman B. Ransone, Jr., *The Office of Governor in the United States* (Tuscaloosa: University of Alabama Press, 1956).

ample opportunity to be heard. Skillfully used, the power of publicity can be more influential than any formal power. Legislators must respect the governor's greater access to the communication media and hence to the minds of their constituents.

In addition to the influence inherent in the office of governor, a governor will also be an important figure in his party, perhaps even its dominant figure. In states with competitive two-party systems, the program of the governor is likely to be identified in the public's mind as the program of his party. Legislators know that they will carry that same party label into the next election. In some measure they will share with the governor the responsibility for the success or the failure of his program because of their common party label. It may be sufficient for a governor to tell his party leaders in the legislature that he feels that his prestige is at stake on a particular measure and that he expects the support of the party faithful. The governor can thus be instrumental in bringing to bear upon the legislature all the cohesive forces described earlier that are associated with party. In the urban industrial states, where party lines reflect socioeconomic, religious, and ethnic affiliation, the governor can exercise great power over legislators in his party by making any issue a party issue, and thereby activating these underlying affiliations. Given the absence of divided government, gubernatorial influence in lawmaking appears strong in a competitive two-party state. Of course, when a governor in a competitive two-party state faces a legislature controlled by the opposition party, the fact that the governor's program is linked to the fortunes of his party operates to reduce his influence over the legislature rather than strengthen it. The more his program bears a party label, the more likely it is to activate the cohesive forces of the party in opposition to the governor.

In the one-party states where party appeals in themselves are insufficient, the astute use of patronage and pork is indispensable in securing support for the governor's program. Pork can include construction contracts, roads, parks, hospitals and other institutions, state insurance contracts, and innumerable other items. It is to one-party states, with their rural economies, lower family incomes, and poorly educated work forces, that state jobs look most attractive and local pork is most important. Frank Sorauf reports that patronage jobs in urban industrial economies are insecure and unattractive, at best "short term desperation job alternatives." [70] But in economically depressed states, including large parts of the South, state jobs are more highly valued.[71]

[70] Frank J. Sorauf, "The Silent Revolution in Patronage," *Public Administration Review,* 28 (1960): 30.
[71] Robert B. Highsaw, "The Southern Governor—Challenge to the Strong Executive Theme," *Public Administration Review,* 19 (1959): 7.

It is apparent that the legislative influence of governors varies from state to state and varies over time within states. Ira Sharkansky has attempted to isolate the factors that influence the success of state executive agencies and governors in getting legislatures to fund their budgetary requests.[72] It is interesting to note some of the key findings about interaction between governors and legislatures: (1) The governor's support appears to be a critical ingredient in the success enjoyed by executive agencies in their budgetary requests to the legislature. Legislatures respond more to governors' recommendations than to agency requests. Agencies with the largest budget expansions enjoyed the greatest gubernatorial support. (2) The governors who enjoyed the greatest budgetary success in the legislature tended to be governors who could be reelected. Governors with high-tenure potential were better able to elicit legislative cooperation in funding requests than those who could not expect to remain in office because of constitutional limitations on their terms.

Another study of the success of governors in passing their legislative programs in a number of states produced the following interesting conclusions: [73] (1) Governors appear more successful in competitive two-party states where they hold a small majority in the legislature than in one-party states where their party holds an overwhelming majority in the legislature. We might think that the more seats the governor had to spare, the more successful he would be, but this is not the case. Apparently the governor is better able to rally support within his own party when he has only a modest majority; when his party has a large majority, he has a more difficult time holding the support of various factions within his party. (2) A governor is more successful when he wins a large popular vote in a general election. Moreover, his success in the legislature is also closely related to his showing in the primary election. Apparently strong opposition in the party's primary indicates factionalism within the party and the resulting inability of the governor to secure the support of party members in the legislature.

LEGISLATURES IN STATE POLITICS

At least three general propositions about state leigslatures emerge from the discussions in this chapter. First of all, state legislatures reflect the socioeconomic environment of their states. Levels of urbanization, in-

---

[72] Ira Sharkansky, "Agency Requests, Gubernatorial Support, and Budget Success in State Legislatures," *American Political Science Review,* 62 (December, 1968): 1220–31.

[73] Sarah P. McCally, "The Governor and His Legislative Party," *American Political Science Review,* 60 (December, 1966): 923–42.

come, and education in the fifty states help to explain many of the differences one encounters in state legislative politics: the level of legislative activity, the degree of interparty competition, the extent of party cohesion, the professionalism of the legislature, the nature of legislative conflict, the level of interest group activity and influence, the nature of legislative relations with the executive, and so on. Of course, there are some unique features of legislative politics in each of the fifty states based upon particular events, individuals, or historical experiences. But generally, the characteristics of a state's legislative system are closely linked to a state's environment.

Second, it seems safe to say that most state legislatures function as "arbiters" of public policy rather than as "initiators." Policy initiation is the function of the governor, the bureaucrat, and the interest group. It is principally these elements that develop policy proposals in the first instance; legislatures are placed in the role of responding to the stimulus provided by these groups. The structure of legislatures clearly reflects their deliberative function. Their rules and procedures and their leadership and committee systems do not lend themselves to policy initiation so much as they lend themselves to deliberation, discussion, and delay. The size and complexity of state government has reached a scale where expert knowledge rather than lay enlightenment is the crucial ingredient in policy formation. The state budget, for example, perhaps the single most important policy-making document, is drawn up by bureaucrats subordinate to the governor and modified by the governor before submission to the legislature. Legislatures make further modifications but seldom do they undertake to rewrite an executive budget. Legislatures are still critical obstacles through which appropriation and revenue measures must pass; they are still the scenes of bloody battles over the ends for which public money is to be spent. Yet before legislative deliberation, the agenda for decision making has already been drawn up, the framework for conflict has already been established, and the issues have already been placed in particular bills. Sophisticated lawmakers are aware of their function as arbiters rather than as initiators of public policy. As one of them put it: "We're the policy-making body of the state government, and basically we should give leadership necessary to meet the problems the state faces. But in practice it comes from the executive branch." [74]

A third general proposition about legislatures is that they function to inject into public decision making a parochial influence. Legislatures function to represent locally organized interests, interests that are manifested in local rather than statewide constituencies. Legislators have deep roots in their local constituencies. They have the religious and ethnic affiliations of

[74] Quotation from Wahlke et al., *The Legislative System*, p. 255.

their constituents, they have lived among them for most of their lives, and they meet them frequently in their businesses and clubs. The process of recruiting legislators is carried on at the local level. State legislators clearly function to represent local interests in state politics.

Governors
in state politics

THE MANY ROLES OF A GOVERNOR

The governor is the central figure in American state politics. In the eyes of many Americans, the governor is responsible for everything that happens in his state during his term of office, whether or not he has the authority or the capacity to do anything about it. Governors are expected to bring industry into their states, prevent prison riots, raise teachers' salaries, keep taxes low, reduce unemployment, see that the state gets its fair share of defense contracts from Washington, remove "chiselers" from the welfare roles, prevent violence in big cities, speed up highway construction, bring tourists into the state, and prevent the busing of black and white school children. These public expectations far exceed the powers of governors. In many ways the expectations placed upon the governor resemble those placed upon the president. But few governors have the powers in state political systems that the president has in the national government. Like the president, the governor is expected to be his state's chief administrator, chief legislator, leader of his party, ceremonial head of his government, chief ambassador to other governments, and leader of public opinion.

As *chief administrator*, he must try to achieve coordination within the state's bureaucracy, oversee the preparation of the state's budget,

Chapter six

162

and supervise major state programs. He must resolve conflicts within his administration and troubleshoot where difficulties arise. He must be concerned with public scandal and endeavor to prevent it from becoming public, or act decisively to eliminate it if it does. The public will hold him responsible for any scandal in his administration, whether he was a party to it or not. The public will hold him responsible for the financial structure of the state, whether it was he or his predecessors who were responsible for the state's debts.

Yet, as we shall see in this chapter, the formal administrative powers of a governor are severely restricted. Many of the governor's administrative agencies are headed by elected officials or independent boards or commissions, over which the governor has little or no control. His powers of appointment and removal are severely restricted by state constitutions. Despite a generation of recommendations by political scientists and public administrators that the governor's control over his administration should be strengthened, governors still do not have control over their administration that is commensurate with their responsibility for it.

As *chief legislator,* the governor is responsible for the major statewide legislative programs. There is a general public expectation that every governor will put forward some sort of legislative program, even a governor committed to a "caretaker" role. The governor largely determines what public issues will be considered by the legislature. By sending bills to the legislature, the governor is cast in the role of the "initiator" of public policy decisions. And if he wants to see his legislative proposals enacted into law, he must also persuade legislators to support them. In other words, he must also involve himself directly in legislative decisions and become an "arbiter" in public policy as well. Yet the governor has very few formal powers over legislation. He can call special sessions of the legislature, and he has the power to veto bills passed by the legislature (except in North Carolina where the governor has no veto power). In thirty-five states it requires a two-thirds vote to override a veto rather than a simple majority. Yet these formal powers do not by themselves make a governor a state's "chief legislator."

Governors also function as *leaders of their party.* The governor's office carries great prestige in any state, and no man becomes governor without considerable political resources of one kind or another. The program of the governor is likely to be identified in the public's mind as the program of its party. To some extent, everyone who runs for public office under the same party label as the governor has a stake in his success. Since all who run under the party's label share its common fortunes, and since its fortunes are often governed by the strength of its gubernatorial candidate, there will always be a tendency for loyal party members to support their governor. However, governors do not have the power to deny party nominations to recalcitrant legislators in their own party. Party nominations are determined at the local level in the American states. The governor has little formal authority over members of his own party.

Ceremonial duties occupy a great deal of a governor's time. Yet a governor is seldom able to mobilize the symbolic and ceremonial power of his office on behalf of state goals in the same way that the president can mobilize the power of his office on behalf of national goals. Emotional ties to state government are not at all comparable to those associated with the national government, not even in the South.

The governor is the *chief negotiator with other governments* in the American federal system, a variation on the diplomatic role of the president. Governors must negotiate with their local governments on the division of state and local responsibilities for public programs, and with other state governments over coordinating highway development, water pollution, resource conservation, and reciprocity in state laws. Increasingly, governors must undertake responsibility for negotiation with the national government as well. The governor shares responsibility with United States senators in seeing to it that his state receives a "fair share" of defense contracts, highway monies, educational monies, poverty funds, and so on.

Finally, the governor is a *leader of public opinion* in his state. He is the most visible of state officials. His comments on public affairs make news, and he is sought after for television, radio, and public appearances. He is able to focus public opinion on issues he deems important. He may not always be able to win public opinion to his side, but at least he will be heard.

If the governor has little formal authority to deal with the complex problems of his state, what political resources are available to him to make the most of his leadership? How can he provide the leadership required for the development of the major state programs for education, welfare, highways, taxation, and so on? How can he control his administration, get his bills passed, and negotiate effectively with the federal government? Why is the governor a leader instead of a figurehead? How does he make his influence felt in questions of public policy?

Much of the rest of this chapter is an attempt to come to grips with these questions. But it is clear at the outset that the governor's power rests largely upon his abilities of persuasion. His power depends upon his ability to persuade administrators over whom he has little authority, legislators who are jealous of their own powers, party leaders who are selected by local constituents, federal officials over whom the governor has little authority, and a public that thinks he has more authority than he really has. Thus, the role of a governor is, above all, that of a persuader—of his own administrators, state legislators, federal officials, party leaders, the press, and the public.

THE MAKING OF A GOVERNOR

As the central position in American state politics, the governorship is a much sought after office. The prestige of being called "governor" for the rest of one's life, and the opportunity to use the office as a steppingstone to the United States Senate, or even the presidency or vice-presidency of the United States, is extremely attractive to men of ambition in American politics.

There are many types of governors, just as there are many different constituencies in the United States. The urbanity and concern for international affairs which was displayed by Governor Nelson Rockefeller is a totally different political style from the folksy, provincial approach displayed by Governor Lester Maddox of Georgia. Many governors have been the sons of families of great wealth, who have chosen public service as an outlet for their energies—the Roosevelts, the Harrimans, the Rockefellers, the Scrantons. Some have been men with successful business careers behind them, such as George Romney of Michigan, former president of American Motors. Others have been men of the people, who have emphasized, or exaggerated, their humble beginnings —Huey Long of Louisiana, Al Smith of New York, "Old Gene" Talmadge of Georgia. The southern "populist" governors, however, have generally disappeared, to be replaced by more urbane and moderate men— Reubin Askew of Florida, Dale Bumpers of Arkansas, and Jimmy Carter of Georgia. Only George C. Wallace of Alabama remains as heir to the populist tradition, and his appeal extends to many working-class whites throughout the nation. Governor Edmund G. Brown, Jr. of California won the office once held by his father "Pat" Brown, who defeated Richard M. Nixon in 1962. Governor Ella T. Grasso of Connecticut was the first woman to win a governorship whose husband had not preceded her in the office. Governor James B. Longley of Maine is the first Independent candidate to win a governorship in nearly fifty years. Governors have been movie actors (Ronald Reagan of California), restaurant owners (Lester Maddox of Georgia), and even party bosses (David Lawrence of Pennsylvania). But the majority of governors have been lawyers by profession. (The predominance of lawyers in public office is explained in Chapter 5). The advent of television has apparently increased the accent on youth and good looks among state governors. The median beginning age among governors has declined over the last few decades.

Historically, presidents were chosen from among the ranks of America's state governors, particularly the governors of the larger states. But recently the importance of international affairs in American politics has detracted somewhat from the popular image of the governorship as a training ground for the presidency. Governors tend to be associated with domestic rather than foreign policy questions. Men such as Nixon, McGovern, Humphrey, Kennedy, Goldwater, and Johnson found the United States Senate a good place to promote their campaigns for presidential nominations. Some scholars have attributed the decline in the number of governors selected as presidential candidates to a general decline in the popularity of governors. But a closer examination of the "vulnerability" of governors reveals that governors seeking reelection are just as successful today as in years past.[1] *Approximately two-thirds of all incumbent governors who seek reelection are returned to office.* This rate of success has remained roughly constant over the decades. So governors are no more "vulnerable" today than in the past, and we must conclude that recent senatorial accession to the presidency is the result of other factors, perhaps the increased role of Washington in domestic affairs and the increased attention given to war and international affairs in presidential politics.

Governors, unlike state legislators, usually come to their office with considerable experience in public affairs.[2] "Promotion" from a statewide elective office, particularly lieutenant governor or attorney general, is the most well-worn path to the governorship. For example, one study of governors holding office showed that twenty-one had previously served in a statewide elective office, including attorney general, lieutenant governor, public service commissioner, comptroller, secretary of state, and state auditor.[3] Experience in the state legislature was also quite common among these fifty governors—twenty-one had served in their state legislatures at some time before becoming governor. Eight of the fifty governors had been both legislators and holders of statewide elective office. Four governors had served in the state judiciary before assuming office. Eleven governors had experience in local government. Five governors had experience in Congress, and seven had experience in the executive branch of the national government. In fact, only five of the fifty governors had no prior experience in public office. The annual salary of governors in 1975 ranged from a low of $10,000 in Arkansas to a high

---

[1] Stephen Turrett, "The Vulnerability of American Governors, 1900–1969," *Midwest Journal of Political Science,* 15 (February, 1971): 108–32.

[2] See Joseph A. Schlesinger, *How They Became Governor* (East Lansing: Michigan State University Press, 1957).

[3] *Book of the States, 1965–66* (Lexington, Ky.: Council of State Governments, 1965).

of $85,000 in New York. The average salary is between $35,000 and $40,000.

What do governors do *after* they leave office? The typical governor wins office in his mid-forties, yet he can expect to hold office for only four to eight years. His future political ambitions are an important factor in his behavior in office. A significant number of exgovernors, 18 to 20 percent, are appointed to federal cabinet-level posts, and another 12 to 15 percent win election to the U.S. Senate.[4] Some accept judgeships (5 to 6 percent). Others try for the presidency or the vice-presidency. But most governors running for the presidency or angling for a vice-presidential nomination have ended up as "also rans." Over half of the nation's exgovernors return to private life (often because the U.S. Senate seats in their state are in the firm grip of incumbents and the opposition party controls the White House and federal appointments).

In recent years more governors have been Democrats than Republicans. Only in 1966 and 1968 was this tide reversed, and the GOP held more governor's chairs than the Democratic party (see Table 6–1).

EXECUTIVE POWER IN STATE GOVERNMENT

Frequently we speak of "strong" and "weak" governors. Yet it is difficult to compare the power of one governor with that of another. To do so, one must examine the constitutional position of the governor, his powers of appointment and removal over state officials, his ability or inability to succeed himself, his powers over the state budget, his legislative influence, his position in his own party and its position in state politics, and his influence over interest groups and public opinion in the state.

Let us examine first of all the governor's constitutional position in state government. In many ways the organization of American state government resembles political thinking of one hundred or two hundred years ago. This colonial experience emphasized "fear of the executive" and resulted in state constitutional restrictions on a governor's term of office, his ability to succeed himself, his control over appointments and removals, the proliferation of separate boards and commissions to govern particular state programs, and long overlapping terms for the members of these boards and commissions. The Jacksonian era of "popular democracy" brought with it the idea that the way to insure popular con-

---

[4] Joseph A. Schlesinger, "The Politics of the Executive," in Herbert Jacobs and Kenneth Vines, eds., *Politics in the American States*, 2nd ed. (Boston: Little, Brown and Company, 1972), p. 213.

TABLE 6.1   Democratic and Republican Margins in Elections for Governor

	1964	1966	1968	1970	1972	1974
Alabama	—	D-63.4	—	D-74.5	—	D-85.0
Alaska	—	R-50.0	—	D-52.4	—	D-50.4
Arizona	D-53.2	R-53.8	R-57.8	R-50.9	—	R-58.3
Arkansas	D-57.0	R-54.3	R-52.4	D-61.7	D-75.8	D-65.6
California	—	R-57.6	—	R-52.8	—	D-51.5
Colorado	—	R-54.0	—	R-52.5	—	D-53.8
Connecticut	—	D-55.7	—	R-53.8	—	D-60.1
Delaware	D-51.4	—	R-51.5	—	D-51.3	—
Florida	D-56.1	R-55.1	—	D-56.9	—	D-61.1
Georgia	—	R-47.4*	—	D-59.3	—	D-68.9
Hawaii	—	D-51.1	—	D-57.6	—	D-54.6
Idaho	—	R-41.4	—	D-52.2	—	D-72.9
Illinois	D-51.9	—	R-51.1	—	D-51.2	—
Indiana	D-56.2	—	R-52.8	—	R-57.2	—
Iowa	D-68.0	D-55.3	R-54.0	R-51.0	R-58.4	R-58.6
Kansas	R-50.9	D-54.8	D-52.2	D-54.3	D-62.7	R-50.3
Kentucky	D-50.7	—	R-51.2	—	D-50.6	D-53.6
Louisiana	D-60.7	—	D-100.0	—	D-57.2	—
Maine	—	D-53.1	—	D-50.1	—	Ind-39.5
Maryland	—	R-49.6	—	D-65.7	—	D-63.5
Massachusetts	R-50.3	R-62.6	—	R-56.7	—	D-55.9
Michigan	R-55.9	R-60.5	—	R-50.4	—	R-51.6
Minnesota	—	R-52.6	—	D-54.0	—	D-64.6
Mississippi	D-61.9	—	D-65.0	—	D-100.0	—
Missouri	D-62.1	—	D-61.1	—	R-55.2	—
Montana	R-51.3	—	D-53.6	—	D-54.1	—
Nebraska	D-60.0	R-61.5	—	D-53.9	—	D-59.3
Nevada	—	R-52.2	—	D-48.1	—	R-50.2
New Hampshire	D-66.8	D-54.0	R-52.4	R-46.0	R-41.6	R-50.9
New Jersey	—	D-57.4	—	R-59.7	—	D-67.6
New Mexico	D-60.2	R-51.7	R-50.2	D-51.3	—	D-50.6
New York	—	R-54.6	—	R-52.4	—	D58.6
North Carolina	D-56.6	—	D-52.7	—	R-51.1	—
North Dakota	D-55.7	—	D-54.8	—	D-5.10	—
Ohio	—	R-62.2	—	D-54.2	—	R-50.2
Oklahoma	—	R-55.7	—	D-48.4	—	D-63.8
Oregon	—	R-55.3	—	R-55.6	—	R-55.1
Pennsylvania	—	R-52.1	—	D-55.2	—	D-54.5
Rhode Island	R-61.1	R-63.3	D-51.7	D-50.1	D-52.9	D-78.4
South Carolina	—	D-58.2	—	D-51.7	—	R-52.1
South Dakota	R-51.7	R-57.7	R-57.6	D-54.8	D-60.0	D-53.6
Tennessee	—	D-81.2	—	R-52.0	—	D-55.9
Texas	D-73.8	D-72.8	D-56.5	D-53.6	D-48.1	D-62.6
Utah	D-57.0	—	D-68.6	—	D-69.1	R-50.0
Vermont	D-64.9	D-57.7	R-55.0	R-57.0	D-55.4	D-49.4
Virginia	D-47.9	D-47.9	—	R-52.5	—	R-50.4
Washington	R-55.8	—	R-53.2	—	R-53.2	—
West Virginia	D-54.9	—	R-50.9	—	R-54.7	—
Wisconsin	R-50.6	R-53.5	R-52.6	D-54.2	—	D-55.7
Wyoming	—	R-54.3	—	R-62.8	—	D-55.8

*Republican candidate Howard Calloway won the popular vote but failed to obtain the necessary majority; Democratic candidate Lester Maddox was elected by the state legislature.

trol of state government was to elect separately as many state officials as possible. The Reform movement of the late nineteenth and early twentieth centuries led to merit systems and civil service boards, which further curtailed the governor's power of appointment.[5] Not all of these trends were experienced uniformly by all fifty states, and there are considerable variations from state to state in the powers that governors have over the state executive branch. Figure 6–1 is an example of a "weak" executive type of state administrative organization. Many important state offices are governed by boards or commissions whose members may be appointed by the governor with the consent of the state senate but for long overlapping terms, which reduces the governor's influence over members of these boards and commissions. Figure 6–2 is an example of a "strong" executive type of state government organization. Only the governor and lieutenant governor and legislature are elected directly by the people. The governor appoints the heads of all major state agencies for a term that is coterminous with his own.

Fortunately, the trend toward separately elected officials and independent boards and commissions appears to be on the wane. In recent years "administrative efficiency" has emerged as the central theme in state government reorganization proposals. Reorganization has emphasized a reduction in the number of departments, more functional integration of state programs, and more power in the governor's office. Yet even though the trend may be toward more streamlined state government organization, it is clear that separately elected officials and independent boards and officials will be around for a long time. Political parties and public officials develop a stake in the continued existence of separately elected public offices; separately elected offices provide more party nominations for the party faithful. Moreover, as we observed in Chapter 3, many interest groups prefer to be governed by boards and commissions that are independent of executive authority. They feel they have more influence over independent boards than those that come directly under a governor's authority. There is often the assumption that boards and commissions enable divergent interests to be represented in the governing of state agencies. Groups are thereby permitted to have a voice in state programs in which they are interested.

Another component of a governor's influence is his ability or inability to succeed himself in office. Turnover in governors' offices is quite high: ten states have a two-year term for the office of governor, and forty states have a four-year term. However, several of the states providing for a four-year term forbid the incumbent to succeed himself. Turnover

---

[5] For a description of the Reform movement in state and local government see Chapter 9.

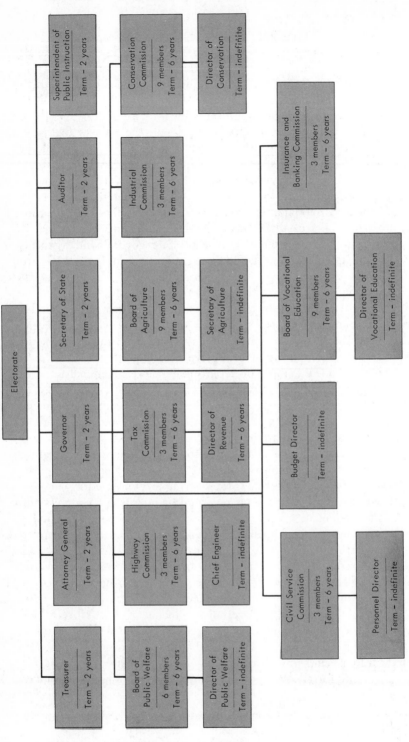

FIGURE 6–1 "Weak" executive type of state administrative organization.

Source: Frederic A. Ogg and P. Orman Ray, *Introduction to American Government,* 13th ed. by William H. Young (New York: Appleton Century-Crofts, 1966), pp. 772–73. Reproduced by permission of the publisher.

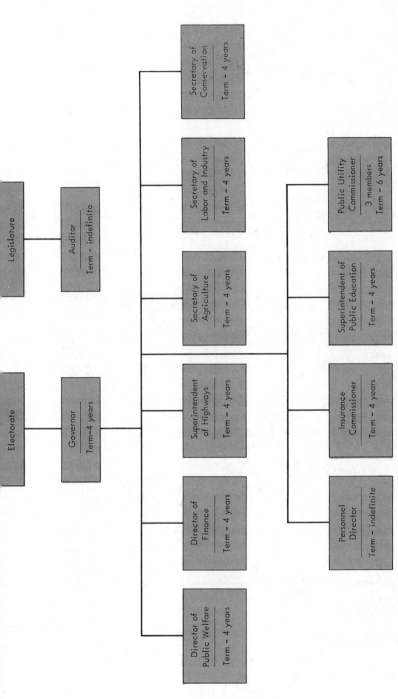

FIGURE 6-2 "Strong" executive type of state administrative organization.

Source: Frederic A. Ogg and P. Orman Ray, *Introduction to American Government,* 13th ed. by William H. Young (New York: Appleton-Century-Crofts, 1966), pp. 772–73. Reproduced with permission of the publisher.

figures suggest that minor elected state officials have longer tenures in office than governors. Apparently a typical secretary of state, state treasurer, or state auditor can expect to stay in office longer than the governor (lieutenant governor and attorney general are positions of high turnover like the governor), and this long tenure for minor elected officials further reduces the governor's control over them.

It is possible to rank the states according to the power that a governor derives from his tenure in office. Governors with the highest "tenure power" are those who are elected for a four-year term and are permitted to succeed themselves indefinitely. Seventeen states fall into this category (see Table 6–2). Governors with the lowest "tenure power" are those who have only two-year terms. The Twenty Second Amendment to the U.S. Constitution suggests that most Americans believe in restricting executive tenure at the presidential level, and many states have similar restrictions on their governors. However, these constitutional

TABLE 6.2   Tenure Provisions for Governors

Four-Year Term, No Restrictions on Re-election

Arizona	Illinois	New York
California	Iowa	North Dakota
Colorado	Massachusetts	Washington
Connecticut	Michigan	Wisconsin
Hawaii	Minnesota	Wyoming
Idaho	Montana	

Four-Year Term, Restricted to Two Terms

Alabama	Maine	Oklahoma
Alaska	Maryland	Oregon
Delaware	Missouri	Pennsylvania
Florida	Nebraska	South Dakota
Indiana	Nevada	Texas
Kansas	New Jersey	Utah
Louisiana	Ohio	West Virginia

Four-Year Term, Consecutive Re-election Prohibited

Georgia	North Carolina
Kentucky	South Carolina
Mississippi	Tennessee
New Mexico	Virginia

Two-Year Term, No Restrictions on Re-election

Arkansas	Rhode Island
New Hampshire	Vermont

SOURCE: *Book of the States, 1974-75*, p. 147.

restrictions can be circumvented by a very powerful governor. When Governor Wallace of Alabama was restricted by his state's constitution to a single four-year term, his wife ran in his place, with Wallace openly avowing that if she were elected he would run the state. Apparently the voters of Alabama were quite willing to accept this arrangement despite the obvious circumvention of the Alabama Constitution. Lurleen Wallace won an overwhelming victory at the polls; later the constitution was amended.

THE GOVERNOR'S MANAGERIAL POWERS

Perhaps the most important managerial power is the power to appoint subordinate officials. Personal appointment of subordinates does not guarantee their responsibility, but there is a greater likelihood that an official appointed by a governor will be someone whose values coincide with those of the governor. Of course a governor is subject to many different pressures in exercising his appointing power; often he must pay off political debts or win the support of a political faction by his selection. Salary limitations and the shortness of tenure make it exceedingly difficult to find capable men for positions of high responsibility in state government. But it is safe to infer that a governor who can name his major department heads is stronger than a governor who cannot. As we have already seen, many department heads in state government are popularly elected, and many departments are headed by elected or appointed boards or commissions over whom the governor has relatively little control.

Political scientist Joseph Schlesinger compared the governors' appointive powers in all fifty states. Taking sixteen major governmental functions in every state, he scored each according to the relative influence, in formal terms, which the governor has over the appointment of the head of each agency handling these functions.[6] If the governor can appoint an agency head without the need for legislative confirmation, this gives him strong appointive power. The need for legislative confirmation by one or both houses reduces the governor's formal appointive power; and of course, if an agency head is appointed by a separate board rather than the governor, this further reduces his appointive power. Finally, if an agency head is separately elected by the people, the governor has no formal authority over his appointment. Schlesinger classified the fifty states according to the degree to which the governor had

[6] These functions are finance, agriculture, attorney general, auditor, budget officer, conservation, comptroller, education, health, highways, insurance, labor, secretary of state, tax commissioner, treasurer, and welfare.

formal appointive powers within the executive branch of government
(see Table 6–3). States that have had major constitutional revisions

TABLE 6.3   Appointive Powers of Governors

Very Strong	Strong	Moderate	Weak	Very Weak
Tennessee	Arkansas	Alabama	Maine	Florida
New Jersey	California	Missouri	Oregon	Texas
Pennsylvania	Connecticut	Washington	Nevada	Colorado
Maryland	Idaho	West Virginia	Wisconsin	Georgia
New York	Kentucky	Alaska	Louisiana	Mississippi
Hawaii	Michigan	Nebraska	New Hampshire	North Dakota
Indiana	Minnesota	Rhode Island	North Carolina	New Mexico
Massachusetts	Ohio	Utah	Kansas	South Carolina
Virginia	South Dakota	Iowa	Wyoming	Oklahoma
Illinois	Vermont	Montana		Arizona
	Delaware			

SOURCE: Council of State Governments, *Book of the States, 1974-75.*

in recent years, such as New Jersey, New York, and Tennesee, rate high.
This is a reflection of the extent of management reform in these states.
The reason why Tennessee ranks so high is that its governor is the only
elected officer (with the exception of three public utilities commissioners),
and most of the other major positions in state government are filled by
him without the need for legislative approval. However, even in Tennessee, the secretary of state, treasurer, and comptroller are chosen by
the legislature rather than the governor. At the other extreme, Colorado's
governor has weak appointive powers not only because Colorado's secretary of state, attorney general, treasurer, and auditor are popularly
elected but also because major departments, such as agriculture, labor,
health, and so on, are headed by civil service appointees. North Dakota's
governor has weak appointive powers because, in addition to the usual
elective offices, the tax commissioner and the commissioner of agriculture, labor, and insurance are also elected positions.

Restrictions on a governor's power of appointment are further complicated by restrictions on his power of removal. A common statutory
or constitutional provision dealing with the governor's removal power
states that removal must be "for cause only"; that is, the governor must
provide a clear-cut statement of charges and an opportunity for an open
hearing to the employee he is trying to oust. This process is often un-
pleasant, and governors seek to avoid it unless they have strong evidence of incompetence, fraud, or mismanagement. When a governor's

removal powers are limited "for cause only," it is next to impossible to remove a subordinate for policy differences. Of course a governor may request an officeholder to resign, even when the governor's removal power is limited, and such a request may be honored by the officeholder in preference to continued unhappy relationships with the governor's office or in fear of the governor's ability to mobilize public opinion against him. As a final resort, a determined governor with influence in the legislature can always oust an official by a legislative act, which abolishes the office or agency the official heads and replaces it with another; this device is sometimes called a "ripper bill."

Certain elected state officials, notably the lieutenant governor and the attorney general, often use their positions to advance their own candidacy for the governorship or the U.S. Senate, thus creating further problems for a governor, particularly when their ambitions are in competition with his own. Lieutenant governors, of course, have few substantive duties in state government, other than the ceremonial one of presiding over the state senate. But the attorney general has more influence —his legal opinions have great importance for a governor's program. Governors are often bound by statute to conform to the attorney general's legal opinion in interpreting state laws and constitutions.

The governor's control over patronage is another potential source of executive power in state government. A governor can win the support of party chairmen throughout the state by providing them with jobs to dispense to "deserving" party workers. This provides prestige and power to party chairmen within their communities, and they are expected to return the favor by supporting the governor. Patronage jobs are particularly important in depressed economies. In the one-party states of the South, for example, with their rural economies, lower family incomes, and poorly educated work forces, state jobs look most attractive. But patronage jobs in urban industrial economies are insecure and unattractive.[7] A large number of state jobs on highways and public works are lower paid, menial positions, which are not very attractive in a wealthy state. Other state jobs require specialized skills and training and do not lend themselves to patronage appointments. Patronage has declined in recent years in importance not only as a product of economic development but also as a result of the growth of civil service systems. A great expansion of state civil service systems occurred after 1935, as a result of the requirement of the federal Social Security Act of that year that states participating in national grants under that law must install civil service systems for employees in the federally aided public as-

---

[7] Frank J. Sorauf, "State Patronage in a Rural County," *American Political Science Review*, 50 (1956); 1046.

sistance, insurance, and health programs. Civil service coverage is now required in state agencies financed even in part by federal grants-in-aid. This national requirement inspired many states to extend civil service coverage to a large number of their own employees. Today more than half of all state employees are under civil service.

Civil service systems, particularly those administered by independent civil service commissions, significantly reduce executive control over program administration. There is a persistent tendency for civil service systems to be routine, mechanical, and unimaginative. Job classification schemes, to which recruitment, qualifications, and pay scales are closely tied, become so rigid with time that executives have little flexibility in recruiting really talented people to state government. Executives whose authority to promote, hire, and fire their employees is severely curtailed can hardly be expected to obtain maximum effort and cooperation from their employees. Even the public administration experts, who originally supported the civil service movement and the removal of state jobs from the governor's authority, are beginning to recommend that the power over personnel administration be returned to the governor.

THE GOVERNOR'S FISCAL POWERS

The state budget is the most important policy document in state government. The governor's control over the state budget is perhaps his most formidable power. While the legislature must enact the state budget into law, and no state monies may be spent without a legislative appropriation, in practice the greatest amount of control over state government rests with the governor and his budget staff. The governor has full responsibility for the preparation of the budget and its submission to the legislature in a majority of states, but in some states he shares this responsibility with a civil service appointee or an appointee of someone other than himself, and in other states he shares the power to prepare the budget with popularly elected officials or members of the legislature (see Table 6–4).

Budget making involves bringing together the requests of all existing state agencies, calculating the costs of new state programs, estimating the probable income of the state, and evaluating these costs and income estimates in the light of program and policy objectives. The final budget document is submitted to the legislature for its adoption as an appropriations measure. No state monies can be spent without a legislative appropriation, and the legislature can make any alterations in the state budget that it sees fit. Potentially, then, a legislature can control any

Table 6.4   Budget Powers of Governors

	Full Responsibility	
Alabama	Maryland	Oklahoma
Alaska	Massachusetts	Oregon
Arizona	Michigan	Pennsylvania
Arkansas	Minnesota	Rhode Island
California	Missouri	South Dakota
Colorado	Nevada	Tennessee
Delaware	New Hampshire	Utah
Florida	New Jersey	Vermont
Hawaii	New Mexico	Virginia
Idaho	New York	Washington
Illinois	North Carolina	West Virginia
Iowa	North Dakota	Wisconsin
Kentucky	Ohio	Wyoming
Maine		

	Responsibility Shared With A *Civil Service Appointee*	
Connecticut	Kansas	Montana
Georgia	Louisiana	

	Responsibility Shared With *Legislature*	
Mississippi		
Texas		

	Responsibility Shared With Independent *Office or Agency*	
Indiana	South Carolina	
Nebraska		

SOURCE: *Book of the States, 1974-75.*

activity of the state government through its power over appropriations, but as a practical matter, the legislature seldom reviews every item of the governor's budget. In practice, budgets tend to reflect the views of those responsible for their preparation, namely, the governor. Thomas Anton summarizes the role of state agencies, budget officers, governors, and legislatures in budget making as follows: "A peek into the decision-making black box in most states, I submit, would probably reveal a system in which operating agency heads consistently request more funds, executive and/or legislative reviewers consistently reduce agency requests, governors consistently pursue balanced budgets at higher expenditure levels, and legislatures consistently approve higher appropriations while engaging in frequent disputes with the governor over revenues." [8]

The pressure for budget increases comes from the request of agency officials. Most agency officials feel compelled to ask for more money each year. According to Anton, requesting an increase in funds "affirms the significance and protects the status of agency employees, assures clientele groups that new and higher standards of service are being pursued aggressively," [9] and gives the governor's office and the legislature something to cut that will not affect existing programs. The governor's budget staff generally recognizes the built-in pressure to expand budgets. The budget staff see themselves as "cutters." As Allen Schick describes it: "The agencies, anticipating a cut, overestimate their needs and pad the budget, while the budget office, in the conviction that the budget is padded, make deep cuts in the agency's estimates." [10] Agencies press for budgetary expansion with better programs in mind, while the governor's budget staff tries to reduce expenditures with cost cutting in mind.

While most states have executive budget systems, and the governor is responsible for the activities of his budgetary staff, the governor's actual control over state spending is limited in many ways. First of all, it is quite common to "earmark" in state constitutions and laws certain funds for particular purposes, such as gasoline taxes for highways. The earmarking device provides certain agencies with an independent source of income, thus reducing the governor's control over operations. In addition, Anton writes: "The governor will probably come to his position without any direct experience in dealing with state finance. His own inexperience will thus provide a sharp contrast to the wisdom of the old hands who occupy administrative and legislative positions of influence, and who will probably regard the governor as an outsider—a 'new boy' come to meddle in their affairs. Moreover, since the average length of service for most governors is less than five years, the old hands can constantly think of the 'new boy' as someone who is likely to be gone from the scene far in advance of their own departure." [11] It is not easy for a governor to master the "constitutional limitations, marvelously incoherent divisions of financial accountability, incomprehensible budget documents, and, worst of all, an intricate maze of general funds, special

---

[8] Thomas J. Anton, "Roles and Symbols in the Determination of State Expenditures," *Midwest Journal of Political Science*, 11 (February, 1967): 36; see also Thomas J. Anton, *The Politics of State Expenditure in Illinois* (Urbana: University of Illinois Press, 1966).

[9] Anton, "Roles and Symbols," p. 29.

[10] Allen Schick, "Control Patterns in State Budget Execution," *Public Administration Review*, 24 (1964): 99.

[11] Anton, "Roles and Symbols," p. 32.

funds, revolving funds, loan funds, trust funds, federal funds, all con-
spired to shroud the state's financial situation in mystery." [12]

Governors have little influence over many items of state spending.
Over fifty percent of state finances come from special "earmarked" funds.
What is left, "general fund expenditures," is also largely committed to
existing state programs, particularly welfare and education. Governors
typically campaign on platforms stressing both increased service and
lower taxes. Once in office, however, they typically find it impossible to
accomplish both and very difficult to accomplish either one. Often new
programs planned by a governor must be put aside, because money must
be found to educate more students who are entitled to an education
under existing programs; or money must be found to pay the welfare
costs of additional clients who are entitled to care under existing programs; or money must be found to raise the salaries of state personnel
who are administering existing programs. The result is that social and
economic conditions really "determine" expenditures, and governors have
little flexibility in budget making. Anton feels that governors must focus
most of their attention on revenue, which typically must be increased
just to keep pace with existing programs. "Governors may be regarded
as 'money providers' or as 'budget balancers'; only infrequently can they
be viewed as 'decision makers' in the determination of state expenditures." [13] (See Chapter 18 for further discussion.)

THE GOVERNOR'S LEGISLATIVE POWERS

The responsibility for initiating major statewide legislative programs falls
upon the governor. The governor's programs are presented to the legislature in various governor's messages and in his budget. Much of the governor's power over the legislature stems from this power as party leader
of public opinion.[14] However, the governor's veto power is a source of
formal authority over legislature and deserves special attention. Only in
North Carolina does the governor have no veto power at all. In some
states, the veto power is restricted by giving the governor only a short
time to consider a bill after it has passed the legislature, by permitting
a simple majority of legislative members to override the veto, or by requiring vetoed bills to reappear at the next legislative session. In other
states, governors have the added power of the item veto, they are given
longer periods of time to consider a bill, and a two-thirds vote of both

[12] Ibid., p. 33.
[13] Ibid., p. 34.
[14] See Chapter 5, "The Governor in the Legislature," pp. 157–61.

houses of the legislature is required to override a veto rather than a simple majority. Thus, it is possible to rank states according to the strength of the governor's veto; this is done in Table 6–5.

TABLE 6.5   The Governors' Veto Powers

Very Strong		Strong	Medium	Weak
Alaska	Minnesota	Alabama	Florida	Indiana
Arizona	Mississippi	Arkansas	Idaho	Maine
California	Missouri	Kentucky	Massachusetts	Nevada
Colorado	Nebraska	Tennessee	Montana	New Hampshire
Connecticut	New Jersey	West Virginia	New Mexico	North Carolina
Delaware	New York		Oregon	Rhode Island
Georgia	North Dakota		South Carolina	Vermont
Hawaii	Ohio		Texas	
Illinois	Oklahoma		Virginia	
Iowa	Pennsylvania		Washington	
Kansas	South Dakota		Wisconsin	
Louisiana	Utah			
Maryland	Wyoming			
Michigan				

SOURCE: *Book of the States, 1974-75.*

What factors affect a governor's success in winning support for his legislative program? Sarah McCally Morehouse studied legislators' support for gubernatorial proposals in sixteen different sessions in twelve northern and western states.[15] She concluded:

1. Party competition in a legislative district does *not* affect a legislator's support for the governor.
2. Governors receive greater support from legislators who are elected from districts which voted heavily for the governor.
3. The greater the party organization's role in selecting a legislator, the greater support he gives to a governor of his party.

Her studies discount socioeconomic characteristics of legislative districts as major determinants of support or opposition to a governor's proposals.

Since we have already discussed the governor's power over the legislature in Chapter 5, let us turn to a consideration of the legislature's power over executive departments. Professor Deil S. Wright asked 933

[15] Sarah McCally Morehouse, "The State Political Party and the Policy-Making Process," *American Political Science Review*, 67 (March, 1973): 55–72.

department and agency heads from all fifty states a series of questions about legislative versus gubernatorial influence in their departments.[16] One question asked the agency heads to judge whether the governor or the legislature exercised greater control over the affairs of this department. As Table 6–6 indicates, more agency heads felt that the legislature

TABLE 6.6   Administrators, Attitudes of American State on Political Relationships

	Percentages (N=933)
Who Exercises Greater Control over Your Agency's Affairs?	
Governor	32
Each About the Same	22
Legislature	44
Other and N.A.	2
	100
Who Has the Greater Tendency to Reduce Budget Requests?	
Governor	25
Legislature	60
Other and N.A.	15
	100
Who Is More Sympathetic to the Goals of Your Agency?	
Governor	55
Each About the Same	14
Legislature	20
Other and N.A.	11
	100
What Type of Control Do You Prefer?	
Governor	42
Independent Commission	28
Legislature	24
Other and N.A.	5
	100

NOTE: For the source of data and the survey instrument containing the precise wording of the questions, see Deil S. Wright and Richard L. McAnaw, "American State Administrators: Study Code and Marginal Tabulations for the State Administrative Officials Questionnaire" (Iowa City, Iowa: Department of Political Science and Institute of Public Affairs, January 1965), mimeographed, 40 pp. Tabled percentages may not add to 100 because of rounding.

SOURCE: Deil S. Wright, "Executive Leadership in State Administration," *Midwest Journal of Political Science*, 11 (February, 1967), 4.

[16] Deil S. Wright, "Executive Leadership in State Administration," *Midwest Journal of Political Science*, 11 (February, 1967): 1–26.

exercised greater control over their departments than the governor. Agency heads also felt that the legislature was more likely to reduce their budget requests than the governor, and that the governor was more sympathetic to the goals of their agency than the legislature. Agency heads generally preferred gubernatorial control to control by the legislature, but many agency heads seemed to prefer independence from either direct gubernatorial or direct legislative control.

THE GOVERNOR AS POLITICAL LEADER

The governor is the most visible figure in state politics. He commands the attention of press, radio, and television. He has a greater opportunity than any other state official to exercise leadership by persuasion. An attractive governor who is skillful in public relations can command support from administrators, legislators, local officials, and party leaders through public appeals to their constituents. Politicians must respect the governor's greater access to the communications media and hence to the minds of their constituents. An effective governor not only understands the broad range of issues facing his state but also is able to speak clearly and persuasively about them. A governor's reputation as leader, however, stems not only from what he says but also from what he does. His reputation must include a capacity to decide issues and to persist in his decision once it is made. A reputation for backing down, for avoiding situations that involve him in public conflict, or for wavering in the face of momentary pressures invites the governor's adversaries to ignore or oppose him. A sense of insecurity or weakness can damage a governor's power more than any constitutional limitation. A governor can also increase his influence by developing a reputation for punishing his adversaries and rewarding his supporters. Once his reputation as an effective leader is established, cooperation is often forthcoming in anticipation of the governor's reaction.

Governors are also the recognized leaders of their state parties. In a majority of states, it is the governor who picks the state party chairman and who is consulted on questions of party platform, campaign tactics, nominations for party office, and party finances. The amount of power that a governor derives from his position as party leader varies from state to state according to the strength, cohesion, and discipline of the state parties. A few governors have been able to build strong party organization in their states and have gained power through partisan appeal. In urban industrial states, where party lines reflect socioeconomic, religious, and ethnic divisions, the governor can exercise great power by an appeal to party loyalty. Of course in one-party states, particularly in the South and the Midwest, the party mechanism is not really an effective instrument of gubernatorial power. Governors in one-party states must rely upon personal organizations or factional support. As we observed earlier, one-party states are really no-party states. The governor must negotiate with individuals and factions in the legislature on an issue-by-issue basis to accomplish his program.

There are at least three limitations to the power that a governor derives from his role as party leader. First of all, a governor cannot deny party renomination to disloyal members. City and county leaders and state legislators hold their positions by their own efforts and owe the governor nothing. Party machinery is localized; it responds to constituency demands, not the voice of the governor. Second, the frequency of divided control, where the governor faces the legislature dominated by the opposition party, requires him to bargain with individuals and groups in the opposition party. If he has acquired a reputation for being too "partisan" in his approach to state programs, he will find it difficult to win over the necessary support of opposition party members. Finally, the use of patronage may make as many enemies as friends. An old political maxim states that "For every one patronage appointment, you make nine enemies and one ingrate."

OTHER EXECUTIVE OFFICES

The lieutenant governor's office in many states is looked upon as a campaign platform for the governorship. Lieutenant governors are said to have a two- or four-year head start for the top job. The lieutenant governor's formal duties are comparable to those of the vice-president of the United States; in other words, lieutenant governors have relatively little to do. The two basic functions of the office are to serve in direct line of succession to the governor and replace him in the event of a vacancy in that office, and to be the presiding officer of the state senate. Since lieutenant governors generally have political ambitions of their own, they seldom make good "assistant governors" who will submerge their own interests for the success of the governor's administration. Unlike the vice-president, lieutenant governors are separately elected and are sometimes members of the governor's opposition party. Some efforts have been made to reduce the boredom of the lieutenant governor's office by assigning him membership on various boards and commissions. Lieutenant governors are frequently members of pardon and parole boards, boards of education, and so on.

The office of attorney general has more real powers and responsibilities than that of lieutenant governor. Attorneys general are elected in forty-two states, and appointed in the other states, usually by the governor. The attorney general is the chief legal counsel for the state. He represents the state in any suits to which it is a party. He acts as legal counsel for the governor and for other state officials. The legal business of state agencies is subject to his supervision. The source of the attorney general's power comes from his quasi-judicial duty of rendering formal written opinions in response to requests from the governor, state agencies, or other public officials regarding the legality and constitutionality of their acts. His opinions have the power of law in state affairs unless they are successfully challenged in court. The governor and other officials are generally obliged to conform to the attorney general's legal opinion until a court specifies otherwise. He renders authoritative interpretations of state constitutions, laws, city ordinances, and administrative rulings.

The attorney general also has substantial law enforcement powers. Most states allow the attorney general to initiate criminal proceedings on his own motion, and nearly all states assign him responsibility for handling criminal cases on appeal to higher state courts or to federal courts. In some states the attorney general has supervisory powers over law enforcement throughout the state.

Most states have elected treasurers, and treasurers in other states are appointed by either the governor or the legislature. Treasurers are custodians of state funds: collecting taxes, acting as paymaster for the state,

TABLE 6.7   Number of States with Elected Executive Officials

Governor	50
Lieutenant Governor	43
Attorney General	42
State Treasurer	39
Secretary of State	38
Superintendent of Education	20
State Auditor	17
Public Utilities Commission	12
Agriculture Commissioner	11
Controller	10
Insurance Commissioner	8
Labor Commissioner	5
Tax Commissioner	2
Highway Commissioner	1
Natural Resources Commissioner	1

SOURCE: *Book of the States, 1974-75.*

and administering the investment of state funds. The principal job of the treasurer is to make payments on departmental requisitions for payrolls and for checks to be issued to those who have furnished the state with goods or services. Generally, the department's requests for checks must be accompanied by a voucher showing the proper legislative authority for such payment. Generally, requests for payment must also be accompanied by a statement from the auditor's or the comptroller's office that legislative appropriations are available for such payment. Thus the treasurer's office works in close relation to another executive office of importance: that of auditor or comptroller. The principal duty of the office of state "auditor" is that of insuring the legislature that expenditures and investment of state funds have been made in accordance with the law. This function is known as a "postaudit" and occurs after state expenditures have been made. The primary duty of the office of the state "comptroller" is to insure that a prospective departmental expenditure is in accordance with the law and does not exceed the appropriations made by the legislature. This "preaudit" occurs before any expenditure is made by the treasurer. Public administration experts consider the comptroller's job of preaudit to be an executive function, and they urge that the comptroller be appointed by the governor. On the other hand, the job of postaudit is essentially a legislative check on the executive, and students of public administration generally feel that the auditor should be elected or appointed by the legislature. However, there is still some confusion in state organizations about the separate functions of auditors and comptrollers—some auditors do "preauditing" and some comptrollers do "postauditing."

Another interesting state office is that of secretary of state. Thirty-eight states elect secretaries of state. Like the lieutenant governor, the secretary of state has very little to keep him busy. He is the chief custodian of state records and, in the case of several states, "keeper of the great seal of the commonwealth." He keeps many state documents filed in his office, including corporation papers. He also supervises the preparation of ballots and certifies election results for the state. The keeping of documents and the supervision of elections does not involve much discretionary power, since these activities are closely regulated by law.

Courts, crime, and correctional policy

POLITICS AND THE JUDICIAL PROCESS

Courts are "political" institutions because they attempt to resolve conflicts among men. Like legislative and executive institutions, courts make public policy in the process of resolving conflict. Some of the nation's most important policy decisions have been made by courts rather than legislative or executive bodies. In recent years the federal courts have taken the lead in eliminating segregation in public life, insuring the separation of church and state, defining relationships between individuals and law enforcers, guaranteeing individual voters an equal voice in government, and establishing the right of women to obtain abortions. These are just a few of the important policy decisions made by courts—policy decisions that are just as significant to all Americans as those made by Congress or the president. Courts, then, are deeply involved in policy making, and they are an important part of the political system in America. Sooner or later in American politics, most important policy questions reach the courts.[1]

In resolving conflict and deciding about public policy, courts func-

[1] For a discussion of courts as political institutions, see Herbert Jacob, *Justice in America* (Boston: Little, Brown and Company, 1965); and Henry J. Abraham, *The Judicial Process* (New York: Oxford University Press, Inc., 1962).

Chapter seven

tion very much like other government agencies. However, the *style* of judicial decision making differs significantly from legislative or executive decision making. First of all, courts rarely initiate policy decisions. Rather, they wait until a case involving a policy question they must decide is brought to them. However, the vast majority of cases brought before courts do not involve important policy issues. Much court activity involves the enforcement of existing public policy. Courts punish criminals, enforce contracts, and award damages to the victims of injuries. Most of these decisions are based upon established law. Only occasionally are important policy questions brought to the court. This "passive" character of the judicial process restricts the policy initiative of judges; neither legislators nor executives suffer from such restrictions. In defining the judicial process, Carl Brent Swisher observed that a court "determines the facts involved in particular controversies brought before it, relates the facts to the relevant law, settles the controversies in terms of the law, and more or less incidentally makes new law through the process of decision." [2]

Courts also differ from other government agencies in that *access* to them is governed by a special set of requirements. An interested individual or group must have an attorney and sufficient money to bear the expense of the court suit. Courts must accept "jurisdiction," which means that a dispute must meet judicial criteria of a "case" or the courts cannot settle it. A case must involve two disputing parties, one of which must have incurred some real damages as a result of the action or inaction of the other. For example, an individual who objects to the state welfare program cannot take his objection to a court unless he can show that the program inflicted some direct personal or property damage on him.

The *procedures* under which judges and other participants in the judicial process operate are also quite different from procedures in legislative or executive branches of government. Facts and arguments must be presented to the courts in the manner specified. Generally these communications are quite formal, and legal skills are generally required to provide written briefs or oral arguments that meet the technical specifications of the courts. While an interest group may hire a public relations firm to pressure a legislature, they must hire a law firm to put their arguments into a legal context. Decorum in courtrooms is rigorously enforced in order to convey a sense of dignity; seldom do legislatures or executive offices function with the same degree of decorum.

Courts must direct their decisions to *specific cases*. While higher courts sometimes depart from particular cases and announce general policy positions, most courts refrain from general policy statements and limit their

[2] Carl B. Swisher, "The Supreme Court and the Moment of Truth," *American Political Science Review*, 54 (December, 1960): 879.

decisions to the particular circumstances of a case. Rarely do the courts announce a comprehensive policy in the way the legislature does when it enacts a law. Of course, the implication of a court's decision in a particular case is that future cases of the same nature will be decided the same way. This implication amounts to a policy statement; however, it is not as comprehensive as a legislative policy pronouncement, because future cases with only slightly different circumstances might be decided differently.

Perhaps the most important distinction between judicial decision making and decision making in other branches of government is that judges must not appear to permit political consideration to affect their decisions. Judges must not appear to base their decisions on partisan considerations, to bargain, or to compromise in decision making. Legislators and governors may base their decisions on party platforms or on their estimate of what will win in the next election, but such considerations are not supposed to influence judges. The *appearance of objectivity* in judicial decision making gives courts a measure of prestige that other governmental institutions lack. While it is true that judges have fewer direct ties with political organizations than legislators or governors, they are, of course, subject to social, economic, and political pressures just as other men are. Judges hold socioeconomic and political views just as everyone else, and they would be less than human if these views did not affect their decision; but it is important that a large portion of the American public perceive judges as unaffected by personal considerations. Court decisions become more acceptable to the public if they believe that the courts have dispensed unbiased justice.

These distinctive features of the judicial process—a passive appearance, special rules of access, specialized legal procedures, decorum, focus on particular cases, and appearance of objectivity in decision making—help to provide essential support for judicial decisions and thus enable the courts to play an influential role in the political system. These distinctive features help to "legitimize" the decisions reached by the courts; that is, they help to win popular acceptance of these decisions.

Legal traditions are influential in court decisions. English common law has vitally affected the law of all of our states except Louisiana, which was influenced by the Napoleonic Code. English common law developed in the thirteenth century through the decisions of judges who applied their notions of justice to specific cases. This body of judge-made law grew over the centuries and is still the foundation of our legal system today. Legislated statutes take precedence over common law, but the common law is applied by the courts where no statutory provisions are relevant. The degree to which statutory law has replaced common law varies among the states according to the comprehensiveness of state statutes and codes. Common law covers both criminal and civil law, although for the most part, the common law of crimes has been replaced by comprehensive criminal codes in the states.

THE STRUCTURE OF COURT SYSTEMS

State courts are generally organized into a hierarchy similar to that shown in Figure 7–1. The courts of a state constitute a single, integrated judicial system; even city courts, traffic courts, and justices of the peace are part of the state judicial system.

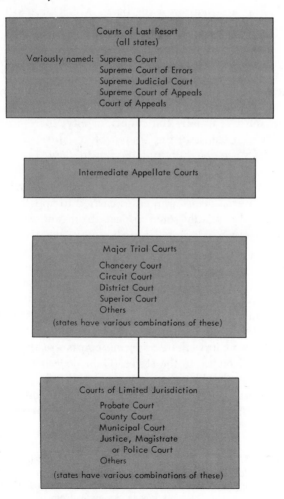

Courts of Last Resort
(all states)

Variously named: Supreme Court
Supreme Court of Errors
Supreme Judicial Court
Supreme Court of Appeals
Court of Appeals

Intermediate Appellate Courts

Major Trial Courts

Chancery Court
Circuit Court
District Court
Superior Court
Others
(states have various combinations of these)

Courts of Limited Jurisdiction

Probate Court
County Court
Municipal Court
Justice, Magistrate
or Police Court
Others
(states have various combinations of these)

FIGURE 7–1 The structure of state and local courts.

At the lowest level are minor courts presided over by justices of the peace, magistrates, or police judges, who frequently have little formal training. These courts are concerned principally with traffic cases, small claims, and misdemeanors, although they may hold preliminary hearings to determine whether a person accused of a felony shall be held in jail or placed under bond. These grassroot courts have often bred distrust for the law because of their incompetence, their reliance upon the fee system, or their direct links with partisan politics.[3] Many justices of the peace have no training in the law.[4] There are frequent complaints about collusion between justices of the peace and local police in the maintenance of "speed traps" for collecting heavy fines from out-of-town motorists. Many "J.P.'s" are paid on a fee basis, which means that the J.P. is paid for the number of convictions he obtains; this has led to the cynical observation that "J.P." signifies "judgment for the plaintiff."

Major trial courts of general jurisdiction—sometimes called district courts, circuit courts, superior courts, chancery courts, county courts, or common pleas courts—handle major civil and criminal cases arising out of statutes, common law, and state constitutions. The geographic jurisdiction of these courts is usually the county or city; there are about fifteen hundred major trial courts in the United States. Juries are used in these courts, and judges are generally qualified in the law. These courts handle criminal cases involving felonies and important civil suits. Almost all cases decided by state courts originate in these major trial courts; trial courts make the initial decision in cases carried to appellate and supreme courts and may also handle some appeals from minor courts. Although trial courts are courts of original jurisdiction rather than appeal courts, they are the only courts most individuals ever face.

Every state has a court of last resort, which is generally called the supreme court. These courts consist of three to nine judges, and most of their work is devoted to cases on appeal from major trial courts, although some states grant original jurisdiction to supreme courts in special types of cases. Since they consider questions of law rather than questions of fact, they sit without jury. State supreme courts are the most important and visible judicial bodies in the states. Their decisions are written, published, and distributed like the decisions of the U.S. Supreme Court. Judges can express their views in majority opinions, dissenting opinions, or concurring opinions. These courts get the most controversial cases

[3] See Arthur T. Vanderbilt, *The Challenge of Law Reform* (Princeton: Princeton University Press, 1955).

[4] On the other hand, Henry J. Abraham quotes a Philadelphia chief magistrate as saying: "A law degree doesn't make a magistrate more qualified. Living with people is more essential than going to a law library to find out what it's all about ... If you take Purdon's law books away from them (lawyers), they're out of business." Abraham, *The Judicial Process*, p. 130.

and those with the most at stake, since these cases are most likely to be appealed all the way to the state's highest court. To relieve supreme courts of heavy case burdens, many of the more populous states maintain intermediate courts of appeal between trial courts and courts of last resort.

There is no appeal from the state supreme courts, except to the U.S. Supreme Court on federal constitutional grounds. This means that state supreme courts have the final word in the interpretation of state constitutions and laws. These courts seldom hesitate to exercise judicial review over state legislative acts.

Special courts can always be found in addition to those already mentioned, notably in large cities. These specialized courts handle domestic relations, juvenile delinquency, the probation of wills, small claims, and so on. It is interesting to note that many of the more populous urban states have created very complex court structures with many specialized types of courts.

THE MAKING OF A JUDGE

Political debate over methods of selecting judges in the states has been carried on for many years. In writing the federal Constitution, the Founding Fathers reflected conservative views in establishing an independent federal judiciary, whose members were appointed by the president for life terms and were not subject to direct popular control. Jacksonian views of popular election were strong in the states, however, and today a majority of state judges are directly elected by the people on partisan or nonpartisan ballots. Table 7–1 shows the several ways in which judges are selected. Most states elect their judges, some in partisan elections and some in nonpartisan elections in which candidates for the bench do not carry party labels. In four states, judges are chosen by their legislatures, and in eleven states, they are appointed by the governor. Other states have adopted the "Missouri plan," in which governors appoint judges on the recommendations of a select committee, and after the judge has been in office for a year or more, the voters are given the opportunity to retain or oust the appointed judge.

The argument for selecting judges by appointment rests upon the value of judicial independence and isolation from direct political involvement. Critics of the elective method feel that it forces judges into political relationships and compromises their independence on the bench. This is particularly true if judicial elections are held on a partisan rather than a nonpartisan ballot, where judges must secure nomination with the support of party leaders. Moreover, it is argued that voters are not able to evaluate

TABLE 7.1 · Methods of Judicial Selection in the States*

Partisan Election	Election by Legislature	Nonpartisan Election	Appointment	Missouri Plan
Alabama	Rhode Island	Arizona	California	Alaska
Arkansas	South Carolina	Florida	Connecticut	California
Georgia	Vermont	Idaho	Delaware	Colorado
Illinois	Virginia	Kentucky	Hawaii	Iowa
Indiana		Maryland	Indiana	Kansas
Louisiana		Michigan	Kansas	Missouri
Mississippi		Minnesota	Maine	Nebraska
New Mexico		Montana	Massachusetts	Oklahoma
New York		Nevada	New Hampshire	Tennessee
North Carolina		North Dakota	New Jersey	Utah
Pennsylvania		Ohio	Wyoming	
Tennessee		Oklahoma		
Texas		Oregon		
West Virginia		South Dakota		
		Washington		
		Wisconsin		

*Some states fall into more than one category because judges at different levels of their court system are selected by different systems.

SOURCE: *Book of the States 1974-75.*

"legal" qualifications—knowledge of the law, judicial temperament, skill in the courtroom, and so on. Hence, judges should be appointed, rather than elected by voters. Attorneys, bar associations, and judges themselves prefer an appointive method in which they are given the opportunity to screen candidates and evaluate legal qualifications prior to appointment.

Actually it is not possible to "take judges out of politics." Selection by appointment or by the Missouri plan removes the selection of judges from *party* politics, but simply places the selection in different political hands. Instead of party leaders, the governor or the bar association become the principal actors in judicial selection. Party leaders are assumed to be familiar with the wishes of attorneys. It is not clear which influence leads to "better" judges, or whether "better" judges are those more sensitive to community values or more trained in legal procedures. Interestingly, states with competitive two-party systems are not necessarily the same states that select their judges through partisan elections. Some of the competitive states appoint as well as elect their judges.

Although most states elect their judges, in practice many judges come to the bench in elective states through the appointment procedure. The apparent paradox comes about because even in elective states, governors generally have the power to make interim judicial appointments when a judgeship is vacant because of the retirement or death of a judge between elections. An interim-appointed judge must seek election at the next regular election, but by that time he has acquired the prestige and status of a judge, and he is unlikely to be defeated by an outsider. Many members of the judiciary in elective states deliberately resign before the end of their term, if they are not seeking reelection, in order to give the governor the opportunity to fill the post by appointment. It is interesting to note that over half of the supreme court judges in states that elect their judiciary come to the bench initially by means of appointment. In practice, then, the elective system of judicial selection is greatly compromised by the appointment of judges to fill unexpired terms.

Another feature of the elective system of judicial selection, which often escapes attention, is that few incumbent judges are ever defeated in running for reelection. The majority of judges seeking relection are unopposed by anyone on the ballot, and fewer than 10 percent of the judges seeking relection are ever defeated.[5] This suggests that even in states with elective systems of judicial selection, judges are still separated from the normal political recruitment process. Judges enjoy more stability and independence from popular control than do legislators or governors.

The Missouri plan is an interesting attempt to combine the elective and appointive systems of selection. The Missouri plan calls for a select committee of judges, attorneys, and laymen to make nominations for judicial vacancies. The governor appoints one of the committee's nominees to office. After the judge has served at least one year, his name is placed on a nonpartisan ballot without any other name in opposition. "Shall judge (the name of the judge is inserted) of the (the name of the court is inserted) be retained in office. Yes ——— No ———." If the voters vote yes, the judge is then entitled to a full term of office. If the voters vote no, the governor must select another name from those submitted by his nominating committee and repeat the whole process. In practice, a judge is hardly ever defeated under the Missouri plan, in part for the same reasons that make it difficult to defeat an incumbent judge (see preceding discussion). Moreover, since "you can't beat somebody with nobody," running under the referendum feature of the Missouri plan is the equivalent of being unopposed. One study reports that only one judge in 179 Missouri plan elections has been defeated—and that one under very extraordinary circumstances.[6] The effect is to place judicial selection

---

[5] Jack Ladinsky and Alan Silver, "Popular Democracy and Judicial Independence," *Wisconsin Law Review* (1966): 132–33.

[6] Richard A. Watson and Rondal G. Downing, *The Politics of the Bench and Bar: Judicial Selection under the Missouri Nonpartisan Court Plan* (New York: John Wiley & Sons, Inc., 1969).

in the hands of the judges or attorneys who compose the nominating committee and the governor, with only a semblance of voter participation. Reformers argue that the plan removes judges from politics and spares the electorate the problem of voting on judicial candidates when they know little about their professional qualifications. Actually, the Missouri plan has *not* resulted in the selection of better-qualified judges,[7] although the plan remains very popular among reformers.

Perhaps the most ironic aspect of the debate over judicial selection methods is that there seems to be very little difference in the kinds of men who are elevated to judgeships by different methods. One study comparing appointed, elected, and Missouri-plan judges concluded that, among judges selected under different systems, there were few differences in their educational qualifications, experience, or social background (except that judges selected by state legislatures were more likely to have been state legislators).[8] More importantly, a careful study comparing decisions of state supreme courts selected by different methods shows no significant relationship between method of selection and judicial decision making.[9] Courts selected by partisan or nonpartisan elections, appointed by governors or legislators, or selected under the Missouri plan, show no clear and consistent trends in deciding for the state when it is a party to the case, or for criminal defendants, or for corporations, or for superior or inferior economic interests.

Republicans have fared better in capturing judgeships than in winning legislative seats or governors' chairs. Stuart Nagel reports that Republicans outnumber Democrats almost two to one in judicial posts.[10] Of course, the one-party Democratic states have Democratic judges just as one-party Republican states have Republican judges; but Republicans do surprisingly well in winning judgeships in the competitive states, proportionately much better than Republican candidates for the legislature or governorship in these states. Most of the judges selected in nonpartisan elections refuse to identify themselves with a political party, as do nearly all the judges selected under the Missouri plan. Judges selected in partisan elections, of course, usually do not hesitate to identify themselves as Republicans or Democrats.

[7] Ibid., Chapter 6. See also Larry L. Berg et al., "The Consequences of Judicial Reform," *Western Political Quarterly*, 28 (June, 1975): 263–80.

[8] Bradley Cannon, "The Impact of Formal Selection Processes on Characteristics of Judges—Reconsidered," *Law and Society Review*, 13 (May, 1972): 570–93.

[9] Burton M. Atkins and Henry R. Glick, "Formal Judicial Recruitment and State Supreme Court Decisions," *American Politics Quarterly*, 2 (October, 1974): 427–49.

[10] Stuart Nagel, "Unequal Party Representation in State Supreme Courts," *Journal of the American Judicature Society*, 44 (1961): 62–65.

JUDICIAL DECISION MAKING

Conflict in state supreme courts, as measured by the number of divided opinions, is less frequent than in the U.S. Supreme Court. Dissenting votes are reported on more than half of all U.S. Supreme Court decisions, but state judges dissent in very few cases. The Council of State Governments reports that the rate of dissent in the state supreme courts is less than 10 percent in more than half of the states.[11] In only a few states is the rate of dissent regularly more than 20 percent—California, New York, Ohio, Michigan, and Pennsylvania. Public disagreement is somewhat more frequent in competitive party states where judges of both parties are represented on the court.

The infrequency of dissenting opinions may obscure a great deal of conflict in state courts. Supreme Court justices write dissenting opinions in order to keep alive a point of view that may serve as a basis for a majority decision by a later court. Well-written dissenting opinions on the U.S. Supreme Court attract the attention of scholars, judges, attorneys, and law students throughout the nation. They can have an important impact on legal thinking even though they represent a minority view on the Court. But seldom do state supreme courts attract enough attention to merit the writing of dissenting opinions. At the state level many judges feel that dissenting opinions are useless. Moreover, many judges feel that a lack of unanimity damages judicial prestige and may tend to destroy the myth of certainty within the law.

Criminal appeals account for nearly one-third of the work load of state supreme courts.[12] But less than two percent involve civil liberty issues; apparently these issues are frequently shifted to federal courts. The largest proportion of state supreme court decision making involves economic interests. A large number of cases involving economic interests result from the important role of the states in the allocation of economic resources. All states regulate public utilities, including water, electrical companies, gas companies, and public transportation companies. The insurance industry is state-regulated. Labor relations and workmen's compensation cases are frequently found in state courts. Litigation over natural resources, real estate, small-business regulations, gas, oil, lumber and mining, alcoholic beverage control, racing, and gambling all reflect the importance of state regulation in these fields. There is a correlation between the kinds of economic litigation decided by state

[11] *Workload of State Courts of Last Resort* (Chicago: Council of State Governments, 1962).

[12] Burton M. Atkins and Henry Glick, "Determinants of Issues in State Courts of Last Resort," *American Journal of Political Science* 20 (February, 1976).

supreme courts and the socioeconomic environment of the state.[13] Supreme courts in poorer, rural states spend more time on private economic litigation (wills, trusts, estates, contracts, titles, etc.), while courts in urban industrial states wrestle with corporate law and governmental regulation of large economic interests. Judges are also called upon to make decisions in political controversies—disputes over elections, appointments to government positions, and jurisdictional squabbles between governments. These cases may constitute 5 to 10 percent of the work load of the courts.

What is the impact of the party affiliation of the judges in court decision making? Party affiliation probably has little impact in decisions in lower trial courts, where much of the litigation has little to do with policy making. But at least two studies have shown party affiliation to be an important influence on state supreme court decision making.[14] Stuart Nagel found that Democratic judges differed from Republican judges by deciding more frequently:

1. For the defense in criminal cases;
2. For the administrative agency in business regulation cases;
3. For the claimant in unemployment compensation;
4. For finding a constitutional violation in criminal cases;
5. For the government in tax cases;
6. For the tenant in landlord-tenant cases;
7. For the consumer in sale-of-goods cases;
8. For the injured in motor vehicle cases;
9. For the employee in employee injury cases.

These decisions suggest that Democratic judges were more in sympathy with the consumer, the workingman, and the defendant in criminal cases, and less in sympathy with business and utilities seeking to avoid public regulation. These are the kinds of attitudes that we might expect Democrats to express, although there is no evidence that the party itself influences these judges. Rather it is likely that the judges' social, economic, and political views influence both their decisions on the court and their decision to affiliate with the Democratic or Republican party. Sidney Ulmer traced the influence of party affiliation on judges' decisions in the Michigan Supreme Court, particularly in workmen's compensation and contributory negligence cases involving attitudes toward labor. He found that Democratic judges are more likely to hold with the working-

13 Ibid.

14 Stuart Nagel, "Political Party Affiliation and Judges' Decisions," *American Political Science Association,* 55 (1961): 843–51; and Sidney Ulmer, "The Political Party Variable on the Michigan Supreme Court," *Journal of Public Law,* 11 (1962): 352–62.

man in these cases, while Republican judges are more likely to decide in favor of the company.

What is the effect of social and ethnic group membership on judges' decisions? Judges, like other decision makers, generally belong to higher social and economic groups; white, Anglo-Saxon Protestants are disproportionately represented among state judges. Stuart Nagel found that judges who were members of ethnic minority groups in America were more likely to decide (1) for the defense in criminal cases, (2) for finding a violation in criminal constitutional cases, and (3) for the wife in divorce cases than were judges with white, Anglo-Saxon background.[15] He also found a difference in the decisions of Catholic and non-Catholic judges. Catholic judges tended to decide (1) for the defense in criminal cases, (2) for the administrative agency in business regulation cases, (3) for the wife in divorce settlement cases, (4) for the debtor in debtor-creditor cases, and (5) for the employee in employee injury cases. Nagel's studies suggest that party influence in judicial selection, with its tendency to grant representation to religious and ethnic groups in proportion to their electoral influence, may help to bring about decisions that reflect popular values.

On the whole, courts tend to be very conservative political bodies. Judicial activism on behalf of social reform in the U.S. Supreme Court is a relatively recent phenomenon. Historically, the Supreme Court was considered a bastion of conservatism, and state courts continue to be viewed as very conservative institutions. Doubtlessly, the heavy reliance that courts place on precedents in decision making is partly responsible for the conservatism of court decisions. State courts feel more bound by earlier precedents than the U.S. Supreme Court and consequently are committed to a more conservative posture. Yet reliance upon precedents cannot be the whole explanation of judicial conservatism, because state judges appear to evidence conservative attitudes even when they are off the bench. Stuart Nagel reports that not only do the judges evidence a great deal of conservatism in their off-the-bench views, but also conservatism seems to make a difference in case decisions.[16] When Nagel compared judges having conservative off-the-bench attitudes with judges having liberal attitudes, the two groups differed significantly. Judges with higher liberal scores decided more frequently (1) for the defense in criminal cases, (2) for the administrative agency in business regulation cases, (3) for the injured party in motor vehicle accident cases, and (4) for the employee in employee injury cases. In other words, con-

[15] Stuart Nagel, "Ethnic Affiliation and Judicial Propensities," *Journal of Politics*, 24 (1962): 92–110.

[16] Stuart Nagel, "Off-the-Bench Judicial Attitudes," in *Judicial Decision-Making*, edited by Glendon Schubert (Glencoe, Ill.: The Free Press, 1963).

servative judges were more likely to find for the state in criminal cases, against the state in business regulation cases, and in favor of insurance companies and employers in cases brought against them.

Additional evidence of state-court conservatism is found in state-court reaction to the U.S. Supreme Court's liberal decisions in *Escobedo* v. *Illinois* and *Miranda* v. *Arizona*.[17] In *Escobedo*, in 1964, the Supreme Court ruled that individuals were entitled to confer with their attorney as soon as a police investigation "has begun to focus on a particular suspect."[18] But guidelines were vague about when "the process shifts from investigatory to accusatory," and standards for determining the voluntariness of waiver of right to counsel were also unclear. Only four state supreme courts (California, Oregon, Rhode Island, and West Virginia) applied Escobedo in a liberal fashion; thirty-seven courts restricted its interpretation to the narrow facts surrounding the *Escobedo* case; nine courts did not confront the question. Indeed, the failure of state courts to extend fully the right of counsel after *Escobedo* led to the U.S. Supreme Court's decision in *Miranda* two years later, which laid down a very specific set of rules governing police questioning of suspects (an accused person must be informed immediately of his right to remain silent, that any statement he might make would be used against him, that he had a right to the presence of counsel, and that the state would provide free counsel if he could not afford it.)[19] But even after *Miranda* (which many state courts openly criticized), the question arose over whether the decision should be applied retroactively to persons already convicted. The U.S. Supreme Court was silent on the issue. Only the Pennsylvania, North Dakota, and West Virginia courts applied the decisions retroactively; forty-seven state courts refused to do so. In short, there is ample evidence that unless the U.S. Supreme Court clearly states its views, state supreme courts will interpret its decisions conservatively.

Judicial decision making is also influenced by judges' perceptions of their own role. The great debate of American jurisprudence centers about whether judges should make law in their decisions or whether they should limit themselves to interpreting the law. Great legalists have argued the merits of activism versus self-restraint in judicial decision

---

[17] This evidence is well-developed in Neil T. Romans, "The Role of State Supreme Courts in Judicial Policy-Making: Escobedo, Miranda and the Use of Judicial Impact Analysis," *Western Political Quarterly*, 27 (March, 1974): 38–59.

[18] *Escobedo* v. *Illinois*, 378 U.S. 478 (1964).

[19] *Miranda* v. *Arizona*, 384 U.S. 436 (1966).

making for more than a century.[20] Of course, popular debate about judicial activism is generally focused on the U.S. Supreme Court, but state court judges must also come to grips with this question. Henry Glick undertook to interview state supreme court judges in four states to ascertain their views of their roles in decision making.[21] About half of the judges interviewed opted for the more restrained role of "law interpreter":

> "We interpret the law. That is our function. We're not authorized to write the law. We can only act in one way: that is to be solely interpreters of the law. The moment he steps out of the role of interpreter, he violates the Constitution which separates the legislative from the judiciary."

Less than one-quarter saw themselves as "lawmaker":

> "Inevitably a judge makes law as does a legislative body. No matter how you decide a case you're making law. Whether you say yes or no in a case, you're making law. . . . Judges always make law and always will."

And some judges were characterized as "pragmatists":

> "When you're a judge, you're part legislator, executive, and judge. You're a creature of all three branches of government when you make a decision. All sorts of things come into consideration."

In summary, judicial decision making is influenced by interest group activity, political party affiliation, social and ethnic ties, religious affiliations, and the liberal and conservative views of judges.[22] This does not mean that "judicial impartiality" is nonexistent or that judges are as free as legislators or governors to write their social and political views into the law. Judges participate in the game of politics as players as well as umpires, but they are limited by the rules of the game, the decisions of legislatures and governors, and public expectations about the way judges ought to behave.

[20] Jerome Frank, *Law and the Modern Mind* (New York: Coward-McCann, Inc., 1930); Benjamin N. Cardozo, *The Nature of the Judicial Process* (New Haven: Yale University Press, 1921); and Roscoe Pound, *Justice According to Law* (New Haven: Yale University Press, 1951).

[21] Henry Glick, *Supreme Courts in State Politics* (New York: Basic Books, Inc., Publishers, 1971). The quotations are from state supreme court judges, 39–42.

[22] For a further exploration of judicial roles, including the "law applier," "law extender," "mediator," and "policy maker," see Victor Eugene Flango et al., "The Concept of Judicial Role: A Methodological Note," *American Journal of Political Sciences*, 19 (May, 1975): 277–90.

CRIME IN THE STATES

Crime rates are the subject of a great deal of popular discussion. Very often they are employed to express the degree of social disorganization or even the effectiveness of law enforcement agencies. Crime rates are based upon the Federal Bureau of Investigation's *Uniform Crime Reports*, but the FBI reports are based on figures supplied by state and local police agencies. (See Table 7–2.) The FBI has succeeded in establishing a uniform classification of the number of serious crimes per 100,000 people that are known to the police—murder and nonnegligent manslaughter, forcible rape, robbery, aggravated assault, burglary, larceny, and theft, including auto theft. But record keeping is still a problem, and one should be cautious in interpreting official crime rates. They are really a function of several factors: the diligence of police in detecting crime, the adequacy of the reporting system tabulating crime, and the amount of crime itself. Yet the evidence seems inescapable that crime in the United States is increasing at a rapid pace.

Crime rates are related to urbanization and economic development in the states.[23] The nation's highest crime rates are in California, New York, and Nevada, and its lowest are in North Dakota and Mississippi. Generally, the urban industrial high-income states have higher crime rates than the rural agricultural low-income states. Urbanization and economic development involve certain social complications: a certain

TABLE 7.2   **Crime Rates in the United States Offenses Known to the Police (Rates per 100,000 Population)**

	1960	1965	1970	1975
Murder and non-negligent manslaughter	5	5	8	10
Forcible rape	9	12	18	26
Robbery	60	172	172	209
Aggravated assault	85	110	162	215
Burglary	506	659	1,068	1,429
Larceny	1,028	1,321	2,066	2,473
Auto theft	182	256	454	461
Total crimes against person	160	199	360	459
Total crimes against property	1,716	2,235	3,599	4,363

SOURCE: FBI, *Uniform Crime Reports,* 1960-1975.

[23] See Thomas R. Dye, *Politics, Economics, and the Public* (Chicago: Rand McNally & Co., 1966), pp. 219–22.

degree of unemployment seems inevitable; the transition from rural to urban life creates many social problems; social isolation and hostility are frequent by-products; traditional value systems and social control are undermined and not immediately replaced by other values and institutions. All these traditions are associated with crime. Figure 7–2 shows the relationship between urbanization and crime rates in the states. Nevada is the most deviant state; it has a much higher crime rate than its degree of urbanization would suggest. Crime rates in Nevada suggest that crime is also related to gambling. Nevada has the most permissive gambling laws of any state in the nation.

Police statistics vastly understate the real amount of crime. Citizens do not report many crimes to police. The National Opinion Research Center of the University of Chicago asked a national sample of individuals whether they or any member of their household had been a victim of crime during the past year. This survey revealed that the actual amount of crime is several times greater than that reported by the FBI. There are more than twice as many crimes committed as reported to the police. The number of forcible rapes was more than three and one-half times the number reported, burglaries three times, aggravated assaults and larcenies more than double, and robbery 50 percent greater than the reported rate. Only auto theft statistics were reasonably accurate, indicating that most people call the police when their cars are stolen.[24]

Interviewees gave a variety of reasons for their failure to report crime to the police. The most common reason was the feeling that police could not be effective in dealing with the crime. This is a serious comment about police protection in America today. Other reasons included the feeling that the crime was "a private matter," that the offender was a member of the family, or that the victim did not want to harm the offender. Fear of reprisal was mentioned much less frequently, usually in cases of assaults and family crimes.

POLICE PROTECTION IN THE STATES

State, county, and municipal governments are all directly involved in law enforcement. Every state has a central law enforcement agency, sometimes called the state police, state troopers, state highway patrol or even Texas Rangers. At one time, state governors had only the National Guard at their disposal to back up local law enforcement efforts, but the coming of the automobile and intercity highway traffic led to the establishment in every state of a centralized police system. In addition to patrolling

---

[24] See Wesley G. Skogan, "The Validity of Official Crime Statistics: An Empirical Investigation," *Social Science Quarterly*, 55 (June, 1974), 25–38.

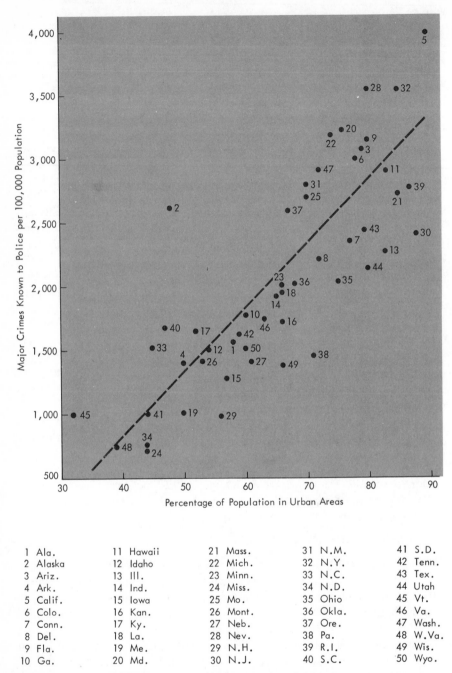

FIGURE 7–2   The fifty states arranged according to urbanization and crime rates.

1 Ala.	11 Hawaii	21 Mass.	31 N.M.	41 S.D.
2 Alaska	12 Idaho	22 Mich.	32 N.Y.	42 Tenn.
3 Ariz.	13 Ill.	23 Minn.	33 N.C.	43 Tex.
4 Ark.	14 Ind.	24 Miss.	34 N.D.	44 Utah
5 Calif.	15 Iowa	25 Mo.	35 Ohio	45 Vt.
6 Colo.	16 Kan.	26 Mont.	36 Okla.	46 Va.
7 Conn.	17 Ky.	27 Neb.	37 Ore.	47 Wash.
8 Del.	18 La.	28 Nev.	38 Pa.	48 W.Va.
9 Fla.	19 Me.	29 N.H.	39 R.I.	49 Wis.
10 Ga.	20 Md.	30 N.J.	40 S.C.	50 Wyo.

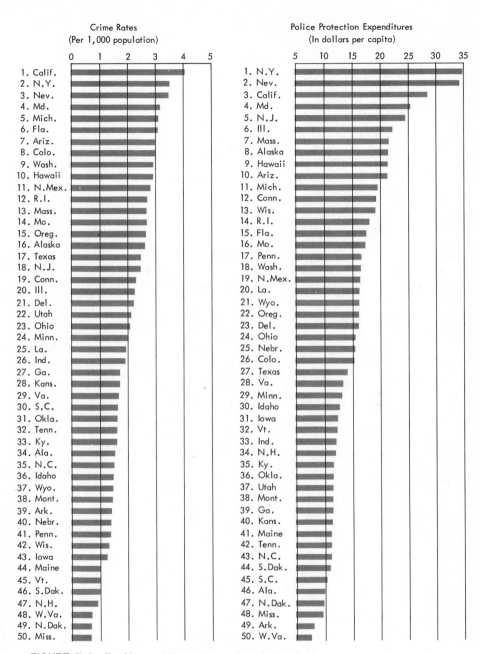

Crime Rates
(Per 1,000 population)

	0	1	2	3	4	5
1. Calif.						
2. N.Y.						
3. Nev.						
4. Md.						
5. Mich.						
6. Fla.						
7. Ariz.						
8. Colo.						
9. Wash.						
10. Hawaii						
11. N.Mex.						
12. R.I.						
13. Mass.						
14. Mo.						
15. Oreg.						
16. Alaska						
17. Texas						
18. N.J.						
19. Conn.						
20. Ill.						
21. Del.						
22. Utah						
23. Ohio						
24. Minn.						
25. La.						

Police Protection Expenditures
(In dollars per capita)

	5	10	15	20	25	30	35
1. N.Y.							
2. Nev.							
3. Calif.							
4. Md.							
5. N.J.							
6. Ill.							
7. Mass.							
8. Alaska							
9. Hawaii							
10. Ariz.							
11. Mich.							
12. Conn.							
13. Wis.							
14. R.I.							
15. Fla.							
16. Mo.							
17. Penn.							
18. Wash.							
19. N.Mex.							
20. La.							
21. Wyo.							
22. Oreg.							
23. Del.							
24. Ohio							
25. Nebr.							

FIGURE 7–3 Rankings of the states: crime and police.

the state's highways, these centralized agencies now provide expert aid and service for local police officers and strengthen law enforcement in sparsely populated regions. Three-quarters of the states have given their central police agencies full law enforcement authority in addition to highway duties: they may quell riots, cooperate with local authorities in the apprehension of criminals, or even intervene when local authorities are unable or unwilling to enforce the law. The size and influence of these agencies vary from state to state. On the whole, however, state police forces constitute a very small proportion of the total law enforcement effort in America. Law enforcement in the nation is principally a local responsibility.

Historically, the county sheriff has been the keystone of law enforcement in the United States. He and his deputies are still the principal enforcement and arresting officers in the rural counties and in the unincorporated fringe areas of many urban counties. In addition, the sheriff serves as an executive agent for county and state courts in both civil and criminal matters, and he maintains the county jail for the retention of persons whose trials or sentences are pending or who are serving short terms of punishment. The sheriff's office is a political one; in every state except Rhode Island he is an elected official. Antiquated fee systems exist in many states in which a sheriff collects a fee for every order, process, warrant, or arrest in which he is involved. Small fortunes can be made by "diligent" sheriffs in one term of office. Constables are elected in most states to perform many of the same functions of sheriffs for rural townships or other subdivisions of the county. Reliance upon the sheriff's office for law enforcement is a characteristic of rural states. Since municipal police forces usually assume the sheriff's law enforcement duties within the boundaries of municipalities, the sheriff's office has seriously atrophied in most urban states; often he is reduced to a process server for the courts.

Urban police departments are the most important instruments of law enforcement and public safety in the nation today. About two-thirds of the nation's population live in municipalities and depend upon municipal police for their protection. City policemen vastly outnumber all other state and county law enforcement officers combined. The urban police department does more than merely enforce the law; it engages in a wide range of activities for social control.

Urban industrial states employ more policemen than rural farm states.[25] We have already seen that urbanization brings about increases in crime rates, so it is not surprising that urbanization also requires an increase in police protection. Urbanization, crime rates, and police protection are all interrelated.

[25] Dye, *Politics, Economics, and the Public,* pp. 223–26.

THE POLITICS OF PROSECUTION

Prosecution is part of the political process. Legislatures and governors enact policy, but its enforcement depends upon the decisions of prosecutors as well as judges. Political pressures are most obvious in the enforcement of controversial policies—gambling laws, Sunday closing laws, liquor rules, laws against prostitution, and other laws that are contrary to the interests of significant segments of the population. But prosecution also involves decision making about the allocation of law enforcement resources to different types of offenses—traffic violations, juvenile delinquency, auto theft, assault, burglary, larceny, and robbery. Decisions must be made about what sections of the city should be most vigorously protected and what segments of the population will be most closely watched. The public prosecutor, sometimes called the district attorney (D.A.) or state's attorney, is at the center of diverse pressures concerning law enforcement.

The political nature of the prosecutor's job is suggested by the frequency with which this job leads to higher political office. Prosecuting attorney is often a stepping-stone to state and federal judgeships, congressional seats, and even the governorship. An ambitious D.A., concerned with his political future, may seek to build a reputation as a crusader against crime and vice, while at the same time maintaining the support and friendship of important interests in the community. The political power of the prosecutor stems from his discretion in deciding (1) whether or not to prosecute in criminal cases, and (2) whether prosecution will be on more-serious or less-serious charges. A prosecutor may decide simply to drop charges ("nol-pros") when he feels adequate proof is lacking or when he feels that police have committed a procedural error which infringed on the defendant's rights. Or a prosecutor may engage in "plea bargaining"—reducing the charges from more-serious to less-serious crimes in exchange for the defendant's promise to plead guilty. Or the prosecutor may reduce charges because he believes it will be easier in court to obtain a guilty verdict on the lesser charge.

Are there any checks on the power of prosecutors? In principle, the *grand jury* is supposed to determine whether evidence presented to it by the prosecutor is sufficient to warrant the placing of a person on trial in a felony case. Ideally, the grand jury serves as a check against the overzealous district attorney, and as a protection for the citizen against unwarranted harassment. However, in practice, grand juries spend very little time deliberating on the vast majority of the cases.[26]

[26] The following discussion relies on evidence presented by Robert A. Carp, "The Behavior of Grand Juries: Acquiescence or Justice," *Social Science Quarterly*, 55 (March, 1975): 853–70.

(A typical grand jury spends only five to ten minutes per case, primarily listening to the prosecutor's recommendation as to how the case should be decided.) Over 80 percent of the cases may be decided on an immediate vote, without discussion among jurors, and almost always with unanimous votes. ("Victimless" sex crimes—prostitution, for example—seems to be the only category of offense that causes disharmony among grand jurors.) Finally, and most importantly, grand juries follow the recommendations of prosecutors in over 98 percent of the cases presented to them. The prosecutor controls the information submitted to grand juries, instructs them in their duties, and is usually perceived by jurors as an expert and relied on for guidance. In short, there is no evidence that grand juries provide much of a check on the power of prosecutors.

CRIME AND THE COURTS

Chief Justice Warren E. Burger has argued persuasively that rising crime in America is partly due to inadequacies in our system of criminal justice. "The present system of criminal justice does not deter criminal conduct," he said in a special State of the Federal Judiciary message. "Whatever deterrent effect may have existed in the past has now virtually vanished." [27] He urged major reform in law enforcement, courts, prisons, probation, and parole.

A major stumbling block to effective law enforcement is the current plight of America's judicial machinery.

> Major congestion on court dockets which delays the hearing of cases months or even years. Moreover, actual trials now average twice as long as they did ten years ago.

> Failure of courts to adopt modern management and administrative practices to speed and improve justice.

> Increased litigation in the courts. Not only are more Americans aware of their rights, but more are using every avenue of appeal. Seldom do appeals concern the guilt or innocence of the defendant, but usually focus on procedural matters.

> Excessive delays in trials. "Defendants, whether guilty or innocent, are human; they love freedom and hate punishment. With a lawyer provided to secure release without the need for a conventional bail bond,

[27] Chief Justice Warren E. Burger, address on the State of the Federal Judiciary to the American Bar Association, August 10, 1970.

most defendants, except in capital cases, are released pending trial. We should not be surprised that a defendant on bail exerts a heavy pressure on his court-appointed lawyer to postpone the trial as long as possible so as to remain free. These postponements—and sometimes there are a dozen or more—consume the time of judges and court staffs as well as of lawyers. Cases are calendared and reset time after time while witnesses and jurors spend endless hours just waiting." [28]

Excessive delays in appeals. "We should not be surprised at delay when more and more defendants demand their undoubted constitutional right to trial by jury because we have provided them with lawyers and other needs at public expense; nor should we be surprised that most convicted persons seek a new trial when the appeal costs them nothing and when failure to take the appeal will cost them freedom. Being human a defendant plays out the line which society has cast him. Lawyers are competitive creatures and the adversary system encourages contention and often rewards delay; no lawyer wants to be called upon to defend the client's charge of incompetence for having failed to exploit all the procedural techniques which we have deliberately made available." [29]

Excessive variation in sentencing. Some judges let defendants off on probation for crimes that would draw five- or ten-year sentences by other judges. While flexibility in sentencing is essential in dealing justly with individuals, perceived inconsistencies damage the image of the courts in the public mind.

Excessive "plea bargaining" between the prosecution and the defendant's attorney in which the defendant agrees to plead guilty to a lesser offense if the prosecutor will drop more serious charges.

The current system of criminal justice is certainly no serious deterrent to crime. Most behavioral research suggests that it is not the severity of punishment that affects behavior, but the establishment of a sure linkage between the errant behavior and the punishment. In other words, crime is more likely to be deterred by making punishment sure, rather than severe. The best available estimates of the ratio between crime and punishment, however, suggest that the likelihood of an individual's being jailed for a serious crime is less than one in a hundred. (See Figure 7–4.) Most crimes are not even reported by the victim. Police are successful in clearing only about one in five reported crimes by arresting the offender. The judicial system convicts only about one in four of the persons arrested and charged; others are not prosecuted, are handled as juveniles, are found not guilty, or are permitted to plead guilty to a lesser charge and released. Only about half of the convicted felons are given prison sentences.

[28] Ibid.
[29] Ibid.

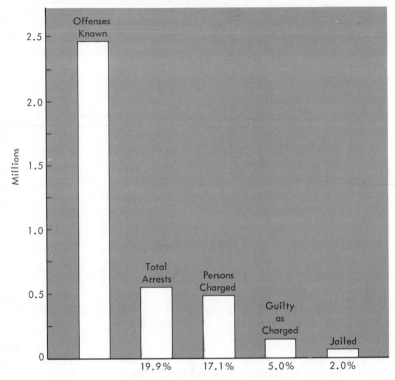

* Actual crime is estimated to be two and one-half times the known offenses.
If the base were actual crime, these percentages would be less than half of
those appearing in the figure. Thus, the number of persons jailed as a
percentage of the actual crime is less than one percent.

FIGURE 7–4   Law enforcement in relation to crime.
Source: Statistical Abstract of the United States, 1970, p. 146.

RIGHTS OF DEFENDANTS

The Warren Court—the Supreme Court of the 1950s and 1960s, under the guidance of Chief Justice Earl Warren—greatly strengthened
the rights of accused persons in criminal cases. Several key decisions
were made by a split vote of the Court and drew heavy criticism from
law enforcement officers and others as hamstringing police in their
struggle with lawlessness. These decisions included:

Mapp v. *Ohio* (1961). Barring the use of illegally seized evidence in criminal cases in the states by applying the Fourth Amendment guarantee against unreasonable searches and seizures. Even if the evidence seized proves the guilt of the accused, the accused goes free because the police committed a procedural error.

Gideon v. *Wainwright* (1963). Ruling that equal protection under the Fourteenth Amendment requires that free legal counsel be appointed for all indigent defendants in all criminal cases.

Escobedo v. *Illinois* (1964). Ruling that a suspect is entitled to confer with counsel as soon as a police investigation focuses on him once "the process shifts from investigatory to accusatory."

Miranda v. *Arizona* (1966). Requiring that police—before questioning a suspect—must inform him of all his constitutional rights including the right to counsel, appointed free if necessary, and the right to remain silent. Although the suspect may knowingly waive these rights, the police cannot question anyone who at any point asks for a lawyer or indicates "in any manner" that he does not wish to be questioned. If the police commit any error in these procedures, the accused goes free, regardless of the evidence of guilt.

It is difficult to ascertain to what extent these decisions have really hampered efforts to halt the rise in crime in America. The Supreme Court under Chief Justice Burger has not extended the rights of accused persons much beyond the Warren Court decisions, nor has it reversed any of these important decisions. Whatever progress is made in law enforcement will therefore have to be made within the current definition of the rights of defendants. It is important to note that Chief Justice Burger's recommendations for a judicial reform center on the speedy administration of justice and not on changes in the rights of defendants.

POLICE AND LAW ENFORCEMENT

Police perform at least three important functions in urban society—law enforcement, keeping the peace, and furnishing services. Actually, law enforcement may take up only a small portion of a policeman's daily activity, perhaps only 10 percent.[30] The service function is far more common—attending accidents, directing traffic, escorting crowds, assisting stranded motorists, handling drunks, and so on. (See Table 7–3). The function of peace keeping is also very common—breaking up fights,

[30] James Q. Wilson, *Varieties of Police Behavior* (Cambridge: Harvard University Press, 1968), p. 18; Arthur Niederhoffer, *Behind the Shield* (New York: Doubleday & Company, Inc., 1967), p. 71.

TABLE 7.3   Citizen Complaints Radioed to Police Vehicles, Syracuse Police Department, June 3-9, 1966[a]

Calls[b]	Number in Sample	Percentage
Information Gathering	69	22.1
Book and check	2	
Get a report	67	
Service	117	37.5
Accidents, illnesses, ambulance calls	42	
Animals	8	
Assist a person	1	
Drunk person	8	
Escort vehicle	3	
Fire, power line or tree down	26	
Lost or found person or property	23	
Property damage	6	
Maintenance of Order	94	30.1
Gang disturbance	50	
Family trouble	23	
Assault, fight	9	
Investigation	8	
Neighbor trouble	4	
Law Enforcement	32	10.3
Burglary in progress	9	
Check a car	5	
Open door or window	8	
Prowler	6	
Make an arrest	4	
Totals	312	100.0

[a]Based upon a one-fifth sample of the week's calls.
[b]Not included are internal calls: those originating with other police officers or purely administrative calls.
SOURCE: James Q. Wilson, *Varieties of Police Behavior* (Cambridge: Harvard University Press, 1968), p. 18.

quieting noisy parties, handling domestic or neighborhood quarrels, and the like. It is in this function that police exercise the greatest discretion in the application of the law. In most of these incidents blame is difficult to determine, participants are reluctant to file charges, and police must use personal discretion in handling each case.

Police are generally recruited from working-class families; only a handful come from middle-class backgrounds, and only a few have more than a high school education. Yet the tasks that they are assigned in society would confound highly trained social scientists. Generally the segment of the population from which police are recruited is more intolerant of unpopular views and authoritarian in its ideas of family and social life. Formal police training emphasizes self-control and caution in dealing with the public, but on-the-job experiences probably reinforce predispositions toward intolerance and distrust of others. The element of danger in the policeman's job makes him naturally suspicious of others. Policemen see much of the "worst kind" of people, and they see even the "best kind" at their worst.

Policemen are engaged in rule enforcement as members of a semi-military organization. They are concerned with authority themselves, and they expect others to respect authority. It is often difficult for even the most well-meaning police officer to develop respect or sympathy for ghetto residents. One policeman described this problem as follows:

> The police have to associate with lower class people, slobs, drunks, criminals, riff-raff of the worst sort. Most of these . . . are Negroes. The police officers see these people through middle class or lower middle class eyeballs. But even if he saw them through highly sophisticated eye-balls he can't go in the street and take this night after night. When some Negro criminal says to you a few times, "you white mother-fucker, take that badge off and I'll shove it up your ass," well it's bound to affect you after a while. Pretty soon you decide they're all just niggers and they'll never be anything but niggers. It would take not just an average man to resist this feeling, it would take an extraordinary man to resist it, and there are very few ways by which the police department can attract extraordinary men to join them.[31]

The policeman's attitude toward ghetto residents is often affected by the high crime rates in ghetto areas. The policeman is suspicious of ghetto residents because crime rates tell him that his suspicions are often justified. Sociologists interviewing policemen in the cities that experienced riots in 1967 reported that policemen accurately perceive the hostility directed at them in the ghettos.[32] Policemen believed that only a small minority of blacks, as compared with a substantial majority of whites, regarded them as friends. Moreover, the police viewed themselves much as blacks viewed them—as unwelcome aliens in the ghetto: they reported feeling isolated in a hostile atmosphere but could not understand why blacks resented them. Finally, antiblack attitudes among the policemen interviewed were fairly strong; for example, 49 percent did not approve of socializing between whites and blacks, and 56 percent were disturbed by the movement of blacks into white neighborhoods.

[31] Wilson, *Varieties of Police Behavior*, p. 43.
[32] *Supplemental Studies for the National Advisory Commission on Civil Disorders* (Washington, D.C.: Government Printing Office, 1968), p. 44.

One commentator described the dilemma of police-ghetto relations as follows:

> First, the police department recruits from a population (the working class) whose numbers are more likely than the average population to hold anti-Negro attitudes; second, the recruits are given a basic classroom training program that is unlikely to change the anti-Negro sentiments; third, the recruit goes out on the street as a patrolman and is more likely than not to have his anti-Negro attitudes reinforced and hardened by the older officer; fourth, in the best departments, the most able officers are soon transferred to specialized administrative duties in training, recruitment, juvenile work, etc., or are promoted after three to five years to supervisory positions; fifth, after five years the patrolman on street duty significantly increases in levels of cynicism, authoritarianism, and generalized hostility to the nonpolice world. Finally, it is highly likely that the worst of the patrolmen will wind up patrolling the ghetto because that tends to be the least wanted assignment.
>
> If this is an accurate description of the urban police system (and my personal observations over the past five years tell me this is so), then the reason is clear why every poll of black citizens shows the same high level of distrust and hostility against policemen.[33]

Policemen do not have the time or inclination to dwell on the social conditions associated with crime—poverty, racism, unemployment, undereducation, high-density living, and so forth. Instead, most policemen adopt a working attitude which Jerome Skolnik refers to as the "rotten-apple" view of man: crime is attributable to the intentions of bad individuals. Skolnik cites one policeman's simple summary: "Poverty doesn't cause crime; people do." [34] This attitude leads the wary policeman to quickly categorize persons on the street who are likely to create a danger to himself and to society—"supicious-looking persons"; emaciated persons who appear to be alcoholics or "junkies"; "known troublemakers"; persons who appear to avoid an officer or who are visibly "rattled" by an officer's presence; loiterers near rest rooms, playgrounds, shopping centers, etc. Many of these cues are automatically applied to blacks.

If police are overly suspicious of blacks, the attitudes of many ghetto blacks toward police are equally hostile. Black novelist James Baldwin writes of police in the ghetto:

> Their very presence is an insult, and it would be, even if they spent their entire day feeding gumdrops to children. They represent the force of the

[33] Burton Levy, "Cops in the Ghetto," in *Riots and Rebellion*, edited by Louis Masotti and Donald Bowen (New York: Sage Publications, 1968), p. 353.

[34] Jerome H. Skolnik, *The Politics of Protest* (New York: Ballantine Books, 1969), p. 259.

white world, and that world's real intentions are simply, to keep the black man corralled up here, in his place. The badge, the gun and the holster and the swinging club make vivid what will happen should his rebellion become overt. . . .

He has never himself done anything for which to be hated—which of us has? And yet he is facing, daily and nightly, people who would gladly see him dead, and he knows it.[35]

Does increased police protection significantly reduce crime? The common assumption is that increased police manpower and increased police expenditures can significantly reduce crime in cities. But, unfortunately, it is very difficult to produce firm evidence to support this assumption. E. Terrance Jones studied crime rates in relation to police manpower and expenditure in 155 cities from 1958 through 1970 and failed to find any evidence to support the more-police-activity-equals-less-crime theory.[36] So many other factors may affect crime rates in cities—size, density, youth, unemployment, race, poverty, etc.—that police activity appears insignificant. Or an increase in police activity may result in increased crime reporting, which tends to obscure any actual reduction in crime in official statistics. Whatever the explanation, the reduction of crime in America appears to be a very elusive goal.

THE GROWING FEDERAL ROLE
IN LAW ENFORCEMENT

Historically, state and local governments exercised principal responsibility for law enforcement in America. The Federal Bureau of Investigation and the Justice Department were charged with the responsibility of enforcing federal law. The federal government employs less than fifty thousand persons in all law enforcement activities, compared with over five hundred thousand state and local law enforcement personnel. Federal prisons contain twenty-five thousand inmates, compared with two hundred thousand in state prisons. Federal involvement in state and local law enforcement, however, is growing.

In the Crime Control and Safe Street Act of 1968, Congress created the Law Enforcement Assistance Administration (L.E.A.A.) within the Department of Justice to channel federal grants-in-aid to the states for use in upgrading state and local law enforcement programs. Most of these

[35] James Baldwin, *Nobody Knows My Name* (New York: Dell, 1962), pp. 61–62.
[36] E. Terrance Jones, "Evaluating Everyday Policies: Police Activity and Crime Incidence," *Urban Affairs Quarterly*, 8 (March, 1973): 267–279.

funds come to the states as "bloc grants" to be employed by the states as they see fit in improving state or local law enforcement. Each state creates a state planning agency responsible for preparing a comprehensive law enforcement and criminal justice plan. The money may be spent on court reform and correctional programs as well as on police protection. Two recurring criticisms of the L.E.A.A. program are that the states do not always channel money into the highest crime areas, and that too much money is spent on "hardware"—special equipment for gadget-minded police chiefs.

STATE CORRECTIONAL POLICIES

Correctional policies vary enormously among the states. States differ in the number of persons committed to prison, correctional expenditures per capita, the care and treatment provided offenders, and the policies governing the parole of prisoners and in many other aspects of penology. Perhaps the explanation for the wide range of state policies in correction lies in the deep division among the American people concerning correctional philosophy. At least four separate theories of crime and punishment compete for preeminence in guiding correctional policies.[37] First, there is the ancient Judeo-Christian idea of holding the individual responsible for his guilty acts and compelling him to pay a debt to society. Another philosophy argues that punishment should be sure, speedy, and commensurate with the crime, and sufficiently conspicuous to deter others from committing crime. Still another consideration in correctional policy is that of protecting the public from lawbreakers or habitual criminals by segregating these people behind prison walls. Finally, there is the theory that criminals are partly or entirely victims of social circumstances beyond their control and that society owes them comprehensive treatment in form of rehabilitation.

Over two million Americans each year are prisoners in a jail, police station, or juvenile home or penitentiary. The vast majority are released within one year. There are, however, about a quarter of a million inmates in state and federal prisons in the United States. These prisoners are serving time for serious offenses: 90 percent had a record of crime before they committed the act that led to their current imprisonment.

If correctional systems could be made to work—that is, actually to rehabilitate men as useful, law-abiding citizens—the benefits to the nation would be enormous. The Law Enforcement Assistance Administra-

[37] See Daniel Glaser, *The Effectiveness of a Prison and Parole System* (Indianapolis and New York: The Bobbs-Merrill Co., Inc., 1964).

tion estimates that 80 percent of all felonies are committed by repeaters—individuals who have had prior contact with the criminal justice system and were not corrected by it.[38] Penologists generally recommend more education and job training, more and better facilities, smaller prisons, halfway houses where offenders can adjust to civilian life before parole, more parole officers, and greater contact between prisoners and their families and friends. But as Daniel Glaser points out: "Unfortunately there is no convincing evidence that this investment reduces what criminologists call 'recidivism,' the offenders return to crime." [39] In short, there is no evidence that men *can* be "rehabilitated," no matter what is done! But prison policies now combine conflicting philosophies in a way that accomplishes *none* of society's goals. They do not effectively punish or deter individuals from crime. They do not succeed in rehabilitating the criminal. They do not even protect the public by keeping criminals off the streets; nineteen out of every twenty persons sent to prison will eventually return to society. Even the maintenance of order *within* prisons, and the protection of the lives of guards and inmates, have become serious national problems. The deaths of forty-three prisoners and guards in Attica State Prison in New York in a bloody riot in 1971 directed public attention to the serious dilemmas of state correctional policy.

Over two-thirds of all prisoner releases come about by means of parole. Modern penology, with its concern for reform and rehabilitation, appears to favor parole releases rather than unconditional releases. The function of parole and postrelease supervision is (1) to procure information on the parolees' postprison conduct, and (2) to facilitate and graduate the transition between the prison and complete freedom. These functions are presumably oriented toward protecting the public and rehabilitating the offender. But states differ substantially in their use of parole: in some states, 90 percent of all releases come about because of parole, while in other states, parole is granted to less than 30 percent of all prisoners. Generally, urban industrial states with higher income and educational levels release a higher proportion of prisoners on parole than rural farm states with lower income and educational characteristics.

What is the effect of correctional expenditures, sentencing policies, and parole systems on *recidivism*—the percentage of released prisoners who return to prison for new crimes? Unfortunately, the weight of evidence suggests *no* relationship between any specific means of handling

---

[38] See Congressional Quarterly, *Crime and the Law* (Washington: Congressional Quarterly Inc., 1971), p. 11.

[39] Glaser, *Effectiveness of a Prison and Parole System*, p. 4.

prisoners and successful rehabilitation. For example, a ten-year study in Georgia comparing inmates released under parole (carefully selected, counseled, and supervised) with inmates given unconditional releases (unselected, uncounseled, unsupervised) showed no difference in the two groups in recidivism.[40] The parole system appears to be worthless. Similarly disappointing results were obtained in a California study comparing parolees given close supervision to those given little supervision; both groups committed the same number of new felonies. Finally, a comparative analysis of expenditures and manpower for corrections, parole, and probation in all fifty states revealed "the almost total absence of linkage between correction variables and recidivism."[41] In summary, prisons do not rehabilitate. If rehabilitation is set as a goal, prisons are bound to be adjudged as failures.

CRIME, DEATH, AND DETERRENCE

Can correctional policies deter crime? This is a difficult question to answer. First of all, we must distinguish between *deterrence* and *incapacity*. *Incapacity* can be imposed by long terms of imprisonment, particularly for habitual offenders; the policy of "keeping criminals off the streets" does indeed protect the public for a period of time, although it is done at a considerable cost ($15,000 to $20,000 per year per prisoner). The object of *deterrence* is to make the certainty and severity of punishment so great as to inhibit potential criminals from committing crimes.

For many years sociologists scorned the notion of deterrence, arguing that many crimes were committed without any consideration of consequences—particularly "crimes of passion"—and that urbanization, density, poverty, age, race, and other demographic factors had more to do with crime than with characteristics of the law. However, recent systematic studies have challenged this view. Sociologist Jack P. Gibbs studied criminal homicide rates and related them to the certainty and severity of imprisonment in the states.[42] The likelihood of imprisonment for criminal homicides (the percentage of persons sent to prison divided by the number of homicides) ranged from 21 percent in South Carolina

---

[40] See Frank K. Gibson et al., "A Path Analytic Treatment of Corrections Output," *Social Science Quarterly*, 54 (September, 1973): 281–91.

[41] Ibid., p. 291.

[42] See Maynard L. Erikson and Jack P. Gibbs, "The Deterrence Question," *Social Science Quarterly*, 54 (December, 1973): 534–51; and Jack P. Gibbs, "Crime, Punishment, and Deterrence," *Social Science Quarterly*, 48 (March, 1968): 515–30.

and South Dakota to 87 percent in Utah. The average number of months served for a criminal homicide ranged from a low of 24 in Nevada to a high of 132 in North Dakota. Gibbs was able to analyze statistically these measures of certainty and severity in relation to homicide rates in the states. His conclusions:

1. States above the median-certainty and median-severity rates have lower homicide rates than states below both medians. Indeed, the homicide rate for low-certainty-rate and low-severity-rate states was *three* times greater than the average rate for high-certainty and high-severity states.
2. Certainty of imprisonment may be more important than severity of punishment in determining homicide rates, but there is conflicting evidence on which of these variables is more influential.
3. Both certainty and severity reduce homicide rates *even after* controlling for all other demographic variables.

Economists have generally confirmed these findings.[43] Their general premise, of course, is that if you increase the cost of something (crime), less of it will be consumed (there will be fewer crimes). Their own studies confirm the deterrent effect of both the certainty and severity of punishment. Economist Gordon Tullock dismisses the notion that "crimes of passion" cannot be reduced by increasing the certainty and severity of punishment:

The prisoners in Nazi concentration camps must frequently have been in a state of well justified rage against some of their guards; yet this almost never led to their using violence against the guards, because punishment—which if they were lucky, would mean instant death, but was more likely to be death by torture—was so obvious and certain.[44]

Tullock argues that to increase the deterrent effect of punishment, potential criminals must be given information about it. Indeed, he suggests, governments might even lie—that is, pretend that punishment is more certain and severe than it is—in order to reduce crime.

One of the more heated debates in correctional policy today concerns capital punishment. Opponents of the death penalty argue that it is "cruel and unusual punishment" in violation of the Eighth Amendment of the U.S. Constitution. They also argue that the death penalty is applied unequally. A large proportion of those executed have been poor, uneducated, and nonwhite. In contrast, there is a strong sense of justice among many Americans that demands retribution for heinous crimes—a life

[43] See Gordon Tullock, "Does Punishment Deter Crime?" *The Public Interest* (Summer, 1974), pp. 103–11.
[44] Ibid., p. 108.

for a life. A mere jail sentence for a multiple murderer or a rapist murderer seems unjust compared with the damage inflicted upon society and the victims. In most cases, a life sentence means less than ten years in prison under the current parole and probation policies of many states. Convicted murderers have been set free, and some have killed again. Moreover, prison guards and other inmates are exposed to convicted murderers who have "a license to kill," because they are already serving life sentences and have nothing to lose by killing again.

Prior to 1972, the death penalty was officially sanctioned by thirty states; only fifteen states had abolished capital punishment.[45] Federal law also retained the death penalty. However, no one had actually suffered the death penalty since 1967, because of numerous legal tangles and direct challenges to the constitutionality of capital punishment.

In 1972, the Supreme Court ruled that capital punishment *as currently imposed* violated the Eighth and Fourteenth Amendment prohibitions against cruel and unusual punishment and due process of law. The decision was made by a narrow 5 to 4 vote of the justices, and the reasoning in the case is very complex. Only two justices—Brennon and Marshall—declared that capital punishment itself is cruel and unusual. The other three justices in the majority—Douglas, White and Stewart—felt that death sentences had been applied unfairly: a few individuals were receiving the death penalty for crimes for which many others were receiving much lighter sentences. These justices left open the possibility that capital punishment would be constitutional if it was specified for certain kinds of crime and applied uniformly.

Since 1972, a majority of states have rewritten their death-penalty laws to try to insure fairness and uniformity of application. Generally, these laws mandate the death penalty for murders committed during rape or robbery, hijacking, or kidnapping; murders of prison guards; murder with torture; multiple murders; etc. Two trials would be held: one to determine guilt or innocence and another to determine the penalty. At the second trial, evidence of "aggravating" and "mitigating" factors would be presented; if there were aggravating factors but no mitigating factors, the death penalty would be mandatory. In 1976, the Supreme Court upheld state laws which were carefully written to insure fairness and due-process in the application of the death penalty. The Court declared that capital punishment itself was not "cruel or unusual" within

---

[45] Alaska, Hawaii, Iowa, Maine, Michigan, Minnesota, New Hampshire, New Mexico, New York, North Dakota, Oregon, Rhode Island, Vermont, West Virginia, and Wisconsin (although in Michigan, New York, North Dakota, Rhode Island, and Vermont there were provisions for certain serious exceptions, for example, killing a prison guard).

the meaning of the 8th Amendment; that the authors of the Constitution did not consider it cruel or unusual; and that the reenactment of the death penalty by so many state legislators was evidence that the death penalty was not considered cruel or unusual by contemporary state lawmakers.

Community political systems

COMMUNITIES AS SETTINGS FOR POLITICS

American communities come in different shapes and sizes, and community politics come in a variety of styles. Generalizing about community politics is perhaps even more difficult than generalizing about American state politics. There are eighteen thousand municipalities in America, seventeen thousand townships, three thousand counties, and a host of other school districts and special districts. Cities range in size from less than one hundred persons to New York's eight million. Two-thirds of the American people live in urban units of local government known as "municipalities," including "cities," "boroughs," "villages," or "towns." Other Americans are served by county or township governments. Moreover, there were 243 metropolitan areas in the United States in 1970; these are clusterings of people and governments around a core city of fifty thousand or more persons. These metropolitan areas are as small as Meriden, Connecticut, with few local governments and only fifty-five thousand persons, or as large as the New York area with six hundred local governments and eleven million people. In short, one may conceive of community political systems as rural counties, country towns, villages, cities of all sizes, or even sprawling metropolitan areas.

Community political systems serve two principal functions. One is that of supplying goods and services—for example, police protection or

Chapter eight

sewage disposal—that are not supplied by private enterprise. This is the "service" function. The other function is the "political" one, that of *managing conflict* over public policy. Of course, the "political" and the "service" functions of local governments are often indistinguishable in practice. A mayor who intervenes in a dispute about the location of a park is managing a local government service, namely recreation, at the same time that he is managing political conflict about whose neighborhood should get the most benefit from the new park. In the day-to-day administration of the service functions of local government, officials must decide a variety of political questions. Where are the facilities to be located? Often the question is where *not* to locate facilities, since many neighborhoods avoid having public facilities for fear that they will displace families, attract "undesirables," or depress local property values. How are public services to be paid for? Which agency or official will be in charge of a particular service? What policies or practices will govern the provision of this service? What level of service will be provided? What will the budget for the service be?

Occasionally, students are led to believe that local governments should be less "political" than state or national governments. Many people feel that it would be best to eliminate "politics" from local government. Historically, this attitude arose in conjunction with the municipal reform movement of the Progressive Era.[1] The reform movement involved a preference for nonpartisan elections, city-manager government, and an "antiseptic," "no-party" style of local government, devoid of the stigma of "politics." A city without politics appealed to many idealists who were disenchanted with boss rule. But the politician who responds to political considerations, in contrast to service considerations, is not necessarily sacrificing the welfare of his community. It is not necessarily true that the community is best served by treating the service function of government as if it were more important or more worthy of government attention than the political one. A politician who undertakes to arrange political compromises and balance competing interests in a community is performing a very important function. Helping people with different incomes, occupations, skin colors, religious beliefs, and styles of living to live together in a reasonably peaceful fashion is a vital task.

COPING WITH COMMUNITY CONFLICT

Government is best suited for managing *conventional* community conflicts—the adoption of the municipal budget, the periodic election of

[1] See Richard Hofstadter, *The Age of Reform* (New York: Alfred A. Knopf, Inc., 1955); and Lorin Peterson, *The Day of the Mugwump* (New York: Random House, Inc., 1961).

municipal officials, requests for rezoning, complaints about municipal services, and the like. But the real test of a political system's capacity to manage conflict occurs with the rise of rancorous conflict—street rioting, disruption over sex education, racial disputes, charges of police brutality, religious objections to school textbooks, and other emotionally charged issues. The distinction between conventional and rancorous conflict is based on the *intensity* of feelings aroused in the community, and not necessarily on the nature of the issue. Issues which would arouse little community interest or conflict in New York or Chicago might break things wide open in Amarillo, Texas, or Parkersburg, West Virginia. Just as American communities come in different shapes and sizes, so do the conflicts that convulse their governments.

What are the sources of community conflicts? Human diversity is the source of all political conflict—differences among men in wealth, occupation, education, ethnicity, race, religion, and style of living. In the United States, there are many rural communities, small towns and cities, and compact surburbs with very homogeneous populations. In these communities, there are few differences among citizens that create permanent lines of cleavage and none that run very deep. Some conflicts occur in these communities, of course, even rancorous ones, but groupings of forces are temporary. In contrast, in most large cities and metropolitan areas there are many different kinds of people living closely together, and there are more lasting cleavages, or "fault lines," which tend to open when controversial issues arise. These cleavages are readily recognized in disputes among upper-, middle-, and lower-income groups; races and ethnic groups; labor and management interests; property owners and nonproperty owners; families with children and those without; suburbanites and city dwellers; and traditional political party divisions.

What factors affect the frequency and intensity of community conflict? Let us consider just three possible conditions which interact to affect the nature of community conflict: size of city, degree of homogeneity of the population, and the extent of community participation.[2]

1. Large cities have greater heterogeneity in their populations and more frequent conflict.
2. But direct citizen involvement in the affairs of large cities is less be-

[2] For some empirical support for these speculations, see Gordon S. Black, "Conflict in the Community: A Theory of the Effect of Community Size," *American Political Science Review* 68 (September, 1974): 1245–61; see also Timothy A. Almy, "Residential Locations and Electoral Cohesion," *American Political Science Review*, 67 (September, 1973): 914–23, who argues that conflict is greater in communities where different social groups are residentially segregated.

cause individuals feel they cannot directly affect community decisions; citizen apathy reduces the intensity of conflict.

3. Thus, larger cities have greater frequency of conflicts but less intensity of conflicts because of lower levels of citizen involvement.
4. Small cities that are homogeneous in social, economic, racial, religious, and political composition will have less conflict.
5. However, if conflict occurs in a small city, it is likely to be more intense because of greater individual participation in community affairs. Where there are fewer voters, the individual feels he has more of a chance of influencing community decisions.
6. The frequency and intensity of conflict will be greatest in small cities that are heterogeneous. Although the popular view of small communities is that they are friendly, homogeneous havens from which the weary can escape the conflicts of large cities, this is not always true. Many of the most bitter community conflicts in recent times— over fluoridation of water, unGodly textbooks in the schools, and civil rights—have occurred in small but heterogeneous towns.

Once a community controversy begins, it follows a fairly predictable pattern of development, regardless of the nature of the issue. At least this is the contention of sociologist James S. Coleman: "It is the peculiarity of social controversy that it sets in motion its own dynamics; these tend to carry it forward in a path which bears little relation to its beginnings." [3] Coleman contends that controversies begin with specific problems and *expand to include general issues*. For example, an objection to certain books in a school library may expand to include criticism of progressive educational philosophy or even religious and moral differences. Rapid expansion of a controversy from the specific to the general occurs more frequently in communities where there are basic socioeconomic cleavages already. Secondly, conflict spreads from the original topic to *new and different issues*. Participants raise these additional issues to gain new allies: for example, "Look here, these developers are the same people who want to cut down our beautiful old trees and ruin the traditional beauty of our town." Finally, a disagreement over policy may *develop personal antagonisms*. A controversy that begins with reasonable arguments tends to heat slowly to the level of personal slander, rumor-spreading, and personal hostility. Coleman believes the development of personal antagonisms is essentially a psychological mechanism: we mentally screen out any "good" qualities in our opponents and progressively see them as totally bad. General cries for the resignation of mayors and councilmen, or the firing of city managers, school principals, and teachers replace earlier specific disagreements. Finally, a dispute becomes totally independent of the original disagreement and takes on a

[3] James S. Coleman, *Community Conflict* (New York: The Free Press, 1957), pp. 9–10.

life of its own. Coleman represented these stages of community conflict as follows:

1. Initial single issue.
2. Disruption of the equilibrium of community relations.
3. Previously suppressed issues against opponent appear.
4. More of opponents beliefs enter into disagreement.
5. Opposition appears totally bad.
6. Personal charges made against opponent.
7. Dispute becomes independent of initial issue.

How do individuals cope with community problems? If you are dissatisfied with the way things are going in your community, you have three choices: (1) resign yourself to the situation, do nothing, and just tolerate it; (2) move away and find a community that provides more satisfactions; (3) stay and make an attempt to change things. Political scientists tend to focus their attention on the people who try to change things, implying that this is the only way to respond rationally to community problems. But economists have developed theories of residential mobility that focus on the individual's choice of community based on a rational calculation of personal costs and benefits.[4] (The theory is most applicable to metropolitan areas where many different kinds of communities are available.) There are recognized negative "push" factors— crime, congestion, noise, overcrowding, racial conflict—and positive "pull" factors—more space, larger houses, better schools, "nice" playmates for the children—both of which affect decisions to move. One might move to the suburbs "for the kids," or move to the city to be close to good restaurants, fine entertainment, cultural events, and specialty shops, or to reduce the trip to work.[5] One can choose *among* suburbs by balancing residential amenities and services against land costs and taxes. In short, economists emphasize rational calculations and freedom of choice, which they assume most citizens possess.

Political scientists deal with the participants in urban politics, sometimes implying that nonparticipation or apathy is irrational, perhaps even unpatriotic. But apathy *is* rational if the costs of organizing and mobilizing political support are high, and if the majority actively favors something you oppose. And "moving out" may not always be possible—particularly for poor people, blacks, and aged. Thus, apathy is rational if any other kind of action is a waste of time, energy, and money, and is very unlikely to bring about significant change.

[4] The widely cited source is Charles M. Tiebout, "The Pure Theory of Local Expenditure" *Journal of Political Economy,* 64 (October, 1956): 416–24.

[5] See George Sabaugh et al., "Some Determinants of Intrametropolitan Residential Mobility," *Social Forces,* 48 (September, 1969): 88–98.

How do people actually respond to community dissatisfactions? Available evidence suggests that, in the face of community problems:

1. Higher-status whites tend either to become politically active or to move out, with political activity somewhat more common.
2. Lower-status whites tend to move out rather than become politically active.
3. Blacks are more likely to become politically active than to move out, probably because of the increased difficulties most blacks face in residential relocation.
4. City residents are more likely to move out, whereas suburbanites are more likely to become politically active.
5. Residents who have just arrived may be "fatigued" by their recent move and choose to be politically active, but citizens of long residence are just as likely to move out as others.

Overall, the tendency to "move away" from urban problems has greatly accentuated the difficulties of the nation's largest central cities.[6] Many of these cities are actually declining in population—losing middle-class whites to their surrounding suburbs. We will return to this problem in Chapters 11 and 13, but it is important to know how individual citizens as well as governments cope with community problems.

COMMUNITIES AS GOVERNMENTAL UNITS

Local government is not mentioned in the U.S. Constitution. Although we regard the American federal system as a mixture of federal, state, and *local* governments, from a constitutional point of view, local governments are really a part of state governments. Communities have no constitutional right to self-government: all of their governmental powers legally flow from state governments. Local governments—cities, townships, counties, special districts, and school districts—are creatures of the states, subject to the obligations, privileges, powers, and restrictions that state governments impose upon them. The state, either through its constitution or its laws, may create or destroy any or all units of local government. To the extent that local governments can collect taxes, regulate their citizens, and provide services, they are actually exercising *state* powers delegated to them by the state in either its constitution or its laws.

All states, with the exception of Connecticut and Rhode Island, have organized *county* governments. In Louisiana, counties are called "parishes," and in Alaska they are called "boroughs." It is difficult to

[6] John M. Orbell and Toru Uno, "A Theory of Neighborhood Problem Solving: Political Action versus Residential Mobility," *American Political Science Review*, 66 (June, 1972): 471–89.

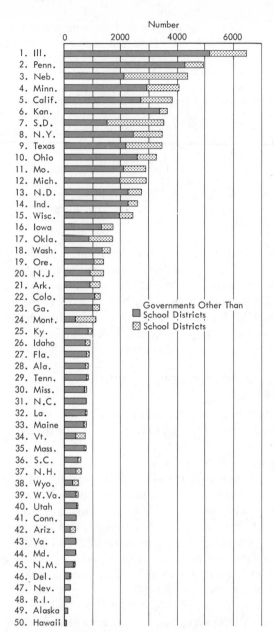

FIGURE 8–1 Local governments in the states.
Source: U.S. Department of Commerce, Bureau of the Census.

generalize about the powers of counties. The average population served by a county government is 59,025, but Loving County, Texas, had only

164 inhabitants in 1970, while Los Angeles County, California, had more than 7 million. The legal powers, organization, and officers of counties also vary a great deal.

TABLE 8.1   Local Governments in the United States

	1967	1962	1957	1952	1972
Counties	3,049	3,043	3,050	3,052	3,044
Municipalities	18,048	17,997	17,215	16,807	18,517
Townships	17,105	17,144	17,198	17,202	16,991
School districts	21,782	34,678	50,454	67,355	15,781
Special districts	21,264	18,323	14,424	12,340	23,885
Total (including States and National Government)	81,299	91,185	102,341	116,756	78,269

SOURCE: U.S. Bureau of the Census, *Census of Government, 1967.*

Perhaps it would be best to begin a description of county government by distinguishing between *rural* and *urban* counties. Obviously there is a great deal of difference between Los Angeles County with 7 million people, Cook County, Chicago, with 5.1 million, and Wayne County, Detroit, with 2.7 million, and the more than eight hundred rural counties in the nation with populations of 10,000 or less. Traditionally, the rural county was the most important unit of local government: it handled such essential matters as law enforcement, courts, schools, roads, elections, poor relief, and the legal recording of property deeds, mortgages, wills, and marriages. Rural communities competed with each other for the location of the county seat, because the community named as county seat won social and political prestige, county jobs, a county fair, and preferential treatment in county roads and public buildings. Moreover, many rural dwellers identify themselves as "coming from" a particular county. The county seat attracted retail business: farm markets were generally located in county seats, where a farmer could transact both public and private business. Rural county government provided an arena for a folksy, provincial, individualistic, "friends and neighbors" type of politics. Rural county government was the province of laymen and amateurs rather than experts or professionals. Decision making was personalized and informal. Often rural counties resemble urban counties about as much as the old-fashioned country store resembles a modern supermarket.

Although county governments differ markedly in their organization, they generally have (1) a governing body variously called the "county commissioners," "county board," "board of supervisors," or even "judges," which is composed of anywhere from three to fifty elected members; (2) a number of separately elected officials with countywide jurisdictions, such as sheriff, county attorney, auditor, recorder, coroner, assessor, judge, treasurer, engineer, and so on; (3) a large number of special boards or commissions which have authority over various functions, such as the county welfare board, county tax equalization committee, hospital board, library board, and civil service commission, whose members may be elected or appointed by the county commissioners or may even include the county commissioners in an ex officio capacity; and (4) an appointed county bureaucracy in roads, health, welfare, libraries, schools, and so on.

Typically, county officials have the following duties:

Sheriff: maintains jail; furnishes police protection in unincorporated areas; carries out orders of the county court.

Auditor: maintains financial records and tax rolls; authorizes payment of county obligations.

County attorney: serves as chief prosecuting attorney; conducts criminal investigations and prosecutes law violators.

Coroner: conducts medical investigations to determine cause of death; maintains county morgue.

Treasurer or Tax Collector: collects, disburses, and maintains county funds; makes county fiscal reports.

Clerk: registers and records legal documents including deeds, mortgages, plats, marriages, divorces, births; certifies election returns.

Assessor: determines value of all taxable property in the county.

The many separately elected county officials and the surplus of independent boards and commissions in county government are generally considered an obstacle to the emergence of strong executive leadership at the county level. The ability of county governments to assume more important functions and responsibilities, particularly in urban areas, probably hinges upon a reorganization of county government to provide for stronger executive leadership.

County government in urban areas is acquiring many of the responsibilities of city governments, and urban counties are increasingly adopting more streamlined, manager types of government organization. Urban counties may provide recreation, flood control, water supply, sewage disposal, library services, airport facilities, countywide police and fire protection, and other urban services. Urban counties may provide these traditional "city services" to the unincorporated areas of the county, that is, to the areas not within the boundaries of cities, and occasionally to cities as well. (See Chapter 11 for further discussion of the future of county government in metropolitan areas.)

Another interesting unit of local government is the "township" or "town," which is found in about half of the states—the northern states from New England to the Midwest. Southern and western states have made little use of this unit of government. Townships are subdivisions of counties and perform many of the functions of county governments at a grassroots level—schools, elections, road repair, tax administration, fire protection, and even law enforcement through local justices of the peace. Townships are unincorporated, which means they do not have charters from state governments guaranteeing their political independence or authorizing them to provide many municipal services. The jurisdiction of townships may extend over many square miles of sparsely populated rural territory. About 40 million people, or one-fifth of the U.S. population, live under township governments today.

Township governments vary considerably in their powers and organization. Perhaps it would be best to classify them as "towns," and "rural townships," and "urban townships." In the New England states, the "town" is a significant unit of local government, with long traditions and deep roots in the political philosophy of the people of the region. In fact, the New England "town meeting" is often cited by political philosophers as the ideal form of *direct* democracy as distinguished from *representative* democracy. For the town meeting was, and to some extent still is, the central institution of "town" government. The New England town included a village and all of its surrounding farms. The town meeting was open to all eligible voters; it was generally an important social as well as political event. The town meeting would levy taxes, make appropriations, determine policy, and elect officers for the year. Between town meetings, a board of selected men, "selectmen," would supervise the activities of the town—schools, health, roads, care of the poor, and so on. Other officers include town clerk, tax assessors and collectors, justices of the peace, constables, road commissioners, and school board members. Although the ideal of direct democracy is still alive in many smaller New England towns, in the large towns, the pure democracy of the town meeting has given way to a representative system, in which town meeting members are elected prior to the town meeting. Moreover, much of the determination of the towns' financial affairs, previously decided at town meetings, has now been given over to the "selectmen," and many towns have appointed town managers to supervise the day-to-day administration of town services.

Rural townships outside of New England have lost much of their vitality in recent years. The school district consolidation movement (see Chapter 14) has centralized the control of public schools at the county level or in school districts, which span villages and townships. Population decline in America's rural areas has made it difficult for many rural *counties* to operate effectively, let alone smaller rural *townships*.

Some urban townships appear to have a brighter future as units of government than rural townships. This is particularly true in certain suburban areas of larger cities where metropolitan growth has enveloped township governments. Some states, Pennsylvania for example, have authorized urban townships to exercise many of the powers and provide many of the services previously reserved to city governments.

CITIES AS "MUNICIPAL CORPORATIONS"

Nearly 70 percent of the American people live in cities. Legally speaking, cities are "municipal corporations," which have received charters from state governments setting forth their boundaries, governmental powers and functions, structure and organization, methods of finance, and powers to elect and appoint officers and employees. The municipal *charter* is intended to grant the powers of local self-government to a community. Of course, the powers of self-government granted by a municipal charter are not unlimited. A state can change its charter or take it away altogether, as it sees fit. Cities, like other local governments, have only the powers that state laws and constitutions grant them. They are still subdivisions of the state. And, of course, state laws operate within the boundaries of cities. In fact, municipal corporations are generally responsible for the enforcement of state law within their boundaries. But they also have the additional power to make local laws, "ordinances," which operate only within their boundaries. But perhaps the most serious limitation on the powers of cities is the fact that American courts have insisted upon interpreting the powers granted in charters very narrowly. The classic statement of this principle of restrictive interpretation of municipal powers was made by John F. Dillon over sixty years ago and is now well known as "Dillon's rule":

> It is a general and undisputed proposition of law that a municipal corporation possesses and can exercise the following powers, and no others: first, those granted in express words; second, those necessarily or fairly implied in or incident to the powers expressly granted; third, those essential to the accomplishment of the declared objects and purposes of the corporation—not simply convenient, but indispensable. Any fair, reasonable, substantial doubt concerning the existence of power is resolved by the courts against a corporation, and the power is denied.[7]

[7] John F. Dillion, *Commentaries on the Laws of Municipal Corporations*, 5th ed., (Boston: 1911), p. 448.

As Banfield and Wilson point out, "This means that a city cannot operate a peanut stand at the city zoo without first getting the state legislature to pass an enabling law, unless, per chance, the city's charter or some previously enacted law unmistakably covers the sale of peanuts." [8]

The restrictive interpretation of the powers of cities leads to rather lengthy city charters, since nearly everything a city does must have specific legal authorization in the city charter. The city charter of New York, for example, is several hundred pages long. City charters must cover in detail such matters as boundaries, structure of government, ordinance-making powers, finances, contracts, purchasing, bonds, courts, municipal elections, property assessments, zoning laws and building codes, licenses, franchises, law enforcement, education, health, streets, parks, public utilities, and on and on. Since any proposed change in the powers, organization, or responsibilities of cities requires an act of a state legislature amending the city's charter, state legislatures are intimately involved in local legislation. This practice of narrowly interpreting city charters may appear awkward, but its effect is to increase the power of courts and state legislators in city affairs. Courts acquire power from their ability to interpret complex city charters; and state legislators with city constituencies acquire power through the practice of granting a local legislator the courtesy of accepting his views on local legislation that affects only his constituency.

State legislative control over cities is most firmly entrenched in *special act* charters. These charters are specially drawn for the cities named in them. Cities under special act charters remain directly under legislative control, and specific legislative approval for that city and that city alone must be obtained for any change in its government or service activities. Such charters give rise to local acts dealing with small details of city government in a specially named city, for example, "that Fall River be authorized to appropriate money for the purchase of uniforms for the park police and watershed guards of said city." [9] Under special act charters, laws that apply to one city do not necessarily apply to others.

In contrast, *general act* charters usually classify cities according to their size and then apply municipal laws to all cities in each size classification. Thus, a state's municipal law may apply to all cities of less than 10,000 people, another law to all cities with populations of 10,000—25,000, another to cities with 25,000—50,000 people, and so on. These general act charters make it difficult to interfere in the activities of a particular city without affecting the activities of all cities of a similar size category.

[8] Banfield and Wilson, *City Politics*, p. 65.
[9] Ibid., p. 66.

Yet in practice there are often exceptions and modifications to general act legislation. For example, since legislators know the populations of their cities, they can select size categories for municipal law that apply to only one city. The Pennsylvania legislature can pass laws for cities of over 1 million, aware that only Philadelphia falls into this category, and for cities of 500,000 to 1 million, aware that only Pittsburgh falls into this category.

Optional charter laws provide cities with some choice in the structure and organization of their governments. Such laws generally offer a choice of governmental forms: strong mayor and weak counsel, weak mayor and strong council, commission, city manager, or some modification of these.

Home rule charters are designed to give cities the power to adopt governmental forms and provide municipal services, as they see fit, without state legislative interference. Home rule charters may be given to cities by state constitutions or by legislative enactments; legislative home rule is considered less secure, since a legislature could retract the grant if it wished to do so. Beginning with Missouri in 1875, more than half the states have included in their constitutions provisions for the issuance of home rule charters. About two-thirds of the nation's cities with populations over 200,000 have some form of home rule.

The intended effect of home rule is to reverse "Dillon's rule" and enable cities to "exercise all legislative powers not prohibited by law or by charter." In other words, instead of preventing a city from doing anything not specifically authorized, home rule permits the city to do anything not specifically prohibited. The theory of home rule grants sweeping powers to cities; however, in practice, home rule has not brought self-government to cities. Home rule provisions in state constitutions range from those that grant considerable power and discretion over local affairs, to provisions that are so useless that no city has ever made use of them. First of all, these constitutional provisions may be too cumbersome or vague for effective implementation. In some states, cities feel that it is easier to use the general law charters, particularly if they provide for optional forms of government, than to use the cumbersome procedures for obtaining home rule. Another important limitation on home rule is the distinction between "self-enforcing" and "non-self-enforcing," or "permissive," home rule provisions in state constitutions. Non-self-enforcing home rule provisions merely permit the state legislature to grant home rule to its cities; cities cannot acquire home rule without legislative action. Only about a dozen states have "self-enforcing" home rule provisions, which enable cities to bypass the state legislature and adopt home rule for themselves. Finally, home rule may be limited by court interpretations of the language of the constitutional provisions granting power to home rule in cities. Constitutional provisions may grant to home rule cities the power to make "all laws and ordinances relating to municipal concerns," or the "powers of local self-government," or all powers "in respect to municipal affairs." Of course, ordinances passed under home rule authority cannot be in conflict with state law. Courts must distinguish between municipal and statewide concerns. In cases where doubt exists, legal traditions of municipal law require that courts resolve the doubt in favor of the state and against local powers of home rule. State legislatures can intervene in local affairs in home rule cities by simply deciding that a particular matter is of statewide concern.

The politics of home rule often pits reform groups, city mayors, and administrators against state legislators and large municipal taxpayers. State legislators are generally wary of giving up their authority over cities. Rural legislators have little reason to support city home rule, and even city legislators seldom welcome proposals to give up their authority over local bills. Sometimes city employees with good access to the legislature will oppose giving a mayor or a city manager too much control over their employment. Taxpayer groups may fear that home rule will give the city the ability to increase taxes. Local bills may be pictured as a distraction to legislators by reformers, but many legislators enjoy the power that it brings them in local affairs and welcome the opportunity to perform legislative services for their constituents. And so, even with reapportionment adding to the number of urban legislators, the League of Women Voters, good-government groups, and mayors may still be frustrated in their attempts to achieve genuine home rule for American cities.

Courts figure prominently in municipal politics. This is because of the subordinate position of the municipal corporation in the hierarchy of governments, and legal traditions, such as Dillon's rule, which narrowly interpret the power of local governments. The power of courts over municipal affairs grants leverage to defenders of the *status quo* in any political battle at the local level. Proponents of a new municipal law or municipal service not only must win the battle over whether a city *ought* to pass the new law or provide the new service but also must win the legal battle over whether the city *can* pass the law or provide the service. Limitations and uncertainties abound about the validity of local enactments. Legal challenges to the authority of the city to pass new regulations or provide new services are frequent. The city attorney becomes a key official because he must advise the city about what it can or cannot do. Not only must the city obey the federal constitution, but it is also subject to the restraints of the state constitution, state laws, its municipal charter, and of course, Dillon's rule. The result is to greatly strengthen courts, attorneys, and defenders of the *status quo*.

FORMS OF CITY GOVERNMENT

American city government comes in three structural packages. There are some adaptations and variations from city to city, but generally one can classify the form of city government as mayor-council, commission, or council-manager. Approximately 51 percent of American cities have the mayor-council form of government; 6 percent have the commission form; and 43 percent have the council-manager form.

The nation's largest cities tend to function under the *mayor-council* plan. This is the oldest form of American city government and is designed in the American tradition of separation of powers between legislature and executive. One may also establish subcategories of "strong" or "weak" mayor forms of mayor-council government. A strong mayor is one who is the undisputed master of the executive agencies of city government and who has substantial legislative powers in the form of budget making, vetoes, and opportunity to propose legislation. Only a few cities make the mayor the sole elected official among city executive officers; it is common for the mayor to share budgetary and administrative powers with other elected officials. Yet many mayors, by virtue of their prestige, persuasive abilities, or role as party leader, have been able to overcome most of the weaknesses of their formal office. Mayor Daley of Chicago must deal with a fifty-member city council, a wide variety of independent boards and agencies like the park district, board of education, and housing authority, a large legislative delegation, and various lesser elected officials. Yet Mayor Daley is the undisputed center of political influence in Chicago.

In recent years, large cities have been adding to the formal powers of their chief executives. Cities have augmented the mayor's roll by providing him with direction over budgeting, purchasing, and personnel controls, and independent boards and commissions and individual councilmen have relinquished administrative control over city departments in many cities. Moreover, many cities have strengthened the mayor's position by providing him with a chief administrative officer, "CAO," to handle important staff and administrative duties of supervising city departments and providing central management services.

The *commission* form of city government gives both legislative and executive powers to a small body, usually consisting of five members. The commission form originated at the beginning of the century as a reform movement designed to end a system of divided responsibility between mayor and council. One of the commission members is nominally the mayor, but he has no more formal powers than his fellow commissioners. The board of commissioners is directly responsible for the operation of city departments and agencies. In practice, one commission

MAYOR COUNCIL FORM

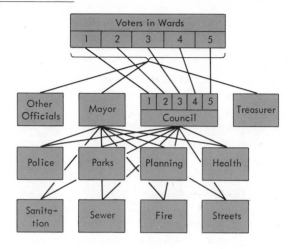

COMMISSION FORM

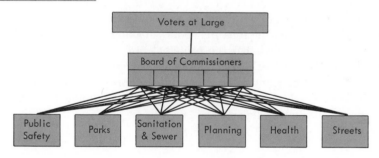

COUNCIL-MANAGER FORM

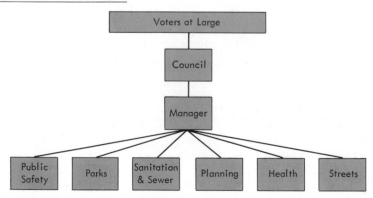

FIGURE 8–2   Forms of city government.
Source: National Municipal League. Reproduced by permission.

235

member will become responsible for the management of a specific department, such as finance, public works, or public safety. As long as the councilmen are in agreement over policy, there are few problems; but when commissioners differ among themselves and develop separate spheres of influence in city government, city government becomes a multiheaded monster, totally lacking in coordination. The results of a commission form of government were generally so disastrous that the reform movement abandoned its early support of this form of government in favor of the council-manager plan.

The *council-manager* form of government revived the distinction between legislative "policy making" and executive "administration" in city government. Policy-making responsibility is vested in an elected council, and administration is assigned to an appointed professional administrator known as a manager. The council chooses the manager and he is responsible to them. All departments of the city government operate under the direction of the manager, who has the power to hire and fire personnel within the limits set by the merit system. The council's role in administration is limited to selecting and dismissing the city manager. The plan is based on the idea that policy making and administration are separate functions, and that the principal task of city government is to provide the highest level of services at the lowest possible cost—utilities, streets, fire and police protection, health, welfare, recreation, and so on. Hence, a professionally trained, career-oriented administrator is given direct control over city departments.

URBAN ENVIRONMENT AND
THE STRUCTURE OF CITY GOVERNMENT

We shall return to the political roles of mayors, managers, and councils in Chapter 10, but let us examine for a moment the social, economic, and political forces shaping the *structure* of city government: that is, the conditions associated with the selection of one of the principal forms of government.

First of all, city-manager government is closely associated with the *size* of cities. Large cities show a distinct preference for the more "political" form of mayor-council government in contrast to the more "efficient" form of council-manager government. (See Table 8–2.) All cities over one million have the mayor-council form of government. Only five of the nation's twenty-six cities with more than 500,000 people have council-manager government: Dallas, San Antonio, Kansas City, San Diego, and Phoenix. The council-manager and commission forms of government are most popular in the middle-sized cities—cities with

TABLE 8.2   Urban Environments and Form of Government

| | | Percentage of Cities | | |
	Number of Cities	Manager	Commission	Mayor-Council
All Cities	(2784)	43	6	51
Size of City				
Over 1,000,000	(6)	0	0	100
500,000 to 1,000,000	(20)	25	0	70
250,000 to 500,000	(27)	48	11	41
100,000 to 250,000	(93)	54	11	35
50,000 to 100,000	(215)	54	7	39
25,000 to 50,000	(439)	54	9	37
10,000 to 25,000	(1072)	46	8	46
5,000 to 10,000	(1112)	34	4	62
Growth Rate				
Large Increase: 15% or more	(359)	59	10	31
Small Increase: 0 to 15%	(152)	39	17	44
Small Decline: 0 to 6%	(77)	30	21	49
Large Decline: 6% or more	(50)	26	36	38
Mobility[1]				
Low: under 12%	(192)	23	22	55
Medium: 12 to 20%	(250)	47	14	39
High: over 20%	(194)	73	9	18
Region				
East	(161)	21	24	55
Midwest	(179)	37	10	53
South	(185)	61	19	20
West	(115)	81	5	14
Educational Level				
High: over 50% High School	(190)	67	10	33
Medium: 40 to 50% High School	(203)	49	12	39
Low: under 40% High School	(247)	33	21	46
White Collar Occupation[2]				
Low: under 35%	(232)	32	20	48
Medium: 35 to 42%	(201)	51	12	37
High: over 42%	(193)	62	13	25
Ethnicity[3]				
Low: under 10%	(213)	54	20	26
Medium: 10 to 20%	(204)	59	11	30
High: over 20%	(223)	32	14	54

[1] Mobility is measured by the percentage of residents who lived in a different county in the previous five years.

[2] White collar occupation is measured by the percentage of persons employed in professional, technical, managerial, clerical, and sales occupations.

[3] Ethnicity is measured by the percentage of persons with foreign-born parents.

SOURCES: Data derived from *Municipal Yearbook,* 1968 (Chicago: National Municipal League, 1968); Robert R. Alford and Harry M. Scoble," Political and Socio-economic Characteristics of American Cities," *Municipal Yearbook,* 1965 (Chicago: National Municipal League, 1965), pp. 82-97.

populations of 25,000 to 250,000 people. Probably, cities with less than 10,000 persons do not have sufficient resources to justify hiring a trained professional city manager, nor in all probability, do they have the administrative problems requiring his expertise. Thus, small cities, like large cities, tend to rely upon mayor-council government, although probably for different reasons.

If the lack of resources and the absence of complex administrative problems in small cities explain the absence of council-manager government in these cities, what explains its absence in larger cities? A common explanation is that the political environment of large cities is so complex, with many competing interests, that these cities require strong *political* leadership, which can arbitrate struggles for power, arrange compromises, and be directly responsible to the people for policy decisions. A large city requires a "political" form of government that can arbitrate the conflicting claims of diverse interests. This implies that in smaller cities there are fewer competing interests, more acceptance of a common public interest, and less division over community policy. A professional city manager would have less difficulty in accepting cues about correct behavior in a small city than in a large city with a complex and political structure. There is a greater degree of consensus on policy direction in a smaller city; therefore, such a city requires a professional administrator rather than a political negotiator. The question is whether or not political skill or administrative expertise is more important in a city, and there is reason to believe that larger cities require political skills more than professional administration.

Growing cities face more administrative and technical problems than cities whose population is stable. There is a strong relationship between population *growth* and council-manager government. (See Table 8–2.) A rapidly growing city faces many adminstrative problems in providing streets, sewers, and the many other services required by an expanding population. This creates a demand for a professional administrator. Population mobility is closely related to manager government. In contrast, the mayor-council form of government is associated with cities having relatively stable populations, in which administrative and technical problems are not quite so pressing, and political conflict is more likely to be well defined and persistent. Council-manager government is more popular in the rapidly growing cities of the West and the South. Table 8–2 reveals that mayor-council government is preferred in Eastern and Midwestern cities, while manager government prevails in the South and especially the West.

Council-manager cities tend to be *middle-class* cities. Cities with large proportions of working-class residents, low-income families, and ethnic minorities are not likely to adopt council-manager government.

Schnore and Alford have presented conclusive evidence, for three hundred suburbs in twenty-five large metropolitan areas, that communities with council-manager government have a smaller proportion of foreign born and persons over sixty-five years of age, a larger proportion of white-collar workers, with a high school education or better, and tend to grow more rapidly in population than communities with mayor-council or commission forms of government.[10] Table 8–2 shows a decrease in manager government associated with an increase in foreign-born population of a city. Table 8–2 also shows that white-collar employees in personnel services, retail stores, and financial establishments, as well as professional people and public administrators, appear to prefer manager government more than blue-collar workers in wholesale trade, transportation, diversified industry, and manufacturing. Blue-collar workers appear to prefer a mayor-council system which provides political channels for the expression of their interests.

Why is it that middle-class communities prefer the manager form of government while working-class communities prefer a mayor-council government? Middle-class citizens, those in white-collar jobs with good educations and reasonably high incomes, are more likely to want government conducted in a businesslike fashion, with a council serving as a board of directors and a city manager as the president of a "municipal corporation." They are primarily concerned with efficiency, honesty, and saving their tax dollars. These values are not necessarily shared by labor, low-status, low-income, ethnic and minority groups, which may prefer a government that grants small favors, dispenses patronage jobs, awards representation and "recognition" to minority groups, and can be held directly responsible by the voters at election time. In a campaign for city-manager government, one usually finds business leaders, newspapers, and civic associations supporting the plan, and labor unions and minority group organizations far less enthusiastic. Party organizations and professional politicians can usually be expected to oppose this plan. Its support generally comes from white-collar, high-income, well-educated, white neighborhoods, and its opposition from low-income, blue-collar, black and ethnic neighborhoods.

Communities with well-organized *competitive party systems* are less likely to have council-manager government than one-party communities or communities in which the formal party organization is weak. States with the highest percentages of medium-sized cities with manager plans are Virginia, North Carolina, California, Texas, and Florida; in con-

[10] Leo Schnore and Robert R. Alford, "Forms of Government and Socioeconomic Characteristics of Suburbs," *Administrative Science Quarterly* (June, 1963), pp. 1–17. See also, John H. Kessel, "Governmental Structure and Political Environment," *American Political Science Review* (September, 1962), 612–21.

trast, states with the highest percentages of mayor-council plans are Indiana, Connecticut, and Ohio. The former states are either one-party states or, in the case of California, states with relatively weak party organization. The states with mayor-council cities are competitive two-party states. It is sometimes argued that the introduction of the manager plan decreases party activity in communities, but it is also true that the presence of strong party organizations may be a significant factor in the defeat of manager plans. Thus, manager government may depress party activity, or strong parties may kill off manager government, or both; but whatever the case, manager government appears incompatible with strong partisan politics in a community. Thus, social, economic, and political forces influence the structure of city government.

THE COMMUNITY-CONTROL CONTROVERSY

In recent years the nation's largest cities have been confronted with a new demand to alter the structure of municipal government—*community control*. *Community control*, which calls for decentralization of large-city bureaucracies and greater neighborhood participation in government, can be applied to law enforcement, sanitation, housing, zoning, and antipoverty programs, although education has been the primary target so far. The demand for greater neighborhood participation in big-city decision making is originating primarily in black ghettos.[11]

Community control is seen by its advocates as a partial solution to a number of problems. First of all, there is the root problem of large, complex, and unresponsive municipal bureaucracies. Decentralization is proposed as a means of making big-city government more responsive to citizen concerns. "Little city halls" located throughout large cities are expected to facilitate greater citizen participation and control over government. Presumably a big-city government would then come to resemble a more manageable small-town or suburban government. Secondly, within black ghettos, there is a sense of powerlessness when the city government itself and the city's institutions in the ghettos— schools, welfare agencies, poverty programs, police, etc.—are controlled and staffed mainly by whites. In such situations, black advocates of community control have posed the analogy of colonialism—where a poor and black population is governed by a larger, remote, unresponsive, and white government. They want control over municipal programs and policies and the hiring and firing of personnel within the ghetto. Thirdly,

[11] See Alan Altshuler, *Community Control* (New York: Pegasus, 1970); Joseph Zimmerman, *The Federated City* (New York: St. Martins, 1972).

community control is advocated as a means of stimulating innovation and diversification in government policy. Community-controlled schools, for example, could experiment with different approaches to education— approaches more suited to the children in the neighborhood. Under decentralization, other municipal services could also be geared to the specific needs of neighborhoods in large cities rather than to uniform, bureaucratic, city-wide standards.

The issue of community control cuts across many conventional liberal and conservative groupings. Liberals who are frequently sympathetic to ghetto needs find themselves in a dilemma over community control, fearing it will lead to segregation rather than integration; conservatives may support community control out of their suspicion of large government bureaucracies. Opponents of "busing" may support community control, hoping that it will serve as an alternative to desegregation of the schools. Blacks who are committed to separatism and are pessimistic about the prospects for integration may support community control, whereas blacks who are committed to integration may oppose it as a step backward in the road toward equality. The strongest opposition to community control has come from municipal employee unions— teachers, policemen, fire-fighters, welfare workers, and others. They perceive neighborhood control as a threat to their jobs, particularly as a threat to the jobs of white city employees working in black neighborhoods.

Community control, however, does not usually mean complete independence. Independence would mean that neighborhoods, including black ghettos, would have to pay for all of their own municipal services. Yet most neighborhoods, particularly black ghettos, do not have the resources to do so. Community control envisions decentralization of urban services and neighborhood participation in policy making, but it does *not* envision exclusive reliance on local resources.

GOVERNING NEW YORK CITY:
WORMS IN THE BIG APPLE

The United States government is the largest of the nation's eighty thousand governments; New York City is the second largest. "The Big Apple" spends over $13 billion a year, more than any other city or state. The problem is that it collects less than $12 billion a year in revenue. The resulting deficits have been piling up over the years— the city is nearly $15 billion in debt and falls deeper into red ink each year. A brief glance at New York's fiscal problems provides us with a good lesson on how *not* to govern a city.

How are New York's debts financed? Like all municipalities, New York City funds its debts by the sale of municipal bonds to banks, investment companies, and private individuals. To help cities keep down the cost of borrowing, the federal government does not tax the interest income on municipal bonds—an attractive incentive for wealthy investors to buy "monies" rather than corporate bonds or stocks. Of course, this is also an advantage to cities: they can usually pay a lower interest rate than corporations because many investors prefer *tax-free*, lower interest to *taxable*, higher interest. So most cities have very little trouble borrowing money. But not New York City—or any other city that fails to balance its budget year after year. The Brooklyn Bridge has been sold too often, and so have New York City bonds. Investors no longer believe that the city will ever be able to balance its budget and pay off its debts. If, as old debts come due, the city cannot borrow anew to pay off these earlier commitments, it will have to default on its obligations, and the result will be *municipal bankruptcy*.

How did the nation's largest city get into such a mess? Underlying New York City's financial difficulties are the socioeconomic problems confronting many large cities: the flight of middle-class families to the suburbs; an influx of the poor and unskilled; an overflow of welfare recipients in the central city; the concentration of social problems—crime, delinquency, poor housing, drug abuse—in the inner city; the special problems of educating large numbers of disadvantaged children in the public school; and so on. The recession of 1974–75 reduced revenues in most of the nation's states and cities, as sales and income-tax revenues declined and property-tax collections were frequently delinquent. Nevertheless, other big cities managed to survive these problems. Perhaps, New York City was the first city to directly confront the possibility of bankruptcy simply because it is the biggest city, and others can be expected to follow the lead of the Big Apple; perhaps there are worms eating away at the core of the other cities as well.

How did the Big Apple become so wormy? In brief, New York City offered so much, to so many, for so little. New York has always taken pride in its treatment of the poor and the oppressed, welcoming wave after wave of new immigrants. From the early days of the Tammany Hall machine, through the flamboyant mayoralities of Jimmy Walker and Fiorello LaGuardia, to the liberal visions of recent mayors Robert Wagner and John Lindsay, the city political organizations catered to the needs (and won the votes) of the city's large needy population. No other city provided such a range of free services and recreation: libraries, parks, and playgrounds; scores of city hospitals; museums and zoos; antipoverty programs and day-care centers; drug treatment programs; and a costly but tuition-free City University of New York open to any city high school graduate, whatever his grades. No other city was as generous to such a large number of city employees (338,000 for a city of eight million): after three years on the job a New York City policeman can earn nearly $18,000 per year, a sanitation worker nearly $16,000, and a full professor at the City University nearly $40,000. But worker productivity is low because supervisory and administrative personnel are in great abundance in relation to police patrolmen, garbage pick-up men, and classroom teachers. (More than one-third of New York City Board of Education employees are nonteachers.) New York City employee pensions are the envy of private as well as public employees everywhere: most city employees can retire at half-pay after twenty or twenty-five years of service. As a result of these many expensive services and benefits, the per capita cost of running New York City is higher than any other city in the nation. (See Table 8–3, left column.) Supporters of New York City point out, however, that New York itself carries many of the burdens that other cities share with state or county governments. For example, most cities shift the costs of welfare and education onto separate county and school-district governments, which are in turn greatly aided by state governments. If we compare all services received by residents of large cities, *combining the expenditures of all governments serving city residents* (see Table 8–3, right column), then New York appears somewhat less expensive relative to other cities.

TABLE 8.3   New York City Expenditures in Comparison with Expenditures of Ten Other Large Cities

| | Per Capita Expenditures, 1973 | |
	City Government	All Governments Serving City
New York City	1,224	1,286
Chicago	267	600
Newark	692	827
Los Angeles	242	759
Philadelphia	415	653
San Francisco	751	1,073
New Orleans	241	431
St. Louis	310	610
Denver	473	721
Baltimore	806	814
Detroit	357	650

SOURCE: U S. Bureau of the Census, *City Government Finances, 1975.*

Typical of other cities, New York is losing much of its middle-class residential tax base. From 1950 to 1970 the white non-Puerto Rican population percentage declined from 87 percent to 65 percent; the black population increased from 10 to 22 percent and the Puerto Rican population from 3 to 11 percent. As the poor arrive, the need for services increases and this requires higher taxes. Higher taxes, together with problems in schools, rising crime, and "antisocial behavior," speeds up the white middle-class exodus from the city. Even many of the nation's large industrial corporations which long maintained their headquarters in Manhattan have been persuaded to leave the city, often at the request of their office employees.

For years under Mayors Robert Wagner and John Lindsay, the city's comptroller, Abraham Beame, managed to postpone fiscal disaster by budgeting gimmicry. Like many cities, New York is required by the state constitution to maintain a balanced budget—obviously an unenforceable requirement. Comptroller Beame simply shifted current expenses, salaries, and supplies, to the capital construction budget, which covers long-term building projects for which the city can borrow money. Other strategies included deliberately overestimating revenues, establishing semi-independent city "authorities" that could borrow money, asking the state and federal governments for "advances" on grants-in-aid, and draining various trust funds. In 1973 Abraham Beame was elected mayor. The fiscal problems that had been swept under the rug by Mayor Lindsay and others came out into the open.

In early 1975 the New York City banks insisted that the city balance its budget and undertake a long-range program to reduce its debts. The banks would no longer lend the city money unless the city displayed greater fiscal responsibility. Mayor Beame called on New York State Governor Carey and President Gerald Ford for assistance, but again was urged to balance the budget to avoid bankruptcy. Mayor Beame eventually proposed a "crisis" budget, reducing expenditures by one billion and laying off 20,000 city employees, including policemen, firemen, and sanitation workers. At the same time he publicly blamed President Ford, the New York City banks, and Republicans in the state legislature for failing to recognize the many social burdens that the city was carrying on behalf of the state and nation. Governor Carey succeeded in getting the New York State legislature to create a Municipal Assistance Corporation ("Big Mac") to convert short-term city debt into long-term debt and to sell to the public bonds that could be backed by specific city revenues.

But the response of the city's powerful municipal employees unions was predictable: sanitation workers walked off the job to protest the firings and so did many policemen and firemen. Garbage piled up on the streets and "Fun City" was grimly relabeled "Fear City." Some observers felt that Beame deliberately chose to concentrate layoffs among the highly visible and well-organized policemen, firemen, and sanitation workers (rather than welfare workers or bureaucrats) in order to increase pressure on the state and federal govenments to come to the rescue of the city. After a series of strikes, demonstrations, and urban turmoil, Mayor Beame began rehiring fired workers. It was clear that the unions had forced Mayor Beame to back down on his "crisis" budget.

The unhappy result, of course, was that "Big Mac" was unable to persuade banks and investors that New York City was really serious about achieving a balanced budget. "Big Mac" was unable to sell bonds for the city. Outstanding city bonds tumbled in value. (A favorite T.V. talk-show joke: offering a contestant a $1,000 New York City bond or one dollar in cash.) Banks and investors continued to refuse additional credit to the city or to "Big Mac" until the city straightened out its finances.

The real financial "crunch" came in the fall of 1975. The city was unable to borrow money, outstanding debts were falling due, and there was not enough cash to pay city employees, welfare recipients, or bondholders. The State of New York itself was also threatened with bankruptcy because banks and investors began to distrust any bonds with a "New York" label. Indeed, the entire market for municipal bonds of cities everywhere began to dry up; investors began to flee the municipal-bond markets; and cities throughout the nation were forced to pay higher interest rates to borrow money. For several hours New York City teetered on the verge of default and bankruptcy until the city's teachers union agreed to lend the city enough money from its pension fund to struggle through for a few more weeks. New York State also appeared headed for bankruptcy. Governor Hugh Carey and Mayor Abraham Beame went to Washington in a last ditch attempt to stave off bankruptcy.

Initially New York's request for federal aid was met with strong presidential opposition. Republican Gerald Ford quickly perceived a campaign issue for 1976—liberal Democratic fiscal irresponsibility leads to bankruptcy. The president threatened to veto any congressional "bail-out" of the city, and his tough stand was widely applauded in the Midwest and West. The *New York Daily News* headlined the President's stand: "FORD TO CITY: DROP DEAD."

While Ford's opposition to federal aid was politically popular, the spector of a New York City and New York State bankruptcy was an economic nightmare. It is estimated that 30 percent of all municipal bonds are from New York City or State, and the "ripple effect" of such a massive bankruptcy might lead to the fiscal collapse of many other cities throughout the nation. Over 500 banks have more than twenty percent of their reserve in New York City or State bonds, and widespread bank closings might occur with default. In a recession-weakened economy, a massive city-state bankruptcy could plunge the nation into a 1930s-style depression.

Eventually, all of the participants in New York's fiscal crisis were forced to come to an agreement. The federal government agreed to provide the city with over two billion dollars in annual revolving credit; sales taxes in the city were increased to nine percent (the highest in the nation); the banks which were holding city bonds were forced to accept delays in principal and interest payments; the city was forced to make additional budget cuts; the unions were obliged to accept additional manpower cuts and to invest some of their pension funds in New York City bonds. But New York's future is still uncertain: increased taxes and reduced services may speed the exodus of taxpaying citizens and corporations from the city, creating more financial problems in the future.

The New York City experience offers many lessons in how *not* to govern a city. There is no single culprit—there is enough blame for every one. Among the more obvious lessons:

1. State governments must find ways to assume some of the financial burdens of central cities and assure that suburbanites will pay some of the costs of concentrating social problems in the inner city.
2. City officials must be responsible in promising benefits and services to their constituents—warning that increased services involve increased taxes.
3. City officials must deal courageously with municipal unions, making it clear what the city can and cannot afford and saying "no" when it is in the public interest to do so.
4. City debt must be handled responsibly—with adequate provision for repayment. Current operating expenses should never be funded through increased debt.

Styles
of community politics

MACHINES AND BOSSES

Machine politics may be going out of style, but something resembling machine politics still exists in many large cities. Party organizations in cities tend to be better organized, more cohesive, and better disciplined than state or national party organizations. Tightly disciplined party organizations, held together and motivated by a desire for tangible benefits rather than by principle or ideology, and staffed by professional politicians, emerged in the nation's large cities early in the nineteenth century. The "machine" style of city politics has historical importance: between the Civil War and the New Deal, every big city had a machine at one time or another, thus it is sometimes easier to understand the character of city politics today by knowing what went on in years past. But a more important reason for examining the machine style of politics is to understand the style of political organization and activity that employs personal and material inducements to control behavior. These kinds of inducements will always be important in politics, and the big-city machine serves the prototype of a style of politics in which ideologies and issues are secondary and personal friendships, favors, jobs, and material rewards are primary.

Chapter nine

The political machine was essentially a large brokerage organization. It was a business organization, devoid of ideologies and issues, whose business it was to get votes and control elections by trading off social services, patronage, and petty favors to the urban masses, particularly the poor and the recent immigrants. To get the money to pay for these social services and favors, it traded off city contracts, protection, and privileges to business interests, which paid off in cash. Like other brokerage organizations, a great many middlemen came between the cash paid for a franchise for a trolley line or a construction contract and a Christmas turkey sent by the ward chairman to the Widow O'Leary. But the machine worked. It performed many important and social functions for the city.[1]

First of all, it personalized government. With keen social intuition, the machine recognized the voter as a man, generally living in a neighborhood, who had specific personal problems and wants. The machine politician avoided abstract and remote public issues or ideologies, and he concentrated instead on the personal problems and needs of his constituents. Lincoln Steffens once quoted a Boston ward leader:

> I think that there's got to be in every ward somebody that any bloke can come to—no matter what he's done—and get help. Help, you understand; none of your law and justice, but help.[2]

The machine provided individual attention and recognition. As Tammany Hall boss George Washington Plunkitt, the philosopher king of old-style machine politics, explained:

> I know every man, woman, and child in the 15th district, except them that's been born this summer—and I know some of them, too. I know what they like and what they don't like, what they are strong at and what they are weak in, and I reach them by approachin' at the right side. For instance, here's how I gather in the young men. I hear of a young feller that's proud of his voice, thinks that he can sing fine. I ask him to come around to Washington Hall and join our Glee Club. Then there's the feller that likes rowin' on the river, the young feller that makes a name as a waltzer on his block, the young feller that's handy with his dukes—I rope them all in by givin' them opportunities to show themselves off. I don't trouble them with political arguments. I just study human nature and act accordin'.[3]

The machine also performed functions of a welfare agency:

[1] See Robert K. Merton, *Social Theory and Social Structure* (Glencoe, Ill.: The Free Press, 1957), pp. 71–81.

[2] Lincoln Steffens, *Autobiography* (New York: Harcourt, Brace & World, Inc., 1931), p. 618; also cited by Merton, *Social Therapy*, p. 74.

[3] William L. Riordan, *Plunkitt of Tammany Hall* (New York: McClure, Phillips & Co., 1905), p. 46.

What tells in holdin' your grip on your district is to go right down among the poor families and help them in the different ways they need help. I've got a regular system for this. If there's a fire in Ninth, Tenth, or Eleventh Avenue, for example, any hour of the day or night, I'm usually there with some of my election district captains as soon as the fire engines. If a family is burned out I don't ask whether they are Republicans or Democrats, and I don't refer them to the Charity Organization Society, which would investigate their case in a month or two and decide they were worthy of help about the time they are dead from starvation. I just get quarters for them, buy clothes for them if their clothes were burned up, and fix them up till they get things runnin' again. It's philanthropy, but it's politics, too—mighty good politics. Who can tell how many votes one of these fires bring me? The poor are the most grateful people in the world, and let me tell you, they have more friends in their neighborhoods than the rich have in theirs.[4]

The machine also functioned as an employment agency. In the absence of government unemployment insurance or a federal employment service, patronage was an effective political tool, particularly in hard times. Not only were city jobs at the disposal of the machine, but the machine also had its business contacts:

Another thing, I can always get a job for a deservin' man. I make it a point to keep on the track of jobs, and it seldom happens that I don't have a few up my sleeve ready for use. I know every big employer in the district and in the whole city, for that matter, and they ain't in the habit of sayin' no to me when I ask them for a job.[5]

Banfield and Wilson argue effectively that it was not so much the petty favors and patronage that won votes among urban dwellers, as it was the sense of friendship and humanity that characterized the "machine" and its "boss."[6] The free turkeys and bushels of coal were really only tokens of this friendship. As Jane Addams, the famous settlement house worker, explained: "On the whole, the gifts and favors were taken quite simply as evidence of genuine loving kindness. The alderman is really elected because he is a good friend and neighbor. He is corrupt, of course, but he is not elected because he is corrupt, but rather in spite of it. His standard suits his constituents. He exemplifies and exaggerates the popular type of a good man. He has attained what his constituents secretly long for."[7]

---

[4] Ibid., p. 52.

[5] Ibid., p. 53.

[6] Edward C. Banfield and James Q. Wilson, *City Politics* (Cambridge: Harvard-M.I.T. Press, 1963), Chap. 9.

[7] Jane Addams, *Democracy and Social Ethics* (New York: 1902), p. 254; also cited by Banfield and Wilson, *City Politics*, p. 118.

The machine also played an important role in educating recent immigrants and assimilating them into American life.[8] Machine politics provided a means of upward social mobility for ethnic group members, which was not open to them in businesses or professions. City machines sometimes met immigrants at dockside and led them in groups through naturalization and voter registration procedures. Machines did not keep out people with "funny" sounding names, but instead went out of the way to put these names on ballots. Politics became a way "up" for the bright sons of Irish and Italian immigrants.

Finally, for the businessman, and particularly for public utilities and construction companies with government contracts, the machine provided the necessary franchises, rights of way, contracts, and privileges. As Lincoln Steffens wrote: "You cannot build or operate a railroad, or a street railway, gas, water, or power company, develop and operate a mine, or cut forests or timber on a large scale, or run any privileged business, without corrupting or joining in the corruption of government." [9] The machine also provided the essential protection from police interference, which is required by illicit businesses, particularly gambling. In short, the machine helped to centralize power in large cities. It could "get things done at city hall."

Political analysts frequently remark that the day of the political machine has passed and that big-city political organizations have radically altered their style of operation. Federal and state welfare agencies now provide the basic welfare services that the bosses used to provide. Large-scale immigration has stopped, and there are fewer people requiring the kinds of services once provided by the machine. Patronage jobs do not look as attractive in an affluent economy, and today civil service examinations cover most governmental jobs anyhow. The middle class was excluded from machine politics, and much of the opposition to the machine came from the middle class. As the middle class grew in American society (today white-collar workers outnumber blue-collar workers), opposition to the machine has grown in every city. Middle-class voters supported reform movements and good-government crusades, which often succeeded in replacing the machine with professional city managers, civil service, reorganized city government, and city admistrations pledged to eliminate corruption and exercise economy and efficiency in government.

Big-city party organizations continue to thrive, although in a somewhat modified form, because they continue to perform important political and social functions in their communities. In a system of "fragmented"

[8] See Elmer E. Cornwell, Jr., "Bosses, Machines, and Ethnic Groups," *Annals of the American Academy of Political and Social Science* (May, 1964), pp. 27–39.

[9] Steffens, *Autobiography*, p. 168.

government in the nation's large cities, these party organizations continue to play an important part in organizing power: that is to say, in "getting things done at city hall." A centralized, well-disciplined party organization helps to overcome the dispersion of power one finds in a normal structure of a big-city government, with its maze of authorities, boards, commissions, agencies, and separately elected officials.

Machine politics will remain with us as long as there is an unmet need to personalize the operations of government, and as long as individuals need services that the formal machinery of government cannot provide. Machine politics will remain as long as people are indifferent to issues and candidates, and can be induced to trade their vote for the small favors that the party organization can offer. And urban party organizations continue to perform important welfare duties, employment services, and petty favors. A survey of precinct politicians in a New Jersey county revealed the following list of services:

1. Help poor people to get work;
2. Help deserving people to get jobs on a highway crew, police force, or fire department or in state positions;
3. Show people how to get their social security benefits, welfare, and unemployment compensation;
4. Help citizens with problems like rent gouging, unfair labor practices, zoning, or unfair assessments;
5. Help one's precinct to get a needed traffic light, more parking space, or more policemen;
6. Run clambakes or other get-togethers for interested people even though no political campaign is involved;
7. Help people who are in difficulty with the law;
8. Help newcomers to this county to get adjusted and get places to live and work;
9. Work with some of the other party's people to reduce the friction and keep the campaign from getting too rough;
10. Help boys with military service problems with advice on the best way to serve.[10]

It is unlikely that these kinds of services will ever go out of style completely. A certain amount of machine politics will be found in every city.

THE BOSS:
RICHARD J. DALEY OF CHICAGO

Mayor Richard J. Daley of Chicago governs the city in the style of traditional politics. (When Mayor Daley himself was asked about his "ma-

[10] Richard T. Frost, "Stability and Change in Local Politics," *Public Opinion Quarterly*, 25 (Summer, 1961): 231–32.

chine," he replied, "Organization, not machine. Get that. Organization, not machine.") In Chicago, few others understand so well the labyrinths of formal and informal power, the complex structure of federal, state, and local government and public opinion, as the mayor. Daley has won election to six four-year terms as mayor of Chicago beginning in 1955. He remains the captain of his old Eleventh Ward Democratic committee, and he is chairman of the Cook County Democratic committee. He picks candidates' slates, runs the patronage machinery, and works his will on nearly all the fifty aldermen who comprise Chicago's city council. Illinois Democratic governors are usually responsive to his wishes, and Chicago's nine-member delegation to the U.S. House of Representatives also acts promptly on Daley's recommendations. The Cook County Democratic delegation to the Illinois legislature is firmly in his hands. No presidential candidate can ignore Daley's political clout, either in the Democratic National Convention or in the general election. Daley may be the most successful mayor in America, not only for his political acumen but also for his ability to manage a great metropolis.

Chicago has had bosses before. There was "Big Bill" Thompson (1915–23, 1927–31), a Republican who left a safe deposit box stuffed with $1.5 million in cash when he died. There was Democratic Ed Kelley (1933–47), who used his power mostly to throw public projects to his personal and political pal, contractor Pat Nash. Chicago has also had reform mayors; one of these was Democrat Martin Kennelley (1947–55), whose good intentions were frustrated by a lack of political judgment and who was unseated by Daley in 1955.

Daley, a Roman Catholic, was born in the impoverished Bridgeport district of Chicago near the stockyards.[11] He sold newspapers on the street as a boy and worked in the stockyards. He worked his way to clerk in the stockyards office and then went at night to the law school at DePaul University. He was appointed secretary to the city council at the age of twenty-five and has remained on the public payroll ever since. He still lives with his large family in his old city neighborhood. In 1936, when a state legislator from Daley's district died, Democratic boss Ed Kelley and ward leader Jake Arvey gave the job to Daley, who gradually worked his way up in the Kelley-Arvey machine. When Adlai Stevenson became governor of Illinois in 1949, he rewarded the Chicago machine by making Daley the state revenue director. But more important to Daley's political power, he was also made county clerk for Cook

<hr>

[11] For an excellent description of the functions of Mayor Daley's political organization in Chicago, see Edward C. Banfield, *Political Influence* (Glencoe, Ill.: The Free Press, 1961). For a hostile account of Mayor Daley by a liberal reformer, see Mike Royko, *Boss: Richard J. Daley of Chicago* (New York: E. P. Dutton & Co., Inc., 1971).

County, which placed him in charge of all the voting machinery in the county and many patronage jobs. Daley's old teacher, Boss Jake Arvey, always felt that a boss should be a "behind-the-scenes operator" and should not run for public office himself, but Daley broke with his old boss Arvey to run for mayor against a Republican reform candidate, who charged scandal and corruption in Chicago in the Democratic government. Daley replied: "If I am elected I will embrace mercy, love, charity, and walk humbly with my God." When he was elected, one commentator observed: "Chicago ain't ready for reform!" From his base in Chicago, Daley quickly made himself the unchallenged leader of Illinois Democrats. Adlai Stevenson was not a "machine" Democrat, and Daley always remained somewhat cool toward Stevenson but was a staunch supporter of Senator John F. Kennedy. Daley was a key supporter and consultant in Kennedy's race for the presidential nomination. On election day, 1960, Daley's machine in Chicago gave Kennedy a margin of 450,-000 votes, giving the crucial state of Illinois to Kennedy, who lost the rest of the state so badly that his statewide edge was only 9,000 votes.

Over his long career, Daley has suffered some defeats among his many victories. In the 1972 Democratic National Convention, Daley-led delegates were unceremoniously ousted from the convention by the dominant McGovern forces. The mayor himself was not even permitted to sit as a delegate. To add to the insult, an anti-Daley candidate, Daniel Walker, won the Illinois Democratic primary and was elected governor. (Walker had once accused Daley of fomenting a "police riot" at the turbulent 1968 Democratic Convention in Chicago; Walker blamed Daley's police, rather than the demonstrators, for the disturbances.) But Daley remained at the helm of the city of Chicago and the Cook County Democratic committee. In 1976, Daley humbled his opponents by winning a large share of the Illinois delegations to the Democratic convention, and defeating incumbent Daniel Walker in the Democratic primary for governor. With the help of the Chicago "machine," a Daley lieutenant, Michael Howlett, defeated Governor Daniel Walker in the Democratic party primary; Walker became the only incumbent governor to be knocked out in a primary election in Illinois in a half century. After twenty years, the Daley machine still appeared in good health.

In an era when successful politicians increasingly reflect the slick "Madison Avenue" image—tall, handsome, glamorous, articulate, at ease with television and press—Mayor Daley is a throwback to an earlier era of municipal politics. Daley looks like an old-time city boss—short and paunchy, with heavy jowls and deep-set eyes. He speaks with "deses" and "dems," but he is smart enough to limit his public appearances to ceremonial occasions. He is not likely to be found exchanging urbane witticisms with Johnny Carson on late-night television. His malapropisms have become legendary: "We will reach greater and greater platitudes of achievement"; "They have vilified me, they have crucified me, yes, they have even criticized me." But these characteristics seem only to endear him to his constituents.

Like other city mayors, Daley's biggest problem today is race relations. Chicago's blacks compose nearly a third of the city's population and half of the public school pupils. Daley remains close to many older black leaders whose support he has always courted, but he is not very close to younger, more militant black leaders like black comedian Dick Gregory of Chicago. Many younger blacks refer to Daley's urban renewal and slum clearance programs as "Negro removal." Many white residents of Chicago have become upset by what they consider Daley's "concessions" to blacks. Yet Daley is in the classic style of the political broker, who continues to try to arrange compromises and win support from both blacks and whites.

Even a liberal critic of Mayor Daley is forced to admit:

> Daley's municipal ambition is backed up, to use the Chicago expression, with political clout. When he wants something done, it gets done. He knows every minuscule aspect of the city, both municipally and politically, knows the balance and has the political power to handle the people who don't measure up. . . . He has managed to keep the machine viable, to bring cost accounting to the city government, to keep up with many reforms in the New Deal tradition, and in the words of one political scientist, "to make the machine a limited instrument for social progress." He has bound together this unnatural consensus at a particularly difficult time, and part of the reason comes from the consensus itself; each member of it is aware of the others and of the counterpressure on the Mayor. This acts as a restraint; they will not push too far for fear of rocking the boat. Part of the reason, too, is that Daley simply works harder than his opponents. He is at early Mass when his enemies are still sleeping, and he is still working on city problems at night when they've all gone to bed or are out drinking. He pays enormous attention to detail; he goes over every job application, to a ridiculously low level. Finally he knows more about the petty details of Chicago than almost any of his critics.[12]

As a political broker, Daley is seldom the initiator of public policy. His approach to policy questions is more like that of an arbitrator between competing interests. When political controversies develop, Daley often waits on the sidelines without committing himself, in the hope that public opinion will soon "crystallize" behind a particular course of action. Once the community is behind a project—and this determination Daley makes himself after lengthy consultations with his political

[12] David Halberstam, "Daley of Chicago," *Harper's Magazine,* August, 1968. Copyright © 1968 by Harper's Magazine, Inc. Reprinted by permission of the author and publisher.

advisers—he then awards his stamp of approval. This suggests that in policy matters many political "bosses" are not so much bosses as referees among interested individuals and groups. The boss is really "apolitical" when it comes to policy matters. He is really more concerned with resolving conflict and maintaining his position and organization than he is with the outcome of public policy decisions.

REFORMERS AND DO-GOODERS

A reform style of politics appeared in the United States shortly after the Civil War to battle the "bosses." Beginning in 1869, scathing editorials in the *New York Times* and cartoons by Thomas Nast in *Harper's Weekly* attacked the "Tammany Society" in New York City, a political organization that controlled the local Democratic organization. William M. Tweed was president of the board of supervisors of New York County, and undisputed boss of "Tammany Hall," as the New York County Democratic committee was called, after its old meeting place on Fourteenth Street. This early reform movement achieved temporary success under the brilliant leadership of Samuel J. Tilden, who succeeded in driving the "Tweed Ring" out of office and went on in 1876 to be the only presidential candidate ever to win a majority of popular votes and then be denied the presidency through the operation of the electoral college. George William Curtis, editor of *Harper's Weekly;* E. L. Godkin, editor of the *Nation,* and Senator Carl Schurz of Missouri laid the foundations for a style of reform politics that continues to have great influence in American cities.[13]

Early municipal reform is closely linked to the Progressive movement in American politics. Leaders such as Robert M. La Follette of Wisconsin, Hiram Johnson of California, Gifford Pinchot of Pennsylvania, and Charles Evans Hughes of New York backed municipal reform at the local level as well as the direct primary and direct election of senators and women's suffrage at the national level. In 1912 social worker Jane Addams, who labored in the slums and settlement houses in New York, sang "Onward Christian Soldiers" at the Progressive party convention in 1912, which nominated Teddy Roosevelt for president. Lincoln Steffens wrote in *The Shame of the Cities* ". . . St. Louis exemplified boodle; Minneapolis, police graft; Pittsburgh, a political industrial machine; and Philadelphia (the worst city in the country), general civic corruption."[14]

[13] See Richard J. Hofstadter, *The Age of Reform* (New York: Alfred A. Knopf, Inc., 1955); and Lorin Peterson, *The Day of the Mugwump* (New York: Random House, Inc., 1961).

[14] Lincoln Steffens, *The Shame of the Cities* (Sagamore Press, 1957), p. 10.

The National Municipal League was formed in 1900 by representatives of reform citizens' associations throughout the country.

From its beginning, reform politics was strongly supported by the native upper-class, Anglo-Saxon Protestant, longtime residents of cities whose political ethos was very different from that which the new immigrants brought with them. The immigrant, the machine that relied upon his vote, and the businessman who relied upon the machine for street railway and other utility franchises had formed an alliance in the nineteenth century, which had displaced the native, old family, Yankee elite that had traditionally dominated northern cities. This upper-class elite fought to recapture control of local government through the municipal reform movement.

Richard Hofstadter described the social, ideological, and political clash between the new immigrants and the Anglo-Saxon Protestant, upper class in the *Age of Reform:*

> Out of the clash between the needs of the immigrants and the sentiments of the natives, there emerged two thoroughly different systems of political ethics . . . one, founded upon the indigenous yankee-Protestant political traditions, and upon middle class life, assumed and demanded the constant, disinterested activity of the citizen in public affairs, argued that political life ought to be run to a greater degree than it was in accordance to general principles, abstract laws, apart from the superior to personal needs. . . . The other system, founded upon the European background of the immigrants, upon their unfamiliarity with independent political action, their familiarity with hierarchy and authority, and upon the urgent needs that so often grew out of their migration, took for granted that the political life of the individual would arise out of family needs, interpreted political and civic relations, chiefly in terms of personal obligations, and placed strong personal loyalties above allegiance to abstract codes of law or morals.[15]

This conflict can still be observed today in American politics. Machine politicians cater to ethnic groups, organized labor, blue-collar workers ("hardhats"), and other white working-class elements of the city. The reform politician appeals to the upper- and middle-class affluent American who is well educated and public service-minded. Reform is popular among liberals, television and newspaper reporters, college professors, and others who consider themselves "intellectuals." It is no coincidence that Mayor Daley of Chicago was born of Irish immigrant parents, while reform Mayor John Lindsay of New York was a wealthy WASP and a scion of one of the city's oldest families.

Reform politics includes a belief that there is a "public interest" that

[15] Hofstadter, *The Age of Reform* (New York: Knopf, 1955), p. 9.

should prevail over competing, partial interests in a city. The idea of balancing competing interests or compromising public policy is not part of the reformers' view of political life. Rather, the reform ethos includes a belief that there is a "right" and "moral" answer to public questions. Conflict and indeed even "politics" is viewed as distasteful. Since reasonable men can agree upon the public interest, municipal government is really a technical and administrative problem rather than a political one. City government should be placed in the hands of those who are best qualified, by training, ability and devotion to public service, to manage public business. These best-qualified men can decide on policy and then leave a separate activity of administration to professional experts. Any interference by special interests in the policies or administration of the best-qualified people would be viewed as corruption.

The objectives of the early reform movement were:

1. The elimination of corruption in public office, and the recruitment of "good men" (educated, upper-income men who were successful in private business or professions) to replace "politicians" (men who were no more successful than their constituents in private life and who were dependent upon public office for their principal source of income).
2. The provision of means by which party machinery could be bypassed in nominations and elections. This meant nomination by petition, and the initiative, recall, and referendum. (Reformers were not really sure about the necessity of this item; it was left to local option in the model city charter.)
3. The reorganization of local government to eliminate many separately elected offices (the "short-ballot" movement) in order to simplify the voter's task and focus responsibility for the conduct of public affairs on a small number of top elected officials.
4. The strengthening of executive leadership in city government—longer terms for mayors, subordination of departments and commissions to a chief executive, and an executive budget combined with modern financial practices.
5. The establishment of "at-large" city-wide constituencies in municipal elections in lieu of "ward" constituencies in order to insure that an elected official would consider the welfare of the entire city in public decision making and not merely his own neighborhood or "ward."
6. The replacement of patronage appointments with the merit system of civil service.
7. The separation of local politics from state and national politics by home rule charters and the holding of local elections at times when there were no state and national elections.
8. The elimination of parties from local politics by nonpartisan elections. (The effect of nonpartisanship is described below in more detail.)
9. The establishment of the council-manager form of government, and the separation of "politics" from the "business" of municipal government.

All these objectives are interrelated. Ideally, a "reformed city" would be one with a council-manager form of government, nonpartisan election for mayor and council, a home rule charter, a short ballot, at-large constituencies, a modern budgeting and financial system, a civil service personnel system, initiative, recall and referendum system, and "good men" at the helm. Later, the reform movement added comprehensive city planning to its list of objectives—official planning agencies with professional planners authorized to prepare a master plan of future development for the city. The National Municipal League incorporated its program of reform into a *Model City Charter*, which continues to be the standard manual of municipal reform.[16] There is reason to believe that the early reformers also opposed immigration (which was very logical, of course, since the immigrant was the backbone of machine politics). Many persons active in municipal reform at the time also supported the passage of the Immigration Act of 1921, reducing immigration to a trickle and establishing quotas heavily weighted in favor of Anglo-Saxon Protestant immigrants and against southern and eastern European Catholic immigrants.[17]

Today reform movements assume a variety of forms.[18] There is, first of all, the "enlightened businessmen's association," which operates outside formal governmental or party structures as a voluntary association, often with paid staffs and researchers. Members of these associations scrutinize local government structure, programs, and expenditures and recommend changes and reforms. Ordinarily, they do not endorse candidates,

---

[16] National Municipal League, *Model City Charter* (Chicago: National Municipal League, 1961).

[17] Andrew D. White, first president of Cornell University, summarized early reform thinking when he wrote in 1890:

What is this evil theory? It is simply that the city is a political body; that its interior affairs have to do with national political parties and issues. My fundamental contention is that a city is a corporation; that as a city it has nothing whatever to do with general political interests; that party political names and duties are utterly out of place there. The questions in a city are not political questions. They have reference to the laying out of streets; to the erection of buildings; to sanitary arrangements, sewerage, water supply, gas supply, electrical supply; to the control of franchises and the like; to provisions for the public health and comfort in parks, boulevards, libraries, and museums. The work of a city being the creation and control of the city property, it should logically be managed as a piece of property by those who have created it, or a real substantial part in it, and who can therefore feel strongly their duty to it. Under our theory that a city is a political body, a crowd of illiterate peasants, freshly raked in from Irish bogs, or Bohemian mines, or Italian robber nests, may exercise virtual control.

Andrew D. White, "The Government of American Cities," in *Forum* (1890); reprinted in Edward C. Banfield, *Urban Government: A Reader in Administration and Politics* (Glencoe, Ill.: The Free Press, 1961).

[18] James Q. Wilson, *The Amateur Democrat* (Chicago: University of Chicago Press, 1963).

participate in election campaigns, or take sides in controversial policy questions. These business and citizens' associations claim to provide "objective" information about taxes, expenditures, services, and administration. This information generally stresses the need for economy and efficiency, lower taxes, or streamlined administration. "Enlightened businessmen" are generally moderate on urban social issues—more liberal than white working-class voters, but more conservative than other reform groups.

A second type of reform movement is the voter education association, which also operates outside the political parties and reviews or evaluates candidates for public office. The League of Women Voters is probably the largest organization of this kind. These organizations are probably more effective in nonpartisan cities or cities in which party organizations are weak than in cities with strong two-party systems. These associations also avoid direct political endorsements, but they are moderately liberal on most policy questions and strongly supportive of a variety of "reforms."

Occasionally, reform movements assume the form of an independent local party. Reform parties, however, usually do not last very long. Since they are committed to "reform," they are prevented by their principles from offering jobs or other material enticements to maintain the continued disciplined support of their party workers. They must rely upon social and ideological rewards, and their supporters often grow tired of these intangible satisfactions. The Liberal party of New York provides an interesting contrast. The Liberal party has had considerable success at the polls and has operated successfully over many years.

Most reform movements are factions operating within existing party organizations, particularly the Democratic party. A reform faction may coalesce around a "blue-ribbon" candidate, usually a man of high social class, high professional achievement, and devotion to public service. He may come from a distinguished old family or be a wealthy and successful businessman with a record of statesmanlike participation in public affairs, and although a loyal party member, he may have no personal identification with local machines or professional politicians. Politics permits him to indulge his fancy for public service and do-goodism.

The prevailing philosophy of the modern reformer is liberal and public regarding. It is a philosophy of *noblesse oblige*—the righteous man's responsibility for the welfare of the poor and downtrodden, particularly the blacks. It is not the broad mass of increasingly affluent white working-class Americans that elicits the reformer's sympathies, but only the most deprived segments of society—the poor, the blacks, the slum dwellers, the sick, the criminal defendants, and so forth. The reformer defies simplistic Marxian interpretations of American politics. Wealth, education, sophistication, and upper-class culture values do *not* foster attitudes of exploitation, but rather attitudes of public service and do-goodism. Reformers are frequently paternalistic toward segments of the masses they define as "underprivileged," "culturally deprived," "disadvantaged," and so forth, but they are not hostile toward them. Indeed, hostility toward such groups as blacks, welfare recipients, and criminal defendants is more characteristic of white working-class masses than it is of upper-class reformers.

Political divisions in American cities do not always take the form of upper classes versus lower classes. Increasingly in urban politics, one finds upper-class liberal reformers allied with certain minority segments of the lower classes, notably blacks, in opposition to white middle-class and working-class masses. Democratic reformers in municipal politics are generally liberal Democrats in national politics, while Republican reformers are frequently supporters of the progressive wing of that party.

Reformers are generally amateurs in politics, in contrast to the professional politicians who constitute the regular party organizations. The "amateur" is more motivated by the ideological and psychological rewards of mixing in government and public affairs; in contrast, the "professional" is interested in tangible rewards—jobs, contracts, public offices. Amateurs are concerned with the great issues facing the nation—war, racism, pollution, poverty. They do not deal with the personal problems confronting individuals, but rather with the broad social problems confronting groups or classes. Reformers view government as an instrument for achieving broad social reforms, and not merely as a source of jobs, buildings and civic improvements, or upward social mobility for gifted individuals from the lower classes. The politics of reform is frequently more ideological than pragmatic. Appeals are made to lofty principles rather than material welfare. All of this, of course, is in direct contrast to the machine style of politics.

Today's reformers differ from earlier reformers in several respects. First of all, they place greater emphasis on the reform of party machinery at all levels of government, rather than the elimination of parties from municipal government. Second, most reformers no longer want to separate national elections from local or state elections; instead, they want local and state politics to become more issue-oriented. Finally, concern for the conditions of blacks in America has led many reformers to reassess their traditional views on government organization and the political participation of the lower classes. Whereas early reformers wanted to discourage lower-class political participation (when white, ethnic, recent immigrants constituted the bulk of the urban lower class), today liberal reformers are attempting to build a coalition with urban blacks. To do so they must encourage black political participation, and this involves structural changes that promote voter turnout and facilitate black access to public office. Reformers are now rethinking their support for "at-large" elections, which frequently dilute black representation on city councils, and reconsidering their insistence on merit systems of appointment, which frequently restrict black access to public employment. Thus reformers, as well as bosses, change over time.

THE FUTURE STYLE OF CITY POLiTICS

Boss Plunkitt once observed that "reform administrations never succeed themselves." Plunkitt realized that the emotional fervor of reform could arouse the public to "throw the rascals out" in moments of righteous concern, but he was confident that, in the long run, organization politics, with its reliance upon personal and material rewards, could outlast the emotional appeal of reform. Reform administrations, he felt, would come and go, but the machine would remain to govern the city with only occasional interruptions. Yet these interruptions occurred with increased frequency in the twentieth century. The machine style of politics still exists, but it has declined noticeably in recent years. City government is vastly more honest, efficient, and democratic than it was a generation ago.

Several factors are generally cited as contributing to the decline of machine politics:

1. The *decline in immigration* and the gradual assimilation of white ethnic groups—Irish, Italians, Germans, Poles, Slavs;
2. Federal *social welfare programs,* which undercut the machine's role in welfare work—unemployment insurance, workmen's compensation, social security, and public assistance have ended the party's monopoly of welfare services;
3. Rising *levels of prosperity* and higher educational levels, which make the traditional rewards of the machine less attractive;
4. The *spread of middle-class values* about honesty, efficiency, and good government, which inhibit party organizations in purchases, contracts, and vote buying, and other cruder forms of municipal corruption. The more successful machines today, like Daley's in Chicago, have had to reform themselves to maintain a good public image;
5. *Structural reforms* such as nonpartisanship, better voting procedures, city-manager government, and—most important of all—civil service which have weakened the party's role in municipal elections and administration.

Patronage was once very useful in maintaining a party organization, attracting voters, financing the party, insuring favorable government actions for party requests, and maintaining discipline within the party's ranks, yet Frank Sorauf has commented on the declining usefulness of patronage in an era of economic prosperity and high levels of employment: "Viewed by most Americans as a short-term desperation job alternative, the patronage position has lost considerable value as a political incentive."[19] Sorauf also notes that patronage runs contrary to the prevailing values of the growing middle class in America: "Patronage is also losing its respectability. Its ethic—the naked political quid pro quo— no longer seems to many a natural and reasonable ingredient in politics . . . the mores of the middle class and image of civil virtue instilled by public education extolled the unfettered, independent voter, rather than the patronage seeking party liner."[20]

But political scientists may have underestimated the continuing usefulness of patronage by defining it only in terms of jobs. If we define *patronage* to include a wide range of tangible benefits—construction contracts, insurance policies, printing and office supplies, architectural services, and other government contracts for goods or services, then patronage may still be important in many communities. Competitive bidding by potential government contractors is required in most states and cities, but it is not difficult to "rig" the process. The fact that the firms that do much of their business with government are also the largest contributors to political campaigns cannot be coincidence. Another source of patronage is the power of courts to appoint referees, appraisers, receivers in bankruptcies, and trustees and executors of estates; these plums require little work and produce high fees for attorneys who are "well-connected." Few cities have ever been able to remove zoning from politics: rezoning property from lower-value classifications (single-family residential) to higher-value classifications (apartments, commercial, industrial) is one of the most important "goodies" available to municipal governments. In addition, municipal construction permits, inspection, and licensing can be slow and cumbersome, or fast and painless, depending on the political resources of the builder-developer.[21]

Something resembling "machine" politics—party organizations held together and motivated by a desire for tangible benefits rather than principle or ideology—continues to thrive in many cities and rural counties. Most machines may not be as centralized, disciplined, or powerful as in a previous era, but as long as the need to personalize government exists

[19] Frank J. Sorauf, "State Patronage in a Rural County," *American Political Science Review*, 50 (1956): 1046–56.

[20] Ibid., p. 1055.

[21] See also Raymond E. Wolfinger, "Why Political Machines Have Not Withered Away and Other Revisionist Thoughts," *Journal of Politics*, 34 (May, 1972): 365–98.

—as long as individuals value small favors, appreciate personal intervention on their behalf with government agencies, need assistance in finding their way around city halls and county court houses, and require help in filing for benefits, obtaining bonds, registering complaints, dealing with the bureaucratic demands of government—political machines will still have a role to play.

NONPARTISANSHIP

The nonpartisan ballot was the most widely adopted reform ever put forward to curb the machines and insure an "antiseptic," "no party" style of politics. Nearly two-thirds of America's cities use the nonpartisan ballot to elect local officials. Reformers felt that nonpartisanship would take the "politics" out of local government and raise the caliber of candidates for elected offices. They believed that nonpartisanship would restrict local campaigning to local issues and thereby rule out extraneous state issues from local elections. They also believed that by eliminating party labels, local campaigns would emphasize the qualifications of the individual candidates rather than their party affiliations.

Nonpartisanship is found in large as well as small cities. Party labels have been removed from local elections in Detroit, Los Angeles, Denver, Dallas, Houston, Boston, Cincinnati, Cleveland, Milwaukee, San Francisco, Seattle, San Antonio, and San Diego. Nonpartisanship is even more widespread than council-manager government. However, there is a tendency for these two forms to be related: 82 percent of all council-manager cities have nonpartisan ballots, while only 49 percent of all mayor-council cities are nonpartisan. (See Table 9–1.)

Party politics is still the prevailing style of local elections in Eastern cities: 76 percent of Eastern cities have partisan elections and only 24 percent have nonpartisan elections. But elsewhere in the nation nonpartisanship prevails: 74 percent of Central cities, 78 percent of Southern cities, and 94 percent of Western cities are nonpartisan. While nonpartisan cities are found in both one-party and two-party states, there is some tendency for competitive two-party states to have a smaller percentage of nonpartisan cities than one-party Democratic or Republican states. Table 9–2, by Phillips Cutright, shows that 56 percent of the cities in competitive states have nonpartisan ballots, compared with 74 percent of the cities in Democratic states and 86 percent of the cities in Republican states. The nonpartisan ballot is also more likely to be adopted in homogeneous middle-class cities, where there is less social cleavage and smaller proportions of working-class and ethnic group members.

TABLE 9.1   Nonpartisanship in American Cities

	Number of Cities Reporting	Percent Partisan	Percent Nonpartisan
All Cities	2,880	35	65
Form of Government			
Mayor-council	1,387	51	49
Commission	174	30	70
Council-manager	1,229	18	82
Population			
Over 500,000	26	42	58
250,000-500,000	25	24	76
100,000-250,000	90	41	59
50,000-100,000	208	32	68
25,000- 50,000	427	33	67
10,000- 25,000	1,057	34	66
5,000- 10,000	1,049	37	63
Region			
East	767	76	24
Central	901	26	74
South	768	22	78
West	444	6	94

SOURCE: International Manager's Association, *Municipal Yearbook, 1968* (Chicago: I.C.M.A., 1968), p. 58.

Cutright reports that there is a tendency for cities with large Catholic populations to retain the partisan ballot; there is also a tendency for cities with heavy factory employment to prefer partisan over nonpartisan elections.[22] However, Cutright's findings are subject to many exceptions: Cleveland, Detroit, and Boston are located in competitive party states and have large working-class populations, large Catholic populations, and deep social cleavages—yet they are officially nonpartisan cities.

To what extent has nonpartisanship succeeded in removing "politics" from local government? Of course, if "politics" is defined as conflict over public policy, then "politics" has certainly not disappeared with the elimination of party labels. There is no evidence that eliminating party ballots can reduce the level of community conflict. If we define "politics" to mean "partisanship," that is, *party* politics, then nonpartisanship may have removed some party influences from local government, although the evidence is by no means clear on this point.

Apparently several types of political systems can be found in non-

[22] Phillips Cutright, "Nonpartison Electoral Systems in American Cities," *Comparative Studies in Society and History* (January, 1963): pp. 212–26.

TABLE 9.2   State Party Systems, Community Cleavage, and Nonpartisanship

State party system	Percent nonpartisan	Number of cities[2]
Competitive states[1]	56	280
Democratic states	74	115
Republican states	86	85
Total	65	480
Religious composition[3]		
High Catholic	56	225
Low Catholic	73	255
Manufacturing levels		
High manufacturing employment	56	218
Low manufacturing employment	73	262

[1]Competitive States: California, Colorado, Connecticut, Delaware, Illinois, Indiana, Kentucky, Massachusetts, Idaho, Michigan, Maryland, Montana, Missouri, New Mexico, New York, Nevada, Ohio, Pennsylvania, Vermont, Washington, West Virginia, Wyoming.

[2]All incorporated cities with 25,000 inhabitants in 1950.

[3]From U.S. Department of Commerce, *Religious Bodies,* 1936 (Washington, D.C.: Government Printing Office, 1941); 1.

SOURCE: Adapted from figures presented in Phillips Cutright, "Nonpartisan Electoral Systems in American Cities," *Comparative Studies in Society and History* (January, 1963).

partisan cities.[23] First of all, in some nonpartisan cities, parties continue to operate effectively behind the scenes in local affairs. Another type of nonpartisan political system is one in which the major parties are inactive, but other formal organizations function very much like parties. Frequently these organizations are civic organizations led by newspapers or business firms. Occasionally liberal or labor groups arise to challenge middle-class civic associations. These organizations may "slate" candidates, manage their campaigns, and even exercise some influence over them while they are in office. These organizations are not usually as permanent as parties, but they may operate as clearly identifiable political entities over a number of years.[24] A third type of nonpartisan political

23 The following discussion relies upon Charles Adrian, "A Typology of Non-Partisan Elections," *Western Political Quarterly,* 12 (June, 1959): 449–58; see also Banfield and Wilson, *City Politics,* Chap. 12.

24 J. Lieper Freeman, "Local Party Systems: Theoretical Considerations and a Case Analysis," *American Journal of Sociology,* 64 (1958). Oliver P. Williams and Charles R. Adrian, "The Insulation of Local Politics under the Non-Partisan Ballot," *American Political Science Review,* 53 (1959): 1052–63. Robert Salisbury and Gordon Black, "Class and Party in Partisan and Non-Partisan Elections," *American Political Science Review,* 57 (September, 1963): 587–97.

system is one in which the Democratic and Republican parties play no role at all and in which there are no local parties or slate-making associations. This is the most common type of nonpartisanship in small cities. Individual candidates select themselves, collect their own money, and create their own temporary campaign organizations. Voting does not correlate highly with party identification, but instead tends to follow a "friends and neighbors" pattern, rather than socioeconomic or partisan lines.

Does nonpartisanship increase Republican influence in city government? It is sometimes argued that the removal of party designations from local elections hurts Democrats by disengaging their traditional support from urban voters—the low-income, labor, ethnic, and black groups that traditionally vote the Democratic ticket. Moreover, the well-educated, high-income groups and interests that are normally Republican have a natural edge in organization, communication, and prestige in the absence of parties. Republicans also have better turnout records in nonpartisan elections.[25] All of this may help to explain why many cities that are heavily Democratic in state and national elections elect mayors and councilmen who are somewhat more conservative. Eugene Lee found that the decline in voter turnout in local (nonpartisan) elections, in contrast to national (partisan) elections, is greatest in Democratic precincts and least in Republican precincts.[26] Williams and Adrian conclude: "A nonpartisan election leads to an increased voice in local affairs for persons who normally vote Republican." [27] Surveys of local officials elected under partisan and nonpartisan systems confirm that nonpartisanship results in the election of more Republicans.[28]

Does nonpartisanship result in "better-qualified" candidates winning public office? Of course, the answer to this question depends upon one's definition of better qualified. Nonpartisanship does result in more high-income, "respectable," older, white, Anglo-Saxon Protestants, with prestige jobs, running for public office.[29] Working-class candidates are disadvantaged by nonpartisanship for several reasons. First of all, as we have already observed, nonpartisanship reduces the turnout of labor, low-income, ethnic, Democratic voters and, consequently, increases the influence of well-educated, high-income, white, Anglo-Saxon Protestant

[25] See Charles E. Gilbert, "Some Aspects of Nonpartisan Elections in Large Cities," *Midwest Journal of Political Science*, 6 (November, 1962): 346–54.

[26] Eugene C. Lee, *Nonpartisan Politics* (Berkeley: University of California Press, 1960).

[27] Williams and Adrian, "The Insulation of Local Politics," p. 1063.

[28] Chester B. Rodgers and Harold D. Arman, "Nonpartisanship and Election to City Office," *Social Science Quarterly*, 51 (March, 1971): 941–45.

[29] Ibid.

Republican voters who continue to come to the polls in nonpartisan elections. In addition, nonpartisanship means the recruitment of candidates will be left to civic associations, or ad hoc groups of one kind or another, rather than Democratic or Republican party organizations. This difference in recruitment and endorsement practices tends to give an advantage to middle-class candidates. Candidates from the lower classes are rarely put forward and endorsed by newspapers and influential civic associations. They seldom receive the kind of public attention in private life that would make their names well known enough to place on a ballot, nor do they have the organizational ties or memberships that would bring them to the attention of civic associations that are recruiting in nonpartisan elections. In contrast, in partisan big-city politics, being a member of a working class, ethnic, or minority group may be a positive advantage. Parties traditionally try to "balance the ticket" with candidates who represent various groups in rough proportion to their voting strength. This practice of having a balanced party ticket with Irish, Italian, Polish, Jewish, and black names on the ballot is thought to add strength to the entire party ticket, since voters will be asked to vote for the party ticket rather than for the individual candidates. Eugene C. Lee reports that the "typical" nonpartisan councilman is a registered Republican, forty-five to fifty years old, who has a professional, managerial, or sales occupation and lives in the "better part of town." [30] He is likely to be a Protestant, a Mason, a member of the chamber of commerce, and a member of a veterans' group, and to have lived in the city for a long time, and to have made his mark in the Community Chest, the Red Cross, or some other civic or welfare association. Of course, there are exceptions to this generalization about nonpartisan candidates. Certainly, in nonpartisan Boston, one is more likely to encounter Irish or Italian Democrats on the city council than Yankee Republicans.

Nonpartisanship contributes to the re-election of incumbent councilmen, particularly when nonpartisanship is combined with at-large elections.[31] Incumbents are more likely to have a name that is known to the voters. Incumbent councilmen in partisan cities are not re-elected as often as incumbents in nonpartisan cities. Moreover, incumbent councilmen running at-large in the city were more likely to be re-elected than incumbent councilmen running from districts. This suggests that it is difficult to hold public officials accountable in a nonpartisan election. The voter does not have the opportunity to hear organized criticisms of in-

[30] Lee, *Nonpartisan Politics*, p. 170.
[31] Charles E. Gilbert and Christopher Clague, "Electoral Participation and Electoral Systems in Large Cities," *Journal of Politics*, 24 (1962): 323–30; James B. Jamison, "Some Social and Political Correlates of Incumbency in Municipal Elections," *Social Science Quarterly*, 51 (March, 1971): 946–52.

cumbent officeholders from an opposition party. When the only challenge to an incumbent officeholder is an unknown name on the ballot, he is more likely to be re-elected than if he is challenged by a candidate backed by an opposition party. The higher rates of re-election in nonpartisan systems suggest that accountability is harder to achieve where party labels are absent.

REFORMISM AND PUBLIC POLICY

What are the policy consequences of reform government? Other things being equal, do reform cities pursue significantly different policies than unreformed cities? Traditionally, political scientists assumed that the reform of city government would bring about changes in public policy. Reform was expected to result in better public services, lower tax rates, more efficient cost-benefits ratios, and more professional administration. But *assumptions* regarding the impact of structural changes on public policy are not a substitute for *systematic investigation* of the actual linkages between political structures and public policies. It is not an easy task to sort out the *independent* effects of reform on public policy from the effects of other urban environmental characteristics that are associated with reform—smaller size, Midwest and Western regions, less ethnicity, more middle-class residents. Urban environmental conditions such as population density, income, occupational structure, poverty, mobility, and property value are *more* influential than the structure of government in determining levels of taxing and spending.[32] However, despite the overriding importance of social and economic conditions in shaping municipal policy, the structure of government—reformed versus unreformed—does have *some* interesting effects on public policy.

There is some evidence, for example, that urban renewal policies may be affected by manager versus mayor government. Political scientist George S. Duggar reports that mayor cities were quicker to respond to the lure of federal money than manager cities and got a faster start on their urban renewal programs.[33] This finding would testify to the political awareness of mayors. On the other hand, Duggar reports that once urban renewal programs were begun, manager cities experienced slightly greater program achievement than mayor cities. Duggan admits that population size is a *more* influential variable in urban renewal achievement than

---

[32] See Chester B. Rogers, *"Environment, System and Social Forces,"* 48 (September, 1969): 72–87.

[33] George S. Duggar, "The Relation of Local Government Structure to Urban Renewal," *Law and Contemporary Problems* (Winter, 1961): 55–65.

governmental structure: greater achievement is associated with greater size. He concludes, however, that governmental structure does have *some* independent effect on urban renewal policies.

The structure of city governments has been found to be related to outcomes in water fluoridation battles. In comparative studies of several hundred cities, sociologists Robert L. Crain and Donald B. Rosenthal found that fluoridation has a better chance of consideration and adoption in cities having a strong executive (a manager or a strong partisan mayor) and a relatively low level of direct citizen participation.[34] Broad popular participation, particularly in the absence of strong executive leadership, frequently spelled defeat for fluoridation. In both mayor and manager cities, partisan electoral systems are marked by the largest proportion of adoptions of fluoridation laws by city councils.

Perhaps the most important systematic study of the policy consequences of reformism is a comprehensive analysis of taxing and spending policies in two hundred American cities with populations of fifty thousand or more by political scientists Robert L. Lineberry and Edmund P. Fowler. They found that reformed cities tended to tax and spend *less* than unreformed cities.[35] Cities with manager governments and at-large council constituencies were *less* willing to spend money for public purposes than cities with mayor-council governments and ward constituencies. (Cities with partisan elections, however, did not actually spend any more than cities with nonpartisan elections.) In short, reformism *does* save tax money.

Lineberry and Fowler also found that environmental variables had an important impact on tax and spending policies. For example, they concluded that:

1. The more middle class the city, measured by income, education, and occupation, the lower the general tax and spending levels.
2. The greater the home ownership in a city, the lower the tax and spending levels.
3. The larger the percentage of religious and ethnic minorities in the population, the higher the city's taxes and expenditures.

What turned out to be an even more important finding in the Lineberry and Fowler study was the difference in *responsiveness* of the two

[34] Robert L. Crain and Donald B. Rosenthal, "Structure and Values in Local Political Systems: The Case of Fluoridation Decisions," *Journal of Politics*, 28 (February, 1966): 169–95.

[35] Robert L. Lineberry and Edmund P. Fowler, "Reformism and Public Policy in American Cities," *American Political Science Review*, 61 (September, 1967): 701–16.

kinds of city governments—reformed and unreformed—to the socioeconomic composition of their populations. Reformed cities (cities with
manager governments, at-large constituencies, and nonpartisan elections)
appeared to be unresponsive in their tax and spending policies to differences in income and educational, occupational, religious, and ethnic
characteristics of their populations. In contrast, unreformed cities (cities
with mayor-council governments, ward constituencies, and partisan elections) reflected class, racial, and religious composition in their taxing
and spending decisions. As Table 9–3 shows, the strength of the correlation between environment and taxing and spending is greater among
unreformed than reformed cities.

**TABLE 9.3   Environmental Characteristics and Tax and Spending Policy in Reformed
and Unreformed Cities**

Relationship between	Correlation between Environmental Characteristics and Taxing and Spending	
	Unreformed Cities	Reformed Cities
TAXES and		
Ethnicity	.62	.34
Private school attendance	.40	.25
Home ownership	−.70	−.44
Education	−.55	−.13
EXPENDITURES and		
Ethnicity	.51	.05
Private school attendance	.46	.08
Home ownership	−.67	−.38
Education	−.49	−.37

SOURCE: Adapted from figures in Robert L. Lineberry and Edmund P. Fowler,
"Reformism and Public Policy in American Cities," *American Political Science Review*, 61
(September, 1967), 701-16.

Reformism tends to reduce the importance of class, home ownership, ethnicity, and religion in city politics. It tends to minimize the role
that social conflicts play in public decision making. In contrast, mayor-
council governments, ward constituencies, and partisan elections permit
social cleavages to be reflected in city politics and public policy to be
responsive to socioeconomic factors. These findings suggest that reformed
cities have gone a long way toward accomplishing the reformist goal—
that is, "to immunize city governments from 'artificial' social cleavages—
race, religion, ethnicity, and so on." Thus, political institutions seem to
play an important role in policy formation.

. . . a role substantially independent of a city's demography. . . . Nonpartisan elections, at-large constituencies, and manager governments are associated with a lessened responsiveness of cities to the enduring conflicts of political life.[36]

In short, reformism makes city governments less responsive to citizens' needs.

The assertion that reformism lessens the responsiveness of city governments was reinforced by an interesting study of the responses of cities to civil-rights-group activity. Political scientist Albert K. Karnig measured the strength of civil rights groups—the National Association for the Advancement of Colored People (NAACP), the National Urban League, the Congress of Racial Equality (CORE), and the Southern Christian Leadership Conference (SCLC)—in 417 cities.[37] He correlated the strength of these organizations with policies generally associated with the needs of poor and black people—low-rent housing, model cities, community-action programs, and neighborhood youth-corp programs. In general, he found the presence of civil rights organizations were related to increased community efforts in these areas. More importantly, however, he found that *reformed governments were less responsive* to civil rights groups in these policy areas than unreformed governments. The associations between civil-rights-group activity and policies favoring the poor and the black were *lower* in cities with nonpartisan elections, manager governments, and at-large elections. This evidence suggests that blacks and other urban minorities have little to gain through reformism.

[36] Ibid., p. 715.

[37] Albert K. Karnig, "Private Regarding Policy, Civil Right Groups, and the Mediating Impact of Municipal Returns," *American Journal of Political Science*, 19 (February, 1975): 91–106.

Participation in community politics

VOTERS IN MUNICIPAL ELECTIONS

The influence of the voter is felt not only on election day but on every day that elected officials act to win his support or avoid his displeasure.

Voter turnout in local elections is substantially lower than in state or national elections. While 55 to 65 percent of the nation's eligible voters can be expected to cast ballots in a presidential election, voter turnouts of 25 to 50 percent are all that can be expected in local elections, even in the nation's largest cities.

Nonpartisanship depresses voter turnout quite substantially. The *Municipal Yearbook* reports that the median voter turnout for partisan cities was 50 percent, while the median voter turnout for nonpartisan cities was only 30 percent. (See Table 10–1.) Partisan campaigns heighten voter turnout, in part because of the greater interest they generate and in part because of the role of party workers in getting out the vote. The difference in voter turnout in partisan and nonpartisan local elections is an important comment on the role of parties in stimulating political participation.

Voter participation in local government can be further reduced by holding municipal elections at odd times of the year when no other state

Chapter ten

TABLE 10.1   Governmental Structure and Voter Turnout in Municipal Elections

	All City Elections	MEAN PERCENTAGE OF ADULTS VOTING Elections Held Concurrently with State or National Elections	Elections Held Independently of Other Elections
Form of election			
Partisan	50	51	41
Nonpartisan	30	43	27
Form of government			
Mayor-council	50	51	44
Commission	38	33	38
Council-manager	27	43	23
Population			
Over 500,000	39	57	20
250,000 to 500,000	37	56	34
100,000 to 250,000	32	50	29
50,000 to 100,000	33	51	29
25,000 to 50,000	33	47	29
All cities over 25,000	33	50	29

SOURCE: *Municipal Yearbook, 1963,* p. 83.

or national elections are being held. A common rationale for holding municipal elections at times other than state or national elections is to separate local issues from state or national questions, but the real effect of scheduling local elections independently is to reduce further voter turnout and to increase the influence of middle-class groups, which vote regularly.

Voter turnout in municipal elections is greater in large than in small cities. Voter turnout in cities with a mayor-council form of government is much higher than in cities with a council-manager plan. In summary, nonpartisanship, council-manager government, and separate municipal elections—all part of the municipal "reform" movement—operate to reduce voter turnout and probably strengthen the influence of middle-class voters at the polls.

Voter turnout in municipal elections is also affected by the social character of cities. We know that *individuals* who are less well educated, less wealthy, more ethnic, and more mobile, vote less often than *individuals* who are educated, wealthy, upper- or middle-class longtime residents of cities. An important study by Alford and Lee, however, reveals that *cities* with larger proportions of poorly educated, ethnic, and mobile populations have *higher* voter turnouts than *cities* with well-educated, middle-class, stable populations. (See Table 10–2.) This apparent paradox is explained as follows:

TABLE 10.2   Socioeconomic Characteristics of Cities and Voter Turnout in Municipal Elections

	MEAN PERCENTAGE OF REGISTRANTS VOTING *(Cities with Nonconcurrent Municipal Elections)*				
	All Cities	East	Midwest	South	West
Ethnicity					
High	51	64	48	53	40
Low	44	—	49	42	43
Education					
High	44	56	45	41	41
Low	52	69	53	45	39
Mobility					
High	42	52	41	43	41
Low	54	67	53	43	41
Age of city					
Old	51	66	52	42	48
Young	43	60	43	43	39
All cities	47	64	48	43	41

SOURCE: Figures reported by Robert R. Alford and Eugene C. Lee, "Voting Turnout in American Cities," *American Political Science Review,* 62 (September, 1968): 796-813.

Voting turnout is higher, not lower, in cities with less well educated populations, perhaps because in those cities political cleavages based on economic interests are more explicit and visible than in middle-class suburbs or other communities likely to have high proportions of college-educated persons. Cities with more stable populations also have higher levels of voting turnout, possibly because of the greater likelihood of integration of the different elements of social and political structure.[1]

In summary, voter turnout in municipal elections can be described as follows:

[1] Robert R. Alford and Eugene C. Lee, "Voting Turnout in American Cities," *American Political Science Review,* 62 (September, 1968): 810.

Low voter turnout is expected with:	*High voter turnout is expected with:*
Nonpartisan electoral systems	Partisan elections with competitive parties
Council-manager form of government	Strong mayor form of government
City elections held separately from state or national elections	City elections held concurrently with state and national elections
Small or middle-sized cities	Large cities
Middle-class, homogeneous cities	Ethnic, heterogeneous cities
Midwestern, western, and southern cities	Eastern cities

EMERGING COALITIONS:
HARDHATS VERSUS LIBERALS AND BLACKS

As we know from Chapter 3, *party voting* is related to income, occupation, education, religion, race, and ethnic origin. Sample surveys and election studies at the state and national levels demonstrate repeatedly that the Republican party draws its voter strength from high-income, well-educated, white-collar, Anglo-Saxon Protestant, and suburban and small-town residents; and in contrast, the Democratic party draws its strength from low-income, poorly educated, blue-collar, black, Catholic, Jewish, and ethnic populations living in larger cities. There is reason to believe that these socioeconomic divisions are influential in partisan elections at the local level as well. Of course, the "class" theory of voting in American politics is subject to many important exceptions. At the national level, there are large numbers of voters whose socioeconomic backgrounds would indicate a tendency to vote the Democratic party, who regularly vote Republican; and vice versa. For this reason, we can only state that lower socioeconomic groups "tend to" vote Democratic, that "by and large" they support Democratic candidates, and that "on the whole" they prefer the Democratic ticket. (See Table 10–3.)

The nation's large, central cities tend to be Democratic, while their suburbs are normally Republican.[2] However, the growing racial problem in the nation's central cities poses a challenge to the Democratic party's winning urban coalition. Working-class whites in large cities may increasingly resent the liberal posture of the national Democratic leadership on such issues as busing, ghetto violence, and street crime. These issues, however, are more likely to cause splits *within* the Democratic party, and

[2] See Oliver P. Williams, Harold Herman, Charles S. Liebman, and Thomas R. Dye, *Suburban Differences and Metropolitan Policies* (Philadelphia: University of Pennsylvania Press, 1964).

it is doubtful that the GOP can make any permanent inroads into Democratic control of the nation's large cities.

The relationships between class and party voting, however, seem to vary according to the size of the city. V. O. Key, in *Public Opinion and American Democracy*, reports that blue-collar and white-collar workers differ more over policy questions in large metropolitan areas than in smaller cities.[3] In smaller cities, the blue-collar workers tended to adopt attitudes similar to those of the white-collar workers, which suggests that class cleavages are not as important in smaller cities as in large metropolitan areas, and hence Democratic and Republican voting is less likely to correlate with socioeconomic class position.[4]

Emerging coalitions between upper-class liberal whites allied with ghetto blacks, in opposition to working-class home-owning whites, can be observed in elections and referenda voting in many large cities. *Referenda voting* is an important aspect of local politics—an aspect not found at the national level. City charters frequently require that referenda be held on all proposals to increase indebtedness or to increase property taxation. These referenda votes provide us with an excellent opportunity to examine the factors influencing voter attitudes toward local government and to test some theories about voting behavior on local issues.

One theory is that a voter in local referenda will try to maximize his family income by weighing the benefits that will come to him from a bond issue against the amount of the tax that will fall on him as a result of the expenditure.[5] Nonproperty owners, having nothing to lose by the expenditure and something to gain, however small, can be expected to favor the passage of bond and expenditure referenda. (Renters seldom realize that landlords will pass the tax increase on to them in higher rent.) Property owners should be far less willing to favor municipal expenditure proposals. Wilson and Banfield examined returns on thirty-five expenditure proposals, voted in twenty separate elections in seven cities, and their findings give strong support to the theory that property owners and nonproperty owners differ consistently over municipal expenditure proposals. The voters in nonhomeowning districts almost invariably supported all expenditure proposals. (See Table 10–3.) Homeowners show a greater distaste for public expenditures that are financed from property taxes than nonhomeowners.

[3] V. O. Key, Jr., *Public Opinion and American Democracy* (New York: Alfred A. Knopf, Inc., 1961), pp. 116–18.

[4] See also Edward C. Banfield and James Q. Wilson, *City Politics* (Cambridge: Harvard-M.I.T. Press, 1963), Chap. 16.

[5] The following discussion of voter behavior on referenda relies heavily upon James Q. Wilson and Edward C. Banfield, "Public Regardingness as a Value Premise in Voting Behavior," *American Political Science Review*, 58 (December, 1964): 876–87.

TABLE 10.3   Referenda Voting Behavior of Four Major Economic Groups, Cook County, Illinois

Group	PERCENT "YES" VOTE	
	County hospital	Welfare hospital
High income homeowners		
Winnetka	64	76
Wilmette	55	70
Lincolnwood	47	64
Middle income homeowners		
Lansing	30	54
Bellwood	21	55
Brookfield	22	51
Middle income renters		
Chicago ward 44	65	71
Chicago ward 48	61	72
Chicago ward 49	64	74
Low income renters		
Chicago ward 2	88	73
Chicago ward 3	87	76
Chicago ward 27	87	78

SOURCE: James Q. Wilson and Edward C. Banfield, "Public Regardingness as a Value Premise in Voting Behavior," *American Political Science Review,* 58 (December, 1964): 878.

Up to this point, the Wilson and Banfield findings tend to support the theory that voters in municipal referenda act rationally in pursuit of their own economic self-interest. However, Wilson and Banfield came up with some very interesting, contrasting findings when they examined the voting behavior of large and small property owners. One might suppose that the more property a voter has, the less likely he is to favor public expenditures that increase his tax rate, since the more property he owns, the higher his tax bill. The owner of a $50,000 home, for example, probably gets no more benefit from a new city zoo than does the owner of a $10,000 one, yet his share of the tax increase is five times as much. Moreover, since many municipal health and welfare facilities will probably never be used by high-income families, these families have added reason to oppose such facilities if they are acting solely on behalf of their own economic self-interest. However, these expectations are *not* borne out by the voting returns. Wilson and Banfield found that the *higher* the family income and value of their property, the *greater* the support for public expenditures in municipal referenda: that is, higher-income groups and the owners of more valuable property can usually be counted upon to support rather than oppose public expenditures—in contrast to lower-income families and owners of less valuable property.

Banfield and Wilson offer an explanation: support for public expenditures is a function of a liberal, "public-regarding" ethic, which is rooted in upper- and middle-class values. Banfield and Wilson argue effectively that "public-regardingness," in contrast to "private-regardingness," is part of the middle-class, white, Anglo-Saxon Protestant subculture in America. The public-regarding voter has a conception of the public interest which inspires him to support measures that benefit the whole community, whether or not they produce specific rewards for himself. In contrast, private-regarding voters—lower-income, working-class, Irish, Italian, Polish and other eastern European, white voters—tend .to vote against public expenditures that do not directly benefit them. Blacks are much more likely to support public expenditures than low-income whites; both black renters and homeowners are more favorable to all proposals than white ethnic voters, although black homeowners are somewhat less enthusiastic than black renters. Jews tend to support public expenditures as much as upper-income Anglo-Saxon homeowners. Wilson and Banfield summarize their public-regardingness theory as follows:

> Each subcultural group, we think, has a more or less distinctive notion of how much a citizen ought to sacrifice for the sake of the community, as well as of what the welfare of the community has constituted; in a word, each has its own idea of what justice requires and of the importance of acting justly. According to this hypothesis, the voter is presumed to act rationally; the ends he seeks are not always verily self interested ones, however. On the contrary, depending upon his income and ethnic status they are more or less public-regarded.[6]

Whether one accepts Banfield and Wilson's "public-regardingness" explanation or not,[7] their findings are important: (1) nonhomeowners give greater support to proposals for public spending than homeowners; (2) among homeowners, wealthy families support public expenditures more than middle- or low-income families; (3) white Anglo-Saxon Protestants, blacks, and Jews tend to support public expenditures more than Irish, Italian, Polish, or other eastern European ethnic voters.

The emerging coalition between affluent, educated, upper-class whites and ghetto blacks may turn out to be an important force in urban

[6] Wilson and Banfield, "Public Regardingness," p. 885.

[7] This explanation is disputed in Raymond E. Wolfinger and John Field, "Political Ethos and the Structure of City Government," *American Political Science Review*, 60 (June, 1966): 306–26; and Roger Durand, "Ethnicity, Public-Regardingness and Referenda Voting," *Midwest Journal of Political Science*, 16 (May, 1972): 259–68.

politics in the coming decade. Working-class ethnic whites see themselves increasingly threatened by both blacks and white liberals on the issues of busing, welfare, crime, and violence.

THE RECRUITMENT OF
COUNCILMEN AND COMMISSIONERS

The typical councilman or county commissioner is a local businessman who is respected in his community and active in civic organizations. He is more likely to be a small businessman with many contacts among his constituents—retail merchants, real estate brokers, insurance agents, and so on; seldom do executives of large corporations concern themselves with local affairs, although they may encourage lower management personnel to do so. In other words, councilmen are recruited from lower-middle-class groups in a community and not from the community's leading men in industry or finance. Councilmen serve because of the prestige it gives them or because of the free advertising and public contacts for their businesses. With the exception of a few very large cities, the pay of councilmen is very nominal. The councilman's job is a part-time one; it is a "community service," which he undertakes in addition to his occupation or business.

City councils in larger cities may be quite different from councils in smaller cities. First of all, they are likely to have more members; moreover, members are more likely to be elected by wards rather than at-large. Since the pay is higher and the opportunity for political advancement is greater in a large city council, one is more likely to find lawyers and professional politicians on these councils than on the councils of smaller cities. Since there is more conflict in larger communities, there is more likelihood of open disputes and divided votes at council meetings. In contrast, council meetings in smaller communities are likely to be very dull affairs, with most decisions being made unanimously. Any disagreement or factionalism is not likely to be expressed openly at council meetings but is resolved prior to an official meeting through consultation and discussion.

The composition of a council will generally reflect the composition of the community itself. In communities with well-educated, affluent residents, councilmen may come from upper-middle-class backgrounds; whereas in predominantly working-class communities, councilmen may be independent contractors or store owners or even blue-collar workers.[8] Typically, councilmen are attorneys, realtors, engineers, insurance brokers,

---

[8] See Bryan T. Downes, "Municipal Social Rank and the Characteristics of Local Political Leaders," *Midwest Journal of Political Science,* 12 (November, 1968): 514–37.

sales managers, professors or high school teachers, salesmen, and proprietors of local businesses.

A majority of American cities elect their councilmen in nonpartisan elections in "at-large" (city-wide) districts. This reflects the success of the reform movement (described in Chapter 9) and the widespread acceptance of the idea of nonpartisanship in municipal government (described in this chapter). Most city councilmen are elected for four-year terms. Specifically, 50 percent of all cities elect their councilmen for four-year terms; 10 percent for three-year terms; and 38 percent for two-year terms. The terms of councilmen overlap in 66 percent of American cities; in these cities only a portion of the council seats are filled in any particular election. Presumably, overlapping terms insure continuity in the deliberations of the council.

At-large districts are designed to promote a city-wide approach to municipal problems among councilmen. Table 10–4 reveals that 59 percent of American cities elect their councilmen at-large, 25 percent by wards, and 14 percent by a combination of at-large and ward constituencies. Reformers believe that ward constituencies encourage parochial views, neighborhood interests, "log-rolling," and other characteristics of "ward politics." These "undesirable" characteristics occur because councilmen are responsible to local majorities in the particular sections or wards

TABLE 10.4   At-Large and Ward Elections for City Council

	Number of Cities	PERCENTAGE OF COUNCIL ELECTIONS			
		At-Large	Wards	Combination	Other
All Cities	2,823	59	25	14	3
Form of Government					
Mayor-Council	1,378	44	32	21	3
Commission	165	85	12	0	3
Council-Manager	1,207	70	20	8	2
Population					
Over 500,000	26	35	31	31	3
250,000 to 500,000	26	58	19	23	0
100,000 to 250,000	89	53	28	17	2
50,000 to 100,000	211	50	26	22	2
25,000 to 50,000	402	60	24	13	3
10,000 to 25,000	1,031	60	26	11	3
5,000 to 10,000	1,038	83	10	6	1

SOURCE: *Municipal Yearbook, 1968,* p. 59.

from which they are elected. In contrast, councilmen elected at-large are responsible to city-wide majorities; this should encourage impartial, cosmopolitan, and community-wide attitudes. Moreover, in council-manager cities, it is argued that the manager can be more effective in serving the "general good" of the whole community if he is responsible to councilmen elected at-large rather than by wards. (Seventy percent of manager cities elect councilmen at-large, compared to only 44 percent of mayor-council cities.) Occasionally, it is even argued that at-large elections result in the selection of "better men" for the council, although recent research suggests that there are no significant differences in the social status, occupations, or experience of councilmen elected at-large and by wards.[9]

Blacks and other minorities may be disadvantaged by at-large elections. Commenting on reformed cities, Banfield and Wilson note the dilemma faced by black councilmen facing re-election in an at-large system:

> Without a strong Negro vote he cannot hope to be re-elected, and to get a strong Negro vote he must . . . be aggressive on at least some racial issues. But he must also have the support of the press and the civil associations in order to be re-elected, and he will not have this unless he is "reasonable" from the standpoint of conservative, middle-class whites.[10]

On the basis of this analysis, it appears that minority groups, especially blacks, are generally better represented in a partisan ward system of elections. Given the prevalence of residential segregation, this system seems to assure genuine black representation. But it is difficult to document the charge that at-large elections invariably discriminate against blacks. A study of blacks elected to city councils in New Jersey revealed that half were elected in at-large systems and 70 percent were elected in constituencies where blacks were in a minority.[11] Perhaps at-large elections discriminate against blacks only in those cities where racial conflict is prevalent and voting along racial lines is common. Sociologist Lee Sloan writes that "if black Americans today were to seek governmental reform in local politics, they could perhaps do worse than ask for a repeal of certain institutional arrangements established and defended in the name of good government."[12]

[9] John Rehfus, "Are At-Large Elections Best for Council-Manager Cities?" *National Civic Review* (May, 1972): pp. 236–41.

[10] Edward C. Banfield and James Q. Wilson, *City Politics* (Cambridge, Mass.: Harvard University Press-MIT Press, 1963), p. 308.

[11] Leonard A. Cole, "Electing Blacks to Municipal Office: Structural and Social Determinants," *Urban Affairs Quarterly*, 10 (September, 1974): 17–39.

[12] Lee F. Sloan, "Good Government and the Politics of Race," *Social Problems*, 17 (Fall, 1969): 161–75.

A surprising number of councilmen are initially *appointed* to their office to fill unexpired terms of resigning councilmen. Kenneth Prewitt reports that 24 percent of 435 councilmen interviewed in eighty-seven West Coast cities were initially appointed to office. Those appointed were likely to be personal friends of councilmen or likely to have held some other city job. Finally, 80 percent of incumbents running for re-election are successful. Voluntary retirement is the most common exit from community politics. Prewitt observes that "the election system provides advantages to those citizens who already have social and political resources; to those favorably located in the network of friendships which play such an important part in city politics; to those whose apprentice roles identify them as likely candidates for political office; to those who have natural organizational ties and support; and, finally, to those already in office if they chose to stand for re-election." [13]

ARE COUNCILMEN RESPONSIBLE POLICY MAKERS?

According to orthodox theory about city government, the city council is supposed to "make policy" for the city. But, of course, the actual policy-making role of councilmen varies a great deal from city to city. Councilmen have more formal power in commission or weak mayor form of government, where the council itself sometimes appoints officials, prepares the budget, supervises departments, and performs other administrative tasks. But in other cities—particularly strong mayor or manager cities—the council merely oversees city affairs. In these cities, the function of the council may be principally the representation of the interests of local constituents—forwarding complaints, making inquiries, pushing for new sidewalks or streetlights, and so forth. This may be particularly true in a ward system.[14]

Contrary to orthodox theory, Adrian found that councilmen do *not* serve as either general policy innovators or general policy leaders. When councilmen do take a stand on public issues, they are more likely to oppose a proposal than to support one. Adrian describes a typical response of the council to a community problem, as follows:

[13] Kenneth Prewitt, *The Recruitment of Political Leaders: A Study of Citizen-Politicians* (Indianapolis: The Bobbs-Merrill Co., Inc., 1970), p. 148.

[14] Williams and Adrian report one ward councilman's speech at a Michigan city council meeting as follows: "You bastard, you had three more blocks of black-topping in your ward last year than I had, you'll not get another vote from me until I get three extra blocks." Oliver P. Williams and Charles Adrian, *Four Cities* (Philadelphia: University of Pennsylvania Press, 1963), p. 264.

When the bus companies came to the councils from time to time asking for fare increases, each councilman would deplore the trend toward higher fares and poorer service, but since the only discernible alternative to refusing the rate increase was a discontinuance of service, almost all councilmen voted in favor of the request. In each of the cities, study committees of lay citizens were appointed to seek solutions to the bus problem. . . . In each case, the council gratefully, and with little discussion, accepted the proposed solutions.[15]

Adrian concludes that the role of the council is one of a largely passive body, granting or withholding its approval in the name of the community, when presented with proposals from a leadership outside of itself. The outside leadership consists of a manager, city departments, the planning commission, citizen groups, or private enterprise.[16]

Many councilmen have little interest in a political career and serve out of a sense of public service (frequently at considerable personal expense in time and energy). "Volunteerism" is widespread in American cities;[17] It is probably most prevalent in suburban middle-class communities. Volunteers see their service as a sacrifice, and they are relatively immune from direct constituency pressure. Threats to oust them at the next election have little meaning. Only insofar as they tend to have the attitudes and characteristics of their constituents can they be said to be "representative." Constituents cannot really hold volunteers accountable by threatening them with defeat at the next election. "I don't really give a damn whether I am re-elected or not" is a common response.[18] Moreover, the attitude of "volunteerism" results in councils that are "(a) more likely to vote against what they see as majority opinion; (b) less likely to feel under pressure from the public; (c) less likely to consider the upcoming election when choosing among policy alternatives; (d) less likely to facilitate group access to the council, and (e) less likely to perform services to constituents."[19]

The problem of political accountability in local politics, then, is aggravated by several factors:

1. *The frequency of appointment to elected office.* It is probable that as many as one-quarter of the nation's councilmen initially came into

---

[15] Adrian, "Leadership and Decision-Making," p. 212.

[16] Of course, councilmen themselves are not likely to agree that their role is a passive one. They like to think of themselves as policy innovators—men of vision and leadership—who follow their own convictions in public affairs regardless of what others want them to do. See Downes, "Municipal Social Rank."

[17] See Kenneth Prewitt, "Political Ambitions, Volunteerism, and Electoral Accountability," *American Political Science Review*, 64 (March, 1970): 5–17.

[18] Ibid., p. 7.

[19] Ibid., p. 11.

office by appointment rather than election. They are appointed, usually by the mayor, to fill unexpired terms.

2. *The effective constituency is very small.* Given the low turnout in municipal elections, and the small constituencies served by a councilman, only a very few votes are required to elect a man to office. (One estimate is that only 810 votes are required to elect an average councilman in a city of 13,000.) A councilman's personal friends, immediate neighbors, business associates, fellow church members, and acquaintances at the Rotary Club may be enough to get him elected.

3. *The infrequency of electoral defeat.* Incumbents running for re-election are hardly ever defeated. It is estimated that 80 percent of incumbent councilmen running for re-election are returned to office.[20] (When they are defeated, it is frequently in groups, when several incumbents are turned out of office at once owing to a specific community controversy.) Councilmen are not likely to be preoccupied with voter preferences.

4. *The frequency of voluntary retirement from elected office.* (The vast majority of councilmen voluntarily retire from office, over half of them after two terms.) Officeholders simply conclude that the obligations of office exceed the rewards.

All these factors, together with the attitude of volunteerism, tend to remove municipal government from direct citizen control. We are reminded of Schlesinger's warning: "No more irresponsible government is imaginable than one of high-minded men unconcerned for their political futures."[21]

CITY COUNCILS AND PUBLIC POLICY

Despite this evidence of a lack of electoral accountability in local politics, some factors may compel councilmen to reflect the will of their constituents in policy making. First of all, volunteerism may be less prevalent in large cities with competitive, partisan elections. We know that big-city councilmen are more likely to be attorneys and professional politicians, to aspire to higher office, and to spend more time on city affairs; we might infer from this that they would be more directly concerned with their constituents' views.

Secondly, we know that councilmen tend to reflect, in their own socioeconomic background, the characteristics of their constituents. This does not *insure* that councilmen share the same attitudes as their constituents on all matters; indeed, the experience of being a public official

[20] John J. Kirlin, "Electoral Conflict and Democracy in American Cities," *Journal of Politics*, 37 (February, 1975): 262–69.

[21] Joseph A. Schlesinger, *Ambition and Politics* (Chicago: Rand McNally & Co., 1966), p. 2.

itself can help to shape a councilman's views and give him a different perspective on public affairs than his constituents. But if councilmen have deep roots in their communities (many social contacts and group memberships; shared socioeconomic, ethnic, racial, and religious characteristics with their constituents), they may reflect these in their policy making, whether they are consciously aware of these "constituency influences" or not. The effects of shared community life may be very influential in shaping decision making in small, homogeneous communities where uniformity of outlook may amount to compulsion. In short, although "electoral accountability" may have little direct influence over councilmen, "belief sharing" may still assure some congruence between the views of community residents and the views of their councilmen.[22]

There are strong relationships between a community's socioeconomic environment, the perceptions and attitudes of its councilmen, and the public policies that are adopted. Perhaps the most comprehensive study of city councils is the Stanford University City Council Research Project —a study, directed by Heinz Eulau, of eighty-seven councils and nearly 500 councilmen in San Francisco Bay region.[23] The summary volume, *The Labyrinths of Democracy*, systematically identifies relationships between community needs and resources; the goals, perceptions, and policy positions of councilmen; and public expenditures for planning and amenities.[24] The researchers find that the policy "maps" of city councilmen (their perceptions of conditions and goals for the future) were in accord with public-spending patterns. They conclude:

> It has been the burden of our argument that the systematic study of public policy cannot be content with correlating indicators of environmental challenges or indicators of resources capability to policy outcomes. Rather, it is our *assumption* that policy development is greatly

---

[22] See David R. Morgan, "Political Linkage and Public Policy: Attitudinal Congruence Between Citizens and Officials," *Western Political Quarterly* (June, 1973): 209–23.

[23] Heinz Eulau and Kenneth Prewitt, *The Labyrinths of Democracy* (Indianapolis: The Bobbs-Merrill Co., Inc., 1973). Other volumes include Robert Eyestone, *The Threads of Public Policy* (Indianapolis: The Bobbs-Merrill Co., Inc., 1971); Kenneth Prewitt, *The Recruitment of Political Leaders* (Indianapolis: The Bobbs-Merrill Co., Inc., 1970); Betty Zisk, *Local Interest Politics: A One-Way Street* (Indianapolis: The Bobbs-Merrill Co., Inc., 1973) and numerous articles.

[24] Unfortunately, these two areas of public spending amounted to less than 25 percent of city spending and accounted for less than half of the "important" problems perceived by councilmen. Thus, the test of these relationships is somewhat flawed. The work is also difficult to understand because of the authors' use of obscure terms and elaborate classification schemes which do not fit well with the data. See Judith V. May, "Urban Legislators and Public Policy," a review essay in *Urban Affairs Quarterly*, 10 (June, 1975): 487–96.

influenced by the predictions, preferences, orientations, and expectations of policymakers—in short, by the political process itself. [Italics mine] [25]

Note that the idea of councilmen *independently* directing the course of public policy is merely an "assumption." Of course, councilmen's ideologies are associated with policy outcomes, but both councilmen's ideologies and policy outcomes are also associated with the social and economic conditions in cities. There is no convincing attempt to sort out the *independent* effect of councilmen's ideologies on public policy from the effect of socioeconomic conditions. However, in a separate volume from the same study, *The Threads of Public Policy*, Robert Eyestone places aggregate measures of councilmen's views on "zoning problems," "development problems," and "amenities problems" in a comparative perspective [26] with population density, property value, city size, and growth rate, to see which of these factors has the greatest impact on city spending. The results seem to undermine much of the emphasis placed on a councilman's independent role in policy making: "For all (cities), population density is overwhelmingly the best predictor." Indeed, *population density* alone explained 72 percent of variation among cities in spending for "amenities," with councilmen's attitudes contributing nothing of statistical significance in explaining these expenditures. *Growth rate* explained 72 percent of the variation in core cities in "planning" expenditures; only in some suburbs did councilmen's attitudes independently affect planning expenditures.

In short, relationships between community environment, councilmen's attitudes, and public policy undoubtedly exist. But councilmen's attitudes seldom stray far from the constraints placed upon them by their communities' populations, needs, and resources.

CITY MANAGERS IN MUNICIPAL POLITICS

When council-manager government was first introduced as part of the municipal reform movement, managers were expressly admonished not to participate in community "politics." Early supporters of manager government believed in the separation of "politics" from "administration." [27] Politics, not only partisanship but policy making as well, should be the exclusive domain of the elected city council. The manager was hired by the council to carry out its policy directives, and the manager could be

---

[25] Heinz Eulau and Robert Eyestone, "Policy Maps of City Councils and Policy Outcomes," *American Political Science Review*, 62 (March, 1968): 143.

[26] Statistically speaking, a multiple regression problem.

[27] Leonard D. White, *The City Manager* (Chicago: University of Chicago Press, 1927).

removed by the council by majority vote at any time. This belief in the separation of policy making from administration was intended to produce "nonpolitical," efficient, and economical government, which middle-class supporters of the reform movement valued so highly. Popular control of government was to be guaranteed by making the manager's tenure completely dependent upon the will of the elected council.

But after a few years of experience with manager government in America, it became increasingly apparent to the managers themselves that they could not escape responsibility for policy recommendations. It turned out to be very difficult in practice to separate policy making from administration. The first code of ethics of the International City Managers Association (ICMA) stated flatly that "no manager should take an active part in politics." Managers agreed that they should stay out of partisan politics and election campaigns, but there was a great deal of debate about the role of managers in community policy making. In 1938, the ICMA revised its code of ethics to recognize the positive role of managers in policy leadership.[28]

Today we are likely to find varying role orientations among city managers. Some see themselves as "policy managers," providing community leadership through their recommendations to their councils on a wide variety of matters. Others see themselves as "administrative managers," restricting themselves to the supervision of the municipal bureaucracy and avoiding innovative policy recommendations, particularly in controversial areas. In the Stanford City Council Research Project, both types of managers were found:

> Political types believe the manager should innovate and lead on policy matters. Further, they endorse direct participation on issues of community conflict and controversy, drawing back only on the question of political campaigning for city councilmen. In contrast, administrative types take a much more limited view of the manager's policy role. Ambivalent about innovation and leadership on policy matters, these managers readily reject involvement in community politics. Administrative managers prefer, in short, a neutral definition of the policy role.[29]

Probably a majority of professionally trained city managers today see themselves as "policy managers." Better-educated managers who have had experience in different cities and who aspire to move to larger cities and assume greater responsibilities are unlikely to settle for a restricted, ad-

[28] See Harold A. Stone, Don K. Price, and Kathryn H. Stone, *City Manager Government in the United States* (Chicago: Public Administration Service, 1940).

[29] Robert O. Loveridge, *City Managers in Legislative Politics* (Indianapolis: The Bobbs-Merrill Co., Inc., 1971), p. 110.

ministrative, role.[30] However, managers without professional training in city administration, or those with engineering degrees, who have lived most of their lives in their own communities and who expect to remain there, may be more likely to accept a fairly narrow administrative role.[31]

While most managers see themselves as policy leaders, most councilmen see managers in their traditional role of administrators.[32] This means that a prudent manager will not wish to *appear* to be a policy maker even when he is. He seeks to have others present his policy proposals to the community, and he avoids the brasher methods of policy promotion. Like any successful politician, he tries to avoid taking public stands on the more controversial issues facing the community. His dependence upon the council for his job prevents him from being too extreme in policy promotion. Managers can push their councils, but they can seldom fight them with any success. Open disputes between the manager and his council are usually resolved by the dismissal of the manager. Managers who assume strong policy-leadership roles have shorter tenures than those who do not. As Adrian explained:

> There appeared to be a psychological advantage to the manager if he could place himself in the position of defending a policy developed by these individuals or groups. He would take a strong stand, but would use protective coloration of saying, "Professional planners tell me. . . ." He would, in other words, take a public position of *leadership* in policy matters, but preferred to attribute policy *innovation* to technical experts or citizens' groups.[33]

Yet, even though managers were providing leadership for their communities, they went to great pains to avoid the public appearance of being the tail that wags the dog—that is, the appearance of making policy for the city council rather than merely executing it.

Nonetheless, the manager is the most important policy initiator in most council-manager cities. Most managers determine the agenda for city council meetings.[34] This permits them to determine the kinds of issues to be raised and the policy options to be considered. The council may not accept everything recommended by the manager, but the manager's recommendations will be given serious consideration. The city manager is

[30] Ibid.

[31] See Timothy A. Almy, "Local-Cosmopolitanism and U.S. City Managers," *Urban Affairs Quarterly*, 10 (March, 1975): 243–77.

[32] Loveridge, *City Managers* Chapters 4 and 8.

[33] Charles R. Adrian, "Leadership and Decision-Making in Manager Cities," *Public Administration Review*, 18 (Summer, 1958): 210.

[34] Deil S. Wright, "The City Manager as a Development Administrator," in *Comparative Urban Research*, edited by Robert T. Daland (Beverly Hills, Calif.: Sage, 1969), p. 219.

the major source of information for most councilmen. The manager prepares the city budget; writes formal reports on city problems, defining the problems and proposing solutions; and advises and educates the council privately as well as publicly.

Thus, managers really have two important roles in community politics: administration and policy making. The administrative role involves the supervision of the municipal bureaucracy; this role requires administrative skills and technical expertise. Managers themselves report that they obtain more personal satisfaction from this role than from any other.[35] The manager directs his personal staff, develops and controls the city budget, and appoints and removes department heads. In most council-manager cities, managers try to guard these powers from direct council interference; these powers are the managers' most important formal resources.

What kind of managers do mayors and councilmen want? Doubtlessly, some mayors and councilmen want to retain a larger policy role for themselves and resent a manager who wants to run the show. These elected officials might try to recruit "administrative managers" by avoiding applicants with forceful personalities, high professional qualifications, and experience in other cities. But we have already suggested that many councilmen are "volunteers" who prefer a passive role in policy making—approving or disapproving proposals brought before them by the manager and others. A weak manager can lengthen council meetings and significantly increase the council's workload. So we should not be surprised to find many, if not most, councilmen welcoming policy leadership from the manager (so long as the manager avoids the appearance of dominating the council). Indeed, one study indicates that a majority of councilmen "expect the manager to take the lead" in budget decisions, hiring and firing personnel, reorganization of city departments, wage and salary negotiations, community improvements, and cooperative proposals with other communities. Only in planning and zoning do councilmen say they want to retain leadership.[36] Presumably these councilmen would try to recruit well-educated, professionally trained, experienced, and mobile managers to their community. However, past manager-council relations in a community may affect recruitment. Some communities may undergo cycles in council-manager relations: a council resentful of a strong manager replaces him with a weak one, only to find that their workload increases, decisions are postponed, complaints of inaction accumulate; and the council decides to find a new, strong manager.

---

[35] *Ibid.*, p. 236.

[36] Alan L. Saltzstein, "City Managers and City Councils: Perceptions of the Division of Authority," *Western Political Quarterly*, 27 (June, 1974): 275–87.

Today, most city managers are professionals who have been trained in university graduate programs in public administration. They are familiar with budgeting and fiscal administration, public personnel management, municipal law, and planning. They tend to move from city to city as they advance in their professional careers. They may begin their careers as a staff assistant to a city official and then move to assistant city manager, then manager of a small town, and later perhaps of a larger city. About three-quarters of all city manager appointments are made from outside the city, and only about one-quarter are local residents, which indicates the professionalism of city management. The turnover rate among the nation's city managers is about 7.5 percent per year. The average tenure of managers who resigned or were removed from office has been about five years.[37]

MAYORS

Today, more than ever before, the nation's cities need forceful, imaginative leadership. The nation's major domestic problems—race relations, poverty, slum housing, violence, transportation, poor schools, fiscal crisis—are concentrated in cities. Mayors are in the "hot seat" of American politics; they must deal directly with these pressing issues. No other elected official in the American federal system must deal face-to-face, eyeball-to-eyeball, with these problems in quite the same fashion as mayors. Next to the presidency, the office of mayor in a big city may be the most challenging job in American politics. In one of his more harried moments, President Lyndon B. Johnson is reported to have said, "Things could be worse, I could be a mayor." [38]

The challenges facing big-city mayors are enormous; however, their powers to deal with these challenges are restricted on every side. Executive power in major cities is often fragmented among a variety of elected officials—city treasurer, city clerk, city comptroller, district attorney, and so on. The mayor may also be required to share power over municipal affairs with county officials. Many city agencies and functions are outside the mayor's formal authority: independent boards and commissions often govern important city departments—for example, the board of education, board of health, zoning appeals board, planning commission, civil service board, library board, park commission, sewage and water board, and so on. Even if the mayor is permitted to appoint the members of the boards and commissions, they are often appointed for a fixed term, and the mayor

[37] *Municipal Yearbook, 1963*, p. 519.
[38] *Newsweek*, March 13, 1967, p. 38.

cannot remove them. The mayor's power over the affairs of the city may also be affected by the many public authorities and special district governments operating within the city, including the public housing authority, urban renewal authority, community action agency (poverty program), sewage and water authority, a mass transit authority, port authority, and so on. Traditionally, school districts have been outside the authority of the mayor or city government. The mayor's powers over city finances may even be restricted—he may share budget-making powers with a board of estimate, and powers over expenditures with an elected comptroller or treasurer. Civil service regulations and independent civil service boards can greatly hamper the mayor's control over his own bureaucrats. The activities of federal and state agencies in his city are largely beyond his control.[39]

Of course, the method of selecting the mayor also influences his powers over city affairs. Nearly a quarter of the nation's mayors are not directly elected by the people of their cities. (See Table 10–5.) These

TABLE 10.5   Term of Office of Mayors in Cities Over 5,000

Form of Government	Percent of Reporting Cities			
	One Year	Two Years	Three Years	Four Years
Mayor-council	2.9	54.2	1.0	41.7
Commission	3.9	19.3	6.4	67.0
Council-manager	21.3	54.6	2.3	24.0
All cities	10.3	51.4	2.0	35.9[1]

[1] An additional 3 percent of reporting cities have five or six year terms for mayors.

SOURCE: *Municipal Yearbook, 1966,* p. 92.

mayors are selected by their city councils or commissions and generally have little more power than other councilmen or commissioners. Their job is generally ceremonial: they crown beauty queens, dedicate parks, lay cornerstones, and lead parades. Mayors may be elected for anything from one to six years, but the two-year and four-year terms are most common in American cities.

The mayor's legislative powers also vary widely. Of course, in all cities he has the right to submit messages to the council and to recom-

[39] Few people realize how hamstrung a mayor may be in dealing with urban problems. For a close-up account of a mayor's problems by the mayor of Milwaukee, see Henry W. Maier, *Challenge to the Cities* (Random House, Inc., 1966).

mend policy. These recommendations will carry whatever prestige the mayor possesses in the community. In cities where the mayor is chosen by the council, he almost always has voting power equal to that of other council members, and more than one-quarter of the mayors who are elected directly have the power to cast a vote on all issues coming before the council. Most mayors preside over meetings of the city council, and this gives them an opportunity to cast votes in case of a tie. Less than one-fifth of the nation's mayors have no voting powers at all on city councils. The veto power over municipal ordinances is another source of legislative strength for the mayor. However, over one-half of the directly elected mayors have no veto power; one-fifth may veto only selected items (usually appropriations). Only one-fifth of the nation's mayors have full veto powers over their councils. Mayors in mayor-council governments are more likely to have veto powers than mayors in commission or council-manager cities. (See Table 10–6.)

TABLE 10.6   Method of Selection and Voting Powers of Mayors in Cities Over 5,000

Form of Government	PERCENT OF REPORTING CITIES WHERE MAYOR IS			PERCENT OF DIRECTLY ELECTED MAYOR VOTING		
	Directly elected	Selected by council	Councilman with highest vote	On all issues	In case of tie	No voting power
Mayor-council	96.6	3.4	0	16.3	58.7	25.0
Commission	77.5	21.2	0.7	92.0	7.0	1.0
Council-manager	50.1	49.1	1.3	54.1	41.3	4.6
All cities	74.5	24.9	0.6	31.7	50.7	17.6

SOURCE: *Municipal Yearbook, 1968,* p. 55.

Another distinction between "strong mayors" and "weak mayors" is made on the basis of their powers of administration. The weak mayor has very limited appointing powers and even more limited removing powers. He has little control over separately elected boards and commissions or separately elected offices, such as clerk, treasurer, tax assessor, comptroller, and attorney. The council, rather than the mayor, often appoints the key administrative officers. No single individual has the complete responsibility for law enforcement or coordinating city administration.

In summary, a mayor's ability to provide strong leadership in his city is limited by fragmented authority, multiple elected officials, limited jurisdiction over important urban services, civil service, state or federal interference, and constraints placed upon his power by "reform" and

TABLE 10.7   Veto Powers of Mayors in Cities Over 5,000

| Form of government | PERCENTAGE OF REPORTING CITIES WHERE MAYOR MAY | | |
	Veto all measures	Veto selected items	No veto
Mayor-council	35.1	33.9	31.0
Commission	11.3	3.5	85.2
Council-manager	6.7	9.4	83.9
All cities	20.8	21.1	58.1

SOURCE: *Municipal Yearbook, 1968,* p. 57.

"good-government" arrangements. Nonetheless, even though it is recognized that mayors have few formal powers to deal with the enormous tasks facing them, it is frequently argued that mayors can and should exercise strong leadership as "political brokers"—mediating disputes, serving as a line of communications, bringing conflicting groups together for reasonable discussions of their differences, and suggesting integrative solutions which diverse groups can accept in coping with the city's problems. In other words, the "ideal" mayor overcomes his limited formal powers by skill in persuasion, negotiation, and public relations. Each "success" in resolving a particular problem "pyramids" his prestige and influence, and he eventually accumulates considerable informal power. He can then direct his energy and power toward accomplishing one or more of the numerous goals set for mayors: reducing racial tensions, providing effective law enforcement, speeding redevelopment and renewal of downtown areas and the relocation of persons living there, improving public schools, constructing low-cost housing, cleaning up the urban environment, finding ways to move people and things about the city speedily and efficiently, and, most of all, finding ways to finance these goals.

But this "ideal" city leadership requires that the mayor possess certain minimum resources: [40]

1. Sufficient financial and staff resources in the mayor's office and in city government generally;
2. City jurisdiction over social-program areas—education, housing, urban renewal, etc;
3. Mayor's jurisdiction within city government over these areas;

[40] Jeffrey L. Pressman, "Preconditions of Mayoral Leadership," *American Political Science Review,* 66 (June, 1972): 511–24.

4. A salary that enables the major to spend full time on the job;
5. Friendly vehicles for publicity, such as newspapers or television stations supportive of the mayor and his goals;
6. Political groups, including a political party, which the mayor can mobilize to attend meetings, parade, distribute literature, etc., on his behalf.

What happens when a mayor is unable to overcome his lack of formal authority in a city? What happens when there is no party organization that can "get things done at city hall," and there is no strong charismatic leader who possesses the charm or salesmanship to "put things across" to the community? Banfield and Wilson provide an excellent summary as to how the lack of city leadership is overcome:

1. To a large extent it is *not* overcome; many things are not done because it is impossible to secure the collaboration of all those whose collaboration is needed.
2. When overcome at all, it is overcome on an ad hoc basis; the mayor, for example, must consider anew with each issue how to get the eight votes he needs in council.
3. Widespread indifference and apathy among the voters mitigates the effect of decentralization of authority to them.
4. The mass communications media are fairly effective in overcoming by salesmanship such decentralization of authority to the voters as remains; causes with strong newspaper support and with big budgets for TV advertising are usually approved at the polls.
5. The devices of salesmanship are extensively used. . . .
6. Measures are frequently compromised so as to "give something to everybody" in order to get them accepted.[41]

In summary, most mayors do not have the formal authority sufficient to deal with the many challenges facing city government. The successful mayor must rely chiefly upon his own personal qualities of leadership: his powers to persuade, to organize, to promote, to sell, to publicize, to compromise, to bargain, and to "get things done." The mayor's role is not usually to initiate proposals for new programs or to create public issues. Nor is his primary concern the administration of existing programs, although he must always seek to avoid scandal and gross mismanagement, which would give his administration a bad public "image." He must rely upon other public agencies, planners, citizens' groups, and private enterprise to propose new programs, and he can usually rely upon his department heads and other key subordinates to supervise the day-to-day administration of city government. The mayor is primarily a promoter of public policy: his role is to promote, publicize, organize, and finance the projects that others suggest.

[41] Banfield and Wilson, *City Politics*, p. 111.

PLANNERS

Professional planners are playing an increasingly important role in community decision making. Today over 90 percent of the cities with populations of ten thousand or more have official planning agencies, although
only about one-third of these cities employ a full-time professional
planner. Nearly all cities with populations over one hundred thousand
employ full-time professional planners.[42]

Early city planners were concerned primarily with the physical development of the city and the use of land.[43] They concentrated on writing
zoning laws, preparing "subdivision regulations" governing the division
of large plots of land into smaller ones, laying out public streets, and
choosing the location of parks, public building sites, public utilities, and
other public facilities.

Early city planning dealt almost exclusively with topics that could
be shown on a map. Planners were trained primarily as engineers or landscape architects. Planners were expected to prepare a *master plan,* or
overall blueprint, for the physical development of the community. The
master plan is a set of maps, information, and policy statements intended
to serve as guides for both public and private decision makers.

In recent years the definition of planning has been broadened to include more than physical and land use planning. Today, planners stress
the interrelatedness of urban life and argue that planning is a continuing
activity which attempts to anticipate human needs and goals, to prepare
for them and guide them into desirable patterns, and to influence and
shape public policy to serve the community's needs and goals most effectively. In addition to land use and physical development considerations,
planners now direct their attention to population projections, economic
conditions, social patterns, life-styles, cultural developments, education,
transportation, and beautification. The phrase *comprehensive planning*
has largely replaced the earlier term *master plan,* in recognition of the
new emphasis on planning as a continuing activity. Obviously this extended definition of planning plunges the planner deep into the political
life of the community.

What formal powers do planners have to influence community
policy? The master plan itself is not legally binding on anyone. Planners
are legally powerless to effectuate their plan themselves—they must rely
on its appeal to policy makers. Mayors and councils can simply file the
master plan away and forget it. However, cities that choose to implement

---

[42] *Municipal Yearbook, 1963,* p. 324.

[43] For an introduction to city planning, see Donald H. Webster, *Urban Planning
and Municipal Public Policy* (New York: Harper & Row, Publishers, 1955).

comprehensive planning and guide physical development by law have a variety of legal tools available to them: (1) zoning ordinances, (2) subdivision regulations, (3) an official map, (4) building and construction codes, (5) locational decisions on public facilities and buildings, and (6) a capital improvement program. Planning agencies often have an important role in all these activities, even though the principal responsibility for these tools of implementation rests with the mayor and council.

Planning commissions usually prepare the *zoning ordinance* for the approval of the council. The zoning ordinance divides the community into districts for the purpose of regulating the use and development of land and buildings. Zoning originated as an attempt to separate residential areas from commercial and industrial activity, thereby protecting residential property values. The zoning ordinance divides the community into residential, commercial, and industrial zones, and perhaps subdivisions within each zone, such as "light industrial" and "heavy industrial," or "single-family residential" and "multifamily residential." Owners of land in each zone must use their land in conformity with the zoning ordinance; however, exceptions are made for persons who have used the land in a certain way before the adoption of the zoning ordinance. An ordinance cannot prevent a person from using the land as he has done in the past; thus, zoning laws can only influence land use if they are passed prior to the development of a community. Many rapidly expanding suburban communities pass zoning ordinances too late—after commercial and industrial establishments are strung out along highways, ideal industrial land is covered with houses, good park and recreational land has been sold for other purposes, and so on.

Since the planning commission prepares the zoning ordinance as well as the master plan, the ordinance is expected to conform with the plan. In many communities, the role of the planning commission is strengthened by the requirement that a city council *must* submit all proposed changes in the zoning ordinance to the planning commission for their recommendation before any council action. The council may ignore the recommendations of the planning commission and rezone areas as they see fit; nevertheless, the requirement that the planning commission review requests for zoning changes doubtlessly contributes to their influence in community development.

Another means of implementing the master plan is *subdivision regulations,* which govern the way in which land is divided into smaller lots and made ready for improvements. Subdivision regulations, together with the zoning ordinance, may specify the minimum size of lots, the standards to be followed by real estate developers in laying out new streets, and the improvements developers must provide, such as sewers, water mains, and sidewalks. Often planning commissions are given direct responsibility for the enforcement of subdivision regulations. Builders and developers must submit their proposed "plats" for subdividing land and for improvements to the planning commission for approval before deeds can be recorded.

The planning commission also prepares the *official map* of the city for enactment by the council. The official map shows proposed, as well as existing, streets, water mains, public utilities, and the like. Presumably no one is permitted to build any structures on land that appears as a street or other public facility on the official map. Many cities require the council to submit to the planning commission for their recommendation any proposed action that affects the plan of streets or the subdivision plan and any proposed acquisition or sale of city real estate. Here again, the recommendation of the planning commission may be ignored by the council, but at least the planners must be listened to.

Finally, comprehensive planning can be implemented through a *capital improvement program.* This program is simply the planned schedule of public projects by the city—new public buildings, parks, streets, and so on. Many larger cities instruct their planning commissions to prepare a long-range capital improvement program for a five- or ten-year period. Of course, the council may choose to ignore the planning commission's long-range capital improvement program in its decisions about capital expenditures, but at least the planning commission will have expressed its opinions about major capital investments.

The federal government has strengthened the position of planning commissions by requiring *planning as a prerequisite to receiving federal money* for public housing, urban renewal, airports, sewage systems, highways, recreation and open space facilities, and even hospitals. Moreover, federal grants are offered to communities for participation in city-wide or regional planning programs. Presumably the federal government's interest in community planning stems from its desire to see that its grant money is not wasted. But these federal requirements for planning greatly strengthened the influence of planners at the local level: without planning, a community would be deprived of federal money in a wide variety of grant-in-aid programs, and much of the cost of planning is paid for by federal planning grants, anyhow. The result is that very few communities today are without planning agencies.

The formal role of planners is advisory, but they can have a substantial influence on community policy. In smaller cities, planners may be preoccupied with the day-to-day administration of the zoning and subdivision control ordinances. They may have insufficient time or staff resources to engage in genuine long-range comprehensive planning. In large cities, the planning staff may be the only agency that has a really comprehensive view of community development. Although they may not have the power to "decide" about public policy, they can "initiate" policy discussion through their plans, proposals, and recommendations. The planners can project the image of the city of the future and thereby establish the agenda of community decision making. Their plans can initiate public discussion over the goals and values to be implemented in the community. The master plan can be a tool for mobilizing public interest in community development.

There are, of course, serious limitations on the influence of planners. First of all, most of the important decisions in community development are made by private enterprise rather than by government. Real estate interests, developers, builders, and property owners make most of the key decisions shaping the development of the community. The most important influence on their decisions is not the action of government but the economics of the marketplace. There is very little evidence that *any* governmental tools—planning, zoning, subdivision control, or capital programming, and so on—can overcome market forces. Property owners will find a way to make the most profitable use of the land, the ideals of the planners notwithstanding. Second, the planners can only advise policy makers; they are just one voice among many attempting to influence public decisions about land use and physical development.

Historically, planning was part of the municipal reform movement. Planners generally showed the antipolitical bias of the reform movement and were deeply suspicious and distrustful of political leaders. Their maps and charts were drawn with little regard to political realities. Yet today many planners are coming to realize that plans are policies and policies spell politics. There is no doubt that planning will reflect politics; the only question is whose politics it will reflect. What values and whose values will become part of the comprehensive plan?

Like reformers, planners tend to be "public regarding"—they are concerned with the welfare of the community as a whole, particularly its most deprived minorities. They are hostile to what they regard as narrow, private-regarding interests, particularly businessmen and developers. They share with reformers a distaste for "politics." David C. Ranney notes that "planners have traditionally distrusted local government, viewing it as a pawn of special interest groups. This distrust is at least partly the result of the relationship between the planning movement and the municipal reform movement." [44]

Planners can play a variety of roles in the policy-making process. [45] One role is that of the pure "technician"—who develops plans strictly

[44] David C. Ranney, *Planning and Politics in the Metropolis* (Columbus, Ohio: Charles E. Merrill Books, Inc., 1969), p. 28.
[45] See Francine Rabinowitz, *City Politics and Planning* (New York: Atherton, 1969).

on the basis of professional planning theory, avoiding political entangle-
ments and remaining aloof from struggles over the acceptance or implementation of plans. The technician-planner emphasizes his neutral
expertise. Another role is that of the "broker"—who acts as confidential
adviser to policy makers and considers the political "marketability" of
his plans and recommendations. Another role is that of the "mobilizer"—
who actively seeks community support for his plans and enlists the backing of civic, business, professional, and service clubs. An even more political role for planners has been proposed in recent years under the
label "advocacy planning." [46] The advocate planner recognizes that plans
must always embody someone's values at the expense of someone else's,
and he expects that various groups in a community will develop and
support alternative plans. The advocate planner is overtly political, particularly on behalf of the poor and the black, and he frequently stresses
social rather than physical planning. Most planners view themselves
primarily as "technicians," although from time to time they will act
as "brokers" and "mobilizers."

Recognition of the political nature of planning has brought about a
gradual shift in the organization of city planning agencies. Historically,
planning agencies were semi-independent commissions, whose members
were appointed from outside the government for long terms. Ordinarily
the mayor could not remove the commissioner. Sometimes their recommendations regarding changes in the zoning and subdivision ordinances
or the capital budget could not be overriden by council, except by a
two-thirds or three-quarters vote. This semi-independent status for planning commissions reflected the reform movement's desire to remove planning from "politics."

Recently the trend has been to organize planning agencies as part of
the city government, directly responsible to the mayor or council. Organizing planners as staff to the mayor and council is expected to make
them more sensitive to community values as they are expressed in the
political process. Norton Long has commented: "This change will both
compel political realism and enrich the end systems of the planners by
forcing them to understand the politician's perspectives and incentives,
and it will jeopardize the planner's capacity to take the long and
detached view. Realism will not be an unmixed blessing, though it is
essential to get a sufficient range of values into the planner's thinking." [47]

[46] Paul Davidoff, "Advocacy and Pluralism in Planning," *Journal of the American Institute of Planners,* 31 (December, 1965): 331–38; and Lisa Peattie,
"Reflections of an Advocate Planner," *Journal of the American Institute of
Planners,* 34 (March, 1968): 80–89.
[47] Long, "Planning and Politics," p. 169.

INTEREST GROUPS

Interest group activity may be more influential in community politics than in state or national political affairs. Since the arena of local politics is smaller, the activities of organized interest groups may be more obvious at the local level. As one local councilman was once quoted:

> Pressure groups are probably more important in local government than they are nationally or in the state, because they are right here. You see them and they see you, and what you do affects them. It's not like in Washington, where half the time a businessman doesn't really know what the result will be for him.[48]

A study of interest group activity in city councils in California discovered that only 16 percent of the 115 councilmen interviewed did not perceive any groups or organizations as "influential" in their city.[49] Sixty-eight percent named two or more groups as influential in their community; and 17 percent were able to name as many as five influential groups. The median number of groups seen as influential by these councilmen was 2.4. By comparison, the median number of active groups perceived by state legislators in a four-state legislative system study were as follows: California—1.15, New Jersey—1.28, Ohio—.90, and Tennessee —.89.[50] In other words, local councilmen in California perceived over twice as much group activity at the local level than legislators in four states perceived at the state level!

At the local level, interest groups frequently assume the form of "civic associations." Few communities are too small to have at least one or two associations devoted to civic well-being, and larger cities may have hundreds of these organizations. In the California study of local councilmen, 94 percent of the councilmen who perceived group activity at the local level named civic associations (service clubs, citizens commissions, improvement associations) as the most influential groups or organizations, which were active and appeared before the council.[51] Only 28 percent of these councilmen named economic groups (merchants, realtors, unions, and so on), and 21 percent named taxpayer associations and reform groups. Actually, these results do not mean that economic interests

[48] Betty Zisk, Heinz Eulau, and Kenneth Prewitt, "City Councilmen and the Group Struggle," *Journal of Politics*, 27 (August, 1965): 633.
[49] Ibid., pp. 618–46. See also Betty Zisk, *Local Interest Politics: A One-Way Street* (Indianapolis: The Bobbs-Merrill Co., Inc., 1973), p. 22.
[50] John C. Wahlke et al., *The Legislative System* (New York: John Wiley & Sons, Inc., 1962), pp. 311–42.
[51] Zisk et al., "City Councilmen," p. 632.

banks, utilities, contractors, real estate operators, bar and club owners, and television and newspaper interests.

Banks often own, or hold the mortgages on, downtown business property. They have an interest in maintaining business, commercial, and industrial property values. Banks are also interested in the growth and prosperity of the city as a whole, particularly large business enterprises who are their primary customers. Bankers are influential because they decide who is able to borrow money in a community and under what conditions. Banks are directly involved in local governments in financing municipal bond issues for public works, school buildings, and so on, and in pledging financial backing for urban renewal projects. Banks are also influential in land development, for they must provide the financial backing for real estate developers, contractors, businesses, and home buyers; hence they are interested in business regulation, taxation, zoning, and housing.

Contractors are vitally interested in city government because the city has the power of inspection over all kinds of construction. Local governments enforce building, plumbing, electric, and other codes, which are of great interest to contractors. Some contractors, particularly road-grading and surfacing companies, depend on public contracts, and they are vitally concerned with both city policy and the personnel who administer this policy. While municipal contracts are generally required by law to be given to the "low bidder" among "responsible" contractors, definitions about what is or is not a "low bid," and who is or who is not a "responsible" contractor, make it important for contractors to maintain close and friendly relationships with municipal officials. It is no accident that builders, contractors, and developers are usually the largest source of campaign contributions for local office-seekers.

Real estate developers are particularly interested in planning, zoning, and subdivision control regulations and urban renewal programs. (Urban renewal programs are discussed at length in Chapter 17.) The success of urban renewal depends upon participation of private developers. When land is cleared, that portion of it not used for public housing or civic improvements is placed on the open market. At this point the ideas of city planners about beautiful, clean, low-cost housing, scenic open spaces, and artistic and cultural amenities must face the economic realities of the marketplace. The land must be sold for as high a price as possible in order to reduce the city's local dollar contribution to the project. It must be sold quickly in order to get the land back on the city's tax rolls. Successful renewal projects generally secure the support of the city's developers before they are even begun. This means that big-city mayors, whether they be Democrats or Republicans, must be on speaking terms with developers and real estate interests.

Newspapers are an important force in community politics.[52] The influence of the press would be relatively minor if its opinions were limited to its editorial pages. The influence of the press arises from its power to decide what is "news," thereby focusing public attention on the events and issues that are of interest to the press. Newspapermen must first decide what proportion of space in the paper will be devoted to local news in contrast to state, national, and international news. A big-city paper may give local news about the same amount of space that it gives to national or foreign news. Suburban or small-town papers, which operate within the circulation area of a large metropolitan daily, may give a greater proportion of the news space to local events than to national and international affairs. Crime and corruption in government are favorite targets for the press. Editors believe that civic crusades, and the exposure of crime and corruption, help sell newspapers. Moreover, many editors and newspapermen believe they have a civic responsibility to use the power of the press to protect the public. In the absence of crime or corruption, newspapers may turn to crusades on behalf of civic improvements—a city auditorium, a cultural center, and the like.

The politics of newspapers can be understood in part by some insight into the economics of the newspaper business. While it is true that, on occasion, some newspapers make financial sacrifices in order to defend the public interest as they see it, in the long run newspapers are businesses and they must consider profit and loss statements like any other business. Only occasionally can a wealthy newspaper owner ignore business considerations and run his paper at a loss. Newspapers get two-thirds of their revenue from advertising. In recent years the newspapers' percentage of all advertising dollars has declined in the face of stiff competition from television. At the same time the cost of newsprint and labor has risen steadily. Many big-city newspapers have either merged or gone out of business in recent years because of a lack of sufficient advertising revenue to offset increasing costs; it was not a lack of readers that brought about their collapse. Moreover, it is important to know that downtown department stores provide the largest source of advertising revenue. Big-city newspapers have been hurt by the flight of the middle class to the suburbs and the declining role of downtown department stores in retail sales in the metropolitan area. In metropolitan affairs, one can expect big-city newspapers to support the position of downtown interests. This means support for urban renewal, mass transit, downtown parking, and other pro-central-city policies in metropolitan affairs. On the other hand, suburban daily and weekly newspapers are supported

---

[52] See Banfield and Wilson, *City Politics*, Chap. 21; and Morris Janowitz, *The Community Press in an Urban Setting* (Glencoe, Ill.: The Free Press, 1954).

by the advertising from suburban shopping centers, and they can be expected to take a pro-suburban position on metropolitan issues.

Newspapers are more influential among middle-class populations than among working-class, ethnic, or black populations. This is a product of differences in reading habits and educational levels between these groups. Newspapers are more influential in the absence of strong party organizations, which would compete with newspapers as channels of communication to the voters. Nonpartisanship, lengthy ballots, numerous referenda, all contribute to the influence of newspapers. Any situation that tends to obscure candidates or issues to the voter contributes to the power of newspapers, since the voter is obliged to rely upon them for information. Newspapers doubtlessly have more influence in local than in state or national politics because of (1) the relative importance in local politics of middle-class groups who read newspapers, (2) the relative obscurity of local politics to the voter in his reliance upon newspapers for information about local affairs, and (3) the relative weakening of party affiliations in local politics.

Any listing of influential interest groups in local politics should include the community's churches and church-related organizations. Ministers, priests, rabbis, and leaders of religious lay groups are frequently participants in community decision making. The Catholic Church and its many lay organizations are vitally concerned with the operation of parochial schools. Protestant ministerial associations in large cities may be concerned with public health, welfare, housing, and other social problems. Ministers and church congregations in small towns may be concerned with the enforcement of blue laws, limitations on liquor sales, prohibitions on horse racing and gambling, and other public policies relative to "vice" and public morality.

THE GROWING POWER OF MUNICIPAL UNIONS

No one has a greater personal stake in municipal government than municipal employees—policemen, firemen, street crews, transit employees, welfare workers, sanitation workers, clerks, secretaries. Their rate of voter turnout in municipal elections is very high, and they are politically influential in small towns and suburbs whether they are organized into unions or not. Municipal employee unions are more influential in large cities, where fragmentation of authority and public acceptance of union activity encourage unions to assert their employees' interests. In New York City, for example, associations of teachers, policemen, firemen, transit workers, social workers, sanitation workers, and so on, have great political significance. Employee work stoppages and other forms of protest occur frequently, even though state law prohibits strikes of municipal employees. The American Federation of State, County, and Municipal Employees, the International Association of Fire Fighters, and the American Federation of Teachers, all AFL–CIO unions, are directly concerned with organization and collective bargaining in public employment. In addition, certain other unions, such as the Transport Workers Union, are organized to bargain on behalf of both public and private employees. In the absence of union representation, public employees may form "professional associations," such as the Fraternal Order of Police and, of course, the National Education Association.

Serious labor relations problems are no longer limited to a few unfortunate large cities like New York.[53] Over the last decade, municipal employee strikes have increased ten-fold, and the problem is certain to grow worse in the near future. Municipal employee unions are rapidly becoming bigger, better-organized, richer, and more militant. They are extending their influence outward from the nation's largest cities, where they are firmly entrenched, to middle-sized and smaller cities and towns.

Most state laws today recognize the right of municipal employees to organize unions and bargain collectively with municipal officials over wages, hours, and conditions of work. However, in contrast to *private* employees, *public* employees are generally prohibited by law from striking. Instead, most state laws stipulate that public employee labor disputes are to go to arbitration—that is, be submitted to neutral third parties for decision. Decisions of arbitrators (or arbitration boards consisting of equal representation from employees and employers, together and with neutral members) may or may not be binding on both the city and union, depending on specific provisions of each state's laws. However, increasing militancy of public employee unions throughout the country have rendered "no-strike" laws practically useless in a heated labor dispute. Policemen, firemen, teachers, sanitation workers, and others, have struck in many large cities and there have been state-wide strikes as well. The unions nullify no-strike laws by simply adding another demand—no legal prosecution of strikers or union leaders—as a condition of going back to work.

The new power of municipal employee unions raises some interesting questions regarding democratic theory. Strikes which threaten the health and safety of a community are qualitatively different than strikes which shut down private business enterprise and threaten only economic dislocation. Strikes of police, firemen, hospital workers, or sanitation workers, for example, must be ended quickly for the safety of the com-

---

[53] Raymond D. Horton, "Municipal Labor Relations: The New York City Experience," *Social Science Quarterly*, 52 (December, 1971): 680–96.

munity; this brings great pressure to bear on public officials to satisfy the demands of strikers, even at the risk of creating serious financial problems for the city. (Strikes by teachers, social workers, maintenance employees, clerks, etc., may cause dislocations, but do not immediately threaten the community's health or welfare.) Elected public officials are theoretically responsible to the majority of citizens who elected them. But the immediate pressure of a small minority of vital municipal employees may force elected officials to sacrifice the long-run public interest.

Yet it is pointless to debate the theoretical problems posed by a strike that threatens public safety and welfare. Such strikes can be expected to occur with increasing frequency in the future. State and local employees, who for generations were paid wages below those for comparable jobs in private enterprise, may soon outstrip private employees in salaries, benefits, pensions, etc. This is not necessarily bad for a community or for the economy in general. However, when municipal labor demands *are* unreasonable, the public must be willing to accept the short-run costs and inconveniences of a strike, rather than suffer the long-run financial plight that results from repeatedly buying labor peace at inflated prices.

Metropolitics:
cities and suburbs

THE ANATOMY OF A METROPOLIS

Two out of every three Americans live in population clusters called metropolitan areas. Most of the nation's population increase is occurring in these metropolitan areas—the increase in metropolitan area population from 1960 to 1970 was 24.4 million, in contrast to a 1.3 million decline in the rest of the United States. (See Table 11–1.) Moreover, most of this increase in metropolitan population is occurring outside the core cities in the nation's booming suburbs. The suburban population of the United States, persons living in metropolitan areas but outside the core city, grew by an amazing 36 percent in a single decade, while the core cities grew only 8.4 percent. Today, American *suburbanites* outnumber either city or rural residents.

What is a metropolitan area? Briefly, a metropolitan area consists of a large central city of fifty thousand or more persons together with the surrounding suburbs, which are socially and economically tied to the central city. The Census Bureau calls a metropolitan area a "Standard Metropolitan Statistical Area" (SMSA) and defines it as a city of fifty thousand or more persons together with adjacent counties which have predominantly urban industrial populations with close ties to the central city. (See Figure 11–1.)

Chapter eleven

TABLE 11.1   Population Growth in Cities and Suburbs of Metropolitan Areas in the United States

| | Total U.S. Population | Metropolitan Areas | | | Outside Metropolitan Areas |
		Total	Central Cities	Suburbs	
1960					
Population (thousands)	179,993	111,886	57,360	54,526	68,107
Percent of U.S. total	100.0	62.2	31.9	30.3	37.8
1970					
Population (thousands)	203,185	136,330	62,193	74,137	66,855
Percent of U.S. total	100.0	67.1	30.6	36.5	32.9
Percentage increase	12.9	21.8	8.4	36.0	−1.9

SOURCE: U.S. Bureau of the Census, *1970 Census of Population,* PC (P3)-3 (Washington, D.C.: Government Printing Office, 1971).

Urban sociologists tell us that the very definition of metropolitan life involves *large numbers* of *different* types of people living *close together* who are socially and economically *dependent* upon one another.[1] *Numbers, density, heterogeneity,* and *interdependence* are said to be distinguishing characteristics of metropolitan life. It is not difficult to envision a metropolitan area as a large number of people living together; we can see these characteristics in metropolitan life from a map or an airplane window. But it is more difficult to understand the heterogeneity and interdependence of people living in metropolitan areas.

The modern economic system of the metropolis is based upon a highly specialized and complex division of labor. We are told that in the simple farm community, a dozen occupations exhausted the job opportunities available to men. An agricultural economy meant homogeneous employment opportunities; that is to say, nearly everyone was a farmer or was closely connected to and dependent upon farming. But in the modern metropolis there are tens of thousands of different kinds of jobs. An industrial economy means highly specialized jobs and accounts for much of the heterogeneity in urban populations. There are wide differences between occupational worlds. It is on the basis of his job that the individual receives an income and his share of the goods and services available in life. Different jobs produce different levels of income, dress, and styles of living. The individual's job shapes the way he looks at the world and his evaluations of social and political events. In acquiring his job, he at-

[1] See especially Scott Greer, *Governing the Metropolis* (New York: John Wiley & Sons, Inc., 1962).

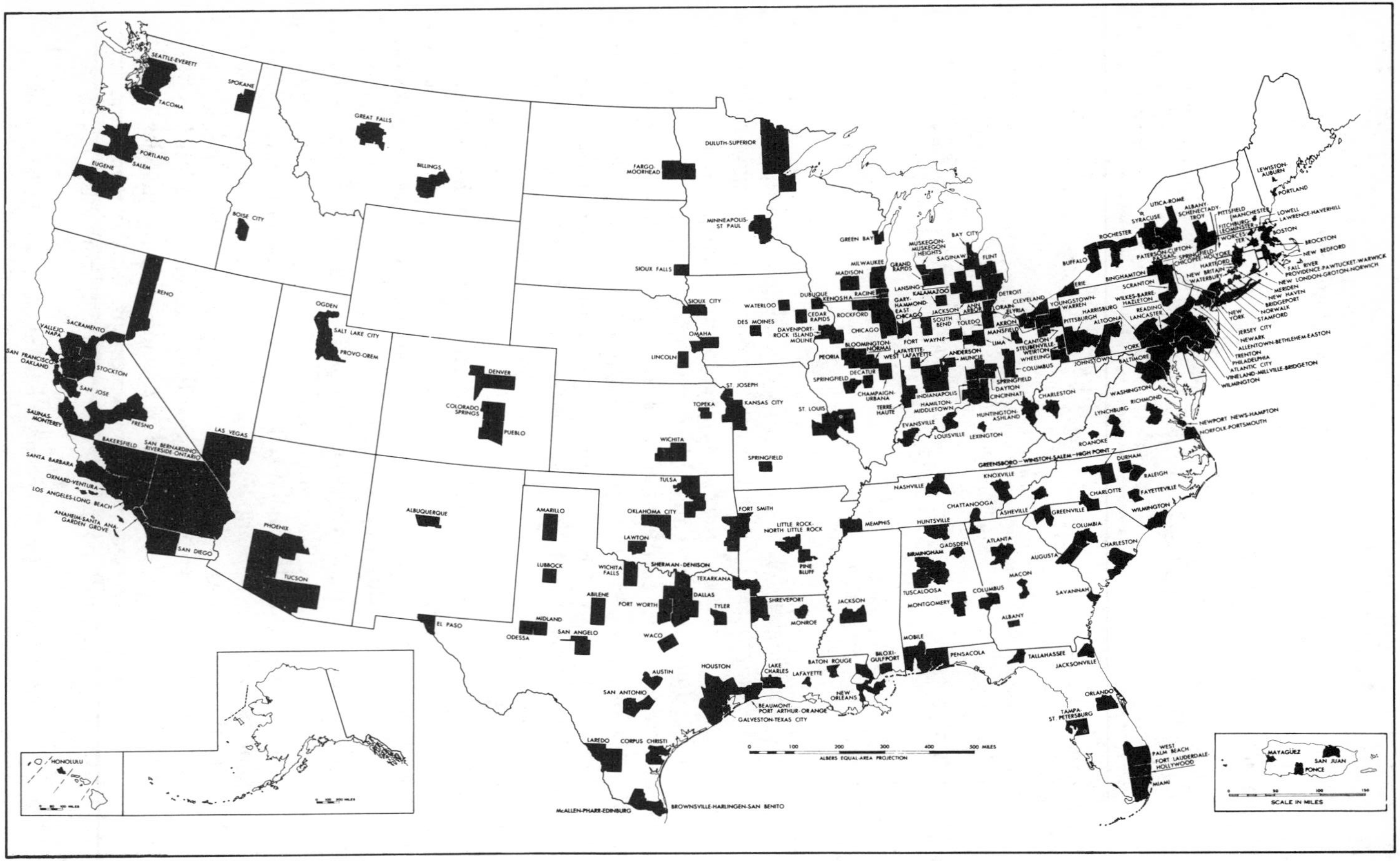

FIGURE 11–1 Standard metropolitan statistical areas.

tains a certain level and type of education that also distinguishes him from those in other jobs with different educational requirements. Differences in educational level in turn produce a wide variety of differences and opinions, attitudes, and styles of living. Metropolitan living concentrates people with all these different economic and occupational characteristics in a very few square miles. This is what is meant by heterogeneity in metropolitan life.

Ethnic and racial diversity are also present. A few decades ago opportunities for human betterment in the cities attracted immigrants from Ireland, Germany, Italy, Poland, and Russia; today, the city attracts blacks, Puerto Ricans, and rural families. These newcomers to the metropolis bring with them different needs, attitudes, and ways of life. The "melting pot" tends to reduce some of this diversity over time, but the pot does not "melt" people immediately, and there always seem to be new arrivals.

People also differ in where they live and how they live. There is a certain uniformity to rural life; day-to-day family life on the farm is remarkably similar from one county to the next. But urban dwellers may live in apartments in the central city or in single-family homes in the suburbs. Some urban dwellers choose a familistic style of life—raising two or more children in their own single-family house, with the wife functioning as a homemaker. Others are less familistic—raising no children or a single child in a rented apartment with the wife holding down a job outside the home.

The list of social, economic, and life-style differences among the people in a metropolitan area is almost endless. Scott Greer writes, "The city is a maze, a social zoo, a mass of heterogeneous social types." [2] Moreover, urban sociologists tell us that people with different social, economic, and life-style characteristics generally live in different parts of a metropolitan area. Physical separation of residences generally accompanies social and economic separation, and so there are "ghettos," "silk-stocking districts," "little Italys," middle-class suburbs, and so on. This physical separation tends to emphasize and reinforce differences among people in a metropolitan area.

But another fundamental characteristic is interdependence. While the traditional farm family was not wholly self-sufficient, its members were much less dependent upon the larger community for employment, goods, and services than is the modern metropolitan dweller. In contrast, urban dwellers are highly dependent upon one another in their daily economic and social activities. Suburbanites, for example, rely upon the central city for food, clothing, newspapers, entertainment, hospitalization,

[2] Ibid., p. 5.

and a host of other modern household needs. More importantly, they rely upon the central city for employment opportunities. Conversely, the central city relies upon the suburbs to supply its labor and management forces. Downtown merchants look to the entire metropolitan area for consumers. This interdependence involves an intricate web of economic and social relationships, a high degree of communication, and a great deal of daily physical interchange among residents, groups, and firms in a metropolitan area. Just as specialization produces diversity among men, it also produces interdependence and the need for coordinated human activity.

Suburbs account for most of the growth of America's metropolitan areas. In the last decade, nearly 20 million Americans moved to the suburbs. Rows upon rows of "ranches," and "split-levels," and "cape cods" now encircle our major cities as if to lay siege to them. No other sector of American life has grown so rapidly. Very few large *central cities* are growing in size; metropolitan areas are growing because their *suburbs* are growing. (See Table 11–1.) This suburbanization is due to technological advances in transportation—the automobile and the expressway. In the nineteenth century an industrial worker had to live within walking distance of his place of employment. This meant that the nineteenth-century American city crowded large masses of people into relatively small central areas, often in tenement houses and other high-density neighborhoods. But new modes of transportation—first the streetcar, then the private automobile, and now the expressway—eliminated the necessity of workers living close to their jobs. Now a man can spend his working hours in a central business district office or industrial plant and spend his evenings in a residential suburb many miles away. The same technology that led to the suburbanization of residences has also influenced commercial and industrial location. Originally industry was tied to waterways or railroads for access to supplies and markets. This dependence has been reduced by the development of motor truck transportation, the highway system, and the greater mobility of the labor force. Now many industries can locate in the suburbs, particularly light industries, which do not require extremely heavy bulk shipment that can only be handled by rail or water. When industry and people move to the suburbs, commerce follows. Giant suburban shopping centers have sprung up to compete with downtown stores. Thus, metropolitan areas are becoming decentralized over time as people, business, and industry spread themselves over the suburban landscape. As Lewis Mumford puts it: "The city has burst open and scattered its complex organs and organizations over the entire landscape." [3]

[3] Lewis Mumford, *The City in History* (New York: Harcourt, Brace, & World, Inc., 1961), p. 34.

TABLE 11.2   Local Governments in Metropolitan Areas

	Number of local governments
Total in 227 SMSAs*	20,703
Municipalities	4,977
Townships	3,255
Counties	404
Special districts	7,049
School districts	5,018
Total in selected SMSAs	
Chicago, Illinois	1,113
Philadelphia, Pennsylvania	876
Pittsburgh, Pennsylvania	704
New York, New York	551
St. Louis, Missouri	474
San Francisco-Oakland, Calif.	312
Portland, Oregon	385
Denver, Colorado	269
Seattle, Washington	268
Indianapolis, Indiana	282
Kansas City, Missouri	272

*Standard Metropolitan Statistical Areas.
SOURCE: U.S. Bureau of the Census, *Census of Governments,* 1972, V, 3.

Another characteristic of metropolitan areas is "fragmented" government. This is another result of suburbanization. Suburban development, spreading out from central cities, generally ignored governmental boundaries and engulfed counties, townships, towns, and smaller cities. Twenty-six metropolitan areas even spread across state lines, and four metropolitan areas of the United States—Detroit, San Diego, El Paso, and Laredo—adjoin urban territory in Canada and Mexico. This suburbanization has meant that hundreds of governments may be operating in a single metropolitan area. Thus, while metropolitan areas are characterized by social and economic interdependence, and consequently require coordinating mechanisms, metropolitan government is generally "fragmented" into many smaller jurisdictions, none of which is capable of governing the entire metropolitan area in a unified fashion.

Governmental fragmentation in metropolitan areas is a function of the size: the larger the metropolitan area, the more fragmented the governmental structure.[4] Fragmentation is also related to the age of settlement and to income levels in the metropolis, although these factors are less in-

[4] See Brett W. Hawkins and Thomas B. Dye, "Metropolitan Fragmentation," *Midwest Review of Public Administration,* 4 (February, 1970): 17–24.

fluential than size. Apparently the older a metropolitan area, the more complex its governmental structure becomes; and the more affluent its citizens are, the more complexity in the form of separate, relatively small units of government can be afforded.

THE WAR BETWEEN CITIES AND SUBURBS

Social, economic, and racial conflict can be observed at all levels of government, but at the metropolitan level, it is most obvious in the conflict that occurs between central cities and their suburbs. At the heart of city-suburban conflict are the differences in the kinds of people who live in cities and suburbs. And city-suburban conflict is at the heart of "the metropolitan problem"; that is, the failure to achieve metropolitan-wide consensus on public policy questions affecting the entire metropolitan area and the failure to develop metropolitan government institutions. It is very difficult to arrive at metropolitan-wide consensus about questions involving desegregation and the busing of students out of their neighborhood to achieve it, mass transit and highway construction, the sharing of welfare costs, the distribution of tax burdens, water supply and sewage disposal problems, planning and zoning, housing policy (including the concentration of blacks in central cities), and a host of other problems. We shall refer to the social, economic, and racial differences between city and suburb as "social distance." This social distance accounts for much conflict between cities and suburbs and constitutes the chief obstacle to the development of metropolitan-wide policies and government institutions.

In describing social-class differences in metropolitan life, political scientist Richard Child Hill observes:

> The unequal distribution of income and social status among groups fosters an unequal system of social relationships in the urban housing market and local government institutions, resulting in differential individual access to housing, neighborhood and "municipal life style." Residential segregation by class and race shapes interaction patterns, friendship ties, marital selection, and social consciousness. The distribution of income and residential location shapes political relationships between collectivities with discordant interests and creates differential access to public goals and services.[5]

Of course, generalizing about cities and suburbs is a dangerous thing. Although we will talk about some common characteristics of cities

[5] Richard Child Hill, "Separate and Unequal: Government Inequality in the Metropolis," *American Political Science Review,* 68 (December, 1974): 1557–68.

and suburbs, students are cautioned that individual suburbs may be quite different from one another (just as there are wide differences between social and economic groups living in central cities). There are, for example, industrial suburbs, residential suburbs, black suburbs, wealthy suburbs, working-class suburbs, and so forth.[6] Nonetheless, a clear perception of the social distance between cities and suburbs is important in understanding metropolitan politics.

Cities and suburbs can be differentiated, first of all, on the basis of *social class*—the occupation, income, and educational levels of their population. The cultured class of an earlier era established "country" living as a symbol of affluence; widespread prosperity has made possible mass imitation of the aristocracy by an upwardly mobile middle-class population. The occupation, education, and income characteristics of persons living in the suburbs of our nation's large metropolitan areas can be clearly differentiated from those of central-city dwellers. The suburbs house greater proportions of white-collar employees, college graduates, and affluent families than any other sector in American life. Table 11–3 contrasts several common measures of social status for American central cities and suburbs.

Status differentials in favor of suburbs are more pronounced in larger metropolitan areas; Leo Schnore reports that status differentials in smaller metropolitan areas are not as great as in larger areas, and sometimes even favor the city rather than the suburbs.[7] However, on the whole, suburban living reflects middle-class values.[8] And social differences between city and suburb are increasing rather than decreasing, as middle-class Americans continue to flee from the central city to the suburbs, and low-income, occupational, and educational groups are concentrated in central cities.

Cities and suburbs can also be differentiated on the basis of *"familism,"* or life-style. Perhaps the most frequently mentioned reason for a move to the suburbs is "the kids." Family after family lists consideration of their young as the primary cause for their move to suburbia. The city is hardly the place for most child-centered amenities. A familistic, or child-centered life-style, can be identified in certain social statistics. One measure is the "fertility ratio," or the number of children born per thousand women from fifteen to forty-four years of age. Another measure is the percentage of women aged fourteen or over who are in the work force. A large number of children per thousand married females of child-

---

[6] See Frederick M. Wirt et al., *On the City's Rim: Politics and Policy in Suburbia* (Lexington: D. C. Heath, 1972).

[7] Leo Schnore, "The Socio-economic Status of Cities and Suburbs," *American Sociological Review*, 28 (February, 1963): 76–85.

[8] See Robert C. Wood, *Suburbia: Its People and Their Politics* (New York: Houghton Mifflin Company, 1958).

bearing age, together with a small proportion of women who work, suggest a family-centered environment. In addition, the single-family, free-standing home is the *sine qua non* of familistic living in an affluent society. Cumulatively, these three life-style measures are said to identify a familistic or child-centered way of life. Table 11–3 shows that (1) there are proportionately more children in the suburbs than in the central cities, (2) a larger proportion of suburban mothers stay at home to take care of these children, and (3) a larger proportion of suburban families are housed in single-family units. The nonfamilistic life-style is characteristic of the central city where there are proportionately fewer children, more apartment living, and greater numbers of employed mothers. A familistic style of life in suburbia suggests the importance of the most fundamental of all child amenities—the school.

Again, it should be pointed out that the suburbs of smaller metropolitan areas are less differentiated from their central cities in terms of life-style than the suburbs of larger metropolitan areas. Smaller cities

TABLE 11.3   Social, Economic, and Life Style Differences Between Cities and Suburbs

	Average for United States	Average for SMSAs	
		Central cities	Suburbs
White-collar occupation, male (percent of work force)	48.2	51.7	56.8
Median family income	$9,590	$9,519	$11,771
Population under poverty level (percent of population)	12.2	13.4	6.3
Families over $25,000 (percent of all families)	4.6	4.6	7.4
Median school year completed	12.1	12.0	12.3
High school graduates (percent)	52.3	50.9	61.9
Nonwhite percentage	11.1	20.6	4.7
Mobility (percent living in different county 5 years ago)	17.1	14.1	18.9
Fertility rate (children ever born per 1,000 females 25-34)	1,986	1,943	2,035
Families with children under 6 (percent of families)	26.1	25.3	27.1
Females in labor force (percent of all females over 16)	41.4	44.5	42.5

SOURCE: U.S. Bureau of the Census.

seem to be able to support a familistic life-style almost as well as their suburbs.

Perhaps the most important difference between cities and suburbs is their contrasting *racial composition*. Black populations in most large cities are growing at a very rapid rate, partly from natural increases and partly from migration from the rural South. New arrivals go into slums, which almost everywhere are located in the oldest part of the central city. The increases in nonwhite populations in large central cities in recent years have been truly astounding. (Table 13–1 shows the increase in nonwhite population percentages of the largest cities in the United States, from 1960 to 1970.) The nonwhite population of most of these cities has doubled and redoubled over the past twenty years. At the same time the white populations of these central cities have been fleeing to the suburbs. Very few large cities gained in white population. The result has been striking changes in the racial composition of central cities.

Many whites have fled to the suburbs to get away from heavy concentrations of blacks in central cities. One reason why many suburbanities may want to remain politically separate from the central cities is that it might make it easier for them to resist "invasion" by blacks. As blacks gain majorities in central cities, they, too, may resist metropolitan governmental consolidation in order to avoid dilution of their political power through merger with white suburbs. The restriction of suburban home sales to whites only and the generally higher costs of suburban homes and property have made it difficult or impossible for blacks to follow whites to the suburbs in any significant number. The nonwhite percentage of all United States suburbs was 4.7 percent in 1970 in contrast to a nonwhite percentage for all central cities of 20.6 percent.

American life is becoming more, not less, segregated over time. These population statistics clearly show that America is building racial "ghettos" in its large central cities and surrounding them with white middle-class suburbs. As the population exodus to the suburbs continues, cities are becoming increasingly bereft of their middle-class, white, high-income, taxpaying populations. Increasingly, nonwhite, low-income, low-education, unskilled, nonfamilistic populations are being concentrated in the central cities. This means we have also concentrated the problems of these people in downtown areas—racial imbalance, crime, violence, inadequate education, poverty, slum housing, and so on. By moving to the suburbs, white middle-class families not only separate themselves from blacks and poor people but also place physical distance between themselves and the major social problems that confront metropolitan areas. This permits them, for the time being, to avoid problems of slum housing, poor schools, expanding welfare rolls, crime and juvenile delinquency, and rioting in the central cities.

POLITICAL DIFFERENCES
BETWEEN CITIES AND SUBURBS

City and suburban social differences are reflected in devergent political patterns in cities and suburbs. In general, large cities are much more Democratic than their suburban rings, which are generally Republican. While temporary shifts may occur from one election to another, this general pattern of Democratic cities and Republican suburbs is likely to prevail for the near future. As long as the national Democratic party represents central-city, low-income, ethnic, labor, and racial constituences, and the Republican party represents middle-class, educated, managerial, white, Anglo-Saxon Protestant constituencies, the political coloration of cities and suburbs is likely to be different. Persons who are leaving cities for the suburbs include a disproportionate number of Republicans. Their places in the cities are being taken by blacks, Puerto Ricans, and poor whites, most of whom are normally Democratic in their politics.

A possible challenge to the Democratic-cities–Republican-suburbs pattern is the increasing affluence of ethnic, working-class populations in America, which permits many of them to buy suburban homes, and leave their central-city neighborhoods. If these new suburbanites retain their ethnic and labor affiliations and traditions of Democratic-party voting, they could make serious inroads into Republican-party strength in the suburbs. However, while some low-income industrial suburbs regularly support the Democratic ticket, on the whole, the Republican suburban vote percentages have suffered very little from the vast increase in suburban population. In fact, the suburban population explosion has saved the Republican party the slow death that it would have experienced if its appeal had been limited to the diminishing ranks of small-town and rural voters. There is no evidence that suburban residence itself affects political behavior.[9] Instead, political differences between cities and suburbs are a product of the different socioeconomic and racial compositions of cities and suburbs.

These party differences pose an obstacle to the consolidation of metropolitan governments. Metropolitan consolidation schemes would place Democratic control of central cities in jeopardy just as they might threaten Republican control of suburban counties. Political leaders, both Democratic and Republican, are not likely to view with favor any proposal that would substitute political insecurity for "a good thing." Re-

---

[9] On suburban voting behavior, see Herbert Hirsch, "Suburban Voting and National Trends," *Western Political Quarterly*, 21 (September, 1968): 508–14; and Frederick M. Wirt, "The Political Sociology of American Suburbia," *Journal of Politics*, 27 (August, 1965): 647–66; Frederick M. Wirt et al., *On the City's Rim: Politics and Policy in Suburbia* (New York: D.C. Heath, 1972).

publican party leaders outside central cities are just as well satisfied with a local one-party system as are the Democrats of the central cities.[10]

POLICY DIFFERENCES
BETWEEN CITIES AND SUBURBS

City and suburban social differences are also reflected in the divergent public policies of city and suburban governments. First of all, there is some evidence that the child-centered character of suburban living produces higher educational expenditures in suburbs than in cities. Suburban parents with high hopes and plans for their children's occupational success tend to focus more concern upon the school system, and spend more money on it per pupil, than city residents. (Of course, in smaller metropolitan areas, where social and life-style differences between city and suburb are slight, differences between city and suburb in educational expenditures are very slight and occasionally run opposite from the expected direction.)

Large central cities show substantially higher operating expenditures per capita than their suburbs. The maintenance of a large physical plant for the entire metropolitan area requires city residents to make higher per capita operating expenditures than those required for suburbanites. In addition, many living costs in suburban communities are shifted from public to private spending (private septic tanks instead of public sewers, private instead of public recreation, and so on). Differences in the public services provided by city and suburban governments are greatest in the area of police protection, recreation, and health. This reflects a concentration in the city of people who are likely to require these public services, in contrast to the suburbs.

The tax bill in suburbs is only slightly lower than in central cities. Taxes had much to do with the migration of the "pioneer" suburbanites, those who moved to the suburbs in the 1930s and 1940s. At that time, suburban living offered a significant savings in property taxation over what were thought to be heavy city taxes. But the tax advantage of the suburbs turned out partly to be a "self-denying prophecy": the more people who fled to the suburbs to avoid heavy taxes, the greater the demand for public services in these new suburban communities, and the higher suburban taxes became to meet these new demands. Yet, the tax bill in most suburbs remains lower than in central cities. The difference in tax burden between city and suburb would be even greater if suburban-

[10] Edward C. Banfield, "The Politics of Metropolitan Area Organizations," *Midwest Journal of Political Science,* 1 (May, 1957): 77–91.

ites did not choose to spend more per public in education than city residents, which produces higher school taxes in the suburbs. The suburbs also manage to limit their indebtedness more than cities, and most of the indebtedness incurred by the suburbs is for school, rather than municipal, purposes.

Finally, it should be noted that policy differences between city and suburb in smaller metropolitan areas do not appear to be as great as policy differences in cities and suburbs in larger metropolitan areas. This corresponds to our earlier point that social and economic differences between city and suburb in smaller metropolitan areas are not as great as in larger metropolitan areas. Of course, it should also be remembered that all these generalizations about cities and suburbs are, indeed, generalizations. Individual cities and suburbs can be found that do not conform to these national patterns.

THE CASE FOR METROPOLITAN CONSOLIDATION

The term *metropolitan problem* has been given to any situation requiring cooperation between city and suburban governments. And there is hardly any governmental activity that has not been identified as a metropolitan problem. Too often civic reformers have tended to limit the discussion of metropolitan problems to the technical problems of providing public services in a metropolis, such as water supply, sewage disposal, transportation, and fire and police protection. But metropolitan problems include all the major social and economic problems confronting American society. Poverty, racial imbalance, slum housing, crime and juvenile delinquency, financial crisis—these problems may be "national" in scope, but they occur principally in the metropolis. In short, the major social problems facing American society are "metropolitan problems." Nor is it possible to argue convincingly that these major social, economic problems are problems of central cities rather than of the entire metropolitan area. John C. Bollens and Henry J. Schmandt, in *The Metropolis*, addressed themselves to this point very effectively:

> Some myopic defenders of suburbia go so far as to say that the major socio-economic problems of urban society are problems of the central city, not those of the total metropolitan community. Where but within the boundaries of the core city, they ask, does one find an abundance of racial strife, crime, blight of housing, and welfare recipients? Superficially, their logic may seem sound, since they are in general correct about the prevalent spatial location of these maladies. Although crime and other social problems exist in suburbia, their magnitude and extent are substantially less than in the central city. But why in an interdependent metropolitan

community should the responsibility of suburbanities be any less than that of the central city dwellers? Certainly no one would think of contending that residents of higher income neighborhoods within the corporate limits of the city should be exempt from responsibility for its less fortunate districts. What logic then is there in believing that neighborhoods on the other side of a legal line can wash their hands of social disorders in these sections?

. . . No large community can hope to reap the benefits of industrialization and urbanization and yet escape their less desirable byproducts. The suburbanite and the central city resident share the responsibility for the total community and its problems. Neither can run fast enough to escape involvement sooner or later.[11]

Many scholars over the years have insisted that "the metropolitan problem" was essentially the problem of "fragmented" government—that is, the proliferation of governments in metropolitan areas and the lack of coordination of public programs.[12] The objective of the metropolitan reform movement of the last thirty years was to reorganize, consolidate, and enlarge government jurisdictions. The goal was to rid metropolitan areas of "ineffective multiple local jurisdictions" and "governments that do not coincide with the boundaries of the metropolis."

Many advantages were claimed for metropolitan governmental reorganization. First of all, the reorganization and consolidation of metropolitan governments was expected to bring about *improved public services* as a result of centralization. Consolidation of governments was expected to achieve many economies of large-scale operations and enable government to provide specialized public services, which "fragmented" units of government could not provide. For example, larger water treatment plant facilities can deliver water at lower per gallon costs, and larger sewage disposal plants can handle sewage at a lower per gallon cost of disposal. Additional specialized public services that could be provided on a metropolitan-wide level are police crime laboratories, central record systems, and central communications systems, which cannot be provided by small suburban police forces.[13]

The problem with this argument is that most studies show that larger municipal governments are *uneconomic* and fail to produce im-

---

[11] John C. Bollens and Henry J. Schmandt, *The Metropolis* (New York: Harper & Row, Publishers, 1965), pp. 249–50.

[12] See Luther Gulick, *The Metropolitan Problem and American Ideas* (New York: Alfred A. Knopf, Inc., 1962). For a more recent summary of the theory of metropolitan consolidation, see Walter A. Rosenbaum and Thomas A. Henderson, "Explaining Comprehensive Governmental Consolidation," *Journal of Politics*, 34 (May, 1972): 428–57.

[13] Robert C. Wood, "A Division of Powers in Metropolitan Areas" in *Area and Power*, edited by Arthur Maass (Glencoe, Ill.: The Free Press, 1959), p. 59.

proved services. Only in very small cities (with populations under 25,000) can economies of scale be achieved by enlarging the scope of government; size does not seem to matter in cities of between 25,000 to 250,000 people; but in cities of over 250,000, further increases in size produce *dis*economies of scale and lower levels of public service per person.[14]

Second, it was argued that metropolitan consolidation would provide the necessary *coordination of public services* for the metropolis. Study after study reported that disease, crime, fire, traffic congestion, air pollution, water pollution, and so on, do not respect municipal boundary lines. The transportation problem is the most common example of a coordination problem. Traffic experts have pleaded for the development of a balanced transportation system in which mass transit carries many of the passengers currently traveling in private automobiles. Yet mass transit requires decisive public action by the entire metropolitan area. Certainly, the city government is in a poor position to provide mass transit by itself without the support of the suburbanites who will be riding on it. And, of course, small suburban governments are totally inadequate to this task. The demonstrated inability of local government to deal with the transportation problem has shifted attention to Washington. Action in many metropolitan areas on mass transit has come to a near standstill, awaiting the helping hand of the federal government. It is argued by some that this sad state of affairs may not have come about if strong, metropolitan-wide governments had been in existence that could have acted effectively to solve the mass transit problem at the local level.

The third major argument for metropolitan consolidation stresses the need to eliminate *inequalities in financial burdens* throughout the metropolitan area. Suburbanites who escaped many city taxes continue to add to the cities' traffic and parking problems, use city streets and parks, find employment in the cities, use city hospitals and cultural facilities, and so on. By concentrating the poor, uneducated, unskilled minorities in central cities, we also saddle central cities with costly problems of public health and welfare, crime control, fire protection, slum clearance, and the like, all the social problems that are associated with poverty and discrimination. We concentrate these costly problems in cities at the same time that middle-class, tax-paying individuals, tax-paying commercial enterprises, and tax-paying industries are moving into the suburbs. Thus, metropolitan-government fragmentation often succeeds in segregating financial

---

[14] For a summary of these studies, see Elinor Ostrum, "Metropolitan Reform: Propositions Denied From Two Traditions," *Social Science Quarterly*, 53 (December, 1972): 474–93.

needs from resources.[15] The result is serious financial difficulty for many central cities. New York's near bankruptcy is an advanced state of a disease infecting many large central cities.

It is also argued that metropolitan government would *clearly establish responsibility for metropolitan-wide policy.* One of the consequences of "fragmented" government is the scattering of public authority and the decentralization of policy making in the metropolis.[16] This proliferation in the number of autonomous governmental units reduces the probability of developing a consensus on metropolitan policy. Each autonomous unit exercises a veto power over metropolitan policy within its jurisdiction; it is often impossible to secure the unanimity required to achieve metropolitan consensus on any metropolitan-wide problem. An opponent of any particular solution need only find, among the countless independent governmental bodies whose consent is required, one that can be induced to withhold its consent in order to obstruct action. The dispersion of power among a large number of governmental units makes it possible for each of them to reach decisions without concern for the possible spillover effects, which may be harmful to other governments or residents of the metropolis.

THE CASE FOR "FRAGMENTED" GOVERNMENT

So long as we view local government exclusively as a mechanism for providing municipal services, the "fragmented" character of metropolitan government will appear to be obsolete and in need of reform.

But the suburbanite does not look upon the efficient provision of public service as the *only* function of local government. Nor does he look upon "the optimum development of the metropolitan region" as a particularly compelling goal. Rather, there are a variety of social, political, and psychological values at stake in maintaining the existing "fragmented" system of local government.[17] First of all, the existence of separate and independent local governments for suburbs plays a vital role in *developing and maintaining a sense of community identity.* The suburbanite identifies his residential community by reference to the local political unit. He does not think of himself as a resident of the "New

---

[15] See Lyle C. Fitch, "Metropolitan Financial Problems," *Annals of the American Academy of Social and Political Science* (November, 1957), pp. 66–73.

[16] See Robert C. Wood, *1400 Governments* (Cambridge: Harvard University Press, 1961).

[17] Oliver P. Williams, Harold Herman, Charles S. Liebman, and Thomas R. Dye, *Suburban Differences and Metropolitan Policies* (Philadelphia: University of Pennsylvania Press, 1965), Chap. 8.

York metropolitan region," but rather as a resident of Scarsdale or Mineola. Even the existence of community problems, the existence of a governmental forum for their resolution, and the necessity to elect local officials heighten community involvement and identity. The suburban community, with a government small in scale and close to home, represents a partial escape from the anonymity of mass urban culture. The institutional apparatus of government helps the suburban community to differentiate itself from "the urban mass" by legislating differences in the size and design of buildings, neighborhood and subdivision plans, school policies, types and quality of public services, and tax expenditure levels.

The political advantages of a fragmented suburbia cannot easily be dismissed. The existence of many local governments *provides additional forums for the airing of public grievances.* People feel better when they can publicly voice their complaints against governments, regardless of the eventual outcome of their grievance. The additional points of access, pressure, and control provided by a decentralized system of local government give added insurance that political demands will be heard and perhaps even acted upon. Opportunities for individual participation in the making of public policy are expanded in a decentralized governmental system.

Maintaining the suburb as an independent political community *provides the individual with a sense of personal effectiveness* in public affairs. The individual can feel a greater sense of manageability over the affairs of a small community. A smaller community helps relieve feelings of frustration and apathy which people often feel in their relations with larger bureaucracies. The suburbanite feels that his vote, his opinion, and his political activity count for more in a small community. He clings to the idea of grass-roots democracy in an organizational society.

Fragmented government clearly *offers a larger number of groups the opportunity to exercise influence* over government policy. Groups that would be minorities in the metropolitan area as a whole can avail themselves of government position and enact diverse public policies. This applies to blacks in the central city as well as white Anglo-Saxon Protestants in the suburbs. Fragmented government creates within the metropolitan area a wide range of government policies. Communities that prefer, for example, higher standards in their school system at higher costs have the opportunity to implement this preference. Communities that prefer higher levels of public service or one set of services over another or stricter enforcement of particular standards can achieve their goals under a decentralized governmental system. Communities that wish to get along with reduced public services in order to maximize funds available for private spending may do so.

Political independence also *allows the suburbanite to insulate himself* from those whose standards and way of life he does not share. Persons who have strived to place physical distance between themselves and those with different cultures and life-styles are unlikely to look with favor on attempts to remove or weaken identifiable boundaries between their communities and communities that are socially dissimilar. It is not necessarily the color of the black doctor who first moves into an all-white suburb that "frightens" the suburbanite. It is the belief that he will be followed by other blacks with "lower" cultural and economic standards. The cultural homogeneity that the suburbanite seeks for himself and his children is better protected when he can make use of the legal machinery of an independent government to maintain this homogeneity by excluding those who might change it. Of course, a suburban government cannot directly discriminate, but it can establish and enforce, through building, zoning, subdivision, and tax ordinances, specific standards that are high enough to make it economically unlikely that a "disrupting" element could enter the community. These formal controls, together with informal pressures on builders, real estate firms, and others, can operate to preserve effectively the cultural uniformity valued so highly in the suburban community.

Racial imbalance and the plight of central-city schools are important forces in maintaining the political autonomy of suburban school systems in the nation's large metropolitan areas. Many suburbanites left the central city to find "a better place to raise the kids," and this means, among other things, better schools. As we have already observed, suburbs generally spend more on the education of each child than central cities. Moreover, the increasing concentration of blacks in central cities has resulted in racial imbalance in center-city schools. Conditions in ghetto schools have long been recognized as a national scandal.[18] Efforts to end de facto segregation within the cities frequently involves busing school children into and out of ghetto schools in order to achieve racial balance. In Chapter 13 we will discuss de facto segregation and ghetto schools in greater detail. But it is important to note here that independent suburban school districts are viewed by many suburbanites as protection against the possibility that their children might be bused to ghetto schools. Autonomous suburban school districts lie outside the jurisdiction of city officials. While it is possible that federal courts may some day order suburban school districts to cooperate with cities in achieving racial balance in schools, nonetheless, the political independence of suburban schools helps to assure that suburban school children will not be used to achieve racial balance in city schools.

[18] Bel Kaufman, *Up the Down Staircase* (Englewood Cliffs, N.J.: Prentice-Hall, Inc., 1964).

"SOLUTIONS" TO THE METROPOLITAN PROBLEM

Let us examine various strategies for metropolitan governmental consolidation in the light of the preceding discussion of the values involved in suburban independence and the need for coordinating governmental activity in metropolitan areas.

The most obvious method of achieving governmental consolidation in the metropolitan area would be for the central city to annex suburban areas. *Annexation* continues to be the most popular integrative device in the nation's metropolitan areas.[19] Approximately three-fourths of the nation's central cities have succeeded in annexing some territory and people over the last ten years. Not all cities, however, have been equally successful in annexation efforts. Opposition to central-city annexation is generally more intense in the larger metropolitan areas. The bigger the metropolis, the more one can expect that suburbanites will defend themselves against being "swallowed up" or "submerged" by the central city. Central cities in smaller urbanized areas experience slightly more success in annexing people than cities in large urbanized areas. Yet size does not appear to be the most influential factor affecting annexation success. Actually, the "age" of a city appears more influential than size in determining the success of annexation efforts. City boundary lines in "older" metropolitan areas are relatively more fixed than in "newer" areas. Perhaps the immobility of boundaries is a product of sheer age. Over time, persons and organizations adjust themselves to circumstances as they find them. The longer these adjustments have been in existence, the greater the discomfort, expense, and fear of unanticipated consequences associated with change.

In general, cities with higher status populations, and fewer minority groups, are able to annex more suburbanites than cities with lower status populations and larger minority groups. Actually, the important variable in annexation success, and probably other efforts at metropolitan consolidation, seems to be the *differential* in status between the central city and its surrounding suburbs. Social class distance favoring the suburbs appears to be a distinct barrier to successful annexation efforts by central cities. Cities are more likely to be successful in annexing persons where there is little social differential between city and suburb.

Three-quarters of the nation's metropolitan areas lie entirely within single counties. From the standpoint of administration there is much to be said for *city-county consolidation*. It would make sense administratively to endow county governments with the powers of cities and to or-

---

[19] The following discussion of annexation activity relies upon Thomas R. Dye, "Urban Political Integration: Conditions Associated with Annexation in American Cities," *Midwest Journal of Political Science*, 8 (November, 1964): 430–46.

ganize them to exercise these powers effectively. Yet, important political problems—problems in the allocation of influence over public decision making—remain formidable barriers to strong county government. Central-city interests can expect representation in consolidated county governments on the basis of population, "one man, one vote," yet suburbanites are likely to fear that consolidation will give city residents a dominant voice in county affairs. Suburbanites may also fear that city-county consolidation may force them to pay higher taxes to help support the higher municipal costs of running the city. Suburbanites may not welcome uniform, countywide policies in taxation or zoning or any number of other policy areas. Suburbanites who have paid for their own wells and septic tanks will hardly welcome the opportunity to help pay for city water or sewer services. Suburbanites with well-established, high-quality public school systems may be unenthusiastic about integrating their schools with city schools in a countywide system, and so on. A variety of policy differences may exist between city and suburb, which will reflect themselves in any attempt to achieve city-county consolidation.

One of the more popular approaches to metropolitan integration is the creation of *special districts or authorities* charged with administering a particular function or service on a metropolitan-wide or at least an intermunicipal level, such as a park, sewage, water, parking, airport, planning, other district or authority. Because the special district or authority leaves the social and governmental *status quo* relatively undisturbed, important integrative demands are met with a minimum of resistance with this device. The autonomy of suburban communities is not really threatened, loyalties are not disturbed, political jobs are not lost, and the existing tax structure is left relatively intact. Special districts or authorities may be preferred by suburban political leaders when they believe it will lessen the pressure for annexation by the central city. Special districts or authorities may also be able to incur additional debt after existing units of government have already reached their tax and debt limits. Thus, special districts or authorities may be able to operate in an area wider than that of existing units of governments and at the same time enable governments to evade tax or debt limits in financing a desired public service.

Yet, experience in cities that have relied heavily upon special districts or authorities has suggested that these devices may create as many problems as they solve. Many special districts and authorities are governed by a quasi-independent board or commission, which, once established, becomes largely immune from popular pressures for change. These agencies may be quite independent of other governmental jurisdictions in the metropolis; their concerns might be water, air or water pollution control, city planning, and so on. Remoteness from popular control or close political responsibility often results in the professional administrators of these authorities exercising great power over their particular function. While authorities and special districts are supposed to be nonprofit governmental agencies, they often act very much like private enterprises, concentrating their resources on those activities that produce revenue and ignoring equally important nonrevenue-producing responsibilities.[20] Independent authorities often borrow money, collect tolls and services charges, and otherwise control their own finances in a manner very much like a private business. The structure of these districts and authorities usually confuses the voters and makes it difficult for the average citizen to hold officials of these agencies responsible for their decisions. Moreover, since these special districts and authorities are usually created for a single purpose, they often come to define the public interest in terms of the promotion of their own particular function—recreation, mass transit, water, parks, and so on—without regard for other metropolitan concerns. This "single-mindedness" can lead to competition and conflict between authorities and other governmental agencies in the region. Sooner or later, the problem of coordinating the activities of these independent authorities of special districts arises. Thus, even from the point of view of administrative efficiency, it is not clear whether the special district or authority, with its maze of divided responsibility, in the long run reduces or compounds the problem of governmental coordination in the metropolis.

Another approach to metropolitan integration is· the *interjurisdictional agreement.* Voluntary cooperative agreements between governments in a metropolitan area are common. Agreements may take the form of *informal,* verbal understandings, or "gentlemen's agreements," which might involve, for example, the exchange between welfare departments of information on cases, or cooperation among police departments in the apprehension of a lawbreaker, or agreements among local fire departments to come to the assistance of each other in the event of a major fire. Agreements may also be *formal* interjurisdictional agreements among governments, perhaps to build and operate a major facility such as a garbage incinerator or a sewage treatment plant. Interjurisdictional agreements may provide for (1) one government performing a service or providing a facility for one or more other governments on a contractual basis, (2) two or more governments performing a function jointly or operating a facility on a joint basis, or (3) two or more local governments agreeing to assist and supply mutual aid to each other in emergency situations.

[20] See Wood, *1400 Governments,* Chap. 4.

One of the attractions of interjurisdictional agreements is that they provide a means for dealing with metropolitan problems on a voluntary basis while retaining local determination and control. Interjurisdictional agreements do not threaten the existence of communities or governments. They do not threaten the jobs of incumbent public officials. Yet at the same time they enable governments to achieve the economies and provide the specialized services that only a larger jurisdiction can make possible.[21]

Metropolitan councils of governments are another form of integration in metropolitan areas. Metropolitan councils are associations of governments or government officials that provide an opportunity for study, discussion, and recommendations regarding common metropolitan problems. Not governments themselves, these councils have no power to implement decisions, but must rely instead upon compliance by member governments. Metropolitan councils provide an arena where officials of metropolitan governments can come together regularly, discuss problems, make recommendations, and, hopefully, coordinate their activities.[22]

Although metropolitan councils started slowly, the federal government provided the major stimulus to their acceptance throughout the nation in 1965, when federal planning funds were made available for metropolitan-wide planning agencies. In recent years, the federal government has gone even further by *requiring* cities in a metropolitan area to obtain the review of a metropolitan-wide planning council in order to qualify for federal grants. Today most metropolitan areas have *some* organization functioning as a metropolitan council of government.[23] Most of these councils, however, are *federally* mandated and funded; without federal intervention, they would probably collapse in many areas.

Generally, metropolitan councils strive for unity in their decisions and recommendations because their recommendations must be acted upon by member governments who are unlikely to implement proposals

[21] Thomas R. Dye, Oliver P. Williams, Harold Herman, and Charles Liebman, "Differentiation and Cooperation in a Metropolitan Area," *Midwest Journal of Political Science*, 7 (May, 1963): 145–55.

[22] The best known councils of government include the Metropolitan Regional Council (New York), Southern California Association of Governments (Los Angeles), Northeast Illinois Planning Commission (Chicago), Southeast Michigan Council of Governments (Detroit), Associated Bay Area Governments (San Francisco), Metropolitan Washington Council of Governments (Washington), East-West Gateway Council (St. Louis), Northeast Ohio Areawide Coordinating Agency (Cleveland).

[23] Frances Frisken, "The Metropolis and the Central City," *Urban Affairs Quarterly*, 8 (June, 1973): 395–422; Melvin B. Mogulof, "Metropolitan Councils of Government and the Federal Government," *Urban Affairs Quarterly*, 7 (June, 1972): 489–507.

they oppose. The result, for the most part, is that studies and recommendations of metropolitan councils are likely to be rather bland. It is very difficult for these councils to deal with the really divisive issues in the metropolis. Since councils have no authority to act upon metropolitan problems, they may be, in the words of Bollens and Schmandt, a "toothless tiger or—even worse—a protector of the inadequate status quo." [24]

CONSOLIDATION BATTLES WON AND LOST

Political realities have frequently overwhelmed the "logic" of metropolitan consolidation. These political realities are deeply rooted in the social, economic, life-style, and racial differences between cities and suburbs described earlier. The record of consolidation referenda in the past decade shows two defeats for every victory. [25] Yet reformers have not been inhibited by the dismal record thus far, and consolidation proposals of various kinds are under discussion in a great many urban areas.

Consolidation involves considerable disruption for public officials—redesigning governmental structure, reordering the authority of various offices, combining offices and agencies, and enlarging the magnitude of government operations. Unless a *large* majority of community influentials are *very* dissatisfied with the current state of affairs, and motivated to actively support consolidation, there is little chance that consolidation efforts will be successful. [26] Consolidation efforts usually begin with the formation of a charter commission to determine the form of the new consolidated government and write a charter for it. Usually the commission includes representatives of both the city and county governments to be consolidated, together with some "citizen" representatives. Sometimes the establishment of the commission itself is the subject of a referendum; interestingly, referenda to establish a commission tend to pass more often than not, even though the final vote on consolidation

[24] See Bollens and Schmandt, *The Metropolis*, pp. 379–80. See Thomas M. Scott, "Metropolitan Governmental Reorganization Proposals," *Western Political Quarterly*, 21 (June, 1968): 252–61; and Advisory Commission on Intergovernmental Relations, *Factors Affecting Voter Reactions to Governmental Reorganization* (Washington, D.C.: Government Printing Office, 1962).

[25] Vincent L. Marando and Carl Whitley, "City-County Consolidation: An Overview of Voter Response," *Urban Affairs Quarterly*, 8 (December, 1972): 181–203.

[26] For an interesting comparison of elite roles in successful (Jacksonville) and unsuccessful (Tampa) consolidation campaigns, see Thomas A. Henderson and Walter A. Rosenbaum, "Prospects for Consolidating Local Government: The Role of Elites in Electoral Outcomes," *American Journal of Political Science*, 17 (November, 1973): 695–720.

is likely to be negative. Establishing a charter commission is more easily obtainable than consolidation itself.

The critical point of the consolidation battle is the referenda vote on the acceptance of the new consolidated-government charter. The form of the vote depends on state law: a "double majority" vote requirement means that a majority "yes" vote must be obtained within the city *and* within the area outside of the city; a "double-count majority" vote requirement means that the vote of city residents is counted twice—once for the city and again for the county because they are also county residents. It is much easier for consolidation to win under the "double-count" requirement. Consolidation campaigns are usually managed by reform groups especially selected for the purpose. They are typically mass-media-oriented campaigns rather than the grass-roots organizational, ward- and precinct-level campaigns of party organizations. Voter turnout is only slightly heavier than that of ordinary municipal elections—ranging from 30 to 60 percent. Contrary to the public pronouncements of reformers, a high turnout does *not* help passage; indeed, there is a slightly better chance of success if turnout is low.

Most consolidation proposals are defeated by *county* residents, that is, suburbanites. The average voter turnout level of suburbanites is much higher than city dwellers and the percentage of "no" votes is much greater in the suburbs than in the city. Thus, overall voter response to consolidation proposals tends to support the notion that suburbanites prefer to maintain their identity and autonomy, their own governmental institutions, and their insulation from city people and problems. They do *not* want the improved public services, coordinated policies, or shared financial burdens that reformers urge upon them. While fear of higher taxes plays a role in suburban opposition, there appear to be many other social and psychological factors at work in helping to preserve suburban autonomy.[27]

The fear of being "submerged" into a large, impersonal, unresponsive government is evidenced by the interesting fact that proposed consolidation charters that stipulate many elected representatives and separately elected administrators (sheriff, tax assessor, etc.) do better at the polls than the "streamline," governmental charters preferred by reformers. In other words, a "Jacksonian" consolidation charter has a better chance of passage than one with a small legislative body and single strong executive.

[27] It is unclear whether greater "social distance" between city and suburbs directly affects referenda voting. See Brett W. Hawkins, "Life-Style Distance and Voter Support of City-County Consolidation," *Social Science Quarterly*, 48 (December, 1967): 325–28; Vincent L. Marando, "Life-Style Distances and Suburban Support for Urban Political Integration," *Social Science Quarterly* (June, 1972): 155–60.

Race is an increasingly important issue in consolidation campaigns. Most successful consolidation efforts have occurred in the South.[28] A common appeal to suburbanites in the South is to vote to join the city to "save" it from black majority rule by "diluting" the black vote. But the issue is complex and cuts both ways. Suburbanites may simply decide to stay out of a consolidated government precisely because it would include many central-city blacks. Blacks were traditionally expected to vote "yes" for economic reasons—to bring valuable suburban property into the tax base of the city. But black support for consolidation will certainly turn to opposition if it appears that blacks will lose power in the outcome.[29]

"METRO" GOVERNMENT

The American experience with federalism at the national level has prompted consideration of federated governmental structures for metropolitan areas. A "metro" government with authority to make metropolitan-wide policy in selected fields might be combined with local control over functions that are "local" in character. Metropolitan federation, in one form or another and at one time or another, has been proposed for many major metropolitan regions in the nation. Yet, with the exception of Toronto, Miami, and Nashville, proposals for metropolitan federation have been consistently rejected by both voters and political leaders. While metropolitan federation promises many of the advantages of governmental consolidation listed earlier—administrative efficiency, economy of large-scale operation, elimination of financial inequalities, and public accountability for metropolitan-wide policy—it seriously threatens many of the social, political, and psychological values in the existing "fragmented" system of local government in the metropolis. Metropolitan federation also poses a problem discussed earlier, that of deciding what is a "metropolitan" problem. In order to allocate functions to a "metro" government in a federation arrangement, one must first determine what is a metropolitan problem in which all the citizens of the area have a responsibility. Let us examine the metro governments of Toronto, Miami,

[28] Notably Miami-Dade County, Fla. (1957); Nashville-Davidson County, Tenn. (1962); Virginia Beach-Princess Ann County, Va. (1962); Jacksonville-Duval County, Fla. (1967); Columbus-Muscogee County, Ga. (1970). However, there have been an equal number of failures in the South: Knoxville-Knox County, Tenn. (1959); Macon-Bibb County, Ga. (1960); Durham-Durham County, N.C. (1971); Richmond-Henrico County, Va. (1961); Memphis-Shelby County, Tenn. (1962).

[29] See Richard L. Engstrom and W. E. Lyons, "Black Control or Consolidation: The Fringe Response," *Social Science Quarterly*, 53 (June, 1972): 161–68.

and Nashville in more detail and then identify sources of political opposition.

It is interesting to note that Toronto's metropolitan federation was *not* adopted by popular referendum in the area, but rather was imposed upon the area by the Province of Ontario.[30] The Municipality of Metropolitan Toronto was created in 1954 by the provincial government, after many years of fruitless negotiations over metropolitan federation between Toronto and its suburbs. The Municipality of Metropolitan Toronto, the new metro government, was given authority over water supply, sewage services, major roads, police, school buildings, metropolitan planning, and mass transit. The metropolitan government is financed by proportional assessments on the tax of the local governments; these local governments retain their tax-collecting duties. They also retain authority over fire protection, street maintenance, garbage collection, and more importantly, public schools. Metropolitan Toronto is governed by a Metropolitan Council. Representation on the council is not accorded on the basis of population but rather on the basis of equality between cities and suburbs.

Miami's metropolitan experiment, the first in the United States, was approved by popular referendum in the area, but only by a bare majority of 26 percent of Dade County registered voters who voted in 1957.[31] They approved a Dade County home rule charter under which the county government became in effect a metro government. The county government assumed a number of functions performed by the local governments in the metropolitan area, including sewage, water supply, transportation, traffic, central planning, and "those municipal functions which are susceptible to area-wide control." All other municipal powers are reserved to the cities, although the county may set minimum performance standards. Vagueness in the charter over precisely what is an area-wide problem has resulted in a great deal of court litigation over the powers of the metro government. The Miami metro plan included council-manager government for the county, to replace the traditional commission form of county government. The Dade County Commission consisted of five members elected at large, five by districts, and one from each city. In its beginning, the commission was badly divided; the first county manager was forced to resign, and controversy and court cases

---

[30] This discussion relies upon Bollens and Schmandt, *The Metropolis*, pp. 477–88; see also Frank Smallwood, *Metro Toronto: A Decade Later* (Toronto: Bureau of Municipal Research, 1963).

[31] This discussion relies upon Edward Sofen, *The Miami Metropolitan Experiment* (Bloomington: University of Indiana Press, 1963); and Edward Sofen, "The Politics of Metropolitan Leadership: The Miami Experience," *Midwest Journal of Political Science*, 5 (February, 1961): 18–38.

surrounded the activities of the county. Miami Beach even attempted to secede from the metropolitan federation. Amendments to the charter that would have crippled the powers of the metro government were defeated at the polls by very slim margins. Opponents of metro included the Dade County League of Municipalities, municipal employees labor unions, several mayors and elected officials, and local chambers of commerce. Metro supporters have been concentrated among Miami's business and political leadership, including the Miami Chamber of Commerce, *The Miami Herald, The Miami News,* the League of Women Voters, and the Dade County legislators. Edward Sofen attributed the narrow victory of the "metro" idea in Miami to the heavy influx of "newcomers" and the absence of strongly entrenched parties or powerful interest groups.

In 1962 the voters of Nashville and Davidson County, Tennessee, approved a metro charter which consolidated the city and the county.[32] Following the defeat of a 1958 consolidation proposal, in which city residents voted three to two in favor of consolidation and suburban residents voted three to two against it, the city of Nashville undertook a very aggressive annexation program in which suburban residents and industries were incorporated into the city without a referendum and probably against their will. Voter approval of the Nashville metro charter is a product of unique and interesting political circumstances in that area. Nashville politics was dominated by Mayor Ben West, an ardent champion of urban causes including reapportionment, urban renewal, and federal and state aid in cities. He headed a strong political organization which was reputedly maintained by the use of patronage. Like many city bosses, West was disliked and distrusted by newspapers, businessmen, and suburbanites. The *Nashville Tennesseean,* long a political foe of Mayor West, portrayed the annexation as an assault on county residents and began a campaign to convince them that metro government would protect them from the evils of the West administration in the city. Thus, metro government was presented to suburbanites as a means to abolish the city and eliminate Mayor Ben West! The city also passed an ordinance levying a ten-dollar tax on all automobiles using the streets of Nashville for thirty days or more. This "green sticker law" raised a storm of protest among suburbanites as "taxation without representation," a storm that reached hurricane proportions when Mayor West ordered the police to arrest and jail suburbanites whose cars were found on the streets of Nashville without green stickers. Thus, prometro forces were able to present metropolitan government to suburbanites as an anticity

[32] This discussion relies upon Brett W. Hawkins, *Nashville Metro* (Nashville: University of Vanderbilt Press, 1966); and Brett W. Hawkins, "Public Opinion and Metropolitan Reorganization in Nashville," *Journal of Politics,* 28 (May, 1966): 408–18.

proposal, which would cripple the city political machine and protect the suburbs from the green sticker tax and the threat of annexation.

The important lesson in the success of the Nashville metro is that it succeeded *not* because of an absence of city-suburban conflict, but because many suburbanites and others who were hostile to the city administration perceived metro government as a means of attacking the city. A metro proposal, which failed when it was presented as a reform, economy, and efficiency proposal, was later successful when it was presented as a political proposal.

Community
power structures

MODELS OF COMMUNITY POWER

Who runs this town? Do the elected public officials actually make the important decisions? Or is there a "power structure" in this community that really runs things? If so, who is in the power structure? Are public officials "errand boys" who carry out the orders of powerful men who operate "behind the scenes"? Or are community affairs decided by democratically elected officials acting openly in response to the wishes of many different individuals and groups? Is city government of the people, by the people, and for the people? Or is it a government run by a small "elite," with the "masses" of people largely apathetic and uninfluential in public affairs? Do people who make the important decisions in business and finance also make the important decisions in urban renewal, public works, education, taxation, public charity, land development, and so on? Or are there different groups of people making decisions in each of these areas, with little or no overlap except for elected officials?

Social scientists have differed over the answers to these questions. Some social scientists, whom we shall refer to as "elitists," believe that power in American communities is concentrated in the hands of relatively few people, usually top business and financial leaders. They believe that this "elite" is subject to relatively little influence from the "masses" of peo-

Chapter twelve

ple. Other social scientists, whom we shall refer to as "pluralists," believe that power is widely shared in American communities among many leadership groups who represent segments of the community and who are held responsible by the people through elections and group participation. Interestingly, both elitists and pluralists seem to agree that decisions are made by small minorities in the community. The idea of direct, individual citizen participation in decision making has suffered with the coming of organizational society and high levels of urbanization and industrialization. Elitists describe a more monolithic structure of power, with a single leadership group making decisions on a variety of issues, while pluralists describe a polycentric structure of power, with different elite groups active in different issues and a great deal of competition, bargaining, and sharing of power among elites.

Let us summarize the points of conflict between elitist and pluralist models of community power. These points have been distilled from a large body of rapidly expanding literature on community power,[1] and they can provide us with a framework for further discussion.

Elitist thinking about community power includes the following ideas:

1. Power stems from roles within the social system of the community. Political power is bound together with social and economic power. Men of wealth and social position in the community will also be men of power.

2. Power is "structured"—that is, power relationships tend to persist over time. Issues and elections may come and go, but the same men will continue to exercise power in the community.

3. There is a reasonably clear and persistent distinction over time between those who exercise power (elite) and those who do not (mass).

4. This distinction is based primarily upon the unequal distribution of control over economic resources in the community. Business and finan-

---

[1] This literature is becoming so voluminous that it seems appropriate to cite only some of the major summary pieces: Thomas J. Anton, "Power, Pluralism, and Local Politics," *Administrative Science Quarterly,* 7 (March, 1963): 425–57; Lawrence Herson, "In the Footsteps of Community Power," *American Political Science Review,* 55 (December, 1961): 817–31; Peter Bachrach and Morton S. Baratz, "Two Faces of Power," *American Political Science Review,* 56 (December, 1962): 947–53; Peter Bachrach and Morton C. Baratz, "Decisions and Nondecisions," *American Political Science Review,* 57 (September, 1963): 632–42; Herbert Kaufman and Victor Jones, "The Mystery of Power," *Public Administration Review,* 14 (Summer, 1954): 205–12; Nelson Polsby, *Community Power and Political Theory* (New Haven: Yale University Press, 1963); Robert Presthus, *Men at the Top* (New York: Oxford University Press, Inc., 1964); Robert Dahl, *Who Governs?* (New Haven: Yale University Press, 1961); Floyd Hunter, *Community Power Structure* (Chapel Hill: The University of North Carolina Press, 1953); Robert Agger, Daniel Goldrich, and Bert Swanson, *The Rulers and the Ruled* (New York: John Wiley & Sons, Inc., 1965); other citations are given in footnotes below.

cial leaders will compose the major part of the "elite." Elected public officials are largely "errand boys" who knowingly or unknowingly respond to the wishes of the dominant economic elite.

5. The elite constitutes a very small proportion of the people in the community. They are not typical or representative of the people of the community in income, education, occupation, or ethnic background. They have higher incomes, better educations, and more prestigious occupations than the "masses" and they come from the culturally dominant ethnic group in America—the white Anglo-Saxon Protestants.

6. There is considerable convergence of power at the "top" of the political system. A diagram of community power would take the shape of a pyramid.

7. Persons in the elite may disagree from time to time, but they share a certain commonality of interests, particularly in support of the basic values that underlie the social system itself.

8. The elite is subject to relatively little influence from the masses. The masses are largely misinformed and apathetic, if not completely alienated, from the community's political system. Of course, the elite is usually benevolent and does not oppress the masses because of a sense of "high-mindedness" and "civic responsibility" and the need to avoid violence and revolution.

In contrast, pluralist thinking involves the following notions:

1. Power is an attribute of individuals in their relationship with other individuals in the process of decision making. An individual has power to the extent that he can get another individual to do something he would not otherwise do, regardless of social positions.

2. Power relationships do not necessarily persist over time. They are formed for a particular decision, and after this decision is made, they disappear, to be replaced by a different set of power relationships when the next decision is made.

3. There is no permanent distinction between "elites" and "masses." Individuals who participate in decisions at one point in time are not necessarily the same individuals who participate at some other time. Many individuals have the *opportunity* to exercise power, whether they choose to do so or not.

4. The distinction between those who participate in a decision and those who do not is based primarily upon the level of interest people have in that particular decision. Individuals can move in and out of the ranks of decision making, simply by becoming active or inactive in politics. Men of wealth and social position are often defeated on community issues by active, skillful leaders who win popular support.

5. Leadership is fluid and mobile. Access to decision making is based primarily upon acquiring the skills of leadership—information about issues, knowledge about democratic processes, skill, organization, and public relations, and so on. Wealth is an asset in politics, but it is only one of many kinds of assets.

6. There are multiple centers and bases of power within a community. Persons who exercise power in some kinds of decisions do not necessarily exercise power in other kinds of decisions. No single elite dominates decision making in all issue areas.

7. There is considerable competition among leaders. Community leaders are not united by any common interest. They seek many divergent policies. Community policy also represents bargains or compromises reached between competing leadership groups.

8. Individuals can participate and make their views felt through their membership in organizations of many kinds. Elections are also important instruments of mass participation in political decisions. Leaders are constantly concerned with public opinion and often refer to it in decision making. Nonparticipation in elections or community affairs may be a product of popular satisfaction with the conduct of leaders.

While these statements describe "ideal" models of elite and pluralist communities, most "real" world communities will probably fall somewhere in between—that is, along a continuum from the monolithic elite model of power to a diffused and polycentric pluralist model. Many social scientists are neither confirmed "elitists" nor "pluralists," but they are aware that different structures and power may exist in different communities. Yet these ideal models of community power may be helpful in understanding the different ways in which community power can be structured. Later we shall suggest some social, economic, and political conditions that may be associated with elite or pluralist power configurations in American communities.

THE ELITE MODEL OF COMMUNITY POWER

European social theory has long been at odds with democratic political writers about the existence and necessity of elites. Gaetano Mosca, in his book *The Ruling Class*, wrote, "In all societies . . . two classes of people appear—a class that rules and a class that is ruled." [2] For Mosca, elitism is explained by the nature of social organization. Organization inevitably results in the concentration of political power in the hands of a few.

[2] Gaetano Mosca, *The Ruling Class* (New York: McGraw-Hill Book Company, 1939), p. 50.

Organized power cannot be resisted by an unorganized majority in which each individual "... stands alone before the totality of the organized minority. A hundred men acting uniformly in concert, with a common understanding, will triumph over a thousand men who are not in accord and can therefore be dealt with one by one." [3] Since organized power will prevail over individual effort in politics, sooner or later, organizations will come to be the more important actors in political life. And organizations cannot function without leaders. In Robert Michels's· words, "He who says organization, says oligarchy." [4] The masses are permanently incapable of running or controlling political organizations. They must cede that power to active, expert, and interested leadership groups. The idea that economic elites will tend to dominate in politics is also found in a great deal of social theory. Mosca wrote that the ruling class will possess "... some attribute real or apparent which is highly esteemed or very influential in the society in which they live." Needless to say, in a capitalist society, control over business and financial resources generally makes one "highly esteemed and very influential."

One of the earliest studies of American communities, the classic study of Middletown, conducted by Robert and Helen Lynd in the mid-1920s and again in the mid-1930s, tended to confirm a great deal of elitist thinking about community powers.[5] The Lynds found in Muncie, Indiana, a monolithic power structure dominated by the owners of the town's largest industry. Community power was firmly entrenched in the hands of the business class, centering on, but not limited to, the "X family." [6] The power of this group was based upon its control over the economic life in the city, particularly its ability to control the extension of credit. The city was run by a "small top group" of "wealthy local manufacturers, bankers, the local head managers of ... national corporations with units in Middletown, and ... one or two outstanding lawyers." Democratic procedures and governmental institutions were so much window dressing for business control. The Lynds described the typical city official as a "man of meager calibre" and as "a man whom the inner business control

---

[3] Ibid., p. 51.

[4] Robert Michels, *Political Parties* (Glencoe, Ill.: The Free Press, 1949).

[5] Robert S. Lynd and Helen M. Lynd, *Middletown* (New York: Harcourt Brace & World, Inc., 1929); and *Middletown in Transition* (New York: Harcourt Brace & World, Inc., 1937).

[6] The "X family," never identified in the Lynds' books, was actually the Ball family, glass manufacturers. Today it is headed by E. F. Ball, Chairman of the Board of the Ball Corporation, Ball Brothers Foundation, Ball Memorial Hospital, Muncie Aviation Corp., Muncie Airport, Inc., and a director of American National Bank and Trust of Muncie, Borg-Warner Corp., Indiana Bell Telephone Co., Merchants National Bank of Muncie, and Wabash College. Ball State University in Muncie is named for the family.

group ignore economically and socially and use politically." Perhaps the most famous quotation from the Lynds' study was a comment by a Middletown man made in 1935:

> "If I'm out of work, I go to the X plant; if I need money I go to the X bank, and if they don't like me I don't get it; my children go to the X college; when I get sick I go to the X hospital; I buy a building lot or house in the X subdivision; my wife goes downtown to buy X milk: I drink X beer, vote for X political parties, and get help from X charities; my boy goes to the X YMCA and my girl to their YWCA; I listen to the word of God in X subsidized churches; if I'm a Mason, I go to the X Masonic temple; I read the news from the X morning paper; and, if I'm rich enough, I travel via the X airport." [7]

W. Lloyd Warner, a noted sociologist, studied Morris, Illinois, in the 1940s, and he describes a somewhat similar power structure to that encountered by the Lynds in Muncie.[8] About one-third of all the city's workers had jobs in "the mill," which Warner says dominated the town:

> The economic and social force of the mill affects every part of the life of the community. Everyone recognizes its power. Politicians, hat in hand, wait upon Mr. Waddell, manager of The Mill, to find out what he thinks on such important questions as "Shall the tax rate be increased to improve the education our young people are getting?"—"Shall the new minister be Mr. Jones or Mr. Smith?"—"Should the city support various civic and world enterprises?"—"Should new industries enter the town and possibly compete with The Mill for the town's available labor supply?" They want to know what Mr. Waddell thinks. Mr. Waddell usually lets them know.[9]

Sociologist August B. Hollingshead studied the same town (sociologists seem to prefer to disguise the names of towns they are studying: Warner called the town Jonesville while Hollingshead called it Elmtown), and his findings substantially confirmed those of Warner.[10]

One of the most influential studies of community politics was sociologist Floyd Hunter's *Community Power Structure*, a study of Atlanta, Georgia.[11] According to Hunter, no one man or family or business dominated "Regional City" (a synonym for Atlanta), as might be true in a

---

[7] *Middletown in Transition*, p. 74.

[8] W. Lloyd Warner et al., *Democracy in Jonesville* (New York: Harper & Row, Publishers, 1949).

[9] Ibid., p. 101.

[10] August B. Hollingshead, *Elmtown's Youth* (New York: John Wiley & Sons, Inc., 1949).

[11] Floyd Hunter, *Community Power Structure* (Chapel Hill: University of North Carolina Press, 1953).

smaller town. Instead, Hunter described several tiers of influentials, with the most important community decisions reserved for a top layer of the business community. Admission to the innermost circle was based primarily on one's position in the business world. These top decision makers were not formally organized but conferred informally and passed down decisions to government leaders, professional personnel, civic organizations, and other "front men." Hunter explained that the top power structure only concerned itself with major policy decisions; there were other substructures—economic, governmental, religious, educational, professional, civic, and cultural—which communicated and implemented the policies at the top levels. These substructures:

> ... are subordinate, however, to the interests of the policy makers who operate in the economic sphere of community life in Regional City. The institutions of the family, church, state, education, and the like draw sustenance from economic institutional sources and are thereby subordinate to this particular institution more than any other. ... Within the policy forming groups the economic interests are dominant.[12]

Top power holders seldom operated openly. "Most of the top personnel in the power group are rarely seen in the meetings attended by the associational understructure personnel in Regional City." [13]

In Hunter's description of community decision making, decisions tend to flow *down* from top policy makers, composed primarily of business and financial leaders, to civic, professional, and cultural association leaders, religious and education leaders, and government officials, who implemented the program; and the masses of people have little direct or indirect participation in the whole process. Policy does not go *up* from associational groupings or from the people themselves. "The top group of the power hierarchy has been isolated and defined as being comprised of policy makers. These men are drawn largely from the businessmen's class in Regional City. They form cliques or 'crowds,' as the term is more often used in the community, which formulate policy. Committees for the formulation of policy are commonplace, and on communitywide issues policy is channeled by a 'fluid committee structure' down to institutional, associational groupings through a lower level bureaucracy which executes policy." [14] According to Hunter, elected public officials are clearly part of the power-level institutional substructure, which "executes" policy rather than formulates it. Finally, Hunter found that this whole power structure is held together by "common interests, mutual

[12] Ibid., p. 94.
[13] Ibid., p. 90.
[14] Ibid., p. 113.

obligations, money, habit, delegated responsibilities, and in some cases, by coercion and force.[15]

While Hunter describes the role of Atlanta's business elite as one of top policy making, a study of businessmen in big-city politics by Peter B. Clark suggests that businessmen are used as prestigious "front men" for policies initiated by civic associations and governmental agencies.[16] Clark argues that big businessmen themselves almost never think up or suggest proposals. Rather, ideas for community action generally come from the professional staffs of various community organizations, for example, a professional hospital director, a civic association staff worker, the newspaper's city editor, or the heads of governmental agencies. Once an idea has been generated at the professional staff level, the next stage is to seek out top businessmen to lend their prestige to the project. A proposal's presentation to the public and submission to city government for ratification is the *final* stage in policy making. If the proposal has been well thought out in advance by the professional staff, and has the support and public backing of prominent businessmen, this final stage may be a mere formality.

In addition to considerations of respect and prestige, business support is also sought because so many community projects require financial investment—public works, urban renewal, schools, streets, auditoriums, hospitals, and so on—and banks and investment firms must be called in to underwrite the bond issues. Businessmen also have technical information which local governments, normally operating without much professional staff, cannot themselves provide. Finally, business support is often sought to disarm potentially influential businessmen who might provide opposition to a proposal if they are not consulted about it in its earliest stages.

The influence of businessmen can be felt even in matters in which they are not directly involved. Many government officials and civic organization workers admit that they anticipate the views of big businessmen in policy decisions even when businessmen are not directly consulted. Clark quotes a civic staff man who explained why a particular community project failed: "This thing wasn't done right. It was just announced. The power structure and the newspaper people weren't checked out. All hell broke loose." [17] Another staff man revealed both his style and his motives when he said: "My method of operation is to touch base early before I raise a question. I do my homework thoroughly to get the controversy

[15] Ibid.

[16] Peter B. Clark, "Civic Leadership: The Symbols of Legitimacy," paper delivered at the 1960 Annual Meeting of the American Political Science Association, New York, September 1960; see also Peter B. Clark, *The Businessman as a Civic Leader* (Glencoe, Ill.: The Free Press, 1964).

[17] Ibid., p. 11.

out of it. Either revise it or throw it out. I have never proposed anything that hasn't been accepted. I don't want to propose anything that would fail." [18]

Several studies have suggested interesting variations on the power elite model. Robert O. Schultze's study of Cibola (Ypsilanti, Michigan) describes shifts in the power structure in that community, resulting from the town's integration into a "national" economy and the appearance of absentee ownership and a new managerial class in the power structure.[19] Schultze contends that in an earlier era of the town's history, locally owned industries dominated the political and economic life of the community. But as local industrialists were replaced by the managers of large national absentee-owned corporations, the power structure became less concentrated. The managers of Cibola's plants had great potential for power within the community, but they were preoccupied with their relationships to their national firms and tended to neglect community affairs. The result was that political power came to rest in the hands of a group of middle-class, local professionals and small businessmen.

THE PLURALIST MODEL OF COMMUNITY POWER

Political science had largely ignored the study of community power prior to the publication of Floyd Hunter's *Community Power Structure*. While sociologists had been developing an important body of literature on community power even before the Lynds' safari to darkest Indiana in the 1920s, community politics remained a "lost world" for political scientists.[20] Political science had been preoccupied with the municipal reform movement, the structure of local government, and the administrative problems of economy and efficiency; they had largely ignored informal structures of power and decision making. Hunter's findings were very discomforting. They suggested that in reality American communities were not governed very democratically. Hunter's research challenged the notion of popular participation in "grass-roots" democracy and raised doubts as to whether or not the cherished values of Jeffersonian democracy were being realized in community life. While admitting that "none of us [political scientists]

---

[18] Ibid.

[19] Robert O. Schultze, "The Role of Economic Dominants in Community Power Structure," *American Sociological Review*, 23 (February, 1958): 3–9; see also Robert O. Schultze, "The Bifurcation of Power in a Satellite Community," *Community Political Systems*, ed. Morris Janowitz (Glencoe, Ill.: The Free Press, 1961).

[20] See Lawrence J. R. Herson, "The Lost World of Municipal Government," *American Political Science Review*, 51 (June, 1957): 330–45.

has moved in with such a study in dynamics of power in a metropolitan community," political scientists Herbert Kaufman and Victor Jones were willing to assert on the basis of their own "administrative experience" that Hunter's study was "at best . . . incomplete; at worst . . . invalid." [21] These political scientists believed that much more competition, access, equality, and popular participation occurred in community politics than the work of the Lynds, Warner, Hollingshead, Hunter, and others implied.

Modern pluralism does not mean a commitment to "pure democracy," where all citizens participate directly in decision making. The underlying value of individual dignity continues to motivate contemporary pluralist thought, but it is generally recognized that the town-meeting type of pure democracy is not really possible in an urban industrial society. The modern pluralist is aware of the rise of giant industrial and financial organizations and the threat they pose to individual liberty. (Historically, liberals perceived the threat to individual liberty to be the concentration of government power; but after the Industrial Revolution, liberals became more concerned with business power and often turned to the government to protect individual rights.) But it is the hope of modern pluralists that "countervailing" centers of power can help to offset corporate power and protect the interests of the individual. Hopefully, competition between big business, big labor, and big government will keep each interest from abusing its power. Pluralism accepts strong government as protection against economic dominance. Likewise, pluralism accepts the growing importance of organized group activity in politics, since it is recognized that the unorganized individual is no match for industrial bureaucracies. A central value in liberal political thought has always been individual participation in decision making. Historically, this meant voting, interest and activity in public affairs, information about public issues, and knowledge about democratic procedures on the part of *individuals*. But to modern pluralists, individual participation has come to mean membership in *organized groups*. In an age of organization, meaningful participation and decision making are said to take place through the individual's membership in groups that make their influence felt in decision making. Interest groups become the means by which individuals gain access to the political system. Government is held responsible not directly by individuals, but by organized interest groups and political parties. Pluralists believe that competition between parties and organized groups, representing the interests of their citizen members, can protect the dignity of the individual and offer a viable alternative to individual participation in decision making.

The pluralist model of community power stresses the fragmentation

[21] Kaufman and Jones, "The Mystery of Power," pp. 205–12.

of authority, the influence of elected public officials, the importance of organized group activity, and the role of public opinion and elections in determining public policy. Who rules in the pluralist community? "Different small groups of interested and active citizens in different issue areas with some overlap, if any, by public officials, and occasional intervention by a large number of people at the polls." [22] Citizen influence is felt not only through organized group activity but also through leaders anticipating the reactions of citizens and endeavoring to satisfy their demands. In addition to the elected public officials, leadership in community affairs is exercised by interested individuals and groups, who confine their participation to one or two issue areas. What are leaders? "Leaders are activists. More precisely they are the most active activists." [23] The pluralist model sees interest and activity rather than economic resources as the key to leadership. Competition, fluidity, access, and equality characterize community politics.

Perhaps the most influential of the pluralist community studies was Robert A. Dahl's *Who Governs?*, a detailed analysis of decision making in New Haven, Connecticut. Dahl chose to examine sixteen major decisions on redevelopment and public education in New Haven and on nominations for mayor in both political parties for seven elections. Dahl found a polycentric and dispersed system of community power in New Haven, in contrast to Hunter's highly monolithic and centralized power structure. Influence was exercised from time to time by many individuals, each exercising power over some issue but not over others. When the issue was one of urban renewal, one set of individuals was influential; in public education, a different group of leaders were involved. Business elites, who were said by Hunter to control Atlanta, were only one of many different influential groups in New Haven. According to Dahl, "The Economic notables far from being a ruling group, are simply one of many groups out of which individuals sporadically emerge to influence the politics and acts of city officials. Almost anything one might say about the influence of the economic notables could be said with equal justice about a half dozen other groups in the New Haven community." [24] The mayor of New Haven was the only decision maker who was influential in most of the issue areas studied, and his degree of influence varied from issue to issue. "The mayor was not at the peak of a pyramid but at the center of intersecting circles. He rarely commanded. He negotiated, cajoled, exhorted, beguiled, charmed, pressed, appealed,

---

[22] Aaron Wildavsky, *Leadership in a Small Town* (Totowa, N.J.: Bedminster Press, 1964), p. 8.

[23] Ibid., p. 282.

[24] Dahl, *Who Governs?* p. 72.

reasoned, promised, insisted, demanded, even threatened; but he most needed support and acquiescence from other leaders who simply could not be commanded. Because he could not command them, he had to bargain." [25]

Aaron Wildavsky's study of Oberlin, Ohio, revealed, if anything, an even more pluralist structure of decision making than Dahl found in New Haven.[26] Wildavsky's study of Oberlin was a reaffirmation of small-town democracy, for in Oberlin, "The roads to influence ... are more than one; elites and non-elites can travel them, and the toll can be paid with energy and initiative as well as wealth." [27] Wildavsky studied eleven community decisions in Oberlin, including such diverse issues and events as the determination of municipal water rates, the passage of the fair-housing ordinance, the division of United Appeal funds, and a municipal election. Wildavsky found "that a number of citizens and outside participants who exercise leadership in most cases is an infinitesimal part of the community," but no person or group exerted leadership in *all* issue areas. To the extent that overlap among leaders in issue areas existed, this overlap involved public officials—the city manager, the mayor, and the city councilmen—who owed their positions directly or indirectly "to expressions of the democratic process through a free ballot with universal suffrage." In addition to public officials, leadership was exercised by individual "specialists," who confined their participation to one or two issue areas. Leaders very often competed among themselves and did not appear united by any common interest. Persons exercising leadership were of somewhat higher social status than the rest of the community, but it was not status or wealth that distinguished leaders from nonleaders, rather it was their degree of interest and activity in public affairs.

A team of Syracuse University social scientists provided additional support for the pluralist interpretation of community power.[28] They compiled a long list of community decisions in Syracuse and identified individuals who participated formally or informally in these decisions. Not one leadership group, but many, were revealed, each one dealing with issues in a separate field, such as health or education. In summing up the results of this massive study, Frank Munger writes:

Only three overall conclusions seem warranted by the materials examined. First, the myth that significant decisions in Syracuse emanate from one

[25] Ibid., p. 204.

[26] Wildavsky, *Leadership in a Small Town*.

[27] Ibid., p. 214.

[28] Frank J. Munger, *Decisions in Syracuse* (Bloomington: Indiana University Press, 1961); see also Linton C. Freeman et al., *Metropolitan Decision-Making* (Syracuse: Syracuse University Press, 1962).

source does not stand up under close scrutiny. Second, there tend to be as many decision centers as there are important decision areas, which means that the decision making power is fragmented among institutions, agencies, and individuals, which cluster about these areas. Third, in reality, there appear to be many kinds of community power, with one differing from another in so many fundamental ways as to make virtually impossible a meaningful comparison.[29]

In many ways New York City is in a class by itself, not only with regard to size but also in the complexity of its government. New York is simply too big, too diverse, to be dominated by a single family, a single industry, or even a small group of business and financial leaders. It came as no surprise when Wallace Sayre and Herbert Kaufman, in their monumental *Governing New York City,* concluded:

> No single ruling elite dominates the political and governmental system of New York City. . . . Most individual decisions are shaped by a small percentage of the city's population—indeed by a small percentage of those who engage actively in politics—because only the participants concerned have the time, energy, skill, and motivation to do much about them. The city government is most accurately visualized as a series of semi-autonomous little worlds, each of which brings forth programs and policies through the interactions of its own inhabitants. . . . New York's huge and diverse system of government and politics is a loose-knit and multi-centered network in which decisions are reached by ceaseless bargaining and fluctuating alliances among the major categories of participants in each center, and in which the centers are partially but strikingly isolated from one another.[30]

Edward Banfield's excellent description of decision making in Chicago also fails to reveal a "ruling elite," although the structure of influence is much more centralized than in New York City.[31] But Banfield finds that Mayor Daley's political organization is at the center of Chicago's influence structure, rather than a business or financial elite. According to Banfield: "Civic controversies in Chicago are not generated by the efforts of politicians to win votes, by differences about ideology or group interest, or by the behind-the-scenes efforts of a power elite. They arise, instead, out of the maintenance and enhancement needs of large formal organizations. The heads of an organization see some advantage to be gained by changing the situation. They propose changes. Other large organizations are threatened. They oppose, and a civic controversy takes place." [32] It is

[29] Ibid.
[30] Wallace Sayre and Herbert Kaufman, *Governing New York City,* paperback edition (New York: W. W. Norton & Company, Inc., 1965), pp. 710, 715–16.
[31] Edward Banfield, *Political Influence* (Glencoe, Ill.: The Free Press, 1961).
[32] Ibid., p. 263.

not usually business organizations that propose changes but "in most of the cases described here the effective organizations are public ones, and their chief executives are career civil servants." While Banfield acknowledged that business and financial leaders played an important role in Chicago politics, they did not really amount to a ruling elite. After studying seven major decisions in Chicago, Banfield concluded that political heads, such as Mayor Daley, and public agencies and civic associations employed top business leaders to lend prestige and legitimacy to policy proposals. The "top leaders" of Chicago—the Fields, McCormicks, Ryersons, Swifts, and Armours—and the large corporations—Inland Steel, Sears-Roebuck, Field's Department Store, and the Chicago Title and Trust Company—were criticized less for interfering in public affairs than for "failing to assume their civic responsibilities." Few of these top leaders participated directly in the decisions studied by Banfield. Banfield admits that this is not proof that the top business leadership did not exercise a great deal of influence behind the scenes. And Banfield acknowledges that the belief in the existence of a ruling elite is widespread in Chicago; he quotes the head of a black civic association as saying: "There are a dozen men in this town who could go into City Hall and order an end to racial violence just like you or I could go into a grocery store and order a loaf of bread. All they would have to do is say what they wanted and they would get it." [33] And Banfield states that top business leaders in Chicago have great "potential for power": "Indeed, if influence is defined as the *ability* to modify behavior in accordance with one's intentions, there could be little doubt that there exist 'top leaders' with aggregate influence sufficient to run the city." [34] However, Banfield maintains that these top leaders do not in fact run the city, for several reasons. First of all, there were many fundamental conflicts of interest and opinion among business leaders. Business leaders do not have sufficient unity of purpose in community politics to decide controversial questions. Second, top business leaders have no effective communication system among themselves which would enable them to act in concert. Third, the top business leaders in Chicago did not have the necessary organization to carry out their plans, even if they could agree on what should be done. Banfield concludes: "The notion that 'top leaders' run the city is certainly not supported by the facts of the controversies described in this book. On the contrary, in these cases the richest men of Chicago are conspicuous by their absence. Lesser business figures appear, but they do not act concertedly: some of them are on every side of every issue." [35]

[33] Ibid., p. 289.
[34] Ibid., p. 290.
[35] Ibid., p. 288.

HOW TO STUDY COMMUNITY POWER

Social scientists have used different methods to study community power. To some extent the differences explain the different findings of elitists and pluralists. Sociologists, including the elitists, insist upon studying the entire social structure of the community, and they view power as a by-product of social and economic position. Persons in a position to control the social and economic life of the community are said to have political power whether they exercise it or not. In contrast, pluralists define power as participation in decision making. Persons are said to have power only when they participate directly in a particular community decision. Pluralists object to the presupposition that people with control over the local and economic resources are necessarily in positions of power:

> ... nothing categorical can be assumed about power in any community. ... If anything, there seems to be an unspoken notion among pluralist researchers that at bottom nobody dominates in a town, so that their first question is not likely to be, "Who runs this community?," but rather, "Does anyone at all run this community?" The first query is somewhat like, "Have you stopped beating your wife?," in that virtually any response short of total unwillingness to answer will supply the researchers with a "power elite" along the lines presupposed by the stratification theory.[36]

The pluralists also object to the elitist presupposition that power relations persist:

> Pluralists hold that power may be tied to issues, and issues can be fleeting or persistent, provoking coalitions among interested groups and citizens, ranging in their duration from momentary to semi-permanent. ... To presume that the set of coalitions which exists in the community at any given time is a timelessly stable aspect of social structure is to introduce systematic inaccuracies into one's description of social reality.[37]

The pluralist also attacks the use of certain sociological methods in community research. According to the pluralists, the interview technique, which was at the heart of Hunter's work, inquired about the *reputation* of power rather than about the *reality* of power.[38] By asking people what they thought about power distributions in the community, Hunter was at

[36] Nelson Polsby, "How to Study Community Power: The Pluralist Alternative," *Journal of Politics*, 21 (1960), 476.

[37] Ibid., 478–79.

[38] Raymond E. Wolfinger, "Reputation and Reality in the Study of Community Power," *American Sociological Review*, 25 (1960), 636–44.

best only conducting a public-opinion poll about power. Hunter was asking about beliefs and reputations; he paid little attention to actual behavior, preferring instead to rely on the ranking of knowledgeable people about how much power other people possessed.

Moreover, Hunter's concern for social structure, the persistence through time of power relations, led him to phrase his questions about influence and leadership in general terms rather than to tie them to particular issues or decisions. For example, both Hunter and Schultze asked the following question:

Suppose a major project were before the community, one that required decision by a group of leaders whom nearly everyone would accept. Which persons would you choose to make up this group—regardless of whether or not you know them personally?

Hunter asked very bluntly: "Who is the biggest man in town?" But pluralists argued that general power rankings can be misleading:

> Most of the reputational researchers, by their failure to specify scopes in soliciting reputations for influence, assume that the power of their leader-nominees is equal for all issues. . . . This is an exceedingly dubious assumption. It is improbable, for instance, that the same people who decide which houses of prostitution are to be protected . . . also plan the public school curriculum.[39]

Pluralists argued that the "reputational technique" results in confusing *status* with *power*. Respondents may offer names of persons who have high status and are well known in the community even though such persons may not actually wield power. A related problem confuses *potential for power* with the *exercise of power*. Respondents may nominate persons who occupy high formal positions in industry or government and could conceivably exercise a great deal of power but who, as a matter of practice, do not. Pluralists believe that the potential for power is not power itself, unless it is actually exercised over specific community decisions. Further, respondents may not have an accurate perception of the distribution of power in a community. The images people have of the decision-making process are more likely to be a product of their personal attitudes toward power than any real conditions prevailing in their communities.

Finally, the pluralists argue that Hunter's research did not adequately inquire about the existence of unity among the "elite." The problem of how much unity among decision makers must exist before we conclude that an elitist structure exists is a very confusing one. Early in the debate Dahl erected a straw man when he said that the test for a rul-

[39] *Ibid.*, p. 638.

ing elite was that *no* competition existed among leaders.[40] It is doubtful, of course, that a society ever existed in which *no* competition prevailed among influentials. It is unreasonable to expect sociologists to prove that members of the elite *always* agree on everything and that they *always* impose their ideas on unwilling masses. On the other hand, to constitute a "ruling elite" a number of persons should have some common attitudes and interests that are distinguishable from the attitudes and interests of non-elites. The question remains, however, *how much* unity among leaders is required in order to verify the existence of an elite? The fault in Hunter's methodology is that he never attempted to test for any commonality of attitudes or interests among his elite members. Instead, he inferred unity of interest from similarity in the class or status background of his elite members. Yet ample evidence is available that business and financial leaders disagree on many things.

Pluralist methods of research, however, are not above criticism either. To the pluralists power means participation in decision making; it means the activities of individuals in relation to other individuals. In Dahl's words: A has power over B to the extent that he can get B to do something that B would not otherwise do." [41] Dahl conceives of power primarily in terms of the behavior of individuals at a specific point in time. His unit of analysis is the individual actor and not the social system. This is a very critical difference in conceptual starting places, and this difference leads directly to contrasting methodologies.

Because the pluralist defines power as decision making activity, it follows that pluralist research into power involves the "decisional technique," that is, a careful examination of a series of concrete public decisions. To study community power, the pluralist first selects a number of "key public decisions" that have received widespread publicity in the community. He then identifies the people who took an active part in making these decisions and obtains a full account of their actual behavior while these decisions were being made. The methodology involves reportorial techniques that have characterized case studies in political science for many years.

But, like that of the elitists, the pluralists' definition of power and their methods of study help to determine their findings and conclusions.[42] First, the case study approach, to which the pluralists are committed, predisposes the researcher to regard each decision as, in part, unique.

---

[40] Robert Dahl, "Critique of the Ruling Elite Model," *American Political Science Review,* 52 (1958): 463–69.

[41] Robert Dahl, "The Concept of Power," *Behavioral Science,* 2 (1957): 202.

[42] Anton, "Power, Pluralism, and Local Politics," pp. 425–57; Bachrach and Baratz, "Two Faces of Power," pp. 947–53.

By examining power in relation to a particular decision, one's findings about power are likely to be tied to particular decisional situations. It is not surprising that the pluralist researcher, after compiling a series of separate case studies, concludes that the exercise of power is situational, that different people exercise power over different decisions, and that generalizations about the exercise of power in different issue areas are unwarranted. The case study method predisposes the researcher to see power in situational terms.

Dahl himself is very pessimistic about the comparability of power studies and the likelihood of developing generalizations about power in communities: "We are not likely to produce—certainly not for some considerable time to come—anything like a single consistent coherent 'Theory of Power.'" [43] In short, the pluralist concept of power and the case study method assume the noncomparability of power relations even before the research has begun.

The pluralist approach also implies that political power is completely reflected in open public decisions. No doubt power is exercised in resolving the well-publicized public issues, but is this the whole story of community power? Bachrach and Baratz argue effectively that power is also exercised when social or political values or institutions limit public consideration to only those issues that are relatively unimportant to the power holders.[44] A is exercising power over B when A succeeds in suppressing issues which might in their resolution be seriously detrimental to A's preferences. In other words, elites exercise power when they prevent issues from becoming public controversies. As Schattschneider explains:

> All forms of political organization have a bias in favor of the exploitation of some kinds of conflict and the suppression of others, because organization is the mobilization of bias. Some issues are organized into politics while others are organized out.[45]

Bachrach and Baratz refer to this phenomenon as "*non*decision making." The pluralist researcher who concentrates his attention on open "concrete decisions" may overlook the possibility that public decision making has been deliberately limited to relatively noncontroversial matters, notwithstanding the fact that there are serious latent conflicts in a community.

[43] Dahl, "The Concept of Power."
[44] Bachrach and Baratz, "Two Faces of Power," pp. 947–53; "Decisions and Nondecisions," pp. 632–42.
[45] E. E. Schattschneider, *The Semi-Sovereign People* (New York: Holt, Rinehart & Winston, 1961).

Nondecision making may take several forms.[46] It may involve de-liberate overt or covert attempts at suppressing issues by powerholders. Powerless people may not even be aware of these efforts to suppress issues; there need be no direct interaction between the elite and the masses in this process. Nondecision making may also occur when middle-echelon public administrators (staff assistants, junior executives, etc.) decide not to raise an issue in *anticipation* of negative reactions by top power holders. But according to Bachrach and Baratz, the most common form of nondecision making is the continuous process of "shaping and reinforcing predominant norms, precedents, myths, institutions, and procedures that undergird and characterize the political process." No political system is really neutral. The reinforcing of a political system in schools, churches, civic groups, political parties, bicentennial celebra-tions, etc., has the effect of suppressing alternative systems and preserv-ing the status quo. These activities can be undertaken by either elites or masses, neither of whom may be fully aware of their effects in rein-forcing the existing distribution of power.

Pluralists, of course, object strenuously to a definition of power that includes "nondecision making." They are unwilling to stray from Dahl's limited definition: "A has power over B to the extent that he can get B to do something he would not otherwise do." Nondecisions are difficult, if not impossible, to research. How can a scholar really ob-serve what is *not* happening? How can we know that A is exercising power over B when B does not know about it, when A and B have no direct contact, and even when A may not be fully aware of what effect his *in*actions are having on B? Bachrach and Baratz reply that the difficulty of research on nondecisions is no excuse for denying their existence.

Another problem in pluralist research is in the selection of "key" public decisions. The pluralist proposes to study public decisions "which are generally agreed to be significant." But what decisions are generally agreed to be significant? The pluralist defines as significant those de-cisions that come before formal governmental bodies. Pluralist methodol-ogy not only overlooks nondecisions but also overlooks private decisions. Pluralist methodology assumes that the significant community decisions are made publicly; yet there is ample evidence that many of the most

---

[46] For an interesting debate over the concept of nondecision making, see Geof-frey Debnam, "Nondecisions and Power: The Two Faces of Bachrach and Baratz," and Peter Bachrach and Morton S. Baratz, "Power and Its Two Faces Revisited," in *American Political Science Review*, 69 (September, 1975): 889–904; see also Richard M. Merelman, "On the Neo-Elitist Critique of Community Power," *American Political Science Review*, 62 (June, 1968): 451–60; Raymond Wolfinger, "Nondecisions and the Study of Local Politics," *American Political Science Review*, 65 (December, 1971): 1063–80.

important decisions in a community are private decisions. Land use and development decisions, industrial location and employment decisions, housing decisions, and many other important economic decisions which profoundly affect every aspect of community life are largely private decisions made with little public visibility. How can the pluralist legitimately exclude these kinds of decisions from his analyses? He cannot claim that such decisions are not made. His only recourse is to distinguish between *public* and *private* decisions and to claim that his interest is in *public* decisions. In other words, his only recourse is to narrow the scope of political science to public decision making. By arbitrarily limiting his subject matter he can escape the responsibility for dealing with private decisions.

Dahl and others acknowledge that the total number of people who are involved in concrete public decisions is a very small minority of the community. For example, Dahl writes: "It is not too much to say that urban redevelopment has been the direct product of a small handful of leaders. . . . The bulk of the voters had virtually no direct influence on the process of nomination. . . . The number of citizens who participate directly in important decisions bearing on the public schools is small.[47] Moreover, all pluralist researchers recognize that persons exercising leadership in each issue area are of higher social status than the rest of the community. These middle- and upper-class people possess more of the skills and qualities required of leaders in a democratic system.

In short, neither the elitist nor the pluralist model of community power is the equivalent of the American ideal of grass-roots democracy— a government of, by, and for the people, in which individuals decide their own future and all have an equal voice in the affairs of their communities.

COMPARATIVE STUDY OF COMMUNITY POWER

Only by comparing structures of power and decision making processes in a wide variety of communities can social scientists learn the actual extent of elitism or pluralism in American community life. Some communities may have concentrated, pyramidal structures of power, while others have diffused, multicentered power arrangements. For example, it is very likely that decision making in Atlanta is much more centralized than decision making in New Haven, Connecticut.

The key to understanding community power lies in identifying

[47] Dahl, *Who Governs?*; see also Presthus, *Men at the Top*, p. 40; and Wildavsky, *Leadership in a Small Town*, p. 265.

different types of community power structures and then relating these to social, economic, and political conditions in communities. For example, we may find that large communities with a great deal of social and economic diversity, a competitive party system, and a variety of well-organized competing interest groups tend to have pluralist decision making systems. On the other hand, small communities with a homogeneous population, a single dominant industry, nonpartisan elections, and few competing organizations may have power structures resembling the elite model.

One of the most important comparative studies of community power is *The Rulers and the Ruled* by Professors Robert Agger, Daniel Goldrich, and Bert Swanson, an intensive study of "power and impotence" in four American communities over a fifteen-year period.[48] These scholars identified four types of power structure, based upon the degree of citizen participation and influence and the degree of competition and conflict among political leaders. (See Figure 12-1.) If many citizens shared polit-

Distributions of Political Power Among Citizens

		Broad	Narrow
Political Leadership	Convergent	Consensual Mass	Consensual Elite
	Divergent	Competitive Mass	Competitive Elite

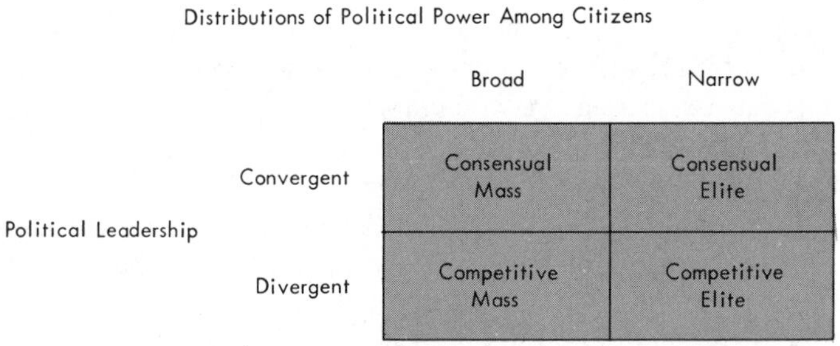

FIGURE 12-1   Types of power structures.
Source: Robert Agger, Daniel Goldrich, and Bert Swanson, *The Rulers and the Ruled* (New York: John Wiley & Sons, Inc., 1946), p. 73. Reproduced by permission.

ical influence and there were two or more competing leadership groups, the community was said to have a "competitive mass" power structure. If many citizens shared political influence and there was little disagreement or conflict among leaders, the community's power structure was termed "consensual mass." If few citizens shared political influence and there was little disagreement among leaders, the power structure was said to be "consensual elite." If few citizens shared political influence, but leaders divided into competing groups, it was said to be a "competitive elite" structure.

[48] Agger, Goldrich, and Swanson, *The Rulers and the Ruled* (New York: John Wiley & Sons, Inc., 1964).

The "consensual elite" structure in *The Rulers and the Ruled* most closely resembles the elite model described earlier, since citizen influence is limited and leaders share a single ideology. The "competitive mass" structure most closely resembles our pluralist model, since many citizens share power and there are competing leadership groups. Of course the "ideal" community is probably the "consensual mass" type, where influence is widely shared among the citizens and there is little conflict among leaders. The municipal reform movement envisions such a community, where democracy prevails and "reasonable men" agree to govern in "the public interest."

The Rulers and the Ruled studies produced many interesting findings about community power. First of all, if leadership changes from competitive to consensual over time, the distribution of power tends to change from mass to elite. In other words, with the disappearance of competition among leadership factions, citizen participation declines, fewer issues are submitted to popular referendum, and the power distribution becomes more elitist. Conversely, when the distribution of power changes from elite to mass, that is, when an increasing number of people begin to "crack" the power structure, political competition is likely to increase.

A competitive mass (pluralist) type of power structure will be more stable over time if the competing leadership groups represent high and low socioeconomic classes than if the competitors represent the same socioeconomic class. Pluralism depends in part upon socioeconomic cleavages in the community being represented by separate leadership groups. When competitive leaders represent the same socioeconomic class, competition can easily disappear over time and the power structure becomes "consensual" rather than "competitive."

The authors found that consensual elite power structures were more likely to occur in communities where the major industries were home owned. Economic leaders of home-owned industries tended to be members of a single group of political leaders in the respective communities, which discouraged political competition. The prominence of these people influenced some groups in their communities to refrain from political activity because they feared illegitimate political sanctions, even though the actual use of these sanctions was relatively infrequent.

POWER AND COMMUNITY: A SUMMARY

What factors are likely to affect the structure of power and pattern of decision making in American communities? Let us conclude with a series of hypotheses that have some support in the available literature but require additional systematic investigation.

1. Homogeneous communities, lacking deep socioeconomic, ethnic, or racial cleavages, have more concentrated power structures than heterogeneous communities. Social cleavages and community conflict are associated with pluralism.[49]

2. An increase in industrialization of economic diversity increases pluralism. Elite structures will be found in communities with single dominant industries more often than in communities with several leading industries.[50]

3. Decision making for metropolitan areas follows pluralist patterns. Elite structures are likely to be found in independent cities that are not part of a metropolitan area. The politics of central cities in metropolitan areas is likely to be pluralistic, while power structures of independent suburbs will usually be more concentrated.[51]

4. As the size of a city increases, decision making becomes more specialized and a multicentered power structure develops. The larger the city, the more likely that elected officials will be able to challenge business and financial leaders as independent sources of power.[52]

5. Older communities are more likely to have elitist power structures than newer, growing communities. Rapid growth and a large influx of "newcomers" reduce the influence of established leadership groups and create competition for leadership.[53]

6. The power structures of southern cities of the United States are usually more elitist than those in other regions of the nation. The tradition of white solidarity on behalf of segregation, the slow development of an industrial economy, and the absence of white ethnic minorities to challenge Anglo-Saxon Protestant dominants has impeded the development of pluralism in southern communities.[54]

7. Nonpartisan elections, council-manager governments, and professional civil services are associated with monolithic power structures.

[49] Miller, "Industry and Community Power Structure," pp. 9–15; and "Decision-Making Cliques in Community Power Structures," pp. 299–310.

[50] Delbert C. Miller and William H. Form, *Industry, Labor and Community* (New York: Harper & Row, Publishers, 1960).

[51] Charles Gilbert, *Governing the Suburbs* (Bloomington: Indiana University Press, 1967).

[52] Schultze, "The Role of Economic Dominants in Community Power Structure," pp. 3–9; and "The Bifurcation of Power in a Satellite Community."

[53] Ernest H. T. Barth, "Community Influence Systems: Structure and Change," *Social Forces*, 40 (October, 1961): 58–63; and Gilbert, *Governing the Suburbs*.

[54] Agger, Goldrich, and Swanson, *The Rulers and the Ruled*; and Hunter, *Community Power Structure*.

Strong political party organizations and a mayor-council form of government are associated with multicenter, pluralistic power structures.

8. Community power becomes less concentrated through time owing to a greater integration of American communities into the national economy. An increase in absentee ownership of industry and increasing urbanization multiplies the number of separate organized interests participating in community politics. Moreover, rising educational levels in the population and the spread of middle-class values stressing popular participation in government reduce the opportunities for a single leadership group to control community politics.[55]

---

[55] David A. Booth and Charles R. Adrian, "Power Structure and Community Change," *Midwest Journal of Political Science*, 6 (1962): 277–96; Roland J. Pellegrin and Charles H. Coates, "Absentee-Owned Corporations and Community Power Structure," *American Journal of Sociology*, 61 (March, 1956): 413–19; and Schultze, "The Role of Economic Dominants in Community Power Structure," pp. 3–9.

Black politics, civil rights, and public order

THE STATES AND SCHOOL DESEGREGATION

The Fourteenth Amendment declares:

> All persons born or naturalized in the United States, and subject to the jurisdiction thereof, are citizens of the United States and of the State wherein they reside. No State shall make or enforce any law which shall abridge the privileges or immunities of citizens of the United States; nor shall any State deprive any person of life, liberty, or property, without due process of law; nor deny to any person within its jurisdiction the equal protection of the laws.

The language of the Fourteenth Amendment and its historical context leave little doubt that its original purpose was to achieve the full measure of citizenship and equality for American blacks. Some Radical Republicans were prepared in 1867 to carry out the revolution in southern society that this amendment implied. But by 1877 it was clear that Reconstruction had failed and that the national government was not prepared to carry out the long, difficult, and disagreeable task of really reconstructing society in the eleven states of the former Confederacy.[1] In

[1] C. Vann Woodward, *Reunion and Reaction: The Compromise of 1877 and the End of Reconstruction* (Boston: Little, Brown and Company, 1951).

Chapter thirteen

what has been described as the compromise of 1877, the national government agreed to end military occupation of the South, give up its efforts to rearrange southern society, and lend tacit approval to white supremacy in that region. In return, the southern states pledged their support of the Union, accepted national supremacy, and, of course, agreed to permit the Republican candidate to assume the presidency after the disputed election of 1876.

·The Supreme Court adhered to the terms of the compromise. The result was an inversion of the meaning of the Fourteenth Amendment so that by 1896 it had become a bulwark of segregation. State laws segregating the races were upheld so long as persons in each of the separated races were treated equally. The constitutional argument on behalf of segregation under the Fourteenth Amendment was that the phrase "equal protection of the laws" did not prevent state-enforced *separation* of the races. Schools and other public facilities that were "separate but equal" won constitutional approval.[2] This separate—but—equal doctrine remained the Supreme Court's interpretation of the equal protection clause of the Fourteenth Amendment until 1954.

As a matter of fact, of course, segregated facilities, including public schools, were seldom if ever equal, even with respect to physical conditions. In practice, the doctrine of segregation was "separate and *un*equal." The Supreme Court began to take notice of this after World War II. While it declined to overrule the segregationist interpretation of the Fourteenth Amendment, it began to order the admission of individual blacks to white public universities, where evidence indicated that separate black institutions were inferior or nonexistent.[3]

Leaders of the newly emerging civil rights movement in the 1940s and 1950s were not satisfied with court decisions that examined the circumstances in each case to determine if separate school facilities were really equal. Led by Roy Wilkins, executive director of the National Association for the Advancement of Colored People, and Thurgood Marshall, chief counsel for the NAACP, the civil rights movement pressed for a court decision that segregation itself meant inequality within the meaning of the Fourteenth Amendment, whether or not facilities were equal in all tangible respects. In short, they wanted a complete reversal of the "separate but equal" interpretation of the Fourteenth Amendment, and a holding that laws *separating* the races were unconstitutional.

The civil rights groups chose to bring suit for desegregation in To-

---

[2] *Plessy* v. *Ferguson,* 163 U.S. 537 (1896).

[3] *Sweatt* v. *Painter,* 339 U.S. 629 (1950); *McLaurin* v. *Oklahoma State Regents,* 339 U.S. 637 (1950).

peka, Kansas, where segregated black and white schools were equal with respect to buildings, curricula, qualifications, and salaries of teachers, and other tangible factors. The object was to prevent the Court from ordering the admission of a black because *tangible* facilities were not equal, and to force the Court to review the doctrine of segregation itself.

On May 17, 1954, the Court rendered its decision in *Brown* v. *Board of Education* of Topeka, Kansas:

> Segregation of white and colored children in public schools has a detrimental effect upon the colored children. The impact is greater when it has the sanction of law, for the policy of separating the races is usually interpreted as denoting the inferiority of the Negro group. A sense of inferiority affects the motivation of a child to learn. Segregation with the sanction of law, therefore, has a tendency to retard the educational and mental development of Negro children and to deprive them of some of the benefits they would receive in a racially integrated school system.[4]

The symbolic importance of the original *Brown* v. *Topeka* decision cannot be overestimated. While it would be many years before any significant number of black children would attend formerly segregated white schools, the decision by the nation's highest Court undoubtedly stimulated black hopes and expectations. Black sociologist Kenneth Clark writes:

> This [civil rights] movement would probably not have existed at all were it not for the 1954 Supreme Court school desegregation decision which provided a tremendous boost to the morale of Negroes by its *clear* affirmation that color is irrelevant to the rights of American citizens. Until this time the Southern Negro generally had accommodated to the separatism of the black from the white society.[5]

STATE RESISTANCE

The Supreme Court had spoken forcefully in the *Brown* case in 1954 in declaring segregation unconstitutional. From a constitutional viewpoint, any state-supported segregation of the races after 1954 was prohibited. Article VI of the Constitution declares that the words of that document are "the supreme law of the land ... anything in the constitution or laws of any state to the contrary notwithstanding."

From a political viewpoint, however, the battle over segregation was just beginning. Segregation would remain a part of American life,

---

[4] *Brown* v. *Board of Education of Topeka*, 347 U.S. 483 (1954).

[5] Kenneth B. Clark, *Dark Ghetto* (New York: Harper and Row, 1965), pp. 77–78.

regardless of its constitutionality, until effective political power was brought to bear to end it. The Supreme Court, by virtue of the American system of federalism and separation of powers, has little formal power at its disposal. Congress, the president, the state governors and legislatures, and the people have more power at their disposal than the federal judiciary. The Supreme Court must rely largely on the other branches of the federal government, on the states, and on private individuals and organizations to effectuate the law of the land.

Yet in 1954 the practice of segregation was widespread and deeply ingrained in American life. Seventeen states required the segregation of the races in public schools. These seventeen states were:

Alabama	North Carolina	Delaware
Arkansas	South Carolina	Kentucky
Florida	Tennessee	Maryland
Georgia	Texas	Missouri
Louisiana	Virginia	Oklahoma
Mississippi		West Virginia

The Congress of the United States required the segregation of the races in the public schools of the District of Columbia.[6] Four additional states— Arizona, Kansas, New Mexico, and Wyoming—authorized segregation upon the option of local school boards. (See Figure 13–1.)

Thus, in deciding *Brown* v. *Topeka,* the Supreme Court struck down the laws of twenty-one states and the District of Columbia in a single opinion. Such a far-reaching decision was bound to meet with difficulties in implementation. The Supreme Court did not order immediate nationwide desegregation, but instead turned over the responsibility for desegregation to state and local authorities under the supervision of federal district courts.

The six border states with segregated school systems—Delaware, Kentucky, Maryland, Missouri, Oklahoma, and West Virginia—together with the school districts in Kansas, Arizona, and New Mexico which had operated segregated schools, chose not to resist desegregation. The District of Columbia also desegregated its public schools the year following the Supreme Court's decision.

Resistance to school integration was the policy of the eleven states of the Old Confederacy. Refusal of a school district to desegregate until it was faced with a federal court injunction was the most common form of delay. Other schemes included state payment of private school tuition in

---

[6] The Supreme Court also ruled that Congress was bound to respect the equal protection doctrine imposed upon the states by the Fourteenth Amendment as part of the due process clause of the Fifth Amendment. *Bolling* v. *Sharpe,* 347 U.S. 497 (1954).

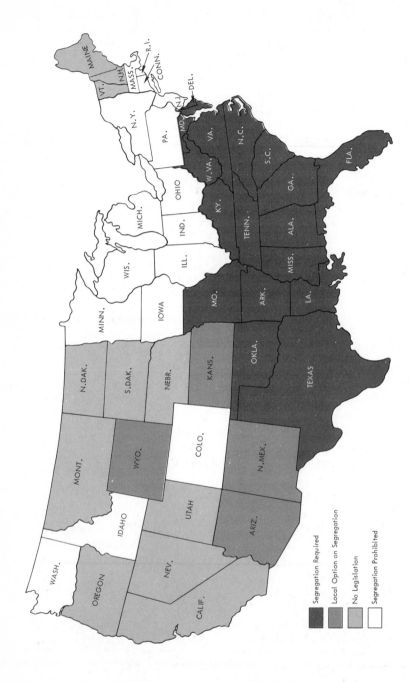

FIGURE 13–1   Segregation laws in the United States in 1954.

Segregation Required

Local Option on Segregation

No Legislation

Segregation Prohibited

lieu of providing public schools, amending compulsory attendance laws to provide that no child shall be required to attend an integrated school, requiring schools faced with desegregation orders to cease operation, and the use of pupil-placement laws to avoid or minimize the extent of integration.[7] State officials also attempted to prevent desegregation on the grounds that it would endanger public safety. State officials themselves precipitated and encouraged violent resistance through attempts to "interpose" and "nullify" federal authority within their states.[8] On the whole, those states that chose to resist desegregation were quite successful in doing so during the ten-year period from 1954 to 1964. In 1964, ten years after *Brown* v. *Topeka*, only about 2 percent of the black school children in the eleven southern states were attending integrated schools. The effectiveness of state policy up to 1964 in resisting the policy of the federal court is an important, although regrettable, comment on the powers of the states in our federal system.

In the Civil Rights Act of 1964, Congress finally entered the civil rights field in support of court efforts to achieve desegregation. Among other things, the Civil Rights Act of 1964 provided that every federal department and agency must take action to end segregation in all programs or activities receiving federal financial assistance. It was specified that this action was to include termination of financial assistance if states and communities receiving federal funds refused to comply with federal desegregation orders. Thus, in addition to *court orders* requiring desegregation, states and communities faced *administrative orders,* or "guidelines," from federal executive agencies, particularly the U.S. Office of Education, threatening loss of federal funds for noncompliance. Acting under the authority of Title VI, the U.S. Office of Education required all school districts in the seventeen formerly segregated states to submit desegregation plans as a condition of federal assistance. "Guidelines" governing the acceptability of these plans were frequently unclear, often conflicting, and always changing, yet progress toward desegregation was speeded up.

The last vestige of legal justification for delay in implementing school desegregation collapsed in 1969 when the Supreme Court rejected a request by Mississippi school officials for a delay in implementing school desegregation plans in that state. The Supreme Court declared that every school district was obligated to end dual school systems "at

---

[7] State laws that were obviously designed to evade constitutional responsibilities to end segregation were struck down in federal courts; but court litigation and delays slowed progress toward integration.

[8] The Supreme Court declared that the threat of violence was not sufficient reason to deny constitutional rights to black children and again dismissed the ancient interposition arguments. *Cooper* v. *Aaron,* 358 U.S. 1 (1958).

once" and "now and hereafter" to operate only unitary schools.[9] The effect of the decision—fifteen years after the original *Brown* case—was to eliminate any further legal justification for the continuation of segregation in public schools.

By 1970 southern school desegregation had proceeded to the point where more black pupils were attending integrated schools in the South than in the North. The Department of Health, Education, and Welfare reported that the percentage of black pupils in the North attending schools which were predominantly black (95 to 100 percent black) was greater than the percentage of black pupils in the South attending such schools. This is an important comparison between the diminishing impact of *segregation by law* in the South and the continuing impact of *de facto segregation* in the North. If the issue is posed as one of "racial isolation," it turns out that by 1970 the efforts of the federal courts and executive agencies in eliminating the last vestiges of segregation by law had reduced racial isolation in the South to the point where it was less than racial isolation in the North.

Thus, the pattern of national enforcement and local resistance in school desegregation suggested that (1) national policy could not be implemented until Congress and the executive branch threatened financial sanctions and (2) state and local resistance could be surprisingly effective in frustrating national policy over a prolonged period of time.

BUSSING AND NEIGHBORHOOD SCHOOLS IN THE SOUTH

As we have noted, southern school officials face both federal court orders and U.S. Office of Education guidelines to end segregated schools and establish unitary school systems. On the surface, this mandate seems clear enough, but is it really? Are southern school districts permitted to operate predominantly black schools in black neighborhoods and predominantly white schools in white neighborhoods? In other words, in establishing unitary school districts, can southern school officials draw school boundaries along neighborhood lines similar to the practice in northern school districts, if the resulting neighborhood schools are racially imbalanced? Or are southern school officials required to bus black and white children out of their neighborhoods in order to achieve a racial balance in each school equivalent to the racial composition of the district at large?

In the important case of *Swann v. Charlotte-Mecklenburg Board of*

[9] *Alexander* v. *Holmes County Board of Education*, 396 U.S. 19 (1969).

Education, the Supreme Court held that southern school districts have a special affirmative duty to eliminate all vestiges of dual school systems, and this responsibility may entail "bussing" and the breakup of neighborhood schools.[10] Where evidence indicates that school districts once segregated students by law, these districts have a special constitutional mandate under the Equal Protection Clause of the Fourteenth Amendment to take whatever steps are necessary, including bussing, to end all traces of dual schools. Moreover, the Court held that the racial composition of a school, in a district that once segregated by law, could be used as prima facie evidence of violation of constitutional rights, and that bussing to achieve racial balance could be imposed as a means of ending all traces of dualism in the schools. The Court was careful in saying, however, that racial imbalance in a school was not in itself grounds for ordering bussing, unless it is shown that some past government action contributed to that imbalance. Thus, the impact of the *Swann* decision falls largely on southern schools.

DE FACTO SEGREGATION
AND BUSSING IN NORTHERN CITIES

In *Brown* v. *Board of Education of Topeka, Kansas*, the Supreme Court stated that segregation had "a tendency to retard the educational and mental development of Negro children and to deprive them of some of the benefits they would receive in a racially integrated school system." The U.S. Civil Rights Commission reported that even when segregation was "de facto," that is, a product of segregated housing patterns and neighborhood schools rather than direct discrimination, the adverse effects on black students were still significant.[11] In northern urban school districts, the Commission reported, predominantly black schools were less likely to have good libraries or advanced courses in sciences and languages than predominantly white schools and more likely to have overcrowded classrooms, poorly trained teachers, and teachers who were dissatisfied with their school assignments. Relying on data supplied by sociologist James S. Coleman in his influential "Coleman Report," [12] the Commission found that black students attending predominantly black schools had lower achievement scores and lower aspiration levels than blacks from similar economic backgrounds attending predominantly

[10] *Swann* v. *Charlotte-Mecklenburg Board of Education*, 39 L.W. 4437 (1971).
[11] United States Commission on Civil Rights, *Racial Isolation in the Public Schools*, 2 vols. (Washington, D.C.: Government Printing Office, 1967).
[12] James S. Coleman, *Equality of Educational Opportunity* (Washington, D.C.: Government Printing Office, 1966).

white schools. When a group of black students in class with a majority of advantaged whites was compared with a control group of blacks attending school with a majority of disadvantaged blacks, the difference in achievement amounted to more than two grade levels. Therein lies the essential argument for ending de facto segregation in northern urban school systems.

Racial isolation of public school pupils is widespread throughout the nation. The U.S. Commission on Civil Rights reported that 75 percent of the black elementary school pupils in seventy-five large cities attended predominantly black schools (those with 90 percent or more black enrollment). However, ending de facto segregation would require drastic changes in the prevailing concept of "neighborhood schools." Schools would no longer be a part of the neighborhood or the local community but rather part of a larger citywide or areawide school system. Inner-city students would have to be bussed to the suburbs and suburban students would have to be bussed to the core city. Finally, the ending of de facto segregation would require school districts to classify students on the basis of race and to use racial categories as a basis for school placement. Although this would supposedly be a benign form of racial classification, nevertheless it would represent a return to both government-sponsored racial classification and the differential application of laws to the separate races (in contrast to the notion that the law should be "color-blind").

The argument for bussing is that it is the most effective method of providing minority groups with equal opportunities in education. Currently, black ghetto schools do not provide the same educational opportunities that are provided in predominantly white outer-city and suburban schools. As a black city councilman in Detroit put it:

> It's pragmatic. We don't have any desire to be close to white people just for the sake of being close to white people. We want the same thing everyone else wants so we can have the same opportunities for our kids to learn and grow.[13]

Blacks have a constitutional right to equal educational opportunities. Bussing is an inconvenience, but it certainly is a minor inconvenience compared with the value of equal educational opportunity. Many proponents of bussing argue that bussing was frequently used in the South to maintain segregation and many black children were bussed past white schools close to their home in order to attend all-black segregated schools. Now it is argued that the same bussing mechanisms should be used to achieve integration rather than segregation. Moreover, many

[13] *Time,* November 15, 1971, p. 64.

supporters of bussing argue that de facto segregation has indeed been abetted by government policies—for example, federal housing programs that build low-income public housing in central cities and promote middle-class home ownership in suburbs; transportation policies that make it easier for affluent, white, middle-class residents to leave the central city for homes in the suburbs while retaining their jobs in the cities, etc.—and, therefore, governments have a clear responsibility to take affirmative steps, including bussing, to integrate public schools. Suburban residents contributed to de facto segregation in the central city when they moved to the suburbs, and now it is only fair that their children be bussed back and forth between the suburbs and the ghettos in order to rectify the resulting racial imbalance.

Opposition to bussing is widespread. Not all of this opposition is "racist." Middle-class parents feel that bussing their children to ghetto schools will expose them to the social problems of ghettos—crimes, drugs, and violence. White parents fear that their children will be exposed to what blacks themselves are trying to escape—the rapes, rip-offs, robberies, and dope addiction that have turned many inner-city schools into blackboard jungles. Middle-class whites who have moved to a suburb because of its school system resent the fact that courts will order their children to be bussed back to the poorer-quality city schools. A Michigan mother argues, "I don't see any reason why they've got a right to come in here and tell me my kids can't use the school I bought and paid for." [14] The greatest opposition to bussing comes when white middle-class children are ordered to attend ghetto schools; opposition is reduced when ghetto children are ordered to attend predominantly white middle-class schools. Most whites do not believe in sending youngsters from a good school to a bad school in order to achieve racial integration. Bussing also destroys the concept of a neighborhood school, where children are educated near their homes under the guidance of their parents. Neighborhood schools are said to stimulate community involvement in the educational process —bringing teachers, parents, and students together more frequently. In addition, bussing involves educational time wasted in riding buses, educational funds spent on buses rather than learning materals, and an unnecessary increase in the risk of accidents to many children.

Proponents of bussing argue that it brings children of different cultures together and teaches them to live and work and play with others who are different from themselves. Sociologist James S. Coleman, whose original studies seemed to support racial balancing efforts, *now* observes that government-mandated, or "forced," bussing, can result in a sizable loss of white pupils in public schools and can actually increase racial

[14] Ibid., p. 57.

isolation and racial tension.[15] Recent studies of bussed black students fail to show any significant improvement relative to white students.[16] It is difficult to justify placing the burden of racial integration of American society on school children; opponents of bussing argue that the parents should first achieve an integrated community and then there would be no need for bussing. Besides, racial balancing does not always result in genuine integration; as one Pennsylvania high school student remarked after a citywide bussing program, "I thought the purpose of bussing was to integrate the schools, but in the long run, the white kids sit in one part of the bus and the black kids in another part." [17]

The question of equality in public education, however, is a constitutional queston that is likely to be resolved by federal courts rather than public opinion, or sociologists, or presidential or congressional action. The Fourteenth Amendment guarantees "equal protection of the laws." If the Supreme Court requires bussing and racial balancing in *all* public schools in order to fulfill the constitutional mandate of the Fourteenth Amendment, then only another amendment to the Constitution specifically prohibiting bussing and racial balancing could overturn that decision.

To date, however, the Supreme Court has not held that there is any affirmative duty of school officials to correct de facto racial imbalances in northern public schools, *unless* racal imbalances are a product of present or pass actions of state or local governments. Most northern cities have no history of direct discrimination by law, and it is difficult to prove that de facto segregation in these cities is a product of any government actions. In *Milligan* v. *Bradley* (1974), the Supreme Court decided by a five to four vote that the Fourteenth Amendment does not require bussing across city-suburban school district boundaries to achieve integration. Where central city schools are predominantly black, and suburban schools are predominantly white, cross-district bussing is not required, unless it is shown that some official action brought about this segregation. The Supreme Court threw out a lower federal court order for massive bussing of students between Detroit and fifty-two suburban school districts. Although Detroit city schools are 70 percent black, none of the Detroit-area school districts segregated students *within* their own boundaries. Chief Justice Burger, writing for the majority, said:

> The constitutional right of the Negro respondents residing in Detroit is to attend a unitary school system in that district. Unless petitioners drew

15 *Newsweek*, September 15, 1975, p. 51.

16 David J. Armor, "The Evidence of Bussing," *The Public Interest* (Summer, 1972), pp. 90–120.

17 *Time*, November 15, 1971, p. 64.

the district lines in a discriminatory fashion, or arranged for the white students residing in the Detroit district to attend schools in Oakland or Macomb counties, they were under no constitutional duty to make provisions for Negro students to do so.[18]

In a strong dissent, Justice Thurgood Marshall wrote:

> In the short run it may seem to be the easiest course to allow our great metropolitan areas to be divided up each into two cities—one white, the other black—but it is a course, I predict, our people will ultimately regret.

Note that this decision applies to city-suburban cross-district bussing. If a federal district court judge in any city, north or south, finds that a deliberate attempt has been made by school officials to draw school attendance lines to further racial separation, he may still order bussing *within* the city to overcome any racial imbalances produced by official action. (In 1974 and 1975, Judge W. Arthur Garrity, Jr. issued such orders in Boston, calling for widespread bussing in that city.) This important decision means that largely black central cities, surrounded by largely white suburbs, will remain de facto segregated because there are not enough white students living within the city to achieve integration.

THE CIVIL RIGHTS ACT OF 1964

The initial objective of the civil rights movement in America was to prevent discrimination and segregation as practiced by or supported by *governments,* particularly states, municipalities, and school districts. But even while important victories for the civil rights movement were being recorded in the prevention of discrimination by governments, particularly in the *Brown* case, the movement began to broaden its objectives to include the elimination of discrimination in all segments of American life, private as well as public. Civil rights was redefined to mean not merely a legal, but an actual, possibility of developing human capacities and sharing in the goods a society has produced and the way of life it has built. This was a more positive concept of civil rights. It involved not merely restrictions on government but a positive obligation of government to act forcefully to end discrimination in public accommodations, employment, housing, and all other sectors of private life.

The Constitution does not govern the activities of private individuals. It is the laws of Congress and the states that govern the conduct of private individuals. When the civil rights movement turned to combat-

---

[18] *Milligan* v. *Bradley* (1974).

ing private discrimination, it had to carry its fight into the legislative branch of government. The federal courts could help restrict discrimination by state and local governments and school authorities, but only Congress, state legislatures, and city councils could restrict discrimination practiced by private owners of restaurants, hotels and motels, private employers, and other individuals who were not government officials.

A new militancy, expressed in Martin Luther King's call for nonviolent direct action, appeared in the civil rights movement in the mid-1950s. Between 1941 and 1954, black protests were primarily in the form of legal cases brought by the NAACP to federal courts; negotiation and bargaining with white businessmen and government officials, often by the National Urban League; and local lobbying on behalf of black constituents by black political leaders in northern communities. But in 1955 the black community of Montgomery, Alabama, began a yearlong boycott with frequent demonstrations against the Montgomery city buses over segregated seating practices. The dramatic appeal and the eventual success of the boycott in Montgomery brought nationwide attention to a local black minister, Martin Luther King, and led to the creation in 1956 of the Southern Christian Leadership Conference. In 1960 black students from the North Carolina Agricultural and Technical College began a "sit-in" demonstration at the segregated Woolworth lunch counter in Greensboro, North Carolina. Soon, "sit-ins" in restaurants, "read-ins" in libraries, "pray-ins" in white churches spread throughout the South, generally under the leadership of the Southern Christian Leadership Conference, which followed "nonviolent" techniques. The Congress of Racial Equality (CORE), which at this time was also committed to the philosophy of nonviolence, initiated a series of "freedom rides" into the South, in which groups of white and black bus travelers attempted to desegregate travel and terminal facilities. Years before, the Supreme Court had held that segregation of interstate travel facilities was unconstitutional, but throughout the South, travel facilities remained segregated. The freedom riders underwent arrest and mob violence in many southern communities. In 1961 President Kennedy was obliged to send four hundred federal marshals to Montgomery, Alabama, to protect the freedom riders.

Perhaps the most dramatic confrontation between the civil rights movement and southern segregationists occurred in Birmingham, Alabama, in the spring of 1963. In support of a request for desegregation of downtown eating places and the formation of a biracial committee to work out the integration of public schools, Martin Luther King led several thousand Birmingham blacks in a series of orderly street marches. The demonstrators were met with strong police action, including fire hoses, police dogs, and electric cattle prods. Newspaper pictures of blacks being attacked by police and bitten by dogs were flashed all over the world. More than twenty-five thousand demonstrators, including Dr. King, were jailed.

The year 1963 was probably the most important for nonviolent direct action. The Birmingham action set off demonstrations in many parts of the country; the theme remained one of nonviolence, and it was usually whites rather than blacks who resorted to violence in these demonstrations. Responsible black leadership remained in control of the movement and won widespread support from the white community. The culmination of the nonviolent philosophy was a giant, yet orderly, march on Washington, held on August 28, 1963. More than two hundred thousand blacks and whites participated in the march, which was endorsed by many labor leaders, religious groups, and political figures. It was in response to this march that President Kennedy sent a strong civil rights bill to Congress, which was later to be passed after his death as the famous Civil Rights Act of 1964.

Again, in 1965, Martin Luther King led a successful nonviolent voting rights march from Selma to Montgomery, Alabama. This march was a protest against a refusal of local southern registrars to register black voters. The hostility of southern segregationists and the failure of state and local authorities to protect the marchers led President Johnson to federalize the national guard and order them to protect the demonstrators. After the march, President Johnson sent another historic civil rights measure to the Congress—the Voting Rights Act of 1965. (See Chapter 3.)

The Civil Rights Act of 1964 passed both houses of Congress by better than a two-thirds favorable vote; it won the overwhelming support of both Republican and Democratic congressmen. It was signed into law on July 4, 1964. It ranks with the Emancipation Proclamation, the Fourteenth Amendment, and *Brown* v. *Topeka* as one of the most important steps toward full equality for the black in America.

The Civil Rights Act of 1964 provides:

  I. That it is unlawful to apply unequal standards in voter registration procedures, or to deny registration for irrelevant errors or omissions on records or applications.

 II. That it is unlawful to discriminate or segregate persons on the grounds of race, color, religion, or national origin in any place of public accommodation, including hotels, motels, restaurants, movies, theatres, sports areas, entertainment houses, and other places which offer to serve the public. This prohibition extends to all establishments whose operations affect interstate commerce or whose discriminatory practices are supported by state action.

III. That the Attorney General shall undertake civil action on behalf of any person denied equal access to a public accommodation, to obtain a federal district court order to secure compliance with the act. If the owner or manager of a public accommodation continued to discriminate, he would be in contempt of court and subject to peremptory fines and imprisonment without trial by jury. This mode of enforcement gave establishments a chance to mend their ways without punishment, and it also avoided the possibility that southern juries would refuse to convict persons for violations of the act.

IV. That the Attorney General shall undertake civil actions on behalf of persons attempting orderly desegregation of public schools.

V. That the Commission on Civil Rights, first established in the Civil Rights Act of 1957, shall be empowered to investigate deprivations of the right to vote, study and collect information regarding discrimination in America, and make reports to the President and Congress.

VI. That each federal department and agency shall take action to end discrimination in all programs or activities receiving federal financial assistance in any form. This action shall include termination of financial assistance.

VII. That it shall be unlawful for any employer or labor union with 25 or more persons after 1965 to discriminate against any individual in any fashion in employment, because of his race, color, religion, sex, or national origin, and that an Equal Employment Opportunity Commission shall be established to enforce this provision by investigation, conference, conciliation, persuasion, and, if need be, civil action in federal court.[19]

FAIR HOUSING

Housing in America is becoming more, not less, segregated. Not only do population figures show that blacks are being concentrated in central

---

[19] Opponents of the Civil Rights Act of 1964 argued that Congress unconstitutionally exceeded its delegated powers when it prohibited discrimination and segregation practiced by *privately owned* public accommodations and *private* employers. Nowhere among the delegated powers of Congress in Article I of the Constitution, or even in the Fourteenth or Fifteenth Amendments, is Congress specifically given the power to prohibit discrimination practiced by *private* individuals. In reply, supporters of the act argued that Congress has the power to regulate interstate commerce. Instead of relying upon the Fourteenth Amendment, which prohibits only *state-supported* discrimination, Congress was relying on its powers over interstate commerce. In unanimous opinions in *Heart of Atlanta Motel* v. *United States* and *Katzenbach* v. *McClung* in December 1964, the Supreme Court upheld the constitutionality of the Civil Rights Act. The Court held that Congress could, by virtue of its power over interstate commerce, prohibit discrimination in any establishment that serves or offers to serve interstate travelers or that sells food or goods previously moved in interstate commerce. This power over commerce included not only major establishments, like the Heart of Atlanta Motel, but also the family-owned Ollie's Barbecue serving a local clientele. *Heart of Atlanta Motel* v. *United States*, 379 U.S. 241 (1964); *Katzenbach* v. *McClung*, 379 U.S. 294 (1964).

cities while whites are fleeing to the suburbs, but even *within* central cities black housing is highly segregated. This separation of racial groups between cities and suburbs, and within cities, is aided by the practices of the private housing industry—builders, mortgage lenders, landlords, and real estate brokers. While the housing industry contends that it is merely reflecting the preferences and financial resources of its customers, the Commission on Race and Housing concluded that "it is the real estate brokers, builders, and mortgage finance institutions which translate prejudice into discriminatory action." [20] The typical housing development concentrates homes in a single price bracket, so that most homeowners live on a street in which the prices of homes do not vary by more than $2,000 or $3,000. Real estate developers contend that the alternative pattern of building high- and low-income houses in the same neighborhood does not appeal to their customers. The result of this practice of building neighborhoods with uniformly priced homes is the creation of social class homogeneity within neighborhoods. This homogeneity even means that whites at different income levels live in different neighborhoods, and, of course, it also means that less affluent blacks are concentrated in areas where low-priced housing is concentrated. Thus, social class segregation of neighborhoods leads to de facto segregation of blacks in residential housing.

But in addition to economically imposed de facto housing segregation, blacks also face a great deal of direct discrimination in the sale and rental of housing. Until recently a large proportion of private housing in America carried racially restrictive covenants in deeds: "No part of the land hereby conveyed shall ever be used, or be occupied by or sold, demised, transferred, conveyed unto, or in trust for, leased, or rented or given to Negroes, or any other person or persons of Negro blood or extraction, or to any person of the semitic race, blood, or origin, which racial description shall be deemed to include Armenians, Jews, Hebrews, Persians, and Syrians." [21] Although racially restrictive covenants are no longer judicially enforceable,[22] the pattern they helped to create still exists.

Government policies have also contributed to housing segregation in America. Under Federal Housing Administration and Veterans Administration housing practices until the late 1950s, some $150 billion in

[20] U.S. Commission on Race and Housing, *Where Shall We Live?* (Washington, D.C.: Government Printing Office, 1958), p. 27.

[21] *Hearings before the U.S. Commission on Civil Rights on Housing in Washington, D.C.* (1958), p. 58; also cited U.S. Commission on Civil Rights, *Racial Isolation in the Public Schools*, I., 21.

[22] *Shelley* v. *Kraemer*, 334 U.S. (1948); *Barrows* v. *Jackson*, 346 U.S. 249 (1953).

mortgage loans, representing more than 15 million housing units, were insured or guaranteed under the "homogeneous neighborhood" policies then in effect.[23] These FHA and VA housing programs were partly responsible for the flight of the white middle class to the suburbs by making home ownership easily available to the middle class. But in addition to the de facto segregation resulting from suburban growth, the FHA and the VA also did nothing prior to 1964 to prevent direct discrimination in the sale of homes. The result was the creation of many all-white suburbs around major urban centers.

Low-rent public housing has been an important source of housing for blacks, but public housing has been confined almost entirely to central cities. The effect of the public housing program, therefore, has been to intensify the concentrations of the poor and nonwhite in the central city. Moreover, even within central cities, local public housing authorities, instead of locating projects on small sites scattered throughout the city, concentrated public housing projects in large blocks located in particular areas of the city, and most frequently in areas of already existing black concentrations.

For many years "fair housing" had been considered the most sensitive area of civil rights legislation. Discrimination in the sale and rental of housing was the last major civil rights problem on which Congress took action. Discrimination in housing had not been mentioned in any previous legislation; even the comprehensive Civil Rights Act of 1964 made no reference to housing. Prohibiting discrimination in the sale or rental of housing affected the constituencies of northern members of Congress more than any of the earlier, southern-oriented, legislation. The real estate industry in America was strongly opposed to restricting the "rights" of property owners "to determine the acceptability and desirability of any prospective buyer or tenant of his property." [24] Moreover, there was reason to believe that a majority of white Americans opposed laws prohibiting discrimination in sale or rental housing. When the California legislature passed a fair housing law, the state's voters replied by overwhelmingly supporting a state constitutional amendment, known as Proposition 14, which prohibited the legislature from abridging the rights of citizens to sell, lease, or rent to the person of their choice. The effect of this constitutional amendment was to nullify the state's fair housing law, and it won a statewide referendum in California by a two to one margin of voters! Later the California Supreme Court held Proposition 14 to be a violation of the Fourteenth Amendment of the United States

[23] U.S. Commission on Civil Rights, *Racial Isolation in the Public Schools*, I., 22–44.

[24] National Association of Real Estate Boards, "Property Owners' Bill of Rights," June 4, 1963.

Constitution and in effect threw out the results of the referendum; but nonetheless the vote itself was clear evidence of widespread popular opposition to fair housing.

Thus, the prospects for a fair housing law were not very good at the beginning of 1968. When Martin Luther King, Jr., was assassinated on April 4, however, the mood of the nation and of Congress changed dramatically, and many felt that Congress should pass a fair housing law as a tribute to the slain civil rights leader. The Civil Rights Act of 1968 prohibited the following forms of discrimination:

> Refusal to sell or rent a dwelling to any person because of his race, color, religion or national origin.

> Discrimination against a person in the terms, conditions or privileges of the sale or rental of a dwelling.

> Advertising the sale or rental of a dwelling indicating a preference or discrimination based on race, color, religion or national origin.

> Inducing persons to sell or rent a dwelling by referring to the entry into the neighborhood of persons of a particular race, religion or national origin (the "blockbusting" technique of real estate selling).

The act applied to all apartments and houses, rented or sold by either real estate developers or by private individuals who used the services of real estate agents. It exempted private individuals who sold their own home without the services of a real estate agent, provided they did not indicate any preference or discrimination in advertising in the sale or rental of a house.

STATE AND LOCAL ANTIDISCRIMINATION LAWS

States and communities in America were active in antidiscrimination legislation long before the federal government got around to its Civil Rights Act of 1964.[25] In 1945 New York passed the first state antidiscrimination law dealing with private employment; this law was similar to Title VII of the federal Civil Rights Act passed nineteen years later. Connecticut and New Jersey passed laws preventing discrimination in public accommodations in 1949; these laws were similar to Title II of the Civil Rights Act. In 1957, New York City adopted a fair housing law similar to the Civil Rights Act of 1968. Thus, the record of states and communities in fighting discrimination in America is not wholly a negative one.

[25] See Duane Lockard, *Toward Equal Opportunity* (New York: The Macmillan Company, 1968).

The typical state fair employment law operates as follows: after a complaint has been filed by an individual, an investigator from the commission tries to determine whether there is probable cause to believe that there is some "unfair" or "unlawful" practice relating to discrimination or segregation in employment; if probable cause is found, informal conciliation is attempted between the commission and the employer; if conciliation is unsuccessful, a formal complaint is issued and a hearing is held, at the conclusion of which the employer may be issued an order requiring him to cease the practice in question; if he refuses to comply, the commission may ask for a court order requiring compliance; if a court order is issued, of course, continued failure to comply would result in contempt of court proceedings with resultant fines or jail sentences. The problem with this approach is that it requires individuals to make complaints before action is taken, and the commission must proceed with one case at a time. Employers are given many opportunities at various stages of the proceedings to cease discrimination in the particular case in question and thereby avoid penalty. The case-by-case approach does not necessarily result in the opening of whole fields of employment to blacks. There are instances in which a single black has been aided in getting employment by a commission order, but few other blacks were subsequently hired. And occasionally, employers may be threatened into hiring less-than-qualified blacks out of fear that refusal to do so would result in costly, time-consuming, and embarrassing legal proceedings.

Fair housing laws are enforced in much the same manner as fair employment laws: each proceeds on complaint, investigation, conciliation, formal notice and hearing, commission orders, and ultimately court sanctions to force compliance. However, most fair housing laws exclude certain housing from their coverage, for example, the rental of rooms within a residence or owner-occupied building (the "Mrs. Murphy" clause) or an even more significant exclusion—sales or rental of single-family homes. Procedural delays are a particularly difficult problem in the enforcement of fair housing laws, since often the home in question is already sold to someone else and taken off the market before a complaint can be processed.

There is reasonable doubt as to whether fair housing laws—federal, state, or local—would ever succeed in breaking up America's ghettos. A crucial problem is the enforcement of fair housing laws. These laws may eliminate overt discrimination, but it is very difficult to detect discrimination when a seller or his agent chooses to mask his prejudice. But perhaps the most important obstacle to the success of fair housing legislation is the economic inability of many blacks to take advantage of it and purchase homes in affluent neighborhoods. Until the income levels of blacks are raised sufficiently to enable them to buy suburban homes, fair housing legislation will remain largely a paper commitment.

There is, yet, no evidence that cities with fair housing laws are any less segregated than those without such laws. This suggests that the economic constraints upon blacks may be more effective in creating ghettos than any direct discrimination that can be eliminated through legislation. Finally, it should be pointed out that established residential patterns are very difficult to reverse. Many blacks and whites become accustomed to prevailing residential patterns. Even if the housing market were open so that housing choice could be freely exercised, there is some question as to whether there would be immediate significant changes in racial patterns of residence.

BLACK POPULATION TRENDS

While blacks constitute only 11 percent of the total population of the United States, they are rapidly approaching a numerical majority in many of the nation's largest cities. Blacks already constitute a majority of the population of Washington, Atlanta, and Newark, and make up more than 40 percent of the population of Detroit, Baltimore, St. Louis, New Orleans, Oakland, Birmingham, and Gary. (See Table 13–1.) They will make up nearly a third of the population of Chicago, Philadelphia, Cleveland, Memphis, and Norfolk. These population trends are bound to have an impact on politics and public policy in these cities.

The two outstanding trends in black population migration in recent decades has been the tendency of blacks to leave the South and to move from rural to urban areas. Census figures show, for example, that while only 27 percent of the nation's blacks lived in urban areas in 1910, 73 percent did so in 1960, and 81 percent did so in 1970. Moreover, in leaving rural areas, blacks tended to concentrate heavily in the central cities of metropolitan areas, rather than in small towns or in metropolitan suburbs. This concentration of blacks in large central cities is a product of the availability of low-priced rental units in older run-down sections of central cities and of discriminatory housing practices of private owners and developers. Of course, underlying the concentration of blacks in run-down sectors of central cities is often a lack of sufficient income to purchase housing in suburbs or in better city neighborhoods. This poverty and unemployment that contributes to the concentration of blacks in "ghettos" is in turn a product of inadequate training and education and low aspiration levels. And problems in education and aspiration are themselves related to a breakdown in family life, delinquency, and crime. Thus, urban blacks face a whole series of interrelated problems in addi-

TABLE 13.1 Nonwhite Population as a Percentage of Total Population, 1960 and 1970, and Percentage Change in White and Nonwhite Population, 1960-70, in 40 Largest Cities in Continental United States

City	Percentage Nonwhite 1950	1960	1970	Percentage of Change 1960-1970 White	Nonwhite
New York	9.8	14.7	23.4	−9.2	61.6
Chicago	14.1	23.6	34.4	−18.6	38.4
Los Angeles	10.7	16.8	22.8	5.4	54.0
Philadelphia	18.3	26.7	34.4	−12.9	25.2
Detroit	16.4	29.2	44.5	−29.1	38.1
Houston	21.1	26.0	26.6	25.6	50.6
Baltimore	23.8	35.0	47.0	−21.4	29.7
Cleveland	16.3	28.9	39.0	−26.5	15.7
Washington, D.C.	35.4	54.8	72.3	−39.4	30.7
Milwaukee	3.6	10.5	15.6	−10.4	69.9
Dallas	13.2	18.7	25.8	14.2	66.3
San Francisco	10.5	18.4	28.6	−15.4	50.5
St. Louis	18.0	28.8	41.3	−31.6	19.1
Boston	5.3	9.8	18.1	−16.5	69.9
New Orleans	32.0	37.4	45.5	−17.6	14.9
San Antonio	7.2	7.9	8.6	9.7	30.6
San Diego	5.5	8.5	11.1	17.2	72.8
Pittsburgh	12.3	16.8	20.7	−18.0	6.0
Seattle	5.8	9.8	12.6	−9.1	43.9
Memphis	37.2	42.7	39.2	21.2	32.3
Buffalo	6.5	13.8	21.3	−20.7	34.1
Phoenix	6.2	8.4	6.7	31.2	52.2
Atlanta	36.6	46.6	51.6	−20.0	37.3
Denver	4.4	7.7	11.0	−.09	60.2
Columbus, Ohio	12.5	19.0	19.0	11.3	30.8
Indianapolis	15.0	23.0	18.4	61.0	38.5
Kansas City, Mo.	12.3	19.3	22.8	.04	37.3
Cincinnati	15.6	22.0	28.0	−17.2	15.9
Minneapolis	1.6	3.2	6.4	−32.5	79.5
Newark, N.J.	17.2	34.4	55.9	−36.7	53.6
Fort Worth	13.1	17.3	20.6	4.4	42.2
Louisville	15.7	21.4	24.0	−14.3	23.4
Long Beach	2.6	5.1	8.2	−.09	100.7
Portland, Ore.	3.5	5.7	7.8	.24	43.3
Oklahoma City	9.3	13.8	16.0	9.1	39.0
Oakland, Calif.	14.5	26.4	40.9	−21.1	52.6
Birmingham	39.9	41.1	42.2	−15.4	−6.5
Norfolk, Va.	27.9	32.6	30.4	−4.5	15.2
Miami, Fla.	16.3	22.6	23.4	13.5	19.3
Omaha	6.7	10.0	10.6	12.8	39.8

SOURCE: U.S. Bureau of the Census, *1970 Census of Population,* Series PC (S1) 2 (Washington, D.C.: Government Printing Office, 1971).

tion to discrimination: poverty, slum housing, undereducation, lack of job skills, family problems, lack of motivation, delinquency, and crime. It is difficult to talk about any one of these problems without reference to them all.

The migration of blacks into cities, particularly in the North, has been accompanied by a heavy out-migration of whites fleeing to the suburbs for a variety of reasons. The total populations of many large central cities have remained stagnant in recent years or even declined slightly; black population percentages have increased because black in-migration has countered the white out-migration. Black birthrates in urban areas have also tended to be slightly higher than those of whites.

Politically, these population trends mean that there will be an increase in organized black participation in urban politics and increasing black importance and power in city administrations. The election of black mayors in Cleveland, Gary, Newark, Detroit, Atlanta, and Los Angeles provides evidence that there will be a rise in the number of black officeholders. Black city councilmen, state legislators, and congressmen are likely to become commonplace in the next few years and evoke little comment from the news media.

However, increasing black percentages in central cities are not likely to lead to black "takeovers," in the sense that black officeholders can afford to ignore or override the interests of white city dwellers. In the first place, whites are going to continue to constitute a majority of the population in most central cities. Second, black candidates are likely to find that there is more political mileage in appealing to white votes by pledging impartiality and promising to be "mayor of *all* of the people." There is little incentive in a strict racist appeal by black candidates, as long as whites remain a substantial proportion of the city voting population.

CONTRASTING STYLES OF TWO BLACK MAYORS: BRADLEY OF LOS ANGELES AND JACKSON OF ATLANTA

Blacks do not occupy public office in America in proportion to their percentage of the nation's population. However, in recent years black candidates have been more successful at the polls than at any time since Reconstruction. Observing the political styles of the black officeholders is an instructive exercise. Most successful black candidates to date have avoided racial militancy, pledging instead to represent "all of the people." Most have avoided positions that would be threatening to whites. They have been generally willing to form electoral and political alliances with white groups.

In Thomas Bradley's successful campaign for mayor of predominantly white Los Angeles in 1973, Bradley projected an image of moderation and reasonableness in racial matters and toughness against crime based on his experience as a former policeman. Bradley's family had moved to Los Angeles from a Texas cotton plantation when Bradley was seven years old. His mother worked as a maid and his father as a waiter and porter to raise their seven children. Bradley won a track scholarship to U.C.L.A. but left college after two years to become a Los Angeles policeman. In 1956, after obtaining a night-school law degree, Bradley was admitted to the practice of law. He retired from the police force in 1961, established a small law practice, and entered Democratic politics. In 1963, Bradley was elected to the city council, the first black to sit in that body in the city's history.

Bradley's first try for the mayor's office was unsuccessful. He challenged the flamboyant Mayor Sam Yorty in 1969 and won an upset plurality over Yorty in the first election. But the city's nonpartisan election law required a second run-off election and a majority vote to win office. At the outset of the run-off campaign Bradley was favored to win; U.S. Senators Jacob K. Javits (R., N.Y.), Robert F. Kennedy (D., N.Y.) and Edmund S. Muskie (D., Ma.) were among the notables from both parties who came to town to support Bradley. Bradley maintained a moderate stance, concentrating his criticism on Yorty's frequent absences from the city. But Yorty launched a blatant campaign aimed at exploiting racial fears; he charged that Bradley was under the control of "black militants and left wing radicals." A population still traumatized by black ghetto rioting of the 1960s gave Yorty a 53 percent victory.

Bradley immediately began campaigning for the next election in 1973, stressing his racial moderation and experience in fighting crime. The first race in 1973 ended again with Bradley and Yorty propelled into a run-off race. Yorty again resorted to his racial tactics. But Bradley projected an image of a pained victim of racism attempting to talk about issues of smog, crime, and mass transit in the face of Yorty's smear tactics. The Bradley campaign was well-financed, with national contributors supporting many professional television commercials. This time Bradley won with 56 percent of the vote. It is estimated that Bradley won nearly half of the white vote in the city, and nearly all of the black vote.

Upon taking office, Bradley established himself as a moderate, hard-working, competent big-city mayor. He worked diligently on behalf of mass transit, crime control, and the revitalization of the city's core. He was elected president of the National League of Cities in 1974. Bradley speaks often of his belief in the American system and has described himself as "a black who believed in the system, who worked

within the system, who fought and prepared himself for new opportunities." [26]

Maynard Jackson's successful 1973 campaign for mayor of Atlanta
was directed more at mobilizing that city's new black majority than at
forging a black, white-liberal coalition. Indeed, for many years, Atlanta
had been governed by just such a coalition—moderate business leaders,
the press, liberal whites, and blacks in alliance against segregationist
elements. Jackson himself had served as Vice-Mayor under a white liberal
Jewish mayor, Sam Massell. But by 1973, Jackson decided to break his
ties with Massell and other white liberals and appeal to the city's 52
percent black majority. He easily defeated Massell to become Atlanta's
first black and youngest (35) mayor.

Jackson is the son of a minister who urged all of his children on to
advanced degrees. Jackson graduated from high school in Atlanta at
fourteen and won a bachelor's degree from predominantly black Morehouse College at eighteen. Jackson went to North Carolina Central University for his law degree and returned to his city to enter politics. He
quickly became visible on the political scene, not only because of his
impressive 300-pound appearance and jovial manner, but also because
of his consistent support of black causes—in rent strikes, employment
disputes, and public housing grievances.

Jackson's election split the traditional "moderate" black-white coalition that had governed the city for so many years. Jackson appeared to
tilt heavily toward the city's black constituency. He tried to fire the city's
competent, professional, white police chief; when he was thwarted by
the courts, he chose an old college chum to serve as commissioner of
public safety ("Super Chief") with jurisdiction over the police chief.
The new commissioner hired assistants who turned out to have police
records. The city's crime rate grew to one of the worst in the nation.
The mayor also presented property owners with a stiff 15-percent increase in taxes. When the city council (half white, half black) reduced
this increase in half, the mayor called the vote "a victory for the rich
against the poor." [27] The *Atlanta Constitution,* long respected for its
opposition to racism, launched an all-out attack on Jackson. But the
Mayor retained his black support with such devices as a spectacular mock
boxing match with world champion Muhammed Ali for black charity.

Atlanta's black population percentage continues to increase as most
new residential development is occurring in the city's surrounding counties. Jackson has been cautious about annexation or the consolidation of

[26] *Current Biography* (1973), p. 55.
[27] *Time,* April 21, 1975.

the few remaining areas of Fulton County not already inside the city. He wants to increase the city's tax base but he does not want to dilute the black voting strength which serves as his base of power.

LIFE IN THE GHETTOS

It is not easy for white middle-class Americans to understand what ghetto life is all about. As Roger Kahn, a white journalist who has tried to understand life in the ghettos, reports:

> Harlem is strange and dark and frightening, and if your skin is white, you are a marked alien. It doesn't matter whether you are a Quaker full of compassion, or a Jew, full of sympathy, or a Baptist, full of guilt, or a Roman Catholic, full of missionary zeal. "Man," they say in Harlem, "long as you white, you ain't one of us, and what you doin' roun' here anyway, white man? Get on back downtown where you belong." [28]

Poll takers and interviewers have a difficult time: "Man, you know why I run first time I see you come? I thought you was fuzz, man, and I was a hustlin' to stash my .45." [29] It is unlikely that many whites, liberal or conservative, understand the full extent of frustration, bitterness, and hatred in America's black ghettos. White conservatives may be shocked to learn that many middle-class values about thrift, hard work, and the sanctity of property are not universally shared with ghetto residents. White liberals may be shocked to learn that racial prejudice is not the monopoly of the white man.

The female-headed black family emerges as one of the striking features of life in the ghetto. Over 25 percent of all black families are headed by women.[30] For the male offspring of a matriarchal ghetto family, the future is often depressing, with defeat and frustration repeating itself throughout his life. He may drop out of school in the ninth grade as a protest to his lack of success. If he fails his armed forces qualification test (and a majority of young men from the ghetto do so), he may never again have an opportunity for further education or job training. Lacking parental supervision, and with little to do, he may get into trouble with the police. A police record will further hurt his chances of getting a job. The ghetto male with limited job skills enters the job market seriously handicapped. His pay is usually not enough to support a family and he has little hope of moving up. He may tie up much of

[28] Roger Kahn, "White Man, Walk Easy," *Saturday Evening Post*, June 13, 1964.
[29] Ibid.
[30] See Daniel P. Moynihan, *The Negro Family: The Case for National Action* (Washington, D.C.: Government Printing Office, 1965).

his income in installment debts for a car, television set, or other conveniences, which he sees in widespread use among middle-class Americans. Because of his low credit rating, he will be forced to pay excessive interests rates, and sooner or later his creditors will garnish his salary. If he marries, he is likely to have at least five children, and he and his family will live in overcrowded, substandard housing. As pressures and frustrations mount, he may decide to leave his family, either because he has found his inability to support his wife and children humiliating, or because only in this way will his wife and children be eligible for welfare payments. Welfare policy again strengthens the role of the female in the black family, because she can get the family on welfare (particularly Aid to Families with Dependent Children) while the male cannot. In fact, his remaining with the family is an obstacle to receiving welfare payments.

Occasionally, the rhetoric of politics suggests that the conditions of blacks in America are worsening, that America is hopelessly "racist," and that there is no possibility of real progress. This is not true. Blacks have made great progress since 1960 in income, jobs, education, housing, and other conditions of life—not only in absolute terms but also in narrowing the gap between themselves and whites. Black leaders can be expected to concentrate on what still must be done to achieve equality in America. But it is important that we do not mistake failure to progress fast enough with failure to progress at all. American society has moved toward equality very rapidly over the last decade. Of course whites have made progress too, and in every measure of "life chances" blacks remain below average white levels. Doubtlessly the progress made by blacks in recent years has been long overdue, and no rate of progress can be considered fast *enough*. But recent progress has been very impressive.

Median black family income was only slightly more than half of the median white family income in the 1950s, but by 1970 black family income had increased to 64 percent of white family income. (See Table 13–2.) In a single decade the proportion of blacks living below the recognized poverty line had fallen from 56 percent of all blacks to 31 percent. Blacks increased their percentage of professional, managerial, sales, clerical, and other white-collar jobs and reduced their percentage of laborers, service workers, and farmers. The proportion of blacks living in substandard housing fell from nearly one-half to less than one-quarter. Blacks also narrowed the gap in education: the proportion of young black males who completed high school rose from 37 percent to over 59 percent in a single decade.

However, there is some disturbing evidence that suggests a slowdown in the march toward equality in the 1970s. Certainly, the recession of 1974–75 had an adverse effect on black economic progress. And blacks

TABLE 13.2   Change in Black-White Life Chances

Median Income of Families

	1947	1960	1968	1970	1972	1974
White	$4,916	$6,857	$8,937	$10,236	$11,549	$13,356
Negro	$2,514	$3,794	$5,590	$ 6,516	$ 6,864	$ 7,808

Median Income of Families of Negro and Other Races as a Percent of White Family Income

Year	%	Year	%	Year	%
1950	54	1964	56	1972	62
1955	55	1966	60	1974	58
1959	52	1968	63		
1960	55	1970	64		

Persons Below Poverty Level

	Millions		Percent of Total	
	Negro	White	Negro	White
1959	11.0	28.5	56	18
1965	10.7	22.5	47	13
1969	7.6	16.7	31	10
1974	7.5	16.3	31	9

Occupation: Negro and Other Races as Percent of All Workers in Selected Occupations

Total	1960	1970	1974
Professional	4	6	7
Medical	4	8	8
Teachers	7	10	9
Managers	2	3	4
Clerical	5	8	9
Sales	3	4	4
Craftsmen	5	7	7
Operatives	12	14	13
Nonfarm laborers	27	24	20
Private household	46	44	41
Other service	20	19	19
Farm	16	11	9

Percent of Persons 25 to 29 Years Old Who Completed 4 Years of High School or More

	Male		Female	
	Negro	White	Negro	White
1960	37	64	42	66
1968	55	78	58	77
1971	59	81	63	80

SOURCE: Bureau of the Census, "The Social and Economic Status of Negroes in the United States," Current Population Reports Series No. 29, p. 23. Updated.

appeared less able to keep up with inflationary pressures than whites. Table 13–2 reveals that even though both black and white family incomes climbed in the early 1970s, the ratio of black-to-white family income dipped from its high of 64 percent in 1970 to 58 percent in 1974. Black poverty has remained at about 31 percent of the black population, while white poverty has continued to decline. However, blacks continue to gain in prestigious occupations and in education.

"AFFIRMATIVE ACTION" OR "REVERSE DISCRIMINATION"?

Aside from bussing, perhaps the most sensitive issue affecting black-white relations in America today is the question of how to achieve equality in education, jobs, and income. The civil rights movement of the 1960s opened new opportunities for black Americans. But equality of *opportunity* is not the same as absolute equality. The problem of inequality today is usually identified as continued differences in black and white median family incomes, differences in the percentages of black and white families living in poverty, differences in the percentages of blacks and whites in professional, managerial, and skilled occupations, and differences between blacks and whites in educational accomplishments.

What public policies should be pursued to achieve equality in America? Is it sufficient that government eliminate discrimination, guarantee "equality opportunity" for blacks and whites, and apply "color-blind" standards to both blacks and whites? Or should government take "affirmative action" to overcome the results of past unequal treatment of blacks—preferential or compensatory treatment that will favor black applicants for university admissions and scholarships, job hiring and promotion, and other opportunities for advancement in life?

The earlier emphasis of government policy, of course, was non-discrimination; although special recruiting techniques, special training, and encouragement of university applicants was stressed, equal employment opportunity ". . . was not a program to offer special privilege to any one group of persons because of their particular race, religion, sex or national origin." [31] This appeared to conform to the original non-discrimination approach of executive orders, beginning with President Harry Truman's decision to desegregate the armed forces in 1946, and carrying through Title VI and Title VII of the Civil Rights Act of 1964 eliminating discrimination in federally aided projects and private em-

[31] See David H. Rosenbloom, "The Civil Service Commission's Decision to Authorize the Use of Goals and Timetables in Federal Equal Employment Opportunity Programs," *Western Political Quarterly,* 26 (June, 1973): 236–51.

ployment. There were no quota systems for black applicants which might result in lower qualified blacks being selected over higher qualified whites for schools, jobs, or promotions.

Increasingly, however, the goal of the civil rights movement shifted from the traditional aim of equality of opportunity through nondiscrimination alone, to *affirmative action* to establish "goals and timetables" to achieve absolute equality between blacks and whites. While carefully avoiding the term *quota*, the notion of affirmative action tests the success of equal employment opportunity by observing whether blacks achieve admissions, jobs, and promotions in proportion to their numbers in the population. One of the first applications of affirmative action occurred in 1967 when the U.S. Office of Federal Contract Compliance issued the "Philadelphia Plan," requiring contractors bidding on federal projects to submit affirmative-action plans including specific percentage goals for the employment of minorities. At first the U. S. Civil Service Commission resisted the imposition of "goals" in federal employment: "This is tantamount to a quota system and is inconsistent with executive orders on equal employment . . . as well as with the concept of the merit system itself." [32] But as pressure developed for greater minority representation, the Civil Service Commission relented somewhat, distinguishing between "quotas" and "goals": "While quotas are not permissible, federal agencies may use numerical guidelines to assess progress toward equal employment opportunity and as one means of deterring the need for additional affirmative action regarding minority employment." [33] The U. S. Office of Education also waffled on affirmative-action requirements for the nation's colleges and universities. In October 1972 it issued guidelines which mandated "goals" for university admissions and faculty hiring of blacks and women. But complaints that white males faced reverse discrimination brought forth a new order in November 1974 that "in all cases the most qualified applicant is the one that should be hired." [34]

Federal policy in this area determines state and local government policy, because state and local governments are recipients of federal funds. But federal policy is ambiguous—perhaps deliberately so. "Quotas" which give preference to blacks because of their race may violate the Equal Protection Clause of the 14th Amendment. Yet federal officials generally measure "progress" in "affirmative action" in terms of the number of blacks admitted, employed, or promoted. The pressure to show "progress" and retain federal financial support can result in prefer-

---

[32] Letter from Civil Service Commission, July 24, 1970, cited ibid., p. 247.

[33] Letter of February 3, 1971; cited ibid., p. 247.

[34] *Washington Post,* November 10, 1974.

ential treatment of blacks and discrimination against whites with equal or better qualifications. It also puts pressure on traditional measures of qualifications—test scores and educational achievement. Blacks argue that these are not good predictors of performance on the job or in school and that these measures are biased in favor of white culture. State and local governments, schools, colleges and universities, and private employers are under pressure to drop these standards.[35] But how far can any school, agency, or employer go in dropping traditional standards? It is not difficult to drop educational requirements for sanitation workers, but what about physicians, surgeons, attorneys, pilots, and others whose skills directly affect health and safety?

The more perplexing question is whether affirmative-action programs discriminate against whites in violation of the Equal Protection Clause of the Fourteenth Amendment. In 1974, Marco DeFunis, Jr., sued the University of Washington Law School because his application was rejected, while blacks with lower grades and test scores were admitted. But the Supreme Court, by a 5-4 decision, decided *not* to decide the issue. (DeFunis had been admitted by a lower federal court order and by the time the case reached the Supreme Court he was near graduation; hence they declared the case moot.) Eventually, however, the Supreme Court will have to rule on this difficult question.

The question becomes even more complex if we try to weigh the costs of some "reverse discrimination" against the value of achieving greater representation of blacks in all echelons of society. Perhaps it is better for society as a whole to make some sacrifices to bring black Americans into the mainstream of economic life—to give them a "stake in society" and hence to sew up the worn fabric of the social system. But who must make these sacrifices—not the established white upper classes, but the sons and daughters of white middle- and working-class families who are in direct competition with upwardly mobile blacks. Must the price of past discrimination against blacks now fall on these young whites? Another problem: can preferential treatment eventually create new injustices for blacks who have been recipients of such treatment? Will it create a facade of equality and representation, while actually patronizing black recipients? Does preferential treatment imply that blacks cannot "make it" without such treatment? Clearly there are sensitive moral and ethical questions surrounding this area of public policy, as well as the constitutional question of equal protection of the laws.

---

[35] See Frank J. Thompson, "Bureaucratic Responsiveness in the Cities: The Problem of Minority Hiring," *Urban Affairs Quarterly,* 10 (September, 1974): 40–68.

VIOLENCE IN AMERICAN CITIES

Civil disorder and violence are not new on the American scene. On the night of December 16, 1773, a group of "agitators" in Boston, Massachusetts, illegally destroyed 342 chests of tea. And violence as a form of political protest has continued intermittently in America to the present day. The nation itself was founded in armed revolution. Yet even though domestic violence has played a prominent role in America's history, the ghetto riots of the 1960s shocked the nation. All these riots involved black attacks on established authority—policemen, firemen, National Guardsmen, whites, in general, and property owned by whites. Three of these riots—Watts, California, in 1965 and Newark and Detroit in 1967—amounted to major civil disorders.

The Watts riot in August 1965 was described in the McCone Commission's report:

> In the ugliest interval . . . perhaps as many as 10,000 Negroes took to the streets in neurotic bands. They looted stores, set fires, beat up white passers-by whom they had hauled from stopped cars, many of which were turned upside-down and burned, exchanged shots with law enforcement officers, and stoned and shot at firemen. The rioters seemed to have been caught up in an insensate rage of destruction. By Friday, disorder spread to adjoining areas, and ultimately an area covering 46.5 square miles had to be controlled with the aid of military authority before public order was restored. . . .

> Of the 34 killed, one was a fireman, one was a deputy sheriff, and one a Long Beach policeman [the remainder were blacks].

> More than 600 buildings were damaged by burning and looting. Out of this number, more than 200 were completely destroyed by fire. The rioters concentrated primarily on food markets, liquor stores, furniture stores, clothing stores, department stores, and pawn shops.[36]

In the summer of 1967, New Jersey's governor proclaimed Newark a city "in open rebellion," declared a state of emergency, and called out the National Guard. For four consecutive days and nights snipers fired at police and firemen, looters made off with the inventories of scores of stores, and arsonists set fire to large portions of commercial property in the black section of that city. More than 4,000 city policemen, state troopers, and National Guardsmen were required to restore order. Before the riot was over, twenty-three persons had been killed, and property damage was widespread. Of the dead, only two were white—a po-

---

[36] Governor's Commission on the Los Angeles Riots, John A. McCone, Chairman, *Violence in the City—An End or a Beginning* (Sacramento: Office of the Governor of California, 1965), pp. 3–5.

liceman and a fireman. Of the black dead, two were children and six were women.

But it was Detroit that became the scene of the bloodiest racial violence of the twentieth century. A week of rioting in Detroit, July 23–28, 1967, left forty-three dead and more than 1,000 injured. Whole sections of the city were reduced to charred ruins and smoke. Over 1,300 buildings were totally demolished and 2,700 businesses sacked. Detroit's upheaval began when police raided an after-hours club and arrested the bartender and several customers for selling and consuming alcoholic beverages after authorized closing hours. A force of 15,000 city and state police, National Guardsmen, and finally federal troops fought to quell the violence. Most of the looted retail businesses were liquor stores, grocery stores, and furniture stores. Many black merchants scrawled "Soul Brother" on their windows in an attempt to escape the wrath of the black mobs. Eventually, homes and shops covering a total area of fourteen square miles were gutted by fire. Firemen who tried to fight fires were stoned and occasionally shot by ghetto residents. Of the forty-three persons who were killed during the riot, thirty-nine were black and ten were white. Among the dead were one National Guardsman, one fireman, one policeman, and one black private guard. Both the violence and the pathos of the ghetto riots were reflected in the following report from Detroit:

> . . . a spirit of carefree nihilism was taking hold. To riot and destroy appeared more and more to become ends in themselves. Late Sunday afternoon it appeared to one observer that the young people were "dancing amidst the flames."

> A Negro plainclothes officer was standing in an intersection when a man threw a Molotov cocktail into a business establishment on the corner. In the heat of the afternoon, fanned by the 20–25 mile per hour winds of both Sunday and Monday, the fire reached the home next door within minutes. As its residents uselessly sprayed the flames with garden hoses, the fire jumped from roof to roof of adjacent two- and three-story buildings. Within the hour the entire block was in flames. The ninth house in the burning row belonged to the arsonist who had thrown the Molotov cocktail. . . .

> . . . employed as a private guard, fifty-five-year-old Julius L. Dorsey, a Negro, was standing in front of a market, when accosted by two Negro men and a woman. They demanded he permit them to loot the market. He ignored their demands. They began to berate him. He asked a neighbor to call the police. As the argument grew more heated, Dorsey fired three shots from his pistol in the air.

> The police radio reported: "Looters, they have rifles." A patrolcar driven by a police officer and carrying three National Guardsmen arrived.

As the looters fled, the law enforcement personnel opened fire. When the firing ceased, one person lay dead. He was Julius L. Dorsey. . . .[37]

The National Advisory Commission on Civil Disorders concluded:

1. No civil disorder was "typical" in all respects . . .
2. While civil disorders of 1967 were racial in character, they were not *inter*racial. The 1967 disorders, as well as earlier disorders of the recent period, involved action within Negro neighborhoods against symbols of white American society—authority and property—rather than against white persons.
3. Despite extremist rhetoric there was no attempt to subvert the social order of the United States. Instead, most of those who attacked white authority and property seemed to be demanding fuller participation in the social order and the material benefits enjoyed by the vast majority of American citizens.
4. Disorder did not typically erupt without pre-existing causes as a result of a single "triggering" or "precipitating" incident. Instead, it developed out of an increasingly social atmosphere, in which typically a series of tension-heightening incidents over a period of weeks or months became linked in the minds of many in the Negro community with a shared network of underlying grievances.
5. There was, typically, a complex relationship between the series of incidents, and the underlying grievances. For example, grievances about allegedly abusive police practices . . . were often aggravated in the minds of many Negroes by incidents involving the police, or the inaction of municipal authorities on Negro complaints about police action.
6. Many grievances in the Negro community resulted from discrimination, prejudice, and powerlessness which Negroes often experience. . . .
7. Characteristically, the typical rioter was not a hoodlum, habitual criminal, or riff-raff. . . . Instead, he was a teenager or young adult, a lifelong resident of the city in which he rioted, a high school drop-out— but somewhat better than his Negro neighbor—and almost invariably underemployed or employed in a menial job. He was proud of his race, extremely hostile to both whites and middle-class Negroes and, though informed about politics, highly distrustful of the political system and of political leaders.
8. Numerous Negro counter-rioters walked the street, urging the rioters to "cool it". . . .
9. Negotiation between Negro and white officials occurred during virtually all of this disorder. . . .
10. . . . Some rioters may have shared neither the conditions nor the grievance of their Negro neighbors; some may have coolly and deliberately exploited the chaos created by others; some may have been drawn into the melee merely because they identified with, or wished to emulate, others.

---

[37] National Advisory Commission on Civil Disorders, *Report* (Washington, D.C.: Government Printing Office, 1968), p. 4.

11. The background of disorder in the riot cities was typically characterized by severely disadvantaged conditions for Negroes, especially as compared with those of whites. . . .
12. In the immediate aftermath of disorder, the status quo of daily life before the disorder generally was quickly restored. Yet despite some notable public and private efforts, little basic change took place in the conditions underlying the disorder. In some cases, the result was increased dislike between blacks and whites, diminished interracial communication, and the growth of Negro and white extremist groups.[38]

ASSESSING THE CAUSES OF RIOTS

One explanation of urban violence is that it is a product of the relative deprivation of ghetto residents.[39] *Relative deprivation* is the discrepancy between people's expectations about the goods and conditions of life to which they are justifiably entitled and what they perceive to be their chances for getting and keeping what they feel they deserve. Relative deprivation is not merely a complicated way of saying that people are deprived and therefore angry because they have less than what they want; it is more complex than that. Relative deprivation focuses on (1) what people think they *deserve*, not just what they want in an ideal sense, and (2) what they think they have a *chance* of getting, not just what they have.

Relative deprivation differs considerably from the *absolute deprivation* hypothesis. The absolute deprivation idea suggests that individuals who are the most deprived are those who are most likely to rise up. Of course, it is true that conditions in America's ghettos provide the necessary environment for violence. Racial imbalance, de facto segregation, slum housing, discrimination, unemployment, poor schools, and poverty all provide excellent kindling for the flames of violence. But these underlying conditions for violence existed for decades in America, and the nation never experienced simultaneous violent uprisings in nearly all its major cities before the 1960s. This suggests that the deprivation itself is not a sufficient condition for violence. Some new ingredients were added to the incendiary conditions in American cities which touched off the violence of the 1960s.

---

[38] Ibid., pp. 110–12.

[39] For a full discussion of the *relative deprivation* explanation as well as alternative explanations, see Dan R. Bowen and Louis H. Masotti, "Civil Violence: A Theoretical Overview," in *Riots and Rebellion*, ed. Masotti and Bowen (Beverly Hills: Sage Publications, 1968). See also James C. Davies, "Toward a Theory of Revolution," *American Sociological Review*, 27 (February, 1962): 6; and Ted Gur, *Why Men Rebel* (Princeton: Princeton University Press, 1970).

Relative deprivation focuses on the distance between current status and expectation level. According to this hypothesis, it is neither the wholly downtrodden—who have no aspirations—nor the very well off—who can satisfy theirs—who represent a threat to civil order. The threat is posed by those whose expectations about what they deserve outdistance the capacity of the political system to satisfy them. Often, rapid increases in expectations are a product of minor symbolic or token improvements in conditions. This leads to the apparent paradox of violence and disorder occurring at the very time that improvements in the conditions of blacks are being made. It is hope, not despair, that generates civil violence and disorder. Masotti and Bowen remark: "The reason why black Americans riot is because there has been just enough improvement in their condition to generate hopes, expectations, or aspirations beyond the capacities of the system to meet them." [40]

Once racial violence has broken out anywhere in the nation, the mass media play an important role in disseminating images of violence as well as the symbols and rationalizations of the rioters. Television offers the rioter a mass audience. It was not unknown for rioters to leave the scene temporarily to hurry to their television sets to see themselves. Moreover, television images may reinforce predispositions to participate and even to legitimatize participation. Television enables blacks in one ghetto to see what blacks in another ghetto are doing, and it explains simultaneous rioting in ghettos across the nation.

THE POLITICS OF RIOTING

Any interpretation of urban violence requires the unraveling of the complex actions and motivations of the participants. Interpretation of riots is a political activity itself: elected public officials concerned primarily with re-establishing order may deliberately de-emphasize the political or racial aspects of rioting, downgrade the seriousness of riots, and brand the participants as "hoodlums," "riff-raff," or "a tiny minority." In contrast, black militants may accentuate the racial character of disorders as well as their seriousness; they may hail riots as "black revolts," "rebellions," or "insurrections." Whites are far more likely to believe that the main cause of civil disorders has been radicals, looters, and other "undesirables," while blacks tend to cite discrimination, unfair treatment by police, unemployment, or poor housing as riot causes.[41]

---

[40] Masotti and Bowen, *Riots and Rebellion*, pp. 24–25.
[41] *Supplemental Studies for the National Commission on Civil Disorders* (Washington: Government Printing Office, 1968).

Blacks and whites also differ on how to prevent violence: whites call for more police control, while blacks call for improvements in socio-economic conditions and the elimination of discrimination.

Our own interpretation is that the ghetto riots of the 1960s were a form of political protest. They expressed the hostility many blacks feel toward white people in general and established authority in particular. To be sure, this form of political protest is a criminal one. And it may be self-defeating. The great majority of the casualities of the riots—the dead and injured—were blacks. And much of the property destroyed belonged to blacks. More importantly, the rioting stimulated a strong law-and-order movement in federal, state, and local politics. Certainly, violence itself is unlikely to solve the complicated problems facing ghetto residents. But the riots were not senseless or without meaning.

Our interpretation of the riots as political protest and the result of "relative deprivation" is buttressed by evidence that a large proportion of ghetto blacks supported the riots.[42] Moreover, the active rioters were not the poorest among ghetto residents. Indeed, the evidence suggests that the rioters were better educated, and had better jobs and higher incomes, than most of their fellow blacks living in the ghettos. Finally, it was noted that rioters were more politically active and racially conscious than nonrioting blacks.

Comparisons of riot and nonriot cities lend additional support to the view that it is *not* absolute deprivation that leads to rioting. Political scientist Bryan T. Downes and sociologist Seymour Spilerman independently concluded in separate studies that objective measures of social and economic deprivation were poor predictors of ghetto violence.[43] The most important difference between riot and nonriot cities was the numerical size of the black population, although population density and recent growth of the black population also contributed to rioting. These conditions may all be related to the development of black community consciousness.

Perhaps the reason for the relative decline in ghetto rioting in 1970s is the realization that this form of political action is useless and self-defeating. No great changes in ghetto life occurred as a result of the rioting in the 1960s. In national politics the primary beneficiaries

---

[42] See ibid., and William McCord and John Howard, "Negro Opinion in Three Riot Cities," in *Riots and Rebellion* edited by Louis H. Masotti and Don R. Bowen (New York: Sage, 1968.)

[43] Bryan T. Downes, "Social and Political Characteristics of Riot Cities: A Comparative Study," *Social Science Quarterly,* 49 (December, 1968): 504–20; Seymour Spilerman, "The Causes of Racial Disturbances," *American Sociological Review,* 35 (August, 1970): 617–49.

appeared to be politicians such as George C. Wallace who espoused a strong law-and-order position. The Johnson, Nixon and Ford administrations did not appear to be moved by the rioting to provide greater assistance to urban ghettos. Indeed, there are many Democrats and Republicans in national politics who would not want to appear to "reward violence" by supporting urban programs in the face of riots.

The politics
of education

DIRECTIONS IN EDUCATIONAL POLICY

The primary responsibility for public education rests with the fifty state governments and their subdivisions. It is the largest and most costly of state functions.

It was in 1647 that the Massachusetts colonial legislature first required towns to provide for the education of children out of public funds. The rugged individualists of earlier eras thought it outrageous that one man should be taxed to pay for the education of another man's child. They were joined in their opposition to public education by those aristocrats who were opposed to arming the common man with the power that knowledge gives. But the logic of democracy led inevitably to public education. The earliest democrats believed that the safest repository of the ultimate powers of society was the people themselves. If the people make mistakes, the remedy was not to remove power from their hands, but to help them in forming their judgment through education. Congress passed the Northwest Ordinance in 1787 offering land grants for public schools in the new territories and giving succeeding generations words to be forever etched on grammar school cornerstones: "Religion, mortality, and knowledge being necessary to good government and the happiness of mankind, schools and the means for education shall ever be

Chapter fourteen

encouraged." When American democracy adopted universal manhood suffrage, it affected every aspect of American life, and particularly education. If the common man was to be granted the right of suffrage, he must be educated to his task. This meant that public education had to be universal, free, and compulsory.

If there ever was a time when schools were only expected to combat ignorance and illiteracy, that time is far behind us. Today schools are expected to do many things: resolve racial conflict and build an integrated society; inspire patriotism and good citizenship; provide values, aspirations, and a sense of identity to disadvantaged children; offer various forms of recreation and mass entertainment (football games, bands, choruses, majorettes, and the like); reduce conflict in society by teaching children to get along well with others and adjust to group living; reduce the highway accident toll by teaching students to be good drivers; fight disease and ill health through physical education, health training, and even medical treatment; eliminate unemployment and poverty by teaching job skills; end malnutrition and hunger through school lunch and milk programs; produce scientists and other technicians to continue America's progress in science and technology; fight drug abuse and educate children about sex; and act as custodians for teenagers who have no interest in education but who are not permitted to work or roam the streets unsupervised. In other words, nearly all the nation's problems are reflected in demands placed on the nation's schools. And, of course, these demands are frequently conflicting.

THE FEDERAL ROLE IN EDUCATION

Currently, the federal government pays only about 10 percent of the cost of education; 90 percent of the cost of public schools is borne by state and local governments. The federal government's role in education, however, is a longstanding one. As already mentioned in the famous Northwest Ordinance of 1787, Congress offered land grants for public schools in the new territories. Then in 1862 the Morrill Land Grant Act provided grants of federal land to each state for the establishment of colleges specializing in agricultural and mechanical arts. These became known as "land-grant colleges." In 1867 Congress established a U.S. Office of Education, which is now a part of the Department of Health, Education, and Welfare. The Smith-Hughes Act of 1917 set up the first program of federal grants-in-aid to promote vocational education and enabled schools to provide training in agriculture, home economics, trades, and industries. In the National School Lunch and Milk programs, begun in 1946, federal grants and commodity donations are made for nonprofit lunches and milk served in public and private schools. In the Federal Impacted Areas Aid Program, begun in 1950, federal aid is authorized for "federally impacted" areas of the nation. These are areas where federal activities create a substantial increase in school enrollments or a reduction in taxable resources because of federally owned property. Federal funds can be used for construction, operation, and maintenance of schools in these public school districts.

In response to the Soviet Union's success in launching the first satellite into space, Congress became concerned that the American educational system might not be keeping abreast of advances being made in other nations, particularly in science and technology. The Russian space shot created an intensive debate over education in America and prompted Congress to re-examine the responsibilities of the national government in public education. "Sputnik" made everyone realize that education was closely related to national defense. In the National Defense Education Act of 1958, Congress provided financial aid to states and public school districts to improve instruction in science, mathematics, and foreign languages; to strengthen guidance counseling and testing; and to improve statistical services—in addition to establishing a system of loans to undergraduates and fellowships to graduate students and funds to colleges, all in an effort to improve the training of teachers in America.

Despite these many individual federal programs in education, before 1965 the overall contribution of the federal government to education was very small. The Elementary and Secondary Education Act of 1965 marked the first real breakthrough in federal aid to education. ESEA is now the largest federal-aid-to-education program. Yet even ESEA cannot be termed a *general* aid-to-education program—one that would assist all public and private schools in school construction and teachers' salaries. The main thrust of ESEA is in "poverty-impacted" schools, instructional materials, and educational research and training.

The Elementary and Secondary Education Act provided for the following:

Title I — Financial assistance to "local educational agencies serving areas with concentrations of children from low-income families" for programs "which contribute particularly to meeting the special needs of educationally deprived children." Grants would be made on application to the Office of Education on the basis of the number of children from poverty-stricken families.

Title II — Grants to "public and private elementary and secondary schools" for the acquisition of school library resources, textbooks, and other instructional materials.

Title III   Grants to public and private schools for "supplementary educational centers and services" including remedial programs, counseling, adult education, specialized instruction and equipment, etc.

Title IV   Grants to universities, colleges or other nonprofit organizations for research or demonstration projects in education.

Title V   Grants to stimulate and strengthen state educational agencies.

Note that the act does include private, church-related schools in some of its benefits, so long as the federal aid money is used for nonreligious purposes within such schools. The greatest amounts of money distributed under ESEA, however, have been to public schools in poverty-impacted areas.

ORGANIZING AND FINANCING PUBLIC SCHOOLS

The fifty state governments, by means of enabling legislation, establish local school districts and endow them with the authority to operate public schools. There are nearly 16,000 local school boards, and 90,000 board members, who are chosen, usually, but not always, by popular election. State laws authorize these boards to levy and collect taxes, to borrow money, to engage in school construction, to hire instructional personnel, and to make certain determinations about local school policy. Yet, in every state, the authority of local school districts is severely circumscribed by state legislation. State law determines the types and rates of taxes to be levied, the maximum debt that can be incurred, the number of days schools shall remain open, the number of years of compulsory school attendance, the minimum salaries to be paid to teachers, the types of schools to be operated by the local boards, the number of grades to be taught, the qualifications of teachers, and the general content of curricula. In addition, many states choose the textbooks, establish course outlines, fix styles of penmanship, recommend teaching methods, establish statewide examinations, fix minimum teacher-pupil ratios, and stipulate course content in great detail. In short, the responsibility for public education is firmly in the hands of our state governments.

State responsibility for public education is no mere paper arrangement. At one time there was no effective way that state governments could insure that local school districts conformed to state policies; there were no enforcement agencies or devices to guarantee that state regulations were enforced. But in recent years, two devices have been utilized effectively by the states to help insure that local districts do not deviate from state standards. The first device is the statewide administrative agency sometimes called the state board of education, the state department of education, or the superintendent of public instruction. The central task of these state administrative agencies is to oversee local school districts and insure that state policies are being implemented. While there are some variations among the states in the power vested

TABLE 14.1   Federal Aid to Education: Major Legislation

1. Elementary and Secondary Education Act, 1965: Cash grants for construction, operation, and maintenance of schools in poverty-impacted public school districts on the basis of the number of children enrolled from poverty-stricken families, and grants to public and private schools for the support of specialized educational facilities.

2. National Defense Education Act, 1958: Financial assistance to states and public school districts to improve instruction in science, mathematics, and foreign languages, to strengthen guidance counseling and testing, and to improve statistical services. Amended in 1963 to include assistance in history, English, civics, geography, remedial reading, and library sciences. (Also included loans to undergraduates, fellowships to graduate students, and funds to colleges to improve training of teachers.)

3. Federally Impacted Areas Aid Program, 1950: Where federal activities create a substantial increase in school enrollments or reduction in taxable resources because of federally owned property, federal funds can be used for construction, operation, and maintenance of schools in public school districts. This program is an outgrowth of defense impacted area aid legislation in World War II.

4. National School Lunch and Milk Programs, 1946: Federal grants and commodity donations for nonprofit lunches and milk served in public and private schools.

5. Smith-Hughes Vocational Education Act, 1917: Federal grants for vocational education to help states and public school districts provide training in agriculture, home economics, trades, and industries.

6. Federal Aid to Colleges and Universities: Although not direct aids to elementary and secondary schools, federal aid to colleges and universities indirectly helps elementary and secondary education by improving the educational climate of the nation. Major sources of federal aid include:
   a. "The GI Bill," providing federal grants for tuition and subsistence for veterans attending institutions of higher education.
   b. Morrill Land Grant Act of 1862, providing states with federal land, the proceeds from which were used to establish land-grant colleges and universities.
   c. Higher Education Act of 1965, providing federal funds for construction of college facilities and to upgrade college libraries.
   d. Medical and Dental Education Program, providing federal funds for construction of facilities and loans to medical and dental students.
   e. Basic Educational Grants.

in these agencies, one trend is common to all the states: state educational agencies are centralizing state control over education.

The operating head of these state agencies, generally called commissioner or superintendent of education, may exercise the most forceful influence over educational policy in the state. In a majority of states these chief school officers are appointed; in other states they are directly elected. The department that this officer oversees provides specialized technical services and information to local school officials; more importantly, it establishes and enforces statewide minimum standards in curriculum, teacher certification, school construction, and many other aspects of school policy and administration.

A second device for insuring the implementation of state educational policies is state grants of money to local school districts. Every state provides grants in one form or another to local school districts to supplement locally derived school revenue. This places the superior taxing powers of the state in the service of public schools operated at the local level. In every state, an equalization formula in the distribution of state grants to local districts operates to help equalize educational opportunities in all parts of the state. Equalization formulas differ from state to state as do the amounts of state grants involved, but in every state, poorer school districts receive larger shares of state funds than wealthier districts. This enables the state to guarantee a minimum "foundation" program in education throughout the state. In addition, since state grants to local school districts are administered through state departments of education, state school officials are given an effective tool for implementing state policies, namely, withholding or threatening to withhold state funds from school districts that do not conform to state standards. The growth of state responsibility for school policy was accomplished largely by the use of money—state grants to local schools.

Increasing state participation in school finance, then, is an indication of increasing centralization of education in the states. In 1900 the state proportion of total public school expenditures in the nation was only 17 percent. In the 1970s, however, state governments have been contributing about 40 percent of total funds for the public schools.

One of the most dramatic reorganization and centralization movements in American government in this century has been the successful drive to reduce, through consolidation, the number of local school districts in the United States. By 1975 this number had been reduced to sixteen thousand. In a thirty-year period, three out of every four school districts had been eliminated through consolidation (See Table 8–1 in Chapter 8.) Support for school district consolidation has come from state school officials in every state. Opposition to consolidation has been local in character.

TABLE 14.2   Federal, State, and Local Contributions to Public Elementary
and Secondary Education

| | Percentage of Revenue Received from | | |
	Federal Sources	State Sources	Local Sources
1974	8.4	39.5	52.1
1970	7.3	40.7	52.0
1967	7.9	39.1	53.0
1963	4.4	39.3	56.4
1960	4.4	39.1	56.5
1957	4.0	39.4	56.6

SOURCE: U.S. Bureau of the Census, *Statistical Abstract of the United States.*

CONFLICT OVER SCHOOL FINANCE:
HAVES AND HAVE-NOTS

Public elementary and secondary schools enroll over 50 million students. Public expenditures for education now amount to more than 5 percent of the nation's total personal income. Over $1,000 per year is spent on the public education of each child. Teachers' salaries have risen dramatically, although the average teacher's salary is still lower than that of most other professions. Teacher-pupil ratios have been lowered on the average to one teacher for every twenty-one pupils.

This impressive record of progress in public education is a tribute to the capabilities of our fifty states. Yet national averages can obscure as much as they reveal about the record of the states in public education. Our federal system provides for the decentralization of educational policy making. Fifty state school systems establish policy for the nation, and this decentralization results in variations from state to state in educational policy. Only by examining public policy in all fifty states can the full dimension of American education be understood.

In 1974 public school expenditures for each pupil ranged from Mississippi's $716 to New York's $1,809. (See Figure 14–1.) The nationwide figure for per pupil expenditures was $1,120.[1] Why is it that some states spend more than twice as much on the education of each child as other states? Economic resources are an important determinant of a state's willingness and ability to provide educational services. Urbanization, education, and, especially, income, correlate significantly with variations among the states in per pupil expenditures for public education. The

[1] U.S. Bureau of the Census, *Statistical Abstract of the United States, 1974* (Washington, D.C.: Government Printing Office, 1974), p. 130.

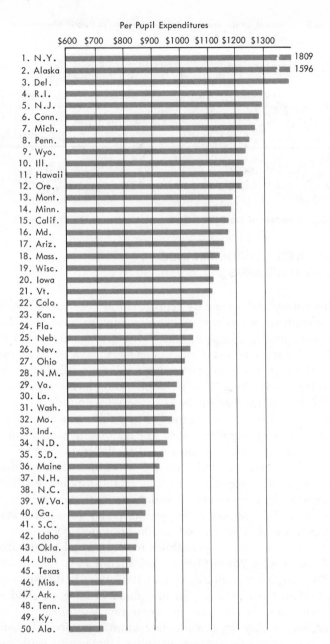

Per Pupil Expenditures

| | $600 | $700 | $800 | $900 | $1000 | $1100 | $1200 | $1300 |

1. N.Y.   1809
2. Alaska   1596
3. Del.
4. R.I.
5. N.J.
6. Conn.
7. Mich.
8. Penn.
9. Wyo.
10. Ill.
11. Hawaii
12. Ore.
13. Mont.
14. Minn.
15. Calif.
16. Md.
17. Ariz.
18. Mass.
19. Wisc.
20. Iowa
21. Vt.
22. Colo.
23. Kan.
24. Fla.
25. Neb.
26. Nev.
27. Ohio
28. N.M.
29. Va.
30. La.
31. Wash.
32. Mo.
33. Ind.
34. N.D.
35. S.D.
36. Maine
37. N.H.
38. N.C.
39. W.Va.
40. Ga.
41. S.C.
42. Idaho
43. Okla.
44. Utah
45. Texas
46. Miss.
47. Ark.
48. Tenn.
49. Ky.
50. Ala.

FIGURE 14–1   Rankings of the states: education.

results are the same even if the southern states are excluded from analysis. Clearly, wealth is the principal determinant of the amount of money to be spent on the education of each child. (See Figure 14–2.)

A central issue in the struggle over public education is that of distributing the benefits and costs of education equitably. Most school revenues are derived from *local* property taxes. In every state except Hawaii, local school boards must raise money from property taxes to finance their schools. This means that communities that do *not* have

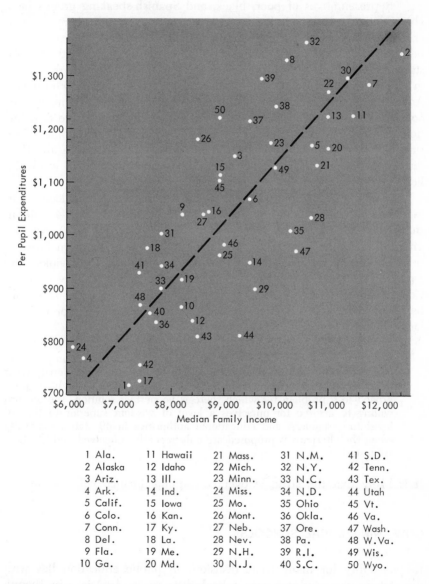

1 Ala.	11 Hawaii	21 Mass.	31 N.M.	41 S.D.
2 Alaska	12 Idaho	22 Mich.	32 N.Y.	42 Tenn.
3 Ariz.	13 Ill.	23 Minn.	33 N.C.	43 Tex.
4 Ark.	14 Ind.	24 Miss.	34 N.D.	44 Utah
5 Calif.	15 Iowa	25 Mo.	35 Ohio	45 Vt.
6 Colo.	16 Kan.	26 Mont.	36 Okla.	46 Va.
7 Conn.	17 Ky.	27 Neb.	37 Ore.	47 Wash.
8 Del.	18 La.	28 Nev.	38 Pa.	48 W.Va.
9 Fla.	19 Me.	29 N.H.	39 R.I.	49 Wis.
10 Ga.	20 Md.	30 N.J.	40 S.C.	50 Wyo.

FIGURE 14–2 The fifty states according to median family income and per pupil expenditure.

much taxable property cannot finance their schools as well as communities that are blessed with great wealth. Frequently, wealthy communities can provide better educations for their children at *lower* tax rates than poor communities can provide at *higher* tax rates, simply because of disparities in the value of taxable property from one community to the next.

Representatives of poor, black, and Spanish-speaking groups have charged that reliance on local property taxation for school finance discriminates against poor communities. The California Supreme Court held that the California system of public school finance, "with its substantial dependence on local property taxes and resultant wide disparities in school revenue, violates the equal protection clause of the Fourteenth Amendment (of the U.S. Constitution)." Note that the argument does not attack the use of property taxes, but rather the inequitable distribution of property tax revenues from one jurisdiction to another. Presumably, if a *state* would collect all property taxes statewide and then distribute the revenues equally among all communities, there would be little objection from have-not groups.

However, the Supreme Court of the United States has declined to intervene in this struggle over educational finance. By a 5–4 vote in *Rodriguez* v. *San Antonio Independent School Board* (1973), the Supreme Court ruled that disparities in property values between jurisdictions relying on property taxes to finance education did *not* violate the equal protection clause of the Fourteenth Amendment. The Supreme Court declined to substitute its own judgment about how schools should be financed for the judgments of forty-nine states. Writing for the majority, Justice Lewis F. Powell said:

> We are urged to abrogate systems of financing public education presently in existence in virtually every state . . . (to declare unconstitutional) what many educators for half a century have thought was an enlightened approach to a problem for which there is no perfect solution. We are unwilling to assume for ourselves a level of wisdom superior to that of legislators, scholars, and educational authorities in 49 states, especially when the alternatives proposed are only recently conceived and nowhere yet tested.

It is likely that the struggle over educational finance will continue.

GOVERNING LOCAL SCHOOLS

Responsibility for many basic decisions in public education lies with the sixteen thousand separate school districts in America. In theory, these school districts are under local control. The people of the local school district are supposed to exercise that control through an elected school board and an elected or appointed superintendent who acts as the chief executive of the community schools. There is some variation to that pattern—in approximately a quarter of the nation's school districts, the boards are appointed rather than elected, usually by city councils, county commissions, mayors, or even judges. In theory, school boards exercise control over curriculum (that is, what should be taught in the schools), buildings and facilities, personnel (including both administrators and teachers), and perhaps most important of all, financing. In practice, however, as we have already seen, the concept of local control over education is heavily circumscribed by both state and federal laws.

American schools face a dilemma in determining who should govern.[2] Aside from the interference of federal and state courts and administrative agencies, there is the recurring problem of "democratization" versus "professionalism." Is a democratically elected board, responsible to the citizens, an appropriate model of goverance for the schools? Or should technical and policy issues be determined by professional educators who possess the necessary technical competence? Or should we continue to attempt to combine these two conflicting notions of governance?

Democratic theory assumes that schools are public institutions which should be governed by the local citizenry through their elected representatives. This was the original concept in American public education developed in the nineteenth century. But as school issues became more complex, the knowledge of citizen school boards seemed insufficient to cope with the many problems confronting the schools—teaching innovations, curricula changes, multimillion-dollar building programs, special educational programs, and so forth. In the twentieth century, the school superintendent and his administrative assistants came to exercise more and more control over day-to-day operations of the schools. Theoretically, the superintendent only implements the policies of the board, but in practice he has assumed much of the policy making in local school districts. He keeps in touch with the university schools of education, devotes full time to his job, receives direct advice from attorneys, architects, accountants, and educational consultants, and generally sets the agenda for school board meetings.

The resulting "professionalism" in education tangles directly with the "democratic" notion of control of schools. There are few meetings

[2] The most comprehensive study of local school politics is Harmon Zeigler and M. Kent Jennings, *Governing American Schools: Political Interaction in Local School Districts* (Boston: Duxbury Press, 1974).

of local school boards which do not involve at least some tug-of-war between board members and the superintendent. (It is interesting to note that in European countries education has long been under the control of professionals, with little or no direct citizen participation in school governance.) Professional educators are frequently disdainful of the laymen who compose the school board: the professionals must patiently explain matters of curriculum, faculties, personnel, and finance to citizen board members who are untrained in the matters about which they must decide. Professional educators often support the idea that "politics" should be kept out of education; to them, this means non-professional, even elected school board members, should not interfere in educational decisions. For example, on the critical question of what should be taught in the public schools, the American Association of School Administrators says: "Curriculum planning and development is a highly technical task which requires special training.... Board members do not have and cannot be expected to have the technical competence to pass on the work of expert teachers in this field." [3]

But school board members and interested citizens generally believe that popular control of education is a vital component of democracy. Schools should be "responsive" to community needs and desires. The "new math," the "look-say" method of reading, sex education, the moral quality of reading material, and many other school problems have inspired increased citizen interest in what is happening in "their" schools. Frequently, citizen criticism has focused on the schools' failure to teach basic skills—reading, writing, and arithmetic. (The verbal and mathematical scores on the national College Board test for high school seniors have dropped each year since 1963.) Another frequent source of citizen concern is the perceived retreat of the schools from traditional moral values. These issues have in turn raised the underlying question—who should govern our schools, professional educators or interested citizens?

ARE SCHOOL BOARDS RESPONSIBLE POLICY MAKERS?

Even if we accept the notion that schools should be governed by a democratically elected board, how can we know whether board members are accurately reflecting their constituents' desires and aspirations? Like most decision makers, school board members are unrepresentative of their constituents in socioeconomic background. Specifically, board members are more often male, white, middle-aged, better educated, more prestigi-

---

[3] Cited in Thomas H. Eliot, "Toward an Understanding of Public School Politics," *American Political Science Review*, 52 (December, 1959): 1132–50.

ously employed, Republican, Protestant, and have lived in the county longer than their constituents.[4] They come disproportionately from "educational families"; three-fifths of all school board members have relatives in education, usually their spouse. Moreover, at least three-fifths of school board members report that they were first prompted to run for the school board by friends already on the board; this suggests a perpetuation of similar kinds of people on school boards. One-quarter of the nation's school boards are appointed, not elected; but even in elected boards at least one-quarter of the members originally came to the board as appointees to replace individuals who left the board with unexpired terms. Seldom are incumbents defeated for re-election; two-thirds of board members who leave office do so voluntarily. The average tenure of board members is about five years, compared to over eight years for superintendents. School board members do not ordinarily aspire to, or gain, higher political office. All of this suggests "volunteerism" among board members and difficulty in holding members accountable through the threat of electoral defeat.

Another problem: usually only a small proportion of a community's voters appear interested in school politics. It is estimated on the average that less than one-third of eligible voters turn out for school board elections. Voter turnout at school bond and tax referenda shows no ground swell of interest in school affairs. Perhaps even more interesting is the finding that the larger the voter turnout in a school bond referendum, the more likely the defeat of pro-educational proposals.[5] In general, the best way to defeat a school bond referendum is to have a large turnout. Proponents of educational expenditures are better advised to work not so much for a large turnout as for a better informed and more educationally oriented electorate.

However, it appears that in more politically competitive school districts, school board members have closer ties to their constituents, they listen more closely to citizen groups, and they are more likely to challenge the dominance of the superintendent. Board members are more "responsive" to citizen demands when elections are partisan and competitive and when there is a history of forced turnover. These conditions are more likely to be found in large cities with elected boards than in small towns or suburbs. In short, a "politicized" board is more responsive to citizen demands, while a "depoliticized" board is more easily dominated by the superintendent.

But the real dilemma remains unsolved: can democratically elected,

[4] Harmon Zeigler and M. Kent Jennings, *Governing American Schools*, p. 27. Based on a national sample of school board members.

[5] See Patricia Sexton, "City Schools," *Annals of the American Academy of Social and Political Science*, 352 (March, 1964): 95–106.

responsible school boards do a better job of educating America's youth than a professional educational bureaucracy? Political scientists Zeigler and Jennings conclude:

> In spite of the obvious perils, political decisions are—as long as we remain committed to democracy—logically superior to technical decisions.[6]

But educationist C. A. Bowers writes:

> When a school's moral responsibility to the student is not sacrificed to political expediency, education can become a humanizing process . . . as long as the "conventional wisdom" legitimizes control of the schools through political strife . . . is it possible to define the purpose of education in terms that elevate and enhance the well-being of the individual and not in terms of the self-proclaimed need of contending interest groups?[7]

The struggle for power over the schools between interested citizens, school board members, and professional educators has now been joined by still another powerful force—the nation's burgeoning new teachers' unions. Most of the nation's two million teachers are organized into either the older, larger National Education Association (NEA) or the smaller but more militant American Federation of Teachers (AFT), an affiliate of the AFL–CIO. Until recently the NEA was considered a "professional" organization of both teachers and administrators. But today state and district chapters of the Classroom Teachers Association, formed out of the NEA, are demanding collective bargaining rights for their members and even threatening to strike to achieve them. Since its origin, the AFT had espoused the right to organize, bargain collectively, and strike, in the fashion of other labor unions. The AFT is small in numbers but its membership is concentrated in the nation's largest cities where it exercises considerable power. Both AFT and NEA chapters have shut down schools to force concessions by superintendents, board members, and taxpayers —not only in salaries and benefits, but also in pupil-teacher ratios, classroom conditions, school discipline, and other educational matters. As the teachers' unions grow stronger, the traditional question of whether citizens or professional administrators should run the schools will be made more complex: what role should teachers' unions have in determining educational policy?

[6] Harmon Zeigler and M. Kent Jennings, *Governing American Schools*, p. 253.
[7] C. A. Bowers, *Education and Social Policy: Local Control of Education* (New York: Random House, Inc., 1970), pp. 4–5.

HIGHER EDUCATION

Federal aid to colleges and universities comes in a variety of forms. Historically, the Morrill Act of 1862 provided the groundwork for federal assistance in higher education. In 1890, Congress activated several federal grants to support the operations of the land-grant colleges, and this aid, although very modest, continues to the present. The GI Bills following World War II and the Korean War (enacted in 1944 and 1952, respectively) were not, strictly speaking, aid-to-education bills, but rather a form of assistance to veterans to help them adjust to civilian life. Nevertheless, these bills had a great impact on higher education in terms of the millions of veterans who were able to enroll in college. In 1966 Congress finally acted to make veterans' education benefits a permanent program for "all those who risk their lives in our armed forces."

Federal support for scientific research has also had an important impact on higher education. In 1950, Congress established the National Science Foundation to promote scientific research and education. NSF has provided fellowships for graduate education in the sciences, supported the development of science institutes and centers at universities, funded training institutes for science teachers at all levels, and supported many scientific enterprises and research projects. In 1965, Congress established a National Endowment for the Arts and Humanities, but funded these fields at only a tiny fraction of the amount given to NSF. In addition to NSF, many other federal agencies—the Department of Defense, the Atomic Energy Commission, the Office of Education, the Public Health Service, and so forth—have granted research contracts to universities for specific projects. Thus, research has become a very big item in university life.

The federal government directly assists institutions of higher education through a series of higher education acts. These acts authorize federal grants and loans for construction and improvement of both public and private higher education facilities; and they provide for federally insured student loans and scholarships, funds for library materials and specialized equipment, grants to expand university extension programs, and grants to strengthen colleges that "are struggling for survival and are isolated from the main currents of academic life."

In 1972, Congress added a new "basic educational opportunity grant" program. The program was intended to offer any college student in good standing a money grant each year to be calculated on the basis of the amount his family could reasonably be expected to contribute to his educational expenses. To date, however, the administration of the program has been clumsy: applications are difficult, the family contribution schedule is complex, and accurately determining family assets is probably impossible. The program is potentially very costly, but each year Congress and the President have severely limited the funds available. As a result, the number of students aided has been small, and the maximum grant itself has been cut to less than $500. Congress also authorized a government-guaranteed loan program that sought to encourage private banks to make low-interest loans to students. The federal government would pay the interest charges while the student was in school and would guarantee repayment in the event the student defaulted on the payment after graduation. But again, results of the program were disappointing: banks found the interest rates too low and administrative details too cumbersome, student defaults ran higher than expected; consequently, the number of student loans has fallen far below expectations.

States have been involved in public higher education since the colonial era. State governments in the Northeast frequently made contributions to support private colleges in their states. The first state university to be chartered by a state legislature was the University of Georgia in 1794. Before the Civil War, northeastern states relied exclusively on private colleges, and the southern states assumed the leadership in public higher education. The antebellum curricula at southern state universities, however, resembled the rigid classical studies of the early private colleges —Greek and Latin, history, philosophy, literature, and so forth.

It was not until the Morrill Land Grant Act of 1862 that public higher education began to make major strides in the American states. Interestingly, the eastern states were slow to respond to the opportunity afforded by the Morrill Act to develop public universities; eastern states continued to rely primarily on their private colleges and universities. The southern states were economically depressed in the post-Civil War period, and leadership in public higher education passed to the midwestern states. The philosophy of the Morrill Act emphasized agricultural and mechanical studies, rather than the classical curricula of eastern colleges, and the movement for "A and M" education spread rapidly in the agricultural states. The early groups of midwestern state universities were closely tied to agricultural education, including agricultural extension services. State universities also took over the responsibility for the training of public school teachers in colleges of education. The state universities introduced a broad range of modern subjects in the university curricula—business administration, agriculture, home economics, education, engineering. It was not until the 1960s that the eastern states began to develop public higher education (notably the State University of New York multicampus system).

Today public higher education enrolls three-quarters of the nation's college and university students. Perhaps more importantly, the nation's leading state universities can challenge the best private institutions in academic excellence. The University of California at Berkeley, the University of Michigan, and the University of Wisconsin are deservedly ranked with Harvard, Yale, Princeton, and Columbia.

The organization and governance of public higher education varies a great deal from state to state. In every state, however, public higher education is separated to some degree from elementary and secondary education. Most states have established boards of trustees (or "regents") with authority to govern the state universities. One of the purposes of the boards is to insulate higher education from the vicissitudes of politics. Prominent citizens who are appointed to these boards are expected to champion higher education with the public and the legislature, as well as set overall policy guidelines for colleges and universities. In the past, there were separate boards for each institution and separate consideration by the governor's office and the legislature of each institution's budgetary request. But the resulting competition has caused state after state to create unified "university system" boards to coordinate higher education. These university system boards consolidate the budget requests of each institution, determine system-wide priorities, and present a single budget for higher education to the governor and the legislature. The stronger and more independent the university system board, the less likely that universities and colleges throughout the state will be distributed to cities and regions in a pork barrel fashion by legislators seeking to enhance their local constituencies.

But the key factor in university politics is the university president. He is the chief spokesman for higher education, and he must convince the public, the regents, the governor, and the legislature of the value of state universities. The president's crucial role is one of maintaining support for higher education in the state; he frequently delegates administrative responsibilities for the internal operation of university to the vice-presidents and deans. Support for higher education among the public and its representatives can be affected by a broad spectrum of university activities, some of which are not directly related to the pursuit of knowledge. A winning football team can stimulate legislative enthusiasm and win appropriations for a new classroom building. University service-oriented research—developing new crops or feeds, assessing the state's mineral resources, advising state and local government agencies on administrative problems, analyzing the state economy, advising local school authorities, and so forth—may help to convince the public of the practical benefits of knowledge. University faculty may be interested in advanced research and the education of future Ph.D.s, but legislators and their constituents are more interested in the quality and effectiveness of undergraduate teaching.

The faculty of the nation's 2,500 colleges and universities—over two and one-half million strong—traditionally identified themselves as professionals with strong attachments to their institutions. The historic pattern of college and university government included faculty participation in policy making—not only in determining academic requirements but also in budgeting, the hiring and firing of personnel, building programs, etc. But government by faculty committee has proven cumbersome, unwieldy, and time-consuming in an era of large-scale enrollments, multimillion-dollar budgets, and increases in the size and complexity of academic administration. Increasingly, concepts of public "accountability," academic "management," cost control, and centralized budgeting and purchasing have transferred power in colleges and universities from faculty to professional academic administrators.

The traditional organization for faculty has been the American Association of University Professors (AAUP); historically, this group has confined itself to publishing data on faculty salaries and officially "censoring" colleges or universities that violated long-standing notions of academic freedom or tenure. (*Tenure* is the practice that a faculty member who has demonstrated his competence by service in a college or university position for three to seven years cannot thereafter be dismissed except for "cause"—a serious infraction of established rules or dereliction of duty, provable in an open hearing.) In recent years, the AFT has succeeded in convincing some faculty that traditional patterns of *individual* bargaining over salaries, teaching load, and working conditions in colleges and universities should be replaced by *collective* bargaining in the style of unionized labor. The American Federation of Teachers has only a few thousand college or university members, but its existence has spurred the AAUP on many campuses to assume a more militant attitude on behalf of faculty interests. Faculty collective bargaining is complicated by the fact that faculty continue to play some role in academic government—choosing deans and department heads, sitting on salary committees, etc.

READING, WRITING, AND RELIGION

The First Amendment to the Constitution of the United States contains two important guarantees of religious freedom: (1) "Congress shall make no law respecting an establishment of religion...," and (2) "Or prohibiting the free exercise thereof." The Due Process Clause of the Fourteenth Amendment made these guarantees of religious liberty applicable to the states and their subdivisions as well as to Congress. Most of the debate over religion in the public schools centers around the "no establishment" clause of the First Amendment rather than the "free exercise" clause. However, it was respect for the "free exercise" clause that caused the Supreme Court in 1925 to declare unconstitutional an attempt on the part of a state to prohibit private religious schools and to force all children to attend public schools. In the words of the Supreme Court: "The fundamental theory of liberty upon which all governments in this Union repose excludes any general power of the state to standardize its children by forcing them to accept instruction from public teachers only. The child is not the mere creature of the state." [8] It is this decision that protects the entire structure of private religious schools in this nation.

A great deal of religious conflict in America has centered around the meaning of the "no establishment" clause, and the public schools have been the principal scene of this conflict. One interpretation of the clause holds that it does not prevent government from aiding religious schools or encouraging religious beliefs in the public schools, so long as it does not discriminate against any particular religion. Another interpretation of the no establishment clause is that it creates a "wall of separation" between church and state in America, which prevents government from directly aiding religious schools or encouraging religious beliefs in any way.

The Catholic Church in America enrolls over half of all private school students in the nation, and the Catholic Church has led the fight for an interpretation of the no establishment clause that would permit government to aid religious schools. As Catholic spokesmen see it, Catholic parents have a right to send their children to Catholic schools, and since they are taxpayers, they also expect that some tax monies should go to the aid of church schools; to do otherwise, they argue, would discriminate against parents who choose a "God-centered" education for their children. Those who favor government aid to religious schools frequently refer to the language found in several cases decided by the Supreme Court, which appears to support the idea that government can *in a limited fashion* support the activities of church-related schools. In *Cochran v. Board of Education* (1930), the Court upheld a state law providing free textbooks for children attending both public and parochial schools on the grounds that this aid benefited the *children* rather than the Catholic Church and hence did not constitute an "establishment" of religion within the meaning of the First Amendment.[9] In *Everson v. Board of Education* (1947), the Supreme Court upheld the provision of school bus service to parochial school children at public expense on the grounds that the "wall of separation between church and state" does not prohibit the state from adopting

---

[8] *Pierce v. The Society of Sisters,* 268 U.S. 510 (1925).

[9] *Cochran v. Board of Education,* 281 U.S. 370 (1930).

a general program which helps *all* children, regardless of religion, to proceed safely to and from schools.[10] These cases suggest that the Supreme Court is willing to permit some forms of aid to parochial school *children* that indirectly aids religion, so long as this is not directly used for the teaching of religion.

However, the Supreme Court has also voiced the opinion that the no establishment clause of the First Amendment should constitute a "wall of separation" between church and state. In the words of the Court:

> Neither a state nor the federal government can set up a church. Neither can pass laws which aid one religion, aid all religions, or prefer one religion over another. Neither can force nor influence a person to go to or to remain away from church against his will, or force him to profess a belief or disbelief in any religion. No person can be punished for entertaining or professing religious beliefs or disbeliefs, for church attendance or nonattendance. No tax in any amount, large or small, can be levied to support any religious activities or institutions, whatever they may be called, or whatever form they may adopt to teach or practice religion. Neither a state nor the federal government can, openly or secretly, participate in the affairs of any religious organizations or groups, and vice versa.[11]

One of the most important Supreme Court decisions in the history of church-state relations in America came in 1971 in the case of *Lemon v. Kurtzman*.[12] The Supreme Court held that it was unconstitutional for a state to pay the costs of teachers' salaries or instructional materials in parochial schools. The Court acknowledged that it had previously approved the provision of state textbooks and bus transportation directly to parochial school children. But the Court held that state payments to parochial schools involved "excessive entanglement between government and religion" and violated both the establishment and free exercise clauses of the First Amendment. State payments to religious schools, the Court said, would require excessive government controls and surveillance to insure that funds were used only for secular instruction. Moreover, the Court expressed the fear that state aid to parochial schools would create "political divisions along religious lines . . . one of the principal evils against which the First Amendment was intended to protect."

Religious conflict in public schools also centers around the question of prayer and Bible-reading ceremonies conducted by public schools. The

[10] *Everson* v. *Board of Education*, 330 U.S. 1 (1947).
[11] Hugo Black, majority opinion in *Everson* v. *Board of Education*, 330 U.S. 1
[12] *Lemon* v. *Kurtzman*, 403 U.S. 602 (1971).

practice of opening the school day with prayer and Bible-reading ceremonies was once widespread in American public schools. Usually the prayer was a Protestant rendition of the Lord's Prayer, and Bible reading was from the King James version. To avoid the denominational aspects of these ceremonies, the New York State Board of Regents substituted a nondenominational prayer, which it required to be said aloud in each class in the presence of a teacher at the beginning of each school day:

> Almighty God, we acknowledge our dependence upon Thee, and we beg Thy blessings upon us, our parents, our teachers, and our country.

New York argued that this prayer ceremony did not violate the no establishment clause, because the prayer was denominationally neutral and because student participation in the prayer was voluntary. However, in *Engle* v. *Vitale* (1962), the Supreme Court stated that "the constitutional prohibition against laws respecting an establishment of a religion must at least mean in this country it is no part of the business of government to compose official prayers for any group of the American people to recite as part of a religious program carried on by government." [13] The Court pointed out making prayer voluntary did not free it from the prohibitions of the no establishment clause; that clause prevented the *establishment* of a religious ceremony by a government agency, regardless of whether the ceremony was voluntary or not:

> Neither the fact that the prayer may be denominationally neutral, nor the fact that its observance on the part of the students is voluntary can serve to free it from the limitations of the establishment clause, as it might from the free exercise clause, of the First Amendment, both of which are operative against the states by virtue of the 14th Amendment. . . . The establishment clause, unlike the free exercise clause, does not depend on any showing of direct governmental compulsion and is violated by the enactment of laws which establish an official religion whether those laws operate directly to coerce nonobserving individuals or not. [14]

One year later, in the case of *Abbington Township* v. *Schempp*, the Court considered the constitutionality of Bible-reading ceremonies in the public schools. [15] Here again, even though the children were not required to participate, the Court found that Bible reading as an opening exercise in the schools was a religious ceremony. The Court went to some trouble in its opinion to point out that they were not "throwing the

[13] *Engle* v. *Vitale*, 370 U.S. 421 (1962).
[14] Ibid.
[15] *Abbington Township* v. *Schempp*, 374 U.S. 203 (1963).

Bible out of the school," for they specifically stated that the study of the Bible or of religion, when presented objectively as part of a secular program of education, did not violate the First Amendment, but religious *ceremonies* involving Bible reading or prayer, established by a state or school, did so.

The politics of transportation, housing, and urban affairs

CONFUSION IN URBAN POLICY

Urban life has come under severe criticism in recent years. A newspaperman describes the dangers of the modern city:

> whose air grows fouler and more dangerous by the day, whose water is threatened increasingly by pollution, whose mobility is undermined by accumulations of vehicles and withering transit, whose educational systems reel under a growing variety of economic, social, and national emergencies, and whose entire pattern is assuming an ominous shape and sociological form, with well-to-do whites in their suburban cities ringing poverty-ridden minority groups widening at the core.[1]

Even the President has bemoaned:

> Our chronic inability to provide sufficient low and moderate income housing, of adequate quality, at reasonable price.

> The special problem of the poor and the Negro, unable to move freely from their ghettos, exploited in the quest for the necessities of life.

[1] Mitchell Gordon, *Sick Cities: The Psychology and Pathology of American Urban Life* (Baltimore: Penguin Books, Inc., 1963), p. 3.

Chapter fifteen

Increasing pressures on municipal budgets, with large city per capita expenditures. . . .

The high human costs: crime, delinquency, welfare loads, disease, and health hazards. This is man's fate in those broken neighborhoods where he can "feel the enclosure of the flaking walls and see through the window the blackened reflection of the tenement across the street that blocks out the world beyond."

The tragic waste, and, indeed, the chaos that threatens where children are born into the stifling air of overcrowded rooms, and destined for a poor diet, inadequate schools, streets of fear and sordid temptation, joblessness, and the gray anxiety of the ill prepared.

And the flight to the suburbs of more fortunate men and women who might have provided the leadership and the means for reversing this human decline.[2]

If things are really this bad, why do many millions of Americans insist on living in metropolitan areas and many more move there every year? The American metropolis is today's land of economic opportunity. People are attracted to cities because they provide greater numbers of jobs as well as greater freedom of occupational choice. Metropolitan living means higher incomes and higher standards of living. In addition to more material things, they offer greater opportunities for the "good life." Metropolitan dwellers are better educated on the average than nonmetropolitan residents. Metropolitan areas have more and better schools at all educational levels, better housing, better hospitals and health care, a greater variety of entertainment, far more institutions of fine arts—libraries, museums, art cinemas, symphonies, and ballet.

The critical deficiency in federal urban policy is that there are no concrete goals or clear priorities in the hundreds of separate programs affecting cities. James Q. Wilson writes about federal urban policy:

"We do not know what we are trying to accomplish. . . . Do we seek to raise standards of living, maximize housing choices, revitalize the commercial centers of our cities, end suburban sprawl, eliminate discrimination, reduce traffic congestion, improve the quality of urban design, check crime and delinquency, strengthen the effectiveness of local planning, increase citizen participation in local government? All these objectives sound attractive—in part, because they are rather vague—but unfortunately they are in many cases incompatible." [3]

Despite the emphasis in federal urban programs on the physical characteristics of cities, however, most observers now acknowledge that

[2] President Lyndon B. Johnson, Message to Congress on the Model Cities Program, January 26, 1966.

[3] James Q. Wilson, "The War on Cities," *The Public Interest* (Summer, 1966), p. 10.

"the urban crisis" is not primarily, nor even significantly, a physical problem. It is not really housing, or highways, or urban rebuilding that lie at the heart of urban discontent. Instead, when we think of the challenges confronting cities, we think of racial tension, crime, poverty, poor schools, residential segregation, rising welfare rolls, and fiscal crisis— in short, all the major domestic problems facing the nation. In an urban society, *all* domestic problems become urban problems.

HUD—FEDERAL HOUSING AND URBAN DEVELOPMENT PROGRAMS

The Department of Housing and Urban Development (HUD) is the federal agency concerned primarily with public housing, mortgage insurance, urban renewal, community facilities, mass transit, and related programs, whose objective is better houses and improved communities. HUD administers federal programs in housing and urban affairs which were begun in the 1930s. The organization of HUD reflects the structure of these major federal programs:

> *Federal Housing Administration*
> FHA programs of mortgage insurance
>
> *Federal National Mortgage Association*
> FNMA ("Fannie Mae") secondary mortgage market operations for federally insured mortgages
>
> *Housing Assistance Administration*
> Low-rent public housing programs for low-income families
>
> *Urban Renewal Administration*
> Federal programs for slum clearance, urban renewal, and planning assistance
>
> *Community Facilities Administration*
> Federal grants and loans to municipalities for sewer, water, mass transit, and other public works

The Federal Housing Administration was created in 1934 to guarantee private mortgages against default by the individual home buyer, thereby enabling banks, savings and loan associations, and other lending agencies to provide long-term, low-interest, low down-payment mortgages for Americans wishing to buy their own homes. After checking the credit rating of the prospective home buyer, the FHA insures the private mortgage lender—bank, savings and loan company, insurance company, and so forth—of repayment of the loan in case the home buyer defaults. This reduces the risk and encourages mortgage lenders to make more loans at lower interest rates, lower down payments, and longer repayment periods. While these advantages in borrowing assist middle-class home buyers, note that the *direct* beneficiaries of the FHA program are the banks and mortgage-lending companies who are insured against losses. The FHA also establishes minimum building standards for homes it insures and thereby has raised the general quality of middle-class housing. The FHA adds a small charge to each mortgage to finance a revolving fund to repay defaulted mortgages. However, the record of Americans in mortgage repayment is so good that FHA has consistently returned premium payments to the U.S. Treasury.

The FHA has been extremely successful in promoting home ownership among millions of middle-class Americans. Millions of families have financed their homes through FHA-insured mortgages, and millions more have financed their homes through mortgages insured by the Veterans Administration. A great many of these mortgages financed *suburban* homes. In fact, the success of FHA and VA programs may have contributed to the deterioration of the nation's central cities by enabling so many middle-class white families to acquire their cherished homes in the suburbs and leave the city behind. The FHA is an entirely federally administered program, but its impact on city and suburban governments should not be underestimated.

The Housing Act of 1937 established a federal public housing agency, later named the Housing Assistance Administration, to provide low-rent public housing for the poor who could not afford decent housing on the private market. The public housing program was designed for persons without jobs or incomes sufficient to enable them to afford home ownership, even with the help of the FHA. The Housing Assistance Administration does not build, own, or operate its own housing projects; rather, it provides the necessary financial support to enable local communities to provide public housing for their poor if the communities choose to do so. The Housing Assistance Administration makes loans and grants to *local* housing authorities established by local governments to build, own, and operate low-cost public housing. Local housing authorities must keep rents low in relation to their tenants' ability to pay. This means that local housing authorities operate at a loss, and the federal government reimburses them for this loss. No community is required to have a Public Housing Authority; it must apply to the Housing Assistance Administration and meet federal standards in order to receive federal financial support.

POLITICS OF PUBLIC HOUSING

Public housing has always been involved in more political controversy than the FHA. Real estate and building interests, which support the FHA because it expands their number of customers, have opposed public housing on the grounds that it is socialistic and wasteful. While in theory public housing serves individuals who cannot afford private housing, private real estate interests contend that public housing hurts the market for older homes and apartments. In addition, owners of slum dwellings seldom welcome competition from federally supported housing authorities. Political difficulties have also been encountered in the location of public housing units. Many Americans will support public housing for low-income persons, so long as it is not located in their neighborhood. A majority of public housing occupants are black, and this automatically involves public housing in the politics of race.[4]

In recent years many of the earlier supporters of public housing, including minority groups, labor, social workers, charitable organizations, and big-city political organizations, have expressed doubts about the effects of public housing. Public housing, while providing improved living conditions, failed to eliminate poverty, ignorance, family disruption, juvenile delinquency, crime, and other characteristic troubles of the slums. Very often, the concentration of large numbers of poor persons with a great variety of social problems into a single, mass housing project compounded their problems. The cost of central-city land required many big cities to build high-rise housing buildings of ten to twenty stories. These huge buildings frequently became unlivable—crime in the hallways, elevators that seldom worked, drugs and human filth in halls and stairways, families locking themselves in and alienating themselves from community life. Huge housing projects were impersonal and bureaucratic, and they often failed to provide many of the stabilizing neighborhood influences of the old slums. Children could be raised in public housing projects and never see a regularly employed male head of a household going to and from work. The behavior and value patterns of problem families were reinforced.[5]

Moreover, removing thousands of people from neighborhood environments and placing them in the institutionlike setting of large public housing developments very often increased their alienation of separation from society and removed what few social controls existed in the slum neighborhood. A family living in public housing and successful in finding employment and raising its income level faced eviction to make room for more "deserving" families. Finally, black groups often complained that public housing was a new form of racial segregation, and, indeed, the concentration of blacks among public housing dwellers does lead to a great deal of de facto segregation in housing projects.

[4] For an analysis of public housing projects, see Leonard Freedman, *Public Housing* (New York: Holt, Rinehart & Winston, 1969).

[5] For the story of the virtual collapse of public housing in St. Louis, see Eugene J. Meehan, "Looking the Gift Horse in the Mouth," *Urban Affairs Quarterly* (June, 1975): 423–63.

Requests by cities for federal aid for public housing have far exceeded the amount of money appropriated by Congress. The result in most cities is a long list of those persons who are eligible for public housing for whom no space is available. An estimated two million people live in public housing in America, but ten million people are probably eligible for public housing under current standards.

To alleviate the shortage of public housing and to correct some of the problems involved in large-site housing projects, Congress authorized three new approaches to supplement public housing—a rent subsidy program, a dispersed public housing site program, and a "turn key" program of acquiring new public housing. The rent subsidy program authorizes federal grants to local housing authorities to provide cash grants to families living in substandard housing, thus enabling them to rent decent private housing facilities. The dispersed public housing site program will provide federal grants to local housing authorities to enable them to purchase single homes or apartment buildings throughout the community for operation as public housing units. The "turn key" program enables local housing authorities to purchase completed housing projects from private builders. The purpose of these programs is to speed up the availability of public housing units and, perhaps more importantly, to eliminate dependence upon large, institutionlike public housing facilities and achieve more dispersal of public housing residents throughout the community.

URBAN RENAISSANCEMANSHIP

In the Housing Act of 1937, the idea of urban renewal was closely tied to public housing. Slum residences were to be torn down as public housing sites were constructed. But in the Housing Act of 1949, the urban renewal program was separated from public housing, and the federal government undertook to support a broad program of urban redevelopment to help cities fight a loss in population and to reclaim the economic importance of the core cities. After World War II, the suburban exodus had progressed to the point where central cities faced slow decay and death if large public efforts were not undertaken. Urban renewal could not be undertaken by private enterprise because it was not profitable; surburban property was usually cheaper than downtown property, and it did not require large-scale clearance of obsolete buildings. Moreover, private enterprise did not possess the power of eminent domain which enabled the city to purchase the many separately owned tracts of land to insure an economically feasible new investment.[6]

[6] For a general discussion of urban renewal by a number of experts, see James Q. Wilson, ed., *Urban Renewal* (Cambridge-M.I.T. Press, 1966).

To save the nation's central cities, the Urban Renewal Administration was authorized to match local monies to acquire blighted land, clear off or modernize obsolete or dilapidated structures, and make downtown sites available for new uses. The federal government does not engage in these activities directly, but makes available financial assistance to local urban renewal authorities for renewal projects. When the sites are physically cleared of the old structures by the local urban renewal authority, they can be resold to private developers for residential, commercial, or industrial use, and two-thirds of the difference between the costs of acquisition and clearance and the income from the private sale to the developers is paid for by the federal government. In other words, local urban renewal authorities sustain a loss in their renewal activities and two-thirds of this loss is made up by federal grants; the rest must come from local sources. However, the local share may include noncash contributions in the form of land donations, schools, streets, or parks.

No city is required to engage in urban renewal, but if cities wish federal financial backing, they must show in their applications that they have developed a "workable program" for redevelopment and the prevention of future blight. They must demonstrate that they have adequate building and health codes, good zoning and subdivision control regulations, proper administrative structures for renewal and other government services, sufficient local financing and public support, and a comprehensive plan of development with provisions for relocating displaced persons.

Urban renewal is best understood from an economic standpoint. For example, an urban renewal agency may undertake a project as follows:

Project Costs	
Land acquisition	$ 8 million
Demolition, relocation	1 million
Provision of new public facilities	1 million
Total	$10 million
Proceeds from sale of land	
to private developer	4 million
Net project cost (loss)	6 million
Contributions	
Federal grant for 2/3 of net cost	4 million
Local contributions in cash	
or services	2 million
Total	$ 6 million

The key to success is to encourage private developers to purchase the land and make a heavy investment—in middle- or high-income housing or in commercial or industial use. In fact, before undertaking a project, urban renewal authorities frequently "find a developer first, and then see what interests him." The city cannot afford to purchase land, thereby taking it off the tax rolls, invest in its clearance, and then be stuck without a buyer. Moreover, the private developer must be encouraged to invest in the property and thus enhance the value of the central city. For example, on the project mentioned above, if a private developer can be persuaded to invest an additional $20 million beyond his purchase price in the construction of housing or business or industry, the value of the land would rise to $24 million. A ten-mill city tax on $24 million returns $240,000 per year, instead of the $80,000 that the city received on a ten-mill tax on the original value of $8 million. So over time a city can more than pay off its own investment in urban renewal by increased tax returns from renewed property and hence make a "profit." Thus, many people can come out of a project feeling successful—the city increases its tax base and annual revenues, the private developer makes a profit (in part because he acquired land at only 40 percent of its cost), and mayors can point to the physical improvements in the city that occurred during their administration.

Moreover, there are many favorable "spillover effects" of a successful urban renewal project:

1. Each project stimulates jobs, not only during demolition and construction but also later in servicing the new housing, business, or industry.
2. The city increases its ability to attract and maintain middle-class residents as well as business and industry.
3. Universities, hospitals, cultural centers, etc., can be built or expanded when all or part of an urban renewal project is turned over to public purposes.
4. Downtown areas can be revitalized and attract private development in areas adjacent to urban renewal projects.

However, there are also drawbacks to urban renewal. The concern for "profit" frequently leads to fiscal conservatism on the part of urban renewal authorities. They do not undertake to renew the very worst slum areas because of the excessive costs involved and because private developers may not wish to go into these areas even after renewal. More importantly, the financial considerations often dictate the choice of profitable middle- or upper-income housing or commercial or industrial use of renewed land, rather than low-cost private or public housing development. Developers make more profit on the former types of investments, and the city gets better tax returns. The effect of urban renewal is frequently to redistribute land from lower-income to higher-income purposes.

Relocation is the most sensitive problem in urban renewal. The vast majority of people relocated by urban renewal are poor and black. They have no interest in moving simply to make room for middle- or higher-income housing, or business or industry, or universities, hospitals, and other public facilities. Even though relocated families are frequently given priority for public housing, there is not nearly enough space in public housing to contain them all. They are simply moved from one slum to another. The slum landowner is paid a just price for his land, but the renter receives only a small moving allowance, averaging about one hundred dollars. Urban renewal officials assist relocated families in finding new housing and generally claim success in moving families to better housing. But frequently the result is higher rents,[7] and urban renewal may actually help to create new slums in other sections of the city. Small businessmen are especially vulnerable to relocation. They often depend on a small, well-known neighborhood clientele, and they cannot compete successfully when forced to move to other sections of the city.

Political support for urban renewal has come from mayors who wish to make their reputation as rigorous proponents by engaging in large-scale renewal activities that produce impressive "before" and "after" pictures of the city. Businessmen wishing to preserve downtown investments and developers wishing to acquire land in urban centers have provided a solid base of support for downtown renewal. Mayors, planners, the press, and the good-government forces have made urban renewal politically much more popular than public housing.

Originally, liberal reform groups and representatives of urban minorities supported urban renewal as an attack on the slum problem. Recently, however, they have become disenchanted with urban renewal, complaining that urban renewal has not considered the plight of the slum dweller. Too often, slum areas have been cleared and replaced with high-income residential developments or commercial or industrial developments that do not directly help the plight of the slum dwellers. Urban renewal authorities are required to pay landowners a just price for their land, but slum dwellers who rent their apartments are shoved about the city with only a minimal amount of support from the "relocation" division of urban renewal authority. Downtown areas have been improved in appearance, but usually at the price of considerable human dislocation.[8]

---

[7] See Chester Hartman, "The Housing of Relocated Families," *Journal of the American Institute of Planners*, 30 (November, 1964): 266–86.

[8] For a scathing attack on urban renewal, see Jane Jacobs, *The Death and Life of Great American Cities* (New York: Random House, Inc., 1961).

DOT—PUBLIC HIGHWAY POLICY

Few inventions have had such a far-reaching effect on the life of the American people as the automobile. Henry Ford built one of the first gasoline-driven carriages in America in 1893, and by 1900 there were eight thousand automobiles registered in the U.S. The Model T was introduced in the autumn of 1908. By concentrating on a single unlovely but enduring model, and by introducing the assembly line processes, the Ford Motor Company began producing automobiles for the masses. By 1921 there were over 20 million cars in existence, and the auto industry was established in the United States. Today there are over 110 million registered motor vehicles in the nation, one for every two persons living in the country; and the automobile population is increasing faster than the human population. The automobile and trucking industry ranks as the largest and wealthiest in the United States. It represents 10 percent of the gross national product.

The provision of public highways is the second most costly function, after education, of state and local governments. Highway politics are of interest not only to the automotive industry and the driving public but also to the oil industry, the American Road Builders Association, the cement industry, the railroads, the trucking industry, the farmers, the outdoor advertising industry, and the county commissioners, taxpayer associations, ecologists and conservationists, and neighborhood improvement associations. These political interests are concerned with the allocation of money for highway purposes, the sources of funds for highway revenue, the extent of gasoline and motor vehicle taxation, the regulation of traffic on the highways, the location of highways, the determination of construction policies, the division of responsibility between federal and state and local governments for highway financing and administration, the division of highway funds between rural and urban areas, and many other important outcomes in highway politics.

It was in the Federal Aid Road Act of 1916 that the federal government, through its Bureau of Public Roads (now the Department of Transportation—DOT), first provided regular funds for highway construction under terms that gave the bureau considerable influence over state policy. For example, if states wanted to get federal money, they were required to have a highway department, and to have their plans for highway construction approved by the Bureau of Public Roads. In 1921, federal aid was limited to a connected system of principal state highways, now called the "federal aid primary highway system." Uniform standards were prescribed and even a uniform numbering system was added, such as "US 1," or "US 30." The emphasis of the program was clearly rural.

Later the federal government also designated a federal aid "secondary" system of farm-to-market roads and provided for "urban extensions" of primary roads, in addition to the federal aid for the primary highway system. Federal funds for primary and secondary and urban extension roads, commonly called "ABC funds," are determined by three separate formulas, but all take into account area, population, postal routes, and mileage. These federal ABC funds are matched fifty-fifty by the states. In the use of their federal funds, states make the surveys and plans, let the contracts, and supervise the construction, but only with the approval of the U.S. Bureau of Public Roads. All ABC funds remain under the administrative control of the states, who are responsible for their operation and maintenance. All payments to contractors for work done on any federal project are made by the states; the Bureau of Public Roads makes very few direct payments.

In 1956, Congress authorized a national system of interstate and defense highways ("I" highways)—now the most important feature of the federal highway policy. At that time, Congress provided for its completion by 1972, and allocated the costs on the basis of 90 percent federal and 10 percent state. The Federal Highway Act of 1956, as amended,

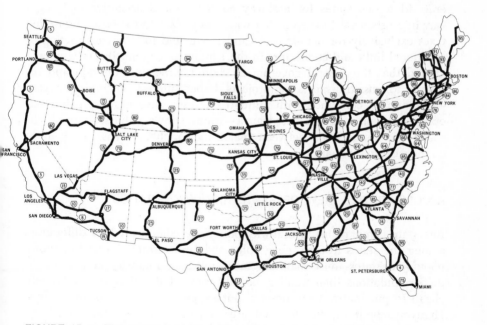

FIGURE 15–1 The national system of interstate and defense highways.
Source: U.S. Department of Transportation, Federal Highway Administration.

authorizes 42,500 miles of highway, designed to connect principal metropolitan areas and industrial centers, and thereby shifts the emphasis of federal highway activity from rural to urban needs. Figure 15–1 shows the I highway system as it will look upon its completion. Although the system will constitute less than 2 percent of the total surface in the nation, it is expected to carry over 20 percent of all highway traffic. The Department of Transportation has been given strong supervisory powers, including the selection of routes (it can even transfer interstate mileage and funds out of a noncooperative state), but administration and execution are still left to state highway departments. Federal monies are paid to the states, not to the contractors, as the work progresses. The Federal Highway Trust Fund is responsible for the orderly scheduling of federal aid and the phasing out of reimbursement requests for the states. Delays and postponements have pushed back the expected completion date of the I highways system to the late 1970s.

Controversy has already developed about what to do with federal highway funds after the completion of the I highway system. The federal gasoline tax of four cents per gallon is a good revenue producer—nearly $6 billion per year in the early 1970s. These funds are currently deposited in the Federal Highway Trust Fund for disbursement as federal aid to the states for highway construction. Automotive and highway interests want to keep it that way. They want to use federal gasoline taxes exclusively for maintenance and repair and for the construction of additional links and connectors in the I highway system. But others have argued that the federal government should direct its attention and resources to mass transportation projects. Urban interests, including mayors and planners, combined with railroad interests, have urged greater federal investment in urban mass transit—trains, subways, busses—and high-speed rail connections between major metropolitan areas, particularly on the eastern seaboard.

A COMPARATIVE VIEW OF STATE HIGHWAY POLITICS

Interstate comparisons in highway policy are complicated by differences among the states in area, geography, soil, and terrain. Large but thinly populated states must maintain more miles of highway in relation to their populations than smaller, heavily populated states. It is relatively cheap to put highways in deserts, but expensive to do so in mountains. Highways built in climates that are subject to freezes, snowfalls, and rainfalls require more maintenance and repair than highways located in less rigorous climates. In short, nature, as well as economics and politics, contributes to variation in highway policy among the states.

The principal source of highway finance is highway-user revenue. Federal highway aid constitutes about 30 percent of all highway funds, but most of the remaining 70 percent comes from taxes and fees levied upon highway users. The state gasoline tax alone accounts for approximately half of all highway receipts. All states levy gasoline taxes of six to nine and one-half cents per gallon. The second most important highway revenue source is the motor vehicle registration fee.

The segregation of these highway-user revenues from general state revenues is an article of faith among highway interests. The theory is that such taxes insure that the cost of highways is paid by the user. As highway revenues have grown, highway interests have pressed for legal and even constitutional principles preventing the use of these revenues for anything except highway purposes. Today, more than half the states have constitutional provisions restricting the diversion of highway-user revenue to nonhighway purposes, and many other states restrict diversion by statute or administrative practice. This policy guarantees a continuous flow of road-building funds and, in effect, gives highways preferential treatment over other public programs. Urban industrial states are far more likely to divert highway receipts to nonhighway purposes than the rural agricultural states.

Highway expenditures do not guarantee a good highway system, but they do provide a rough index of the extent to which supporters of highways have succeeded in obtaining public funds for their objectives. Per capita highway expenditures in the states are significantly related to urbanization: increases in urbanization result in a *decrease* in per capita highway expenditures.[9] In other words, rural agricultural states spend more per capita on highways than urban industrial states. Not only do rural farm states spend more per capita on highways, but they also spend more in relation to their personal income. The federal government relieves some of the burden of highway financing in rural states by giving them proportionately more funds than it gives to urban states. But federal monies notwithstanding, rural states still expend more effort for highways than urban states. Whether one prefers to measure highway efforts in per capita expenditures or in relative terms, the tendency for rural agricultural states to emphasize highways is unmistakable. (See Figure 15–2.)

Quite clearly, rural politics are much more highway-oriented than urban politics. Part of the reason for this may be the problems of rural politics a few years ago. Rural roads disturb relatively few individuals, while metropolitan highways involve uprooting thousands of outraged

[9] See Thomas R. Dye, *Politics, Economics, and the Public* (Chicago: Rand McNally & Co., 1966), pp. 157–61.

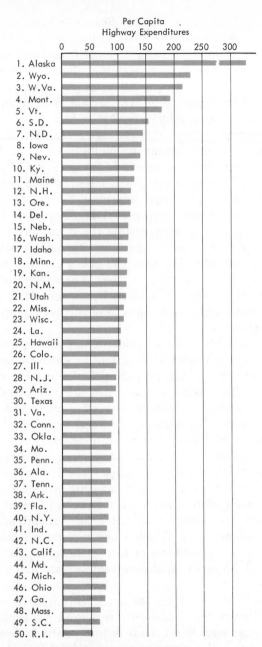

FIGURE 15–2 Rankings of the states: highways.

residents and irate businessmen. Freeways are a good idea when they run through somebody else's backyard. Mileage is much cheaper and faster to build in rural areas; urban highways require more years and more money per mile.

THE METROPOLITAN TRANSPORTATION MESS

To date, expressways have failed in alleviating the transportation problems in large cities. City planners, transportation specialists, and nearly all who have studied the modern city's traffic picture readily agree that the only way to relieve traffic congestion and preserve central cities is to get people out of private automobiles and into public transit, that is, "to move people, not vehicles." [10] Technological and economic evidence points to rail transit as the only reasonable way to move persons in and out of the central city at rush hours. Automobiles on expressways can move about two thousand people per lane per hour, buses can move between six thousand and nine thousand, but rail systems can carry up to sixty thousand persons per hour. In other words, one rail line is estimated to be equal to that of twenty or thirty expressway lanes of automobiles in terms of its ability to move people.

Of course, as most commuters know all too well, privately owned commuter railroads are in generally deplorable operating condition and even worse financial condition. The average citizen has a tremendous investment in his automobile; the automobile has become a status symbol and even a way of life for the nation's suburbanites. Few Americans want to see their heavy financial investment sit in a garage all day. Americans clearly prefer private automobile transportation and costly expressways to mass transit, regardless of the arguments of transportation experts. The result is that existing private mass transit facilities have been steadily losing customers over the last two decades. As their operating costs increase and their patronage declines, many private bus and rail carriers resort to raising fares, reducing service, and putting off maintenance—all of which simply turns away more customers and accelerates the downward spiral. Very often service is poor and equipment is dirty and uncomfortable. Spokesmen for commuter railroads insist that the fault is not theirs—that they must compete with automobiles operating on publicly subsidized, multimillion-dollar expressways. The individual American cannot be lured away from his beloved automobile and the privacy and convenience he thinks it gives him.

It is virtually impossible for the nation's major cities to continue to rely upon automobile transportation over expressways to handle pro-

[10] See Francis Bello, "The City and the Car," *The Exploding Metropolis* (New York: Fortune Magazine, 1957).

jected increases in transportation needs. Most of our cities are already experiencing expressway traffic jams at rush hours and a resulting increase in time and cost to the average automobile commuter. Needless to say, the cost of mass transit facilities on a *per capita* basis is small compared with the cost of expressway building. Some pilot projects in New York, Philadelphia, San Francisco, and Boston found that it was necessary to provide public subsidies to commuter rail companies or to have city governments acquire these facilities at a loss if commuter service was to be restored. The cost of such public subsidies is very small in comparison with the cost of building and maintaining expressways. Thus, mass transit is a considerable saving to most cities, even if fares do not meet operating expenses. Moreover, these pilot projects indicated that new, speedier, more comfortable, air-conditioned, high-capacity trains with fewer stops and more frequent time schedules, together with an expensive advertising campaign, could lure many riders back to public transportation.

Mass transit facilities, while cheaper than expressways, are still quite costly, particularly for cities that do not already have commuter rail service. Proponents of greater federal aid for mass transit argue that cities and states do not have sufficient resources to build mass transit facilities. They argue that mass transit is cheaper than expressway construction and that expressways can never handle predicted traffic increases, anyhow. They emphasize the costs of traffic jams in time and wages lost and their economic impact on central cities. They point out that privately owned mass transportation facilities fail to show profits and that, therefore, these companies are not in a position to make improvements in equipment, facilities, and services at fare levels that would attract riders. Rural opposition stresses the increased centralization at the federal level that would be involved in federally aided mass transit. They object to the idea that the entire nation, including rural areas, should be asked to contribute to solving transportation problems of the nation's cities. Although the federal government contributes heavily to the expressway construction, they believe that states and communities should bear the cost of mass transit by themselves. Moreover, they are doubtful about the feasibility of convincing Americans that they should give up the convenience of their automobiles for mass transit.

To date, federal activity under the Urban Mass Transportation Act has largely been limited to financing urban mass transportation planning. For the most part, pleasant, rapid, convenient, and efficient mass transit continues to be a planner's dream, and federal, state and local policy continues to emphasize automobile transportation and expressway construction.

THE URBAN "CRISIS" RECONSIDERED

For many years now statesmen, scholars, and commentators have bemoaned the nation's urban "crisis." The cities are portrayed as centers of poverty, racial conflict, crime and deliquency, poor housing, inadequate education, ill health, white flight, pollution and congestion, and so forth. As Edward C. Banfield notes, "We are told on all sides that the cities are uninhabitable, that they must be torn down and rebuilt, or new ones must be built from the ground up, that something drastic must be done—and soon—or else." [11] But despite the real and persistent problems of urban life, the urban "crisis" is more a product of our rising standards and expectations about life in America than it is a product of any actual deterioration of city life. As Banfield observes:

> The plain fact is that the overwhelming majority of city dwellers live more comfortably and conveniently than ever before. They have more and better housing, more and better schools, more and better transportation, and so on. By any conceivable measure of material welfare the present generation of urban Americans is, on the whole, better off than any other large group of people has ever been anywhere. What is more, there is every reason to expect that the general level of comfort and convenience will continue to rise at an even more rapid rate through the foreseeable future.[12]

People come to cities precisely *because* they are congested. If they were not congested, they would not be cities and they would not be worth coming to. It is well within our technological know-how to drastically lower pollution levels. Yet we have not done so because the problem is not sufficiently serious to stimulate us into action. If there were a real "crisis"—people dying on the streets from asphyxiation—then we would certainly act on the pollution problem. The rush-hour traffic problem—so frequently referred to in terms of "crisis," "strangulation," and so forth—could be solved *if* people would trade the luxury of their own private cars for mass transit. (An even easier solution would be the staggering of business hours of downtown offices and businesses.)

Poverty and racial discrimination are more widespread outside central cities than inside them. Of course, unlike people living in rural areas and small towns, the poor and the black in cities live closely together and develop a collective consciousness and sense of identity. Their rhet-

---

[11] Edward C. Banfield, *The Unheavenly City* (Boston: Little, Brown and Company 1970), p. 3.
[12] Ibid., pp. 3–4.

oric, behavior, and politics call attention to the poverty and racial discrimination that still exist in urban life, and to the extent that this activity stimulates additional action on the part of governments and citizens, it is perhaps desirable. But it is also true that this activity makes us more *aware* of existing poverty and racial discrimination. And our expectation today is that any level of poverty or discrimination must be eliminated.

Police brutality was once defined as cops beating prisoners with nightsticks. Today it is defined as unexplained questioning and searching or the use of disrespectful language by police. A generation ago a majority of students dropped out of high school before graduation. But it was not until the 1960s, when three-quarters of all students graduated, that the "dropout" problem was cited as a problem, and each year the proportion of high school graduates is rising.

Edward C. Banfield writes: "To a large extent . . . our urban problems are like the mechanical rabbit at the racetrack which is set up to keep just ahead of the dogs no matter how fast they may run. Our performance is better and better, but because we set our standards and expectations to keep ahead of performance, the problems are never any nearer to solution. . . ." [13] Perhaps it is a good thing that we set ever higher standards for ourselves, because we are constantly spurred to improve the quality of life in America. However, there are dangers in this —we may mistake failure to progress as fast as we would like for failure to progress at all. The first danger in such a misinterpretation is that we will rush into a series of ill-considered and wasteful public programs that make matters worse rather than better. These programs may be presented in such a way as to lead people to believe that all their daily problems of life will soon be solved for them by the government. When it turns out that these programs fail to do so, disillusionment and bitterness set in. It is not so much the wasted public funds that constitute a loss as it is the dashed hopes and the loss of confidence that result.

Perhaps a more important danger is that society will be blamed for all the problems that beset individuals, and individuals will be excused from all effort to improve their own lives. Available energies will be devoted to finding governmental programs to solve individual and family problems, and all forms of social dependency will increase. Individuals will come to assume *less* responsibility for their own lives, whereas the traditional democratic value was to encourage individuals to shape their own lives.

Finally, there is danger that people will take the rhetoric of "crisis,"

[13] Ibid., pp. 21–22.

"racism," and so on, seriously and will overlook the tremendous progress that society has made. They may conclude that society is "not worth saving" and that they no longer have confidence or trust in their government or nation.

The politics
of poverty and welfare

POVERTY IN AMERICA

Political conflict over poverty begins with disagreement about its definition. Proponents of programs for the poor frequently make high estimates of the number of poor; they view the problem of poverty as a persistent one, even in an affluent society; they contend that many millions of poor people suffer from hunger, exposure, and remediable illness and that some of them even starve to death. Their definition of the problem almost mandates immediate and massive public programs. Others minimize the number of poor in America; they see poverty diminishing over time without major public programs; they view the poor in America as considerably better off than the middle class of fifty years ago and even wealthy by the standards of most other societies in the world; and they deny that individuals need to suffer from hunger, exposure, remediable illness, or starvation if they make use of the services and facilities available to them. This definition of the problem minimizes the need for massive public programs to fight poverty.

According to the U.S. Social Security Administration there are about 24 million poor people in the United States, or about 12 percent of the population. These are the number of Americans falling *below* the annual cash income level required to maintain a decent standard of liv-

Chapter sixteen

ing. This definition of poverty was derived by careful calculation of costs of food, housing, clothing, and other items for rural and urban families of different sizes. The dollar amounts are flexible to take into account the effect of inflation; these amounts can be expected to rise each year with the rate of inflation. In the mid-1970s the poverty line for an urban family of four was approximately five thousand dollars per year.

There are several problems in this definition of poverty. First of all, it does not account for regional differences in the costs of living, or climate, or accepted style of living. Second, it does not account for family assets—for example, a family that owns its own home does not usually devote as much income to housing as a family that rents. Third, there are many families and individuals whose particular circumstances may place them officially among the poor but who do not think of themselves as "poor people"—students, for example. Doubtless there are others whose income is above the poverty line but who have special problems—sickness, for example—which leave them impoverished. Finally, the official definition of poverty does not recognize the problems of those who spend their incomes unwisely. If money goes for liquor or dope or expensive cars, or if money is siphoned off by loan sharks, impoverished relatives and friends, or high prices charged by ghetto store owners, then even a reasonably high income family can live in poverty. Yet despite these problems, the Social Security Administration definition has provided the best available estimate of poverty in America.

How poor is "poor"? There is reason to believe that the 24 million Americans living in official poverty do not all suffer hardship and privation.[1] About 45 percent own cars, 42 percent own their own homes, and more than 50 percent have some savings. Nearly 80 percent of the poor have television sets, and 75 percent have refrigerators or freezers. Over 75 percent have hot water, access to a telephone for receiving calls, a kitchen with cooking equipment, a flush toilet and a bath. Yet the diets of the poor are nutritionally bad, whether from ignorance or poverty. The poor do not seek medical attention except in emergencies. The result is a great deal of preventable illness and malnutrition.

Who are the poor? Poverty occurs in many different kinds of families and in all environmental settings. The incidence of poverty varies sharply among groups living under different circumstances, however, and several groups experience poverty in greater proportions than the national average. (See Table 16–1.) First of all, the likelihood of *blacks* experiencing poverty is three times greater than that of whites; the percentage of the black population of the United States falling under the

[1] Herman P. Miller, "The Dimensions of Poverty," in *Poverty as a Public Issue*, ed. Ben B. Seligman (New York: The Free Press, 1965).

TABLE 16.1   Percentage of Population Below
Poverty Level

Total	11.6
White	8.9
Black	31.4
Central Cities	14.4
Suburbs	7.1
Rural	14.4
Under 25	16.1
25-65	8.5
Over 65	15.7
Families with male head	7.1
Families with female head	34.4
Less than 8 years school	21.3
8 years school	11.4
High school graduate	8.1
College graduate	3.1

SOURCE: U.S. Bureau of the Census, Current
Population Reports, Series P-60, "Money Income
and Poverty Status" (Washington: Government
Printing Office, 1975).

poverty line is 31.4 compared with 8.9 percent for the white population. Second, *female-headed families* experience poverty far more frequently than male-headed families; 34.4 percent of all female-headed families live below the poverty line. Third, the *aged* experience more poverty than persons of working age. While we think of poverty as a characteristic of persons living in large, central-city ghettos, *rural* families actually experience as much poverty as central-city families. On the other hand, central cities have more poverty than their surrounding suburbs.

Are the poor disappearing? In 1937, Franklin D. Roosevelt, in his second inaugural address, said, "I see one-third of a nation ill-housed, ill-clad, ill-nourished." Since that time the American political and economic system has succeeded in reducing the proportion of poor to less than 12 percent. Table 16–2 provides a closer look at the change in the number and percentage of poor over the last fifteen years. All these figures account for the effect of inflation, so there is no question that the number and percentage of the population living in poverty is declining, despite increases in the population. Over the long run, both black and white poverty is declining, but the rate of decline among blacks has not been as great as the rate of decline among whites. In-

TABLE 16-2 Changes in the Number of Poor

	1959 Millions	1963 Millions	1963 Change from 1959	1967 Millions	1967 Change from 1963	1969 Millions	1969 Change from 1967	1975 Millions	1975 Change from 1969
Total	39.5	36.4	−2.0	27.8	−6.5	24.3	−3.5	24.2	−0.4
White	28.5	25.2	−3.0	19.0	−6.8	16.7	−2.3	16.3	−2.4
Nonwhite	11.0	11.2	+0.4	8.8	−5.9	7.6	−1.2	7.9	+3.9
Percentage of total population	22.4%	19.5%	−3.4%	14.2%	−5.3%	12.2%	−2.0%	11.6%	−0.6%

SOURCE: U.S. Bureau of the Census, *Current Population Reports*, Series P-60, "Money Income and Poverty Status," (Washington: Government Printing Office, 1975).

deed, recessions have occasionally reversed the decline and added to black poverty. Poverty has not declined in the 1970s as rapidly as in the 1960s.

POVERTY AS RELATIVE DEPRIVATION

It is also possible to define poverty as "a state of mind"—some people think they have less income or fewer material possessions than most Americans, and they believe they are entitled to more. Their sense of deprivation is not tied to any *absolute* level of income. Instead, their sense of deprivation is *relative* to what most Americans have and what they, therefore, believe they are entitled to. Even fairly substantial incomes may result in a sense of relative deprivation in a very affluent society; commercial advertising and the mass media portray the life of the "average American" as one of high levels of consumption and material well-being.

Today the poor are not any more deprived relative to the nonpoor than in the past. However, they *feel* more deprived—they perceive the gap to be wider and they no longer accept the gap as legitimate. Blacks are overrepresented among the poor; the civil rights movement made blacks acutely aware of their position in American society relative to whites. Thus, the black revolution contributed to a new awareness of the problem of poverty in terms of relative differences in income and conditions of life.

Defining poverty as relative deprivation really defines it as *inequality* in society. As Victor Fuchs explains:

> By the standards that have prevailed over most of history, and still prevail over large areas of the world, there are very few poor in the United States today. Nevertheless, there are millions of American families who, both in their own eyes and in those of others, are poor. As our nation prospers, our judgment as to what constitutes poverty will inevitably change. When we talk about poverty in America, we are talking about families and individuals who have much less income than most of us. When we talk about reducing or eliminating poverty, we are really talking about changing the distribution of income.[2]

Thus, eliminating poverty defined as relative deprivation would mean achieving absolute equality of incomes and material possessions in America.

Let us try to systematically examine poverty as relative deprivation. Economists have already provided us with a way of measuring income

[2] Victor R. Fuchs, "Redefining Poverty and Redistributing Income," *The Public Interest* (Summer, 1967), p. 91.

distributions within political systems.[3] Income inequality can be measured by a Gini coefficient or a Gini index, which ranges from a plus 1.00 (theoretically perfect inequality) to 0.00 (theoretically perfect equality). Income inequality is greatest in Mississippi and least in Utah. (See Figure 16–1.) In general, income inequality is greater in the southern, rural,

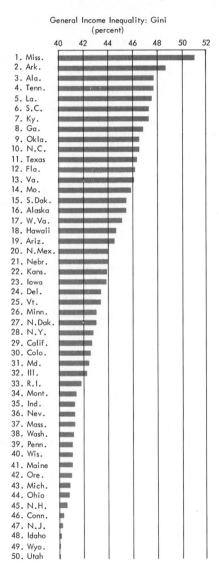

FIGURE 16–1 Rankings of the states: inequality.

[3] James Morgan, "The Anatomy of Income Distributions," *The Review of Economics and Statistics*, 44 (August, 1962): 270–80.

and poorer states. Income distributions are more equalized in the wealthy, urban, industrialized states.

Inequality in America is decreasing over time. However, the rate of decrease is not very rapid. Certainly poverty as relative deprivation is not disappearing at the same rate as absolute poverty. Table 16–3 divides all American families into five groups—from the lowest one-fifth of personal income to the highest one-fifth—and shows the percentage of total family personal income received by each of these groups over the years. (If perfect income equality existed, each fifth of American families would receive 20 percent of all family personal income, and it would not be possible to rank fifths from highest to lowest.) The poorest one-fifth received 3.5 percent of all family personal income in 1929; in 1974, however, this group had increased its percentage of all family personal income to 5.4. (Most of this increase occurred during World War II.) The highest one-fifth received 54.4 percent of all family personal income in 1929; in 1974, however, this percentage had declined to 41.0. This was the only income group to lose in relation to other income groups. The middle classes improved their relative income position even more than the poor. Another measure of income equalization over time is the decline in the percentage of income received by the top 5 percent in America. The top 5 percent received 30.0 percent of all family personal income in 1929, but only 15.3 percent in 1974. The Gini coefficient of income inequality declined from .49 to .38 in that same time period. There is no doubt that income differences in America are decreasing over the long run, although there has been no equalization thus far in the 1970s.

It is unlikely, however, that income differences will ever disappear completely—at least not in a society that rewards skill, talent, risk, and ingenuity. If the problem of poverty is defined as relative deprivation—that is, *inequality*—then the problem is not really capable of solution. Regardless of how well off the poor may be in absolute terms, there will always be a lowest one-fifth of the population that receives something less than 20 percent of all income. Income differences may decline over time, but *some* differences will remain, and even minor differences can acquire great importance and hence pose a "problem."

SOCIAL INSURANCE
AND UNEMPLOYMENT COMPENSATION

In the Social Security Act of 1935, the federal government undertook to establish the basic framework for welfare policies for all levels of gov-

TABLE 16.3 Percent Distribution of Family Personal Income[1] by Quintiles and Top 5 Percent of Consumer Units,[2] Selected Years, 1929-74

Quintiles	1929	1941	1947	1954	1962	1968	1974
Lowest	3.5	4.1	5.0	4.8	4.6	5.7	5.4
Second	9.0	9.5	11.0	11.1	10.9	12.4	12.0
Third	13.8	15.3	16.0	16.4	16.3	17.7	17.6
Fourth	19.3	22.3	22.0	22.5	22.7	23.7	24.1
Highest	54.4	48.8	46.0	45.2	45.5	40.6	41.0
Total	100	100	100	100	100	100	100
Top 5 percent	30.0	24.0	20.9	20.3	19.6	14.0	15.3
Gini concentration ratio	.49	.44	.40	.39	.40	.37	.38

[1] Family personal income includes wage and salary receipts (net of social insurance contributions), other labor income, proprietors' and rental income, dividends, personal interest income, and transfer payments. In addition to monetary income flows, it includes certain nonmonetary or imputed income such as wages in kind, the value of food and fuel produced and consumed on farms, net imputed rental value of owner-occupied homes, and imputed interest. Personal income differs from national income in that it excludes corporate profits taxes, corporate saving (inclusive of inventory valuation adjustment), and social security contributions of employers and employees, and includes transfer payments (mostly governmental) and interest on consumer and government debt.

[2] Consumer units include farm operator and nonfarm families and unattached individuals. A family is defined as a group of two or more persons related by blood, marriage, or adoption, and residing together.

SOURCE: U.S. Bureau of the Census, *Current Population Reports*, Series P-60, Number 80, Number 99.

ernment. State and local welfare activities are greatly influenced by federal policies begun in the Social Security Act of 1935.

This Act placed great reliance on *social insurance* to supplement and, it was hoped, eventually to replace *public assistance*. The distinction between a *social insurance program* and a *public assistance* program is an important one, which has on occasion been a major political issue. If the beneficiaries of a government program are required to have made contributions to it before claiming any of its benefits, and if they are entitled to the benefits regardless of their personal wealth, then the program is said to be financed on the *social insurance* principle. On the other hand, if a program is financed out of general tax revenues, and if the recipients are required to show they are poor before claiming its benefits, then the program is said to be financed on the *public assistance* principle.

One of the key features of the Social Security Act is the Old-Age, Survivors, and Disability Insurance (OASDI) program; this is a compulsory social insurance program financed by regular deductions from earnings, which gives individuals a legal right to benefits in the event of certain occurrences that cause a reduction of their income: old age, death of the head of the household, or permanent disability.[4] OASDI is based on the same principle as private insurance—the sharing of a risk of the loss of income—except that it is a government program that is compulsory for all workers. OASDI is not public *charity*, but a way of compelling people to provide *insurance* against a loss of income. OASDI now covers about nine out of every ten workers in the United States. Both employees and employers must pay equal amounts toward the employees' OASDI insurance. Upon retirement, an insured worker is entitled to monthly benefit payments based upon his age at retirement and the amount he earned during his working years. However, average monthly payments are really quite modest: in the early 1970s the average monthly amount for a retired worker with a wife age sixty-five was less than $300. So OASDI has not eliminated poverty from the ranks of the retired in America.

OASDI also insures benefit payments to survivors of an insured worker, including his widow if she has dependent children. But if she has no dependent children, her benefits will not begin until she herself reaches retirement age. Finally, OASDI insures benefit payments to persons who suffer permanent and total disabilities that prevent them from working more than one year. However, on the whole, payments to sur-

[4] The original act did not include disability insurance; this was added by amendment in 1950.

vivors and disabled workers are just as modest as those provided retired workers.

OASDI is a completely federal program, administered by the Social Security Administration in the Department of Health, Education, and Welfare. But OASDI has an important indirect effect on state and local welfare programs, by removing people in whole or in part from welfare roles. By compelling people to insure themselves against the possibility of their own poverty, social security has doubtlessly reduced the welfare problems which state and local governments would otherwise face.

The second feature of the Social Security Act was that it induced states to enact unemployment compensation programs through the imposition of the payroll tax on all employers. A federal unemployment tax is levied on the payroll of employers of four or more workers, but employees paying into state insurance programs that meet federal standards may use these state payments to offset most of their federal unemployment tax. In other words, the federal government threatens to undertake an unemployment compensation program and tax if the states do not do so themselves. This federal program succeeded in inducing all fifty states to establish unemployment compensation programs. However, the federal standards are flexible and the states have considerable freedom in shaping their own unemployment programs. In all cases, unemployed workers must report in person and show that they are willing and able to work in order to receive unemployment compensation benefits, and states cannot deny workers benefits for refusing to work as strikebreakers or refusing to work for rates lower than prevailing rates. But basic decisions concerning the amount of benefits, eligibility, and the length of time that benefits can be drawn are largely left to the states.

PUBLIC ASSISTANCE

A third major feature of the Social Security Act was its public assistance provision. The OASDI and unemployment compensation programs were based upon the insurance principle, but the federal government also undertook to help the states provide assistance payments to certain needy persons. Today, the federal government directly aids three categories of welfare recipients—the aged, the blind, and the disabled. The federal government also provides *grants to the states* to assist the fourth and largest category—families with dependent children. Within broad outlines of the federal policy, states retain considerable discretion in the Aid to Families with Dependent Children (AFDC) program in terms of the amounts of money appropriated, benefits to be paid to recipients, and rules of the program, such as rules of eligibility. Each state may choose to grant assistance beyond the amounts supported by the national government. Each state establishes its own standards to determine "need." As a result, there is a great deal of variation among the states in ease of access to welfare rolls and in the size of welfare benefits. (See Figure 16–2.)

It is important to note that the federal government aids only four categories of welfare recipients. Only dependent children or persons who are aged, blind, or disabled fall within the categories of recipients eligible for federal support. Aid to persons who do not fall into any of these categories but who, for one reason or another, are "needy," is referred to as "general assistance." General-assistance programs are entirely state-financed and state-administered. Without federal participation, these programs differ radically from state to state in terms of the persons aided, the criteria for eligibility, the amount and nature of benefits, and the administration of financing. The average general assistance payment is lower than comparable payments in federally supported programs.

States also continue to maintain institutions to care for those individuals who are so destitute, alone, or ill that money payments cannot meet their needs. These institutions include state orphanages, homes for the aged, and homes for the ill. They are, for the most part, state-financed as well as state-administered. Persons living in these tax-supported institutions normally are not eligible for federal assistance, although they may receive old-age payments for medical care received in a nursing home. This feature of federal welfare policy has provided incentive for the states to turn their indigent institutions into nursing homes. The quality of these homes and of the people employed to care for their residents varies enormously from state to state.

Federal standards for state AFDC programs, which are established as a prerequisite to receiving federal aid, allow considerable flexibility in state programs. Federal law requires the states to make financial contributions to their public assistance programs and to supervise these programs either directly or through local agencies. Whatever standards a state adopts must be applicable throughout the state, and there must be no discrimination in these welfare programs. The Social Security Administration demands periodic reporting from the states, insists that states administer federally supported programs under a merit system of employment, and prevents the states from imposing unreasonable residence requirements on recipients. But in important questions of administration, standards of eligibility, residence, types of assistance, and

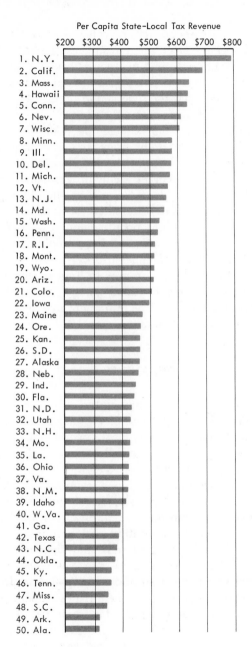

Per Capita State-Local Tax Revenue

FIGURE 16–2 Rankings of the states: welfare.

amounts of payments, the states are free to determine their own welfare programs.

Public assistance recipients are generally eligible for participation in a variety of social service programs. These include Medicaid, public housing, school lunch and milk, manpower training, Office of Economic Opportunity antipoverty programs, various educational and child-care programs and services, and the food stamp program.

The *food stamp program* now distributes billions in federal monies to improve food and nutrition among the poor. Eligible persons may purchase food stamps, generally from county welfare departments, at a small fraction of their value in foodstuffs. The stamps may then be used to purchase food at supermarkets. This program has mushroomed very rapidly since its origins, with expansions in eligible population and increases in the costs of food. Eligibility for food stamps now extends to many persons who are not poor enough to qualify for public assistance. Eligibility is determined by a complex formula which has allowed some fairly affluent families to receive stamps. Indeed, one proposed reform of this costly program is to limit participation only to the poor. Federal expenditures for food stamps are rapidly approaching federal expenditures for the AFDC program, making food stamps a major subsidy for low-income families.

PUBLIC HEALTH, MEDICARE, AND MEDICAID

Public health and sanitation are among the oldest functions of local government. Keeping clean is still one of the major tasks of cities today, a task that involves many different local governmental agencies in street cleaning, sewage disposal, garbage collection, and the provision of clean water supply. Very often these services are taken for granted in the United States, but in underdeveloped countries of the world, health and sanitation are still major tasks. Local public health departments are directly concerned with the *prevention* of disease. They engage in a compulsory vaccination, immunization, and quarantine, as well as regulatory activity in the processing of milk and the safeguarding of water supplies. In more recent years, these agencies have become concerned with the difficult problems of air and water pollution. In addition to the preventive activities of the public health departments, state and local governments also provide extensive, tax-supported hospital care. State and local governments provide both general and specialized hospitals, health centers, and nursing homes, and very often subsidize private hospitals and medical facilities as well. New York City operates twenty-two hospitals, twenty-seven health centers, employing over 40 thousand people. This is the nation's largest city hospital system, but almost every community subsidizes hospital facilities in some way. City and county hospitals and heavily subsidized private hospitals are expected to provide at least emergency care to indigent patients.

Health and hospital care are also supported by state governments. State health departments generally supervise local health departments, distribute state grants to local health departments, and provide health services in areas where there are no local health facilities. Generally, local health departments need state monies in order to operate effectively. But perhaps the states' greatest impact on public health is the provision of specialized state hospitals for tuberculosis, mental illness, and so on. These specialized hospitals are managed directly by the states and are supposed to supplement local hospital care by providing facilities that local governments could not afford.

In nearly every community, decision making in health and hospital matters is firmly lodged in the hands of leaders of the local medical associations. These local physicians, men of prestige and influence in community leadership structures, believe that questions of public policy should be determined predominantly by the doctors as a group, through their local medical society. Often professional social workers and health workers have chafed under the reins of the physicians; they sometimes contend that the doctors insist on a private practice approach where public measures are critically needed.

The federal government is also deeply involved in public health. The U.S. Public Health Service, now part of the Department of Health, Education, and Welfare, is one of the oldest agencies of the federal government, having been created in 1798 to provide medical and hospital care for merchant seamen. Today, the service provides medical care and hospital facilities to many categories of federally aided patients; enforces quarantine regulations; licenses biological products for manufacture and sale; engages in and sponsors medical research; and, most important of all, administers federal grant-in-aid programs to states and communities for the improvement of health and hospital services. Federal grants-in-aid are available to promote the construction of hospitals, nursing homes, diagnostic centers, rehabilitation centers, medical schools, and other medical centers.

In 1965, Congress enacted an historic, comprehensive medical care act for persons over sixty-five, which became known as "Medicare." Medicare provides for prepaid hospital insurance for the aged under Social Security, and low-cost voluntary medical insurance for the aged under federal administration. Medicare includes (1) a compulsory basic health insurance plan covering hospital costs for the aged, which is financed through payroll taxes collected under the social security system;

and (2) a voluntary but supplemental medical program that will pay doctors' bills and additional medical expenses, financed in part by contributions from the aged and in part by the general tax revenues. So far, only aged persons are covered by Medicare, but efforts to extend compulsory government medical insurance to all persons may prove successful in the near future.

In 1965, Congress also passed a medical assistance program (Medicaid) which provided federal funds to enable states to guarantee medical services to all public assistance recipients. Each state operates its own Medicaid program. Unlike Medicare, Medicaid is a welfare program designed for needy persons; no prior contributions are required, and recipients of Medicaid services are generally welfare recipients. States can extend coverage to other medically needy persons if they choose to do so. The cost of this program has far exceeded all original estimates, which suggests that the poor in America require much more medical attention than they have received in the past.

What accounts for differences among the states in welfare policy? All available evidence indicates that economic development is significantly related to welfare policy in the states.[5] A state's income is the single most important variable determining the level of welfare benefits. In terms of welfare payments, it is far better to be poor in a wealthy state than in a poor one. (See Figure 16–3.)

Poorer states have larger proportions of their populations on public assistance rolls, and poorer states have lower welfare benefit payments. This means they pay smaller amounts of money to larger numbers of people. Even though the federal formula does not offset disparities among the states in welfare payment levels, it does offset disparities among states in the burden of welfare costs. The federal government pays a larger share of public assistance costs in poorer states, while requiring richer states to share a greater portion of their public assistance costs. Federal percentages of the total public assistance expenditures *decline* with increases in state income levels.

What effect does pluralism—party competition and voter participation—have on welfare policies in the states? The traditional assumption in the political science literature was that pluralism in a political system increased the benefits to the masses, particularly the poor. It was assumed that competition and participation would make governments more responsive to the interests and needs of the have-nots. And, indeed, it is true that welfare benefits are higher in those states with greater party competition and higher voter turnouts. But these states are

[5] Thomas R. Dye, *Politics, Economics and the Public* (Chicago: Rand McNally & Co., 1966), pp. 115–48.

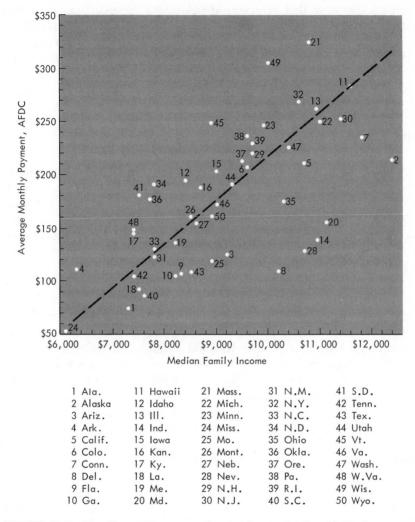

FIGURE 16–3 The fifty states arranged according to median family income and average monthly payments, AFDC benefits.

1 Ala.	11 Hawaii	21 Mass.	31 N.M.	41 S.D.
2 Alaska	12 Idaho	22 Mich.	32 N.Y.	42 Tenn.
3 Ariz.	13 Ill.	23 Minn.	33 N.C.	43 Tex.
4 Ark.	14 Ind.	24 Miss.	34 N.D.	44 Utah
5 Calif.	15 Iowa	25 Mo.	35 Ohio	45 Vt.
6 Colo.	16 Kan.	26 Mont.	36 Okla.	46 Va.
7 Conn.	17 Ky.	27 Neb.	37 Ore.	47 Wash.
8 Del.	18 La.	28 Nev.	38 Pa.	48 W.Va.
9 Fla.	19 Me.	29 N.H.	39 R.I.	49 Wis.
10 Ga.	20 Md.	30 N.J.	40 S.C.	50 Wyo.

also the more economically developed states with higher income, urbanization, and education levels. It is difficult to sort out the effect of pluralism from the effect of economic development on welfare benefits. However, several scholars have employed complex statistical analysis to assess the *independent* effect of pluralism on public policy.[6] The evidence

[6] See Dye, *Politics, Economics, and the Public;* and Richard E. Dawson and James A. Robinson, "Inter-Party Competition, Economic Variables and Welfare Policies in the American States," *Journal of Politics,* 25 (May, 1963): 265–89.

supports the view that economic development is *more* influential *than* party competition or voter participation in determining welfare policies. In other words, states devote more money to helping have-nots because they have more economic resources to do so, and not necessarily because of political competition or participation. Competition and participation, however, do have *some* independent effect liberalizing welfare benefits.[7]

THE WELFARE MESS

Public assistance turned out to be, politically, one of the most unpopular programs ever adopted by Congress. It is disliked by the national, state, and local legislators who must vote the skyrocketing appropriations for it; it is resented by the taxpayers who must bear the ever-increasing burdens of it; it is denounced by the officials and caseworkers who must administer it; and it is accepted with bitterness by those who were intended to benefit from it.

First of all, dependence upon public assistance in America is increasing at a very rapid rate. (See Figure 16–4.) Whether or not it is the public assistance program itself that encourages dependency, one thing is certain: more Americans depend upon public assistance today than ever before, despite a healthy national economy. Certainly our public assistance programs have not succeeded in reducing dependency. In the last decade the number of welfare recipients has doubled, and public assistance costs have quadrupled. Interestingly, it is *not* the programs for the aged, blind, or disabled or even the general assistance programs, that have incurred the greatest burdens. It is the Aid to Families with Dependent Children (AFDC) program which is the largest, most expensive, and most rapidly growing of all welfare programs, and the most controversial.

Most of the growth in welfare rolls has occurred during periods of high employment; it cannot be attributed to economic depression. The acceleration has occurred because more people are applying for public assistance. They have been aided by the activities of civil rights and welfare rights organizations, Office of Economic Opportunity-supported community action groups, and comparable groups, which have informed eligible persons of the law and encouraged them to apply for

[7] See Charles Cnudde and Donald J. McCrone, "Party Competition and Welfare Policies in the American States," *American Political Science Review*, 58 (September, 1969), 858–66. For a full discussion of the problems of assessing the relative effects of political and economic forces on public policy, see Thomas R. Dye, *Understanding Public Policy* (Englewood Cliffs, N.J.: Prentice-Hall, Inc., 1972), Chap. 11. See also Gary L. Tompkins, "A Causal Model of State Welfare Expenditures," *Journal of Politics*, 37 (May, 1975): 392–416.

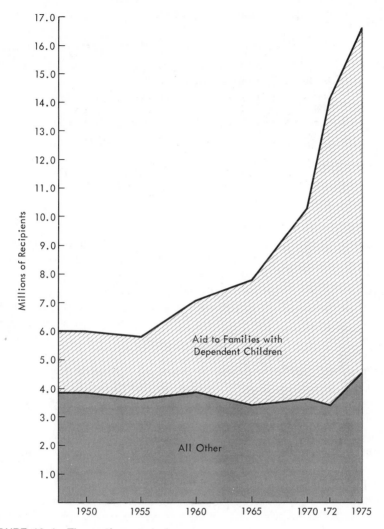

FIGURE 16–4 The welfare explosion.

assistance. Increases in assistance levels, relaxation of eligibility requirements, and a more sympathetic attitude on the part of welfare administrators have also contributed to the increase in welfare rolls. So, also,
has the movement of persons from southern and rural areas, where
welfare administration is tighter, to northern urban areas, where access
to welfare rolls is less restricted.

Despite increased dependency upon welfare and the growing burden
of welfare costs, a majority of the nation's poor do *not* receive public
assistance. There were 24 million poor people in America in 1975, yet

TABLE 16.4   Growth of Public Assistance Programs

	Total	AFDC	Other
	(Millions of Recipients)		
1950	6.0	2.2	4.0
1955	5.8	2.2	3.5
1960	7.0	3.1	4.0
1965	7.8	4.4	3.5
1970	10.4	6.7	3.8
1972	15.0	10.8	4.2
1975	16.5	11.6	5.0

only 16.5 million were on welfare rolls. Many of the nation's poor are *working poor* who are ineligible for welfare assistance because they hold jobs, even though these jobs pay very little.

Not only does welfare fail to assist many of the nation's poor, it does not provide enough in the way of assistance to recipients to raise them out of poverty. While welfare benefits differ from state to state, in every state the level of benefits falls well below the recognized poverty line.

Operating policies and administration of welfare have produced a whole series of problems, including disincentives to family life and work. Until recently, most states denied AFDC benefits if a man was living with his family, even though he had no work. This denial was based on the assumption that an employable man in the household meant that children were no longer "dependent" upon the state. Thus, if a man lived with his family, he could watch them go hungry; if he abandoned them, public assistance would enable them to eat. Moreover, an unmarried mother could get on welfare rolls more easily than a married mother, who had to prove she was not receiving support from her husband. These rules have been relaxed in recent years, but it is still more difficult for whole families to get on public assistance than fatherless families.

In most states, if a recipient of assistance takes a full-time job, assistance checks are reduced or stopped. If the recipient is then laid off, it may take some time to get back on the welfare roll. In other words, employment is uncertain, while assistance is not. More importantly, the jobs available to most recipients are very low-paying jobs which do not produce much more income than assistance, particularly when transportation, child care, and other costs of working are considered. All these facts discourage work.

Welfare administration is made difficult by the heavy load assigned to caseworkers, many of whom are recent college graduates. They spend much of their time determining eligibility, computing payments, and filling out an avalanche of proper forms. With case loads averaging up to 100 families or 200 families, their contacts with recipients must be hurried, infrequent, and impersonal. Caseworkers are unable to develop any close bonds of friendship or rapport with persons in need of help. Recipients often come to view caseworkers with distrust, or worse. The strain on caseworkers is very great; big-city welfare departments report high turnover among caseworkers each year.

Fraudulent welfare claims are a source of concern for federal and state administrators. The U.S. Office of Management and Budget cites survey studies which indicate that 40 percent of all welfare claims under the AFDC program are inaccurate.[8] About 10 percent of AFDC recipients are not eligible for any payment, 23 percent are receiving greater payments than they should, and another 8 percent are underpaid. The food stamp program experiences about the same proportion of ineligibles and overpayments as the AFDC program. Most of these inaccuracies are technical errors rather than outright fraud.

Social dependency and disincentives to work are magnified by the "pyramiding effect" of separate public assistance and social service programs. A family on the welfare rolls is generally entitled to participate in the food stamp program, to receive health care through Medicaid, to gain access to free or low-rent public housing, to receive free lunches in public schools, and to receive a variety of other social and educational benefits at little or no cost. These benefits and services available to the poor are not counted as income, yet the nonpoor must pay for similar services out of their own earnings. If a family head on welfare takes a job, he not only loses welfare assistance, but, more importantly perhaps, becomes ineligible for food stamps, Medicaid, public housing, and many other social services.

One study reported that a family of four in New York City would have to earn more than $7,000 per year to live as well as a family receiving just four basic social benefits—public assistance, food stamps, school lunches, and Medicaid.[9] The report argues that the level of benefits from multiple social programs discourages work unless the anticipated earnings are $8,000 or more. The study also reported that female-headed families were far better off than male-headed (or "intact") families because of

[8] *The Budget of the United States Government,* 1975 (Washington, D.C.: Government Printing Office, 1974), pp. 128–29.

[9] Report prepared for the Joint Economic Subcommittee on Fiscal Policy, released July 8, 1973, reported in Congressional Quarterly, *The Future of Social Programs* (Washington, D.C.: Congressional Quarterly, 1973), p. 87.

eligibility rules for various social programs. Another estimate by the U.S. General Accounting Office places the total value of all social services available to an urban family of four on welfare at over $11,000 per year. Thus, only a fairly well-paying job would justify going off the welfare rolls.

However, many of the popular stereotypes about welfare recipients are unjustified.[10] Most welfare recipients are unemployable because of age, physical disability, lack of skills, or preschool children in the home. There is no feasible way to "put them to work." The vast majority of recipients are not "chiselers" but are in real need. Few women "have babies just to get on welfare"; in most states an additional child raises welfare payments by little more than one dollar a day. Few people move to the liberal states just to get more welfare money; over three-quarters of New York City's welfare recipients were born there.

Nevertheless, reform of the current welfare system is high on the agenda of national decision making. Some form of "guaranteed annual income"—direct cash payments to the poor, prorated against earned income—may eventually replace the clumsy patchwork programs of AFDC, food stamps, general assistance, Medicaid, etc. Reform will also increase federal responsibilities for welfare (perhaps making welfare an exclusively federal responsibility) and reduce the burdens on states and communities. It will probably assist working as well as nonworking poor and equalize welfare benefits throughout the nation. But difficulties will remain. The costs of a "guaranteed annual income" may turn out to be three or four times greater than the costs of the current welfare system. Congress will be under great political pressure to raise. the minimum guarantee each year. Moreover, it is not certain whether this expansion of welfare will increase social dependency in America and further undermine incentives to work. Work or training requirements in welfare programs have always proved difficult to administer. It is conceivable that such an expansion in welfare assistance would encourage dependency by making the acceptance of such assistance a common family practice, extending well up into the middle class.

THE WAR ON POVERTY

In attempting to identify the causes of poverty in America, economist and former presidential advisor John Kenneth Galbraith distinguished

---

[10] See Joe R. Feagin, "America's Welfare Stereotypes," *Social Science Quarterly*, 52 (March, 1972): 921–33.

between "case poverty" and "area poverty."[11] Case poverty is largely a product of the personal characteristics of affected persons. Some persons have been unable to participate in the nation's prosperity because of old age, illiteracy, inadequate education, lack of job skills, poor health, inadequate motivation, or racial discrimination. Area poverty is a product of economic deficiencies relating to a particular sector of the nation, such as West Virginia or much of the rest of Appalachia, and large parts of rural America. Urbanization, industrialization, and technological development appear to have passed up many of these areas, creating high rates of unemployment and large numbers of low-income families. People in these "depressed areas" suffer many of the problems of case poverty, because the two types of 'poverty are not mutually exclusive. But both case poverty and area poverty differ from the "mass poverty" of the 1930s or the mass poverty predicted for capitalist societies by Marxian doctrine. Today's poverty afflicts only a minority of Americans, but it does not disappear even when the economy expands and the nation is prosperous.

The federal government campaign against area poverty is centered in the Economic Development Act of 1965.[12] It authorizes grants and loans for public works, development facilities, technical assistance, and other activities to help economically depressed areas and to stimulate planning for economic development. In this act, the responsibility is placed upon local and state governments to apply for economic development assistance from the Economic Development Administration and to create multicounty and multistate development areas and districts for the purposes of planning economic development.

The Appalachian Regional Redevelopment Act of 1965 is another federal approach to the problem of area poverty. The name *Appalachia* denotes an eleven-state region centering around the Appalachian mountains from southern New York to middle Alabama. It is generally conceded to be the largest economically depressed area in the nation, although it does contain "pockets of prosperity." The focus of the Appalachia Act is upon highway construction, which is believed necessary to open up the region to economic development, although it may make it even easier for the residents to leave.

As an approach to case poverty, the federal government finances

[11] John Kenneth Galbraith, *The Affluent Society* (Boston: Houghton Mifflin Company, 1958); another influential book in the development of antipoverty policy in the Kennedy-Johnson years was Michael Harrington, *The Other America* (New York: The Macmillan Company, 1963).

[12] For an excellent summary of public policies in the war on poverty, see James E. Anderson, "Poverty, Unemployment, and Economic Development: The Search for a National Anti-Poverty Policy," *Journal of Politics*, 29 (February, 1967): 70–93.

Comprehensive Employment and Training Act (CETA) programs, which authorize federal grants to state employment agencies and private enterprise for on-the-job training programs to help workers in depressed areas, or elsewhere, acquire new job skills. Originally the act called for matching funds on a fifty-fifty basis by state governments after the first two years of the program; [13] but when it appeared certain that states would drop the program altogether rather than share its costs, the federal government amended the act to authorize 100 percent federal financing. It seems safe to conclude that state and local governments would not undertake manpower training programs for unskilled workers without full federal financial support.

The most important legislation in the "war on poverty" was the Economic Opportunity Act of 1964.[14] This Act established the Office of Economic Opportunity (OEO) directly under the President with authority to support varied and highly experimental techniques for combating poverty at the community level. The focus was upon case poverty, and the objective is to help the poor and unemployed become self-supporting and capable of earning adequate incomes, by bringing about changes in the individuals themselves or in their environment. The strategy was one of "rehabilitation, not relief." OEO had no authority to make direct grants to the poor as relief or public assistance. All its programs were aimed, whether accurately or inaccurately, at curing the causes of poverty rather than alleviating its symptoms.

The Economic Opportunity Act established several programs oriented toward young people. The strategy appeared to be aimed at breaking the cycle of poverty at an early age. The Job Corps was designed to provide education, vocational training, and work experience in rural conservation camps for unemployable youths between the ages of sixteen and twenty-one. Another program for teen-age youths was the Neighborhood Youth Corps. It was designed to provide some work, counseling, and on-the-job training for youths who are living at home. A Work-Study Program helped students from low-income families remain in school by giving them federally paid part-time employment with cooperating public or private agencies. Many universities and colleges were participants in this program; they benefit from the federally paid labor, and students benefit from the part-time jobs created.

The core of the Economic Opportunity Act was a grass-roots Community Action Program to be carried on at the local level with federal

---

[13] First passed in the administration of President John F. Kennedy, the original legislation was the Manpower Training and Development Act of 1962.

[14] For a description of the programs under the Economic Opportunity Act, see Joseph A. Kershaw, *Government against Poverty* (Chicago: Markham, 1970).

financial assistance, by public or private nonprofit agencies. Communities were urged to form a "community action agency," composed of representatives of government, private organizations, and, most importantly, the poor themselves. It was originally intended that OEO would *support antipoverty programs* devised by the local community action agency. Projects might include (but were not limited to) literacy training, health services, homemaker services, legal aid for the poor, neighborhood service centers, manpower vocational training, and childhood development activities. The act also envisioned that a community action agency would help *organize the poor* so that they could become participating members of the community and avail themselves of the many public programs designed to serve the poor. Finally, the act attempted to *coordinate federal and state programs for the poor* in each community.

Community action was to be "developed, conducted, and administered with the maximum feasible participation of the residents of the areas and members of the groups served." This was one of the more controversial phrases in the act itself. Militants within the OEO administration frequently cited this phrase as authority to "mobilize" the poor "to have immediate and irreversible impact on the communities." This language implied that the poor were to be organized as a political force, by federal antipoverty warriors using federal funds. Needless to say, neither Congress nor the Democratic administration of President Lyndon Johnson intended to create rival political organizations in communities that would compete for power with local governments. But some OEO administrators thought that the language of the act gave them this authority.

Community action agencies were expected to devise specific antipoverty projects for submission to Washington offices of OEO for funding. The most popular of these projects was Operation Head Start—usually a cooperative program between the community action agency and the local school district. Preschool children from poor families were given six to eight weeks of special summer preparation before entering kindergarten or first grade. Another popular antipoverty project was the Legal Services Program. Many community action agencies established free legal services to the poor to assist them in rent disputes, contracts, welfare rules, minor police actions, housing regulations, and so on. Other kinds of antipoverty projects funded by OEO included family-planning programs—the provision of advice and devices to facilitate family planning by the poor; homemaker services—advice to poor families on how to stretch low family budgets; manpower training—special outreach efforts to bring hard-core unemployed into more established manpower programs; "Follow Through"—to remedy the recognized failures of Head Start and continue special educational experiences for poor children after they enter school; "Upward Bound"—educational counseling for poor children; and so forth.

The typical Community Action Agency was governed by a board consisting of public officials (perhaps the mayor, a county commissioner, a school board member, public health officer, etc.), prominent public citizens (from business, labor, civil rights, religious, and civil affairs organizations), and representatives of the poor (in some cases elected in agency-sponsored elections but more often hand-picked by ministers, social workers, civil rights leaders, etc.). A staff was to be hired, including a full-time director, and paid from an OEO grant for administrative expenses. A target area would be defined—generally it was the low-income area of the county or the ghetto of a city. Neighborhood centers were established in the target area, perhaps with general counselors, employment assistance, a recreation hall, a child-care center, and some sort of health clinic. These centers assisted the poor in contacting the school system, the welfare department, employment agencies, the public housing authority, and so on. Frequently, the centers and the antipoverty workers who manned them acted as intermediaries between the poor and public agencies. The jargon describing this activity was "outreach."

The Office of Economic Opportunity was always the scene of great confusion. New and untried programs were organized at breakneck speed. There was a high turnover in personnel. There was delay and confusion in releasing funds to local community action agencies. There was scandal and corruption, particularly at the local level. Community action agencies with young and inexperienced personnel frequently offended experienced governmental administrators as well as local political figures. Congressional action was uncertain, the project's life was extended for a year at a time, and appropriations were often delayed. But most damaging of all, even though programs were put in operation, there was little concrete evidence that these programs were successful in their objectives, that is, in eliminating the causes of poverty.

The Office of Economic Opportunity was "reorganized" by the Nixon Administration, transferring its educational and manpower training programs—the Head Start program, the Job Corps, and Manpower Training —to other federal agencies and relegating OEO to the status of a "laboratory agency." In 1973, President Nixon recommended that OEO be abolished, that federal support for local community action agencies be discontinued, and that remaining programs, including legal services, be transferred to other agencies. Congress has not yet acted decisively on the future of OEO, although the courts have prevented the President from discontinuing OEO on his own initiative. Nonetheless, the future of Economic Opportunity programs looks very bleak.

The demise of the economic opportunity programs cannot be attributed to political partisanship. The war on poverty had become the unpopular stepchild of the Johnson Administration long before LBJ left office. The reasons for the failure of this effort to implement a curative strategy are complex.

Daniel P. Moynihan summarized the community action experiences as follows:

> Over and again the attempts by official and quasi-official agencies (such as the Ford Foundation) to organize poor communities led first to the radicalization of the middle-class persons who began the effort; next to a certain amount of stirring among the poor, but accompanied by heightened radical antagonism *on the part of the poor* if they happened to be black; next to retaliation from the larger white community; whereupon it would emerge that the community action agency, which had talked so much, been so much in the headlines, promised so much in the way of change in the fundamentals of things, was powerless. A creature of a Washington bureaucracy, subject to discontinuation without notice. Finally, much bitterness all around.[15]

---

[15] Daniel P. Moynihan, *Maximum Feasible Misunderstanding: Community Action in the War on Poverty* (New York: The Free Press, 1969).

The politics
of budgeting and taxation

TAX POLICY:
BEARING THE BURDENS OF GOVERNMENT

Federal, state, and local governments in the United States take about 40 percent of the nation's income in taxes and revenues. The largest share of this total tax bite, about two-thirds, goes to the federal government. But states and communities collect over one-third of all government revenues, and revenue raising presents states and communities with important political choices. Decisions must be made about how much revenue is to be raised, how it will be raised, from whom it will be raised, and how great a financial burden will be imposed. These decisions often embroil states and communities in their most important political battles.

The U.S. Constitution places very few restrictions on the power of the states to tax; it prohibits states, without the consent of Congress, from levying taxes on imports and exports; and by implication it prohibits states from using the taxing power to deny to citizens equal protection of the law or due process of the law. State constitutions, however, frequently restrict state taxing powers. These state constitutional restrictions often include maximum rates, prohibitions on incomes or sales taxes, prohibitions on progressive rates, and prohibitions on classification schemes. These restrictions, of course, are generally the product of politi-

Chapter seventeen

TABLE 17.1 Total Government Revenues, 1902-1975

	Amount in Billions	Federal Percentage	State-Local Percentage	Percentage of National Income
1902	1.7	38.5	61.5	8.2
1913	3.0	32.3	67.7	8.6
1922	9.3	45.7	54.3	14.7
1932	10.3	21.6	78.4	24.2
1940	17.8	39.3	60.7	21.8
1950	66.7	80.3	19.7	27.6
1960	153.1	65.2	34.8	36.7
1965	202.9	62.0	38.0	39.4
1970	342.6	63.9	36.1	40.6
1975	540.0	65.0	35.0	43.9

SOURCE: U.S. Bureau of the Census, *Statistical Abstract of the United States.*

cal victories by taxpayers who have succeeded in writing their views on taxes into state constitutions. In addition to taxes, states and communities also derive revenue from compulsory insurance payments, income from public businesses, fines, rents, and charges, and more importantly, grants-in-aid from the federal government. As we shall see, these non-tax revenues are an important part of state and local government finance.

Important changes have occurred in tax and revenue policies in America in the last few decades. In 1902 total government revenues amounted to only $1.7 billion. States and communities collected more revenue than the national government: 61.5 percent of all government revenues were raised in the states, while the federal government accounted for only 38.5 percent of all revenues. And total government revenues amounted to only 8 percent of the nation's income. Seven decades later, public revenue collections in the United States had risen to over 540 billion. Perhaps more important than dollar increases is the fact that governments now take about 40 percent of the national income. This means that the *burden of government finance has grown much faster than the nation's income.*

Another important change is the change in the relative position of federal versus state-local revenue collections. Wars, depressions, and threats of war have resulted in *the shifting of financial emphasis from the states and communities to the national government.* The national government in 1970 collected about 64 percent of all revenues, while states and communities collected the remaining 36 percent.

Important changes have also occurred in the last fifty years in *the types of taxes relied upon by state and local governments.* At the turn of the century, general property tax reigned as the only really important source of both state and local revenue. In theory, at least, all property within a community was assessed at market value and a single uniform rate of tax was applied. In practice, however, property assessments fell far below true market value, and they were not uniform from one county or municipality to the next; assessments varied from as high as 75 percent of fair market value to as low as 10 percent. Some property was specifically exempted from property taxation—for example, the property of government agencies and religious institutions. Some property, especially personal property such as furniture and automobiles and intangible property such as stocks and bonds, was simply hidden from the assessors. The property tax on real estate provided most state and local revenue.

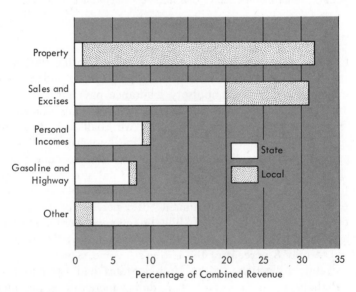

FIGURE 17–1   State and local tax sources.

Today, *property taxes continue to be the major source of revenue for local governments.* Intangible property, such as stocks and bonds and personal property, has gradually been dropped from the local tax property rolls, either legally or illegally, but real estate is relatively easy to find and it cannot be easily moved about. A local sales tax can result in merchants moving beyond city boundaries, and a city income tax can speed the population exodus to suburbia. Because of the dependence of local governments on property taxation, the role of this tax in the total state-local revenue system in America remains significant. States that turn over government functions to communities will have a total tax structure that is heavily dependent on property taxation. States that assume more direct responsibility for public services will depend somewhat less on property taxation.

While the property tax is the most important source of revenue for local communities, *the general sales tax is now the most important source of tax revenue for state governments.* Consumers are a notoriously weak pressure group, and opposition by retailers can usually be squelched by state kickbacks of a certain percentage of a tax for the retailers' efforts in collecting it. It is difficult for taxpayers to count pennies dribbled away two or three at a time; the tax does not involve obvious payroll deductions, as in income taxation, or year-end tax bills, as in property taxation. The burden of the sales tax is not as visible as the income or property taxes, even when large items are purchased, and the purchaser usually considers the tax as part of the item's cost. By 1975 all but five states had imposed a general sales tax. (See Table 17–2.)

In 1911 Wisconsin passed the first modern, enforceable state income tax. Many states fell in line after the national government began taxing income in 1913. Like the general sales tax, the income tax can produce a great deal of revenue. *Most of the states now have an individual income tax.* A few of these are flat rates of 2 or 4 percent of taxable in-

TABLE 17.2   States Without Sales and Income Taxes in 1975

States without General Sales or Gross Receipts Taxes	States without Individual Income Taxes	States without Corporate Income Taxes
Alaska	Connecticut*	Nevada
Delaware	Florida	Texas
Montana	Nevada	Washington
New Hampshire	New Hampshire*	Wyoming
Oregon	New Jersey	
	South Dakota	
	Tennessee*	
	Texas	
	Washington	
	Wyoming	

*These states tax income from interest, dividends, or capital gains, but not wage income.

SOURCE: U.S. Bureau of the Census, *Statistical Abstract of the United States 1975.*

come, but most are graduated and progressive like the federal individual income tax. Rates of progressive state income taxes may run from a modest 1 to 4 percent (Missouri) to a steep 2 to 14 percent (New York). A few states do not tax all income, but only income from interest, dividends, and capital gains. The corporate income tax is even more popular than the individual income tax; all except six states taxed corporate income in 1970. (See Table 17–2.)

A COMPARATIVE VIEW
OF STATE TAX SYSTEMS

What accounts for differences in tax policy among the states? Total state-local tax revenues vary from a high of nearly $800 per person in New York to a low of $300 in Alabama. (See Figure 17–2.) This means that per capita tax levels of some states are over twice as high as those of other states. Some states rely heavily on their local governments and upon property taxation to supply needed revenue. Some states rely heavily on grants-in-aid. Tax burdens, that is, taxes in relation to personal income, also vary considerably among the states. Available evidence suggests that a state's level of economic development is the most important influence on state-local revenue policies.[1]

First of all, let us examine the effect of economic development on levels of taxation in the states.[2] There is little doubt that the ability of the states to raise tax revenue is a function of their level of economic development. Figure 17–3 is a scatter diagram showing the closeness of the relationship between tax revenues and median family income among the states. It shows that as family incomes go up, per capita taxes collected by state and local governments also go up.

The concept of tax *burden* generally refers to taxes paid in relation to personal income; because of differences among the states in income levels, states with the highest *levels of taxation* are not necessarily the same states with the highest tax burdens. The total tax burden in a state is measured by "total state and local tax revenues as a percentage of personal income." The state-local tax burden averages 12 percent of personal income in the United States. Among the fifty states, high levels of in-

---

[1] Thomas R. Dye, *Politics, Economics, and the Public* (Chicago: Rand McNally & Co., 1966), Chap. 7.

[2] Levels of *revenue* refer simply to amounts of money per person raised from all sources. Levels of *taxation* refer to amounts of money per person raised through taxation and exclude monies from federal grants-in-aid, insurance premiums, rents and charges, and utility and store receipts.

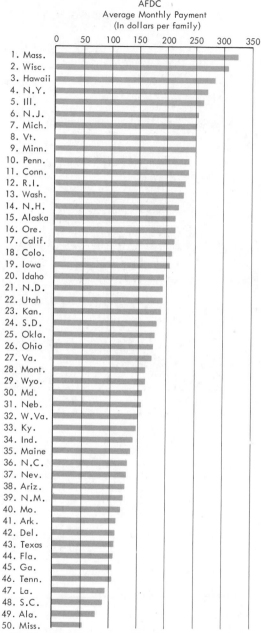

AFDC
Average Monthly Payment
(In dollars per family)

| | 0 | 50 | 100 | 150 | 200 | 250 | 300 | 350 |

1. Mass.
2. Wisc.
3. Hawaii
4. N.Y.
5. Ill.
6. N.J.
7. Mich.
8. Vt.
9. Minn.
10. Penn.
11. Conn.
12. R.I.
13. Wash.
14. N.H.
15. Alaska
16. Ore.
17. Calif.
18. Colo.
19. Iowa
20. Idaho
21. N.D.
22. Utah
23. Kan.
24. S.D.
25. Okla.
26. Ohio
27. Va.
28. Mont.
29. Wyo.
30. Md.
31. Neb.
32. W.Va.
33. Ky.
34. Ind.
35. Maine
36. N.C.
37. Nev.
38. Ariz.
39. N.M.
40. Mo.
41. Ark.
42. Del.
43. Texas
44. Fla.
45. Ga.
46. Tenn.
47. La.
48. S.C.
49. Ala.
50. Miss.

FIGURE 17–2   Rankings of the states: taxation.

dustrialization usually reduces the burdens of taxation; industrialized states can collect a great deal of tax monies without taking a very large

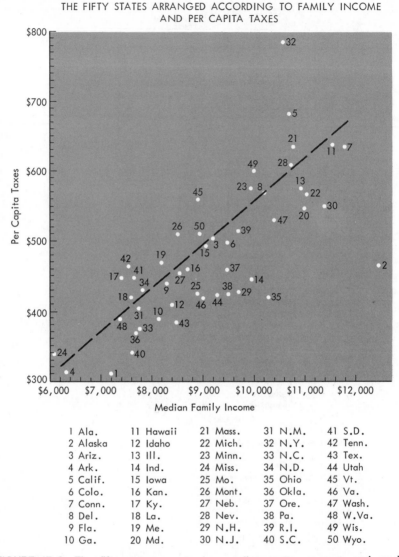

THE FIFTY STATES ARRANGED ACCORDING TO FAMILY INCOME AND PER CAPITA TAXES

1 Ala.	11 Hawaii	21 Mass.	31 N.M.	41 S.D.
2 Alaska	12 Idaho	22 Mich.	32 N.Y.	42 Tenn.
3 Ariz.	13 Ill.	23 Minn.	33 N.C.	43 Tex.
4 Ark.	14 Ind.	24 Miss.	34 N.D.	44 Utah
5 Calif.	15 Iowa	25 Mo.	35 Ohio	45 Vt.
6 Colo.	16 Kan.	26 Mont.	36 Okla.	46 Va.
7 Conn.	17 Ky.	27 Neb.	37 Ore.	47 Wash.
8 Del.	18 La.	28 Nev.	38 Pa.	48 W.Va.
9 Fla.	19 Me.	29 N.H.	39 R.I.	49 Wis.
10 Ga.	20 Md.	30 N.J.	40 S.C.	50 Wyo.

FIGURE 17–3 The fifty states arranged according to tax revenue and median family income.

percentage of personal income.[3] Apparently the way to lower the tax burden in a state is to attract industry. High tax burdens are not necessarily a product of high tax levels, although, of course, there is some relationship between these variables. Yet, high tax levels in an urbanized,

[3] Dye, *Politics, Economics, and the Public,* pp. 188–91.

industrialized, high-income state may not necessarily be accompanied by a heavy tax burden. It is possible to have low tax levels that, because of the lack of industry and low income levels, may be very burdensome—that is, quite high in relation to low incomes.

Another important difference between richer and poorer states is in the degree of decentralization in state and local finance and administration. Local governments tend to play a greater role in the collection of taxes and the provision of public services in urban, high-income states, while state governments collect a greater portion of revenue and provide more services in rural, low-income states. Earlier, we observed that state governments in poorer rural states undertake more direct responsibilities in education, welfare, and highways. Low levels of economic development tend to force decentralization upon these states. Wealthy urban states can afford to let local governments shoulder more responsibilities.

TYPES OF TAXES AND TAX POLITICS

The politics of taxation center about the question of who actually bears the burden or "incidence" of a tax, that is, which income groups must devote the largest proportion of their income to taxes. Taxes that require high-income groups to pay a larger percentage of their incomes in taxes than low-income groups are said to be *progressive,* while taxes that take a larger share of the income of low-income groups are said to be *regressive.*

Economists estimate that, in general, state and local tax systems are regressive.[4] Certainly the revenue systems of state and local governments are more regressive than that of the federal government, which relies heavily upon the progressive individual and corporate income tax. This means that, in general, if a particular governmental function is financed through state and local revenue systems rather than federal revenues, it is being financed on a regressive rather than progressive revenue basis. Thus, much of the political debate over "federalism," that is, over which level of government, state or federal, should provide a particular governmental service, concerns the fact that the federal government tax structure is generally progressive, while the state and local tax structures are generally regressive.

Property taxes are quite regressive. This conclusion is based on the assumption that the renter actually pays his property taxes through increased rentals levied by the landlord, and the further assumption that

---

[4] George A. Bishop, "Tax Burdens by Income Class," *National Tax Journal,* 14 (1961).

high-income groups have more wealth in untaxed forms of property. Since the property tax is the foundation of local tax structures in every state, it is reasonable to conclude that states that rely largely upon local governments for taxes and services are relying more upon regressive tax structures. Yet, in defense of property taxation, it is often argued that no other form of taxation is really feasible for local governments. Local sales and income taxes force individuals and businesses to leave the communities levying them; real estate, on the other hand, is less easy to move about and hide from local tax assessors. Real estate taxes are the only type of taxes that can be effectively collected by relatively untrained local tax officials.

Revenues from property taxation depend upon the property wealth of a community. Dependence upon property taxation means that wealthier communities will be able to raise more funds with less burden on taxpayers than communities without much property wealth. In other words, reliance on property taxation results in inequalities in burdens and benefits between wealthier and poorer communities. This is an important problem in states where local school districts carry the major share of the costs of education. Wealthy school districts are able to provide more school funds with less sacrifice than poor school districts, and hence "equality of educational opportunity" may vary a great deal among communities in the same state.

The burden of property taxes depends upon the ratio of assessed value of property to the fair market value of the property; the rate at which assessed property is taxed, which is usually expressed in mills, or tenths of a percent; and, finally, the nature and extent of tax exemptions and reductions for certain types of property. The ratio of assessed value to full market value may be quite low, sometimes less than 10 percent, and it may vary from one community to the next, even in those states requiring uniform assessment ratios throughout the state. The failure of communities to have periodic and professional tax evaluation means that taxes continue to be levied on old assessment figures, even while market values go up. The result, over time, is a considerable lowering of assessment ratios, and therefore taxes, on older homes and businesses and industries. Newer residents, whose sale price is generally known to tax assessors and who must therefore pay taxes on the uniform assessment ratio, are generally much more favorable toward re-evaluation of property for assessment purposes. There are very few communities in which a suggestion of a re-evaluation will not set off a heated debate between those who are enjoying a low assessment and those who are not. When a community tampers with re-evaluation or a change in the ratio of assessed to market value, it threatens to change the incidence or distribution of tax burdens within a commnuity. If new tax revenues are needed, it is much easier to simply increase the rate or millage to be applied against the assessed value of property. Many communities face state restrictions on maximum tax rates, or they are required to submit any proposed increase in tax rates to the voters in a referendum. These restrictions are usually favored by low-tax forces which have succeeded in obtaining legislation at the state level that impairs the taxing abilities of local governments.

Some categories of property are exempt from taxation; these usually include properties that are used for nonprofit, charitable, religious, educational, and other public purposes. Occasionally such exemptions are attacked by those who feel that they are, in effect, subsidies to the exempted organizations; this is particularly true regarding exemptions for religious property. Exemptions for educational or public properties sometimes work a hardship on communities in which large public facilities or educational institutions are located. But the exemptions that arouse the greatest controversy are usually those given by state or local governments to new business and industry, in an effort to induce them to locate in the state or community granting the exemption.

State and local *sales and excise taxes* are generally regressive, but not as regressive as property taxes.[5] The regressivity of sales taxation is based upon the assumption that low-income groups must devote most, if not all, of their income to purchases, while high-income groups devote larger shares of their income to savings. However, many states exclude some of the necessities of life from sales taxation, such as packaged food bought in supermarkets, in order to reduce the burden of sales taxation on the poor. Yet, on the whole, sales taxation remains more regressive than income taxation.

States generally rely more heavily on sales taxation than on income taxation. However, reliance upon one or the other type of tax varies from state to state. The decision to place primary reliance upon sales or income taxation is one of the most important policy choices facing state government. The yield from both types of taxation can be quite large.

There are several arguments on behalf of sales taxation in the states. The first is that sales taxation is the only major source of revenue left to the states—local governments must rely on property taxes, and the federal government has placed such a heavy tax burden on incomes that taxpayers will not countenance an additional state bite out of their paychecks. Moreover, sales taxes are not as visible as income or property taxes, since sales taxes are paid pennies at a time. Generally, the customer considers the sales tax as part of the price of an item. Taxpayers never add up the total they have paid in sales taxes, so sales taxation ap-

[5] Bishop, "Tax Burdens by Income Class."

pears to be a relatively "painless" form of taxation. In addition, sales taxes insure that low-income groups who benefit from public services will share in the costs of government. Actual hardships for the poor from sales taxes can be reduced by excluding food and other necessities from taxation, but the poor will pay taxes when purchasing other consumer items. Finally, sales taxes are useful in reaching mobile populations, that is, tourists, commuters, and transients—persons who derive benefits from a host state but who would not otherwise help pay for these benefits.

In contrast, progressive state *income taxes* are defended on the principle of ability to pay; that is, the theory that high-income groups can afford to pay a larger percentage of their income into taxation at no more of a sacrifice than that required of low-income groups to devote a smaller proportion of their income to taxation. The principle of a graduated income tax based on ability to pay, a principle accepted at the federal level in 1913 with the passage of the Sixteenth Amendment, together with the convenience, economy, and efficiency of income taxes, is generally cited by proponents of income taxation. Sales taxes are more difficult to administer, and some retailers may pocket tax funds unless a state has a considerable force of auditors to oversee sales tax collection.

Occasionally, *state lotteries* or legalized gambling are suggested as an alternative to direct taxation. More than half the states receive income from horse racing, gambling, or lotteries. Nevada leads the way with nearly a quarter of its revenue coming directly from gambling taxes. But only Nevada has generalized legal gambling; most states restrict gambling to pari-mutuel betting on the racetrack. The total revenues raised from such sources, however, make up less than 5 percent of all state-local revenues. Recently several states started public lotteries as a means of raising public money. But there are problems involved in this area. First of all, lotteries do not bring in very much money. Second, the administrative costs, including prize money, may run as high as 50 percent of the gross revenue. This compares very unfavorably with the estimated 5 percent cost of collecting income taxes and with the only slightly higher cost of collecting sales taxes. Finally, it seems likely that lotteries are *very* regressive, with low-income groups doing most of the gambling. Perhaps the only justification is that people will gamble anyhow and it is better for the state to reap the benefits than for organized crime to do so.

THE POLITICS OF BUDGETING

Too often we think of budgeting as the dull province of clerks and statisticians. Nothing could be more mistaken. Budgets are political documents which record the struggles of men over "who gets what." The budget is the single most important policy statement of any government. There are few government activities or programs that do not require an expenditure of funds, and no public funds may be spent without budgetary authorization. The budget sets forth government programs, with price tags attached. Determining what goes into a budget, that is, the budgetary process, provides a mechanism for reviewing government programs, assessing their cost, relating them to financial resources, making choices among alternative expenditures, and determining the financial effort that a government will expend on its program. Budgets determine what programs are to be reduced, increased, initiated, or renewed. The size and shape of the budget is a matter of serious contention in the political life of any state or community. Governors, mayors, administrators, legislators, interest groups and citizens all compete to have their policy preferences recorded in the budget. The budget lies at the heart of the political process.

The budgetary process begins with the governor or mayor's office sending to each governmental agency and department a budget request form, accompanied by broad policy directives to agency and department heads about the size and shape of their requests. Very often these budget requests must be made six to twelve months prior to the beginning of the fiscal year for which the requests are made; governmental fiscal years usually run from July 1 to June 30. After all requests have been submitted to the budget office, the serious task of consolidating these many requests begins. Individual department requests are reviewed, revised, and generally scaled down; often departments are given more or less formal hearings on their budget request by the budget director. The budget agency must also make revenue estimates based upon information it obtains from the tax department. Finally, budget requests and revenue estimates must be prepared. A great many decisions may already have been made by the time the budget director submits the tentative budget to the governor or the mayor for his approval. But a governor or a mayor must decide whether his budget is to be balanced or not; whether particular departmental requests should be increased or reduced, in view of the programs and promises important to his administration; whether economies should involve overall "belt tightening" by every agency or merely the elimination of particular programs; or finally, whether he should recommend the raising of new taxes or the incurring of additional debt, and if so, what kinds of taxes or debts should be requested. These decisions may be the most important that a mayor or a governor makes in his term of office, and he generally consults both political and financial advisers—budget and tax experts, party officials, interest group representatives, and legislative leaders. Ordinarily, these difficult decisions must be made before the governor or the mayor presents his budget message to the legislature. This budget message explains and defends the final budget presented by the chief executive to his legislative branch.

The governor's budget generally appears in the lower house of the legislature as an appropriations bill, and it follows the normal path of any bill. It is assigned to a ways and means committee or an appropriations committee, which often holds hearings on the bill and occasionally re-shapes and revises the executive budget. After the house committee reports the appropriations bill and it is passed by the lower house, it is then sent to the upper house where it repeats essentially the same steps. How a governor's budget fares in the legislature generally depends upon his general political power, public reactions to his recommendations, the degree of support he receives from department heads, who are often called to testify at legislative budget hearings, his relationships with key legislative leaders, and the effectiveness of interest groups that favor or oppose particular expenditures. After it is passed in identical form by both houses, the final appropriations measure is sent to the governor for his signature. If the governor has an item veto, he can still make significant changes in the budget at that time; however, most governors are obliged to accept the final appropriations measure, which provides basic authority to spend money for the fiscal year. Of course, agencies granted the authority to spend a particular amount are not required to do so, and if the funds are not available, agencies may be forced to spend less than their appropriation. However, no agency may spend more than its appropriation for particular programs.

What forces are actually involved in the budget-making process? First, there is ample evidence that budgeting is a very *conservative* process—that is, if one defines the term conservative to mean preservation of the *status quo*.[6] Invariably, the forms provided by the budget office require departments to prepare budget requests alongside of last year's expenditures. Decision makers generally consider last year's expenditures as a base. Consequently, active consideration of budget proposals is generally narrowed to new items or requested increases over last year's base. The attention of governors and legislators, and mayors and councils, is focused on a narrow range of increases or decreases in a budget. A budget is almost never reviewed as a whole every year, in the sense of recon-sidering the value of existing programs. Departments are seldom required to defend or explain budget requests that do *not* exceed current ap-propriations; but requested increases in appropriations require extensive explanation, and they are most subject to downward revision by higher political officials. The "incremental" nature of budgeting creates some

[6] For a discussion of the budgetary process at the federal level, see Aaron Wildavsky, *The Politics of the Budgetary Process* (Boston: Little, Brown and Company, 1964).

interesting informal rules of the budget game. Thomas Anton summarizes some of these budgetary folkways: [7]

1. Spend all of your appropriation. A failure to use up an appropriation indicates that the full amount was unnecessary in the first place, which in turn implies that your budget should be cut next year.
2. Never request a sum less than your current appropriation. It is easier to find ways to spend up to current appropriation levels than it is to explain why you want a reduction. Besides, a reduction indicates your program is not growing and this is an embarrassing admission to most government administrators.
3. Put top priority programs into the basic budget, that is, that part of the budget which is within current appropriation levels. Budget offices, governors and mayors, and legislative bodies will seldom challenge programs which appear to be part of existing operations.
4. Increases that are desired should be made to appear small and should appear to grow out of existing operations. The appearance of a fundamental change in a budget should be avoided.
5. Give the budget office, chief executive, and the legislature something to cut. Normally it is desirable to submit requests for substantial increases in existing programs and many requests for new programs, in order to give higher political authorities something to cut. This enables them to "save" the public untold millions of dollars and justify their claim to promoting "economy" in government. Giving them something to cut also diverts attention away from the basic budget with its vital programs.

Budgeting is very *political*. As Aaron Wildavsky was told by a federal executive, "It's not what's in your estimates, but how good a politician you are that matters." [8] Being a good politician involves (1) the cultivation of a good base of support for one's requests among the public at large and among people served by the agency, (2) the development of interest, enthusiasm, and support for one's program among top political figures and legislative leaders, and (3) skill in following strategies that exploit one's opportunities to the maximum. Informing the public and one's clientele of the full benefit of the services they receive from the agency may increase the intensity with which they will support the agency's request. If possible, the agency should inspire its clientele to contact governors, mayors, legislators, and councilmen and help work for the agency's request. This is much more effective than the agency's trying to promote for its own requests.

Finally, as we have already seen, socioeconomic conditions further

---

[7] For an excellent description of budgetary politics in a state, see Thomas J. Anton, *The Politics of State Expenditures in Illinois* (Urbana: University of Illinois Press, 1966).

[8] Wildavsky, *Politics of the Budgetary Process*, p. 19.

reduce the alternatives for budgetary action. Very often, local governments *begin* the budgetary process by estimating the amount of revenues that can reasonably be expected from the existing tax base, various service charges, and intergovernmental revenues; this estimate then becomes the ceiling for all budget requests. This practice, together with the conservative tendency of accepting past expenditure levels, seriously curtails policy change. This may be part of the reason why governors and mayors have a difficult time bringing about significant policy changes, and it contributes to the public's view of "politics as usual" and a feeling that nothing can be done, regardless of who is elected.

Budgeting is also quite *fragmented*. In most of the states there is a great deal of constitutional and statutory "earmarking" of revenues. A common example is the earmarking of gasoline tax revenues for highway purposes. This practice fragments the budget and reduces executive control over the allocation of public funds.

Finally, budgeting is *nonprogrammatic*. For reasons that accountants have so far kept to themselves, an agency budget typically lists expenditures under ambigous phrases: "personnel services," "contractual services," "travel," "supplies," "equipment." Needless to say, it is impossible to tell from such a listing exactly what programs the agency is spending its money on. Obviously such a budget obscures policy decision by hiding programs behind meaningless phrases. Even if these categories are broken down into line items (for example, under "personnel services," the line item budget might say, "John Doaks, Assistant Administrator $15,000"), it is still next to impossible to identify the costs of various programs. Reform-oriented administrators have called for budgeting by programs for many years; this would present budgetary requests in terms of end products or program packages, like aid to dependent children, vocational rehabilitation, administration of fair employment practices laws, highway patrolling, and so on. Chief executives generally favor program budgeting because it will give them greater control over the policy. But very often administrative agencies are hostile toward program budgeting; it certainly adds to the cost of bookkeeping, and many agencies feel insecure in describing precisely what it is they do. Wildavsky points out that there are some *political* functions served by nonprogram budgeting. He notes that . . .

> agreement comes much more readily when the items in dispute can be treated in dollars instead of basic differences in policy. Calculating budgets in monetary increments facilitates bargaining and logrolling. It becomes possible to swap an increase here for a decrease there or for an increase elsewhere without always having to consider the ultimate desirability of the programs blatantly in competition.[9]

[9] Ibid., p. 136.

Program budgeting also provides the opportunity for the introduction of performance standards in the bugeting process. "Performance budgeting" usually involves the designation of some unit of service, for example, one pupil, one hospital patient, or one welfare recipient, and the establishment of standards of service and costs based upon a single unit of service. A common example of performance budgeting is found in school systems where pupils are designated as a basic unit of service and standards for numbers of teachers, supplies and materials, auxiliary personnel, building floor space, and many other cost items are calculated on the basis of number of pupils to be served. Thus, standards may allocate teachers on the basis of 1 to 25 students, or a full-time principal for every 250 students, or a psychologist for every 1,000 students, or twenty dollars' worth of supplies for every student, and so on. These formulas are used to determine the allocation of resources at budget time. One political consequence of the use of formulas in performance budgeting is the centralization of budgetary decision making. Departments are merely asked to provide the number of pupils or patients or recipients or other units of service they expect to serve in the coming fiscal year. A central staff of budget analysts then determines allocations through the application of formulas to the service estimates provided by the departments. Many departments, accustomed to less bureaucratic procedures, feel that the use of formulas is mechanical and inflexible. But it is not surprising in a large and complex bureaucracy to see the search for equitable patterns in the distribution of resources leading to the use of formulas applied throughout the system. Often, however, once a formula has been established, it is difficult to change or adjust the formula even from one year to the next. Performance budgeting places great power in the hands of the staff personnel budget offices who devise the formulas. Performance budgeting is generally favored by economy-minded groups, particularly businessmen who are familiar with the application of unit cost procedures to manufacturing enterprises.

Thomas Anton has examined the respective roles of the governor, state agencies, budgetary commission, and legislature in the development of the Illinois budget.[10] Agency budget requests are generally much higher than last year's appropriations. The executive budgetary commission makes heavy cuts into agency requests. The governor makes additional cuts to bring his budget into balance. But the general assembly proceeds to restore many of the cuts in agency requests. The final budget is much higher than last year's appropriations, but much lower than agency requests.

[10] Thomas J. Anton, "Roles and Symbols in the Determination of State Expenditures," *Midwest Journal of Political Science*, 11 (February, 1967): 27–43.

MONEY, POWER, AND "REVENUE SHARING"

Federal grants-in-aid are money payments made by federal agencies to state and local governments for carrying out programs of interest to the federal government. Federal grant-in-aid programs are established by Congress under its power to "tax and spend for the general welfare." One-sixth of all state-local revenue comes from the federal government in grants-in-aid. We have already described federal grant programs in education, welfare, housing and urban renewal, and highways, but there are more than two hundred federal grant-in-aid programs currently in operation, which cover a tremendously wide variety of programs. It is true that states and communities administer these programs and generally match federal funds from their own fiscal sources, but federal grants-in-aid usually involve federal intervention in policy making, through minimum standards and "guidelines." Federal agencies retain the right to approve or disapprove grant applications submitted by states and local governments. The federal grant-in-aid system has entailed many problems. Some of these were described in Chapter 2 in our discussion of federalism. The current grant-in-aid structure is a haphazard collection of hundreds of separate programs, each with its own policies, its own requirements and procedures, and its own funding. There are no clear priorities in the federal grant-in-aid system. It is uncoordinated and bureaucratic. Excessive red tape in grant preparation, approval, and funding from Washington creates lengthy program delays and uncertainty. The system restricts the ability of state and local officials to determine their own priorities. The system is unresponsive to the needs of specific communities because guidelines and funding do not take account of local situations.

The State and Local Fiscal Assistance Act of 1972 was a true landmark in American federalism; it established a general revenue-sharing program—the turnover of a certain amount of federal tax revenues to state and local governments with few or no strings attached.

Shared revenues are allocated to each state on a formula based on three factors: population, tax effort by state and local governments, and the income level of the population. One-third of the amount allocated to each state may be retained by the state government, but two-thirds are distributed to local governments according to the same factors used to determine the state's allocation. The effect of this formula is to reward poorer states which tax their populations heavily.

There are very few restrictions on the use of this money; it may be used for police and fire protection, sewage and garbage disposal, pollution abatement, transportation, parks and recreation, and most other recognized state-local functions. The act denied the use of these funds to meet federal matching requirements in education or welfare because of the heavy federal support already being given to these areas. This general revenue sharing will not replace any of the established grant-in-aid programs.

Proponents of revenue sharing, including many big-city mayors, argue that the federal government is better at collecting revenue than state or local governments—particularly big cities, with their limited jurisdiction over tax bases. The federal government is not really in competition with anyone for residents or industry, as are state and local governments. The federal individual and corporate income tax is an effective, progressive producer of large amounts of revenue, in contrast to state and local property and sales taxes. Moreover, state and *local* taxable resources are unequally distributed among jurisdictions; federal revenues can help equalize disparities between communities.

Although state and local officials admire the tax collecting capabilities of the federal government, they generally believe that the national government cannot undertake itself to provide basic public services—police and fire protection, garbage disposal and sewage treatment, pollution abatement, public transportation, recreation, libraries, etc. Moreover, difficulties with the haphazard and bureaucratic system of federal grants-in-aid in housing, urban renewal, antipoverty programs, manpower training, welfare, education, etc., convinced many governors and mayors that they could do a better job themselves in confronting domestic problems if federal money were made available with no strings attached. In other words, while the federal government is better at collecting revenue, states and communities are better at spending it. Hence, proponents of revenue sharing argued that it combines the best features of each level of government.

Opposition to revenue sharing, as one might expect, is centered in Washington. Congressmen do not like to see a system develop in which they are cast in the unpopular role of tax collector, while state and local officials have all the "fun" of determining how to spend the money. Even conservative congressmen who dislike the centralized bureaucracy in Washington are fearful of separating the spending function from the taxing function. They believe that the decisions to spend money must be accompanied by the burdens of collecting it, or else spending would become irresponsible. They are joined in their opposition to revenue sharing by some liberal congressmen who fear that state and local officials do not share their definition of national purposes and priorities. These congressmen wish to retain the power to control federal funds in Washington. And, of course, the Washington bureaucracy itself, even under a President who supports revenue sharing, is a major source of opposition to the proposal.

Research on the effects of revenue sharing shows that the funds do indeed reward low-income states and cities which make high tax efforts.[11] However, many states and cities which have budget surpluses are receiving shared revenues from a federal government which itself is running heavy deficits. Most shared-revenue funds have gone to maintain basic city services—police, fire, streets, sanitation, public buildings. Liberal critics of the program have complained that very little money has gone into social service programs. They also charge that enforcement of non-discrimination provisions is difficult when federal funds are spread so widely to so many cities and so many functions.

Power and money tend to go together in American politics. Power in the federal system has flowed toward Washington over the decades, largely because Washington had the superior taxing powers and therefore the money to deal more effectively with the nation's major domestic problems. Revenue sharing promises to revitalize state and local governments by providing new access to financial resources. If Congress refrains from adding strings over the years to shared revenues (a big "if"), states and communities will acquire both money and power to deal with domestic issues. This is why revenue sharing is potentially a great landmark in American federalism: it offers the hope that states and communities can slow the flow of power to Washington. Of course, the balance of power in American federalism can only be stabilized if states and communities use their new-found money and power wisely and effectively in dealing with the challenges confronting the nation.

[11] For a summary of several studies made by Brookings Institution and the Government Accounting Office, see Congressional Quarterly, *Weekly Report*, September 27, 1975: 2053–59.

Index

Index